Human Corporation for Sustainable Development

Claus Luttermann

# Human Corporation for Sustainable Development

## Corporate Finance, Financial Reporting, and Value Creation

Springer

Claus Luttermann
Chair of International Business Law
Cath. University of Eichstätt-Ingolstadt
Ingolstadt, Bayern, Germany

ISBN 978-3-032-07614-4 ISBN 978-3-032-07615-1 (eBook)
https://doi.org/10.1007/978-3-032-07615-1



This Springer imprint is published by the registered company Springer Nature Switzerland AG
The registered company address is: Gewerbestrasse 11, 6330 Cham, Switzerland

*In Memoriam*

Marianne und Wilhelm
Luttermann

# Preface

*"The foundation of law is humanity."*

*Albert Schweitzer (1923, pp. 93, 352)*

People can bring good into the world. For this purpose, the corporation as a human corporation is an ingenious legal instrument for sustainable value creation. In the face of uncertainty, for responsible entrepreneurs in developing sustainable corporations, it is about corporate finance and financial reporting (accounting, auditing) in all business activities, across spaces and times – to fulfil demand and for reaching new shores or unknowns. Jurisprudence shapes human living conditions for everyone as the entrepreneur of one's own life in the midst of lives. For a better world, where human, economy and environment live in harmony.

We should think and act holistically again. The corporation is an essential element of a human constitution of freedom as a culture of responsibility. A legal institution, with which prosperity can be generated individually and generally in a sustainable way. But the law of the corporation is withering away, dominated by tragically efficient souls, constrained in formal constructions, promoted by neoclassical emptiness ("economic analysis of law"), establishing law-free zones with a monopoly of valuation and AI (the "numbers game", Levitt (1998)) that seize silent power over the financial markets and all of us.

My work, which I laid the foundation for at the University of Münster in Westphalia, Germany, and at UC Berkeley (1995–1996) with the juridical analysis of the economy (Luttermann (1998)), has moved forward (Luttermann, see examples below). Corporations and capital markets are a field of law worldwide. This is in fact clear and evidenced by countless scandals since the famous works by Brandeis (1914) and Berle and Means (1932), global accounting fraud such as Enron Corp. with the dissolution of its auditor Arthur Andersen LLP (2001), the world debt crisis, being rampant since the fall of Lehman Brothers Inc. (15.09.2008), and the accompanying upheavals of our time. In order to create a better world, in the plenty of life and imagination, instead of numbers, it is about the people, the actual life circumstances (facts) and the reasonable foundation of a sustainable *Vermögensordnung* (order of assets, Luttermann (2015)).

All in all, this is to be established with the human corporation with substance through real values and trust in reciprocity, internationally grounded and ensured (please note: power only respects countervailing power). This requires, even on the shoulders of giants, the work of many people. Where we for a whole, aware of our limits, undertake the universal approach, we do this because some of us "(lest our true aim be lost for ever) … should venture to embark on a synthesis of facts and theories" (Schrödinger (1944) p. 1). A basis for human existence, which we can develop in a complementary way.

Law is practised ethics: This applies to the human corporation as it does to all people in every language, the organ of the spirit. Using a language other than your own, which "you think you can handle", is like a river that "suddenly becomes wild and dangerous again" (Canetti (1981) p. 64). A bold venture into – comparative – law, languages and translation (from Latin *translatio*, to transfer from one to another). Overall, for a better world, it is to promote the dialogue of cultures for sustainable development and cooperation in complementarity.

The human will to freedom clears the way. Thanks to my family, Prof. Dr. Karin, Lauritz and Clara Luttermann, who enrich the journey wonderfully.

Ingolstadt, Germany
Pythagorio, Greece

Claus H. Luttermann

2025/2024

## References


Berle, A. A., & Means, G. C. (1932). *The modern corporation and private property*. The Macmillan Company.

Brandeis, L. D. (1914). *Other people's money and how the bankers use it*. Frederick A. Stokes Company Publishers.

Canetti, E. (1981). Dialog mit dem grausamen Partner. In Canetti, *Das Gewissen der Worte*. Fischer Verlag.

Levitt, A. (1998). *The "numbers game"*, 28.09.1998. https://www.sec.gov/news/speech/speecharchive/1998/spch220.txt (accessed: 15.09.2025).

Luttermann, C. (1998). *Unternehmen, Kapital und Genußrechte: Eine Studie über Grundlagen der Unternehmensfinanzierung und zum internationalen Kapitalmarktrecht*. Mohr Siebeck.

Luttermann, C. (2003). In *Münchener Kommentar zum Aktiengesetz* (2nd ed., Vol. 5/1). CH Beck Verlag.

Luttermann, C. (2008). Die Erosion der Freiheit. *Frankfurter Allgemeine Zeitung (FAZ)*, 23.06.2008, p. 22.

Luttermann, C. (2010). Juristische Analyse von Ökonomie, Staat und Gesellschaft. *Zeitschrift für Rechtspolitik (ZRP), 43*, 1–4.

Luttermann, C. (2015). Corporate Law and the *Vermoegensordnung* (Order of Assets). *European Business Law Review (EBLR), 26*, 31–48.

Schrödinger, E. (1944). *What is life?* Cambridge University Press (ed. 1992).

Schweitzer, A. (1923). *Kultur und Ethik*. CH Beck Verlag (ed. 1990).

**Competing Interests** The author has no competing interests to declare that are relevant to the content of this manuscript.

# Content Overview

# Contents

# Part I
# We, the Entrepreneurs

# Chapter 1
# Incorporate Substance for a Better World

"How can we escape from this prison of textism, of legal mathematics and geometrical concepts?"*

*Bernhard Großfeld*

## Contents



*Grossfeld, Dreaming law: comparative legal semiotics, 2010 German Law Publishers, Stuttgart, p. 265. On this Luttermann, Editorial, 3(1) Comparative Law and Language (2024) I-II, journal ed. by Trento University, Italy (https://teseo.unitn.it/cll). See below, e.g., 5.5.5, 5.6 and 9.9. Luttermann (1998) pp. 210-237 (financial theory).




C. Luttermann, *Human Corporation for Sustainable Development*,
https://doi.org/10.1007/978-3-032-07615-1_1

## 1.1 About the Beginning

The human mind (German *Geist*) and energy (*Tatkraft*) can change the world for the better. With human rights and climate change, it is about the transformation of the economy. The corporation as a human corporation, formed with substance and led responsibly (see 2.2.2), ingeniously provides a financial instrument for this purpose (see 2.5.1). Good governance has to be established in a sustainable way as a field of law through reasonable financing and valuation, financial reporting and auditing (principle of reasonableness).[1] On the basis of science and supported by technology, the human being makes reasonable decisions morally in the centre of life:[2] Jurisprudence guides the way to the law as practised ethics. Globally, it is about an entrepreneurial culture of responsibility (*unternehmerische Verantwortungskultur*, see 1.3.1), individually and in community.

Everyone is an entrepreneur of life. In practice, it is primarily about a new way of thinking. Humans, the economy and the environment have to be reconciled overall. This is demanded by reason, the dominion of which as a constitution of liberty, where individualism and the greater good do not contradict but reinforce each other, is still lacking.[3] This liberty is fundamental for human life in peace and prosperity, in which creation is also preserved for following generations (intergenerational justice).[4] With the intellectual level, it also encompasses the economic basis, the practical dimension of our existence. Naturally, this is accompanied by the responsibility evolving from the self-determined action of every single human for her or his effects on the environment. Developing in the community of life. Remember the universality of the objectives and principles of the Charter of the United Nations (see 1.2).

For that, it is essential to maintain the balance as we progress. Through reason, measure and mean, to bring freedom and responsibility into harmony. But we waste mind and resources for trumpery and vanity, even for war and warlike purposes. Carelessly, as if everything were infinite. In a world of shams and debt systems (fiat money), misdirecting real assets, aggravating massive imbalances, privatizing profits without performance for the few, and socialising losses. Thoughtlessly, as if there

[1] Fundamentally Luttermann (1998), Unternehmen, Kapital und Genußrechte (Companies, capital and profit participation rights), esp. on the *Prinzip der Angemessenheit* (principle of reasonableness) pp. 1-11, 135-176, and 465-485.

[2] Morals being regarded as a theory of law (*Rechtslehre*, Latin *iurisprūdentia*): Kant (1795), on eternal peace (the categorical imperative), inspired by ancient Greek philosophy (Aristotle, see 3.9). Cf. on the reverence for life Schweitzer (1923) and (1931–1945), Luttermann (2013) and (1998). Overall below, esp. chapters 8 and 9.

[3] See on the theory of moral sentiments Smith (1759/1790$^{6}$), on the constitution of liberty Hayek (1960) and Sen (2007) on identity and violence.

[4] Overall ICJ, Advisory Opinion, 23.07.2025 (https://www.icj-cij.org/sites/default/files/case-related/187/187-20250723-adv-01-00-en.pdf, accessed: 25.08.2025), e.g. para. 156: "present generations are trustees of humanity tasked with preserving dignified living conditions and transmitting them to future generations." See below 1.2 and 1.4.2, also 6.1.3.

were no tomorrow. Irresponsibly. Modern economic sciences, according to the idea of justice, with the humanities and natural sciences are in place for the transition to a modern economy.[5] What keeps us busy instead of sustainably promoting general wealth in a fair competition of ideas while cooperatively protecting our home, the earth?

It is time to change. This does not require reinventing the wheel, but using it reasonably. Jurisprudence offers practical ethics for the creation of value (*Wertschöpfung*). Tie in power, ascertain the limits of the effectiveness of state organisation and come up with solutions so people can develop freely and altogether as responsible entrepreneurs of their lives by virtue of mind, imagination and reason. Incorporated – as laid out here – in a reasonable legal system for good governance, financing and valuation of corporations; in the broader sense within a global asset order (*Vermögensordnung*, see 1.6 and chapter 8). The human corporation functions as a sustainable financial instrument essentially through sustainable valuation and financial reporting with auditing.

## 1.2 To Lasting Peace and Prosperity

Humans may establish and secure their prosperity in peace through the law. Practical reason therefore strives for lasting peace and avoids the destructive germ of injustice. For Immanuel Kant, this culminates in the following duty: Act in a such way that you can want your maxim to become general law (so-called categorical imperative – German original: *Kategorischer Imperativ*); thus everlasting peace is not an empty idea, but an continuous task for each and everyone.[6] This confidence in a moral predisposition towards goodness in humans, to conquer evil, was extended by Albert Schweitzer with regard to all our relations to our environment as "veneration for life" (*Ehrfurcht vor dem Leben*).[7] Law, meaningless, id est non-existent without ethics, is established as practised ethics. Substance and sustainability go hand in hand with this (see 2.2.3).

Muir Woods, the forest of gigantic redwoods on California's Pacific coast north of San Francisco, still conveys this sense of life. There, giant trees rise into the sky that were already digging their tender roots into the ground before the time of the Magna Carta Libertatum (1215) and have since been seeking the sun. Steadfast witnesses, defying all storms and fires through time, demonstrating the force of life. A place of natural worship, where a person may feel unity as a whole and breathe a

[5]Phelps (2007). Cf., giving an introduction to ecological economics, Costanza, Cumberland, Daly et al. (2015). Basically Sen (2009), from p. XI (on Adam Smith and the "nature of the present economic crisis"). See chapters 6 to 9.

[6]Kant (1795), appendix II. [at the end].

[7]Schweitzer (1923), Kulturphilosophie I and II. On this Luttermann (1998) pp. 139-144, and Luttermann (2013). Cf. in historical perspective Nussbaum (2013), generally on the topic of luck (*Glück*) versus self-sufficiency (*Selbständigkeit*).

whiff of eternity. It was here that in May 1945 more than five hundred delegates from around fifty nations met in Cathedral Grove, a natural dome of living trees, for the first peace conference after the Second World War. This conference signed the Charter of the United Nations in San Francisco (Herbst Theatre, Civic Centre) on June 26, 1945.

This Charter of the United Nations (UN Charter), together with the International Court of Justice, encompasses our topic. It is about lasting peace and human rights, the interaction of different societies (equally sovereign states) in a system of balance of power (the "Westphalian system"),[8] and actually about a new world order (i.e., about war and peace, see esp. chapters 8 and 9). With the Universal Declaration of Human Rights (1948), the UN Charter forms *de lege lata* the basis for peace, after two World Wars had, within one human lifetime, brought "untold sorrow to mankind": A world constitution of law, to unite our strength to "maintain international peace and security" and "to develop friendly relations among nations based on respect for the principle of equal rights and self-determination of peoples".[9] In order to create "conditions of stability and well-being" for this goal, the United Nations, as Article 55 UN Charter in Chapter IX on "International Economic and Social Cooperation" put it, is to promote:

> "a. higher standards of living, full employment, and conditions of economic and social progress and development;
> b. solutions of international economic, social, health, and related problems; and international cultural and educational cooperation; and
> c. universal respect for, and observance of, human rights and fundamental freedoms for all without distinction as to race, sex, language, or religion."

This is our foundation, which sustains humans and their environment. All nations have pledged to fulfill these goals (Art. 56 UN Charter). This is the basis on which people may live and do business, develop ideas, form societies (partnerships, corporations) and cooperate. – The International Court of Justice (ICJ, The Hague), the highest world court, confirms this basically in its landmark decision of July 23, 2025[10] by expressively declaring the protection of human and environmental rights an international obligation. On request of the General Assembly of the United Nations from 2023,[11] it delivered an advisory opinion on "Obligations of states in respect of climate change", underscoring

[8] Designated after the peace treaties of Münster and Osnabrück, two cities in the German region of Westphalia, which ended the cruel Thirty Years' War (1618-1648) that had devastated large parts of Europe, so-called Peace of Westphalia (*Westfälischer Frieden*). See Kissinger (2015) pp. 3-4, 68; cf. Kampmann (2021).

[9] Art. 1 and Preamble.

[10] ICJ, Advisory Opinion: Obligation of states in respect of climate change (see https://www.icj-cij.org/sites/default/files/case-related/187/187-20250723-adv-01-00-en.pdf, and documents related to the procedure https://www.icj-cij.org/case/187, both accessed: 25.08.2025), jurisdiction in accordance with Art. 96 UN Charter and Art. 65 ICJ Statute ("legal question"). Basically below 1.6, 2.2 and Luttermann (1998) pp. 135-145, 465-485, Luttermann (2010a).

[11] UN General Assembly, Request for an advisory opinion, resolution 77/276 of 29.03.2023 (https://digitallibrary.un.org/record/4008332?v=pdf, accessed: 25.08.2025).

"the urgent and existential threat posed by climate change".[12] The Court, under the applicable international law,[13] materially focusses:

> "The Charter of the United Nations is a pillar of contemporary international law. Its purposes include achieving international co-operation in solving international problems of an economic, social, cultural or humanitarian character (Article 1). Climate change is a global problem which manifests itself in all these and other fields of concern for the United Nations."[14]

The Court continues that the "protection of the environment and the protection of human rights have been generally recognized as interdependent",[15] and that the climate system should be protected "for the benefit of present and future generations of humankind, on the basis of equity" (intergenerational equity);[16] likewise, the German Constitutional Court speaks of *Generationengerechtigkeit* (intertemporal justice).[17] Overall, it is – as the International Court of Justice puts it – about the legal consequences for "States" and with respect to "peoples and individuals", which are to be determined accordingly: in order to prevent significant environmental harm; due diligence (*gebotene Sorgfalt*) lege artis (i.e. according to "the best available science" and technological information and measures),[18] and the duty to cooperate apply (see 6.1). The International Court of Justice, in its advisory opinion on climate change as "an existential problem of planetary proportions", concludes:

> "A complete solution to this daunting, and self-inflicted, problem requires the contribution of all fields of human knowledge, whether law, science, economics or any other." And the Court expresses "the hope that its conclusions will allow the law to inform and guide social and political action to address the ongoing climate crisis."[19]

Around the globe, this is the field for human corporation, economy and environment (juridical analysis).[20] A universe of diversity in unity, for imagination and fair competition through reliable information, id est financial reporting and valuation in terms of

---

[12] ICJ, Advisory Opinion, ibid., para. 73. More details below 6.1.1.

[13] Charter of the United Nations, Climate change treaties (UNFCCC, Kyoto Protocoll, Paris Agreement: see below 1.4.2), UN Convention on the Law of the Sea, other environmental treaties, customary international law etc., see ICJ, Advisory Opinion, 23.07.2025, ibid., paras. 113-173.

[14] ICJ, Advisory Opinion, 23.07.2025, ibid., para. 115.

[15] ICJ, Advisory Opinion, 23.07.2025, ibid., para. 144, referring to the Stockholm Declaration of 1972 and to the Paris Agreement; on that see below 1.4.2.

[16] ICJ, Advisory Opinion, 23.07.2025, ibid., paras. 155-157 (referring to the UNFCCC and to the Paris Agreement, on both see below 1.4.2) and paras. 161, 374.

[17] German Bundesverfassungsgericht (BVerfG), 29.04.2021 (1 BvR 2656 et al.), ECLI:DE:BVerfG:2021:rs20210324.1bvr265618; on this below 1.4.2.

[18] See ICJ, Advisory Opinion, 23.07.2025, ibid., paras. 280-289, 347, also, e.g., paras. 136-137, 214, 254 and 347 with 158, 180, and 293-294 (precautionary principle); also below, e.g., 1.4.2, 4.2.2, 6.1 and chapter 9.

[19] Overall ICJ, Advisory Opinion, 23.07.2025, ibid., para. 456. Cf. basically Luttermann (1998) pp. 135-145, 465-485, and Luttermann (2010a): juridical analysis of the economy, state and society, see below, e.g. 1.6, 6.7.3, 7.3.2 and 8.2.2 with chapter 9.

[20] Ibid.

sustainability (*Nachhaltigkeit*, see 2.2.3, also 4.11.4, 5.2.4). In order to promote lasting peace and general prosperity, complementarily as climate partners (*Klimapartner*).[21] The issue is the development of good governance, finance and valuation for sustainable value creation (*Wertschöpfung*). Again, we need not re-invent the wheel, id est the corporation, but we do need to learn how to use it with reason. That is what human corporation, sustainable finance and financial reporting are about.

## 1.3 Reporting for Business: Corporation, Finance, and Networking

### *1.3.1 Capital, Competition, and Confidence*

Promote common values rather than purely private profits: Is it about squaring the circle? – The economic mind is a vivid element of our civilisation. This source feeds prosperity and progress, ideas of business. However, without capital, an idea merely remains an idea. Basically, we are dealing with practical company financing (*Unternehmensfinanzierung*). People transform ideas into practice in projects and enterprises (corporations). These are financed with capital. Linguistically, the word derives from Latin *caput*,[22] *capitis*, meaning main sum, stock, in contrast to payments made on this in the case of utilization by third parties. In general, capital is thus a sum of money meant to show a profit (dividend, interest) and given for this purpose; in terms of sustainability, it should be real money in substance (*Substanz*, cf. on fiat money 1.4.3).

In the form of corporate financing, this denotes the quintessence of market economy with the contractually agreed share in entrepreneurial success (profit, loss). In the market, entrepreneurs (*Unternehmer*) compete with their ideas and business models (*Geschäftsmodellen*) for the – best possible – financing of their enterprise (project). Investors are in search of investment objects, id est opportunities with the best possible return (return on investment). Overall, the issue is assets (*Vermögenswerte*), questions of valuation and reporting, on the optimal allocation of limited resources through acquisitiveness (*Erwerbsstreben*). If capital is invested, this is therefore done out of self-interest, while at the same time the general good is promoted. This is described as

[21] Luttermann (2022): climate partners of a cooperative world asset order (*Weltvermögensordnung*), see below, e.g., 6.1, and esp. chapters 8 and 9.

[22] Cf. from ancient India the Sanskrit word *kapalam* (कपलम्, Ved. a half, a part [https://sanskritdictionary.com], *Kapalam* కపాలం noun: Skull [https://dictionary.tuteehub.com], German *Schädel*). See also in English the term "live stock" (*lebendes Inventar, Viehbestand*) used in agriculture, which is quantified by the number of heads in a herd.

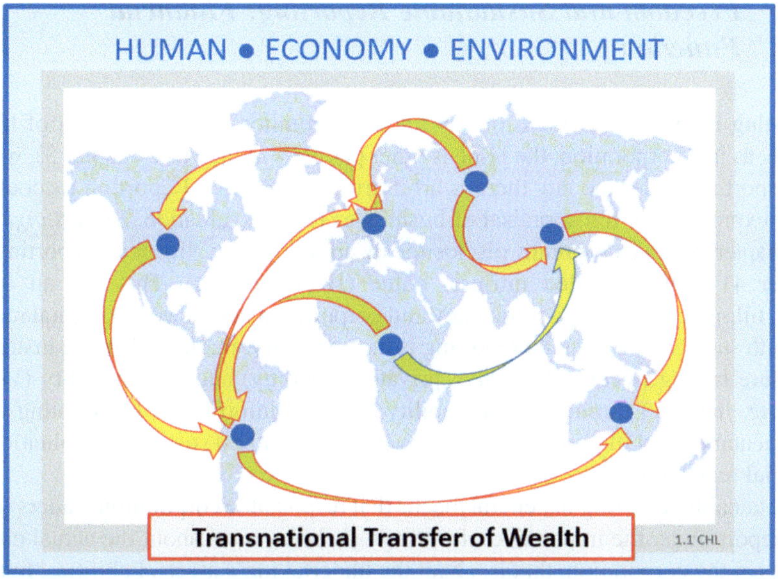


**Fig. 1.1** Business activities (corporations) and global transfer of risk and wealth

the "invisible hand" by Adam Smith,[23] by everyone promoting the greatest possible gain on his occupation. Own profit, whatever that may be, continues to have a particularly motivating effect and serves both the cause of freedom and the common good.

This is integrated into the constitution of liberty, a culture of responsibility (*Verantwortungskultur*). Basically, it is about participation in prosperity, both on a small scale (the autonomous individual) and on a large scale (the national economy, *Volkswirtschaft*): the transfer of wealth and risk (see Fig. 1.1).[24] Capital markets worldwide are orderly events (*geordnete Veranstaltungen*, see 2.6.1). Investors provide the money on a contractual basis for investment purposes, not short-term speculation. Investors place it at the disposal of the entrepreneur or corporation they can trust.[25] In practice, capital in short means: real money plus trust. Corporation leaders build trust through substantial business, the transaction and success – actual and potential – of which is sustainably documented (corporate disclosure). Sustainable reporting on the result (profit or loss) of business activity is key for successful entrepreneurs (investors) and corporations. In fair competition, the business and its success depend on sustainable reporting (valuation).

---

[23] Smith (1776/1789[5]) pp. 571-573 (chapter II).

[24] Overall with 1.4.3, 1.6.2, 8.4.2 and chapter 2. Basically on the order of assets (*Vermögensordnung*) and transfer of wealth and risk Luttermann (2012) and (2015a). See also chapters 8 and 9.

[25] See below 1.5.2, Luttermann (2010b) and chapter 6.

### *1.3.2 Freedom and Sustainable Reporting: Financial Function*

Reporting is the core element of any legal community as a constitution of liberty. Where, as in a corporation, the issue is other people's money (see chapter 3), without true reporting under the law there is arbitrariness (*Willkür*). Reporting (accounting) as the expression of the appraisal of businesses (law of valuation, *Bewertungsrecht*, see chapter 5) and corporate disclosure (accounting law, financial reporting, see chapter 4) treats so-called intrinsic value (*Werthaltigkeit*). This has an overall effect, filling the forms of contract law and corporation law as well as capital markets law with substance. Financial reporting is the necessary, market-adequate instrument to ensure lasting freedom (*Freiheit*, private autonomy) and responsibility (*Verantwortung*, liability) through accountability: verified information (accounting as the documentary proof of good corporate governance),[26] id est sustainable valuation and financial reporting.

Sustainable reporting in general means that responsible corporation leaders (directors) report under the imperative of truth (*Wahrheitsgebot*) about the actual circumstances of the corporation, that is, about the undertaking's assets, liabilities, financial position and profit or loss. With the questions of valuation (*Bewertungsfragen*), this naturally includes the environmental and human rights situation, that is, ecological and social aspects. What is decisive with the actual circumstances are simply facts in the sense of the law of evidence (*Beweisrecht*). It is essential that the existence, the law of the corporation and its economic development (e.g., restructuring, mergers & acquisitions) are shaped by valuation and accounting law: This determines *what* is valued as assets and *how*. That is the quintessence (*Inbegriff*) of a corporation as a legal person. It is only in this way that the corporation becomes comprehensible in its existence as a legal person (see 3.1 and chapter 4) and responsibly manageable in its business operations.

The corporation is a form of financing, a financial instrument. It brings together investors as shareholders (equity) and creditors (debt) in the same boat: a community of chance and risk, i.e. a venture community (*Wagnisgemeinschaft*), the seating plan of which is arranged according to profit (chance) and loss (risk) by the law in form of contracts. Accordingly, the investors finance the corporation (financial function). Sustainable reporting, id est reliable valuation and information, builds the necessary trust in the – generally anonymous – capital markets, on the basis of which the investors can make their decision in a fair comparison of the competitors (corporations).[27] This is what keeps the market alive. Through sustainable financial reporting, it becomes an efficient instrument of resource allocation. Sustainability basically means: factual verifiability of the information (valuation) in the sense of truth (*Wahrheit*, see 1.4.1, 2.6.3).

---

[26] See below, e.g. 8.3.2 and already Luttermann, in each case the chapter 7, in du Plessis, Großfeld, Luttermann et al. (2007), 1st ed., (2012), 2nd ed., and (2017), 3rd ed.

[27] See below 2.4.2.

### 1.3.3 Cooperation and Digital Networking

It is particularly under the conditions of competition that co-operation can be advantageous. People are diverse with regard to their talents and possibilities. Together, it is possible, as the idiom goes, to "move mountains" which otherwise would seem insurmountable (see complementarity, chapter 9). Speaking in terms of political regulation, this is the idea of subsidiarity, which the European Union is based on: The larger unit (only) provides support where the task makes demands on the smaller unit that it cannot fulfill (Art. 5 TEU). The principle of capacity building (*Hilfe zur Selbsthilfe*) is formed in co-operation: it supports the individual economically through partially co-operative business operations (e.g. production, purchase or sales). This optimizes the power of free entrepreneurs and the whole in the form of a network; recently also globally in the "disrupting digital business" and the so-called "token economy" (e.g., DAOs, see 3.7).[28]

From an evolutionary point of view, it is the common purpose (*gemeinsamer Zweck*) that makes a corporation or partnership. Formalised under corporate law, this common purpose determines the contractual relation of the rights and obligations of the individual towards the whole. Originally, there was a comprehensive partnership of life, economy and assets that was based on familiarity (*Vertraulichkeit*, Lat. *familiaritas*): the family (kin, *Sippe*) with one coffer (*Kasse*) to which all members contributed and from which the common needs were met. From this, partially co-operative societies developed, including outsiders (non-kin, *Nichtverwandte*), where the own assets (capital) were insufficient. This kind of community then assumes a separate existence, with the economic purpose overriding the personal ties. Consensual communities of interest evolve, with promotional capital contribution (fund assets, *Sondervermögen*) serving the stipulated purpose (undertaking, corporation; see in more detail 2.3.3 and 3.7).[29]

Information, formal bookkeeping (*Buchführung*) and reporting (accounting, financial reporting) thus becomes necessary: towards the external investors for profit (and loss) sharing in separate asset spheres, in particular in the legal person (corporation), which is impersonally designed (French *société anonym*), but for which responsible human involvement is indispensable (see 7.3.1). Although increasing financing through debt (leveraging) shifts the weight to the detriment of the non-shareholders, financial theory and practice curtail valuation to the advantage of the shareholders (so-called "shareholder value"). What is lost out of focus is the fact that as a community of venture (*Wagnisgemeinschaft*), designed for the longer term, the investors of a corporation are sitting in the same boat, so to speak; and in the final instance all of us are "lenders of last

[28] See also 1.5.3 and 1.6.1, cf. 8.5. About perspectives chapter 9.

[29] See on the principle of separation (*Trennungsprinzip*) below 1.4.1, 2.4.3 and 3.6.5. Altogether Luttermann (1998), from p. 135, pp. 148-176 and from 177. Cf. below in 7.4.1 (USA).

resort". This is proven by the global crises in environment, human rights and finance,[30] the solution of which requires and demands sustainable co-operation (networking).

## 1.4 Climate Change: Corporations, Catastrophes, and Chances

### *1.4.1 Work of Man: Realities of the Corporate Fiction*

We are dealing with the work of man (*Menschenwerk*), entrepreneurship (*Unternehmertum*) and scientific insights. The creative mind can do good if it is – in a constitution of liberty – based on reason and responsibility (cf. Greek *phrónesis*, *Vernünftigkeit*, see 9.1). This motif provides the confidence to master the challenges of any time and to take hold of its chances and opportunities. This comprises the development of entrepreneurial instruments such as the corporation, global financial markets and co-operative structures. Embedded in an order of liberty, in order to shape the changes necessary in the face of elementary crises in a fair and sustainable way. For liberty, Schiller wrote, also requires its master:[31] an entrepreneurial culture of responsibility, which can be practised by everybody and is guaranteed by a reasonable system of financial reporting (accounting, auditing, i.e. valuation law – *Bewertungsrecht*).

This makes the corporation an ingenious construction: As a legal person (fiction, *Fiktion*, also so-called juridical person), it cannot be seen, but only grasped in its accounting view[32] in the assets legally assigned to it (*Sondervermögen*, see 1.3.3 and chapter 4). As a creation of the law, the corporation cross-culturally unites generally three structural principles:[33]

(1) Entrepreneurs as human beings (natural persons) wanting to take opportunities while reasonably limiting the risks are first and foremost offered limitation of liability through the corporation as a legal person (*Juristische Person*, principle of separation).[34]

[30] Basically Luttermann (2008) and (2010a).

[31] German original by Friedrich Schiller (1781), 1. act, 2. scene: "Auch die Freiheit muss ihren Herrn haben".

[32] More details below 2.4.2, 3.1 and chapters 4 and 5.

[33] More details below 2.4.3. On the origin of the legal person as a kind of "replica" (*Nachbildung*) of the natural person (*Mensch*) see below 7.3.1.

[34] Note that the principle of separation is not unbreakable (e.g., "piercing the corporate veil") and is a rather recent development, which traditionally hardly applied (see, e.g., 3.6.2, 3.2.3 and 1.3.3). On the basic problem of periodisation (instead of a total balance – *Gesamtbilanz*) and definite distributions in the case of a corporation see 3.6.4.

(2) At the same time, risks can be divided, in particular in consolidation (*Konzernbildung*), through the proliferation of legal entities (multiple legal subjectivity, multipersonality).
(3) The corporation is the eternal asset holder (*ewiger Vermögensträger*), an enduring entrepreneurial form of organisation ("immortality", permanence).

This shows the ingenious financial character – the financial function (see 1.3.2) – of the modern corporation (joint-stock company, *Aktiengesellschaft*): Through stock market listing (*Börsennotierung*, so-called publicly held corporation), the corporation transforms the short-term capital of many investors into long-term financing for important businesses (corporations). The company's financing is secured, while individual investors are free to withdraw their capital (investment) by selling their shares (stocks, see 2.5.1). This kind of ingenious sustainability (conversion) provides a solid financial basis for sustainable projects, for modern corporation (i.e. the human corporation). Especially as the aforementioned conversion (transformation of time periods) also applies in principle to marketable debt securities. The bondholder "is distinctly an investor",[35] too, and so are investors in hybrid financial instruments (see 8.3.2). Overall, we see and speak of the so-called *Wagnisgemeinschaft* (venture community, see 1.3.2).

Corporate business thus takes many forms and may be used in different ways. A wide field, for good or evil. We all know that fire may make life warm or destroy it. What is crucial is responsible action, here of the corporate leaders. The "visible hand", described by Alfred Chandler as "the managerial revolution in American business",[36] works globally: In our world of global capital economy with much light and darkness, gigantic wealth and huge poverty, fascinating technological progress and devastating power of destruction. It is time to change direction. Corporations and financial markets are no phenomena on another planet. The insights of our civilisation have to be utilised for the whole. Humankind is facing at least two existential challenges, the so-called global financial crisis and climate change; let us take a look at the latter first.

### 1.4.2 Science and Liberty: Climate Protection as an Existential Task

The basic issue is the preservation of the existence and liberty of humans. Earth offers us the natural resources. This is powerfully described by Sally Ride, astrophysics expert and astronaut. The earth is surrounded by a really thin royal-blue line,

[35] See already Isaacs (1923) 201, at 210, Uhlman (1938) and McDaniel (1988). Luttermann (1998) pp. 21-23, 145-162 and 471-485 (also from p. 327: corporate debt relationships, relational contract), Luttermann (2003) Einf BilanzR recitals 26-43. See also below 3.5.4 and, on the liable capital (*Haftkapital*), 3.6 (esp. 3.6.5).

[36] On the visible hand Chandler (1977). See Fig. 2.1.

the earth's atmosphere; this is its and our spacesuit: "about as thick as the fuzz on a tennis ball. So narrow, a strong gust of interplanetary wind could blow it all away … it's everything that separates us from the vacuum of space. If we didn't have that atmosphere, we wouldn't be here, and if we do anything to destroy that atmosphere, we won't be here."[37] – This refers to the effect of the anthropogenic greenhouse emissions, in particular through the use of fossil fuels. In its Article 2, the Paris Agreement from 2015, following the United Nations Framework Convention on Climate Change (UNFCCC 1994), specifies:[38]

> "1. This Agreement, in enhancing the implementation of the Convention, including its objective, aims to strengthen the global response to the threat of climate change, in the context of sustainable development and efforts to eradicate poverty, including by:
> (a) Holding the increase in the global average temperature to well below 2°C above pre-industrial levels and pursuing efforts to limit the temperature increase to 1.5°C above pre-industrial levels, recognizing that this would significantly reduce the risks and impacts of climate change;
> (b) Increasing the ability to adapt to the adverse impacts of climate change and foster climate resilience and low greenhouse gas emissions development, in a manner that does not threaten food production; and
> (c) *Making finance flows consistent with a pathway towards low greenhouse gas emissions and climate-resilient development.*[39]
> 2. This Agreement will be implemented to reflect equity and the principle of common but differentiated responsibilities and respective capabilities, in the light of different national circumstances."

This is demanded by reason: the enlightened man, progressing in his thirst for knowledge, makes use of the best possible insights in a holistic way. With the epochal turning point of Nicolaus Copernicus (1473–1543), who introduced our heliocentric view of the world,[40] investigation of nature and the critical mind of the modern era arose, which are still bearing us on today. – *Sapere aude!* – This is, expressed in the once common European language of Latin, the light of all women and men, for all people, born equal and free; expressed in English: Have courage and make use of your own reason; and it is the law, that "has seen the beginning of an evolution toward recognition of the inherent

---

[37] Ride, quoted after: Sherr (2014) pp. 310 and 311.

[38] Source: https://unfccc.int/sites/default/files/english_paris_agreement.pdf. On the 17 Sustainable Development Goals (SDGs) of the United Nations below 8.5, on the meaning of "sustainability" (*Nachhaltigkeit*) below 2.2.3. With chart on the regulatory structure of transnational climate protection law from a European perspective Luttermann (2003) recitals 17-47 (25). See ICJ, 23.07.2025, above 1.2.

[39] Here highlighted in italics by the author. See the UN environment programme (UNEP) finance initiative with Principles for Responsible Investment (PRI) and the Net-Zero Asset Owner Alliance (NZAOA: www.unepfi.org/net-zero-alliance); also the Principles for Responsible Banking (PRB: www.unepfi.org/banking/bankingprinciples, both accessed: 25.08.2025). Cf. European Union, e.g., the Corporate Sustainability Reporting Directive (EU) 2022/2464 (CSRD), see chapter 4, and the Corporate Sustainability Due Diligence Directive (EU) 2024/1760. Overall Luttermann (2021) and esp. chapters 2, 3, 6 and 7.

[40] Copernicus (1543), De revolutionibus orbium coelestium.

rights of Nature to exist, thrive and evolve".[41] Science and its faculties with discipline offer us the common basis to comprehend (*ergründen*), to bring something into order (*etwas in eine Ordnung bringen*), to conclude (*schlussfolgern*) and in particular to uncover errors. Initially, of course, what propels us is an aspiration: What is true?

This question, naturally hand in hand with the idea of justice (*Gerechtigkeit*), stirs the human soul. It also refers to the actual circumstances (*tatsächliche Verhältnisse*, facts). As the imperative for truth (*Gebot der Wahrheit*), it provides the measure for our life circumstances with nature, markets and corporations, in economy and law (accounting law), for good corporations, financing and leadership. The enlightened human being continues to ask questions and to investigate. The protection of our environment is part of this. Globally, reasons and effects of climate change are being investigated by scientists and assessed, among others, by the UN Intergovernmental Panel on Climate Change (IPCC) as a whole.[42] Science, not fear-mongering, facilitates reasonable solutions. Greenhouse gas emissions are, according to current knowledge, to be regarded as harmful and predominantly irreversible, to the detriment of global warming. This is the reason for the transition to the carbon neutrality of economy and society.[43]

The European Union has led the way, aspiring to create the first carbon-neutral continent by 2050. To this end, the European Union has announced the "Green Deal" (2019), establishing a valuation system based on the law of capital markets, with reporting obligations, intended – in the sense of Article 2 No 1c Paris Agreement[44] – to direct investment in "green" financial instruments.[45] This demonstrates – along with all the questions to be asked – the core function of sustainable reporting for the human corporation, for the so-called "ecological-social transformation of economy and society" (see 4.2.3, 4.11.4). Good governance, finance and valuation for a better world. The European Commission introduced the "Clean Industrial Deal" (2025), a bold "business plan" that "brings together climate action and competitiveness under one overarching growth strategy".[46] All of this has to be included in the constitution of

---

[41] UN, Harmony with Nature: Rights of Nature Law and Policy, with multifarious examples, also on Nature as a special "entity" (legal personality *sui generis*, see: http://www.harmonywithnatureun.org/rightsOfNature/, accessed: 25.08.2025). See below 6.1. Basically on reason Kant (1784).

[42] Basically ICJ, Advisory Opinion, 23.07.2025, see above 1.2; current: www.ipcc.ch.

[43] Ibid., cf. above Art. 2 No. 1. (c) of the Paris Agreement 2015. See in the USA the opposite standpoint of the Trump administration: U.S. President, Executive Order "Putting America first in international environmental agreements", Jan. 20, 2025 (www.whitehouse.gov), to withdraw from the Paris Agreement of 2015, joining Iran, Libya and Yemen as the only countries worldwide outside the agreement; cf. the withdrawal from the Paris Agreement during President Trump's first term in office, 04.11.2019 (https://2017-2021.state.gov/on-the-u-s-withdrawal-from-the-paris-agreement, accessed: 25.08.2025). See also below 6.7.2 (SEC Climate Disclosure Rules), 8.2.3. and 8.4.3.

[44] See quote above.

[45] See 1.5.3 and 2.2.1 on the EU taxonomy, a classification system for so-called "sustainable business activities" (*nachhaltige Wirtschaftsaktivitäten*). Luttermann, L. (2025) with a European opening balance (*Eröffnungsbilanz*) for 2023 on the transformation process.

[46] EU Commission, The Clean Industrial Deal: a joint roadmap for competitiveness and decarbonisation, 26.02.2025, COM(2025) 85 final, 1. Introduction. Cf. Draghi report: The future of European competitiveness, 09.09.2024.

liberty. For the European Union, the common values in the humanistic sense are laid down with the rule of law (*Rechtsstaatlichkeit*), subsidiarity and self-responsibility (Art. 2 to 6 TEU).

An almighty central power (*Zentralgewalt*) is thus irreconcilable even with the noble goal of climate protection (principle of reasonableness, see 1.1).[47] Experience has shown that cooperation (subsidiarity and complementarity, see chapter 9) works better than a commanding intelligence. Young and future generations must be included. The Climate Change Act (*Klimaschutzgesetz*) laid down by the German legislator after the Paris Agreement was sharpened by the German Federal Constitutional Court (*Bundesverfassungsgericht*), along with the United Nations IPCC emissions budget: the timely reduction of carbon emissions (greenhouse gas, GHG) is necessary to guarantee the liberty of the generations to come (*Generationengerechtigkeit*, inter-temporal justice).[48] That sounds good. Living at others' cost (debt mentality) is not an option for a human community. However, how reliable are insights hitherto regarding the rule of law overall?

### 1.4.3 Economy and Greed: Global Financial (Debt) Crisis

Humans and their environment have moved to the centre of consciousness, where they belong and where they always were, albeit widely ignored. Even today in practice fatally and systematically dwarfed to so-called "consumers" (*Verbraucher* from Latin *consumere* for to consume, deplete, destroy).[49] Humans in their dignity, however, are beings working, thinking and doing business for their existence and progress. In the diversity of life, what is coming to the forefront is the massive economisation of practically all life domains, directly or indirectly, through financial markets (pension plans, property management, currencies, debt and interest policies etc.) This is accompanied by religiously loaded fundamentalism, as, e.g., a key player of the financial industry simply placarded: banks serve a social purpose and are "doing God's work".[50] – Are we falling back behind Enlightenment with such strays?

---

[47] Leading the way Brandeis, dissenting, in *Olmstead v. U.S.*, 277 U.S. 438, 479 (1928), see below 8.2.3. Cf. controversial U.S. President Donald Trump, who "has chosen", as Kagan, J. (with whom Sotomayor and Jackson, JJ., join), dissenting, in *Trump v. Wilcox*, 605 U.S. ___ (2025), writes, "to take the law in his own hands" and not "leaving to this Court the prerogative of overruling its own decisions"; on this below 8.2.3 (with more references). See also below 6.7.2 and 7.7.

[48] German Bundesverfassungsgericht (BVerfG), 29.04.2021 (1 BvR 2656 et al.), ECLI:DE:BVerfG:2021:rs20210324.1bvr265618. Now also ICJ, Advisory Opinion, 23.07.2025 (https://www.icj-cij.org/sites/default/files/case-related/187/187-20250723-adv-01-00-en.pdf, accessed: 25.08.2025) paras. from 155, 161 (intergenerational equity), see above 1.2.

[49] See on that in more detail 2.2.2. Already Luttermann (2015c) 805, 809-10.

[50] Lloyd Blankfein, CEO and Chairman Goldman Sachs Group, Inc., 09.11.2009, quoted from: https://dealbook.nytimes.com/2009/11/09/goldman-chief-says-he-is-just-doing-gods-work/?mcubz=1 (accessed: 25.08.2025). Overall see chapter 6 (esp Figs. 6.1 and 6.3) and chapter 9.

This has long been taking place in the global "financial crisis" (*Weltschuldenkrise*). An outgrowth of the financial industry and the so-called "modern" corporation, led by the creed of "creating shareholder value".[51] In short: humans acting in an uncontrolled way as the creators of values – but only for the select group of "shareholders" with ruthless behavior in the pursuit of personal profit. This is in the focus of our considerations. In neoclassical financial theory and capital market practice, the instrument is systematically the valuation vehicle of the added so-called "fair value" (more precisely: "shareholder value").[52] With huge leeway for valuation practically through the uncontrollable inclusion of the future, that is, of arbitrarily shaped expectations (hopes), which, presented in mathematical formulas, in fact have the appearance of being exact: the same corporation in this way can easily be presented as being far more valuable. Such hope values (*Hoffnungswerte*) are widespread in the practice of great numbers of manipulated figures (*Zahlenwerke*) called "financial reporting" – till the great breakdown.[53]

We are currently experiencing this in the enduring world debt crisis (*Weltschuldenkrise*, so-called "financial crisis"). A systematic disaster economy, reducing humans to a purposefully rational economic creature (*homo oeconomicus*), as has become clear since the fall of the investment bank Lehman Brothers Holdings, Inc. (September 15, 2008): Gigantic debts (leveraging), phony financial instruments with global securitisation chains and pyramid systems (derivates, Ponzi schemes), masses of admittances (toxic assets) in the accounts of corporations, central banks, shadow banks and other rubbish dumps (see chapter 6). Systematic valuation manipulation (*Bewertungsmanipulation*), the unscrupulous actors of which produce ridiculous profits. The coup is: Profits are privatised, losses socialised to the detriment of states, *vulgo* their liable citizens (tax payers, savers). The politics of boundless debts and insubstantial monetarisation (fiat money) with quantitative easing (inflation, high-debt deficit spending) and – tendentially – zero or even negative interest act dominant.

Basically, this is a variety of age-old greed, wisely described by John Kenneth Galbraith in his "Short history of financial euphoria". Highlighting the "brevity of the financial memory", he focuses: "The world of finance hails the invention of the wheel over and over again, often in a slightly more unstable version. All financial innovation involves, in one form or another, the creation of debt secured in greater or lesser adequacy by real assets."[54] This means the infinite reappearance of uncontrolled leverage. With this, abuse becomes tangible. Through the corporation and its financial constructions and policies, profits (real assets) and losses (liability) are transferred in an inappropriate but efficient way among the capital investors. A gigantic transfer of

---

[51] Book of the same name by Rappaport (1986), 2nd ed. (1997).

[52] Basically Luttermann (2009) and chapter 6. Overall Bernstein (1993).

[53] Luttermann (2006) and Luttermann (2010b). See below, esp. chapters 4 to 7.

[54] Galbraith (1994) p. 19. Cf. Stiglitz (2010) and Tooze (2019) with details on the "world financial crisis" since 2008; see also below, e.g., 1.5.2.

assets (*Vermögenstransfer*, wealth), in the last instance to the detriment of the whole. This awareness offers great opportunities for the good.

## 1.5 Human Corporation: From Fictions to Facts for Sustainable Finance and Valuation

### *1.5.1 Valuation Law for Good Governance*

Corporations as a form of organisation (legal entity, *Rechtsträger*) for economic activity are globally a multifaceted phenomenon for permanent enterprises (companies) and specific projects (project companies). What stands out is corporate governance as the essence of the allocation of legal powers within the "modern corporation". In theory and practice shaped globally in the way of neoclassical economics, its main focus is on the powers of the corporate directors and of shareholders interest,[55] making the model of shareholder primacy predominant with its creation of "shareholder value" (i.e. short-term profit maximisation) as generally so-called "fair value". In contrast, the interests of the bondholders and of various other corporate groups (stakeholders) seem marginal, including a liberal "social entity" concept (long-term prosperity).

Both perspectives illustrate the ongoing discourse regarding the nature of the corporation, usually phrased as: "What is a corporation?" – This is not a formal legal question, to an even lesser degree are technical questions of financing or economics implied. Rather, as the reference to different interests shows, what is important is *what* is expected of a corporation. This depends on standpoint and perspective, on awareness. Capitalist acquisitiveness (*Erwerbsstreben*) operates in the web of relationships between economy and state as the relevant institutions.[56] The perspective changes with the position taken. William T. Allen sums it up in the following way: "in defining what we suppose a public corporation to be, we implicitly express our view of the nature and purpose of our social life. Since we do disagree on that, our law of corporate entities is bound itself to be contentious and controversial."[57] – So, does this mean that the field and the consequences remain curtailed by the mighty, capricious so-called "zeitgeist"?

[55] Outstanding Michigan Supreme Court case *Dodge v. Ford Motor Co.*, 204 Mich. 459, 507 (Mich. 1919), 170 NW 668: "A business corporation is organized and carried on primarily for the profit of the stockholders. The powers of the directors are to be employed for that end." See *Revlon v. MacAndrews & Forbes Holdings, Inc.*, 506 A.2d 173, 182 (Del.Supr. 1986), and Lipton (2025) on "shareholder primacy". Cf. Hansmann and Kraakman (2001) on "the end of history for corporate law".

[56] Cf. in the classic discourse Riechers (1996).

[57] Allen (1992) 261, 281. Allen was the Chancellor of the Delaware Court of Chancery (1985-1997). See above, e.g., 1.2, also below 2.1, 3.8 and 6.1.

In any case, reason and awareness demand focusing the valuation of the corporation in the legal sense, as will be elaborated on for the human corporation later in this book with its essential financing function (*Finanzierungsfunktion*).[58] This means that the law, especially the traditional corporate law and capital markets law, need to be adequately designed and measured in a new way with the idea of law (*Rechtsidee*). This may initially come as a surprise as the financing of a company (corporate finance) and questions of valuation are usually regarded as a domain of economics and the world of numbers (e.g., accounting or financial reporting and auditing, rating, appraisal report), where jurisprudence has little to contribute.[59] This fails to recognise the essential, the content necessary for a sound order and fair business practice. In valuation, and probably there only, can we grasp the interests at work in a reasonable as well as a sustainable way and discipline them: from fictions to facts, the sound basis for sound business within a community organised in the unity of freedom and responsibility, id est "the constitution of liberty" (Hayek).

For only where, id est only when and insofar as the foundations of the valuation are made transparent and in particular binding standards (*Maßgaben*, norms) are set, can valuation be freed from arbitrariness and be what is required in legal relations: valuation as a legal act (*Rechtsakt*); this also applies to financial reporting and auditing (see 1.5.2). This is true overall, what is needed is a sound valuation law (*Bewertungsrecht*). To avoid any misunderstanding: From a market economy perspective, the parties to a contract are required to negotiate the value ratio (*Wertverhältnis*) of their performance and consideration (*Leistung und Gegenleistung*), expressed in the price (*Preis*). Questions of valuation also pertain to this for a corporation, but they also go beyond. As there is a general lack of market prices for many so-called "assets" (*Vermögenswerte*), arbitrariness reigns in financial reporting (accounting, auditing) as well as in appraisal reports (*Bewertungsgutachten*) and the like without valuation law. In their famous focus on "The modern corporation and private property", Berle and Means talked about a "corporate system" as a "major social institution".[60] In this context, they called "control of accounting" a "powerful weapon", saying:

> "So long as accounting standards are not hardened, and the law does not impose any specific canons, directors and their accountants may frame their figures, within limits, much as they choose."[61]

Like Louis D. Brandeis already wrote in his famous book "Other people's money and how the bankers use it", the timeless insight: "the disclosure must be real" and to

---

[58] See below 2.6.3, 3.5.3 and 3.5.6.

[59] Cf. focused, interdisciplinary in the following, esp. chapters 3 to 5. Basically Luttermann (1998), esp. pp. 1-11, 135-145, and 465-485 (principle of reasonableness) and pp. 145-176 (corporation finance); in practice Luttermann (2023a) and Luttermann (2023b). See also below, e.g. 1.6, 2.6 (sustainability) with chapter 6 (global capital markets), 7.3 (corporate reality) and chapters 8 and 9. Cf. Mestmäcker (2007).

[60] Berle and Means (1932, 1967) p. 3.

[61] Berle and Means (1932, 1967) p. 182.

"be effective, knowledge of the facts must be actually brought home to the investor".[62] Otherwise, financial instruments of all types (equity, debt, hybrids, derivatives) – and thus, it should be emphasised, the corporate financial function itself – are, as Berle and Means put it, "substantially meaningless".[63] Berle and Means thus described the core content, not only the substance of corporate financing, but the substance of the modern corporation in general. At the same time, we see the requirements for a just, sound order for corporations and capital markets. In essence, it is about facts instead of fictions. This designates the core in both "good" and "bad". The lack of a meaningful valuation system opens paths for abuse right up to the persistent disaster economy, at the same time marking out the solution through a reasonable valuation law (*Bewertungsrecht*).

This is here undertaken with a legally sound, fact-based concept of sustainable financial reporting, which, however, requires essential change in thought and practice. Hitherto, so-called "corporation law" (*Gesellschaftsrecht*) has been regarded as the supreme discipline, generally in a narrowed perspective with regard to organisational law, without the crucial consideration of the financing and valuation of corporations, id est the material content of a corporation (so-called "accounting law", *Bilanzrecht*).[64] However, both belong together, like form and substance, legally and factually. This must be taken into focus, for sustainable entrepreneurship and fair competition, as well as against ideological usurpation and reduction of the corporation. Good governance builds on valuation law for the corporation, designed and established as a whole: a human corporation for entrepreneurs.

### 1.5.2 Individual Responsibility and Substance: A Concept of Trust

Basically, for a human corporation, i.e. good governance, finance and valuation, it is all about trust. This marks the beginning and the end in human relationships, which include corporate governance and finance as well as control. Confucius says that trust is the foundation on which true effectiveness initially becomes possible.[65] In life, trust grows through personal contact. In the – increasingly digital – world of business, this is lacking, in particular in global capital markets and in the anonymity of the corporation and its financiers (stockholders, bondholders). This is treated in the scope of the principal-agent theory, transcending economics and institutional studies anywhere that

---

[62] Brandeis (1914) p. 104.

[63] Berle and Means (1932, 1967) p. 183. See below 8.3.2.

[64] Cf. relevant books as well as courses (programmes) at law faculties: accounting law (financial reporting, auditing), appraisal of businesses or the like hardly features there at all. See below, e.g., 3. 5.1, 7.3, 8.3.1 and chapters 4 and 5. In interdisciplinary perspectives Berle (1938) and (1928), Großfeld (2000), Luttermann (1996), Großfeld and Luttermann (2005).

[65] Confucius, Analects (Lunyü), book XIX, 10. Cf. Fig. 1.2.

problems of information have an effect (e.g., asymmetry, moral hazard, agency costs): classically in the separation of ownership and control with theories of property rights, finance (capital or ownership structure) and management in the corporation (joint-stock companies).[66]

Reporting is the key for trust-building (*Vertrauensbildung*), but is widely neglected. Reporting, shaped in a sustainable way in the sense of the imperative of truth (see chapter 4), provides reliable information on the situation of the assets and liabilities (*Vermögenslage*), financial position (*Finanzlage*) and profit or loss (*Ertragslage*) of the corporation. This information is the expression of personal responsibility: The corporation leaders (directors, *Rechnungsleger*) give account regarding the result, the situation and the perspectives of their business dealings in the reporting period up to the reporting date. The English word *report* (from Old French *raport* and Latin *re-portare*) means "give a formal account" – here as a fact-based disclosure to the investors that actually brings home the "knowledge of the facts" to be effective.[67] Reporting is a legal act, not a marketing event. Current law (valuation law) is meant to prevent succumbing to human weakness and make the figures seem better than they are in fact.[68] Sustainable reporting breaks through anonymity and serves to control power. It forms the basis for sustainable financing of sustainable economic activity (*nachhaltige Wirtschaftstätigkeit*) – both urgently needed.

Jurisprudence should integrate this into a comprehensive concept of trust (*Vertrauen*) and control (*Kontrolle*) for corporations and projects in the sense of sustainability, id est verifiability (*Nachprüfbarkeit*, see 5.2.4 and Fig. 1.2). With this, the complete field of financing undertakings (*Unternehmensfinanzierung*) must be ordered in a suitable way, in the last instance for a global order of assets (*Vermögensordnung*).[69] Thereby it becomes clear that in practice we are always dealing with a corporation as a juridical person (*company, corporation*), that is financed by private and/or public financiers, id est investors that need to be informed. A community of venture (*Wagnisgemeinschaft*) founded on contracts and capital. For marketable forms of financing (stocks, bonds, hybrids etc.), investors have to rely on an adequate general framework of protection within the complex power structure of the market in making use of their freedom of contract. The core of such a

[66] Jensen and Meckling (1976). Cf. U.S. President Franklin D. Roosevelt (Message from the President to the Congress, The White House, March 29, 1933, 73rd Congr., 1st Sess., Cong. Rec. – Senate 937) on "the ancient truth that those who manage banks, corporations, and other agencies handling or using other people's money are trustees acting for others." See overview in chapter 3.

[67] See above in 1.5.1 on Louis D. Brandeis (1914) p. 104; on this in more detail below, e.g. 3.3, 7.4.3 and 7.6.3 with chapters 4 and 5. On the meaning 2.4.2 (*re-portare*).

[68] Leffson (1987) pp. 152-153 and 55. Cf. Eisenberg (1976) p. 196.

[69] See below 1.6, 3.6.5 and chapter 8.

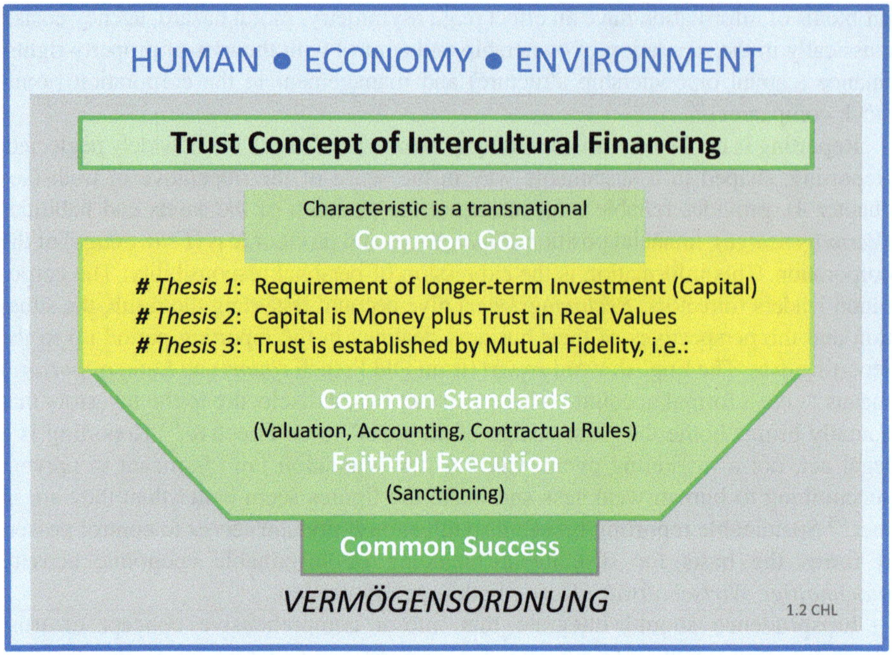


**Fig. 1.2** Human corporation, market and the trust concept of intercultural financing (*Vermögensordnung* – order of assets; in details chapter 5 and, interculturally, below, e.g. 1.6, 2. 2.2 with chapters 8 and 9. On the denotation of "asset" (*Vermögen*) see chapter 8 (footnote 3))

framework is a robust valuation law of the corporation for adequate information of the investors through financial reporting and auditing (real disclosure).[70]

This needs to be considered cross-culturally for a reasonable order of our world (see 1.6.3), which is in upheaval. The results of speculative manias and shortsighted disaster economics (*Katastrophenwirtschaft*), the timeless "financial euphoria"[71] – highlighted again in the so-called world financial crisis (*Weltschuldenkrise*) since 2008 by "the banks and their dangerous balance sheets" with "toxic or unsellable" assets[72] – prove, in particular in view of socio-ecological realities, first and foremost: the urgency of a fundamental reform towards a sustainable, substantial economy. Capital markets, enterprises (projects) and structures of financing are widely transnational in a multipolar world, id est intercultural. Within this framework, the human corporation works institutionally with limitation of liability, the necessary equivalent of which is increased transparency. Legal structures that are sustainable all-round

[70] See below 2.4.2 and 8.3.2. Luttermann, Claus (2003) Einf BilanzR recitals 29 and 26-43. Cf. Brandeis (1914) p. 10.

[71] Galbraith (1994). Comprehensive Aliber, Kindleberger, McCauley (2023). See also chapter 6.

[72] See, e.g., Tooze (2019), esp. chapter 13 (fixing finance) with the citations on pp. 291 and 315.

form the basis for developing sustainable financing globally – for corporations, cooperation and beyond.[73] Let us affirm the core elements (see Fig. 1.2):

(1) What is characteristic for a corporation or project and its responsible parties is a common purpose (in German so-called *gemeinsamer Zweck*).[74] In order to reach this goal, reasonably longer-termed financial means are necessary in the process of financing the corporation or project, id est: sustainable investments (capital, assets).
(2) Capital is, practically spoken, real money plus trust in real values.[75] This substance is characterised through its connection to values: Material assets (*Sachwerte*) like natural resources (precious metals, rare earths, water etc.) and technical know-how (e.g. patents) instead of the insubstantial business world with counterfeit money (fiat money), debt orgies and eventually fraudulent financial constructions.
(3) Trust is based on individual responsibility. This means personal trust and mutual fidelity (see 1.6.1). In widely anonymous structures (corporations, global capital markets, digitisation), trust is inevitably founded and preserved through the corporate directors on common standards (sound rules of valuation, accounting, contract), their faithful application (compliance) and control (auditing), if necessary also effective sanctions.

So, this is what must be developed: The human corporation, its good governance, finance and valuation demands faithful action in dealing with the money of other people in a sustainable order of assets (*Vermögensordnung*).[76] In Western legal tradition, this is provided through the practice according to the established rules of civil procedure (*Zivilprozess*). The court procedure (*Gerichtsverfahren*) always takes effect anyway (e.g., in an action for liability) in case of a dissent regarding the correctness (*Ordnungsmäßigkeit*) of a material valuation. This is what the action of the leaders responsible, id est each corporate director, is guided by legally, this is what they must adjust their business practices and their financial reporting to (so-called "compliance"). Truth is the imperative, built procedurally on facts and clear communication (see 4.12.3). Accordingly, the concept of trust (*Vertrauenskonzept*, see

[73] Overall chapters 8 and 9 with 3.7.

[74] See below 2.3.3, 3.7 and basically with historical development analysis tracing back to Roman law and embracing modern institutional economics (Coase, North) and contract law: Luttermann (1998) pp. 145-162. See also Luttermann (1998): financing corporations (pp. 163-176), equity in German accounting law (pp. 177-191) and in a comparative law analysis financing corporations in the USA (pp. 195-452) with: equity an hybrid securities (pp. 238-357) and accounting law (pp. 358-452).

[75] See below 2.7, 8.1 (the "common good") and chapter 6: banking on trust. Luttermann (2019) on trust and intercultural investment.

[76] See below 1.6 and 2.7.

Fig. 1.2) is conceived and implemented as civil-procedural valuation (*zivilprozessuale Bewertung*)[77] for a culture of responsibility.

### *1.5.3 Networks: On Human Prosperity in Digitised Societies*

The corporation thus fits into the world of modern networks for human prosperity. Cooperation shows itself in human history as a liberal idea for success. In digitised societies, it opens up new dimensions worldwide for individual and general prosperity. Digitisation creates new realities, alliances and networks through technical standards. Globally, this aims at information and communication, the safeguarding and exchange of data (e.g., distributed ledger technology, DLT), entrepreneurially across all traditional industries with digital business models (disrupting digital business).[78] It is about value chains (*Wertschöpfungsketten*) and transformation, but principally about power, id est the control of power. For what simply seems or is addressed as a "technical" standard soon turns out to be a yardstick, the new gatekeeper in a market. Artificial intelligence (AI), self-learning algorithms conquer fields, and may promote and challenge humans (e.g., corporate directors).[79]

The corporation, as a creation of the law itself a virtual reality (juridical person), is central here. A corporation comes into being, exists and decays according to valuation rules (*Bilanzstatut*).[80] Rules of valuation are a gigantic steering tool (*Lenkinstrument*) for global capital flows (see 4.8, 8.2.2). It is clear that for this reason the private so-called "IASB", a special interest organisation, strive for the establishment of its so-called "International Financial Reporting Standards" (IFRS) as the "global language of finance": A world monopoly of valuation.[81] The revolution of the empire of finance is driven technically. The magic formula is the "eXtensible Business Reporting Language" (XBRL). This computer language is the basis for electronic data transfer, gathers bookkeeping, accounting, and auditing. XBRL defines the structure of documents, classifies business relations and generates deals according to defined measures (taxonomies). Such hierarchies of presentation are displayed in specific systems of order such as the "IFRS".

---

[77] See below 4.6.4, 4.6.5 and 4.10.2, chapter 5. Founded in civil procedure Luttermann (2023b), esp. recitals 22-35 and, e.g., already Luttermann (2003) Einf BilanzR recital 2 and § 264 HGB recitals 20, 125-169.

[78] Cf. the work of the same title by Wang (2015). See also below, e.g., 3.7 on the network structure of a decentralised autonomous organisation (DAO).

[79] See below 9.6, 3.5.6 and chapter 6.

[80] See below 8.4.2. Fundamentally Luttermann (2015a).

[81] See below 4.11. Sunder (2010): "the *pied piper* of financial reporting"; cf. already (in March 2010) on "the monopoly question": Luttermann (2010c). Basically Luttermann (2011b); Luttermann (2023a) recitals 83-85 (and 86-100). See below 3.5.6 and overall chapter 4, esp. on regional "IFRS" 4.8.6 and 4.8.7 (European "IFRS").

The development has tremendous force, its developers gain unprecedented power. Information is recognised as a production factor besides the classical canon of land (natural resource), labor and capital – controlled by corporations as virtual gatekeepers.[82] Capital markets, economy and society as a whole are building on data exchange. Whoever determines the sign systems (*Zeichensysteme*), determines the content and hence thinking and acting. XBRL can be used with different programmes. In this respect, contents remain untouched. Readers of financial statements can access the data, e.g., for one's own balance sheet analysis (*Bilanzanalyse*). The technical form, however, only provides what its creators laid down in the design. At the same time, it creates pressure towards a uniform accounting world, in order to be compatible for data exchange with investors, suppliers, authorities. Accordingly, the taxonomy defines what data and contents a XBRL-instance gathers. With "XBRL/IFRS", a global standard for electronically based accounting and auditing, for information as such is established.

It is about the prosperity of the world, about us all: Who sets the standard of valuation? Who supervises? – The key question gains worldwide significance with the ecological transformation of economy and society. The private special interest organisation "IASB" here also turns to a monopoly: an "International Sustainability Standards Board" (ISSB) sets so-called "IFRS Sustainability Standards" ("IFRS S") operating "on the same footing as financial reporting".[83] The paradigm change towards sustainability of the economy in the European Union (EU), which is instrumentalising the financial system for this with its Green Deal, is supported by a "technically robust classification system" (the EU taxonomy): It is supposed to create clarity about which business activities count as "green" or "sustainable".[84] The components are so-called "technical valuation criteria". They are supposed to guarantee equal treatment of relevant business activities in certain sectors, if these contribute to one or more of the fixed environmental goals to the same degree (Art. 9 EU Sustainability Regulation).[85] Accordingly, a certain "degree of ecological

---

[82] See, e.g., Deutscher Bundestag (German Parliament), Enquete-Kommission Zukunft der Medien in Wirtschaft und Gesellschaft, final report, 22.06.1998, *Bundestag-Drucksache* 13/11004, from p. 36. Cf. Lessig (2001), esp. pp. 267-68.

[83] The IFRS Foundation Trustees announced the creation of the ISSB on 03.11.2021 (www.ifrs.org/groups/international-sustainability-standards-board, see the quotation: home.kpmg/xx/en/home/insights/2021/11/sustainability-reporting-climatechange-issb.html, both accessed: 25.08.2025). Cf. basically the opposite standpoint of the Trump US-administration, above 1.4.2 and below 6.7.2, overall 4.8.6 (regional "IFRS"). On the long-standing rejection of "IFRS" in the USA below 4.8.5, 7.8.3 and 4.11.4.

[84] Regulation (EU) 2020/852 of 18 June 2020 on the establishment of a framework to facilitate sustainable investment, and amending Regulation (EU) 2019/2088, OJ EU 22.6.2020, L 198/13 (EU Sustainability Regulation), recital 5. In detail Luttermann (2021). Directive (EU) 2024/1306 of 29.04.2024 amending Directive 2013/34/EU as regards the time limits for the adoption of sustainability reporting standards for certain sectors and for certain third-country undertakings, OJ L, 2024/1306, 8.5.2024. Overall below 4.8.

[85] Regulation (EU) 2020/852, ibid., recital 45, see on benchmarking also recital 39.

sustainability of an investment" applies (Art. 1 No. 1 EU Sustainability Regulation).[86]

How is this determined? – What is clear is this: Systems of criteria for entrepreneurial valuation questions are, in particular in digitised societies (including currencies), a powerful valuation apparatus for assets (*Vermögen*), for the qualification and distinction of "good and evil". This should not be glossed over by harmless-sounding remarks that it is only about "technical" procedures. Practically, it is about the core function of any business activity: the distribution of and the participation in present and future prosperity. Materially, the standard setters as the aforementioned gatekeepers are decisive (see 4.11.3: opinion embedded in code). This makes it all the more necessary to begin here – finally – with the core instrument of the corporation as a financial institution. And this not only in a technical-formal way (corporate law as organisational law), but substantially regarding its finances (*Finanzverhältnisse*), id est its assets (valuation law, see 3.2). This is a global field.

## 1.6 Jurisprudence for Global Prosperity: *Vermögensordnung*

### *1.6.1 The Nature of Institutions, Subsidiarity, and Humanity*

How can mankind, prosperity and power be ordered in a reasonable way? – The spirit of humanity, naturally inherent to everyone and embodied in the United Nations Charter,[87] can pave the way. Institutions must serve the idea of justice in human community, otherwise they lack legitimacy. This comprises the society, economy and the law, as the corporation shows. Materially, it is about financing, valuation and transfer of prosperity, about liberty and responsibility: A *Vermögensordnung* (order of assets), to be established globally if possible for general prosperity (Latin *prosperitas*) as the basis for the happiness of human beings.[88] Adam Smith wrote about the wealth of nations, whose main drive is the striving of the human being to improve his economic circumstances and his social rank.[89] Jurisprudence provides a reasonable legal framework that curbs the egotisms in – also juridical – persons (corporations) for a constitution of liberty.[90]

---

[86] On the transformation process with data for 2023 from banking regulation Luttermann, L. (2025): a European opening balance (*Eröffnungsbilanz*).

[87] See above 1.2 and 1.4.2. On the UN Agenda 2030 below 6.1 with 8.2.1 and 8.5.

[88] Fundamentally Luttermann (2015a) and (2015b), Luttermann (2012).

[89] Corresponding to natural rights, cf. already in his lectures on Jurisprudence Adam Smith (1762/1766), p. 8 (see, e.g., from p. 331 onwards, on the self-interest of the person, supply and demand), then elaborately on the wealth of nations Smith (1776/1789$^5$).

[90] Basically the work of the same name by Hayek (1960).

**Fig. 1.3** Regulatory framework for sustainable business activities of corporations and capital markets

It is all about human dignity (human rights), the human being as a natural entrepreneur. A global order of assets (*Vermögensordnung*), in traditional wording conceived of as *international* and, more far-reaching, *intercultural*, may establish a sustainable global economy and prosperity (see chapters 8 and 9). As the basis for a permanent peace that is not merely a dream of peoples and philosophers,[91] but in practice formed by humans – as already highlighted: the law as practised ethics (German: *Recht ist praktizierte Ethik*, see 1.1 and 1.2). Based on our reasoning, we may practically focus, for this and the journey of transition in economy and societies, on three core elements:

(1) the imperative of fidelity (*Treuegebot*),
(2) the imperative of truth (*Wahrheitsgebot*) and
(3) the subsidiarity principle (*Prinzip der Subsidiarität*).

Essentially, it is about attitude (Adam Smith: "moral sentiments"), with subsidiarity being institutionally based. We have to start concretely with the humans, precisely because with the corporation, an abstract creation of the law (juridical person), we are dealing with a global wealth system. The golden rule of human community – through all cultures, times and even wars, as Hugo Grotius clairvoyantly grasped it in his path-breaking book "De jure belli ac pacis" (On the law of war and peace, 1625), – is the imperative of fidelity (*ex fide bona*): Do not inflict on another person what you yourself regard as a wrong. Fidelity (*Treue*) as the expression of "trust in reciprocity" (*Vertrauen auf Gegenseitigkeit*). Where fidelity, mutual trust, ends, human relations end.[92] This comprises life and its circumstances, its order globally

[91] Kant (1795): On eternal peace. See, e.g., Corporate Sustainability Due Diligence Directive (EU) 2024/1760, recital 7: "All businesses have a responsibility to respect human rights, which are universal, indivisible, interdependent and interrelated." Basically Luttermann (1998) pp. 135-145, 465-485, Luttermann (2010a) and (2013).

[92] Grotius (1625/1950) pp. 597 and 549 (with reference to Aristotle).

as an order of assets (*Vermögensordnung*) and at the same time their valuation, actually and legally (valuation law, financial reporting). Numbers are at best an expression of adequate valuation (see 1.6.3).

The universal imperative of fidelity (*Treuegebot*) is accompanied by the imperative of truth (*Wahrheitsgebot*). Both are primordially required in legal relations and mark the essence of law, the idea and basis of justice (*Gerechtigkeit*). In the legal sense, it is about facts, the actual circumstances (*tatsächliche Verhältnisse*), in the contract explicitly about the duties of the parties with performance (*Leistung*) and consideration (*Gegenleistung*) as a value ratio (*Wertverhältnis*), and overall the material content of the legal relation (valuation law). Procedurally, this is related to the imperative of truth with the law of evidence (*Beweisrecht)* which shapes the law as a whole, for effective legal protection of the asset positions (*Vermögenspositionen*) through judicial review and sustainability; this includes procedural law (*Prozessrecht*) and enforcement law (*Vollstreckungsrecht*).[93] Overall, humans decide as institutionally acting individuals, whether "good or evil" comes into the world. From this evolves a reasonable global economic law (*Weltwirtschaftsrecht*), the human basis for a sustainable world order.[94]

Private law (*Privatrecht*) and law of nations (international law – *Völkerrecht*) are the components. The liberal legal order of the civil society, in which assets are attributed to the responsibility of a legal subject (human being, juridical person) while at the same time being distinct from other spheres of assets (*Vermögenssphären*), is jointly – also in the sense of statehood – built with the principle of subsidiarity. It supports the individual as a whole and vice versa, overall – as Adam Smith focused – serving the realisation of the common good: Tasks are always solved at the individual (lower) level, as long as the help of a common (higher) level is not required (i.e., in short: "help towards self-help").[95] This substantially characterises a market economy, which is liberally – from people for people – formed out of self-responsibility (*Eigenverantwortung*) and a public spirit (*Gemeinsinn*), the *sensus communis*, id est bridling egotisms and state centralism.

Reason thus requires treating human affairs sustainably. At the same time, this reminds us that sustainability (*Nachhaltigkeit*, see 5.2.4) is not a fad, but the epitome of humanity. Business activities and environmental protection do not tolerate any exceptions. In fact, they are even elementary for a balance that establishes lasting peace through a sustainable order of assets (*Vermögensordnung*): The law as lived reciprocal ethics, as laid out in the concept of trust.[96] However, "humanity" does not designate our very nature, as Erasmus explains, but the morality of a human being worthy of his nature.[97] This is what we have to instruct and implement institution-

[93] See in detail chapters 4 and 5.

[94] Luttermann (2015b). See also chapters 8 and 9.

[95] See 1.5.2 and 1.6.3. An example for a commonwealth of nations organised by the principle of subsidiarity is the European Union, see Art. 5 Treaty of the European Union.

[96] See above 1.5 with Fig. 1.2.

[97] Erasmus of Rotterdam (1517) p. 68, in German: *"Humanität" legt nicht schon unsere Natur dar, sondern die seiner Natur würdige Gesittung eines Menschen*. Cf. below 9.9 on the art of life.

ally. In a structure that guides and protects investments like the "invisible hand" (Adam Smith) into reasonable uses – with the corporation through sustainable financial reporting.

### *1.6.2 Reporting for Good Governance, Finance, and Valuation (Value Creation)*

Financial reporting appears to many to be a side issue. But remember, is it not essentially, as John Stuart Mill explains in a pioneering way, about the "Civil, or Social Liberty: the nature and limits of the power which can be legitimately exercised by society over the individual."[98] – Law and the economy in fact as a "constitution of liberty" (F.A. von Hayek), with statehood being founded and delimited for increasing prosperity on the whole through free development of personal creativity that is as great as possible. Overall, Adam Smith works: a social system that draws on the diversity of all people. The law promotes and balances this efficacy by determining the institutional framework, here the rules of the corporation. Financial reporting is the core element as the necessary account of the dealings with other people's money, whereby liability is limited. We will thus focus on the specifics within the larger picture.

The ecological transformation of the economy as a paradigm shift, termed "Green Deal" by the European Union, is taking hold of economy and society. The approach of sustainable regulation of the financial markets has a broad effect (see, e.g., 4.2, 4. 9.2). Guiding principles and institutional core elements are not new. For the balance required in progress, already dealt with overall,[99] they remain to be further developed with a sustainable valuation law for the well-led corporation. Good governance is condition and expression of a good corporation (microeconomics) and a good economy (macroeconomics). From the perspective of the theory of state, it was already Wilhelm von Humboldt who marked the limits of the effectiveness of the state and the education of humans as its most noble task.[100] Resulting innovations drive a modern economy with change (*Wandel*) and insecurity (*Unsicherheit*), which – beyond neoclassical theory "having no people in it" – as good economy characterises "challenge and personal development" as "the essence of the good life".[101] Here, the European enlightened humanism works.

---

[98] Mill (1859) p. 1, and esp. chapter 4.

[99] Luttermann in du Plessis, Großfeld, Luttermann et al. (2007), chapter 7; see already Luttermann (1998) and Luttermann (2003) Einf BilanzR recitals 1-45, Luttermann (2023b) recitals 39-44. On the green paradigm shift (sustainability) Luttermann (2023a) recitals 17-47.

[100] Humboldt (1792) on ideas for an attempt to determine the limits of the state's effectiveness.

[101] Phelps (2007) 543, 552 and 555. Cf. on depersonalisation in the corporate development see 3. 5.4, 3.7 and 3.8 with chapter 7.

This comprises the social integration of the individual into the business world, as entrepreneur, investor, employee (e.g., for a private pension plan). Through this, in the constitution of liberty prosperity is created and participation in it secured. The financing of a corporation or project (capitalism) proves to be a critical core mechanism, whose contractual substance (assets) is to be protected by a reasonable legal system with sound valuation law at its core. For practically, it is all about the transfer of wealth (assets), id est focused in the juridical analysis of the economy: power control (*Machtkontrolle*), wealth sharing (*Wohlstandsteilhabe*) and the preservation of creation (*Schöpfungsbewahrung*).[102] In the dynamic, transnational economy of global capital markets, supply chains and groups, this demands adequate solutions. Hitherto, politically, the perspective of national state and national economy dominates: In transnational investment, the overall assets of a national economy (order of assets) has an advantage or disadvantage in relation to another national economy (order of assets).[103] We must think further on.

In fact, a sustainable valuation law (good valuation), is essential from a microeconomic and macroeconomic point of view. Proprietary positions are characterised by substantial content in the sense of a sustainable measure (*Maß*, e.g., gold standard),[104] which demands procedural security in the sense of sustainability (*Nachprüfbarkeit* – verifiability, see 5.2.4). The two things are united through a robust valuation law founded on the imperative of truth with regard to the law of evidence, for reasonable corporation finance in globally fairly ordered capital markets: In valuation, facts (substantial data) are required and hope values (hypothetical data) to be avoided, id est sustainable reporting instead of soft information. Reliable information is needed: For sustainable investments in sustainable business activities of corporations and projects, not for short-sighted speculation.[105] Good finance and good valuation determine each other reciprocally and form the basis of good corporate governance in accordance with legal requirements, i.e. sustainable value creation.

For this, it is necessary to establish an adequate legal framework (see Fig. 1.3). A *Vermögensordnung* (order of assets) as an investment protection law and at the same time as an institutional engine for sustainable investments, overall a world economic law (*Weltwirtschaftsrecht*) for a global wealth system (intercultural order of assets, see 8.4.2). With this, the challenge is taken into focus. Any economic unit and legal order (e.g., state, company or corporation) basically is an order of assets. The task is always fair valuation, harmonisation and coordination through legally effective provision. Valuation law and thus sustainable reporting form the core for individually and institutionally shaping the entrepreneurial success of a modern business

[102] See, e.g., 7.3.2 and chapter 9. Luttermann (1998) pp. 465-485 and from 139, Luttermann (2010a) 1, 4. See Figs. 5.1, 5.3 and 6.3 (juridical analysis of the economy), Fig. 8.1 (humanity).

[103] Basically above 1.6.1 and chapter 8 (esp. 8.4.2). See already Großfeld and Luttermann (1993).

[104] See below 5.3.4. Luttermann (2008).

[105] Already on that above 1.3.1 and overall chapter 6.

(corporation) in the sense of sustainability; this applies in particular with a view to a so-called “green” economy.

### *1.6.3 Intercultural Cooperation and World Order*

We need to think holistically for sound solutions. That is our natural task with the global order in a multipolar world. Especially for sustainable politics of peace, because the just and equitable “functioning of the global economic system”[106] is key and so is the human corporation for the economic system worldwide (see 8.5). The principle of subsidiarity (see 1.5.2) lends itself to meaningful design, as required – in the sense of jurisprudence – by the people, environment, economy and society. Sustainability (*Nachhaltigkeit*), in the scientific and legal sense (see 5.2.4), designates the actual circumstances accessible and at the discretion of human insight and reason. At stake are life circumstances in their reality and diversity in widely global – financial – markets. We need to be aware that *weltanschauung* and knowledge – probably “irresistibly prejudiced” – grasps one (our!) excerpt of the world, which we may easily take for the whole.[107] Its coordination is a kind of ongoing research project for finding solutions that are as sustainable as possible.

Peace, best for the whole world, sustainably created through a global wealth system, thus requires comparative law (*Rechtsvergleichung*). This means it is cultural research over the complete range of scientific disciplines,[108] guided by jurisprudence for justice as the idea of the law (cf. rule of law – German *Rechtsstaatlichkeit*). The necessary valuation law must not be reduced to numbers: They do not prove anything, they are the “sign of completed limitation”.[109] What is essential is the reality (German *die tatsächlichen Verhältnisse*), id est concrete facts and science (*lege artis*) as a common basis worldwide (see 1.4.2). Numbers are only the result of the editing of realities in methods, models, mathematical formulas. In questions of valuation, they systematically (mis-)lead to manipulation, as – proven over and again[110] – is massively the case in the capital markets with corporations. What must always be the guiding principle is truth with justice (*Gerechtigkeit*) as the idea of law (*Rechtsidee*),

---

[106] Cf. Kissinger (2015) pp. 365-374 (cit. p. 369), focussing on p. 8: “Any system of world order, to be sustainable, must be accepted as just – not only by leaders, but also by citizens”. See below chapter 8 (esp. 8.5) and chapter 9 with Fig. 9.1.

[107] See below 3.8. On the psychology of weltanschauungen Jaspers (1919/1954) p. 142. Cf. Sen (2007) pp. 49-58.

[108] Luttermann (2023a) recitals 21, 24-25, 34-35 and 43, Luttermann (2023b) recitals 22-32 and 50-58.

[109] Spengler (1918) p. 77 (the decline of the west); simultaneously for cross-cultural similarities Sen (2007) pp. 49-50. Großfeld (2019) pp. 76-77. Overall Luttermann (1999).

[110] See above 1.5.2 and below, e.g., 3.5.3 (with Berle and Means), 4.6.1 and chapter 6. Overall Aliber, Kindleberger, McCauley (2023) and Stiglitz (2010). Basically Galbraith (1994).

which connects and supports us everywhere, as the imperatives of fidelity and truth demand for practical implementation.

Being strong in good means responsibly striving for the truth.[111] It is necessary to establish a global business law as an adequate legal framework. The legal order and thus the world of business is an order of assets (*Vermögensordnung*) that needs to be calibrated transnationally. This is demanded by global crises. Jürgen Habermas[112] speaks of the global society as an involuntary community of risk and conflict settlement "on the ground of" unfettered communication (i.e. information). We can shape things concretely for general prosperity in cooperation, in the awareness of joint responsibility and complementarity (see chapters 8 and 9): The valuation and financing of a corporation is regularly based on sustainable information (reporting) as an influential production factor. In order for this gigantic potential to blossom globally in enterprises, reason demands a Copernican turn to the imperative of truth.[113]

## 1.7 On the Road for a Better World

We shall make an attempt to bring more light (truth) into the world of the human corporation for the sake of sustainable business activity (human corporation). The corporation, as a universal phenomenon of entrepreneurial activity, may elevate all our lives through prosperity in the sense of a sustainable development of environment, economy and society – to ensure due care with regard to human rights and the environment (due diligence). Sustainable financial reporting of the corporation as a legal process is practically universal as a key for accessing the global field with the imperative of truth. The use of resources is generally to be understood in financial terms for the sustainable transformation and development of the economy: Financing and valuation of enterprises and projects require sustainability, so they can serve as the necessary foundation for responsible business activity (good governance, duty of care).[114]

Law, economics and environment belong together, ordered in their material content as the constitution of entrepreneurial freedom. The question of chaos or order pervades human life. Both comprise form and content, probably intrinsic to our nature. However, in general, in the words of Erwin Schrödinger, there is a natural

[111] Cf. Mengzi (Mencius), book IV A, 12 and 19 as well as book I B, 14.

[112] Habermas (1996) p. 398.

[113] Luttermann (2011a) 330. See also chapters 8 and 9. Basically Luttermann (2003), esp. Einf BilanzR recitals 1-3, 37 and commentaries on § 264 HGB in Luttermann (2003) p. 765-830. See Fig. 7.3.

[114] Basically Williams (2021). See below 8.4.3 and Luttermann, L. (2024) with a fundamental governance concept that captures the duty of care (*Sorgfaltspflicht*) of corporate directors as sustainable financial due diligence (*Finanzsorgfalt*). Cf., e.g. *Garfield v. Allen, 277 A.3d 296* (Del. Ch. 2022).

tendency of things to devolve into disorder – but life seems to be based "partly on existing order that is kept up" (order based on order).[115] A motivation for development and sustainability. Practically, as described, in the world of business and law, we are dealing with human weakness (greed). In the corporation, denoted by Ambrose Bierce "an ingenious device for obtaining individual profit without individual responsibility",[116] this becomes tangible. We need to grasp, establish and implement the corporation as a truly human corporation, id est draw it out of the mythical world of "numbers" (games), out of the darkness of indeterminacy, establishing it in reality with facts and verifiability (valuation law);[117] this applies in particular in view of mathematical-digital abstractions.

This is the reason of the law (*ratio legis*) and the job of its actors, to create clarity (determinacy, transparency) through facts, and substance and information through sustainable reporting. The imperative of truth forms the rock on which financing and valuation, the sustainable business operation of the corporation is built. With this, it is possible to establish the necessary unity of entrepreneurial freedom (private autonomy) and entrepreneurial responsibility (duty of care, liability). The resulting investment protection (*Investitionsschutz*) serves as an incentive for sustainable investment, while at the same time protecting those responsible (corporate directors, auditors) in respective enterprises and projects from unwarranted liability. In particular, however, in this way the trust required at the practical level can be built up. The law as practiced ethics, as the measure for any "production factor" facilitates prosperity globally through an order of assets. Overall, good is strengthened.

This is what is intended by our journey. In order to grasp the "ingenious device" of the corporation in its essence and to transform the corporation – in the sense of jurisprudence (*ratio legis*) – through reasonableness (*Vernünftigkeit* – Greek *phrónesis*) universally into a sustainable instrument, the focus lies on: the development of the human corporation with sustainable finance (chapters 2 and 3), based on a sound system of real valuation, control and disclosure (chapters 4 and 5) and, above all, on personal responsibility (chapters 6 and 7); this leads on the whole to a – global – *Vermögensordnung* ("order of assets") through complementarity, with human (*dem Menschen*) autonomously in the centre, accompanied by a transition to sustainable living conditions (*Lebensverhältnissen*) with new "minds and measures" (chapters 8 and 9).

---

[115] Schrödinger (1944) p. 68.

[116] Bierce (1911), corporation, *n*.

[117] See below, esp. 4.11.4, 5.2.4 and overall chapter 6 in the light of (hyper-)speculation. Luttermann (2010b).

## References


Aliber, R. Z., Kindleberger, C. P., & McCauley, R. N. (2023). *Manias, panics and crashes: A history of financial crises* (8th ed.). Palgrave Macmillan.

Allen, W. T. (1992). Our schizophrenic conception of the business corporation. *Cardozo Law Review, 14*, 261–282.

Berle, A. A., Jr. (1928). *Studies in the law of corporation finance*. William S. Hein & Co.

Berle, A. A. Jr., & Means, G. C. (1932, 1967). *The modern corporation and private property* (2nd ed.). Harcourt, Brace & World.

Berle, A. A., Jr. (1938). Accounting and the law. *The Journal of Accountancy, 65*, 368–378.

Bernstein, P. L. (1993). *Capital ideas: The improbable origins of modern Wall Street*. Free Press paperback ed.

Bierce, A. (1911). *The devil's dictionary*, first published by Doubleday, Page & Co. (in 1906, partly) and by Arthur F. Bird (in 1907 as: *The cynic's word book*).

Brandeis, L. D. (1914). *Other people's money and how the bankers use it*. Frederick A. Stokes Company Publishers.

Chandler, A. D. (1977). *The visible hand: The managerial revolution in American business*. Harvard University Press.

Confucius. (1914/2013). *Analects (Lunyü – Gespräche)*. German translation by Richard Wilhelm (3rd ed.). marixverlag.

Copernicus, N. (1543). *De revolutionibus orbium coelestium*. Johannes Petreius.

Costanza, R., Cumberland, J. H., Daly, H., Goodland, R., Norgaard, R. B., Kubiszewski, I., & Franco, C. (2015). *An introduction to ecological economics* (2nd ed.). CRC Press.

du Plessis, J. J., Großfeld, B., Luttermann, C., Saenger, I., & Sandrock, O. (2007). *German corporate governance in international and European context* (1st ed.). Springer.

du Plessis, J. J., Großfeld, B., Luttermann, C., Saenger, I., Sandrock, O., & Casper, M. (2012). *German corporate governance in international and European context* (2nd ed.). Springer.

du Plessis, J. J., Großfeld, B., Luttermann, C., Saenger, I., Sandrock, O., & Casper, M. (2017). *German corporate governance in international and European context* (3rd ed.). Springer.

Eisenberg, M. A. (1976). *The structure of the corporation: A legal analysis*. Little, Brown and Co.

Erasmus of Rotterdam. (1517). *Querela pacis (The complaint of peace)*. German: *Die Klage des Friedens*. Diogenes, 2017.

Galbraith, J. K. (1994). *A short history of financial euphoria*. Viking Penguin.

Großfeld, B. (2000). Global accounting: Where internet meets geography. *American Journal of Comparative Law, 48*, 261–306.

Großfeld, B. (2010). *Dreaming law: Comparative legal semiotics*. German Law Publishers.

Großfeld, B. (2019). *Schritte über Grenzen: Rechtsvergleichende Kulturerfahrung*. Lit Verlag.

Großfeld, B., & Luttermann, C. (1993). Rechtsfähigkeit und Qualifikation ausländischer Gesellschaften im Internationalen Steuerrecht. *Praxis des Internationalen Privat- und Verfahrensrechts (IPRax), 13*, 229–231.

Großfeld, B., & Luttermann, C. (2005). *Bilanzrecht (Accounting Law): Die Rechnungslegung in Jahresabschluß und Konzernabschluß nach Handelsrecht und Steuerrecht, Europarecht und IAS/IFRS* (4th ed.). CF Müller Verlag.

Grotius, H. (1625). *De jure belli ac pacis*. German translation by Walter Schätzel, *Vom Recht des Krieges und des Friedens*. Mohr Siebeck, 1950.

Habermas, J. (1996). *Die Einbeziehung des Anderen: Studien zur politischen Theorie*. Suhrkamp.

Hansmann, H., & Kraakman, R. (2001). The end of history for corporate law. *The Georgetown Law Journal, 89*, 439–468.

Hayek, F. A. von (1960). *The constitution of liberty*. University of Chicago Press.

Humboldt, W. von (1792). *Ideen zu einem Versuch, die Grenzen der Wirksamkeit des Staats zu bestimmen*, first published by Eduard Trewendt, 1851.

Isaacs, N. (1923). Business security and legal security. *Harvard Law Review, 37*, 201–213.

Jaspers, K. (1919/1954). *Psychologie der Weltanschauungen* (2nd ed.). Piper, 1994.

Jensen, M. C., & Meckling, W. H. (1976). Theory of the firm: Managerial behavior, agency costs and ownership structure. *Journal of Financial Economics, 3*, 305–360.
Kampmann, C. (2021). The Treaty of Westphalia as peace settlement and political concept. In M. Weller, M. Retter, & A. Varga (Eds.), *International law and peace settlements* (pp. 64–85). Cambridge University Press.
Kant, I. (1784). Beantwortung der Frage: Was ist Aufklärung? *Berliner Monatsschrift*, 481–494.
Kant, I. (1795). *Zum ewigen Frieden (On eternal peace)*. Friedrich Nicolovius.
Kissinger, H. (2015). *World order: Reflections on the character of nations and the course of history*. Penguin Books.
Kricheldorf. (2014). *Erkenntnisse und Irrtümer in Medizin und Naturwissenschaften*.
Leffson, U. (1987). *Die Grundsätze ordnungsmäßiger Buchführung* (7th ed.). IDW-Verlag.
Lessig, L. (2001). *The future of ideas: The fate of the commons in a connected world*. Vintage Books.
Lipton, A. (2025). The legitimation of shareholder primacy. *Journal of Corporation Law* (forthcoming, also: European Corporate Governance Institute, Law Working No. 826/2025). https://papers.ssrn.com/sol3/papers.cfm?abstract_id=5120765 (accessed: 25.08.2025).
Luttermann, C. (1996). Über Buchführung und Bilanzrecht: 502 Jahre nach Erscheinen der "Summa de arithmetica, geometria, proportioni et proportionalita" von Luca Paciuolo. In J. Baetge, D. Börner, K.-H. Forster, & L. Schruff (Eds.), *Festschrift for Rainer Ludewig* (pp. 595–626).
Luttermann, C. (1998). *Unternehmen, Kapital und Genußrechte: Eine Studie über Grundlagen der Unternehmensfinanzierung und zum internationalen Kapitalmarktrecht*. Mohr Siebeck.
Luttermann, C. (1999). Dialog der Kulturen: Vergleichendes Handels- und Kapitalmarktrecht im Sprachspiegel. In U. Hübner & W. F. Ebke (Eds.), *Festschrift for Bernhard Großfeld* (pp. 771–789). Verlag Recht und Wirtschaft.
Luttermann, C. (2003). In B. Kropff & J. Semler (Eds.), *Münchener Kommentar zum Aktiengesetz* (Vol. 5/1, 2nd ed.). CH Beck Verlag.
Luttermann, C. (2006). Unternehmenskontrolle und Bilanzmanipulation nach anglo-amerikanischen Mustern (IAS/IFRS und U.S., GAAP'), *Die Wirtschaftsprüfung (WPg), 59*, 778–786.
Luttermann, C. (2008). Über Vertragsverhältnisse und Bewertungsrecht: Geld, Zeitwert und internationaler Goldstandard. *Finanz-Betrieb (FB), 9*, 193–204.
Luttermann, C. (2009). "Fair Value": Mythos, Methoden und Maß international. *Recht der Internationalen Wirtschaft (RIW), 55*, 1–11.
Luttermann, C. (2010a). Juristische Analyse von Ökonomie, Staat und Gesellschaft. *Zeitschrift für Rechtspolitik (ZRP), 43*, 1–4.
Luttermann, C. (2010b). Regulierungsperspektiven: "War und ist die Finanzkrise die Folge von Hyperspekulation?". *Österreichisches Bank-Archiv (Zeitschrift für das gesamte Bank- und Börsenwesen – Journal of Banking and Financial Research, ÖBA), 58*, 444–448.
Luttermann, C. (2010c). Die Monopolfrage – Otto Sandrock zum 80. Geburtstag. *Recht der Internationalen Wirtschaft (RIW), 56*(3/March: "Die erste Seite"), p. I.
Luttermann, C. (2011a). Kopernikanische Wende zum Wahrheitsgebot oder eine europäische Ratingagentur nach US-Mustern? *Europäisches Wirtschafts-und Steuerrecht (EWS), 22*, 330–333.
Luttermann, C. (2011b). Europäische Gesellschaften zwischen Weltmonopol (IFRS/XBRL) und Freiheitsverfassung. *Juristenzeitung (JZ), 60*, 965–972.
Luttermann, C. (2012). Internationale Vermögensordnung, Insolvenzrecht und Schulden(transfer)-systeme. *Zeitschrift für Wirtschaftsrecht (ZIP), 34*, 305–313.
Luttermann, C. (2013). Recht als praktizierte Ethik und unternehmerische Verantwortungskultur. In E. Weber (Ed.), *Albert Schweitzer – Hundert Jahre Menschlichkeit: Spital Lambarene (1913–2013)* (pp. 74–76). Deutscher Hilfsverein für das Albert-Schweitzer-Spital in Lambarene e.V.

Luttermann, C. (2015a). Corporate law and the *Vermoegensordnung* (order of assets). *European Business Law Review (EBLR), 26*, 31–48.
Luttermann, C. (2015b). Über Idee und Methodik eines internationalen Investitionsschutzes (Vermögensordnung) durch Privatrecht und Völkerrecht. *Zeitschrift für Europarecht, Internationales Privatrecht und Rechtsvergleichung (ZfRV), 56*, 274–282.
Luttermann, C. (2015c). Kapitalmarktrechtliche Information bei Finanzprodukten (PRIIP), Privatautonomie und Vermögensordnung. *Zeitschrift für Wirtschaftsrecht (ZIP), 37*, 805–814.
Luttermann, C. (2019). Perspectives of infrastructure project finance: Intercultural investment, connectivity and trust. *Finance: Theory and Practice (Финансы: теория и практика), 23*, 27–37.
Luttermann, C. (2021). Grüner Paradigmenwechsel für Unternehmensfinanzierung, Vermögensanlage und Bewertungsrecht. *Recht der Internationalen Wirtschaft (RIW), 67*, 191–200.
Luttermann, C. (2022). Klimapartner einer kooperativen Weltvermögensordnung, *Recht der Internationalen Wirtschaft (RIW), 68* (10/October), p. I (editorial, "Die erste Seite": https://online.ruw.de/suche/pdf/riw/riw-10-2022-id3f3bdcf9c541ac4fde57cadb3ca5968.pdf, accessed: 25.08.2025)
Luttermann, C. (2023a). Unternehmensbewertung im Spannungsfeld von Rechts- und Wirtschaftswissenschaft. In K. Petersen, C. Zwirner, & G. Zimney (Eds.), *Handbuch Unternehmensbewertung* (3rd ed., pp. 163–202). Bundesanzeiger Verlag.
Luttermann, C. (2023b). Juristische Anforderungen an eine ordnungsmäßige Unternehmensbewertung und an ein Bewertungsgutachten. In K. Petersen, C. Zwirner, & G. Zimney (Eds.), *Handbuch Unternehmensbewertung* (3rd ed., pp. 653–682). Bundesanzeiger Verlag.
Luttermann, L. (2024). Unternehmensführung: Nachhaltige Finanzinformation (U.S. SEC Climate Rules/EU), Wertschöpfung und Bankenfinanzierung. *Recht der Internationalen Wirtschaft (RIW), 70*, 410–422.
Luttermann, L. (2025). Nachhaltige Wirtschaftsaktivitäten: Eine europäische Eröffnungsbilanz aus Finanzdaten der Bankenregulierung. *Recht der Internationalen Wirtschaft (RIW), 71*, 26–43.
McDaniel, M. W. (1988). Bondholders and stockholders. *Journal of Corporation Law, 13*, 205–315.
Mengzi (Mencius). (2012). *Von der Freiheit des Menschen (On the freedom of men)*. German translation by Richard Wilhelm 1921. marixverlag.
Mestmäcker, E.-J. (2007). *A legal theory without law: Posner v. Hayek on economic analysis of law*. Mohr Siebeck.
Mill, J. S. (1859). *On liberty*. John W. Parker.
Nussbaum, M. C. (2013). *The fragility of goodness: Luck and ethics in Greek tragedy and philosophy* (2nd ed.). Cambridge University Press.
Phelps, E. (2007). Macroeconomics for a modern economy. *The American Economic Review, 97*, 543–561.
Rappaport, A. (1986). *Creating shareholder value: The new standard for business performance*. Free Press (2nd ed. 1997: Creating shareholder value: a guide for managers and investors).
Riechers, A. (1996). *Das "Unternehmen an sich": Die Entwicklung eines Begriffes in der Aktienrechtsdiskussion des 20. Jahrhunderts*. Mohr Siebeck.
Schiller, F. von. (1781). *Die Räuber (The robbers)*. Metzler.
Schrödinger, E. (1944). *What is life? The physical aspect of the living cell*. Cambridge University Press.
Schweitzer, A. (1923). *Kultur und Ethik (Kulturphilosophie I and II)*. CH Beck Verlag, 1990.
Schweitzer, A. (1931–1945). *Kulturphilosophie III*. CH Beck Verlag, 1999 (Part 1/2) and 2000 (Part 3/4).
Sen, A. (2007). *Identity and violence: The illusion of destiny*. Penguin Books.
Sen, A. (2009). *Introduction to Adam Smith, The theory of moral sentiments* (pp. VII–XXVI). Penguin Books.

Sherr, L. (2014). *Sally Ride: America's first woman in space*. Gale.
Smith, A. (1759/1790[6]). *The theory of moral sentiments, Edinburgh* (6th ed.). Penguin Books, 2009.
Smith, A. (1762/1766). *Lectures on Jurisprudence* (The Glasgow Edition; eds. Meek, Raphael, and Stein). Oxford University Press 1978 (reproduction 1982 by Liberty Fund).
Smith, A. (1776/1789[5]). *An inquiry into the nature and causes of the wealth of nations, London* (5th ed.). Bantam Classic Edition, 2003.
Spengler, O. (1918). *Der Untergang des Abendlandes: Umrisse einer Morphologie der Weltgeschichte* (33.-47. ed.). CH Beck Verlag, 1990.
Stiglitz, J. E. (2010). *Freefall: America, free markets, and the sinking of the world economy*. W. W. Norton & Company.
Sunder, S. (2010). IFRS monopoly: The pied piper of financial reporting. *Accounting and Business Research, 41*, 291–306.
Tooze, A. (2019). *Crashed: How a decade of financial crisis changed the world*. Penguin Books.
Uhlman, R. E. (1938). The law of hybrid securities. *Washington University Law Quarterly, 23*, 182–207.
Wang, R. "Ray" (2015). *Disrupting digital business*. Harvard Business Review Press.
Williams, C. A. (2021). Fiduciary duties and corporate climate responsibility. *Vanderbilt Law Review, 74*, 1875–1916.

# Part II
# The Sustainable Finance Function of the Corporation

# Chapter 2
# The Human Corporation and a Sustainable Financial System

> "Civil society would become a scene of bloodshed and disorder" without the enforcement of "the practise of this virtue (of justice)".*
>
> *Adam Smith*

## Contents



*Smith (1759/1790[6]), The theory of moral sentiments, Edinburgh, 6th ed., here: Penguin Books, New York 2009, p. 401. Cf. Augustine of Hippo, *De civitate Dei* (The city of god), written 413 to 426, IV, 4: So what else are states (kingdoms – German: *Reiche*), if they lack justice, but large gangs of robbers?



C. Luttermann, *Human Corporation for Sustainable Development*,
https://doi.org/10.1007/978-3-032-07615-1_2

## 2.1 Understanding the Corporation and Politics

Corporations are a global phenomenon, an entrepreneurial instrument that is subject to state regulation, id est national law in the traditional sense of *lex societatis*:[1] the human corporation lives in valuation law (*lex aestimatio*, see 8.4.2). The corporation (from Latin *corpus*, body) counts as an entity: "a body of people that has been given a legal existence distinct from the individuals who compose it."[2] A legal entity as an entirety (*Gesamtheit*) authorised by law for a certain purpose (*Zweck*), id est: a common purpose (*gemeinsamer Zweck*).[3] It is prominent in large companies, founded through a statute, in former times a royal charter, by now mostly through registration and designed in manifold ways. This means that the corporation (joint stock company) is of eminent importance both economically and socially,[4] therefore it is the topic of politics. It is described as "a work of irreconcilable contrasts, imbued into it through political history as well as through the history of economics and the history of ideas."[5]

We remain optimistic, in particular as time circumstances have a causal effect, and reason may have a guiding function. No one, neither human nor corporation, exists through themselves alone, everything is connected. – Speaking with Johann Wolfgang von Goethe (in translation): "As everything weaves itself into a whole, one working and living in the other!"[6] – A guiding light for people and the environment, for the human corporation and a meaningful so-called "socio-ecological" transformation of the economy (see chapters 1 and 8). Every era poses tasks and challenges to be solved by its actors, in order to win the future. Earlier insights are of help here. Walther Rathenau, a leading German entrepreneur (AEG AG) and minister in the Weimar Republic, regarded the large undertaking in the midst of financial people as "one member in the economic whole of the country, even the world"[7] in its

---

[1] Subject matter of private international law (*Internationales Privatrecht*) as conflict of laws (*Kollisionsrecht*). See below, e.g., on the international allocation of assets 4.4.4 with 4.8 and 8.4.2 with Fig. 8.3 (*lex aestimatio*, valuation statute) as well as Fig. 8.3 (*lex societatis*).

[2] Brown (1993) p. 515 (corporation). Cf. Latin *corporare* to form the body (German *zum Körper bilden*). On that below 7.3.1.

[3] See above 1.5.2, below 2.3.3, 3.7. Fundamental Luttermann (1998) pp. 145-162.

[4] See above chapter 1, below, esp., chapters 3 and 6.

[5] Klein (1904) p. 54 (German original). Cf. above 1.5.1.

[6] Translation. German original: Goethe (1808), *Nacht* (night), Faust: *"Wie alles sich zum Ganzen webt! Eins in dem andern wirkt und lebt!"*.

[7] Rathenau (1922) pp. 16-17.

orientation towards the common good. This is reflected in the doctrine of the "enterprise as such" (*das Unternehmen an sich*), oscillating in the web of different interests,[8] generally addressing the question of the interest of the enterprise:[9] Whom does the corporation serve?

The discussion revolves around capitalism, the great social projects of democracy and communism, it falters between liberalism and socialism, comprising practically all facets of political economy. Philosophical world view (*Weltanschauung*) meets life realities, marking the corporate purpose, the relations between participants (shareholder, bond-holder, employee, etc.) and formulating guidelines for corporate governance. Ideas and ideologies are mingled, misjudged, disseminated – legally consolidated or factually fixed. The arc spans to the present of the so-called "socialism with Chinese characteristics",[10] propagated by the Chinese president Xi Jinping and coined by Deng Xiaoping (1904–1997), the architect of modern China (see 2.3.1). Overall, creative destruction (Schumpeter) is at work, in newspeak: disrupting digital business, and economics in the main "has become a technical, often arcane calling".[11] But it needs much more since in reality peace and humanity are essential. In order to establish a better world, we need to balance interests reasonably. Basically, it is all about power and control.

After the inferno of the Second World War, abridged neoliberalism blossomed, for which a certain individual capitalism is a synonym for the torch of liberty: the social responsibility of business is to increase its profits (shareholder value theory).[12] The visible hand is called state deregulation, outstandingly represented by Margaret Thatcher (1979–1990) and Ronald Reagan (1981–1989); the enemy defeated in 1991 was the planned economy of the Soviet Union: after this so-called "end of history"[13], this neoliberalism triumphed with Bill Clinton (1993–2001), who brought investment and commercial banks together to maximise their returns.[14] The change of corporations described by Berle and Means, the "master instrument

---

[8]Overview by Laux (1998).

[9]See already above 1.5.

[10]Introducing Boer (2021).

[11]Heilbroner (1992) p. 323. Cf., e.g., Wang (2015) p. 13: disrupting digital business as "a passion for transformation".

[12]Basically Rappaport (1986); review of the 2nd ed. by Luttermann in (2000) *Die Aktiengesellschaft (AG), 45*, 143. Cf. on Milton Friedman, also the limits of capitalism, below 7.3.3 and 8.2.2; note also below 4.11.4, 4.12.3 and 5.3.5 (creating shareholder value), overall esp. chapter 6.

[13]Fukuyama (1992).

[14]Under repeal of the Banking Act of 1933 (so called Glass-Steagall Act) by the Financial Services Modernization Act of 1999 (so called Gramm-Leach-Bliley Act).

of civilization" (Veblen), gained ground with the separation of ownership and control under the corporate system, designated "plutocracy" by Walther Rathenau.[15] The modern term "corpocracy" names the financial lobby as political deciders,[16] a global network of multi-corporate enterprises and a vast concentration of property (power).[17] Worldwide, criticism of capitalism, and inequality are on the increase.

Idea and potential of the corporation as a sustainable financial institution are curtailed, although they are universally needed. Our very foundation, the Earth and the stipulations of human community (cf. Art. 55 UN Charter),[18] is eroding. Poverty and climate change testify to a globally urgent need for action, which is in fact widely recognized. The European Union is undertaking a socio-ecological reform of the largest internal market of the world for a new strategy of growth (Green Deal). This green paradigm change far exceeds so-called "corporate social responsibility" (CSR), the Anglophone offshoot of the common good–related *"Unternehmen an sich"* (Rathenau). Sustainability is a paradigm about to be translated into an overall concept of sustainable economic activity (human corporation, see Fig. 8.1). A kind of never-ending story. But as said bevor: For this, there is no need to reinvent the wheel; instead we have to learn to make appropriate use of it.

## 2.2 Humanity: Good Governance, Finance, and Valuation

### *2.2.1 The Green Paradigm Shift and the Human Corporation*

The development of good governance for the human corporation overall, based on sound finance and valuation, is our objective and goal. To this end, a scientific attempt is made to name foundations that are binding and viable for humans. This also applies to environmental issues. In the form of life circumstances (*Lebensverhältnisse*), they not only concern, but encompass practically everybody as well as the economy and society as a whole. Here, we are only just at the beginning. The green paradigm shift, the sustainable so-called "socio-ecological" transformation of the economy (Clean Industrial Deal, see 1.4.2), marks a time change for humankind. A hopefully Copernican turn towards reason and truth in all life circumstances. This demands and

[15] Berle and Means (1932, 1967) p. 4. Cf. Rathenau (1918) pp. 112-131.

[16] Jeremey Grantham, 01.07.2011: www.finews.ch/news/finanzplatz/6121-jeremy-grantham-ueber-die-us-finanzlobby-gold-und-den-naechsten-crash (accessed: 22.08.2025). Cf. Galbraith (1994), Wedel (2009) p. 205: "The challenge for the public is to try to preserve the accountability and transparency that is needed in a democratic society.", and Applebaum (2024), from p. 43 on "international kleptocracy".

[17] Vitali, Glattfelder, Battiston (2011); cf. Coffee (2001). See below 3.5.6, 3.7 (big asset managers) and 6.2.3, 6.5.1 and 7.3.1 (common ownership and control).

[18] Overall see above 1.2 and below 6.1 with ICJ, Advisory Opinion: Obligations of states in respect of climate change, 23.07.2025 (https://www.icj-cij.org/sites/default/files/case-related/187/187-20250723-adv-01-00-en.pdf, accessed: 22.08.2025).

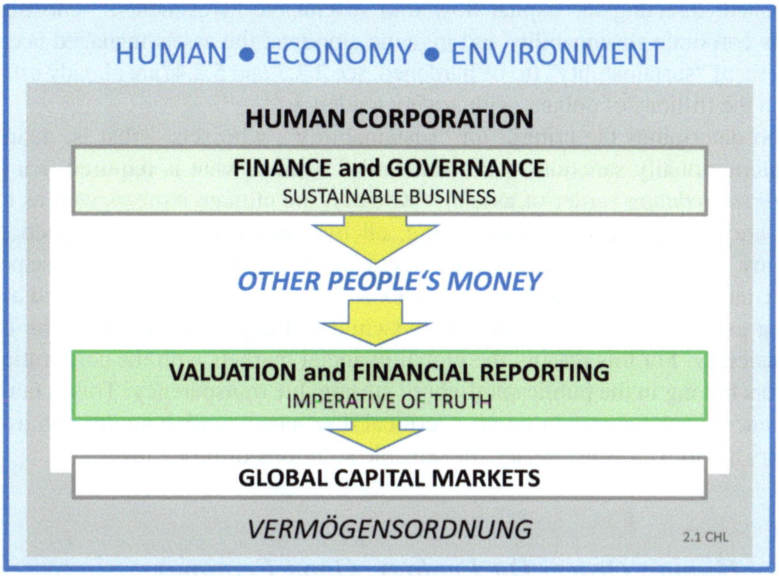


**Fig. 2.1** Financing and governing a human corporation with other people's money (See on global justice chapter 8 (with Fig. 8.1))

requires thinking and acting comprehensively, responsibly on the basis of the actual situation in the sense of sustainability (i.e. facts, science, and verifiability: see 4.1 with Fig. 7.3, and Fig. 2.1).

The corporation is thus central in its elementary financial function (*Finanzfunktion*, see Fig. 2.1 with 2.5). Its global dominance as an instrument for undertakings and projects predestines it as the motor for the reasonable transformation of the economy. Ecologically, the goal is climate neutrality of any business activity involving greenhouse gases. The European Union is aiming to achieve this by 2050 through the transition to "a modern, resource-efficient and competitive economy", which no longer emits any net greenhouse gases and dissociates economic growth from the use of resources (so-called "Green Deal").[19] To this end, a sustainable financial system is to be

[19] EU Commission, The European Green Deal, 11.12.2019, COM(2019) 640 final, 1. Introduction. See basically on the UN Paris Agreement above 1.4.

established, directing the capital flow into sustainable investments.[20] Globally, the issue is corporate sustainability and gigantic amounts; the assets managed according to criteria of "sustainability" (to be hardened, see 2.2.3 and 5.2.4) are already estimated to be in the trillions of dollars, with arising tendency.[21]

Who determines the criteria for "sustainability", who sets – that is, guarantees and internationally sanctions – the standards? In fact, what is required is a global *Vermögensordnung* (order of assets).[22] Clearly, the climate issue as well as human rights are affecting every human being, all life circumstances and aspects of the economy. This makes it too important (lucrative) to not be subject to diverse policies and business practices. The Earth is our existence. This has to be preserved also for coming generations, for the future is our child in the present. We bear the overall responsibility. For this reason, the global financial markets with the corporation and its actors belong in the public spotlight of sustainable transparency. This is taught by experience for the common good. A critical discourse – a dialogue of cultures (see chapters 8 and 9) – is necessary for sensible solutions of problems.

### 2.2.2 *Human Order: On Ecology, Good Economy, and Reasonableness*

With people and the environment, it is a question of a good economy. This means the search for a good, a just life overall. In general and in practical terms of the idea of justice, it is about the concept of human order. Enlightened humanism does not regard the personal concept of a good life (individualism) and the general design of a good economy (common good) as opposites. Both are reciprocally necessary conditions for effectively establishing a just order (rules, institutions) sustainably overall and for the whole. Friedrich Carl von Savigny (1779–1861),[23] a great German legal scholar, describes the rule that determines the free, secure space for the effectiveness of each individual, namely the law (droit, *das Recht*): It is only by accepting this that humans may exist as free creatures, promoting themselves and each other.

This sets modern references, encompassing economic and ecological requirements. A human being works in the external world, and it is necessary, for the individual as well as in general, to recognize the laws of life (*"Gesetze des Lebens"*).[24] The core of

[20] In accordance with Regulation (EU) 2020/852 of 18.06.2020 on the establishment of a framework to facilitate sustainable investment, OJ EU 22.06.2020, L 198/13, on this Luttermann (2021).

[21] See Global Sustainable Investment Alliance (www.gsi-alliance.org) and its Global Sustainable Investment Review. Morningstar Investor is reporting USD 3.2 trillion assets in global sustainable funds (29.01.2025: https://www.morningstar.com/sustainable-investing/global-esg-fund-flows-increase-q4, retrieved: 22.08.2025).

[22] See below 2.7, above 1.5.2 and 1.6 and chapter 8.

[23] Savigny (1840) pp. 331-332. Cf., e.g., below 5.3.3 and 7.3.1.

[24] Ibid., p. 333 and overall pp. 331-333.

human community is thus understood as order, where legal relations between persons and as a state constitution are comprehensively described.[25] Education of humans and the limitations of the state are correlated. We have already seen that evolutionarily in the context of the history of ideas.[26] The life circumstances (*Lebensverhältnisse*) with individual entrepreneurship and the general environmental conditions of course go beyond national-economic areas (*national-volkswirtschaftliche Gebiete*, see 3.7, 8. 4.2). There may be different royal roads. In any case, economy and society go together, and the corporation and financial markets belong in the center of our efforts: for the good economy of a just, sustainable community. Humans and the environment need to be reconciled.

What is required is a culture of responsibility (*Verantwortungskultur*) that is generally established and has to be practised individually. In general, the principle of appropriateness (*Prinzip der Angemessenheit*) holds, the sense of moderation (cf. doctrine of the mean) as the guiding principle. Drawing on the realm of European Enlightenment and Indian and Chinese thinkers, Albert Schweitzer (1875–1957) formulated the ethical maxim of his cultural philosophy: "I am life that wants to live, in the midst of life that wants to live" (so-called veneration for life).[27] This precedence of reason over nature and attitude (*Gesinnung*), formulated in view of the epochal catastrophe of the (first) World War, marks a universal precept. It may guide how to deal with the environment, sustainable leadership, financing and valuation of companies (corporations), self-interest promoting the common good.[28] Does that in essence not sound like the world of thought in which practically even Friedrich Carl von Savigny (as just described) and – as is well-known – Adam Smith were already working?

Under the idea of justice, this leads to the order of a good economy, creating material prosperity as the basis for responsible action of human beings that is in unison with nature and human rights. This is what we have to learn. Humans should not – as is widely disparagingly the case – to be called "consumers"[29] (*Verbraucher*), id est a person which literally "squanders, destroys, or uses up" (from Latin *consumere*). Humans should be educated as sustainably thinking entrepreneurs of their life, sustainably ordering their own existence, integrated into the whole of a sustainably organised society. This may be termed the generally required "socio-ecological" transformation of economy, society and state (human corporation). It complements the Industrial Revolution, the beginning of which is usually dated to around the middle of the eighteenth century. A green revolution? – In the knowledge of living above our natural resources, it seems more like an act of reason. Scientific insight is therefore essential. Good intentions are not sufficient.

---

[25] Hayek (1991) pp. 178 et seq.

[26] See chapter 1 and below 6.2. Cf. already Luttermann (2007/2017) in: du Plessis, Großfeld, Luttermann et al. (3rd ed.) pp. 433-437 (9.2).

[27] Schweitzer (1923) p. 330.

[28] Overall Luttermann (1998) pp. 139-144 and Luttermann (2013a).

[29] Brown (1993) p. 490 (consumer).

With the environmental goals, as marked out by United Nations and European Union,[30] the restructuring of business activities is about humans, nature and technology in their complexity. Sustainability as an ordering principle must be proven through solid results of scientific research.[31] Holistically integrated into the cosmos of rules, it functions as a yardstick. A wide, open field. Ecological economics, e.g., is "an attempt to recapture the spirit of integrated, interactive analysis of problems that defined the early history of science".[32] Jurisprudence goes even further in order to retain the balance in the transition to something new. In any case, the green concept must not be abused (greenwashing), not congeal into religious dogmatism. Critical rationalism,[33] legal comparison and intercultural dialogue[34] open up pathways.

### 2.2.3 *Transparency: Sustainability or How Does the Corporation Work?*

We are on a great journey that will continue. The search for better economic business activity, in essence for a better world, for prosperity in social and personal life, this all remains as a challenge. It has possibly become greater through nature and at the same time more solvable than ever with the possibilities human civilisation (including technologies etc.) has at its disposal worldwide (see 9.6 on generative artificial intelligence). This includes the economy, the financial markets and corporations. They are all too important to be left to one-sided interests. Our existence and progress are linked to them. The overall necessary framework, measure and substance in practice, right up to the independent control (and sanctioning) in the case of controversy (misuse), is provided to humans as creatures doing business by the law as practiced ethics, individually as well as institutionally.[35] Accordingly, we need to focus.

Sustainability acts as the key to purpose, understanding and implementation. More recently, according to the Brundtland Report on environment and develop-

---

[30] See above 2.2.1 and chapter 1.

[31] See, e.g., Kricheldorf (2014) and Lowenstein (2000).

[32] Costanza, Cumberland, Daly et al. (2015) p. 28. Cf. basically Heilbroner (1992) p. from 16 (18) and 311.

[33] E.g., Popper (1987), esp. p. 63, with the insight that is guiding for the entire field of our knowledge that there is no authority that is above criticism (German original: *dass es "keine Autorität gibt, die über jede Kritik erhaben ist"*).

[34] Fikentscher (2004), Großfeld (2019) and Luttermann (1999a). On the overview Reimann and Zimmermann (2006), Siems and Yap (2024). On Islamic finance Luttermann (2009), on intercultural investment Luttermann (2019) and (2020). See below, esp. chapter 9.

[35] See above 1.2 and Luttermann (2013a).

ment, the motto has been "producing more with less".[36] More insight is provided already by language. Conceptually, sustainability in general denotes "the quality of being sustainable", meaning to be "supportable, bearable" and "able to be upheld or defended", from the verb *sustain* (Latin *sustinere*) to "maintain at the proper level or standard", to "provide for the life or needs of", to "support as valid, correct, or just", id est to substantiate, to "be adequate as a ground or basis for".[37] So it is all about maintaining, supporting and protecting what nature and law conform with, and showing a human order that is just. What needs to be clarified is the following: What can essentially be regarded as "sustainable"? And consequently, to what degree do concrete companies, projects, financial instruments provide "sustainable" investments for a corresponding business activity?

In particular, however, the "corporation" itself must be clarified as an institutional basis. It is a question of its character, its chances and limitations, the conditions of its use as a sustainable – financial – instrument for entrepreneurially sustainable business activity (*nachhaltige Wirtschaftstätigkeit*) in the transnational context of international and global markets. This is where its function is to sustainably support enterprises and projects. In order for this to be the case, the corporation has to be well managed, financed and valuated (good corporate governance, see Fig. 4.2). How can this and the green paradigm change, the great restructuring into a good economy and society, be successful globally, as long as the essential tool, the corporation, is hardly working in a reasonable way? If it is not understood or ensured how it is to be handled appropriately? – Thus we are practically working on the key for clarifying, to put it succinctly, the following question: How does the corporation work?

In some places, this may sound banal or be similarly torn to pieces. Is that surprising? Hardly, as so much is at stake. Nobody should be naïve enough to expect that there are no policies sailing in the wake of the epoch-making restructuring in the direction of climate protection and sustainable economy – even under the flag of science. The corporation, coveted as well as elementary, is practically a universal plaything. This is proved by the experience of many generations. Since the turn of the millennium alone, this has been powerfully illustrated world-wide in the uncovering of numerous accounting scandals,[38] gigantic shifts in assets (so-called "shareholder value") and tax manipulations (e.g. Luxemburg Leaks, Panama Papers, Paradise Papers, and offshore companies). See the world debt crisis since 2007 – the "sinking of the world economy" (Stiglitz) – right up until the present: The breeding ground is made up of insecurity paired with human greed.[39]

Essentially, what is lacking is transparency. This means it is the reporting of the corporation that is lacking, as named here: *sustainable financial reporting*. The

[36] United Nations, Report of the World Commission on Environment and Development: Our Common Future, 04.08.1987 (https://digitallibrary.un.org/record/139811?v=pdf).

[37] Brown (1993) p. 3163 (sustain).

[38] The – relatively few – well-known cases include, e.g., Enron, WorldCom, Lehman Brothers, Parmalat, Tesco; see also chapters 4 to 6.

[39] Overall Stiglitz (2010), esp. pp. 147-183. Basically Galbraith (1994).

disclosure of reasonable, reliable information is paramount for the economy and society as described. Without this information, neither the corporation (microeconomics) nor the financial system (macroeconomics) can function in a sustainable way. Joseph Stiglitz writes, "markets on their own seem not able to provide the proper amount of transparency, which is why government has to step in and *require* the disclosure of information" by means of "good accounting systems", it is "really about deception".[40] This does not come as a surprise, long since having been known and demanded (see esp. chapters 3 to 5), but failed politically time and again.[41] For sustainability, markets and the corporation need to be taken into focus in a comprehensive perspective.

## 2.3 Corporate Practice: Some Highlights on World Order

### *2.3.1 China Building a Digital New Silk Road (Pax Sinica)*

Corporate practice appears as a phenomenon of human communities worldwide. It is not so much a question of a specific legal form, but rather a matter of logical construction. The concept of a corporation (legal person) and characteristic structures of its organisation[42] are revealed – also in a historico-cultural way – as a basic pattern in the public and private context. This is illustrated in particular by the People's Republic of China, where a market-based order encounters a gigantic empire shaped by state socialism. Politically driven in a strict regime by the Communist Party through Deng Xiaoping‘s strategy change since 1978: Economic reforms, accession to the World Trade Organization (2001), system building (BRICS, China-CEEC) and reaching for natural resources in Africa, South and Central America, Russia.[43] Citizens and corporations are to be trained in a system of supervision and rating (Social-Credit-System).[44]

Amidst urgent structural problems (corruption, rural exodus, debt ratios), President *Xi Jinping* opened China cautiously for foreign investors, buying strategic

[40] Stiglitz (2010) p. 156.

[41] Luttermann (1999b) with numerous English-language references and Luttermann (2003), esp. Einf BilanzR and § 264 HGB. See also chapters 6 and 7.

[42] Details below, esp. chapters 3, 4 and 7 (corporate directors).

[43] See for more details: www.brics-info.org and www.china-ceec.org/eng. Cf. critically, e.g., Bräutigam (2009) and French (2014). On Chinese debt contracts with foreign governments Gelpern, Horn, Morris et al. (2021).

[44] On the social credit system and China's rule of law Marianne von Blomberg in Everling (2020) pp. 111-137, cf. Chang (2015).

assets (corporations) in Europe, opening up new markets for his own companies. With the Going-Global-Strategy, he relies on regulation for growth and prosperity,[45] so that the people will continue to desist from demanding political participation. The key project is the OBOR-Strategy (One Belt, One Road) initiated by Xi in 2013 after the model of the ancient Silk Road: The goal is to form an economic area encompassing Asia and Europe, Africa and Oceania with 5 billion people for global economic development in the new world order – traditionally with the Chinese sun for "All Under Heaven"[46] (*Pax Sinica*).[47] In economies (states) participating, value creation processes are tied to Chinese standards, infrastructures and institutions (e.g., an Infrastructure Investment Bank) as well as global trade and financial systems on the basis of the digital Renminbi (eRMB, Gold).[48] China's drive to wire the world ideologically in its favor.[49]

State interests and entrepreneurship are channelled. This concerns more than 150,000 state-owned enterprises (SOEs) including 75 of the world's largest corporations (Fortune Global 500). The government makes use of this for capital-intensive infrastructure construction industries, to "achieve social goals" beyond profitability in order to maintain "social stability" and "control over key elements of society".[50] It forces so-called private entrepreneurs to follow the course of the state.[51] Accordingly, also in China corporate governance, finance and valuation are changing in peculiar ways. Even where familiar-sounding terms such as "Corporate Social Responsibility" (CSR) are encountered, success and SOE-efficiency are related to the political ecosystem. This means: "The Chinese government is the primary resource allocator of the economy, and is expected to build a harmonious society through initiatives in promoting employment and employee benefits, training and education, environmental protection, and poverty alleviation"; this makes the "social enterprise theory" a plausible reason for Chinese SOEs.[52]

This leads to questions of valuation ("substance over form"), the more so as clear demarcation is lacking. From a Western perspective, Chinese corporations seem hybrid, where private investors have a financial share and even the right to vote in SOEs (mixed ownership). However, what does "private" actually mean under an omnipotent state regime? Corporations may be designed adequately, as the stock

---

[45] On this Wendy Wu, 01.03.2017: www.scmp.com/news/china/economy/article/2074875/xi-jinping-joins-calls-more-control-financial-risks (accessed: 22.08.2025). IWF, Resolving China's Corporate Debt Problem, WP/16/203.

[46] Kissinger (2015) p. 222. Cf. the phrase "all under the sky".

[47] See Maçães (2020), Xi (2014) pp. 349-359 and Maliszewska, van der Mensbrugghe (2019); on developments: http://beltandroad.hktdc.com/en/belt-and-road-basics (accessed: 22.08.2025). On the socialist rule of law Xu (2019).

[48] So-called Gold Trade Notes, overall Luttermann (2017).

[49] Cf. on the digital Silk road Hillman (2021).

[50] Lin, Lu, Zhang and Zheng (2020) pp. 31-55 (esp. 1. and 2.2.).

[51] See www.economist.com/business/2021/07/24/china-offers-a-masterclass-in-how-to-humble-big-tech-right (accessed: 22.08.2025).

[52] See Lin, Lu, Zhang and Zheng (2020) p. 7. Cf. below 8.2.3.

market launch of Alibaba at the New York Stock Exchange in 2014 demonstrated. Allegedly, some few persons around founder Jack Ma were in control in concern-like structures (partnerships, variable interest entities) with "questionable long-term legitimacy, evidence of potentially conflicted related party transactions, and takeover defence arrangements".[53] As the Financial Times summed up for potential investors: "You don't own it".[54] The Chinese government stopped the stock market launch of Alibaba's financial daughter Ant Group (Alipay) in 2020 two days before the date pointing to "gaps" in disclosure requirements; a restructuring of the "private" Fintech-giant with state-backed firms was the result.[55]

The government intervenes where it sees interests defined as the "common good" (creation of social value) endangered. This is shown by the stock market launch of Chinese digital firms in the USA for e-commerce, the media and services (e.g. Didi Global Inc.) as well as technology producers (e.g., BYD Semiconducter); companies seeking offshore-listing require a cybersecurity review.[56] Obviously the strategic issue is data control and power in the global economy. This is illustrated by Alibaba pioneeringly with its Electronic World Trade Platform (eWTP) established with government instruments (standard setting, arbitration courts, digital currency electronic payment – eRMB) along the new Silk Road: a Chinese trade cosmos as a mixture of capital, corporatism and totalitarianism with its own pulse beat, excluding competitors.[57] – A brave new world?

### *2.3.2 Big Business in the World (Pax Americana)*

In the USA, the country of the proverbially "unlimited opportunities", the recent history of the corporation was shaped for the world. In the course of railway construction, which developed the continent in the Californian gold rush (1849), entrepreneurs such as Leland Stanford with his "Chinese coolies" (Central Pacific Railroad) stand out.[58] The "Big Business" reaching out globally in a monopoly-like manner are characterised by magnates such as the major ship-owner Cornelius

[53] MSCI ESG IVA Report: Alibaba Group Holding Ltd., 15.9.2014 (https://www.msci.com/research-and-insights/paper/msci-esg-iva-report-alibaba-group-holding-ltd, accessed: 22.08.2025)). Overall Luttermann (2014).

[54] Financial Times, 10.09.2014, p. 7.

[55] Julie Zhu, Reuters, 01.09.2021 (www.reuters.com/technology/exclusive-chinese-state-firms-take-big-stake-ants-credit-scoring-jv-sources-2021-09-01, accessed: 22.08.2025).

[56] Cyberspace Administration of China (http://www.cac.gov.cn): to address risks for data to be "affected, controlled, and maliciously exploited by foreign governments"; cf. The Economic Times, 10.07.2021: https://economictimes.indiatimes.com/news/international/business/china-tightens-rules-on-foreign-ipos-in-new-blow-to-tech-firms/articleshow/84301041.cms, and Reuters, 24.08.2021: www.reuters.com/world/china/china-halts-over-40-ipos-amid-regulatory-probe-2021-08-23 (both accessed: 22.08.2025).

[57] European Union Chamber of Commerce in China, The road less travelled: European involvement in China's Belt and Road Initiative, 2020. Cf. Xu (2019).

[58] Rayner (2008).

Vanderbilt, John D. Rockefeller (Standard Oil Company) and his banker J.P. (John Pierpont) Morgan. Capitalists, termed "robber barons", heaping up gigantic riches with their corporations in private empires;[59] right until today some of them work for public welfare through philanthropic foundations, like the steel tycoon Andrew Carnegie (see Carnegie Corporation of New York – known as the Carnegie Foundation).

It is well known: Where there is a lot of light, there is also a lot of shadow (Goethe).[60] It is about valid life circumstances, here in particular the capital market culture of financing, valuation and the organisation of corporations. The U.-S. Congress reacted to the evolving trusts and monopolies with the Sherman Antitrust Act of 1890. The U.S. Supreme Court ruled in 1911 that the Standard Oil Company, by then organised in a powerful holding, was to be dismantled into more than thirty individual companies.[61] A milestone of competition law, the light of which is now – all the more so with the rise of AI (see 9.6) – also capturing the corporate giants of the internet age like Alphabet Inc. (Google), Amazon.com Inc. or Meta Platforms Inc. (Facebook) illegally monopolising digital technologies.[62] History seems to be repeating itself. "Equal opportunities" (Alexis de Tocqueville) have been described as "that form of society, no matter what political classification, in which every man has a chance and knows that he has it."[63] A community whose most effective element for the law appears to be, as Lawrence M. Friedman put it: "current emotions, real economic interests, concrete political groups".[64]

Thus, phenomena and perspectives oscillate in the USA as a federal republic with fifty states (corporation laws), which are in competition with each other. After the First World War, speculation and greed blossomed in the boom of the Golden Twenties, collapsing in the stock market crash in 1929 and bringing the Great Depression in its wake. President Franklin D. Roosevelt aimed at stronger control of corporations and capital markets with his "New Deal" (Securities Act 1933, Securities Exchange Act 1934) through uniformly valid mandatory disclosure

---

[59] Josephson (1934).

[60] German original: Goethe (1773), 1. act. See below 9.5.

[61] *The Standard Oil Company of New Jersey et al. v. United States*, 221 U.S. 1. Cf. historically on the development of corporations below 3.6.2.

[62] See, e.g. Toria Rainey, 07.10.2019, https://www.bu.edu/articles/2019/break-up-big-tech/ and Mihir A. Desai, 20.02.2023, https://www.washingtonpost.com/opinions/2023/02/20/big-tech-meta-google-amazon/ (both accessed: 22.08.2025), also below 6.2.1. On legislative action U.-S. Congress, Amendment to H.R. 3825, 21.06.2021 ("Ending Platform Monopolies Act"). Cf. antitrust cases *United States et al. v. Google LLC*, 2024 WL 3647498 (D.D.C. Aug. 5, 2024): illegally monopolising the search engine in violation of section 2 of the Sherman Antitrust Act of 1890, and *United States et al. v. Google LLC*, No. 23-108, 2025 WL 1132012 (E.D. Va. Apr. 17, 2025): illegal monopoly in digital advertising technologies, violating sections 1 and 2 of the Sherman Antitrust Act of 1890. See billion fine against Google for abusing its market power: ECJ, 10.09.2024 (C-48/22 P – *Google and Alphabet*, EN) ECLI:EU:C:2024:726.

[63] Lowell (1887) p. 14.

[64] Friedman, L. M. (1985) p. 19.

(accounting, auditing) when dealing with other people's money.[65] However, investor protection through accurate information fails systematically due to lobbyism, which establishes questionable so-called "standards" in the "universe of generally accepted accounting principles"[66] (so-called U.S. "GAAP") instead of more uniform state regulation.[67] The masterminds are powerful organisations of the financial industry (AICPA, FASB, big – meanwhile: only four – auditing firms). Accordingly, trained managers have long since been in control of publicly held corporations with the – globally familiar – phenomenon of the "separation of ownership and control".[68]

In this way, on Wall Street the modern capital markets for the financing (investment) of corporations were shaped for public distribution with so-called "securities", such as stocks, bonds and innumerable hybrid or derived constructs (derivatives) as legal instruments.[69] Used politically in this area, financing theories relating to the valuation of the company and its securities have gained ground globally: "Promoting Global Preeminence of American Securities Markets"[70] with the financial industry promoting self-regulation and "avarice triumphs over prudence" in the battle over regulation.[71] Mathematical methods and models dominate through neoliberal deregulation and corporate management, profiting directly from the valuation games (managerial incentive contracts). Implemented into the market situation, treated as "efficient", is a colourful world of profit maximisation that works through constructed leverage of risk and so-called "assets" (hope values): creating shareholder value. A triumph for a few to the detriment of many, termed as an economy of disaster (see 4.6). Overall, what is at work is greed, the result of which Joseph Stiglitz described as "the great American robbery".[72]

This is shown by the global debt-and-trust-crisis since 2008, in which so-called market values have been floundering: "fair values"? – Rather, alchemy-based valuation techniques, with which great segments of the market (so-called "assets") fizzle out, such as securitized structured financial products (mortgage-backed securities, corporate auction-rate securities). In the accounts of the corporations, billions of

---

[65] Fundamental Brandeis (1914), on this above 1.5.1.

[66] *Godchaux v. Conveyance Techniques, Inc.*, 846 F.2d 306, 315 (5th Cir. 1988).

[67] See also below 4.9.7 (minority opinions in FASB, IASB) and 4.11 (IFRS/XBRL world monopoly of valuation). On the history and development of accounting law (*Bilanzrecht*) in the USA Luttermann (1999b).

[68] Chandler (1977), esp. p. 377 et seq.; cf. Coffee (2001) and Schmalz (2018). Also below 6.2.3 and 6.5.1 with the big money-managers like Blackrock (see 2.5.3). Overall chapters 6 and 8.

[69] Bernstein (1993). Luttermann (1998) pp. 195-237 (corporate finance, basics), pp. 238-354 (financing with hybrid financial instruments). See chapter 6, e.g. 6.2.1, 6.4.3 and 6.5.3 with 8.3.2.

[70] SEC, Report to National Securities Markets Improvement Act 1996.

[71] Stiglitz (2010), esp. pp. 109-110, 147-183.

[72] Stiglitz (2010), ibid. Cf. Luttermann (2006). In detail on the crisis and the loss of credibility Tooze (2019). In historical perspective Aliber, Kindleberger and McCauley (2023), from p. 267. In German, e.g., on Anglo-American valuation theory as one of the causes of the financial crisis Hering, Olbrich and Rollberg (2010); Matschke, Brösel, Toll (2024) from p. 829. Luttermann (2010).

dollars have thus to be written off (so-called “toxic assets”). William Sharpe said in his Nobel Memorial Prize speech that certain financial instruments (stock index futures contract) could bring real markets closer to the idealised world postulated by his balance model of the valuation of property (CAPM).[73] – Making the world be the way you want it? – In this way, his colleagues Merton and Scholes drove our world to the brink in 1998 with their highly leveraged Long-Term Capital Management L.P. (LTCM hedge fonds) disaster.[74] – Note: Hope values (*Hoffnungswerte*)[75] instead of substance curtail essential insights (so-called “cooking the books”).

### *2.3.3 Ancient Times and Societates Publicanorum (Pax Romana)*

Since time immemorial, people have taken risks for chances. Development and progress are based on this. Risks are inherent to entrepreneurial activity and a motivation for forming companies at all: The community of risk of the financiers with a – more or less – common purpose, legally organised and ordered.[76] This is always accompanied by questions of valuation, which recent economy has attempted to grasp with models of valuation and market efficiency, or theories of balance. What brought Harry Markowitz the Nobel Memorial Prize in 1990, garnished as a portfolio theory, was already recommended to capitalists by Cato in Ancient Rome, in the sense of a calculable, limited risk: Instead of financing one ship, it is better to furnish fifty ships with 49 capitalists, who each take the fiftieth part of interest in each ship.[77] An infinite game.

Large, costly projects in logistics and infrastructure, such as shipping, road and canal construction, provide early examples of corporate practices. Cooperations between people have been flourishing for centuries as corporation or union (*Gewerkschaft*), known as the oldest form of association in mining (salt, mineral ores, coal) in the Tridentine colliery customs (*Tridentiner Bergwerksgebräuche*) of 1208. High risk through earth collapse or water ingress into the mines, coupled with uncertain gain and high capital demand, required joint enterprises, risks also being spread through simultaneous operation of several mining fields. It was early overseas trade, between huge chances of profit and dangers such as storm or piracy, that was even more instrumental in promoting the development of modern legal forms, as documented in

---

[73] Sharpe (1991) p. 489.

[74] Lowenstein (2000). Merton and Scholes had received the Alfred-Nobel-Memorial Award for Economics 1997.

[75] In more detail below 3.7.

[76] Overall Luttermann (1998) p. 135 et seq. See below 3.6 (participation in profit and loss, transfer of wealth).

[77] After: Mommsen (1865) p. 863.

the *tabula Amalfitana*. The *commenda* – precursor of the silent partnership (*stille Gesellschaft*) and limited partnerships (e.g., *Kommanditgesellschaft*) – is an association between capitalists (*commendatores*), who entrust goods, money or a ship to an entrepreneur (*commendatarius*).

Capital investment, originally limited to persons (family) connected through *Hausgewalt* (domestic power), became a business in maritime profit already in Roman times (Latin *ad proficuum maris*, German *Geschäft auf Seegewinn*). In the *fenus nauticum* (nautical loan), the investor remits money to overseas locations at his own risk. It is the speculative business (*Spekulationsgeschäft*) of Antiquity, remaining exempt from the Occidental prohibition of interest until the emperor Iustinian (482–565 AD).[78] Albeit, at the time, the conceptual formation of the law, the development of property, financing and entrepreneurial relationships were only in their beginnings. Constructions we are familiar with today, such as private legal communities with the quality of a legal person, do not exist yet with the Ancient Greeks and Romans. In comparing similar basic patterns providing logical solutions for enduring legal questions (*Dauerfragen des Rechts*), the difference in life circumstances should always be taken into consideration.

Accordingly, the Roman *societates publicanorum* (societies of the publicans, German *Gesellschaften der römischen Steuerpächter*), treated by Livius for 215 B. C., attest to a financial system highly developed over centuries in the Roman Empire. The state gave a temporary lease (*Pacht*) on public revenues (e.g., the tenths, port tolls, mines) to prosperous, personally liable citizens (e.g., wholesale merchants, *Großkaufleute*), connected in societies of classical law (*societas*). The *societates publicanorum*, whose quality as a legal person is debated due to a lack of sources, operated the tax leases themselves or underlet them (sublease), collected the public dues, did banking business, trade, shipping, took over and credited military provisions and public building projects. To this purpose, they organised gigantic financial means, and, in exchange for shares in profits, also outside capital (*pars adscripta*), continuing also if members (*socii*) changed, who count as legal entities in their contractual entirety. The *societates publicanorum* were state-supporting, profitable economic enterprises with great political influence.[79] The progressive legal development (*fortschrittliche Rechtsentwicklung*) founded and promoted the power basis of the Roman Empire also in economic terms.

In corporations, manifold ways of cooperation between humans are thus observable, including the corporate character of their organisation. What is central is financing, the sharing of profits and losses. This is essential for private law order formed in view of new living conditions. The origin is the family association (*Familienverband*) as a natural and intimate community, which conducts business activities with joint funds (*gemeinsame Kasse*). This even remains true for the great trading firms at the beginning of the Renaissance, like the Fugger family with Jakob

[78] Overall Luttermann (1998) pp. 136-139. See also below 3.7.

[79] See previous footnote with sources.

Fugger the Rich (1459–1525), one of the wealthiest individuals ever and already with a charity.[80] – However, the need for capital requires entrepreneurs to take in strangers in the form of outside capital or even as associates. In this way, commercial companies (*Erwerbsgesellschaften*) evolve and with them the necessity for regular – financial – reporting on business operations (profit or loss).

## 2.4 Reporting: Legal Person, Structures, and Characteristics

### *2.4.1 Corporation and Corporate Law*

In the private law order, types of contracts for designing and financing communities of risk for lasting enterprises and projects have been developed. Due to the freedom of contract (*Privatautonomie*), anyone may choose among them individually, proverbially taking his place in the same boat: either as a partner with respective capital contribution (shareholder with so-called equity capital) or creditor (non-shareholder with so-called outside capital, debt).[81] Historically, issuing capital to a corporation becomes the essential point of reference of the entrepreneurial activity of the individual, superseding personal involvement. In this way, corporations (*Kapitalgesellschaften*) arise that, as legal persons, are – like a natural person (*Mensch*) – legal entities (*Rechtssubjekte*) with the power to act in legal dealings (*Rechtsverkehr*, pls. note 7.3.1).

What we know: The English term "corporation" goes back to the Late Latin word *corporatio, corporationem* (from *corporare*, to form), occurring in Late Middle English at the end of the sixteenth century for an artificial person as the result of incorporation.[82] Like in the sphere of Roman law, in English tradition the legal personality (*Rechtspersönlichkeit*) of the corporation (legal person) is a privilege endowed through a charter by the sovereign – initially the king or queen (i.e. a royal charter, concession system). Originally, this was meant only for very few entities for purposes in support of the state, such as the organisation of financial institutions and colonial overseas trade. This was part of the tradition described above. The idea of a permanent stock of capital with the issue of shares emerges in the East India Company at the beginning of the eighteenth century. Soon, new foundations by merchants follow, who make use of corporations in the modern sense. Adolf Berle

---

[80]He endowed the "Fuggerei" in Augsburg (Germany) in 1516, a settlement with 52 houses for craftsmen and day laborers in need through no fault of their own, which is still in operation today; considered the world's oldest social housing estate (*Sozialsiedlung*). Steinmetz (2015) and Pölnitz (1949). See also 3.8 and on cooperation above 1.3.3.

[81]Basics above 2.4.2 (*Wagnisgemeinschaft*). See also on self-responsibility below 5.3.3 and 5.3.4; on protection of minority shareholders (resp., bondholders) 5.4.

[82]Brown (1993) p. 956 (corporation). The word "corporation" is attributed to Brooke, who used it in his "Abridgement" of 1586, see Berle (1928) p. 6 (in note 3).

sums up: "Once the difficulties of royal creation, mystic entity, and resulting limited powers have been removed, we shall be not very far from the continental theory, nor very far from the business idea, of what a corporation should be."[83]

The ideas imported from England with common law during the colonial period are the deeper foundation in which the modern American business corporation is rooted. In the United States, newly founded in 1776, corporations emerged in the late eighteenth century through state concession, predominantly for banks, insurance companies as well as for businesses for the development of infrastructure (such as water supply, bridge building).[84] In 1811, the State of New York issued the first General law in the United States for the incorporation of business companies for certain manufacturing purposes, marking the departure from the concession system (*Konzessionssystem*) to the normative system (*Normativsystem*), and also secured this path in the year 1846 constitutionally, like the State of Iowa.[85] The normative system, today common in continental Europe, in which the corporation arises under the fulfilment of the legally normed conditions (*ex lege*), essentially prevailed, having gained ground in most states by the end of the nineteenth century.[86]

The constitutionally federal system of the United States led to different manifestations. Among the federal states, sharp competition arose for securing financial resources.[87] As Justice Louis D. Brandeis writes in his legendary dissent in *Liggett v. Lee*, there was a race "not of diligence but of laxity"[88] with regard to the legal requirements of incorporation. Apart from New Jersey, West Virginia and others, it was in particular the legislation of Delaware – built on the groundbreaking approach of New Jersey in 1875[89] – that gained "liberal" fame. The small state on the East Coast evolved into an anchor point of corporate law development within American economy: *Delaware corporate law* has to some extent virtually become national

[83] Berle (1928) p. 22 (see pp. 1-25 on basics of corporation finance). Comprehensive George Cawston and Augustus Henry Keane, The Early Chartered Companies (A.D. 1296–1858), 1896 (reprint, The Lawbook Exchange, Ltd., Clark, New Jersey 2017).

[84] Between 1796 and 1800, 181 enterprises are said to have received "charters", see Friedman, L. M. (1985) p. 189. Especially on New York see Seavoy (1982), from p. 39.

[85] First Statute, according to which corporations could be founded in Connecticut in 1837 for any legal purpose – albeit limited to twenty years; overall Larcom (1937) pp. 1-3, Seavoy (1982), from p. 65. By the way, New York City was also a "chartered corporation", Friedman, L. M. (1985) p. 188. Cf. for Britain below 2.4.3.

[86] Larcom (1937) p. 3. See below 3.4.2. In Germany, e.g., according to the normative system (*Normativsystem*), a legal entity (*juristische Person*) is created by entry into the commercial register (*Handelsregister*), see § 41(1)(1) AktG (for the *Aktiengesellschaft* – AG) and § 11(1) GmbHG (for the *Gesellschaft mit beschränkter Haftung* – GmbH).

[87] Fees for the incorporation (filing fees) as well as corporate franchise tax, which a federal state collects for the permission to do business on its territory.

[88] *Louis K. Liggett Co. v. Lee*, 288 U.S. 517, 541, 559 (1933); there, from p. 550, generally on the development of the corporation. See also, currently, below 4.11.4 on Delaware and (with 4.11.1 to 4.11.3) so-called "standard setting" for so-called "IFRS" ("IFRS S").

[89] See Buxbaum and Hopt (1988) pp. 115-116.

**Fig. 2.2** Substance for corporate structures, id est "substance over form" (human corporation)

*corporate law,*[90] *and beyond.* This includes curbing the potential for misuse of this legal form through state regulation.

### *2.4.2 Financial Reporting (Substance) for Corporate Structures (Form)*

For companies (projects), the modern corporation – German *Aktiengesellschaft* (AG), Dutch *Naamloze vennootschap* (NV), French *Société Anonyme* (SA), Italian *Società per azioni* (S.p.A.), Spanish *Sociedad Anónima* (SA) – macro-economically provides an ingenious construction (form), which we will be having a closer look at. For sustainable business activity in an individual case as well as for a sustainable financing system as a whole, this includes truthful accounting, id est one based on the actual situation (substance, see Fig. 2.2). This means giving account in terms of sustainable facts about dealing with other people's money (Brandeis).[91] In English, *financial reporting* is often used synonymously for accounting, with the verb "report" deriving from Latin *reportare*, id est, composed of *re-* (back) and *portare* (carry):[92] Responsible corporate leaders in the final instance carry the capital given

[90] See on the Delaware General Corporation Law: Folk (2022). Großfeld (1968) pp. 164-168. See also below 3.4.2.

[91] See below 3.3 (esp. 3.3.3) and, with various perspectives on limited liability, 3.4 to 3.6.5.

[92] Brown (1993) re-entry report, p. 651 (verb) and p. 650 (noun, no. 2.b.), e.g, with a word by Oliver Cromwell from 1534: "Therof shal I not faile to make true raport to his Highnes." See overall on valuation chapters 4 and 5.

back to the investors as well as regular dividends (interest) and indeed substantial information about business success (profit or loss).

Financial reporting denotes financing as the epitome of the corporation for creating a community of venture (*Wagnisgemeinschaft*, see 1.3.2), in which the investors take legally determined positions of their own free will. This leads to specific capital structures (equity, debt), which in a given case are depicted in the accounts. This involves the valuation of the corporation and its financial instruments (securities), in particular the shares (equity securities) and accounts payable (credits, debt or hybrid securities). This is what theory and practice of financing focus on. Value (*Wert*) as a quality, in contrast to quantities, is naturally not a given, but rather an expression of individual and general circumstances.[93] The capital market with its structures – ideally imagined as efficient[94] – is the institution where these circumstances are negotiated and find their expression in prices (*Preise*). The price contractually fixed between parties in an individual deal represents the market value, here, e.g., that of a financial instrument (stock, bond etc.).

However, agreement on the process of valuation may still be lacking. In any case, without sustainable, id est substantially fact-based reporting, no sound valuation and financing of enterprises (projects) can take place. Fundamental for this and therefore for sustainable financing of the corporation are powerful accounting rules, which have to be designed rigorously in a reasonable system. According to the imperative of truth (see 4.4.4), they must be practiced by those responsible (corporate directors, accountants, auditors, see 4.6). Considered as a whole, it is about substance and form: Formally, that means clearly and completely (form), as well as materially, that means truthfully with regard to content and essence (substance). In all this, the imperative of truth provides the yardstick ("substance over form", see Fig. 2.2). Existence and function of the corporation depend on this, in particular participation in its success (profit, loss) as well as liability. Overall, it is about the true-to-fact information of the investors as a legal act (*Rechtsakt*).

Substantial financial reporting (accounting) as described is thus obviously the essential structural element of the corporation, elementary for its sustainable business practice: accounting as the documentary proof of good corporate governance (see chapter 4).[95] Overall, this concerns questions of valuation, which occur in manifold ways in the course of business, processed in bookkeeping and accountancy, ending in financial reporting (accounting, auditing and disclosure). With financing, risk management and publicity of a corporation, they comprise the complete practice of transactions, taxation, restructuring (mergers & acquisitions, insolvency). We are therefore dealing with the essence of the responsible management of a corporation. This includes duties of the corporate directors and questions of the liability of the management. To this end, clear, powerful rules are required in

---

[93] See in more details chapters 4 and 5.

[94] Coffee (2001) p. 4: "efficiency does not necessarily triumph". Cf. overall chapters 6 and 7.

[95] See already Luttermann, chapter 7, in du Plessis, Großfeld, Luttermann et al., 1st ed. (2007), 2d ed. (2012) and 3rd ed. (2017), basically Luttermann (1999b).

the concept of valuation in civil proceedings: required for sustainable finance and in fact out of self-interest for the managers responsible.[96]

This characterises sustainable financial reporting (valuation) in its elementary significance for the functioning of the corporation as a whole. It also shows the way to sustainable business activity. However, awareness is widely still (too) low. At any rate, implementation requires far more effort, as has been clear for a long time. The modern corporation and its financial instruments, wrote Berle and Means (1932) "are substantially meaningless" unless there are "provisions definitely regulating the corporation's accounting (methods)".[97] And, as Melvin Eisenberg (1976) underlines, "the methods by which the numbers are generated must be as objective as possible".[98] In essence this means: sustainable financial reporting, i.e. verified information (see chapter 4). Because it is about people's lives individually (investments) and in society as a whole (equilibrium), not about an abstract "numbers game" in which some irresponsible characters get rich at the expense of the whole.[99] Facts instead of baseless fictitious projections are required.

### 2.4.3 *Legal Characteristics: Principle of Separation, Multipersonality, and Permanence*

The modern corporation is a creation of the law (legal person) as a financial instrument (finance function, see 1.1, 2.5.1), that is, human genius and limits. The legal character provides the measure. This should be taken note of, for financing and financial reporting (auditing) of the corporation partake of it, make reference to it. They can only be designed with the eminent aspects of valuation in a way that makes sense as whole. For this purpose, the following question needs to be clarified fundamentally here first: How is the modern corporation constructed? – We have already seen basic patterns, approaches and predecessors in our consideration of the historical development. There are three features that come to the fore legally in practice and in the perspective of legal comparison, universal "corporation DNA", so to speak: the principle of separation, multipersonality and permanence.[100]

Fundamental for the modern corporation as a legal person is the so-called principle of separation (German *Trennungsprinzip*, see Fig. 2.1: "other people's money"). For the corporation, in more recent times,[101] this is represented by a

---

[96] Altogether above 2.2.2 and below in more details chapters 4 to 7, also 8.3.2. See Figs. 7.1 and 7.2, both on personal responsibility and valuation.

[97] Berle and Means (1932, 1967) p. 183.

[98] Eisenberg (1976) p. 186.

[99] Levitt (1998). Cf. Stiglitz (2010).

[100] Fundamentally above 1.4.1. See also below 3.7 (evolutionarily) and 9.7.

[101] See chapter 3, generally 3.7 (overview) and, e.g., 3.4.1, 3.6.2 and 3.6.5.

special fund (*Sondervermögen*). This comprises all assets on the balance sheet, e.g., land, equipment, patents, accounts receivable, cash and cash equivalents. The term "special fund" denotes that certain assets are separated, in particular from the – other – private funds of the partners and other financers (*Kapitalgeber*, third parties). That is the nature of the principle of separation for a legal person: By being attributed to the legal person, assets (*Vermögen*) legally assume a separate existence with regard to other legal entities (shareholders, third parties) for the corporation. Through legal separation (corporate veil), different property spheres (*Vermögenssphären*) come into being. Each property sphere constitutes its own legal sphere. The attribution is performed in the accounts (see chapter 4).

The accounts represent the attribution of assets to a legal subject – here: the corporation. For the corporation as a legal person, a balance sheet is opened (opening balance), in which all assets and debts have to be listed according to their value and which has to be continued regularly (as a rule each business year) in their development (annual accounts). It is only in and with the picture in the accounts that the corporation becomes tangible, apperceptive (consciously perceptible – German *begreifbar*) as an independent entity:[102] This practically illustrates the "virtual reality" of the legal person (*Rechtsperson*), which is basically a fiction as a creation of the mind (see 7.3.1). The attribution of assets (special fund) also includes the liability situation. The basic tenet is that for the creditors of the corporation, it is only the (special) fund of the corporation that is liable for their commitments (accounts payable);[103] to this extent, the partners (shareholders) are third parties in legal dealings (*Rechtsverhältnis*), id est in external relations of the corporation.

This widely mirrors the circumstances of legal vehicles for the operation of large scale business ventures, as already shown regarding legal development (see 2.3.3). Until the British Companies Act of 1844 granted any venture fulfilling the statutory conditions separate legal existence (joint stock company – normative system), a corporation could only come into being either under a royal charter or by virtue of an act of parliament (see 2.4.1). Otherwise, partnership law obtained, id est for questions of liability, the natural members (humans) had to be identified, which became increasingly difficult with rising numbers and freely transferable shares. The landmark common law decision of the House of Lords in *Salomon v. Salomon & Co. Ltd.* in 1897 marked the corporation as a separate legal entity.[104] However, at that point, in English legal history the "idea that a non-human entity could in law be treated as a subject of rights and duties" had been current for centuries already: Notwithstanding

---

[102] See on details below in chapter 4. In a comprehensive comparative legal analysis of "a true and fair view" in the European Union (Art. 2(3) Directive 78/660/EWG [= Art. 4(3) Directive 2013/34/EU]) with Germany (§ 264(2)(1) HGB, both: *"ein den tatsächlichen Verhältnissen entsprechendes Bild"*), Great Britain and France as well as the USA, see Luttermann (2003) § 264 HGB, recitals 42-169. About retaining the substance under Directive 2013/34/EU: Luttermann (2013b).

[103] For the German *Aktiengesellschaft* (stock corporation) this is explicitly regulated, e.g., in § 1(1)(2) AktG.

[104] *Salomon v. A. Salomon & Co. Ltd.*, House of Lords, 16.11.1897, UKHL 1, AC 22.

persistent critical observation, "the doctrine of limited recourse has, by and large, stood the test of time".[105]

The principle of separation logically leads to two further characteristics of the modern corporation. Due to the principle of separation, a human being (natural person) may multiply legal ownership (*Rechtsträgerschaft*) – factual with both personal and economic identity – through the foundation of legal persons like the corporation (multipersonality, see 7.3.1). As an exception, the recourse to the owner (shareholders) of the corporation can be taken into consideration (so-called "piercing the corporate veil",[106] German *Haftungsdurchgriff*[107]). The third feature goes hand in hand: Having effectively come into being, the corporation as a legally independent organisation whose membership may vary basically has an unlimited existence. That means it operates over time for the permanent pursual of a purpose beyond its founder (permanence) as an "eternal asset holder" (*ewiger Vermögensträger*). Overall, this is the reason for its attractiveness and its problems, in particular in the transnational sphere.[108]

## 2.5 The Corporation as a Sustainable Financial Instrument

### *2.5.1 Function and Structure of the Corporation*

The corporation is itself a financial instrument with regard to its function and structure (so-called financial function, see 1.1 and 1.3.2), which is in the focus. Well, according to the classic question: What is a corporation? – Legally founded, the corporation with its principle of separation serves as an independent organisation (legal person) and asset holder (*Vermögensträger*), as has just been shown. Melvin Eisenberg characterises it as "a profit-seeking enterprise of persons and assets organized by rules" that are largely mandatory (e.g., disclosure), at least for publicly

[105] See overall Grantham and Rickett (1998), citations on p. 4 and p. 5. Gower (2021) part 2.

[106] E.g., in the US: Benjamin Cardozo refusing in *Berkey v. Third Avenue Railway*, 244 N.Y. 602, 155 N.E. 914 (1927); cf. piercing the veil *Kinney Shoe Corp. v. Polan*, 939 F.2d 209 (4th Cir. 1991). In the UK: *Gilford Motor Co. Ltd v. Horne* [1933] Ch 935; *Jones v. Lipman* [1962] 1 WLR 832 (a company used as a "mere façade" concealing the "true facts"). Banoo (2020). Cf. on human rights violations, environmental damage and duty of care owed by a parent company *Lungowe v. Vedanta Resources plc* [2019] UKSC 20.

[107] In Germany (so-called *Durchgriffshaftung*), e.g.: BGH, 14.11.2005 (II ZR 178/03), BGHZ 165, 85 (<openJur 2011, 12132>); with groundbreaking conception of liability BGH, 16.07.2007 (II ZR 3/04 – Trihotel), BGHZ 173, 246 (<openJur 2011, 7477>); BGH, 06.11.2018 (II ZR 199/17), BGHZ 220, 179 (<openJur 2019, 98>). Basically Jung (2002), Luttermann (2008). Early discussion in RG, 22.06.1920 (III 68/20), RGZ 99, 232, 234.

[108] For details see below, esp. chapter 3 and on the measure of valuation 8.4.2 (*lex aestimatio* – valuation statute).

held corporations.[109] It has a binding structure designed to give investors security even in anonymous markets. The German legislator has emphasised that the charter of a joint stock corporation (*Aktiengesellschaft* – AG) may only deviate from the legal regulations if these explicitly allow for this (§ 23(5)(1) *Aktiengesetz* – AktG, German Stock Corporation Act).

But why does the corporation have a basically binding structure? That is the cardinal question of its function. Naturally, the question of the function is predominant, for sensibly the designed structure corresponds to the purpose pursued. The law is not an end in itself. It derives from motives and serves a specific objective (*ratio legis*). It also develops for certain reasons, being set down in relation to a specific purpose. The purpose is overall described as the creator of law as a whole.[110] In short: Rules are the essence of a certain function. As shown in its historical development, the corporation practically evolves as a form of organisation for larger, permanent enterprises (projects) pursued by humans. It is to be financed in the sense of a capital economy on capital markets (with, in economic terms, efficient transaction costs), sustainable and independently of individual preferences. We have already seen this as the venture community of the capitalists,[111] id est, as a reservoir of small and larger sums of capital.

This describes the practical function of the corporation as a financial instrument. Its structural elements are related to this. As a legal person, the corporation is independently equipped with capital (assets), which it has at its disposal for its enterprise (projects). Regardless of the individual change of its financiers (shareholders, bondholders), who may freely come and go via market transactions (*Börsengeschäfte*, i.e. stock exchange dealings etc.). This leads to the ingenious transformation of time periods (*Zeitdauertransformation*): the short-term capital of the financers turns into long-term capital of the corporation, which remains untouched by changes in personal ownership of the shares and bonds.[112] For this to work, binding rules are necessary that are valid as a protective frame and a basis of trust: *corporate law and capital markets law – with sustainable financial reporting being materially the core of both.*

---

[109] Eisenberg (1989) pp. 1486 and 1487. See Klein (1904) p. 5, on the idea of the corporation as an independent *"Geldvereinigung"* (monetary association), noting that the money itself "became an entrepreneur", see below 3.3.4 and 3.8. Cf. on the "code of capital" Pistor (2019).

[110] Jhering (1877), title page: motto.

[111] Above 1.3.2 and 2.4.2. See on the development below 3.7. Basically on risk and profit below 3. 3.4 and Knight (1921/1971) with Coase (1937) and – in terms of more modern institutional economics (information, transaction costs etc.) – North (1992). See Luttermann (1998) pp. 151-162 (on investment, institutions and participation in profit), pp. 465-485 (juridical analysis of the economy, see on this also above 1.6, below, e.g., 4.13, 5.2.2 and 7.3.2 with 9.7). Cf. Coffee (2001) p. 4: "efficiency does not necessarily triumph".

[112] Basically above 1.4.1 in the context of the corporate fiction. See below 3.6 on the liable capital (*Haftkapital*) of the corporation. Cf. the colourful world of private financing of (corporate) start-ups including "overfunding", id est overvaluation. See on sound valuation chapter 5, and overall on corporation finance chapters 3 and 6.

### 2.5.2 *Investment: Sustainable Corporate and Project Finance*

The flipside of this financing of an enterprise (project) is the investment: Capitalists provide capital to the corporation in a market-based way, they invest. The investors are free in the choice of the object of their investment, id est, of the corporation as well as of specific securities – both are financial instruments. They choose via the market (stock exchange) from innumerable possibilities for investment, that is, they make their decision about investment and disinvestment according to their individual preferences. The corporation financed in a capital market-based way is an object of valuation and investment through its securities (stocks, bonds), in which investors gather at will through providing capital – and only capital, no matter if more short-termed or longer-termed, in an anonymous setting (cf. French *Société Anonyme*, SA, and in more languages see 2.4.2).

Remember, what thus stands out is financial reporting (accounting) of the corporation. It exists and operates in its legally organised function as a financial instrument (place of capital collection/object of investment) with the money of other people. This demands binding rules according to which the corporate directors as the persons responsible must give account about their dealings with this invested money (capital/assets) and the results (see 2.4.2). That is at the core of the description that the corporation is "an enterprise, organized by rules".[113] However, it is widely referred to the formal – organisational – corporation law (*Gesellschaftsrecht*), which is uselessly reduced and practiced. Why? – It cannot be stressed enough: Without powerful financial reporting, that is, without mandatory legal rules on material – valuation-law – substance (assets) of the corporation (valuation law), the corporation is at the mercy of the arbitrariness and capriciousness of the corporate directors: and therefore, commonly a worthless shell.

This is generally valid, as developed in the concept of trust for the valuation of assets.[114] It comprises *corporate law and capital markets law as a common base*. What is more: Even if designations (e.g., special purpose vehicle) may vary and deflect, the corporation as a financial instrument forms the core of an enterprise as well as of a project, both financed by private or public investors on global capital markets. Correspondingly, the common separation into "project finance" and "corporate finance" seems to fall short. Basically, the regulatory core of valuation and financial reporting that it has in common with the corporation should be developed in an appropriate way, so that the whole domain of financing can be ordered sustainably.[115] In this way, the sustainable ("socio-ecological") transformation of the economy may succeed.

---

113 Eisenberg (1989) p. 1487.

114 See above 1.5.2 (with Fig. 1.2) and 2.5.1, below 2.7 with chapters 4, 5 and 7. Overall chapters 3 and 6.

115 See Luttermann (2019) and (2020).

### 2.5.3 On Common Ground: Good Communication

The corporation as a financial instrument as well as the capital market, both with an investor-protecting function, are reciprocally related to each other. The connecting link is sustainable financial reporting and auditing, safeguarding accountability regarding entrepreneurial dealing with other people's money. In the market-based structure supply and demand are co-ordinated by presenting sustainable information. This happens in a way appropriate to liberty in a legal order according to generally binding rules under the imperative of truth (*Wahrheitsgebot*).[116] Overall, it is thus a question of good communication through clear language.[117] The market actors depend on reliable data, id est facts instead of "soft information" (hypothetical data), for entrepreneurial efficiency and calculability (see 2.6.2 with Fig. 2.3). This also includes the state and society, as well as transnational and global conflict solving and co-operation.

In a fundamental way, this affects discourse on the corporation, in particular with regard to market efficiency and asset valuation.[118] As shown, as a legal institution the corporation functionally satisfies a financial legal need. The construction should be appropriately oriented toward life circumstances. In classical perspective and wording, the debate, according to Berle und Means, still revolves around the "separation of ownership (by stockholders) and control (by management)". Enhanced again through the "separation of ownership from ownership": This signifies that "the direct stockholders of private companies are typically not end-user investors", but money-managers (e.g., mutual funds, hedge fonds) "whose interests are not necessarily aligned with the interests of long term investors".[119] Practically, huge asset managers (e.g., BlackRock, Vanguard, UBS) and digitalised processes (algorithms) are gaining alarming power. For complete depersonalisation of human relations (responsibility) is gaining ground.[120]

The core of the considerations remains, for it is always about other people's money. Functionally, capital and corporation, its leadership, financing and valuation depend on sustainable financial reporting and auditing. Probably even more so through digital anonymization (depersonalisation). Indeed, we have to go further in our thinking. Market and regulation do not contradict each other (see 2.6.1). What is divisive are one-sided treatments, in particular of market or regulation failure

[116] See above 1.5.2 with 4.4.4 and chapter 9. Overall Luttermann (1998), from p. 135.

[117] See, e.g., below 2.6, 4.12.3 and 7.6.3. Basically Luttermann (2023) recitals 91-95 (business and financial communication), Luttermann, C. and Luttermann, K. (2020) pp. 201-242 (legal linguistics).

[118] See chapter 5 (valuation) and 7.3 (market efficiency). Fundamentally, proceeding from clarification of the misunderstanding of "leverage" (pioneering Modigliani and Miller, 1958), see Luttermann (1998) pp. 219-237. Cf. Coffee (2001) p. 4: "efficiency does not necessarily triumph".

[119] Strine (2014) p. 449. Cf. Coffee (2001) and Jensen (1989/1997). See also below 3.5.5 and chapter 6.

[120] See on artificial intelligence (AI) 3.5.5 and 3.7 (electronic person), esp. in chapter 6 (algorithms) and 9.6.

(Nirvana Fallacy): "markets, morals and law" taken together may expediently "curb traditional and positional conflicts".[121] What remains clear is that human achievement is imperfect. However, it is evident that the essential problem is this: inadequate transfer of property through valuation (number) games in financial instruments. Sensibly powerful rules for corporation and market need to prevent this. Good communication – sustainable financial reporting – for good corporations and projects within a sustainable financial system is required.[122]

## 2.6 Sustainability: Financial Reporting for a Better World

### *2.6.1 Market and Corporation as Orderly Events*

The importance of the financial system affects the whole: Sustainable financial reporting (accounting), id est good governance, finance and valuation of human corporations for a better world. The human corporation as a legal institution led by humans (corporate directors) for a privately organised enterprise operates its financing (business) in a market-based way; this includes valuation and corporate governance. This points to financial theories and legal practice current until now, in particular the efficient market theory with the market doctrine, supported by the U.S. Supreme Court,[123] and the way so-called free markets function. What is a free market supposed to be? – The term is usually, specifically in the diction of neoclassical economic theory, politics, and practice, with an emphasis on the attribute (adjective) "free", misunderstood as a carte blanche.

What is necessary for comprehension of the term corporation is this clarification: the market as an institution is an *orderly* event (*geordnete Veranstaltung*, see 3.3.4), practically its epitome. A market as an institution in general serves the co-ordination (satisfaction) of human needs through supply and demand, to this purpose building on rule-driven action (negotiation, valuation, contract); even on a black market there are certain rules (cf. supply and demand, pricing, sanctions).[124] This rule-drivenness is crucial for the corporation and its business operations. However, Milton Friedman's neoliberal catchphrase that a corporate executive's social responsibility is "to make as much money as possible" [125] (the so-called Friedman doctrine) has

[121] Eisenberg (1989) pp. 1524-1525.

[122] See in more details chapter 4.

[123] *Halliburton Co. v. Erica P. John Fund, Inc.*, 573 U.S. 258 (2014). Leading *Basic, Inc. v. Levinson*, 485 U.S. 224, 108 S.Ct. 978, 99 L.Ed.2d 194 (1988).

[124] See North (1992) in terms of modern institutional economics (information, transaction costs etc.), cf. Coase (1937). Luttermann (1998) pp. 151-162 (on investment, institutions and participation in profit), pp. 465-485 (juridical analysis of the economy; on this also above 1.6, below, e.g., 4.13, 5.2.2 and 7.3.2with 9.7).

[125] Milton Friedman, The New York Times, 13.09.1970: www.nytimes.com/1970/09/13/archives/a-friedman-doctrine-the-social-responsibility-of-business-is-to.html (accessed: 22.08.2025).

wide currency. But Friedman added: "while conforming to the basic rules of the society, both those embodied in law and those embodied in ethical custom".[126] This is disregarded, while it strengthens our position. As opposed to centralism, the market is characterised by voluntary co-operation through co-ordination (cf. 1.7: "order based on order"). The elementary proposition is that both parties to an economic transaction benefit from it, provided it "*is bi-laterally voluntary and informed*".[127]

Thus, humans shape their individual transactions, guided by the rules of the respective market (as an orderly event). Market and corporation are therefore reciprocally related to each other in a social system. This comprises the economy and the society essentially as a legal system (see chapter 8: the *Vermögensordnung*). We have already dealt with this regarding the idea of peace and justice as the constitution of liberty, built on responsibility and reason.[128] Overall, the basic issue is a necessary balance (equilibrium). Practically, for the corporation this means letting the market and corporate activity operate in what Friedrich August von Hayek generally described as a system of liberty under general laws (rules). The green paradigm change affects all business activities (markets), marking out far-reaching goals and objectives. What is therefore required is a sensible measure.

### *2.6.2 Financial Reporting: A Right to Information and the Capital Market Concept*

What should be kept in mind is that sustainable financial reporting (i.e., the law of accounting, valuation and auditing) is at the same time a right to information: the right of the investor to be informed about the assets, liabilities, financial position and profit or loss and the profit situation of the corporation by the persons responsible (corporate directors). Structurally, experience works. For information has at all times been the basis of entrepreneurship and politics, as is illustrated globally by the pre-Babylonian temple economy, the Roman postal system (*cursus publicus*), the capital economy (double-entry bookkeeping and accounting) of Venetian merchants and of the British Empire.[129] Information deficits, balance sheet manipulation ("cooking the books") promote regulation of accounting (i.e., financial reporting and auditing, disclosure).[130] Innovation has minimised the time factor and the data volume of information transmission, in particular digital corporate publicity in the age of the internet.

---

[126] Ibid.

[127] Friedman (1962, 2002) p. 13 (italic in the original).

[128] See above 1.6 (with chapter 8) and 2.5, fundamentally chapter 9.

[129] Overall Luttermann (2003) Einf BilanzR recitals 19-25.

[130] See above 2.4.2 and below 3.3 with chapter 4.

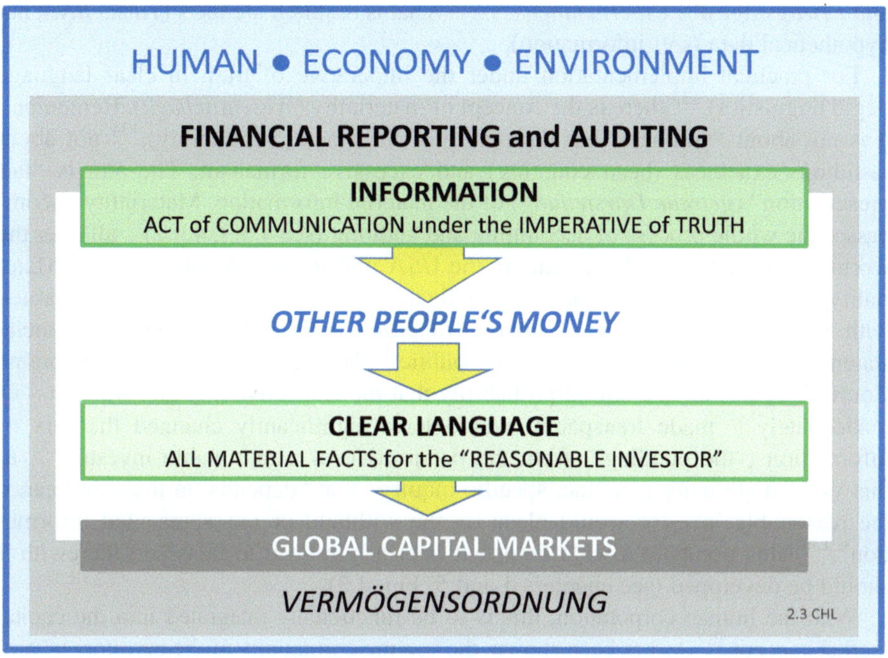


**Fig. 2.3** Information of the reasonable investor through financial reporting in clear language as a legal act (*Rechtsakt;* see also below 4.12.3 (Fig. 4.8) and chapter 5)

However, the measure of quality remains. In the word "information", we recognise Latin *forma* for "form, picture", and *informare* for "to shape, brief", that is, vividly expressed: to "put someone in the picture" (German *"jemanden ins Bild setzen"*). In English, this becomes information (to inform), as an action (*Handlung*) paraphrased as communication of instructive knowledge about certain facts, subjects, events; and in a stricter sense: an account, report, a formal statement.[131] Naturally under the imperative of truth and clarity (*Gebot der Wahrheit und Klarheit*). The claim of those persons with a right to information is to be informed about the entrepreneurial operations in a factually adequate way (legal act, *Rechtsakt*). As is regulated in European law in the general norm Article 4(3) (1) Directive 2013/34/EU for financial reporting, the legal representatives of the corporation (German: *Kapitalgesellschaft*) have to provide "a true and fair view" of the financial status and the profit situation in the annual accounts to this purpose (*"ein den tatsächlichen Verhältnissen entsprechendes Bild der Vermögens-, Finanz-*

[131] Cf. Brown (1993) p. 1364 (inform, information). On clear communication below 4.12.3 (with Fig. 4.8), on clear meaning 7.6.1 and 7.6.3.

*und Ertragslage des Unternehmens"*).[132] What is required are facts (*Tatsachen*), not hypothetical data (soft information).

For practical implementation under the imperative of truth in clear language (legal linguistics),[133] there is the concept of materiality (*Wesentlichkeit*). Remember, it is not about "numbers" but the reality of life (facts, verifiability),[134] not about fastidious exactness (bean counting) and excessive formalism. The aim is "fair presentation" (*getreue Darstellung*) of the material information. Materiality encompasses the whole process of accounting and auditing (see 4.5.3, 4.9.7) – all over the world. Legislation has shaped this in the USA with general legal standards. Materiality in the context of the publicity obligatory in securities trading is interpreted with regard to the recipient horizon (*Empfängerhorizont*), readers of financial statements (the interested, investing public). According to the U.S. Supreme Court, there has to be a strong probability that the respective fact that was not – or inadequately – made transparent would have significantly changed the mix of information ("the pudding") from the perspective of a reasonable investor.[135] In this view, materiality is a "fact-specific inquiry" that "depends on the significance the reasonable investor would place on the withheld or misrepresented information".[136] This points to a wide field, but is clearly related to facts and therewith it should be developed (see chapters 4 and 5, Fig. 4.3).

With the human corporation, this is to be functionally integrated into the capital market concept.[137] As has been shown, the venture community of the investors (shareholders, bondholders: *Wagnisgemeinschaft*) inherent in the life circumstances overall depends on sustainable financial reporting. The classic reduction to the shareholders (corporate law) as the risk bearers (shareholders' equity) misjudges that in the publicly held corporation the shareholders are hardly willing or able to argue their interests effectively. The assets component (*Vermögenskomponente*) of the shareholders property

---

[132] See – also for different languages – Directive 2013/34/EU of 26 June 2013 on the annual financial statements, consolidated financial statements and related reports of certain types of undertakings, repealing Directives 78/660/EEC and 83/349/EEC, OJ L 182, 29.6.2013, pp. 19-76 (German version: DE). Basically Luttermann (2003) § 264 HGB recitals 16-169. See also above 2.4.3 (German § 264(2)(1) HGB), below 7.4.2 (reasonable investor), and Luttermann (2013b).

[133] Luttermann, C. and Luttermann, K. (2020) pp. 201-242, also for a multilingual setting, see in English Luttermann, C. and Luttermann, K. (2021). See below 7.6 on "softness" and reasonable certainty.

[134] See above 1.6.3 (German: *die "tatsächlichen Verhältnisse"*, § 264(2)(1) HGB), chapter 4 (esp. 4.5) with verifiability (valuation law), esp. 4.11.4 and 5.2.4. Cf. overall chapter 6 in the light of (hyper-)speculation.

[135] *Basic, Inc. v. Levinson*, 485 U.S. 224, 231-232, 108 S.Ct. 978, 99 L.Ed.2d 194 (1988), on SEC Rule 10b-5 under § 10(b) Securities Exchange Act 1934 ("materiality" of messages about negotiations regarding fusions). On facts and materiality below 4.5.3.

[136] *Basic*, ibid. (485 U.S. 224), at 240; citing this decision: *Hillson Partners L.P. v. Adage, Inc.*, 42 F.3d 204, 209 (4th Cir. 1994), on the influence of the time factor regarding regulations of materiality (at 214-215). Cf. on the other hand on so-called "soft information" – refuted by the SEC: *Flynn v. Bass Bros. Enterprises, Inc.*, 744 F.2d. 978, 985-6 (3rd 1984). See below 7.6.

[137] See above 1.5, 2.2 and 2.5 to 2.6. Basically Luttermann (1998), from p. 486.

position (*Anteileigentum*, equity, *Eigenkapital*) dominates. Buying shares is widely investment of capital (corporate finance), as for the other investors, creditors (*Fremdkapitalgeber*). Overall, what provides material protection is a legal order in which sustainable financial reporting, id est with effective control by independent auditors (auditing, see 4.9), prevents arbitrary shift of risk and profit.[138]

## 2.6.3 *Perspectives: Attempt at a Legal Clarification*

So we should think of the human corporation as an outstanding development of the human spirit and a chance that should be designed meaningfully and made use of sensibly (human corporation). This holds in a global dimension, seen on an intercultural level (see 2.7). However, as William Shakespeare already put it in the Merchant of Venice, "the world is still deceiv'd with ornament".[139] – So let us strive toward the core of our consideration. The corporation, as a creation of the law[140] and a global capital-market phenomenon, in the characteristics of its financing function provides a universal instrument for effecting good in detail and as a whole. With the help of sustainably organised business activity, practiced responsibly by people transcending ideological reduction and deflection. Basically, the common basis for this is *financial reporting and auditing* as a necessary act, documenting verified corporate management (information function, see chapter 4).

Remember, financial reporting (accounting) is a legal act, not marketing. This holds overall for valuation, accounting and auditing (corporate disclosure, German *Rechnungslegung*). The law must provide the clear measure so that the addressee of the information is in fact "put into the picture" (i.e. informed) by those responsible (see 2.6.2). At the same time, the corporate directors and auditors can take responsibility by providing the necessary evidence (facts) of good corporate governance (due diligence) and good auditing (compliance). For the market-based function of the corporation – with its financing (capitalisation) via the capital markets – their financial reporting (valuation) has to be clarified, legally, for meaningful, sustainable practice, id est for *sustainable finance and financial reporting* (good governance). The following considerations shall serve our further course:

(1) *What is the purpose of financial reporting by the directors of the corporation?* – In short: financial reporting (accounting) intends to inform. Its purpose is to inform the investors through the corporate directors giving account on their dealings with other people's money (accounting as a legal act), for controlling (auditing as a legal act, too), id est: accounting and auditing as verified information for investors

---

[138] See above 1.4.1 and 1.4.3. For details below, esp. 3.5.4 and 3.7.

[139] Shakespeare (1600), act III, scene II (Bassanio).

[140] See for details above 2.4 (historically: 2.3.3), chapter 3 (esp. 3.2.1) and 7.3.

(accountability, finance function of the corporation).[141] That is the *ratio legis* of financial reporting. It requires sustainability of the information (truth, i.e. facts instead of "soft information") in the sense of independent – in the last instance juridical – verifiability of the information (sustainable financial reporting). This is not paid attention to adequately. We will discuss the purpose as a whole, including the following questions.

(2) *Why are sustainable finance, financial reporting and auditing essential for the corporation?* – In short: Because it safeguards that the corporation as a permanent financial instrument (finance function) with its own legal personality (legal subject) and led by corporate directors (humans) functions correctly – despite the human weakness of wanting to make figures seem better than they are. The imperative of truth provides the measure, namely for the numbers and figures (*Zahlen und Zahlenwerke*) and the narrative parts (e.g., name of the balance sheet item, notes). The imperative requires at the same time their verifiability for control (auditing), id est financial reporting and auditing for sustainable value creation (*nachhaltige Wertschöpfung*).[142] This is widely lacking,[143] as in the penetration of the subject matter. It may be watered down through peripheral aspects, such as information for "investment purposes" (cf. "decision usefulness" theory). This becomes clear overall.

(3) *Why should sustainable business activity of the corporation (so-called "green" finance and investment) be integrated into general financial reporting?* – In short: Because the purpose of reporting embraces the complete spectrum (principle of completeness – *Vollständigkeitsprinzip*), id est all financially relevant activity (principle of materiality – *Wesentlichkeitsprinzip*), and is valid independent of type, content or structure of the business activity. That has to be fulfilled by the responsible leaders of any corporation as a legal act under the imperative of truth (see (1) and (2)).[144] Accordingly, it is noteworthy that so-called "green" sustainability, id est in the sense of climate protection and human rights, can lead to special demands for governance, finance and valuation (note basically: "climate risk as a financial risk is relevant")[145] as well as for reporting and auditing; in particular for the prevention of abuse ("greenwashing"). This needs to be made clear.

---

[141] See above 1.3 to 1.5 and below, esp. chapters 4 and 5. Basically Luttermann (2003) and (1998).

[142] See overall above 2.2, 2.4 to 2.6 (with Fig. 2.2: "substance over form") and chapter 1, below esp. chapters 3 and 4.

[143] See in details esp. chapter 6.

[144] See above, esp. 1.7 and 2.2 with chapters 4 and 7.

[145] See below 8.4.3, with 4.5.3. Fundamentally Williams (2021) on corporate climate responsibility and fiduciary duties with more references, see also below 8.4.3. Cf. the position of the Trump administration in the USA, above 1.4.2 (note 31) and below in 6.7.2. Overall for sustainable development and climate risk management UN World Conferences and Office for Disaster Risk Reduction (UNDRR: www.undrr.org, accessed: 22.08.2025).

(4) *How is sustainable finance, financial reporting and auditing to be implemented adequately in practice as legal protection?* – In short: The function of the corporation is faithful action by the enterprise leaders with other people's money in a sustainable order of assets (*Vermögensordnung*). Its legal framework protects the persons involved in case of disagreement about the regularity of a material valuation through the practice of civil proceedings (court). This is what the action of those responsible for leading the enterprise is based on legally and what it has to be related to in an individual case. Truth is the imperative, procedurally built on facts (information, see (1) and (2)). This is what the concept of civil procedural valuation is accordingly based on, which should be established as sustainable financial reporting and auditing,[146] as will be shown overall.
(5) *How can sustainable protection for individual investment, society and nature be established worldwide?* – In short: through an international order of assets (*internationale Vermögensordnung*).[147] With regard to the corporation, this fundamentally concerns the protection of all investments and especially overseas investment in the transnational capital transactions of enterprises and projects. For foreign, private legal subjects (humans, legal persons) invest in the legal domain of another state. This bears on private law and the law of nations and needs to be calibrated with the green paradigm change for climate protection and human rights. Economy and ecology, along with advanced technology (e.g. AI), have to be reconciled through humanity, id est sustainable business activities in a global order (*globale Vermögensordnung*). This is truly a field obviously wide and incomparable,[148] which may be further researched and fertilised through sustainable finance, financial reporting and auditing: for a better world (creation of value).

## 2.7 Concept of Trust: Corporation and Intercultural Reason

Practically, this is a challenge for all those involved. Corporate activity and investment, enterprises and projects naturally transcend borders, traditionally conceived of from the perspective of national economies. Remember, financial reporting (accounting) is not about numbers, but people, business, life circumstances (human corporation). With the corporation, business and financing are constructed transnationally. This means that manifold characters and cultural patterns meet, with complex *Weltanschauungen* having an impact. What may be of help in the necessary dialogue of

[146] See chapters 4 and 5. Basically on the imperative of truth and facts Luttermann (2003) § 264 HGB recitals 125-128, see there also Einf BilanzR recitals 26-45, 60-95 and 107-136. For valuation law practice Luttermann (2023).

[147] Fundamentally above 1.6 with chapter 8.

[148] See chapters 8 and 9.

cultures is an awareness that we are prone to taking our own section of the world for the whole picture, as Karl Jaspers has warned: We may press beyond the world we are experiencing through our knowledge, but even with this knowledge we remain irresistibly prejudiced – what lies beyond we do not see, because we cannot even divine it.[149] What can build bridges is a reciprocal understanding for differentness, in particular through comparative law work.

So what is needed is an intercultural approach to corporate finance, a concept of trust. Intercultural here denotes the leading principle for future-oriented thinking which everybody may contribute to. The practice of international financing of enterprises and projects hitherto in general focusses monolithically on so-called "neoclassical" (Anglo-American-style)[150] theories and models. This involves abridgements and distortions, as evidenced globally in the massive shift of assets (so-called "shareholder value") and the economy of disaster (so-called "financial crisis" etc.). The game is better described as one of greed (debt crisis): creating oceans of debt with worthless instruments while shifting real wealth into own harbours.[151] A multipolar world makes demands that are interculturally more diverse: sustainable legal structures, in order to develop capital markets globally for financing enterprises and projects, for good, sustainable transformation of the economy. Humanity constitutes the foundation of the corporation, for prosperity and peace.

Economy, state and society are failing with simplistic structures lacking in substance. This also applies to the corporation, its leadership, financing and valuation, which are treated here. What needs to be established is the necessary trust between the corporate directors (corporation) and the investors. Capital as the basis of the corporation is *money plus trust* in real values, secured through sustainable financial reporting and auditing (concept of trust and control).[152] This capital of trust (*Vertrauenskapital*) may be formed interculturally and be effective in the necessary transformation of the economy, especially for human rights and environmental protection. This can take place through the common bond that appears to be inherent to all cultures: reason (faculty of reason), id est, the priority of reason.[153] The modern corporation should be treated accordingly as a human corporation; this may result in joint success for enterprises and projects worldwide: reaching the common goal (purpose) in peace and prosperity.

[149] Jaspers (1919, 1994) pp. 17-18 and from 141. Basically Fikentscher (2004), as well as on the dialogue of cultures Luttermann (1999a).

[150] See overall and, e.g., above 2.3.2, below 6.2.1 with chapter 3 (esp. 3.2.3, 3.3.2), chapters 4 and 7.

[151] See chapter 1 (with Fig. 1.1) and, e.g., below 3.2.3, 3.3.3, 3.5.3; comprehensively chapters 6 and 7 (individual banking on trust), with chapters 4 and 5. In a common global perspective chapters 8 and 9.

[152] Basically above 1.5.2 (Fig. 1.2) and, on individual responsibility, chapters 6 and 7. Luttermann (2019) and (2020).

[153] See, e.g., above 2.2.2 with Popper (1987) and Sen (2007) p. 161. Cf. Mengzi (Mencius), book VI A, 7.

# References


Aliber, R. Z., Kindleberger, C. P., & McCauley, R. N. (2023). *Manias, panics and crashes: A history of financial crises* (8th ed.). Palgrave Macmillan.

Applebaum, A. (2024). *Autocracy, Inc.: The dictators who want to run the world*. Random House.

Banoo, S. (2020). *Lifting of the corporate veil: Decoding the doctrine of separate legal personality*. Available at SSRN: https://ssrn.com/abstract=3609245 (accessed: 22.08.2025).

Berle, A. A. Jr. (1928). *Studies in the law of corporation finance*, William S. Hein & Co.

Berle, A. A. Jr., & Means, G. C. (1932, 1967). *The modern corporation and private property* (2nd ed.). Harcourt, Brace & World, 1967.

Bernstein, P. L. (1993). *Capital ideas: the improbable origins of modern Wall Street*. Free Press.

Boer, R. (2021). *Socialism with Chinese characteristics*. Springer.

Brandeis, L. D. (1914). *Other people's money and how the bankers use it*. Frederick A. Stokes Company Publishers.

Bräutigam, D. (2009). *The dragon's gift: The real story of China in Africa*. Oxford University Press.

Brown, L. (Ed.). (1993). *The new shorter Oxford English dictionary on historical principles* (2 Vols.). Clarendon Press.

Buxbaum, R. M., & Hopt, K. J. (1988). Legal harmonization. In M. Cappelletti, M. Seccombe, & J. Weiler (Eds.), *Interpretation through law* (Vol. 4). de Gruyter.

Chandler, A. D. (1977). *The visible hand: The managerial revolution in American business*. Harvard University Press.

Chang, X. (Ed.). (2015). *Society building: A China model of social development* (2nd ed.). Cambridge Scholars Publishing.

Coase, R. H. (1937). The nature of the firm. *Economica, 4*, 386–405.

Coffee, J. C. (2001). The rise of dispersed ownership: The roles of law and the state in the separation of ownership and control. *Yale Law Journal, 111*, 1–81.

Costanza, R., Cumberland, J. H., Daly, H., Goodland, R., Norgaard, R. B., Kubiszewski, I., & Franco, C. (2015). *An introduction to ecological economics* (2nd ed.). CRC Press.

du Plessis, J. J., Großfeld, B., Luttermann, C., Saenger, I., & Sandrock, O. (2007). *German corporate governance in international and European context* (1st ed.) (with Matthias Casper, 2nd ed., 2012, 3rd ed. 2017). Springer.

Eisenberg, M. A. (1976). *The structure of the corporation: A legal analysis*. Little, Brown and Co.

Eisenberg, M. A. (1989). The structure of corporation law. *Columbia Law Review, 89*, 1461–1525.

Everling, O. (Ed.). (2020). *Social credit rating*. Springer.

Fikentscher, W. (2004). *Modes of thought: A study in the anthropology of law and religion* (2nd ed.). Mohr Siebeck.

Folk. (2022). On the Delaware General Corporation Law, by: R. S. Saunders, A. L. Land, J. C. Voss, & C. C. Gardner. Wolters Kluwer.

French, H. W. (2014). *China's second continent: How a million migrants are building a new empire*. Knopf Doubleday Publishing Group.

Friedman, L. M. (1985). *A history of American law* (2nd ed.). Simon & Schuster.

Friedman, M. (1962, 2002). *Capitalism and freedom* (40th Anniversary ed.). University of Chicago Press.

Fukuyama, F. (1992). *The end of history and the last man*. Free Press.

Galbraith, J. K. (1994). *A short history of financial euphoria*. Viking Penguin.

Gelpern, A., Horn, S., Morris, S., Parks, B., & Trebesch, C. (2021). *How China lends: A rare look into 100 debt contracts with foreign governments*. https://ssrn.com/abstract=3886817 (accessed: 22.08.2025).

Goethe, J. W. von (1773). *Götz von Berlichingen*. Printed anonymously.

Goethe, J. W. von (1808). *Faust: Eine Tragödie, Erster Teil*. JG Cotta'sche Buchhandlung.

Gower. (2021). *Principles of modern company law* (11th ed.) by P. L. Davies, S. Worthington, & C. Hare. Thomson Reuters.

Grantham, R., & Rickett, C. (Eds.). (1998). *Corporate personality in the 20$^{th}$ century*. Hart Publishing.

Großfeld, B. (1968). *Aktiengesellschaft, Unternehmenskonzentration und Kleinaktionär*. Mohr Siebeck.

Großfeld, B. (2019). *Schritte über Grenzen: Rechtsvergleichende Kulturerfahrung*, Lit Verlag.

Hayek, F. A. von (1991). *Die Verfassung der Freiheit* (3rd ed.). Mohr Siebeck.

Hillman, J. E. (2021). *The digital Silk Road: China's quest to wire the world and win the future*. Profile Books.

Heilbroner, R. L. (1992). *The worldly philosophers: The lives, times and ideas of the great economic thinkers* (6th ed.). Touchstone.

Hering, T., Olbrich, M., & Rollberg, R. (2010). Zur angelsächsischen Bewertungstheorie als Mitursache der Finanzkrise. In F. Keuper & F. Neumann (Eds.), *Corporate governance, risk management und compliance* (pp. 29–43). Gabler.

Jaspers, K. (1919, 1994). Psychologie der Weltanschauungen (2nd ed.). Piper.

Jensen, M. C. (1989/1997). Eclipse of the public corporation. *Harvard Business Review, 67*(Sept-Oct 1989), revised 1997.

Jhering, R. von (1877). *Der Zweck im Recht* (Vol. 1). Breitkopf & Härtel.

Josephson, M. (1934). *The Robber Barons: The great American capitalists 1861–1901*. Harcourt, Brace & Co.

Jung, P. (2002). *Der Unternehmergesellschafter als personaler Kern der rechtsfähigen Gesellschaft*. Mohr Siebeck.

Kissinger, H. (2015). *World order: Reflections on the character of nations and the course of history*. Penguin Books.

Klein, F. (1904). *Die neueren Entwicklungen in Verfassung und Recht der Aktiengesellschaft*. Manz.

Knight, F. H. (1921/1971). *Risk, uncertainty and profit*, first published by Houghton Mifflin Company, here edition 1971 with an introduction by G. J. Stigler, University of Chicago Press.

Kricheldorf, H. R. (2014). *Erkenntnisse und Irrtümer in Medizin und Naturwissenschaften*. Springer.

Larcom, R. C. (1937). *Delaware corporation*. Johns Hopkins Press.

Laux, F. (1998). *Die Lehre vom Unternehmen an sich: Walther Rathenau und die aktienrechtliche Diskussion in der Weimarer Republik*. Duncker & Humblot.

Levitt, A. (1998). *The "numbers game"*, 28.09.1998. https://www.sec.gov/news/speech/speecharchive/1998/spch220.txt (accessed: 22.08.2025).

Lin, K. J., Lu, X., Zhang, J., & Zheng, Y. (2020). State-owned enterprises in China: A review of 40 years of research and practice. *China Journal of Accounting Research, 13*, 31–55.

Lowell, J. R. (1887). *On democracy and other essays*. Macmillan and Company.

Lowenstein, R. (2000). *When genius failed: The rise and fall of Long-Term Capital Management*. Random House.

Luttermann, C. (1998). *Unternehmen, Kapital und Genußrechte: Eine Studie über Grundlagen der Unternehmensfinanzierung und zum internationalen Kapitalmarktrecht*. Mohr Siebeck.

Luttermann, C. (1999a). Dialog der Kulturen: Vergleichendes Handels- und Kapitalmarktrecht im Sprachspiegel. In U. Hübner & W. F. Ebke (Eds.), *Festschrift for Bernhard Großfeld* (pp. 771–789). Verlag Recht und Wirtschaft.

Luttermann, C. (1999b). *Bilanzrecht in den USA und internationale Konzernrechnungslegung*. Mohr Siebeck.

Luttermann, C. (2003). In B. Kropff & J. Semler (Eds.), *Münchener Kommentar zum Aktiengesetz* (2nd ed., Vol. 5/1). CH Beck Verlag.

Luttermann, C. (2006). Unternehmenskontrolle und Bilanzmanipulation nach anglo-amerikanischen Mustern (IAS/IFRS und U.S. 2.3.3 and "GAAP"). *Die Wirtschaftsprüfung (WPg), 59*, 778–786.

Luttermann, C. (2008). Juristische Person, Konzern und Existenzvernichtungshaftung. *Juristische Arbeitsblätter (JA), 12*, 833–838.

Luttermann, C. (2009). Islamic Finance: Ein Dialog über Recht, Weltwirtschaft und Religionen. *Juristenzeitung (JZ), 64*, 706–715.

Luttermann, C. (2010). Regulierungsperspektiven: „War und ist die Finanzkrise die Folge von Hyperspekulation?". *Österreichisches Bank-Archiv (Zeitschrift für das gesamte Bank- und Börsenwesen – Journal of Banking and Financial Research, ÖBA), 58*, 444–448.

Luttermann, C. (2013a). Recht als praktizierte Ethik und unternehmerische Verantwortungskultur. In E. Weber (Ed.), *Albert Schweitzer – Hundert Jahre Menschlichkeit: Spital Lambarene (1913–2013)* (pp. 74–76). Deutscher Hilfsverein für das Albert-Schweitzer-Spital in Lambarene e.V.

Luttermann, C. (2013b). Neue Bilanzrichtlinie: Europäisches Bewertungsrecht in prozessualer Praxis. *Neue Zeitschrift für Gesellschaftsrecht (NZG), 16*, 1128–1133.

Luttermann, C. (2014). Alibabas Wunderwelt: Perspektiven chinesischer Kapitalmarkt- und Gesellschaftsrechtspraxis. *Recht der Internationalen Wirtschaft (RIW), 60*, 777–784.

Luttermann, C. (2017). VR China: Neues Foreign Investment Law and Gold Trade Notes. *Recht der Internationalen Wirtschaft (RIW), 63*, 255–263.

Luttermann, C. (2019). Perspectives of infrastructure project finance: intercultural investment, connectivity and trust. *Finance: Theory and Practice (Финансы: теория и практика), 23*, 27–37.

Luttermann, C. (2020). Zum Vertrauenskonzept für Interkulturelle Projektfinanzierung: Kapital, Vertrag und Kooperation. In D. Hummel (Ed.), *EU's connectivity in times of Eurasian dynamics, challenges for banking and finance* (pp. 35–48). WeltTrends.

Luttermann, C. (2021). Grüner Paradigmenwechsel für Unternehmensfinanzierung, Vermögensanlage und Bewertungsrecht. *Recht der Internationalen Wirtschaft (RIW), 67*, 191–200.

Luttermann, C. (2023). Unternehmensbewertung im Spannungsfeld von Rechts- und Wirtschaftswissenschaft. In K. Petersen, C. Zwirner, & G. Zimney (Eds.), *Handbuch Unternehmensbewertung* (3rd ed., pp. 163–202). Bundesanzeiger Verlag.

Luttermann, C., & Luttermann, K. (2020). *Sprachenrecht für die Europäische Union*. Mohr Siebeck.

Luttermann, C., & Luttermann, K. (2021). Towards peace in Europe: On legal linguistics, prosperity and European identity – the European Reference Language System for the European Union. *International Journal of Legal Discourse, 6*, 7–41.

Maçães, B. (2020). *Belt and Road: A Chinese world order*. Hurst Publishers.

Maliszewska, M., & van der Mensbrugghe, D. (2019). *The Belt and Road initiative: Economic, poverty and environmental impacts*. World Bank. Policy Research Working Paper 8814.

Matschke, M. J., Brösel, G., & Toll, C. (2024). *Unternehmensbewertung: Funktionen, Methoden, Grundsätze* (5th ed.). SpringerGabler.

Mengzi (Mencius). (2012). *Von der Freiheit des Menschen*. German translation by Richard Wilhelm 1921.

Modigliani, F., & Miller, M. H. (1958). The cost of capital, corporation finance and the theory of investment. *American Economic Review, 48*, 261–297.

Mommsen, T. (1865). *Römische Geschichte* (1. Band, 4th ed.). Weidmannsche Buchhandlung.

North, D. C. (1992). *Institutionen, institutioneller Wandel und Wirtschaftsleistung*. Mohr Siebeck.

Petersen, K., Zwirner, C., & Zimny, G. (Eds.). (2023). *Handbuch Unternehmensbewertung* (3rd ed.). Reguvius.

Pistor, K. (2019). *The code of capital: How the law creates wealth and inequality*. Princeton University Press.

Pölnitz, G. von (1949). *Jakob Fugger: Kaiser, Kirche und Kapital in der oberdeutschen Renaissance*. Mohr Siebeck.

Popper, K. R. (1987). *Auf der Suche nach einer besseren Welt* (2nd ed.). Piper.

Rappaport, A. (1986). *Creating shareholder value: The new standard for business performance*. Free Press (2nd ed. 1997: Creating shareholder value: a guide for managers and investors).

Rathenau, W. (1918). *Von Kommenden Dingen*. S. Fischer (translation by E. and C. Paul: Rathenau, *In days to come*, 1921).
Rathenau, W. (1922). *Vom Aktienwesen: Eine geschäftliche Betrachtung*. S. Fischer.
Rayner, R. (2008). *The associates: Four capitalists who created California*. W.W. Norton & Company.
Reimann, M., & Zimmermann, R. (Eds.). (2006). *The Oxford handbook of comparative law*. Oxford University Press.
Shakespeare, W. (1600). *The merchant of Venice*. Thomas Heyes.
Savigny, F. C. von (1840). *System des heutigen römischen Rechts* (Vol. I). Veit.
Schmalz, M. C. (2018). Common-ownership concentration and corporate conduct. *Annual Review of Financial Economics, 10*, 413–448.
Schweitzer, A. (1923). *Kultur und Ethik (Kulturphilosophie I and II)*. CH Beck Verlag (ed. 1990).
Seavoy, R. E. (1982). *The origins of the American business corporation, 1784-1855*. Greenwood Press.
Sen, A. (2007). *Identity and violence: The illusion of destiny*. Penguin Books.
Sharpe, W. F. (1991). Capital asset pricing with and without negative holdings. *Journal of Finance, 46*, 489–509.
Siems, M., & Yap, P. J. (2024). *The Cambridge handbook of comparative law*. Cambridge University Press.
Steinmetz, G. (2015). *The richest man who ever lived: The life and times of Jacob Fugger*. Simon & Schuster.
Stiglitz, J. E. (2010). *Freefall: America, free markets, and the sinking of the world economy*. W. W. Norton & Company.
Strine, L. E., Jr. (2014). Can we do better by ordinary Investors? A pragmatic reaction to the dueling ideological mythologists of corporate law. *Columbia Law Review, 114*, 449–502.
Tooze, A. (2019). *Crashed: How a decade of financial crisis changed the world*. Penguin Books Great Britain.
Vitali, S., Glattfelder, J. B., & Battiston, S. (2011). The network of global corporate control. *PLoS One, 6*(10), 1–6.
Wang, R. "Ray". (2015). *Disrupting digital business*. Harvard Business Review Press.
Wedel, J. R. (2009). *Shadow elite: How the world's new power brokers undermine democracy, government, and the free market*. Basic Books.
Williams, C. A. (2021). Fiduciary duties and corporate climate responsibility. *Vanderbilt Law Review, 74*, 1875–1916.
Xi, J. (2014). *China regieren (the governance of China)*. CBT China Book Trading.
Xu, L. (2019). The changing perspectives of Chinese law: Socialist rule of law, emerging case law and the Belt and Road initiative. *The Chinese Journal of Global Governance, 5*, 153–175.

# Chapter 3
# Corporation Finance: Real Disclosure, Profit, and Liability

"Much of the opposition to a system of freedom under general laws arises from the inability to conceive of an effective co-ordination of human activities without deliberate organization by a commanding intelligence."*

*Friedrich August von Hayek*

## Contents



*Hayek, Die Verfassung der Freiheit, 3rd ed. 1991, Mohr Siebeck, Tübingen, p. 229 (The constitution of liberty, 1960, The collected works of F.A. Hayek, XVII, ed. by Hamowy, The University of Chicago Press, 2011).



C. Luttermann, *Human Corporation for Sustainable Development*,
https://doi.org/10.1007/978-3-032-07615-1_3

## 3.1 On Truth, Economic System, and Magic Flutes

"This portrait is enchantingly beautiful" sings Tamino, the prince in The Magic Flute, when he is shown a picture of Pamina, the daughter of the Queen of the Night. Wolfgang Amadeus Mozart, the unique composer of this famous opera (*Die Zauberflöte*),[1] conveys the magic to listeners through his music. The fairytale, with diverse characters in a scintillating whole, is meant to enchant people and capture their imagination. It uses number symbolism (three) in the text, translated into many languages, and in the music, which needs no translation. Music beyond words. A masterpiece of timeless art that fascinates people all over the world. The world we are talking about.

A similar kind of magic is also at work in the global economy, on the business stage and especially on the capital markets. Of course, at first sight, it is so-called "hard facts", money, that ring here: business financing and investment (corporate finance), figures dominate, cool calculation. – But what is the real situation? – Quite simply, it is like on all markets: busy comings and goings, pied pipers all over! Not magnificent like Mozart's bird catcher Papageno. On behalf of publicly held corporations, paid storytellers, fundraisers are on their way, seeking for one catch: other people's money. Rather simple, professional players with figures in the "numbers game" (e.g., mathematical formulas, models and valuations, ratings, financial reports),[2] bent on sending one message to the investing audience: "a beautiful portrait", id est – in competitive terms – the prettier picture of their corporation on the capital markets.[3]

[1] Mozart, The Magic Flute, Act 1, Scene 1 (Tamino's tenor aria), first performance 30.09.1791 in Vienna (Austria).

[2] Levitt (1998).

[3] For the elementary meaning in theory and practice below 3.2.2, 3.5.5 and 3.6.1; also in 3.8 and 3.9. One should be aware of incentive systems, limits of law (accounting) and expectation gaps, see, e.g. 3.3.4, 3.5.2 and 3.5.3. Fundamentally Luttermann (2015a) and Luttermann (2003) recitals 123-133. On comparative perspectives, esp. reforming the "modern" corporation Vagts (1966), and overall on the dialog of cultures, e.g., above 1.6.3, below 3.8 and Luttermann (1999b).

However: The participants in the global financial markets require faithful information about the financial position and performance of a corporation.[4] The numerous accounting scandals that have been revealed since the epic fall of Enron Corporation and its auditing company Arthur Andersen LLP (2001),[5] as well as dubious financial engineering and valuation mounting in the world-wide economic crisis (*Weltschuldenkrise*), continuing ever since, have destroyed trust – the epitome of capital in human affairs (see 1.5.2). We are experiencing a period of massive changes, authoritarian regimes with war in Europe again, and of climate change (see chapter 1), facing a turning point: Acting in an ethically responsible way is part of human nature and climate protection at the same time as part of entrepreneurship – it is for humans the essence of a free order worth living.

The economic system hitherto, built on debts ("leveraging"), future profits and fantasy values (so-called "fair value"), provides no solid basis. Financial instruments, increasingly with ecological content right up to greenwashing (malpractice, fraud), have become complex and abstract (structured finance); misleading due to lack of transparency, misinformation, difficult to detect (cf. overall the human factor, see 6.1.2). They inflate accounts and produce pseudo-profits. Who can understand this? – Basically, they are the paper resource of the financial industry for covertly shifting risks, while at the same time producing magnificent profits, fees and bonuses for those involved – as long as business flourishes. Manipulation gains ground, valuations of billions denominated in US dollars and other currencies (fiat money) burst like bubbles.[6] From mountains of debt, we are staring into an abyss: corporations, financial markets, economies are suffering and collapsing.

Remember, this is attributed to Mozart: The music is not in the notes, but in the silence in between. Where ethically responsible action is lacking, deficits will accumulate. We have already shown this and will ground the corporation more strongly in theory and practice in the following as a human corporation. What is fundamental for this is to clarify financing and valuation with the imperative of truth (*Wahrheitsgebot*). Because "true and fair" accounting and auditing, id est sustainable valuation and reporting on a transcultural basis, is the documentary proof of good corporate governance: the verified information of investors (see chapter 4: *Bilanzwahrheit*). It is the means and chance to build up confidence and success for investments, id est sustainable value creation.[7] – How about if we build up trust internationally?

---

[4] See above 2.6.2 (information function) and chapter 4 (accounting, disclosure).

[5] Luttermann, *Der Fall Enron entzaubert die amerikanischen Bilanzregeln* (The Enron case debunks American accounting rules), Handelsblatt, 30.01.2002, p. 10. See Levitt (1998) and Luttermann (1999a).

[6] Cf. data on the Troubled Asset Relief Program (TARP) by the U.S. Treasury: https://home.treasury.gov/data/troubled-asset-relief-program (accessed: 22.08.2025). See overall, e.g., above 1.4, below 4.1 to 4.3, and chapter 6.

[7] Basically above 1.5.2 with chapters 5 and 6, as well as chapter 7 (personal responsibility) and chapter 9 (complementarity).

## 3.2 Truthfully Building Investors' Trust in a Corporation

### *3.2.1 Facing Reality: Have You Ever Seen a Corporation?*

Let us take a look at reality. Uncertainty is our capricious companion in life. Corporate leaders and investors have to face and to deal with a kind of Janus Bifrons, the Ancient Roman god of all beginnings, choices and transitions, presenting two faces looking into opposite directions: chance and risk (see 3.3.4). Both are ambiguous designations. From the perspective of the law, "risk" is of particular interest regarding liability. Talking pictures, the literal meaning of risk probably derives from Vulgar Latin *resecum* (possibly from Arabic *risq*) for "cliff", symbolically "to run into danger". In the world of merchants in former times, it was this that constituted the danger of shipping goods, as we have already seen in corporate history.[8] Times may change, but the basic patterns remain largely the same under the sun.

Still, acting in business, realising a chance, achieving any goal, usually means taking risks. This is characteristic of an enterprise: undertaking[9] something risky without – to some measurable or even immeasurable extent[10] – knowing the outcome. Corporate directors owe fiduciary duties and have to act in good faith on an informed basis (cf. so-called business judgement rule, duty of care).[11] Internationally, we can see that the legal development of the financing of businesses fundamentally strives for a form with limited liability for capital. The basic idea of limited holdings of equity capital as a venture which is "calculable" due to its limitation at the same time appeals to a larger audience. Over a century ago, Frederic Pollock and Frederic W. Maitland remarked: "Every system of law that has attained a certain degree of maturity seems compelled by the ever increasing complexity of human affairs to create persons who are not men (…)."[12]

That artificial person is the corporation (UK: public company limited by shares; cf. Dutch *de naamloze vennootschap*, French *la société anonyme, German die Aktiengesellschaft*, Italian *la società per azioni*, Portuguese *a sociedade anónima*, Spanish *la sociedad anónima*). This practically denotes our topic, the human

[8]See above 2.3.3 and with modern technology and circumstances chapters 6 and 9 (esp. 9.6: AI, genetic engineering).

[9]Cf. to undertake something, in German *etwas unternehmen* (from older *undernim*) and Old English *underniman* (cf. the verb *nim*), "take on, begin an undertaking, enterprise etc.," also "enter into a formal agreement, make oneself responsible, for a person etc., carry on a business, ready to undertake an enterprise, esp. one involving some danger or risk"; cf. the verb *take* (late Old English) for "to seize, grasp, catch, to get possession of, begin to grow, gain acceptance, succeed – make, do, perform". Overall Brown (1993) pp. 3206-3208 (take) and p. 3476 (undertake).

[10]Knight (1921) pp. 19-20.

[11]*Smith v. Van Gorkom*, 488 A.2d 858 (Del. 1985), at 872-73. On directors' fiduciary duty with a "novel theory": *Garfield v. Allen*, 277 A.3d 296 (Del. Ch. 2022), discussed by Wilson Corley (2024). Cf. *Meade v. Christie*, 974 N.W.2d 770 (Iowa 2022). According to corporate climate responsibility Williams (2021). Luttermann (1998), from p. 518.

[12]Pollock and Maitland (1982) p. 486.

corporation. It is globally about good governance of the corporation, its financing and valuation. Goal and motivation are clear in view of uncertain life circumstances. For the permanent success of an enterprise (project), the leaders responsible for a corporation build the necessary trust sustainably through truthful information: sustainable financial reporting (auditing, see 2.6.2). However, the path is obstructed by questionable, arbitrarily designed practices, theories, models and data frameworks in systematic deficiency and manipulation. There is already a legion of well-known cases, still the evil "numbers game" continues (see 3.2.2). – Therefore, let us start pragmatically with a simple question:

*Have you ever seen a corporation, say American Telephone & Telegraph (AT&T) Inc.?*

To be sure, many people use their services every day, pay for them and also know how to place orders in the local store or meanwhile via the internet. But: Who is the "AT&T" corporation? – Originally founded[13] in 1885 and having become a multinational conglomerate holding company, it has been and still is an agent in business transactions only as a legal person (entity), a creation of the law. We cannot see it, cannot touch it. Legal persons only exist as an idea or a legal system, as a "fiction" of the law (Friedrich Carl von Savigny).[14] In the landmark decision *Dartmouth College v. Woodward* in 1819, John C. Marshall, Chief Justice of the U.S. Supreme Court, had already put it similarly this way: As a distinct legal person, the corporation is "invisible, intangible, and existing only in contemplation of law".[15]

The significance of this is often forgotten. For at the same time, corporations (companies) as legal entities (*Juristische Personen*) – numbering sheer incalculable millions worldwide – do in fact exist as the actual bearers of the economy, practically the epitome of the business world. They can – by law like any natural person (human being) – take part in legal transactions, make contracts, acquire property, go to and be taken to court. However, this in no way contradicts Marshall and Savigny. For it is always humans (as organs of the legal person) acting for the corporation, namely its executives (board of directors) and shareholders or their proxies (general meeting).[16] So as the answer to our question we can put to record: No one ever has seen a "corporation".

[13]As the successor of the original Bell Telephone Company, founded in 1877 by Alexander Graham Bell, a co-founder also of AT&T, meanwhile headquartered in Dallas, Texas.

[14]Savigny (1840) pp. 85, 236, 239. See also below 7.3.1.

[15]4 Wheat. 518, 636 = 17 U.S. 518, 636 (1819).

[16]See chapter 7 (esp. 7.3.1 on origins) and – in times of AI – 9.6 to 9.8. Cf. Berle (1929) p. 189: "Corporation law, at least in the Anglo-Saxon system, is peculiarly a matter of fiction. Commencing with the corporate fiction itself, it next asserts that the relationship between a corporation and its stockholders is one of contract. But few stockholders have ever seen a corporate charter and by-laws; and their consent to them has to be fictitiously implied." See also below 3.5.4.

### 3.2.2 Handling the "Invisible" Reasonably

How does this work? – In a practical sense, accounting (bookkeeping) provides us with the instrument to deal with something invisible. An instrument that at first glance may appear to be both technically formal and magical (see 3.1 with Mozart). But is forming the epitome of the corporation, id est its substance as – like the natural person – an independent actor within the legal and economic order: financial reporting (annual accounts). In these accounts, the assets (e.g., inventory, patents, real estate) as well as the liabilities (equity/capital) legally allocated to a corporation are reflected, as set out above (see 2.4.3). In the representation of its accounts, the corporate enterprise becomes mentally and legally tangible as a legal person (*Juristische Person*).

The issue for the corporation and its responsible directors in the financing of the corporation is a reasonable legal order (see Fig. 7.1). The same applies to the investors, whose money (capital) is at stake. Accounting (financial reporting, auditing) is a field of its own within the law. In general terms, it is about the law of business accounting.[17] This can be seen in the word "accounting" conceptually: "To account" (from Latin *accomp[u]tare*) means to give a counting, a reckoning of something (e.g. money).[18] As shown for the word "reporting", used synonymously (financial reporting),[19] accountability comprises corporate governance and the control of this power. That is the reason why good corporate governance and sustainable value creation (*Wertschöpfung*) in a market economy – combining liberty (*Freiheit*) and responsibility (*Verantwortung*) – requires verified financial reporting of the corporation (see 2.6.2).

This shapes the corporation as a permanent financial instrument, as already shown (see 2.5). With its structure of legal organs (*Organe*) and assets (*Vermögen*), it is naturally modelled on the human being (see 7.3.1). The corporation as a legal entity bears assets and liabilities. Besides people (natural persons), this makes the corporation the legal structural element of the property and liability system in the constitution of liberty. By means of the financial statements (accounts), stating in words (names of the balance sheet items, notes etc.) and numbers the corporation's assets, liabilities and performance, a picture of the corporation evolves. Remember: It is only in this accounting picture that we can grasp the corporation in reality, conceptually and regarding assets (in terms of capacity),[20] deal with it in legal transactions (markets). Valuation and liability revolve around this accounting picture.

This functionally characterises the corporation as a whole, in any walks of life. Accounting law (accounting and auditing) is the foundation of valuation law

---

[17] On the basics of accounting and the law Berle (1938). On Berle's efforts to make accounting an integral part of legal doctrine Luttermann (1998) pp. 396-398.

[18] Brown (1993) p. 651 (l.c., 3 – s.v. report), pp. 84-88 (account – accounting).

[19] See above 2.6.2 and overall chapter 4.

[20] On the denotation of "asset" (German *Vermögen*) see below 8.1 (footnote 3).

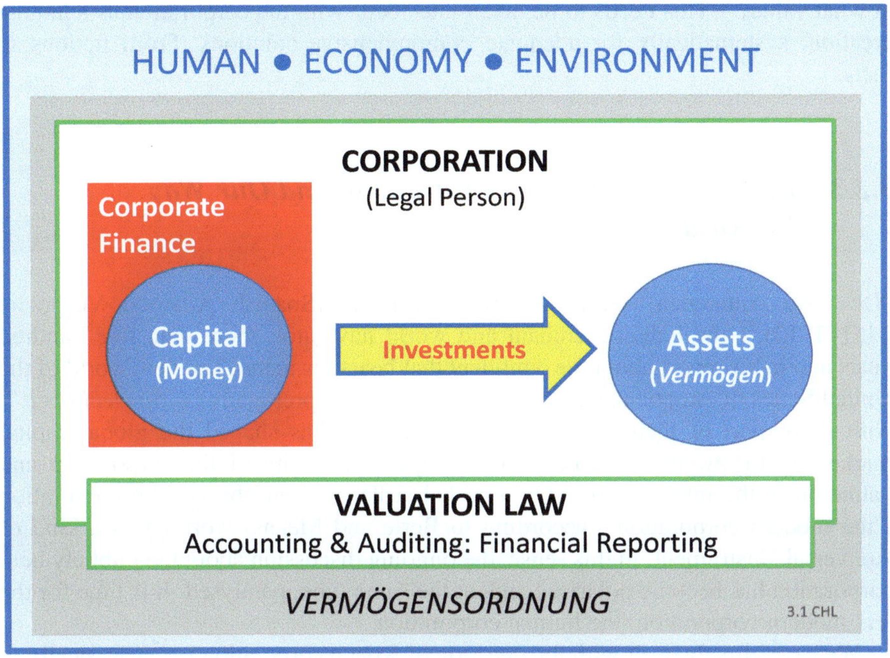


**Fig. 3.1** Corporation, finance (investment), and the valuation law

(*Bewertungsrecht*, see Fig. 3.1). A wide field and indeed the core of so-called corporation law and capital markets law, even of the economy and society as a whole. This encompasses the governance and control of the corporation. The law of accounting (appraisal) is meant to keep the person accountable from succumbing to human weakness and making results look more positive.[21] The core function of financial reporting (valuation) is to be adequately implemented in order for the corporation to be made meaningful use of. For this to be possible, it needs primarily to be understood, systematically structured and practically established. With the imperative of truth (*Wahrheitsgebot*), reasonably characterising a moderate measure. Based on the idea of justice under the rule of law, which applies for everyone on the basis of facts (substance).

It is procedurally guaranteed from independent norm-setting over factually adequate practical application with according control up to effective legal protection, including sanctions. With this, previous deficits have become surmountable, in particular valuation manipulations, which in the corporation are still a widespread basic flaw. Of course, we know from our own experience: If two people see the same thing, their perceptions need not be identical. So what is *true*, then? – Regarding the rendering of accounts, this concerns financial reporting in a fundamental way: What counts as an asset, what as a liability, what is to be classed as what? And, above all:

[21] Leffson (1987) pp. 55 and 152-153.

at what value? – This needs to be taken into focus with the corporation as a human creation, systematically for adequate comprehensive solutions: From fictions to facts.

### *3.2.3 Reflecting Corporate Construction and Our Way Forward*

"De nova Antarctica" wrote Amerigo Vespucci (Spanish Américo Vespucio, 1451–1512),[22] the Italian merchant and world navigator, more than five hundred years ago in his report about the continent that bears his name. The new world of the United States of America, whose pragmatic language prerogative (*"Sprachhoheit"*) with the export of their law and legal concepts[23] has shaped the global capital markets in the twentieth century, also shapes the reality of the corporation and valuation in the internet era.[24] On a global scale, we can observe the corporation ("the modern corporation", according to Berle and Means) working as a kind of "universal" instrument. In this sense, the ongoing discussion about the publicly held corporation has become polarised and, at the same time, paralysed. It is time for the real modern corporation: the human corporation.

We have already dealt with the question of what a corporation is.[25] Classically, it is about the capital structure (on the balance sheet), id est of "equity or shareholders' capital" (*Eigenkapital*) and "debt capital" (*Fremdkapital*). With the title of the pioneering work by Berle and Means, "private property", that is, the position of the "equity" of the corporation's balance sheet, is in focus. This characterises economic life on the wrong track of "shareholder value".[26] Compared to the shareholders and their agents (directors), other financiers and their positions (debt) lead a life in the shadows – not least academically. From a historical point of view, that may be understandable, but it shortens the horizon unreasonably. This applies in particular to the questions of liability and valuation of the corporation, the shift of risk and profit (wealth), which are so central to entrepreneurial practice (corporate governance) and investor protection.

Traditional concepts and patterns of thought and action have to be reconsidered. When around the year 1500, Amerigo Vespucci explored the *Mundus Novus*, in the

---

[22] Mundus Novus, printed by Matthi Hüpfuff, Straßburg 1505, as a translation of "Von der Nüwen welt".

[23] Großfeld (2019) p. 29. Cf. Macron, Initiative for Europe, 26.09.2017: https://www.diplomatie.gouv.fr, and Pécresse: www.welt.de/debatte/kommentare/plus236121956/Frankreich-Valerie-Pecresse-Im-schlimmsten-Fall-droht-Europa-die-Unterwerfung.html (both accessed: 22.08.2025). On linguistic imperialism Phillipson (1992). On multilingualism Luttermann, C. and Luttermann, K. (2021).

[24] In global perspective Luttermann (2000).

[25] Above 2.5.1. Cf. on "free market" in 2.6.1.

[26] See below 3.4.4, 3.6.2 and 3.6.5.

European "old world" the development of the mathematical perspective took place that is now dominating the capital markets of the world in the internet era with the patterns of Wall Streets' global financial industry. For a sound valuation law, we need to proceed further in our thinking. The corporate person is a linguistic analogy to the natural person (see 7.3.1). Metaphorically, it is seductive to make equations and abridgements. As he pierced the corporate veil, Benjamin N. Cardozo wrote: "Metaphors in law are to be narrowly watched, for starting as devices to liberate thought, they end often by enslaving it."[27] The issue was an abusive group relationship of parent corporation and subsidiary, an area which is characterised by corporate constructions worldwide.

So we can put on record: In order to establish a comprehensive, reasonable legal system and practice, we must dissolve the fossilised shells of the corporation, id est its governance, financing and valuation. We have already paved the way for developing new territory. This also includes reconsolidating seemingly familiar terrain. In any case, we need to broaden our view. For our purpose, we will proceed to clarify corporation and valuation under the imperative of truth, designed as a good deal here and everywhere (see 2.2.2), through: sustainable financial reporting (chapter 4) and valuation (chapter 5) as well as responsible governance (chapters 6 and 7). This lays the ground for a global order of assets, a *Vermögensordnung* and beyond (chapters 8 and 9). To this end, we will continue to take a closer look behind-the-scenes of the modern corporation.

## 3.3 Dealing with Other People's Money

### *3.3.1 Corporate Business, Capital Markets, and Finance for Profit*

What is expedient is the idea of the corporation as an instrument of risk financing (see 3.2.1, 3.5.4). It is well known to everyone that corporations are key figures in the business world. Although they are invisible, we deal with them internationally. As a legal person and financial instrument, the corporation is a structural element of the legal system and hence, of the economy globally.[28] In view of the uncertainty of future developments, business is generally conducted in legal forms with limited liability. The global model for this is the publicly held corporation (*börsennotierte Aktiengesellschaft*, here abbreviated as: corporation). Central issues are therefore the amount of capital of the corporation, contractually provided, the duty of care of its directors as well as valuation law, and law concerning liability. Climate change, the development of sustainable economic activities through transformational processes

[27] Cardozo in *Berkey v. Third Avenue Railway* 244 NY 84 (1926), at 94. Cf., e.g., Lim (2014), Payne (1997); on tort liabilities of corporate groups Lipton (2014).

[28] See above 3.2.2 and 2.5, further 1.7, 2.7 and chapters 8 and 9.

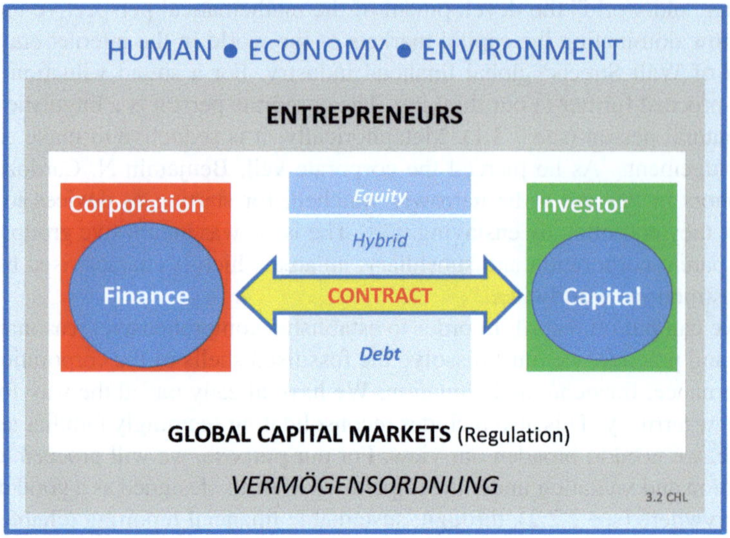


**Fig. 3.2** Financing of a corporation on the basis of contracts

in the economy, in undertakings (corporations) and society, affects this area as a whole.[29]

While exploring the public disclosure (financial reporting, accounting) we are dealing with the financing of corporations (*Unternehmensfinanzierung*, corporate finance). The corporation has to finance its business transactions. Capital is its means of existence. Private entrepreneurs and investors provide the capital (see Fig. 3.2). They strive for profit, id est, return on the capital they invest (ROI). Financial instruments of the corporation are traded at the stock exchanges. These are international market places for fast mass capital transfer, and at the same time, they constitute the nuclei of economic development – as we are witnessing since the beginning of the internet age (*Internetzeitalter*) at the turn of the twenty-first century: the magical triumvirate of virtual reality consisting of capital (fiat money), corporation and digitisation.[30] Aren't these three epic "fictions" at work? – Investors operate worldwide. In the middle of the nineteenth century, e.g., when political restructuring brought troubled times across Europe, European investors purchased securities of private railroad companies in the United States worth more than $1 billion.[31]

New York City then flourished on Wall Street as the new financial center with global reach. This is reminiscent of Renaissance Venice (in present-day Italy) as a center of finance and world trade (Levant, Silk Road). The first investment banking

[29] See overall chapters 1 and 2. Fundamental Williams (2021), Luttermann (2023) recitals 17-47, and Luttermann, L. (2024) and (2025).

[30] Cf. above 1.4.1; Luttermann (2000) and (2008). See also below 5.3.4 on the source and measure of value.

[31] Overall Luttermann (1998) pp. 238-268.

firms in the new world, some are well known even today (e.g., Lehman Brothers [founded 1850], Kuhn, Loeb & Co. [1867], Goldman Sachs [1869]), served as agents above all for capital magnates from England, the Netherlands, Germany, France and Switzerland. This was the birth of modern Wall Street (i.e., modern corporation), as Alfred D. Chandler put it 1977 in his revealing study "The visible hand" on the formative years of modern capitalism (from the 1850s until the 1920s):

> "As soon as the American capital market became centralized and institutionalized in New York City, all the present-day instruments of finance were perfected; so too were nearly all the techniques of modern securities marketing and speculation. Bonds became the primary instrument to finance railroad construction."[32]

This already shows the importance of the bond markets (debt) for the financing and valuation of companies (corporations). Their volume is traditionally many times that of the stock markets (equity), in spite of the fact that they are overshadowed by the latter, also in legal terms (see 3.2.3, 2.5.2). New York's Wall Street became the epitome of the so-called "capitalism" (from capital, Latin *capitale*, based on *caput* for head, see 1.3.1): hotbed and epicenter of economic theory and practice of the twentieth century,[33] influencing corporations worldwide. World War I in Europe (1914–1918) brought a great boom for the USA through flight capital from Europe as well as through production, first for the war, then for reconstruction: the heyday of the Roaring Twenties. It resulted in the epic Wall Street Crash of 1929 and the Great Depression that followed.

### *3.3.2 Banks, Capital as Credit, and Crisis*

While the British Empire disappeared on account of the war, the USA had gained supremacy with Wall Street in world finance. Of course, the City of London continued as a vivid part of the "Anglo-American economic entente"[34] (see 7.2.1). Just look at the Bretton Woods system of fixed exchange rates (1944 by Keynes, White)[35] and the rise of the Euromarkets in London.[36] What remained overall was greed. With its escape from reality, as Joseph Schumpeter identified "recurrent mania" as "a normal feature of business life",[37] it had long since become rooted in

---

[32] Chandler (1977) pp. 91-92. See also below 3.6.2.

[33] Insightfully, Bernstein (1993). Overall on corporate finance Brealey, Myers, Allen, and Edmans (2025).

[34] Roberts and Kynaston (2002) p. 184. More recently Tooze (2019) pp. 79-84 and chapter 23.

[35] John Maynard Keynes (UK Treasury) and Harry Dexter White (US Treasury) are considered the architects of the system; see Roberts and Kynaston (previous footnote).

[36] Comprehensively Lomax and Gutmann (1981).

[37] According to, altogether instructive, Galbraith (1994) p. 67. In detail Schumpeter's perspectives on capitalism Schumpeter (1947/2018), esp. on greed (*Habgier*), e.g., p. 172: *"Der praekapitalistische Mensch ist tatsächlich nicht weniger ‚raffend' als der kapitalistische Mensch."*, i.e. man is by nature "acquisitive" (avidly, greedy, rapacious).

the USA as well. In manifold ways, it has shaped the construction of the country, the Wall Street Panic of 1907, the era of high-yield junk bonds in the 1980s, massive manipulations of markets (the "numbers game") with the financial crisis since 2007/2008 and up until the present (the spirit seems to be at work even in the White House). Massive supply of paper (financial instruments, fiat money) chases limited supply of goods (substance, real values).[38]

Basically, the expansion of information asymmetries and credit (so-called "leverage", see 3.3.3) are key: Capital ideas, which established "the frantic, raucous capital markets".[39] This reign belongs in the spotlight of research and politics, where it had already been before the World War. Practically, the expansion of credit fuels speculative manias.[40] This is not the place to engage in the continuing discourse of economic specialists on that (so-called monetarists, Keynesians etc.). However, it is that time in which motives and current law for real disclosure (financial reporting) for the modern corporation are rooted. In the aftermath of the Panic of 1907, U.S. Congress (Pujo Committee) undertook the so-called "Money Trust" investigation, uncovering a massive concentration of wealth (*Reichtum*) and manipulative control of banks and the New York Stock Exchange by a few people (180 individuals) in 1913.[41] This is the circle out of which in the very same year the questionable so-called "Federal Reserve System" (FED) in the United States is privately established.[42] There is a lack of substantial reform.

It is only later after the stock market crash on New York's Wall Street in 1929 that fundamental reforms are undertaken in the Great Depression by U.S. President (1933–1945) Franklin D. Roosevelt in his New Deal (see 3.3.3). This means that for nearly a generation, the evil game ("house of cards") was continued, in spite of its deficiencies being known. Thanks to "the brevity of the financial memory" in the population and the actors of the financial industry, who know how to make use of this with the creation of debt (*Schulden*, i.e., bank notes, financial instruments): "the wonderful process of enrichment".[43] This merely means that stock markets and the speculation with corporations and their "securities" as financial instruments are fuelled, to the detriment of others. In practice every businessman, every corporation works with capital that belongs to others. That means they are dealing predominantly with "other people's money".

This takes us straight to the core. Louis D. Brandeis, American lawyer and later associate justice on the U.S. Supreme Court (1916–1939, called "the people's

---

[38] After Galbraith (1994) pp. 53-69. Cf. Schumpeter (1947/2018) p. 115, saying that Capitalism is in its essence an evolutionary process. On corporate crises, legal systems and economic development Milhaupt and Pistor (2008).

[39] Bernstein (1993) p. 305.

[40] Aliber, Kindleberger, and McCauley (2023) pp. 67-92.

[41] Pujo, Arsene, Report of the Committee Appointed Pursuant to House Resolutions 429 and 504 to Investigate the Concentration of Control of Money and Credit, February 28, 1913.

[42] Prins (2014) pp. 17-39.

[43] Galbraith (1994) pp. 2 and 11-24 (19).

lawyer"), showed the way in his famous book "Other people's money and how the bankers use it" (1914). Even before the First World War, this made him the spiritus rector of U.S. President (1913–1921) Woodrow Wilson. Factually in accordance with the insights of the Pujo Committee in U.S. Congress, it was already in his election campaign that he took up some of the ideas of Brandeis for his reform programme for strengthening the economy (so-called "New Freedom": banking reform, tariff reduction, elimination of monopolies and trusts). Wilson freely stated:

> "The great monopoly in this country is the monopoly of big credits. So long as that exists, our old variety and freedom and individual energy of development are out of the question. A great industrial nation is controlled by its system of credit. Our system of credit is privately concentrated. The growth of the nation, therefore, and all our activities are in the hands of a few men who, even if their action be honest and intended for the public interest, (...) necessarily, by very reason of their own limitations, chill and check and destroy genuine economic freedom. This is the greatest question of all, and to this statesmen must address themselves with an earnest determination to serve the long future and the true liberties of men."[44]

Whatever Wilson, whose election campaign was financed by leading bankers,[45] did as President (esp. to hand over the currency monopoly to the "quasi-private" Federal Reserve System),[46] what we know is this: Credit (capital) is of elementary importance for the corporation and its legal order. This is what the financial systems at least of Western culture are now based on. Let us take a look at the macro-economic dimension. Louis D. Brandeis was concerned with free competition. His central point was that the investment bankers, the so-called "money trust", were acting in concert with businessmen (associated banks, trust companies, life insurance companies) to create and control trusts in America's then key industries (e.g., railroads, public service, industrial corporations). Brandeis noted: "The power and the growth of power of our financial oligarchs comes from wielding the savings and quick capital of others."[47] – The big money-managers, like today.[48]

---

[44] Wilson (1913) p. 79. Cf. quotation by Brandeis (1914) p. 1.

[45] Like, e.g., Jakob Schiff (see Prins (2014) pp. 27 and 39, generally pp. 29-32), senior partner of the investment bank Kuhn, Loeb & Co. as well as father-in-law of Paul M. Warburg, appointed by U.S. President Wilson to the Federal Reserve Board.

[46] The U.S. Supreme Court in *Trump v. Wilcox*, 605 U.S. ___ (2025), 145 S. Ct. 1415, 1415 (2025) (per curiam): "The Federal Reserve is a uniquely structured, quasi-private entity that follows in the distinct historical tradition of the First and Second Banks of the United States." See also below 6.2.1.

[47] Brandeis (1914) p. 18.

[48] Also called asset management or investment management companies (e.g., BlackRock, Vanguard Group, UBS, Fidelity Investments, Morgan Stanley, Goldman Sachs), see below 2.5.3 and chapter 6.

### 3.3.3 *Reporting for Trust: "Full and Real Disclosure" (New Deal)*

This coins the economy, built inextricably on liberty and responsibility together in a capital-market way with the corporation under the imperative of truth. In a concept of trust and control through sustainable financial reporting (see 1.5.2 and 2.7), so that the invisible corporation and its human actors become adequately comprehensible. With the bankers, Louis D. Brandeis brought the financial industry, its financial instruments (bonds, stocks, hybrids) and its abuses into focus. He believed that "the creation of a civilized existence could be done, if all citizens participated in the workings of their societies."[49] All in all, concern is basically with power and control of power. This was true not only then, but, irrespective of time, also remains so today and will do so in the future. It all revolves around capital and disclosure (publicity).

Generally, banks provide and increase the supplies of credit (paper wealth) und therefore in reality leverage (shift of profits, wealth).[50] Politically, this seems precarious. As John Kenneth Galbraith generally notes: "Only after the speculative collapse does the truth emerge."[51] Thus, it is only after the stock market crash of 1929 in the Great Depression that the psychological strain becomes strong enough for the idea of corporate disclosure to come to the fore. The – pretty much the same – financial industry with its financial instruments that, in a more modern guise, is fueling the global debt crisis in the internet era, also lead to a call for action in those days. Brandeis's criticism was not directed at limiting the bank profits legally or at thoughtfully preventing investors from making (potentially) unfavourable deals. His remedy against abuses is full and real disclosure of the facts to the investor.[52] Brandeis states this graphically:

> "Publicity is just commended as a remedy for social and industrial diseases. Sunlight is said to be the best disinfectant; electric light the most efficient policeman."[53]

The law and its actors have to provide for sufficient light in capital dealings. This idea of information forms the basis of the U.S. capital market laws, which President Franklin D. Roosevelt established in his New Deal. These three cornerstones of federal legislation are particularly noteworthy: the Securities Act of 1933 (regulating the offer and sale of securities), the Securities Exchange Act of 1934 (regulating the exchange of securities and founding the Securities and Exchange Commission – SEC – as the federal regulator of securities markets), and the Trust Indenture Act of

---

[49] Strum (1984) p. 406. On Brandeis also below in 7.4.3.

[50] See above 3.3.2 and below 3.6; cf. on facts below 7.7.3.

[51] Galbraith (1994) p. 17. See also chapter 6.

[52] Brandeis (1914) pp. 101-105.

[53] Brandeis (1914) p. 92. Cf. Gower (2021) 22-001, on disclosure as the fundamental principle and basic safeguard underlying the Companies Act ever since 1862: "If the public and the members were enabled to find out all relevant information about the company, this, thought the founding fathers of our company law, would be a sure shield". See here chapters 4 and 5 with 7.7.3.

1939 (supplementing the Act of 1933 in case of the distribution of debt securities).[54] Still today, these acts form the legal basis of the capital markets, also for the regulation of accounting and auditing by the SEC.[55] That has long since been mostly forgotten, as has the *coup de main* at the time with which the financial industry regained its position of power on those subjects as early as 1938,[56] having since then secured it in spite of all crises: disclosure on the basis of private standard setting, which we will take a closer look at.[57]

But first of all, the focus is on the relevant motives of legislation, the *ratio legis*. We have seen, it was a rocky path that lead there. It was the excesses of the financial industry, including the Wall Street Panic of 1907 and the Wall Street Crash of 1929, that cleared the field for new ways, id est state regulation. U.S. President Franklin D. Roosevelt, in his message to Congress regarding the draft of a Securities Act, rejected the idea that the Federal Government should undertake any action which could be interpreted as the examination or guarantee of the value or profitableness of newly issued securities. Yet, he then made clear:

> "There is, however, an obligation upon us to insist that every issue of new securities to be sold in interstate commerce shall be accompanied by full publicity and information, and that no essentially important element attending the issue shall be concealed from the buying public. This proposal adds to the ancient rule of caveat emptor, the further doctrine, 'Let the seller also beware.' It puts the burden of telling the whole truth on the seller. It should give impetus to honest dealing in securities and thereby bring back public confidence."[58]

President Franklin D. Roosevelt concluded his address with these words:

> "What we seek is a return to a clearer understanding of the ancient truth that those who manage banks, corporations, and other agencies handling or using other people's money are trustees acting for others."[59]

With these words, he made the leitmotif formed by Brandeis into the legal measure for practice. Roosevelt and Brandeis were united in striving for the ideal to ensure fair dealing on the capital markets. However, Brandeis' deeply ingrained aversion against "bigness" as such, particularly in the form of large conglomerations of economic power, was never shared by President Roosevelt. For the latter, the need for regulation did not concern "bigness" as a problem. To him, the cardinal question in his campaign against abuses and for "trustee" integrity in those dealing with other

---

[54] See in more detail below 3.6, esp. from 3.6.2.

[55] On, e.g., SEC climate rules Luttermann, L. (2024) and (2023).

[56] See SEC, Accounting Series Release (ASR) No. 4, Administrative policy on financial statements, and already, e.g., 1935 in the case *Norther States Power Company*: Chatov (1975) pp. 107-132; cf. SEC Commissioner Healy (1938). Overall Luttermann (1998) pp. 375-395 (setting standards for financial reporting), pp. 395-405 (business accounting law), and pp. 405-440 ("Generally Accepted Accounting Principles" – GAAP in the USA).

[57] See 3.5.6 and chapters 4, 5. Overall Luttermann (1998), esp. pp. 358-452, Luttermann (1999a).

[58] Message from the President to the Congress, The White House, March 29, 1933, 73rd Congr. 1st Sess., Cong. Rec. – Senate 937, also printed in McCormick (1948) pp. 20-21. Cf. Berle below 7.7.3.

[59] Ibid. Cf. for European law below 4.4.4 with 4.5 and 4.6.

people's money was the following: *Who* exercises control and *to what ends*?[60] – We know that the control of any corporation and its directors always depends on "true and fair" accounting, id est sustainable financial reporting under the imperative of truth (see chapter 4).

### 3.3.4 Finance for Profit: Incentive Systems, Prudence, and Balance

Basically, it is about capturing the reality of the corporation (i.e., to record, to account for). The control function runs into a void and fails where those responsible do not – as U.S. President Franklin D. Roosevelt said – tell "the whole truth" in dealing with other people's money. This strengthens our concept of trust and control (see 1.5.2), oriented in financial reporting under the imperative of truth towards the "actual circumstances" (facts) of the corporation.[61] This is the common basis of those involved in the capital-market financing of corporations (projects). A community of risk, forming itself – as already described (see 1.3.2) – for the financing of the corporation, in an order of legal transactions, in order to gain uncertain profits with a certain amount of risk.

What do risk and profit stand for? – Both are experienced differently by individual people, naturally and culturally, manifold aspects playing a role here. This is what valuations and investments are based on, too. People look for a hold and for certainty (cf. financial instruments called "securities", *Wertpapiere*). That is why in corporate affairs the corporate directors must exercise the duty of care (from Latin *cura*)[62] and why the corporation's financial instruments (shares, bonds, hybrids) are traded at the stock markets, where rules apply (regulation, so-called "standards"). For the economy, Frank H. Knight has placed this fundamentally within the scale of tension he termed "risk, uncertainty and profit". Proceeding from "the individual psychology of valuation", to which we shall come later,[63] people and markets work with the imperfection and asymmetries of knowledge:

---

[60] Elliott Roosevelt (Ed.), F.D.R.: his personal letters, after Bedts (1964) p. 141 (under the aspect of the Public Utility Holding Company Act 1935). See also Nicholas (2004).

[61] See above 2.4.2, 2.6.2. Comparatively on "a true and fair view" Luttermann (2003), § 264 HGB, recitals from 42 and 83-169 (European law). The same applies under the new Directive 2013/34/EU: Luttermann (2013).

[62] Secure (Latin *securus*), as *se-* plus *cura* (to care), untroubled, free from doubt or distrust, feeling sure or certain, confident in expectation; see Brown (1993) p. 2753 (secure). Security (Latin *securitas*), a certificate attesting ownership of stock, the financial asset represented by such a document; see Brown, ibid., p. 2754 (security). Cf., e.g. *Garfield v. Allen*, 277 A.3d 296 (Del. Ch. 2022) and on sustainable disclosure (facts) below 7.7.3.

[63] See overall chapters 4 and 5.

> "The essence of the situation is action according to *opinion*, of greater or less foundation and value, neither entire ignorance nor complete and perfect information, but partial knowledge."[64]

In the financing of a corporation, there is a system of incentives. We take risks in order to take the opportunity of having chances for profit. A chance that is more or less certain, that means probable and thus determinable, must present stimulus psychologically sufficient for the accompanying risk to be taken. In the financing of corporations, it is precisely these constellations of chance and risk – lawfully defined in a specific financial instrument – that are being traded and accepted (i.e. contractually agreed upon). Accordingly, the opportunity of gaining profit for the investor stands against the possibility of losing invested capital. That is literally Janus Bifrons at work (see 3.2.1). Being prepared to take a risk is rewarded or, from an economic perspective: remunerated through the risk interest rate (so-called *Risikozins*).[65] Such positively experienced incentives motivate the actors of the markets, which operate as orderly events (see 2.6.1).

The economy and legal order are incentive systems. Logical thinking serves the optimisation of benefit, goal-oriented in the use of cognition and knowledge (information), here: in the financing of a corporation. Basically, we see with Adam Smith that every individual that employs his capital "necessarily endeavours so to direct that industry, that its produce may be of the greatest possible value": This at the same time unintentionally – "led by an invisible hand" – promotes the annual revenue of the society, id est the public interest.[66] This function is regarded as the "benchmark model" of a market economy ("perfect liberty"),[67] more precisely: within the law as the "constitution of liberty", as Hayek put it, emphasising the importance of individualism and information in the economic process.[68] Sustainable financial reporting here systematically serves the adequate protection of the market participants acting responsibly.

This includes prudence (principle of conservatism – *Vorsichtsprinzip*) as an elementary part of the concept of information (real disclosure).[69] For incentives trigger expectations. If these are subjectively disappointed, this needs to be objectified, in order to identify "expectation gaps" (so-called *Erwartungslücken*). This applies to any system, id est also to financial reporting as a legal order (*Vermögensordnung*, see 1.6):

---

[64]Knight (1921) p. 199.

[65]Legal systems set or accompany such incentives and are themselves incentive systems. Luttermann (1998) pp. 18-19, 21-24 (on contracts as chance-risk constellations).

[66]Smith (1776/1789$^5$) p. 572 (book IV, chapter II). Cf. Coffee (2001) p. 4: "efficiency does not necessarily triumph".

[67]Krueger, Introduction to Smith: The wealth of nations (preceding footnote) p. XXIII.

[68]Hayek (1960). See more details in the following sections.

[69]On prudence (duty of care), e.g., below chapter 4 (e.g. 4.5.4, 4.6.3 to 4.6.5, 4.8.2 to 4.8.5, 4.9.5), chapters 6 (6.4) and 7; on information (clear language) above 2.6.2, esp. with a "risk passport" (*Risikopass*) for financial instruments below 6.6.5 and Luttermann (2001b) 1901, 1904–1905; cf. meanwhile Regulation (EU) No 1286/2014 on so-called "key information documents".

Whoever demands too much from the law will struggle with the results.[70] Thus, President Roosevelt rightly avoided examining or guaranteeing the value or profitableness of securities, underlining the necessity of real disclosure under the imperative of truth.[71] What is necessary is integrating the market forces involved systematically in an ethically consolidated market balance, making use of it for necessary control of the corporation through financial reporting and auditing (sustainable information and wealth creation).

## 3.4 Limited Liability: Legal Capital of the Corporation and Beyond

### *3.4.1 Liability: Capital and Liquidity (Insolvency)*

Being liable for one's debts is the ethos of entrepreneurial responsibility. The points of reference are capital and liquidity (*Liquidität*, solvency), the two go together. Capital is an indispensable part of the corporation's existence, as already shown, forming the basis of its business. What counts in business ("going concern", *Unternehmensfortführung*) is liquidity. Viewed practically: A liquidity crunch (*Liquiditätsklemme*) is a severe problem – even up to the point as a reason for insolvency proceedings (*Insolvenzgrund*). Everyone knows from experience what a lack of cash means. Liquidity hits corporations in their central vein, the capital basis. This is what business, liability and valuation fundamentally relate to. Limited liability means: the rights of the corporation's creditors are restricted to the assets of the company, which are separate from the assets of the corporation's shareholders (principle of separation).[72]

The corporation as a financial instrument is thus privileged, and therefore also its members (shareholders). They are legally protected, though not to an unlimited degree (e.g., see "piercing the corporate veil" – *Haftungsdurchgriff*).[73] However, there are generally developed financing rules, established in particular in and according to the above-mentioned insolvency law in order to avoid a legal process of bankruptcy (*Insolvenzverfahren*). Any corporation conducts its business under the proviso of the legal order that official pressure will be exerted in the case of deficient

---

[70] Details below 4.5.6. Basically Luttermann (2003) Einf BilanzR recitals from 123 (on "expectation gaps" – *Erwartungslücken*, i.e. limits of law); cf. Luttermann (1998) pp. 16-21.

[71] See above 3.3.3 and chapter 4.

[72] Fundamentally 1.4.1 and 2.4.3 (principle of separation). Cf. overall Gower (2021), chapter 2, discussing advantages and disadvantages of incorporation.

[73] In principle, only the assets of the corporation are liable for the liabilities of the corporation; see, e.g., in Germany explicitly § 1(1)(2) AktG and § 13(2) GmbHG. On the – in more recent times – rare cases of recourse to the shareholders (piercing the corporate veil, *Durchgriffshaftung*) see in details Coffee, Gilson, Quinn (2022) pp. 215-245, above 2.4.3 and structurally below 3.6.

business financing. Accordingly, in the last instance, a corporation that is no longer able to meet its financial obligations (*Zahlungspflichten*) can be taken off the market. This traditional hammer of insolvency law aims at the liquidation of the remaining corporation assets in order to meet at least some of the creditors' demands (pro-rata portion in bankruptcy). Of course, troubled companies can be financially reorganised and restructured (*Sanierung*) in line with the market and the law (i.e., also contractually agreed).

Such rules are generally part of market economy systems. Germany, for instance, has had such an insolvency law since 1999. Based on experiences in the United States, it follows a line which is praised as "conforming to the market", incorporating ideas of the so-called "economic analysis of the law".[74] – Whatever this 1995may mean,[75] the decisive point here is: In order to institute insolvency proceedings (*Insolvenzverfahren*), there has to be a reason for opening them (*Eröffnungsgrund*) that is based on the individual financial situation (see § 16 German Insolvency Code, *Insolvenzordnung* – InsO). The law names three facts of the case: the general reason of "insolvency", if the debtor is not able to meet his financial obligations when they are due (§ 17 German InsO, *Zahlungsunfähigkeit*). In the case of imminent insolvency, it is "foreseeable"[76] that the debtor will not be able to fulfill his financial obligations at the time they are due (see § 18 German InsO, *drohende Zahlungsunfähigkeit*). Here, the focus in both cases is on liquidity.

For corporations (legal persons), the third reason for the opening of insolvency proceedings is over-indebtedness (*Überschuldung*). According to legal definition, this is the case if the assets (*Vermögen*) of the debtor no longer cover his obligations (*Verbindlichkeiten*, § 19(2)(1) German InsO). This relates to the accounted capital structure and questions of valuation. The debtor's assets may only be used for going concern values (*Fortführungswerte*, instead of the lower liquidation value) if the continuation of the company is intended and the company seems viable economically (see § 19(2)(2) German InsO, so-called "going concern" – *Unternehmensfortführung*).[77] Over-indebtedness, however, may also be the case when there is a positive prognosis for continuation. This is to prevent a company from continuing business in the face of lacking personal liability even if the assets are not sufficient to cover the debts.[78] In a case of over-indebtedness the covering funds (cover capital – *Deckungskapital*) have to be

[74]Balz in Balz and Landfermann (1995), esp. pp. XXXVI, XXXIX and XLIV-XLV; on the legal comparative part explanation to the government draft, printed in Balz and Landfermann, ibid., pp. 53-54.

[75]See 1.5.1 and Luttermann (1998) pp. 465-485, Mestmäcker (2007). On the juridical analysis of economics below, e.g. 5.2.2, 6.7.3, 7.3.2 and 7.4.1, also 8.2.2 and 9.7.

[76]Cf. on this constituent fact of probability theory and value theory Luttermann (1998), from p. 229.

[77]Explanation government draft (to § 23), in: Balz/Landfermann (1995) p. 93. Cf. in the European Union as a general financial reporting principle Art. 6 no. 1(a) Directive 2013/34/EU: "the undertaking shall be presumed to be carrying on its business as a going concern", implemented e.g. in the German Commercial Law, § 252(1) no. 2 HGB. See below 3.5.1.

[78]*Deutscher Bundestag*, *Bericht Rechtsausschuss* (report, legal committee of the German Bundestag on § 23(2)), in: Balz/Landfermann (1995) ibid.

determined in the ratio of "assets" and "liabilities" on the basis of insolvency law. In any case, the fact of over-indebtedness coins a capital structure rule. Apart from the state of liquidity, this is the barometer for a corporation regarding insolvency law.

In the normal course of business, the basic pattern works: The investment of capital forms assets in the corporation, binds capital (capital commitment, *Kapitalbindung*: current assets, fixed assets; cf. nominal capital, *Nennkapital*, see 3.4.3). Capital commitment is generally commended in the sense of creditor protection (*Gläubigerschutz*). Together with the traditional shareholders' capital (equity, *Eigenkapital*) that is intended as a static (stable) basis of liability, it forms the legal capital system (see 3.4.2). The dilemma is: Investment at the same time leads to illiquidity. Corporations as dynamic enterprises require liquid means (money), precisely in order to be able to serve creditors dutifully ("in good time"), to carry on and extend business (in short: "Cash is king!"). Both aspects have to be structurally coordinated. It is here that accounting and valuation (financial reporting) take fundamental effect.

### 3.4.2 Ideas and Developments of Legal Capital

Almost everything about legal capital, Manning and Hanks wrote, "is a little peculiar".[79] Of course, one could remark, it's all about the energy-laden relationship of the shareholders and creditors (bondholders) of a corporation: They have interests as opposite as fire and water, don't they? – Well, that depends. – We have already treated the complex and will continue to do so, in order to sound out the legal framework for viable solutions. As shown, in the corporation as a financial instrument with sustainable financial reporting functional and legal issue is capital, id est, the capital structure (*Kapitalstruktur*). In law and practice, we find more or less different concepts. This requires particular attention in our consideration of the United States, which often seem quite monolithic from the outside. However, corporation law (legal capital) is developed and practiced in manifold ways in the fifty federal states (*Bundesstaaten*).

The idea of the corporation is situated in the federalist field of tension, in the midst of the sociopolitical reality.[80] Let us first take a look at the breeding ground. The framework of ideas imported during the colonial era from England with the common law is the deeper foundation in which the modern American business corporation, with its global radiation, is rooted. In the late eighteenth century, corporations developed in the USA through state concessions (*Konzessionssystem*), the majority for banks, insurance companies as well as for companies for the creation of an

[79] Manning and Hanks (1990) p. 1. According to Manning and Hanks (2013) p. 1, more than twenty years later, it still "is somewhat peculiar".

[80] See above 1.5.1 and chapters 2 and 6. Cf. in our times of climate change Lipton (2025) and Strine (2025). See chapter 8.

infrastructure (water supply, bridge construction).[81] In 1811, the State of New York passes the first general law in the United States for the incorporation of business companies for certain fabrication purposes. This marks the turn from the concession system to the normative system (*Normativsystem*, see 2.4.1). In 1837, Connecticut passes a statute according to which corporations may be founded for any legal purpose, limited, however, to a period of 20 years. New York, like Iowa (see Art. VIII. Const. of the State of Iowa, 1998), secures the freedom of foundation even in its constitution (see Art. X Const. of the State of N.Y., 2025).

The federal order, indeed, entailed different versions of corporations (i.e., limited liability, *Haftungsbegrenzung*). In Ohio and Minnesota, for instance, there was double liability of shareholders, Illinois forbade corporations to have shares in other companies. By the end of the nineteenth century, the normative system had taken hold in most of the fifty states.[82] They competed sharply for the limited financial resources for companies (corporations). In the legal demands of incorporation, the federal states conducted a race, as Louis D. Brandeis writes in his famous dissent in *Liggett v. Lee*, "not of diligence but of laxity".[83] Besides, e.g., Arizona, Dakota, Nevada, New Jersey, New Mexico and West Virginia implementing laws with more or less "liberal features", it was the laws of Delaware, based on the important approach of New Jersey of 1875,[84] which gained "liberal" fame. Favored by its location near the financial and political centers Washington, Philadelphia, New York and Boston, the small state developed into a focal point of corporate law development – as already seen in the realm of financial reporting (see 2.4).

All in all, American federalism seems "laboratory-like", because in the general structure one state can experiment with legal constructions by way of "trial and error", as Justice Brandeis put it: "one of the happy incidents of the federal system".[85] This competitive character of the law, id est in the sense of Friedrich August von Hayek, "competition as a discovery procedure", is consciously tended. It promotes the community of the United States. In order to unify the law of corporations, the American Bar Association presented the Model Business Corporation Act (MBCA) in 1950. With regard to structure and content, it is based on the Illinois Business Corporation Act of 1933, leading to the MBCA (2016 Revision), which has since been updated.[86] The Model Acts are designed as practical guidelines for the revision of the laws of individual states. They cover widespread opinions on the

---

[81]Friedman (1985) p. 189, speaks of 181 charters for companies for the period of 1796-1800. For the following Luttermann (1998) pp. 238-357 (§ 8, with further details and references).

[82]Comprehensively Larcom (1937) and Seavoy (1982). On "double liability" *Anderson v. Abbott*, 321 U.S. 349 (1944). As a rationale for limited liability Smith (2009).

[83]288 U.S. 517, 541, 559 (1933).

[84]Buxbaum in Buxbaum and Hopt (1988) pp. 115-116.

[85]In *New State Ice Corp. v. Liebmann*, 285 U.S. 262, 311 (1932).

[86]In detail: https://www.americanbar.org/groups/business_law/resources/model-business-corporation-act/ (accessed: 22.08.2025). Cf. European Model Company Act (EMCA), for final publisher version 2017: https://papers.ssrn.com/sol3/papers.cfm?abstract_id=2929348 (accessed: 22.08.2025).

adequate adaptation of the different commercial and social interests projected onto the modern business corporation,[87] including its legal structure. Many federal states (36, as of 2024) have adopted the MBCA into their legislation in a more or less modified way.[88]

We are thus looking at diversity and may put on record: There is no such thing as *the* corporation, rather, the term covers quite different constructions. But help is on its way. Let us take a closer look at the legal framework. Two fundamentally different concepts of capital structure form the landscape of corporation law in the United States: Legal capital, which is generally considered to be an essentially statically operating model, in order to protect creditors, whose gaze is directed at the balance sheet assets for fear "of an ultimate liquidation Armageddon";[89] this is what the statutes are based on. Apart from this widely influential model dynamics of the enterprise lead to – we call it the Californian way – further models, focusing on "the prospective lender's primary interest (…) in the economic prospects" of the corporation[90] (see 3.4.5).

### *3.4.3 Legal Capital System: Stated Capital, Par Value, Surplus (MBCA)*

First, there is the traditional basic concept of the legal capital system. It has a wide distribution and is akin, e.g., to company law in Germany (*Mindestkapital* – minimum capital). For the protection of the corporate creditors, the system is based on the idea of insolvency in the corporate treasury (assets) as well as on a rule for limiting the distribution of company assets to shareholders (*Aktionäre*). The idea of creating a permanent capital base for corporations through the issue of shares with par value (as a fixed number of a currency) appeared in common law under King William III as early as the beginning of the eighteenth century.[91] Generally, a creditor "is more likely to be paid, and is thus better off, the more assets the debtor has on the payment

[87] Goldstein and Hamilton (1983).

[88] American Bar Association (ABA), April 23, 2024: www.americanbar.org/news/abanews/aba-news-archives/2024/04/aba-launches-new-mbca-resource-center (accessed: 22.08.2025). Recent enactments and amendments, e.g., Alabama (2019), Colorado (2019), Florida (2018), see (above footnote 85) with an overview (www.americanbar.org). Cf. largely adopted according to ABA, Model Business Corporation Act annotated, 3rd. ed., vol. 1, as of 1995 Supp., p. XLI, in: Arkansas (1987), Florida (1989), Georgia (1989), Indiana (1986), Iowa (1989), Kentucky (1988), Mississippi (1988), Montana (1991), New Hampshire (1992), North Carolina (1990), Oregon (1987), South Carolina (1988), Tennessee (1988), Utah (1992), Vermont (1993), Virginia (1985), Wisconsin (1990). See on MBCA and Delaware corporate law Gorris, Hamermesh and Strine (2011).

[89] Manning and Hanks (1990) p. 18, from there also the following quote.

[90] Ibid. Manning and Hanks (2013) p. 23 (and still, p. 24, on: "an ultimate liquidation Armageddon").

[91] Berle (1928) p. 13, with mention of the East India Company.

date".[92] Practically, this means, as shown with the insolvency law: cash to meet the obligation (see 3.4.1).

In essence, it is about the ethical unity of liberty and responsibility (liability). In the modern era, "stated capital account" as a balance-sheet item designates the permanent (proprietary) capital in the corporation. It basically comprises the sum of the par value shares issued at least at the par value determined in accordance with the memorandum and articles of association. In addition, there is a part of the remuneration, determined by the board of directors, for issued no-par value shares, representing merely a fraction of the complete series issued.[93] The "par value" idea is directed at a fair contribution of each partner to the company basis, while no payments to the shareholders are allowed to be made from the stated capital (*Nennkapital*). Overall, it is about a balance of interests. Besides the "stated capital account", there is the umbrella term "surplus" as a balance sheet item. But this is not uniform. Individual jurisdictions divide the surplus into different items shown separately for identification and qualification of the source of profit.

This has led to the development of different variations of the legal capital systems.[94] Let us first think of the initial case, which, regardless of the source of profit, has only the comprehensive balance-sheet item "surplus" (medieval Latin *superplus*, German *Überschuss, Mehrerlös*). Justice Louis D. Brandeis[95] wrote on this principle in a tax law case:

> "The term 'surplus' as employed in corporate finance and accounting, designates an account on the books, representing the net assets of the corporation in excess of all liabilities, including its capital stock."

This principle also holds for the "stated capital/surplus" concept. A characteristic example is the New York Business Corporation Law. It allows dividends or other payments (*Auszahlungen*), as long as subsequently the net assets of the corporation are still at least equal to its – more closely defined – stated capital (cf. German *Grundkapital*, the aggregate par value of all shares outstanding).[96] Net assets refers to the difference between accounted assets and accounted liabilities. If the examination shows that payments would make the accounted net assets fall below the

---

[92]Manning and Hanks (2013) p. 13. Cf. on minimum capital in Germany § 7 AktG (AG, *Grundkapital* – basic or stated capital: 50.000 EUR), § 5(1) GmbHG (GmbH, *Stammkapital* – capital stock: 25,000 EUR; cf. without that minimum capital the so-called *Unternehmergesellschaft* – UG, § 5a GmbHG, a counterpart to the British Limited Company – Ltd.).

[93]See, e.g., New York Bus. Corp. Law § 506(a) and Mod. Bus. Corp. Act (1969) § 2(j).

[94]Overview in Manning and Hanks (2013) pp. 77-80 („surplus"-types) pp. 80-84 (stated capital statutes); there, apart from the types briefly treated above, the following types are highlighted, p. 83: stated capital/net profits statutes (New Jersey), and, pp. 83-84, stated capital/current net profits statutes (Delaware).

[95]In *Edwards v. Douglass*, 269 U.S. 204 (no 2.), 214 (1925), on § 31(b) Revenue Act 1917. Cf. on surplus determination (stock repurchases, dividend payments) *In re The Chemours Company Derivative Litigation* C. A. 2020-0786-SG (Del. Ch. Nov. 1, 2021).

[96]N.Y. Bus Corp Law (2021) §§ 510(b), 102(a)(12).

amount determined in the item "stated capital account", transfer of value to the shareholders is not allowed. For this would mean that the liable capital of the corporation (*haftendes Kapital*), which is considered to be permanent, is touched (cf. the so-called balance sheet-stated capital/surplus test, or for short: bankruptcy/insolvency or equity test).[97]

Practice has exposed some dark sides to this concept working with rigid balance sheet ratios, when in the economic crisis between the two World Wars unprofitable "assets" (so-called *Vermögenswerte*) of American railways no longer satisfied the claims of the creditors.[98] In addition, there were different interests in several classes of shareholders competing for payment potential (e.g. senior and preferred shareholders), as well as the differentiated demands for information of modern capital markets on the development of entrepreneurial activity. Attention was directed at laying open the sources of profit according to the dynamic criteria of profit and loss account, particularly the earned surplus, a particular kind of surplus as a payable resource; increasingly, cash flows are moving into focus (cf. valuation methods of "discounted cash flow" – DCF).[99] A range of stated capital/earned surplus statutes developed. Basically, a new type that works with a large number of surplus accounts shown individually on the balance sheet.

Common in use is the so-called capital surplus account (or "paid in surplus account"). It comprises in particular those proceeds (*Erlöse*) that are made for newly issued par-value shares over and above the par-value, or which are not assigned to the stated capital account when securities (shares) without par-value are issued. Finally, the sum of the earned surplus account is shown in the balance scheme. This is where this type gets its name from. For its variants generally allow for payments to equity holders under the basic condition that there is no insolvency (cf. 3.4.1), only up to the amount of disposable net profits. An example of such a regulation is provided by the Model Business Corporation Act in its version of 1979, which served as a model for numerous Federal States (e.g., Arizona, Connecticut, Georgia, Hawaii, Indiana, Kentucky, Maine, New Hampshire, Rhode Island, South Carolina, Vermont, Washington D.C.).[100]

---

[97] See in detail Manning and Hanks (2013) pp. 68-69, following the classical case of *Wood v. Dummer*, 30 F. Cas. 435 (C.C.D. Me. 1824) (no. 17, 944) on distributing corporate assets to the shareholders, Manning and Hanks (2013), from p. 36.

[98] Manning and Hanks (2013) p. 81. On the denotation of "asset" (German *Vermögen*) see below 8.1 (footnote 3).

[99] Manning and Hanks, ibid. Cf., e.g. *In re ISN Software Appraisal Litigation*, C.A. No. 8388-VCG (Del. Ch. Aug. 11, 2016); *SourceHOV Holdings Inc. v. Manichaean Capital LLC*, No. 215, 2020 (Del. Ch. Jan. 22, 2021).

[100] In more detail Manning and Hanks (2013) pp. 81-83 (and 85-86). Chronology of the MBCA Booth (2000). Cf. in detail Lipson and Hamermesh (2020). See American Bar Association, Corporate Laws Committee (CLC) of the Business Law Section, responsible for reviewing, revising, and updating the MBCA (current: www.americanbar.org/groups/business_law/about/committees/corporate-laws/). On the revised version RMBCA 1984 and MBCA 2016 see below 3.5.2.

This therefore remains generally representative for recognising problems and ways of solution for adequate financing and governance of corporations. This relates to our topic of sustainable financial reporting (valuation) with the central as well as timeless question of the distributions to shareholders (*Ausschüttungen*, esp. dividends). James Hanks, co-author of the standard work on "Legal capital", speaks of "the vacuity of traditional legal capital statutes", the reform process of the Model Business Corporation Act (amendments 1980, 1984 revision), focussing the following aspects with the fundamental works by Bayless Manning:

> "First, all pro rata payments to shareholders on account of their shares – whether by dividend, redemption, other reacquisition, or partial liquidation – have the same economic effect on the corporation (a decrease in its assets, typically cash) and on the shareholders (no change in each shareholder's percentage of shares owned). Therefore, there should be no difference in their legal treatment. Even a non-pro rata share acquisition by the corporation offers no more opportunity for board misbehaviour than issuing shares in exchange for a parcel of land or a computer-software program of uncertain value.
>
> Second, it makes no economic sense to base, even in part, the amount of assets that a corporation has the power to distribute on arbitrary and economically irrelevant figures like par value and its derivative, stated capital.
>
> Third, there is no difference between 'treasury shares' – shares that the corporation issues but later reacquires (whether through redemption or repurchase) – and shares that are authorized but never issued. Therefore, treasury shares serve no conceptual purpose and should be abolished."[101]

## 3.4.4 *Trust Fund Theory, Loopholes, and Criticism*

The aspects mentioned show the foundations and developments of the legal capital system, untouched by the particularities of the individual jurisdiction. The corporation may distribute dividends or other payments to its shareholders. It can also repurchase shares for which there were special blocking regulations as treasury shares. Just as in that case,[102] the blocking of payments valid for stated capital account in the sense of the trust fund theory was meant to bind a certain amount of recoverable assets (*Haftungsmasse*, liable capital) in the treasury of the corporation (payout block, *Ausschüttungssperre*). Justice William Story 1824 in *Wood v. Dummer* made some fundamental statements about the "capital stock" of an insolvent bank. In his words, this was to be seen as a pledge or trust fund for the payment of the debts the corporation had contracted.[103]

---

[101] Hanks (2011) 211, 213. On surplus determination (for stock repurchases, dividend payments) *In re The Chemours Company Derivative Litigation* C. A. 2020-0786-SG (Del. Ch. Nov. 1, 2021). Cf. on "shareholder primacy" Lipton (2025).

[102] On the regulation of "treasury shares" in connection with the concepts of "stated capital" and "par value" Fletcher, § 5080.80.

[103] *Wood v. Dummer*, 30 F. Cas. 435, at 436 (C.C.D.Me. 1824) (no. 17, 944); in more detail Manning and Hanks (2013), from p. 36, Ballantine and Hills (1935) 229, from p. 231. Cf. below 3.5.1.

The legal capital system is thus a concept for building up trust in the financial capacity of the corporation. The existence of nominal capital (*Grundkapital*, e.g., §§ 6 and 7 German Stock Corporation Act) which is, however, not objectively fixed, is traditionally aimed at protection: of the corporate creditors (debt capital – *Fremdkapital*) against the corporate shareholders (equity capital – *Eigenkapital*), of older ownership rights against more recent preferred share rights, as well as – in an unfortunately abbreviated understanding (cf. 3.4.5) – of the shareholders (accurate: all investors) in general against mismanagement and impairment of their investment and its earning power (*Ertragskraft*).[104] What is most important in this respect is the assumption that current and potential investors (creditors, shareholders as financiers) orient their decisions regarding a corporation which is privileged through limited liability along the lines of its reference numbers shown in the accounts (financial reporting). The stated capital is regarded as "a nominal, arbitrary, and economically irrelevant number",[105] while having strong signal function.

The regulatory concepts for paying back invested capital to the shareholders in the legal capital system apply within the field of tension between the protection of the creditors and entrepreneurial flexibility and freedom (entrepreneurial freedom – *Unternehmerfreiheit*). They can run more or less emptily. There are some obvious weak points: for instance, an intentionally low nominal value of the par-value shares accepted by the relevant company law. The complete profit over the nominal amount is then considered as paid-in surplus, which the company may dispose of (divest) without the restrictions usually valid for capital stock. What is also remarkable is the increased issue of shares without par-values, overvaluation of investment in kind (so-called "watered" stock) or systematically a transfer of wealth (via distribution), for which the stock capital is reduced according to the regulations for the payment of dividends (share byback). Of course, what remains possible and particularly most important is the transfer of wealth practiced generally through systematic valuation manipulation (so-called "creating shareholder value").[106]

Even when the capital surplus account is exhausted, payment potential may be created through a revaluation surplus equal to the market value of the corporation's property, the worth of which is higher than its book value. The assets are determined by the board of directors, in the traditional comprehension and practice not necessarily according to sound general accounting principles (cf. so-called "GAAP"). It is supported – essentially similar to the capital structure of "equity" (*Eigenkapital*) and "debt" (*Fremdkapital*) in the corporation (leverage)[107] – by the business judgment

[104] Ballantine and Hills (1935) 229, 233, with reference to the judgement of the Californian Supreme Court in *Martin v. Zellerbach* (38 Cal. 300 (1869)), which illustrates well the trust fund theory.

[105] Hanks (2011) 211, 213.

[106] See also 3.6.5, overall chapters 4 and 5. On "shareholder primacy" Lipton (2025).

[107] See 3.3.3, 3.5.1 and 3.6.2 to 3.6.3.

rule.[108] This procedure points to the previously mentioned predominant view. Legislators hardly ever included the determination of "stated capital", "surplus account" etc. in their overall concept, at least they did not link them explicitly to the valid standards of accounting. The persons responsible were probably expected to behave in a "reasonable manner".[109]

In view of the possibilities of circumvention and their perception in economic practice, criticism was repeatedly voiced regarding the legal capital system and the corporation (limited liability) itself. At the dawn of the twentieth century and the Wall Street Panic (1907), Ambrose Bierce, American author and journalist, institutionally described the corporation as an "ingenious device for obtaining individual profit without individual responsibility".[110] In the 1940s, U.S. President Franklin D. Roosevelt in the ground-breaking New Deal based his demand for corporate disclosure (financial reporting) on the ancient rule of caveat emptor,[111] and there was the pithy saying: "The 'trust fund' of yesterday is the sterile dollar sign of today."[112]

A good example of the criticism is Robert W. Hamilton, reporter for the Model Business Corporation Act Revision Project in the United States, who writes that the concepts of "par value" and "stated capital" offer relatively little which would make them attractive for the situation today. At best, they were historical curiosities, which provided hardly any true protection to creditors. He believed that experienced lawyers aiming at maximal flexibility for their "corporate creations" had skewed them. At worst, they were confusing or even misleading.[113] This kind of criticism of the legal capital system, widely regarded as inefficient,[114] had a lasting effect.

---

[108] Thus *Randall v. Bailey*, 23 N.Y.S.2d 173 (Sup.Ct. 1940), *affirmed*, 288 N.Y. 280, 43 N.E.2d 43 (Ct.App. 1942). Cf., e.g., *Garfield v. Allen*, 277 A.3d 296 (Del. Ch. 2022), *Meade v. Christie*, 974 N.W.2d 770 (Iowa 2022) and Luttermann (1998) pp. 327-329. One manifestation of the business judgement rule has been adopted in Germany in the definition of the duty of care (*Sorgfaltspflicht*) and responsibility (*Verantwortlichkeit*) of corporate directors (*Vorstandsmitglieder*) in § 93(1)(2) AktG. See Luttermann (1998) pp. 517-525. Cf. below chapter 7.

[109] Thus for Californian General Corporation Law of 1931 Ballantine/Sterling, quoted after Ackerman and Sterrett (1976) 1052, 1080.

[110] Bierce (1911), corporation, *n*.

[111] See above 3.3.3.

[112] Hills (1935), 1334, 1343. However, the scope of the "trust fund doctrine" is often not realized; see already *Hospes v. Northwestern Manufacturing & Car Co.*, 50 N.W. 1117, 1119-20 (S.Ct. Minn. 1892). Cf. on financial provisions of the MBCA: Hackney (1957).

[113] Hamilton (1987) p. 123 (1996, p. 147); cf. on revisions (MBCA, RMBCA) below 3.5.2. See Hanks (2011) pp. 211, 212-213.

[114] Thus, e.g., Fletcher, § 5080, and in the same vein the detailed criticism by Manning and Hanks (2013) pp. 91-95 as well as Ackerman and Sterrett (1976).

### 3.4.5 *The Californian Way: Ideas, Rigid Tests, and Shareholder Distribution*

It was the Californian legislators who first dared to break the ground in turning away the mental patterns regarding the corporation, the traditional way of handling its financial structure (legal capital, see 3.4.1 to 3.4.4), so firmly anchored by legal experts in and through generations. The General Corporation Law (CA Corp Code),[115] which took effect on January 1, 1977 in California, renounces the legal capital system for the regulation of distributions of the corporation to its shareholders. This means that the protection patterns of the trust described (such as par value, stated capital, paid-in surplus and treasury shares) fall into disuse. Their place is taken by the balance-sheet item retained earnings (net earnings) as well as financial tests. They were valid for any distribution of the corporation or its subsidiaries to the corporation's shareholders (until 2012; cf. 3.4.6).

On the whole, the concept of capital structure with its rules of payout (distributions) is based on the current financial state of a corporation. According to the parliamentary commission called into being by the Californian legislator for the reform, this serves the purpose both of protecting creditors and shareholders and limiting dividends and repurchase of shares in a sensible way.[116] Harold Marsh and Roy Finkle,[117] both decisively involved, note as the guiding principle: creating a legal framework which, in transcending the form selected for a particular transaction, refers to its essential content (i.e., "substance over form"). With regard to the domain treated here, this superficially means: with balanced rights and duties (liability) between directors and shareholders (investors), the restrictions for dividends depend more on the financial state of the corporation than on accounts that may be manipulated. This is meant to provide the creditors with corporate structures of realistic minimum protection.[118] This sounds good, but in fact it is the valuation that is essential (see chapters 2, 4 and 5). The reform remains a milestone in this direction.

The basic line for any distribution is marked by a liquidity test (CA Corp Code § 501, equity insolvency test, basically see 3.5.1). According to this, distributions are forbidden if or through which a company is or becomes incapable of fulfilling its due liabilities. The core of the Californian protection concept is constituted by two financial tests, according to which, on the basis of accounting data, the following

---

[115] California Corporations Code, Title 1, Corporations, Div. 1 General Corp. Law, added by Stats. 1975, c. 682, § 7. See Ackerman and Sterrett (1976). On the Californian environment Buxbaum in Buxbaum and Hopt (1988) p. 122.

[116] Report of Assembly Select Committee, see Marsh and Finkle (1995), vol. 3, Appendix A-120 (on § 500). See also on basic elements and the legal development since the 1930s below 5.5.1.

[117] In Marsh and Finkle (1995), vol. 1, § 1.10 (p. 44). Marsh is the author of the draft of the California General Corporation Law, Finkle advised the Assembly Select Committee.

[118] Marsh and Finkle (1995), vol. 1, pp. 44-45, 45-46 and 47. On the liability of preferred shareholders and the directors for „improper distributions": Ackerman and Sterrett (1976), from p. 1090. Cf. critically with initial empirical data Ben-Dror (1983). Basically Luttermann (1998) pp. 479-485. Cf. on "shareholder primacy" Lipton (2025).

holds: First, CA Corp Code § 500(a) allows distributions equal to the retained earnings. In those cases where there are none, or to the degree that the planned payments are higher, paragraph (b) of the regulation takes effect.[119] There, the historical legislator further declared output without payment (in-kind benefit, *unentgeltliche Leistung*) to be admissible, if afterwards:

(1) the assets of the company (without goodwill, capitalized research and development expenditure, prepaid expenses) is at least 25% above the liabilities (without deferred credits to income) and
(2) the current assets are at least equal to the current liabilities.[120]

Requirement (1), also known as the "quantitative solvency test", is generally valid. In contrast, requirement (2), also known as the "liquidity test", only applies to those companies which, like the public corporations we are interested in here, structure their assets into non-current assets (*Anlagevermögen*) and current assets (*Umlaufvermögen*) according to the rules of accounting (cf. U.S. "GAAP").

Share dividends may be paid independently of these tests due to their mentioned exclusion from the term "distribution". This also holds if there are no retained earnings or the liabilities surpass the assets. In the absence of the distribution of tangible assets (*Sachwerten*) of the company, in such a case protection of creditors appeared to be required only in a modified form: a sub-balance (adverse balance – *Unterbilanz*) is to be shown in the account "retained earnings".[121] This is meant to rouse the current creditors and repel potential investors. In CA Corp Code Section 166, the law makes a distinction. It sets off dividends in shares from other "distributions without consideration" of a company to the shareholders. This distinction is crucial. The tests normed particularly in chapter 5 of the Code regarding dividends of other kinds (cash dividends, property dividends) as well as partial liquidations do not hold for share dividends.

One point needs to be highlighted with regard to accounting law (*Bilanzrecht*). In deviation from earlier Californian law, the so-called "generally accepted accounting principles" (U.S. "GAAP") – as far as necessary: consolidated – must have been adhered to. This also holds for the financial tests treated initially, for which, however, there were exceptions and modifications.[122] In legal and business practice,

[119] See CA Corp Code § 500 (2023): any distribution to the corporation's shareholders (Section 166) is permitted if the board of directors has made a good faith determination under subdivision (a) or (b) of paragraph (1).

[120] If the net profits of the two preceding financial years before taxation of income and before expense are on average lower than the average of interest expense for these years, the current assets have to amount to at least 25% more than the short-term liabilities; Cal. Gen. Corp. Law § 501(b)(2), prior to the reform of 2011, with further details.

[121] Thus Ackerman and Sterrett (1976) 1052, 1055 (there fn. 22) and 1057.

[122] Cal. Gen. Corp. Law § 114: "financial statements and accounting items" as well as specifically with "any distribution payable in property" § 500(2)(c); on deviations Ackerman and Sterrett (1976) 1052, 1064-1068. Note: Consistent with "GAAP" assets are valued at their historical carrying cost (*historischer Buchwert*) instead of their current so-called "fair market value".

the so-called "balance sheet and liquidity" test was considered (too) complex and therefore liability-prone (see 3.4.6). Basically, California had established a special position among the U.S. states for more than a generation.[123]

### 3.4.6 California's Relaxed Standards and Personal Liability

The 2011 reform of California's Corporations Code aimed to streamline the legal standards for corporate distributions and dividends. The State Bar of California emphasises in its reasoning that restrictions are to be harmonised with those of other company forms (e.g., California limited liability company) and – in terms of competitiveness (i.e. competitive disadvantage) – with the corporate laws of most federal states.[124] Another main argument in favour of the reform is also that the "Existing Statute imposes unnecessary restrictions on financially healthy corporations, particularly those which have both historical book losses and appreciated property"; they "may have no retained earnings and thus are unable to rely on Section 500(a) of the Existing Statute to make distributions to their shareholders".[125] As the legislative proposal of the State Bar of California put it for the new statute:

> "The Proposed Statute replaces the unnecessarily complicated and rigid balance sheet and liquidity tests in the Existing Statute with tests that permit a corporation to distribute cash or property to shareholders (whether as a dividend or repurchase or redemption of shares) if, after giving effect to the distribution, the value of the corporation's assets equals or exceeds the sum of its liabilities and the liquidation preference of any preferred stock, and provides the corporation with greater flexibility in how to value assets and liabilities."[126]

This balance sheet test replaces the previous two-pronged "balance sheet and liquidity" test. The new balance sheet test is seen as a more flexible test because the corporation's board of directors may base its determination on its own discretion on various methods of valuation (see CA Corp Code Section 500(c)).[127] It should be remembered that even a U.S. Court of Appeals spoke of the "universe of generally accepted accounting principles" (so-called U.S. "GAAP").[128] Unknown expanses that are largely unexplored and undefined. Accordingly CA Corp Code Section 500 (c), the corporation's board of directors is free to determine the "fair market value" of the corporation's assets (instead of historical carrying cost). At the same time, the

---

[123] Cf. Manning and Hanks (2013), from p. 67 (chapter 4).

[124] State Bar of California, Business Law Section of the Corporations Committee, Legislative Proposal (BLS-2011-01), May 7, 2010, p. 7 (Reasons for the Proposal).

[125] Ibid.

[126] Ibid, p. 5 (Proposal). Cf. California Assembly Bill No. 571, signed into law by the Governor of California on September 1, 2011 and effective January 1, 2012.

[127] Quoted in the following paragraph of the text. See on the "discretionary power" of corporate directors below 3.5.3 and 3.5.5, 7.5.2. Basically Berle (1959).

[128] *Godchaux v. Conveyance Techniques, Inc.*, 846 F.2d 306, 315 (5th Cir. 1988), with reference to the U.S. Supreme Court in *Thor Power Tool Co. v. Commissioner*, 439 U.S. 522, 544 (1979).

other option remains that a corporation's board of directors is able to declare a dividend out of retained earnings (retained earnings test). All distributions are – due to common sense and its codification – subject to the same general solvency test as before the reform of 2011 (see 3.4.5 and cf. in 3.5.2).

Thus, for current California corporation law overall, we can put on record: The board of directors, in the case of "any distribution to the corporation's shareholders (Section 166)", shall determine "in good faith" (CA Corp Code § 166). The corporation's board of directors may base its determination that a distribution is not prohibited under CA Corp Code (Section 500 subdivision (c) or under Section 501) on any of the following, as the CA Corp Code Section 500 subdivision (c) regulates:

"(1) Financial statements prepared on the basis of accounting practices and principles that are reasonable under the circumstances.
(2) A fair valuation.
(3) Any other method that is reasonable under the circumstances."

Well, this obviously opens up a conceivably vast field. Is this really expedient? – One reason for the reform of California's corporation law stands out and is also the first to be mentioned: "The Committee [of the State Bar of California] believes that the Proposed Statute is necessary and advisable in order to (i) simplify and clarify the formula pursuant to which corporations may make distributions to shareholders".[129] Clarity (definiteness) is essential for a legal norm (statutory regulation) so that the addressees are able to recognise and fulfil the legal requirement while at the same time excluding arbitrariness (reasonable certainty, see 7.6.3).[130] The reasoning, however, refers (without precise labelling!) to so-called "generally accepted accounting principles" (GAAP), whatever that means,[131] and explicitly to the "actual fair market value of the distributing entity's assets". Both references fail to fulfil the requirement of clarity, which is already shown by the authoritative minority votes (so-called "standard setting"), and also in the case of so-called "fair value", the largely arbitrarily driven and calculated hope values (*Hoffnungswerte*: "future economic benefits").[132]

The Californian reform act is therefore questionable. Differences to the corporate laws of other states, including Delaware law, have been eliminated "and boards of directors will have more flexibility in what they rely on to determine that applicable

[129] State Bar of California, Business Law Section of the Corporations Committee, Legislative Proposal (BLS-2011-01), May 7, 2010, p. 7 (reasons for the proposal); see also, p. 8: on the "potential impact of the overly formulaic approach of the Existing Statute". Cf. above 3.4.5.

[130] See above 1.5.1, 2.5.2 and 2.6.2, for practical implementation esp. chapter 5.

[131] Basically Luttermann (1998) pp. 405-440, and Luttermann (1999a).

[132] See, e.g., 3.5.2 and 3.5.3, 3.6.4 and in detail chapters 4 and 5. See already Levitt (1998) and Luttermann (1999a). Cf., e.g., *Burroughs International Company v. Datronics Engineers, Inc.*, 254 Md. 327, 255 A.2d 341, 342 (Ct. App. Maryland 1969): "Unhappily, the resolution of the problem calls for an involuntary excursion into the terra incognita known to accountants as GAAP."

standards are satisfied".[133] The legislation is commented on as "the sad end of a creative effort by California to stand against the national trend allowing corporations to make distributions until the company reaches the cusp of insolvency".[134] However, personal (and even criminal) liability remains to be observed, if the value determinations of the corporation's directors "are later to be found unreasonable" by judges (courts); sound rules protect the corporation, its shareholders, and its creditors.[135] – Basically, this shows, regardless of legal changes and circumstances, that for the law and practice of the corporation it is always, as we put it according to the imperative of truth (see chapters 4 and 5), in fact: sound valuation for sustainable financial reporting is the yardstick.

## 3.5 Rethinking the Modern Corporation

### *3.5.1 Roots: Holistic Thinking and Acting*

In the law and in practice, the corporation in fact turns out to be quite constant in its diversity: Accounting law (*Bilanzrecht*), id est the law for financial reporting and auditing (sustainable value creation – *nachhaltige Wertschöpfung*), is the core. Basically, the modern corporation is an object of valuation as a financial instrument. This is what its construction and leadership as a form of organisation for permanent financing of enterprises (or projects) is related to. Its presentation on the market (stock market), the trading of its securities, aims at pricing (valuation). This is actually a communicative process (see 2.6.2), requiring certain information (real disclosure). In particular in view of the literal anonymity of the publicly held corporation, quickly gaining even more ground through digitalised processes. Accounting law is valuation law (*Bewertungsrecht*, see Fig. 3.1). At the same time, it is information law that provides the capital market conditions with its legal ground. It is about legal conditions.

This remains largely unnoticed. What is necessary is rethinking. The modern corporation is the sport of economic, socio-politically relevant interests. In spite of, or possibly because of this, it was long held that in the domain of accounts the jurist

---

133 Gallardo (2011).

134 Comment by Franklin A. Gevurtz (McGeorge School of Law, University of the Pacific, Sacramento, CA), 30.09.2011, posted (at 12:08 am) under Gallardo (2011), Comments, 2. Cf. also 3.5.1.

135 See, e.g., Hakim Law Group, 21.07.2017 (https://hakimlawgroup.com/shareholder-distribution-by-california-corporations-important-restrictions-and-standards-you-need-to-know/, accessed: 22.08.2025); cf. below 3.5.2. On "investments" Luttermann (1998) pp. 471-485, and Isaacs (1923) p. 210: "The legal difference between stocks and bonds plays only an indirect and perhaps a minor part". Cf. on "shareholder primacy" Lipton (2025). Please note above 1.4.1.

(*Jurist*) had little say; valuation was considered to be a purely economic question:[136] The elementary dimension, both in individual cases and for the society as a whole a legal vacuum? – And in fact, the domain is correspondingly characterised by legal abstinence, beyond the reign of law and truth. This has been felt long since not only by the actors of the capital markets, but massively by people around the globe. Corporate chicanery (misuse, fraud) "involves false statements about the value of assets (…), and the profit rate", in fact: "Information is withheld or dissembled".[137] The modern corporation is in the centre of the economy of disaster, of authoritarian practices as well as the new environmental and human rights protection (see Green Deal of the European Union and the United Nations).[138] We must think and act holistically in the realm of science, id est also interdisciplinarily, and across borders for human corporation.

The references hitherto provide further orientation. The Californian concept (see 3.4.5) lays less claim to originality than it may seem. Some of the most important building blocks had long been known and in some parts had been in general use. The idea of creditor protection incorporated in the equity insolvency test goes far back in common law: in centuries-old royal statutes and the chancery jurisprudence of the English courts of equity.[139] Today the idea is generally linked to the concept of a living company (so-called "going concern"-premise – *Grundsatz der Unternehmensfortführung*), a principle, that is fundamental to the law and practice of financial reporting and the appraisal of businesses (assets, corporations).[140] In the United States, it was also in the area of protection norms for creditors and individual classes of shareholders that the multitude of independent jurisdictions took effect. Dividend law oriented itself towards the legal capital system. Under the regime of common law and statutory law, a diverse, sometimes in one state even confusing, multitude of rules and tests limiting the payments of companies.[141]

[136] See previous footnotes (with 3.4.6), above 1.5.1, and Germany: Pinner, Proceedings (*Verhandlungen*) of the 34. *Deutscher Juristentag* 1926 (Köln, German Jurists' Conference), vol. 2, 1927, p. 674. See Berle and Means (1932, 1967) p. 271. Cf. Manning and Hanks (2013) p. 70: "The interplay of law and accounting that determine these numbers is exceedingly complex, subtle and difficult." Gower (2021) 22-001: "the fundamental principle underlying the Companies Act has always been that of disclosure." Please note above 1.5.1 and 2.5.2 with chapter 4.

[137] Aliber, Kindleberger, and McCauley (2023) p. 129. Cf. Vagts (1966) 24-25 and from 78 on extending the corporate constituency: the public. Stiglitz (2010), e.g. from p. 147 (156), and from 278.

[138] See ICJ, Advisory Opinion, 23.07.2025 (https://www.icj-cij.org/sites/default/files/case-related/187/187-20250723-adv-01-00-en.pdf, accessed: 25.07.2025), on that and overall above 1.2 and 2.2, below 6.1.

[139] Comprehensively Weiner (1928), Weiner (1929), Weiner and Bonbright (1930).

[140] See 3.4.1 and chapter 4 (reporting, auditing), chapter 5 (valuation). In the European Union as a general financial reporting principle Art. 6 no. 1. (a) Directive 2013/34/EU: "the undertaking shall be presumed to be carrying on its business as a going concern" (in Germany § 252(1) no. 2 HGB); see also recitals 16, 24 of the mentioned Directive.

[141] Weiner (1929) 461, 462-463, distinguishes four main groups, which forbid dividends (1) in the case of existing of imminent insolvency or (2) if remaining net assets falls below a certain amount,

All federal states make use of a form of "equity insolvency test"; and there is an additional variant of the mentioned tests based on accounts, which aim at a certain debt equity ratio of the company (leverage).[142] The same was true of the older Californian legal capital system. It was from this source that the reform was fed. The equity insolvency test according to Cal. Gen. Corp. Law Section 501 (1977) is taken from Section 1501 of the old law. The reform was able to base itself on important earlier work regarding the financial tests. For recognition and regulation, the macro-economic relations and theories, the instability of the supply of credit, and accompanying discourses on the stability of the financial system remain noteworthy right up to the present. Basically, the conflict seems to be one between the private good und the public good, with the question, "who should look out for the public interest?"[143] – We are experiencing that with the world debt crisis and have developed the concept of trust and control,[144] in order to resolve (supposedly) conflicting interests and to guarantee good governance of the corporation systematically overall through sustainable financial reporting and, of course, its corresponding auditing.

As early as the critical period around 1930 with the Wall Street Crash, the Great Depression and President Roosevelt's New Deal initiative, researchers in the United States debated sustainable alternative models to the stated capital system of the "trust fund theory".[145] Still under the ideal of "legal capital", Henry W. Ballantine was instrumental in fixing the California Corporation Law of 1931, which at the time was modern in its balancing of creditor and shareholder protection. The starting point was the already common practice of institutional investors. In deviation from the lawful "legal capital" standard, they agreed on dividend limits in contract with the capital seekers according to the current ratio of assets to liabilities of the company. At that time, scholars were already discussing testing concepts for payments including the security margin of 1:1.25 (ratio of current assets to current liabilities) later implemented in Cal. Gen. Corp. Law Section 500(b)(1). This became the model of the financial tests introduced in California in 1977.[146]

---

or which allow dividends only (3) from the overall net profits since the founding of the company or (4) from the current net profits.

[142] Cf. Manning and Hanks (1990) pp. 64-65 (apart probably from Massachusetts) and Manning and Hanks (2013) p. 69.

[143] Aliber, Kindleberger, and McCauley (2023) pp. 87-92.

[144] On this above 1.5.2 and below chapters 4 to 7. Basically Luttermann (2003) Einf BilanzR recitals 26-43, 107-136, and Luttermann (2003) § 264 HGB recitals 16-21, 42-169 and 207-216.

[145] Overall above 3.4.4.

[146] Ballantine and Hills (1935) 229, 262, with reference to Cal. Civ. Code § 348b; N.C. Cons. Stats. Ann. (1919) § 1179; Ackerman and Sterrett (1976) 1052, at 1053. Cf. also Luttermann (1998) pp. 479-485.

### 3.5.2 *Reflections on Corporations Accounting (Valuation)*

The reform in California, again, set a milestone for the development of the corporation, its security markets, as well for accounting and auditing. It legally establishes the power of the players of the "numbers game", rather inconspicuous in the relation of equity (*Eigenkapital*, assets) and debt (*Fremdkapital*, liabilities) with the accounting ratios (1:1.25; see 3.5.1): a seemingly mathematical precision suggesting a deceptive certainty to the detriment of the actual circumstances, and thus creating expectations, id est reflexively also significant expectation gaps.[147] The corporation is in fact mathematically based, even as a legal form, where it is functionally about financing and accounting.[148] Questions of valuation are usually dealt with in econometrically designed hypotheses, theories and valuation models by the financial industry reaching out globally from "Wall Street". Thus, we will continue in our investigation.

After California had proceeded with its reform concept in 1977, on the federal level the Model Acts of the American Bar Association followed. The breakthrough was achieved with additions to the Model Business Corporation Act in 1980 and then with the Revised Model Business Corporation Act of 1984 (RMBCA) in its version with additions of 1987: It was well-known that by "its very nature, any form of balance sheet test is inherently wholly dependent upon the accounting principles followed in constructing the numbers on both the assets and the liabilities sides of the balance sheet"; however, in fundamental contrast, practically the old attitude dominated that a distinction should be made between "law and accounting".[149] According to the RMBCA, partners to a contract are allowed to select a par value for shares.[150] This may be imperative for a company extending its trade into a state which has a "par value" concept, for instance also for the basis of tax assessment. The reform of 1980 already abstained from the rigid arsenal of the legal provisos that had developed out of stated capital and par value, suffocating entrepreneurial financing business. This signalled the dawn of modern Wall Street's rush to do big business with fancy, complexly structured securities as well as selling stocks, bonds (debentures, notes) and, of course, legions of hybrid financial instruments.[151]

---

[147] See above 3.3.4 and below 4.5.6. Fundamentally Luttermann (1998) pp. 210-237 (*Finanzierungstheorie*: on financing theory), pp. 238-357 (*Finanzierung mit Hybridformen*: financing with hybrid securities). Cf. Coffee, Gilson, and Quinn (2022), chapter III (esp. pp. 164-176), and Williams (2021), fundamental on fiduciary duties according to corporate climate responsibility.

[148] Please note 3.1, 3.5.3 and 3.5.5.

[149] Cf. already 3.5.1. Manning and Hanks (2013), from p. 181 (see Appendix, pp. 223-238: selected Sections). Manning participated in the reform in 1980, 1984 and 1987 in the leading Committee on Corporate Laws of the ABA.

[150] RMBCA § 2.02(b)(iv).

[151] Fundamentally Bernstein (1993) and Luttermann (1998) pp. 238-357, Luttermann (1998) pp. 238-357 (*Finanzierung mit Hybridformen*: financing with hybrid securities). Cf. Aliber, Kindleberger, and McCauley (2023) p. 133. See below 3.6.3 to 3.6.5. On financial engineering see 6.6.4 with Fig. 6.2.

In the RMBCA, centrally, two elements are combined as a standard for payments of any kind ("distributions" according to RMBCA § 1.40(6)): the classic equity insolvency test treated above (see 3.4.5, 3.5.1) and a "balance sheet test" (RMBCA § 6.40(c)).[152] Apart from the liquidity requirement, this combines two components: (1) The payment must not make the assets get less than the liabilities; (2) the liabilities include the complete amount of the rights of the shareholders due in the case of liquidation, which take precedence in relation to the current payment (so-called "adjusted net worth balance sheet test"). This standard aims at creditor protection and balancing out different classes of shareholders. To this end, the corporation's board of directors is – as the later reform of the MBCA 2016 § 6.40 (d) in its updated version also confirms – to apply reasonable practices and principles of accounting, fair valuation or any other method of valuation suited to the circumstances (RMBCA § 6.40(d); cf. CA Corp Code Section 500 subdivision (c), see above 3.4.6), but not necessarily the so-called U.S. "GAAP".[153]

This rule of the Model Act, aimed at creating scope for action, stood in contrast to Californian law, which, with the same intention, refers explicitly to the so-called U.S. "GAAP". In practice, this may lead to drastically different valuations. Choper, Coffee and Gilson illustrate this with the example of the interesting case *Randall v. Bailey*, which was decided according to New York legislation.[154] The revaluation of assets carried out there for the creation of payment potential would also be covered under the RMBCA by the business judgement rule. However, Choper, Coffee and Gilson argued that according to the U.S. "GAAP" in force in Californian law it goes against the principle of the valuation of assets in its initial outlay (cf. so-called "fair value"). The statement "according to U.S. 'GAAP'" is correct. The solution Choper, Coffee and Gilson propose under the RMBCA is, however, questionable. What still stands out is the finding that "the linchpin of the Model Act is how the corporation's assets and liabilities are valued".[155] However, as shown here, this is generally the case with the corporation, and the view that California has solved the problem with the provision of "GAAP" remains misleading.[156] For our

---

[152] Cf. (comparable in an interesting way): Hamilton (1984) p. 114 (*lit.* E., 2. para.), 121 ff. (according to the draft version of 1984) and Manning and Hanks (2013) pp. 187-197 (see Appendix, pp. 223-238, exact wording and official commentary in print).

[153] Cf. Official Comment (to be quoted shortly in the text above) and American Bar Association, Model Business Corporation Act Annotated (3rd ed., vol. I) p. XXXI.

[154] *Randall v. Bailey*, 23 N.Y.p.2d 173 (Sup.Ct. 1940); cf. above 3.4.4. Choper, Coffee, Gilson (1995) pp. 230-231. Overall Coffee, Gilson, and Quinn (2022) pp. 185-198.

[155] Coffee, Gilson, and Quinn (2022) pp. 188-189. Cf. the Delaware Court of Chancery upholding the stock repurchases and dividend payments of a company that used GAAP financial statements to determine the availability of surplus: *In re The Chemours Company Derivative Litigation* C. A. 2020-0786-SG (Del. Ch. Nov. 1, 2021).

[156] Still believing in "GAAP", too: Coffee, Gilson, and Quinn (2022) p. 189. Cf. below 3.5.3 and overall chapter 4.

study, the motives published regarding the RMBCA of 1987 are illustrative; they initially run as follows:[157]

> "The board of directors should in all circumstances be entitled to rely upon reasonably current financial statements prepared on the basis of generally accepted accounting principles in determining whether or not the balance sheet test of section 6.40(c)(2) has been met, unless the board is then aware that it would be unreasonable to rely on the financial statements because of newly discovered or subsequently arising facts or circumstances. But section 6.40 does not mandate the use of generally accepted accounting principles; it only requires the use of accounting principles that are reasonable in the circumstances."

This passage underlines in particular the responsibility of the corporation's board of directors for time-bound reasonable decisions on the basis of current knowledge (see chapters 6 and 7); they are potentially sanctioned for unreasonable payments with liability according to §§ 8.30, 8.33 RMBCA (cf. MBCA 2021 §§ 8.30, 8.32). To this extent, the RMBCA concept goes beyond the static picture of the balance sheet data which are outdated rather quickly, but only in the sense of an exception ("unless"). Overall, after the reform MBCA 2016 it must now be taken into consideration that "the financial provisions of the Act do not use the concept of surplus but do have restrictions on distributions built around both equity insolvency and balance sheet tests."[158] In this way, it is clarified for the balance sheet test that no "particular accounting terminology of a technical nature" is utilized or "particular accounting concepts" are specified: In making determinations, "the board of directors may make judgments about accounting matters."[159] The corporation explicitly is not obliged to make its financial statements on the basis of so-called U.S. "GAAP", with the exception "if it is not otherwise required".[160]

However, the U.S. "GAAP" have been and still are regarded as the foundation: as an authoritative measure in which decisions are as a rule securely grounded, as long as other facts which would call for modifications are lacking. The commentary on the draft version voices the expectation that the U.S. "GAAP" will in most cases provide the basic rule.[161] The authors of the RMBCA of 1987 felt obliged to extend the formulation with a view to the great number of small and closely-held corporations. In contrast to the publicly held corporations, for which according to the Securities Act it is mandatory that they be registered and do their accounting according to "GAAP", the small and closely-held corporations often deviate from

[157] Quoted after Manning and Hanks (1990) pp. 203-204 (2013: 234-235), reprinted in 42 The Business Lawyer (1986) 259. Cf. on the corporation's board of directors' power and authority Coffee, Gilson, and Quinn (2022) pp. 9-10.

[158] MBCA 2021 § 6.40, Official Comment, No 1.

[159] MBCA 2021 § 6.40, Official Comment, No 3.

[160] MBCA 2021 § 16.01, Official Comment, No 3.

[161] In Hamilton (1984) p. 125, Manning and Hanks (2013) p. 235. Cf. Coffee, Gilson, and Quinn (2022) pp. 186-190.

the U.S. "GAAP" or do their accounts solely according to tax law.[162] This has been further explicated as follows:[163]

> "These facts of corporate life indicate that a statutory standard of reasonableness, rather than stipulating generally accepted accounting principles as the normative standard, is appropriate in order to achieve a reasonable degree of flexibility and to accommodate the needs of the many different types of business corporations which might be subject to these provisions, including particular closely-held corporations. Accordingly, the Revised Model Corporation Act contemplates that generally accepted accounting principles are always "reasonable in the circumstances" and that other accounting principles may be perfectly acceptable, under a general standard of reasonableness, even if they do not involve the "fair value" or "current value" concepts that are also contemplated by section 6.40(d)."

The Model Act thus consciously phrases the capital structure rules in a general way. The purpose is probably to open up an independent resource of "other accounting principles" apart from the so-called U.S. "GAAP", whatever that means (see 3.5.3), with the "general standard of reasonableness". Judging by the wording, this intention remains vague right from the start. However, it establishes what was actually intended and has long dominated in practice: an open "regulation" (correctly said: the illusion of regulation) working as a kind of carte blanche or, one could say, a catch-all phrase. This is confirmed by the current version of the MBCA 2016, which explicitly names a wide range of possible methods. In a given case, "a wide variety of methods may be considered reasonable", explicitly "even if any such method might not be a "fair valuation" or "current value" method."[164] – A perplexing position, isn't it?

### *3.5.3 Accounting: Focussing the "Global GAAP"*

The adequate dealing of the legal fiction "corporation"[165] provides a global challenge. Basically, it is about the limits of human cognitive faculties[166] and the will to regulate reasonably. The carte blanche of the MBCA serves a motley, limitless festival of numbers of the financial markets and great dramas surrounding the corporation, under the Shakespearean motto "As you like it". This is the greedy "numbers game" played worldwide with the masses, magic flutes and capital catchers, as illustrated at the beginning with Mozart's enchanting opera (see 3.1),

162 Official commentary, in Manning and Hanks (2013) ibid.

163 Ibid. Cf. on the meaning and determination of "fair value" the Nebraska Supreme Court, relying on the MBCA, in *Bohack v. Benes Service Co.*, 984 N.W.2d 325 (2023), 313 Neb. 409; the Supreme Court of North Carolina, relying on Delaware law, in *Reynolds American Inc. v. Third Motion Equities Master Fund Ltd.*, 379 N.C. 524 (N.C. 2021). In details on appraisal (fair value) see chapter 5.

164 MBCA 2021 § 6.40, Official Comment, No 3 (last paragraph).

165 Basically above 1.4.1, 1.5 and 2.4.3.

166 See also above 1.6.3.

where those responsible pull the strings behind the curtains and cheer on inconspicuous claqueurs. Regulation in the role of the spoilsport, until the partying audience wakes up from its intoxication, staring into the empty ditch. A gigantic gap that not even – more precisely: in particular also – the so-called U.S. "GAAP", themselves a core element of this game world, do not (are not meant to) fill.

A timeless game. In the neoclassical Wall Street and worldwide which John Kenneth Galbraith described as "financial euphoria". At the end of the twentieth century, even before the great global wave of discovered accounting scandals in the course of Enron Corp. and WorldCom, Inc., Arthur Levitt as chairman of the U.S. Securities and Exchange Commission (SEC) spoke of the "widespread, but too little-challenged custom: earnings management", id est: "the motivation to meet Wall Street earnings expectations may be overriding common sense business practices. Too many corporate managers, auditors, and analysts are participants in a game of nods and winks."[167] – Had there not already nearly a hundred years ago been the demand for "full and real disclosure" (New Deal) as the reason for U.-S. Congress to create the SEC in 1934 as the legal regulator for standards of accounting and auditing?[168] – Let us go back in time with Berle and Means (1932) to their "modern corporation" and its financial instruments (securities):

> "The directors have another powerful weapon (…). They have a large measure of control over the company's income account. So long as accounting standards are not hardened, and the law does not impose any specific canons, directors and their accountants may frame their figures, within limits, much as they choose. (…) the directors may route the earnings by merely arranging (the existence of earnings year by year). (…) One of the reasons why the power of the directors in this regard is so wide lies in the fact that accountants themselves have as yet failed to work out a series of standard rules. The reason may be that in the nature of things strict rules are out of question. (…) In result, however, securities like, say participating preferred stock, or income bonds, whose yield is payable only if it is earned, year by year, are substantially meaningless unless [there are] provisions definitely regulating the corporation's accounting. In fact, the more carefully drawn of such securities, where the design is really to protect the holders, include a definition of accounting methods."[169]

The fundamental issue is a clear legal framework securing all investors and preventing the excessive transfer of wealth.[170] This comprises the presentation of the situation regarding assets, finances and profits of the corporation, which has to be ordered sustainably as a whole with financial reporting, as we are undertaking to do

[167] Levitt (1998).

[168] See above 3.3.3, 3.3.4 and 3.4. Cf. on the legal development in Germany Luttermann (2003) Einf BilanzR recitals 56-136, on European law Luttermann (2003) Einf BilanzR recitals 137-208.

[169] Berle and Means (1932, 1967) pp. 182 and 183. Remember that shareholders and bondholders (also hybrids) are investors, see above 1.4.1 with Isaacs (1923) 201, 210. On hybrid financial instruments Luttermann (1998), e.g., 471-482, and De Spiegeleer, Van Hulle, and Schoutens (2014); early research by Hansen (1936) and Uhlman (1938). Cf. overall Coffee, Gilson, and Quinn (2022) pp. 9-22 (directors).

[170] See above 3.1, 1.4.3 and 1.6.2. Please note on the so-called "fair value" in chapter 7, esp. 7.5.2 and 7.6. Cf. Coffee, Gilson, and Quinn (2022) pp. 185-198, on protection against intra-corporate opportunism.

here. In particular in view of "the nature of things", as is the case for all life circumstances that are the object of the law. Whatever Berle und Means may have meant with "strict rules", they aptly remarked that control over accounting is crucial. It is about relevant facts instead of arbitrary mathematical models and fictions. What stands out generally is what Melvin Eisenberg criticised regarding the MBCA – still or already – in 1973: the failure "to employ a methodology appropriate for producing a model".[171] It thus shows that the renouncement of the methodological basic patterns important in the legal capital system, which connects the Model Act and the California General Corporation Law as a mental basis, in practice does not necessarily generate results that are different from the traditional approach.[172]

At the same time, the central importance of accounting (valuation) as a legal domain, comprising corporation law and contract law, in the framework of the financing of corporations becomes clear. And of course, for their purpose of rendering account and providing information through accounting on "other people's money",[173] the U.S. "GAAP" must be methodologically grounded in the general legal standard of reasonableness. In the United States, the trend followed the way paved by California. Meanwhile, most federal states have turned away from the legal capital system, the majority of these jurisdictions having thus adapted their corporate law to one of the versions of the MBCA.[174] The states that, as one might say, are more or less still adhering to the traditional model include Delaware, Texas and New York – three leading jurisdictions within the United States besides California.[175] It remains to be said that the transfer of value to the detriment of the debt holders (bonds, hybrids) may be limited in other ways than by the typical corporate law of federal states as treated here (e.g., by covenants, sound valuation rules).[176]

Basically, it is about the solution of conflicts of the interests involved. What would be expedient is an awareness that questions of valuation are eminent and founded in civil law. Be it in buying and trading securities, in mergers or

[171] Eisenberg (1974) 1407, 1427.

[172] Cf. above 3.5.2. On mathematical arbitrariness above 3.4.3 with 3.1, 3.2.3, and 3.5.2, on a sustainable solution 3.9. Hanks (2011) 211, 213.

[173] In detail above 3.3, below 3.8 and chapters 4 and 8.

[174] The major MBCA 2016 revision has been adopted in some jurisdictions, including Alabama, Florida, Idaho, Iowa, Montana, Virginia. American Bar Association Business Law Section, Corporate Law Committee, on the Model Business Corporation Act (2016 Revision): 72 The Business Lawyer 421-430. See Model Act states and for current information: https://www.americanbar.org/groups/business_law/about/committees/corporate-laws/ (accessed: 22.08.2025).

[175] On Delaware: Gorris, Hamermesh, and Strine (2011) and *In re The Chemours Company Derivative Litigation* C. A. 2020-0786-SG (Del. Ch. Nov. 1, 2021); cf. Clark (2011), according to MBCA and other entity laws, and Fletcher, § 5080.20. On a federal corporation law Karmel (1991).

[176] See 3.6 (esp. 3.6.4). Note: Certain kinds of abusive property transfer or indebtedness, for which a corporation does not receive an appropriate counter-value, are treated in the Uniform Fraudulent Transfer Act or its new version, the Uniform Voidable Transfers Act. Most federal states have adopted one of the two versions. In general the federal Bankruptcy Act applies, which takes effect for creditor protection in the case of the insolvency of a corporation.

transformations, from the shareholder as well as bondholder perspectives or for other forms of financing: this is where the systematic development of valuation law starts for the adequate solution of conflicts; e.g., in the case of a merger, the majority shareholder enters into a contract to the detriment of third parties (minority shareholders and the like), who have to be adequately recompensed for value loss.[177] The necessary measure is provided by sustainable financial reporting (valuation, see chapters 4 and 5). This carries the human corporation and its financing function, systematically integrated into the global order of assets (see chapter 8). For this, let us take a further look at life circumstances.

### *3.5.4 "In a State of Flux": From Rathenau to Berle and Means*

Corporations, as a peculiar creation of law ("fiction"), carry out diverse economic activities worldwide. They require sustainable organisation, especially in times of change and economic transformation. Corporations are traditionally conceived as organisational forms for important enterprises (projects). They are communities of venture (*Wagnisgemeinschaften*, see 1.4.1 and 3.7). As shown, they operate permanently as a financial instrument organised with a legal person of their own (legal entity), in which in a modern guise is oriented toward trading its securities among the public on capital markets (cf. Securities Act, Securities Exchange Act and Trust Indenture Act).[178] Although the markets for debt capital (bonds, *Fremdkapital*, i.e. bondholders) are far larger, the focus is on the equity markets (stocks, *Eigenkapital*, i.e. shareholders), thus on the stock exchange trading and the corporations' shareholders.

However, this is particularly true for larger undertakings (corporations, companies): *"Niemand ist ständiger Eigentümer"* – no one is a permanent owner, wrote Walther Rathenau, the German industrialist (AEG)[179] and statesman (Minister of Foreign Affairs, Weimar Republic),[180] as early as 1918 in his book *Von Kommenden Dingen* (In days to come)[181] on the impersonal form of the joint-stock company (publicly held corporation, *börsennotierte Aktiengesellschaft*). This insight, accompanied by Rathenaus motive of the progressive *"Verdrängung der Habsucht durch*

[177] In detail Luttermann (2023) recitals 48-68.

[178] See 3.3.3 and below 3.5.5.

[179] The former mammoth Allgemeine Elektricitäts-Gesellschaft, Berlin (German General Electric Company), founded by Walther's father Emil Rathenau.

[180] Assassinated 1922 by extreme nationalists because he inaugurated a new policy of reconciliation with Germany's former enemies and carried out the disastrous Versailles resolutions. See Keynes (1919).

[181] Rathenau (1918) p. 141: *"Niemand ist ständiger Eigentümer; ununterbrochen wechselt die Zusammensetzung des tausendfältigen Komplexes, der als Herr des Unternehmens gilt."* English translation by E. and C. Paul: Rathenau, In days to come, London 1921, pp. 120-121.

*Verantwortungsgefühl*" (displacement of greed by a sense of responsibility) in the face of the moral problems of the economy,[182] shows a way for the development of a human corporation. The statement by Rathenau was taken up by Adolf Berle and Gardiner Means[183] in their book "The modern corporation and private property"; at the beginning of the closing chapter ("The new concept of the corporation") – they quote (in translation) Walther Rathenau:

> "No one is a permanent owner. The composition of the thousandfold complex which functions as lord of the undertaking is in a state of flux. ... This condition of things signifies that ownership has been depersonalized. ... The depersonalization of ownership simultaneously implies the objectification of the thing owned. The claims to ownership are subdivided in such a fashion, and are so mobile, that the enterprise assumes an independent life, as if it belonged to no one; it takes an objective existence, such as in earlier days was embodied only in state and church, in a municipal corporation, in the life of a guild or a religious order. ... The depersonalization of ownership, the objectification of enterprise, the detachment of property from the possessor, leads to a point where the enterprise becomes transformed into an institution which resembles the state in character."[184]

Basically this designates a source of conflict still bubbling to this day. This needs methodological clarification. In doing so, the temporal context has to be kept in mind, nowadays in particular the digitalisation of the markets and the concentration of investors (big asset managers).[185] In fact, what actually remains constant is this: In the shares of a joint-stock corporation listed at the stock exchange the asset component (property) is dominant. The member rights (right to vote, right to information etc.) are atomised in the investor public (*Anlegerpublikum*) and/or change frequently and the control function hardly comes into play. The problem is more extensive, however. It comprises structurally all investors (i.e., stockholders and bondholders,[186] including hybrid financial instruments) who gather as a community of venture (*Wagnisgemeinschaft*) to finance a corporation (cf. relational contract law); the holistic view is gaining ground with the global protection of people and the environment, esp. in terms of fiduciary duties (duty of care, see 1.2 and 6.1).[187]

Overall, it is about the reasonable protection of the investors in corporations. We will place this within a comprehensive concept (see 3.6, chapters 4 to 9). Let us therefore continue with Walther Rathenau on the essential issue. He seems virtually

---

[182] Rathenau (1918) p. 141.

[183] Berle and Means (1932, 1967) p. 309.

[184] Compare to the original text: Rathenau (1918) pp. 141-143. See also below 3.7 and, on the origin of the modern corporation (legal person), 7.3.1.

[185] More details in 3.5.5. Cf. Berle (1959): "power without property".

[186] Already Isaacs (1923) and above 1.4.1. Cf. Berle (1928) p. 189 on stockholders, see above 3.2.1.

[187] Fundamental ICJ, Advisory Opinion, 23.07.2025 (https://www.icj-cij.org/sites/default/files/case-related/187/187-20250723-adv-01-00-en.pdf, accessed: 25.07.2025), see below 6.1; according to corporate climate responsibility also Williams (2022). On director's duties to creditors Conaway Stilson (1995). In historical perspective (from classical contract law and neoclassical contract law) on corporate debt relationships (relational contract law) Macneil (1978); cf. McDaniel (1986) and (1988). Overall Luttermann (1998) pp. 311-330 and 471-485 (with further references), Luttermann (2003) Einf BilanzR recitals 26-43. In details below 3.5.6 and 3.6.

timeless, and with his fine sense of economic relations he points towards the future. In his famous essay *Vom Aktienwesen*[188] (On the nature of stocks, 1917), he writes – translated analogously – about "the organic life motions of the economic bodies". Therein, he remarks in German on the necessity of secret reserves, for: "If the company were subject to the changing tide of the times without any internal balance, the fluctuation of value would be lasting and gigantic." We will return to this later as well.[189] Here, let us first listen to Rathenau's conclusion:

> "There would be a return of the situation as it was at the beginning of the capitalist era, when any value became a game sheet, when every rumour, every precipitate piece of news set in motion the imbalanced thermometer of the stock exchange prices, when daily fortunes were won and lost, and in the final instance it was only the small circle of initiates, the movers, shakers and profiteers, who took the advantage."[190]

### 3.5.5 General Rule, Not Casuistry: Handling Fictions and Facts in a State of Flux

Well, Rathenau sounds familiar? – Just think of the dotcom bubble in the late 1990s, caused by excessive speculation of internet-related corporations at the stock markets, and numerous accounting scandals which have been uncovered since the fall of the Enron Corporation on Wall Street at the dawn of the twenty-first century. As a prime witness we already know Arthur Levitt, who in 1998 as Chairman of the U.-S. Securities and Exchange Commission (SEC) denounced systematic manipulation of accounts: "the numbers game", even operated on a quarterly basis (with hope values, consensus estimates etc.). He demanded a change of culture in the rendering of account. He underlined the task of the auditors as "the public's watchdog in the financial reporting process" and spoke of "a gray area where the accounting is being perverted; where managers are cutting corners; and where earnings reports reflect the desires of management rather than the underlying financial performance of the company".[191]

So let us look back to the motives and legal foundations, already developed – also for the SEC – more than two generations before. Following Walther Rathenau, in 1932 Adolf A. Berle and Gardiner C. Means in "The modern corporation and private property" formulate[192] the tenet of the separation of ownership and control. Being written in English, the book had a seminal impact worldwide on corporate governance. Unfortunately, some central statements by the authors regarding the rendering

---

[188] Rathenau (1917, English translation: On the nature of stocks).

[189] See below 3.6 (with 3.7 to 3.9) and chapters 4 to 7. Fundamentally chapter 8 (*Vermögensordnung*).

[190] Rathenau (1917) p. 36 (para. two). Cf. below 5.1 and chapter 6.

[191] Levitt (1998). Overall chapter 4 and Luttermann (1998), from p. 358.

[192] See Rathenau above 3.5.4.

of account have received very little attention.[193] They are made within the context of earlier "Studies in the law of corporation finance" by Adolf A. Berle,[194] who, as one of the "brain trusters" of U.S. President Franklin D. Roosevelt, also had an influence on the reform program of the New Deal. In the vein of corporation publicity intended for the capital markets in the Securities Acts (see 3.3.3), Berle and Means write:

> "Accountancy plays a great part (...) in the market career of the security. It is customary for bankers to rely in making up their statements on accountants' reports, and the integrity of the accountant and the soundness of his method are the greatest single safeguard to the public investor and to the market in general."[195]

This captures the eminent, but hitherto widely underestimated (or simply ignored) core function of accounting, id est financial reporting (valuation) for the capital market; at the same time also for those responsible in the corporation (directors), for auditors and, first and foremost, for the investors, who must be protected (real disclosure, see 3.3.3). This is the purpose of valuation law, id est, in particular accounting law (*Bilanzrecht*, financial reporting, auditing) and, along with this as a general framework of protection, corporation law and capital market law. Regarding the central role of the law for questions of financing, valuation and the "full and fair disclosure" of corporations, id est corporate disclosure (so-called publicity, *Unternehmenspublizität*), which, however, is hardly ever the leitmotif in practice, Berle and Means rightly state:

> "But rules of accounting are not as yet fully recognized rules of law in this field; though it is obvious that the development of the law of corporation finance makes almost mandatory the legal sanction of good accounting practice."[196]

With this statement, Berle and Means describe the situation as it was in their time. Of course, according to their culture, their kind of thinking and acting was trained in common law, which is methodologically based on case law. In the twentieth century, an influential work by Oliver W. Holmes, associate justice of the U.S. Supreme Court, put it this way: "The life of the law has not been logic; it has been experience."[197] This school of thought, influenced by precursors such as John Stuart Mill, combines philosophical principles and pragmatism in an application-oriented way (so-called legal realism). A general order (*allgemeine Ordnung*), the law, is principles-based, not the work of casuists (rules-based, like U.S. "GAAP/IFRS", see 4.8.4). Adam Smith stated that their doctrine is not about, "what a conscientious regard to the general rules of justice would demand of us" and that their books,

---

[193] Cf. above 3.5.1 and 1.5.1.

[194] Berle (1928), see also Berle and Fisher (1932). Cf. Berle and Means (1932, 1967) on disclosure, e.g.: book three, chapter II (pp. 264-277) and chapter III (pp. 278-285).

[195] Berle and Means (1932, 1967) p. 271.

[196] Berle and Means (1932, 1967) ibid. Cf. Eisenberg (1976) chapter 12, on the critical role of the auditor (accountant) in the modern corporation with the "pressure on the accountants to go along", pp. 197-198, points to the fact: "a more flexible auditor can almost always be found". On auditing, control and sanctions below 4.9.

[197] Holmes (1881) p. 1.

therefore, are "as useless as they are commonly tiresome" – "yet upon account of the still greater variety of possible circumstance, it is a chance, if among all those cases there be found one exactly parallel to that under consideration".[198]

In 1928, Adolf A. Berle addressed the publicity of accounts and the fiduciary obligation of the corporate directors: "Requirement of disclosure has to do with facts only, and not with prospects, hopes or estimates."[199] Louis D. Brandeis had already focused on this issue.[200] The following passage by Berle and Means on "accounting and the law" pinpoints the problem, basically still in effect especially in the common law world today, and at the same time indicates the way to go in order to really establish a true and sustainable "modern", id est a human corporation:

> "In fact, the failure of the law to recognize accounting standards is probably due to the lack of agreement among accountants; but year by year certain tenets are forged out, finding their way into the body of standard accounting practice and ultimately into the law. In general the problem revolves around securing a method of accounting which will give an approximately accurate picture of the situation."[201]

This is followed by a two-page list with examples of possible accounting manipulations "for the purpose of showing an abnormal profit".[202] – The field seems infinite and abuse its fertiliser. Generations later the SEC Chairman Levitt casuistically names five case groups from the – still or increasingly – common "accounting hocus-pocus" saying: "Accountants are wise enough to (...) develop principles that allow for flexibility to adapt to changing circumstances. (...) Abuses such as earnings management occur when people exploit this pliancy"; and Levitt "calls for immediate action".[203] The facts since then: an economy of disaster and number games as probably never before in human history with the corporation and financial industry – epically fuelled by the fiat money spending-policy of "quantitative easing". The imperative of truth requires different work for the good, id est also for corporate finance, financial reporting and auditing (valuation, see chapters 4 to 7). Once again, as Joseph Stiglitz nailed it, "the great American robbery", where,

[198] Smith (1790) pp. 395 and 400, see also pp. 401-403 (on ethics and jurisprudence); cf. already Cicero (44 BC) 3 (60) to (74). See above 2.2, chapter 1 with chapters 4 (esp. 4.4.4, 4.8.4), 5 and 7 (esp. 7.8.1). Overall chapters 8 and 9.

[199] Berle (1928) p. 181 (with 187-188).

[200] Brandeis (1914), esp. p. 104: "But the disclosure must be real. (...) To be effective, knowledge of the facts must be brought home to the investor." See overall (with this quote as the leitmotif) chapter 4, and above 3.3.3 (real disclosure).

[201] Berle and Means (1932, 1967) pp. 271-272. Cf. Eisenberg (1976) chapter 12, esp. on the "enormous discretion" given to management "in selecting among competing accounting principles"; see also above 3.5.3, 7.5.2 and Berle (1959): "power without property". Basically on the practice of minority opinions in FASB and IASB Luttermann (1998) pp. 419-421 and below 4.9.7.

[202] Ibid., pp. 272-273.

[203] Levitt (1998), the case groups: "big bath" restructuring charges, creative acquisition accounting, "cookie jar reserves", "immaterial" misapplications of accounting principles, and the premature recognition of revenue.

globally, again "avarice triumphs over prudence".[204] – A never-ending story of a fox keeping the geese?

### 3.5.6 *Sustainability: Big Asset Management and Artificial Intelligence (AI)*

The corporation, as a creation of law, depends fundamentally on sustainability in its existence and financing function. In a capital market, its balance sheet with the accounting valuation stands for this on the basis of the actual circumstances (see chapters 4 and 5). This is shown from an evolutionary point of view by basic patterns and relations of entrepreneurial organisation (see 3.7). Recent developments have moved global digitisation (big data) and powerful asset managers (big money) into focus. They open remarkable dimensions across borders. In times of unprecedented global financial wealth (2024: $477 trillion) and the unfolding "GenAI era" (GenAI for generative AI) with a megahype,[205] the wealth management industry has changed the way of investing in companies. Private public asset managers, some with trillions of US-Dollars in assets under management, shape capital markets, corporations, and widely the thinking and acting of actors in politics, economy and society (see chapters 6 and 9).

It is about values and transformation processes. The relations are manifold and complex, while the asset managers themselves are organised corporatively: Who is behind this? – Let us take three prominent examples: What seems comprehensible is the Norwegian Statens Pensjonsfond (Oslo), the leading sovereign wealth fund (2024: total assets around $1.68 trillion), which invests in thousands of corporations worldwide, "to ensure responsible and long-term management of revenue from Norway's oil and gas resources".[206] A different type of Sovereign Wealth Fund is the China Investment Corporation (Beijing, 2025: total assets around $1.33 trillion), founded in 2007 as "a vehicle to diversify China's foreign exchange holdings and seek maximum returns for its shareholders within acceptable risk tolerance".[207] The private BlackRock, Inc. (New York, 2024: total assets around $11.55 trillions) names as its principles: "BlackRock's purpose is to help more and more people

[204] Stiglitz (2010), esp. pp. 109-183, chief economist of the World Bank (1997-2000) and Nobel Laureat (2001). Cf. Aliber, Kindleberger, and McCauley (2023), esp. pp. 127-169, 321-343 (cf. 7th ed. 2015, pp. 313-368).

[205] See below 6.8.5. Data: Boston Consulting Group (BCG), Global Wealth Report 2023, p. 2; BCG, Global Wealth Report 2024, The GenAI era unfolds, p. 2 (details: 3-4): global wealth growing by 4.3%. Cf. overall on AI below in 9.6 to 9.9.

[206] Government Pension Fund Global (Oljefondet), source: www.nbim.no (12.7.2024). Cf., e.g., Røste (2021), Lastra, Fearnley, and Satragno (2022).

[207] Source: http://www.china-inv.cn/en/, data: www.swfinstitute.org/profile/598cdaa50124e9fd2d0 5ac89 (both accessed: 22.08.2025). Cf. Norris (2016) pp. 192-221, Hembrecht (2013), Li (2009).

experience financial well-being".[208] Sounds good, especially with marked sustainable perspectives. – Who's in control?

The classic perspective (Berle and Means: separation of ownership and control, see 3.5.5) is changing radically. Practically, two or multiple corporate layers take effect, similar to multi-level corporate structures, through which personal responsibility may be overlaid. This enables asset managers to exert an influence on the corporate management of seemingly independent corporations, due to the (parallel) property relations, also relevant with regard to competition law (cf. so-called common ownership, see 6.5.1). The representatives of the big asset managers vote at general meetings of thousands of corporations around the globe, id est acting in concert? – Their votes have weight in whole sectors and beyond, as, e.g., BlackRock openly announces: "We are deeply invested in the success of *all of our stakeholders*" (clients, employees, shareholders, the communities where we operate) and – with the remark that "we run our business *sustainably and responsibly*," – at "the companies we invest in for our clients, we advocate for *sustainable and responsible business practices* that drive *long-term value*."[209]

What counts as "sustainable" and what as "responsible"? – Who sets the standards, where are legitimacy, transparency, independent control: The practice of so-called standard setting through private actors of the financial industry is well-known (see chapters 4 to 6: "IFRS"). The Norwegian GPFG, being a state investment vehicle in the rule of law, may partly function as a model, esp. "in terms of procedural rather than substantive justice".[210] However, it must be said that even there in fact out-dated action patterns of financial risk are practiced.[211] In particular in view of climate change and human rights, thinking and acting have to be sustainable, where in fact climate risk is to be implemented as financial risk: in a really sustainable, financially established culture of entrepreneurship.[212] This involves managing the corporation with decision processes, analysis and management, developed digitally. BlackRock again in their company guidelines: "*Aladdin unifies us*, creating a *common language* for us to interpret the world, the markets, and our clients'

---

[208] Source (accessed: 22.08.2025): www.blackrock.com/corporate/about-us/mission-and-principles; cf. www.bloomberg.com/news/articles/2023-07-14/blackrock-assets-rise-to-9-4-trillion-fueled-by-bull-market?leadSource=uverify%20wall#xj4y7vzkg. See, e.g., Miller (2023), Wigglesworth (2021) and overall below chapter 6.

[209] BlackRock, 5. Principle (font here in italics instead of bold in the original): www.blackrock.com/corporate/about-us/mission-and-principles (accessed: 22.08.2024 and, still unchanged under the Trump-administration, 22.08.2025). Cf. Edmans, Levit, and Reilly (2019).

[210] On the ethics of global investment Clark, Dixon, and Monk (2013) 67.

[211] See Nilsen, Sjåfjell, and Richardson (2019).

[212] Fundamentally Williams (2021), Luttermann, L. (2022), (2024) and (2025). See also chapter 8.

needs."[213] – A reference to Aladdin's magic lamp, an enchanting fairytale like Mozart's magic flute (see 3.1) from Arabian Nights?

What is denoted is our real world. "Aladdin" is an acronym for "Asset, liability and debt and derivative investment network", the data analysis system of BlackRock, which evaluates around a tenth of all assets globally (also investment portfolios of banks, insurances, pension funds) through artificial intelligence.[214] Is artificial intelligence with its black boxes taking over? The digital transformation of the world, massive and disruptive (digital business revolution), changes interactions, organisation and communication on capital markets and in the corporation.[215] In the interconnected economy, algorithms obtain, discussed even as an "electronic person" besides human beings and legal persons.[216] New systems for exchange of values (crypto currencies) and information such as transactional reporting (XBRL global ledger), a world monopoly of valuation (see 1.5.3). However, sustainably it is still about trust, possibly obscured by technology and data floods (see chapter 6) and human responsibility (see chapter 7).

## 3.6 On the Liable Capital (*Haftkapital*)[217] of the Corporation

### *3.6.1 Thinking and Acting with "Virtual" Realities*

Adequately dealing with the corporation as a legal entity (fiction)[218] seems to pose problems even in the digitally virtual era of the internet (*Internetzeitalter*). And yet it is practically used widely, being integrated into the reality of our life and global markets. The corporation appears as an early form of virtual reality that is difficult to grasp. The adjective "virtual" derives from Latin *virtus, virtutis* for power, virtue (*Kraft, Tugend*). It means "effective in respect of inherent qualities", in physics denoting a quantum-mechanical state, the existence of which can be experimentally

[213] BlackRock, 2. Principle (fond here in italics instead of bold in the original): www.blackrock.com/corporate/about-us/mission-and-principles (accessed: 12.7.2024 and, still unchanged under the Trump-administration, 22.08.2025).

[214] Data: www.blackrock.com; cf. https://www.appsruntheworld.com/customers-database/products/view/blackrock-aladdin (both accessed: 22.08.2025). Du (2022).

[215] Already above 2.6.3 (V), below 3.7, 6.8.5 and 9.6. Luttermann (2023) recitals 91-100, see also recitals 86-90 on digitised transformation and valuation.

[216] EU Parliament resolution, 16.02.2017, on Civil Law Rules on Robotics (2015/2103(INL)); EU Commission, Artificial intelligence, 25.04.2018 (https://ec.europa.eu/commission/presscorner/detail/en/IP_18_3362, accessed: 22.08.2025). On electronic persons, robots and personal responsibility Claudia Stancati and Giusy Gallo in Giovagnoli and Lowe (2020) pp. 121-129. Cf. EU AI Act (21.04.2021: COM/2021/206 final). See also below 3.8, 6.8.5 and 9.6.

[217] Overall Luttermann (1998), esp. pp. 133, 530-533, 548-549, and Luttermann (2001a).

[218] See above 3.2.1 and 3.5.3 to 3.5.5, below 7.3.

proved only with difficulty due to the classical law of the conservation of energy (so-called uncertainty relation), and in computing "not physically existing but made by software to appear to do so from the point of view of the program or the user".[219]

In this, we recognise assonances and clues for dealing with the corporation that are already familiar. As "an artificial being" (John Marshall), a creation of the law, which is referred to as "fiction" (Friedrich Carl von Savigny), we can neither see nor touch a corporation (see 3.2.1).[220] World-famous brand names such as Apple Inc., The Coca-Cola Company, Mercedes-Benz Group AG (previously Daimler-Benz AG), Nestlé S.A. and Sony Corporation probably evoke similar associations around the world, in particular certain products, which appear before our inner eye (*sic*!). Buying their products (e.g., mobile phone, soft drink, car, chocolate, TV) also involves something virtual: so-called "money" (fiat money), increasingly in digital transaction (bits and bytes, e-wallet). – But what do we actually purchase with such money when investing in the corporation, the acquisition of corporate securities (*Wertpapiere*), which nowadays no longer have any physical existence? What in fact is the so-called "capital" of the corporation?

We realise how our familiar lifeworld, realities or what we regard as such out of habit, seem to be dissolving. How what is concrete and what is mental is blending together. The dualism of human mental and physical life, for life comprises the body (*den Körper, Leib* – materiality) and the mind (*den Geist*, the soul, *die Seele* – immateriality). This is where we will begin, with the mind taking the lead: The corporation appears as a form of thought, an immaterial construct, a creation of the mind (*Schöpfung des Geistes*) practically implemented in the reality of the economy (see 7.3.1); for a specific entrepreneurial goal (purpose, *Zweck*), focused on the function of financing (see 1.3.3). This is ensured by the balance sheet picture (*Bilanzbild*) emerging in the accounts (financial reporting) of the corporation as a legal person, when according to the principle of separation (*Trennungsprinzip*) certain assets are separated out and attributed to the corporation as an independent legal subject (see 3.1, 2.4.3).[221] This establishes the order of assets (*Vermögensordnung*, see Figs. 3.1 and 3.2, chapters 4, 5 and 8).

Through this, the corporation becomes tangible, id est manageable, in a legal as well as in a practical sense, in its financial statements (*Jahresabschluss,* see, e.g., § 242 and § 264 *Handelsgesetzbuch*, German Commercial Code). The presentation in the financial statements is about the "point of view", which is to be a picture that corresponds to the actual circumstances (cf. "a true and fair view").[222] Overall,

219 Brown (1993) p. 3586 (virtual). Cf. below 3.7, 7.3.1 (origins of the corporation), and overall chapter 9 (with AI).

220 *Trustees of Dartmouth College v. Woodward*, 17 U.S. 518 (1819). See below 7.3.1 and critically Wolfe (2017).

221 Cf. Klein (1904) p. 5, on the idea of the corporation as an independent *Geldvereinigung* (monetary association), noting that the "money" itself "became an entrepreneur" (already above in 2.5.1). Note, however, that at that time "money" was still real (with gold, silver), and not just fiat money as it is today.

222 See altogether chapter 4.

culture-specific aspects, different ways of thinking and different perspectives may operate, which we will come to again later.[223] The world has seen that many times with foreign corporation listing at the New York Stock Exchange, e.g., in the balance sheet picture of the Daimler-Benz AG 1993 under different regulations (see 4.6.3). Remember, the relevant regulations determine what may or must be presented in what way or what gives, as shown (see 3.5.3), the corporate directors a largely free rein.[224] At the same time, illusion techniques and, as it were, visual strategies develop, veiling or deluding about the asset, finance and profit situation in the balance sheet picture – as if in a virtual world (cyber space).

The consequences for the investors (i.e., shareholders, bondholders), however, are all too real: through – contractually – participating in entrepreneurial success (profit, loss) of the corporation, id est through the (share or bond) price development of their securities (financial instruments) and the dividends or interest received (micro-economic). Overall, accordingly, this is in macro-economic terms the shift of assets (wealth, *Vermögensverschiebung*) and of liability right up to the complete scenario of an economy of disaster.[225] This shows that the corporation has not yet been completely thought through and (or) is not properly operated (regulated). In contrast, it is about the actual situation (circumstances, facts – *die tatsächlichen Verhältnisse*), which has to be sustainably represented through financial reporting, id est also in governance, financing and valuation of the corporation.[226] A form without substance is an empty shell. So we will first turn in more detail to entrepreneurial substance.

### 3.6.2 *Corporate Constructions, Financing, and Liability (***Haftkapital***)*

For an adequate solution of conflict situations, a reasonable law of financing, valuation and accounting (auditing) of the corporation provides business transactions with a sound order of assets (*Vermögensordnung*) as a constitution of liberty. This is the basis of good corporate governance, while at the same time being – in the idea of justice (*Gerechtigkeit*) – a sustainable order of liability (*Haftung*) based on responsibility (*Verantwortung*, see chapter 7), the inalienable companion of liberty (*Freiheit*, see 1.3.2, 1.7 and chapter 6). For this, the following has first to be clarified: a corporation has limited liability, as – like any legal subject – it does not have at its disposal unlimited liability mass (*Haftungsmasse*), but only certain assets (*Vermögen*). Here, the fundamental separation of the asset spheres takes effect, classically between

---

[223] Below 3.8, cf. already, e.g., 3.1, 3.3, and chapters 1, 2 and 8.

[224] Overall on legal development and discussion above 3.5 (with further references).

[225] See, e.g., above 2.7 and 3.5.1. In details chapters 6 and 7.

[226] On this see 3.3.4, 2.5 and 2.6.2. In details chapters 4 and 5.

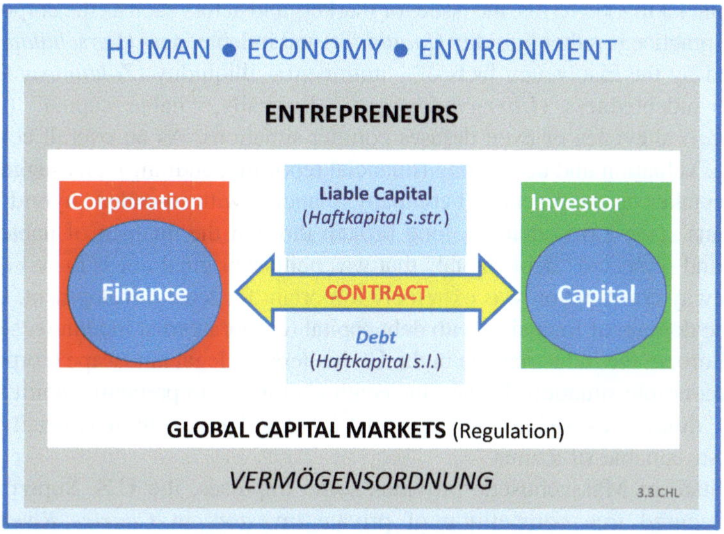


**Fig. 3.3** The liable capital (*Haftkapital*) of a corporation in the strict sense (*sensu stricto*, s.str.) and in the broader sense (*sensu lato*, s.l.)

the corporation and its shareholders (principle of separation).[227] Beyond its equity capital, however, the issue is factually the here so-called "liable capital" of the corporation (*Haftkapital*, see Fig. 3.3).

In general, in the balance sheet assets (*Bilanzvermögen*) of the corporation, the equity capital (*Eigenkapital*) counts as the recoverable assets for the claims of the company creditors (debt capital, *Fremdkapitalposten*). In the traditional dualism of equity capital or debt capital, attribution takes place according to the legal form of the investment (*Kapitalbegebung*).[228] This formal perspective, however, hardly does justice to the diversity and dynamics of business life; even creditors basically enjoy more shine than protection in this view. We have already seen this with unilateral transfer of assets (value, so-called "creating shareholder value", see 3.4.4 and 3.6.5), the targeted encumbrance of debt through a systematically low equity ratio (so-called "leverage") as well as structurally in the discourse about payouts (insolvency tests etc., see 3.4.5 and 3.5). Usually, the relation of "equity" and "debt" is central for measurement, id est the capital structure (debt-equity ratio, *Kapitalstruktur*). This formal approach – also with regard to groups of corporations (separate legal persons as a "MNE") – occurs internationally.[229]

[227] See above 3.4.1, 2.4.3. Cf. Davies (2002) p. 11, Easterbrook, Fischel (1991) p. 11.

[228] Note: Debt capital is particularly attractive in cases (jurisdictions) where the payout (distribution) as a business expense (operating cost – *Betriebsausgabe*) reduces taxes or is otherwise privileged.

[229] Luttermann (1998) pp. 6-19, 177-194 and from 209. Overall Coffee, Gilson, and Quinn (2022), from p. 139 (chapter III). On global or multinational enterprises (MNEs) below in 3.7, 6.5.1 and in terms of accounting, financing and liability below 4.7, 8.4.2. Cf. on the "liability of individuals"

In financial market terms, the issue for markets and actors such as the corporation in dynamic practice is rather liquidity (*Liquidität*) and indebtedness (*Verschuldung*). This is marked by the insolvency facts of – imminent – illiquidity (*Zahlungsunfähigkeit*) and over-indebtedness (*Überschuldung*).[230] Basically, "liable capital" (so-called *Haftkapital*) alleviates or even defuses conflict situations. As an overall concept for financing, valuation and accounting (financial reporting, auditing), this suggestion for a solution takes up the practice of company financing with so-called "hybrid financial instruments" (see 3.6.5) that has long broken through the dualism of liable "equity capital" and protected "debt capital" that was neither original nor is there no alternative. Railway construction was extremely important for legal development. In particular in the domain of financing with debt capital (corporate trust indenture, see 3.6.3). Like in Europe, the industrial age in the USA alters the legal landscape (corporations) via the economic situation. In the nineteenth century, entrepreneurial spirit and "big business" flourish, as we have already seen[231] and will look at in more detail – since it is about sustainable structures.

The State of Massachusetts provides some impulses, the U.S. Supreme Court having secured free competition of private investors in *Charles River Bridge v. Warren Bridge*:[232] a legal toll-bridge license does not prevent the future legislator from licensing a neighbouring bridge which is to be a toll-free bridge, absorbing all the profit. In this way, the new railway companies are able to outdo the older turnpike corporations due to better technology. This process mirrors the uncertainty in legal questions, which accompanies the economic development of the corporation as a form of organisation for large companies (projects). States such as Massachusetts, a center of industrial stock corporations, are initially restrictive. In order to protect the creditors, the corporate character of companies is modified either by law or by the courts. Under certain circumstances, shareholders are even personally liable for obligations of the company. There seems to be a tendency towards personal liability of the shareholders, increasingly giving the joint-stock companies the character of a partnership, with some corporate features and privileges.[233]

---

Conard (1993) pp. 707, 711: "The enterprise concept may prove to be just as troublesome an obstacle to justice as the entity concept.", referring to *Minton v. Caveney*, 364 P.2d 473 (Cal. 1961).

[230] Thus in German law §§ 17, 18 and 19 InsO, see above 3.4.1. Luttermann (2003) Einf BilanzR recitals 117-119. On *Haftkapital* see Luttermann (1998) pp. 133, 530-533, 548-549, and Luttermann (2001a).

[231] See 3.5.2 and 2.3.2; also 7.4.3. From a regulatory perspective on "bigness" 3.3.3.

[232] 36 U.S. 420, 423 (1837).

[233] Kent (quoted in *Charles River Bridge v. Warren Bridge*, ibid., p. 493), according to whom only Rhode Island, New York, Maryland and South Carolina followed this policy to a sensible degree as creditor protection.

The central concern is monopoly-like power in a state through the transformation of individual property into capital of the corporation as eternal proprietor.[234] As a consequence of these policies, massive amounts of capital are transferred to states with a stricter principle of separation, id est limitation of liability (*Haftungsbegrenzung*). As early as 1825, the governor of Massachusetts accordingly appeals to the legislator for a correction of this course, which leads to a so-called more investor-friendly law in 1830.[235] Steps such as this reduce the tension in the financial situation of the railway companies in the face of high initial investments in railway construction and rolling equipment (locos, rail waggons). As in Europe, apart from state support,[236] it is particularly private capital that is needed. In the USA, the railways are the first private companies which can no longer be financed by the often sparsely populated local construction domain. For the simultaneous construction of the numerous lines, it is necessary for great amounts of capital to be raised on a supra-regional (national) level as well as on an international level.

The decisive move comes around the middle of the century, as has been mentioned: Until 1859, more than $1.1 billion are invested in securities of private railway companies, around $700 million of which were raised in the preceding ten years. Political unrest and wars in Europe, with streams of emigrants going overseas, drive European capital into the railway projects in the USA. New York City thrives as a financial center with the Wall Street's financial industry and with it, basic patterns of finance (see 3.3.1). The dominant way of financing contractually via bonds (debentures, notes), particularly mortgage bonds, provides advantages for both parties. By being shareholders, the initiators of railway construction retain control of the company (corporation), the new investors receive regular earnings. However, the new investors want to participate in the success of the capital-hungry railways. In reaction, these offer a range of securities:[237] preferred stocks, profit-related income bonds (participating debentures), convertible securities (bonds).[238]

### 3.6.3 *Hybrid Debt Financing: Corporate Trust Indenture*

Basically, it was then that the ongoing game began to create "innovative" forms of financing through contractual construction, the so-called financial engineering. A practically limitless spectrum in particular of financial instruments with participatory

[234] Warren (1911) pp. 495-496 and 500 (there fn. 1). On the basics see above 2.4.3 (an "eternal asset holder" – *ewiger Vermögensträger*). Cf. Großfeld (1968), from p. 85, and above 2.3.2 on corporations monopolising modern technologies (e.g. Google).

[235] Warren (1911) pp. 494-495.

[236] Ibidem, p. 486 (there fn. 1).

[237] Detailed overview in Huppertz (1930), from p. 12. Cf. Hansen (1936) and Uhlman (1938).

[238] Huppertz (1930), ibid. and from p. 23 (on the strong increase of its use since 1900, with a list of conversion conditions on pp. 25-29). Overall Luttermann (1998) pp. 238-258; cf. conceptually on hybrid securities Luttermann (1998) pp. 258-268.

character, also explicitly containing valuation law elements (contractual terms, clauses, covenants – *Vertragsklauseln*) and thus located in classical capital structure between equity and debt: hybrid debt securities (hybrid financial instruments, today also so-called “mezzanine capital”).[239] Until the turn of the twentieth century, the mortgage bonds of the railways and canal constructors remain the leading items; increasingly, other companies also start financing themselves in a major way by issuing debt securities.[240] Contractually, the corporate trust indenture develops during this time, fixing the conditions of financing. Under the trust indenture, a corporation issues a large number of debt securities for taking out capital; these are consequently of legally identical (*in*dentical!) content.[241]

Partners to the contract are the corporation and an indenture trustee. The latter is involved for the party of the (future) holders of securities in order to see to the conclusion and implementation of the trust indenture. The contract creditors of the corporation are, however, the holders of the debt securities as investors (debt capital of the corporation, in classical term of balance sheet so-called *Fremdkapital*). With the purchase of securities, they join the trust indenture. This construction served the financing of the railways with bonds secured by mortgage (i.e. mortgage bonds).[242] In order to raise the long-term capital required for enterprises which at that time were extremely risky (and in actual fact are still widely so), recourse was taken to the conventional mortgage, id est secured by a land charge (*Grundpfandrecht*) for the security of the investors: real estate as real value (sustainable finance) instead of today’s “numbers game” (in form of fancy models and mathematics with hope values, fiat money etc.). The core problem in the development of the new financial instrument was securing a large number of holders of a series of mortgaged securities, while at the same time retaining the tradability of the individual items.

The involvement of a trustee (so-called “indenture trustee”) solved this problem. A company wanting to issue mortgage bonds confers premises in mortgage and other property eligible to serve as collateral onto the trustee for the protection of the investors (bondholders). The right of lien (*Pfandrecht*) thus runs to the trustee, not to the holders of the secured debt securities (*Schuldverschreibungen*). The bonds remain freely tradable and as a rule enjoy primacy over other creditors. If the corporation deteriorates financially, the current securities holders enjoy the right to

---

[239] See below 3.6.5. Fundamental on hybrid financial instruments Luttermann (1998) pp. 268-357, from p. 421 and p. 453 (§ 7 *Genußrechte*: participating rights on international capital markets). On hybrid securities with more recent practices De Spiegeleer, Van Hulle, and Schoutens (2014); cf. Gower (2021) 31-002.

[240] Gardiner (1931) p. 3 and 5.

[241] Overall Landau and Peluso (2015); Luttermann (1998) pp. 271-291 (corporate trust indenture). Historically, Blackstone (1766), chapter 20 (of alienation by deed), p. 295: “If a deed be made by more parties than one, there ought to be regularly as many copies of it as there are parties, and each should be cut or indented (formerly in acute angles *instar dentium*, but at present in a waving line) on the top or side, to tally or correspond with the other; which deed, so made, is called an indenture.”

[242] Commentaries (1971) of the American Bar Foundation, pp. 5-6.

lien, which the trustee executes for their best, as determined in the contract. From the perspective of the corporation, this construction may, however, also lead into financial straits. The corporation is prevented from issuing further series of mortgage bonds if in a previous issue of securities it was forced to mortgage nearly all the capital assets. This was the original practice.

As an alternative, the open-end corporate mortgage came up, which can be variably valued and, according to trust indenture, allows for the issue of further series. All the same, the market for secured bonds waned particularly with industrial corporations.[243] Instead of the mortgages, investor protection was shifted contractually (macro-economically via marketable financial structures). This meant that at the turn to the twentieth century it was generally unsecured debentures[244] instead of – secured – bonds[245] that moved into the focus of financial planning in the expanding economic domains dependent on flexibility (or at least striving for it).[246] Here, the framework for the protection of investors was also the trust indenture. Based on the indenture trustee, more flexibly negotiable protective clauses developed, e.g., for securing rank in relation to other creditors or in order to exclude extensive debt of a corporation (cf. so-called "leverage").[247]

Since then the construction of the trust indenture has ruled the market for debt securities. The foundation is the Trust Indenture Act of 1939, a federal law which requires corporate bonds and other debt securities to be issued under an indenture agreement approved by the SEC. The great financial crisis of the 1930s with numerous abuses to the detriment of the holders of securities led the U.S. Congress to create norms for identical protection of capital investors in all Federal States (New Deal).[248] Reforms, Model Indentures and State common law have since then formed

---

[243] Commentaries (1971) p. 6.

[244] The term is derived from Latin *debere* (to be obliged, to owe). The term *debentur* was the original term in English law for a formal certificate of indebtedness which came up before the term *bond* (*band*; see following footnote). In the USA, debentures count as evidence for a non-secured debt. The third traditional type of debt securities is the note (cf. Latin *nota*, from *notus, a*: noted), the arbitrary choice of words, however, being problematic. In contrast to bonds and debentures, the note is described as a paper which is usually held until the date of short-term or long-term date of payment and is non-negotiable; thus it is of minor importance to us. Overall Luttermann (1998) pp. 240-241. Cf. Gower (2021) 31-006 and 007.

[245] The term *bond* occurs in Middle English as a regional variant of *band*. In legal language, bond regularly stands for a documented, conditional or unconditional contractual obligation to pay a certain sum of money. See William Shakespeare (1600), act I, scene 3 (Venice, Shylock): "Goe with me to a Notarie, seale me there Your single bond" (cf. "simple bond" – Latin *simplex obligatio*). In the U.S. legal sphere, the bond (also: certificate of indebtedness) is a long-term debt security with a term of at least ten years, which is covered by the issuing corporation in the right of lien through real estate or movables. Overall Luttermann (1998) pp. 239-240.

[246] Commentaries (1971) p. 6.

[247] Commentaries (1971) p. 7. Cf. Landau and Peluso (2015) pp. 36-60, and see below 3.6.4.

[248] See also above 2.3.3; here: Act of Aug. 3, 1939, 53 Stat. 1149, Secs. 301-328, printed in 15 U.S. C. § 77aaa *et seq.*: with more than USD 7.5 million in securities outstanding at any one time. On the legislation procedures *Morris v. Kantor*, 390 F.Supp. 817, 820 *et seq.* (S.D.N.Y. 1975).

the basis for the legal situation. In practice, the trust indenture is considered to be the most "complex" legal document,[249] also known as the "Long Tom" of corporate financing; and although – perhaps for this reason – it is often ignored even by lawyers, the Trust Indenture Act can play a significant role in the restructuring of corporate debt, both domestically and internationally.[250]

### 3.6.4 *Valuation Aspects: Covenants, Principle of Periods, and Transfer of Wealth*

Within this legal framework, individual financial constructions are designed in manifold ways, practically incomprehensible. Creatively, financing is about risk management and in terms of law for corporate directors dealing diligently (duty of care). Covering risks at the same time means shifting risks, that is, also value transfer. Generally, a distinction needs to be made between securities with a certain duty of payment by the issuer, to be fulfilled only in the case of a specified event (fixed income securities), and those for which one or several fluctuating benchmarks form the basis of the calculation of remuneration, which has to be adapted periodically (floating-rate securities). Practically, the borderline may become blurred in the mixed forms if other elements are added, just as in general the valuation of the financial instrument and thus the market price (fair value) as well as the potential for conflict with other investors of the corporation.

Contractual safeguard clauses (*Schutzklauseln*) for limiting economic risks of the investors in debt securities in the course of the entrepreneurial action of the issuer (business covenants) may theoretically be divided into two basic categories with regard to the source(s) of risk: stipulations for protection against risks from general business behaviour (general risk) as well as those from a certain business fact (event risk); practically, overlaps are possible. Conceptually, all stipulations have in common that they are meant to unfold a protective effect, in that after unfolding in the individual case, entrepreneurial freedom of action (*unternehmerischer Freiraum*) of the issuer is more or less limited or designed in a cost-relevant way. Some of the essential agreements often encountered in indentures, pertaining to typical events occurring generally and potentially impairing unsecured investors (debtholders) include:[251]

---

[249] Landau (1995) pp. 47, 52-3 (there fn. 1: "Not entirely whimsically... defined as 'the crystalized fears of five generations of lawyers'."). See on the expanding scope of the trustee's potential liability Landau and Peluso (2015), chapter 3 (from p. 61).

[250] See Shuster (2006), Halbhuber (2017) and Lubben (2022); cf. comparative analysis Ehmke (2018). On the "Long Tom" Manning and Hanks (1990) p. 103 (note: "Long Tom" was the nickname for far-range artillery in World War II). Hanks in Manning and Hanks (2013) p. 101, switched to "Big Bertha", a German synonym: *Dicke Bertha*).

[251] Modified according to Fischel (1989) 131, 135-137; cf. e.g. *McMahan & Co. v. Wherehouse Entertainment, Inc.*, 65 F3d 1044, 1046 (2nd Cir. 1995). Instructive before the backdrop of "high-

(1) Restriction of payments to shareholders, for which specific maximum rates (*Höchstsätze*) are fixed regularly through reference to the profit situation of the corporation (i.e., to financial reporting);
(2) restriction of further liabilities, in particular ones with priority (*Vorrang*);
(3) restriction of the encumbrance of properties and other – significant – assets of the corporation by liens (negative pledge clause);
(4) restriction with regard to the sale of such assets.
(5) Besides this, there are regulations requiring tests for the maintenance of a certain financial situation of the issuer (so-called financial maintenance tests)[252] or imposing certain obligations of public disclosure on him.

Such covenants connected to accounting (so-called accounting-based covenants) constitute central elements in the web of protection. They relate in general to "the keeping of proper financial and accounting records", id est first of all the annual audited statements, with the adherence of certain ratios.[253] The owner of a security may be granted special sales options via covenant (so-called poison puts) to prevent deterioration (*Wertverluste*). Such return rights (*Rückgaberechte*, put options), for example at par quotation, often have a dual trigger, e.g., a fixed event (e.g. a company takeover) and the rating of the security under "investment grade".[254] Finer stipulations automatically granting the owner of a security a higher interest rate in the case of downgrading or failing certain financial figures (accounting data, e.g., a profit target) are also wide-spread (so-called super poison puts); however, these covenants raise the relative price of the securities they make less risky at first glance from an economic perspective. But it must be emphasised, that such special stipulations (event-risk covenants) do not always turn out to stand up in court.[255]

yield corporate debt" (junk bonds) Coffee/Klein (1991). Stipulations in a typical indenture in Landau and Peluso (2015) pp. 36-60. Cf. on protection against intra-corporate opportunism Coffee, Gilson, and Quinn (2022) pp. 185-198, on "shareholder primacy" Lipton (2025).

[252] Cf. generally the discussion above in 3.5.

[253] Landau and Peluso (2015) p. 192, with further covenants, e.g., to "keep true books of record and account", to "file with the trustee balance sheets, income and surplus statements, and other pertinent financial statements", to "inspect the obligor's books". See Section 314(a)(1) of the TIA and on such indenture reporting covenants *Bank of New York v. Bearingpoint, Inc.*, 824 N.Y.S.2d 752 (Sup. Ct. N.Y.County 2006), *United Health Group Inc. v. Wilmington Trust Co.*, 548 F.3d 1124 (8th Cir. 2008).

[254] See Luttermann (1998) pp. 265-268.

[255] See generally 3.6.4. Cf., e.g., *Metropolitan Life Insurance Co. v. RJR Nabisco, Inc.*, 716 F.Supp. 1504 (S.D.N.Y. 1989), at 1516-18: implied covenant on "good faith and fair dealing"; on this *Harris Trust and Savings Bank v. E-II Holdings, Inc.*. 926 F.2d 636, at 642 (7th Cir 1991): "broad and unqualified language". Overall Luttermann (1998), from p. 291, esp. pp. 318-327 (indenture covenants, interpretation), from p. 412 (recognition as debt or equity security), and from p. 421 (balance sheet-based clauses). On court decisions: Deitz, McDonald, Graebner, and Togawa Mercer (2019). *Audax Credit Opportunities Offshore Ltd. v. TMK Hawk Parent, Corp.*, 150 N.Y.S.3d 894 (N.Y. Sup. Ct. 2021), *Bayside Capital Inc. v. TPC Group Inc.*, Adv. Pro. No. 22-50372 (Bankr. D. Del. July 6, 2022).

The situations of conflict are aggravated through the principle of periodisation (accrual accounting, *Prinzip der Periodisierung*).[256] This pertains to accounting law (financial reporting, auditing). The economic success of an enterprise can, in the last instance, only be determined after the termination of the corporation through a total balance (*Gesamtbilanz*): This comprises the complete duration of business activity, id est, the success of the enterprise (profit or loss). Due to the uncertain nature of future business developments, payments to shareholders of the corporation on the basis of the annual accounts (profit in a stated period) are basically arbitrary. For it means that, subject to the principle of separation, the company's creditors are ultimately deprived of some of the liable assets (*Haftkapital*). It thus seemed historically questionable to fix an earlier date for the distribution of profits to the partners with the annual accounts. In partnership, where personal liability may alleviate the problem to a certain extent, short-term company contracts were meant to help. The limited partners (*Kommanditisten*) had the general legal obligation to replace lacking assets in the case of bankruptcy by earlier profits.[257]

The idea of the corporation as an independent asset holder (*Vermögensträger*) is alien to such a procedure. It is designed for profits from long-term capital-intensive enterprises with corresponding risk-profiles. Investors in return expect short-term and ultimate dividends as shareholders who may leave the corporation at any time by selling their shares. The custom which had developed in trading practice, id est, distributing profits and losses in unlimited partnerships (*Personengesellschaften*) according to the annual balance sheet, also spread to corporations (limited companies, *Kapitalgesellschaften*). The law tacitly accompanied this development. The recognition of the annual balance sheet as an interim balance sheet logically follows the development of the principle of separation between shareholders and the corporation as a juridical person. It was the recognition of the separate legal personality that was suspect from a contemporary perspective: periodical distribution of profits seemed all the more dubitable as shareholders were only responsible for debts of the company to the limit of their signed share.[258] Therefore, jurisprudence, grounded in Roman legal thinking, assumed a duty of the shareholders to pay back received payments in the case of insolvency of the corporation (*compagnie*).[259]

The development led to renouncing the "organic" (total) financial statement (total balance, *Gesamtbilanz*).[260] This promoted company law and accounting law, leading to the form familiar to us now: the annual financial statement (*Jahresabschluss*) of a corporation as the legal basis for distributions (esp. dividends). According to

[256] Fundamentally Luttermann (1998) pp. 165-166. See above 1.4.1.

[257] Overall Luttermann (2003) Einf BilanzR recitals 62-66.

[258] Renaud (1863) p. 569, does, however, speak in favour of periodical distribution from the net gains, reserve or redemption funds (cf. p. 588). Luttermann (2003) Einf BilanzR recitals 62-66 and 67-95 (development of German laws since 1794). Cf. Lipton (2025) on "shareholder primacy".

[259] Pöhls (1842), from p. 235.

[260] Spanning the entire life cycle of a company (corporation), in German also called the *Totalbilanz*.

Article 218 of the General German Commercial Code of 1861,[261] the shareholder was in no case obliged to "give back the interest and dividends he had received in good faith". The Prussian Corporation Act of 1843 already ruled out the refunding of interests and dividends paid to shareholders even in the case of insolvency; the payments had to be made from the "surplus profit".[262] The consequence of being allowed to calculate and distribute the profit definitively on the basis of an annual financial statement is, however, linked to the principle of separation. The 1857 Nuremberg minutes of the draft of the German Commercial Code rightly highlight this as a "strong, but unavoidable privilege of the joint-stock companies".[263] The idea of privileging still influences current corporation law globally.

### *3.6.5 Sustainable Finance: The Liable Capital of the Corporation (***Haftkapital***)*

This much can be determined: In England, we have already seen the recognition of the company (corporation) as "at law a different person" in *Salomon v. Salomon & Co Ltd.* (1897) according to the Companies Act 1862, which is still a landmark decision.[264] The case went round the world or, more precisely, round what is now the Commonwealth of Nations in a controversial debate. But the case had "become one of the cornerstones of the entire edifice of corporate law".[265] The doctrine of the separateness of legal personality, and hence limited recourse (principle of separation, *Trennungsprinzip*), stood the test of time: It has never been doubted and has even been extended to the separate companies of a group (corporate group, *Konzern*), id est group relationships (*Konzernverhältnisse*).[266] Limited recourse may be limited in individual cases through "the lifting of the corporate veil" (see 1.4.1, 2.4.3). In

[261] In German: *Allgemeines Deutsches Handelsgesetzbuch* (*ADHGB*).

[262] Section 18 Prussian Corporation Act (*Preussisches Aktiengesetz: "reine Überschuss"* – pure surplus). Cf. on the term "surplus" above in 3.4.3.

[263] In the German original: *"ein erhebliches, wenn auch nicht zu vermeidendes Privilegium der Aktiengesellschaften"*. Cf. Barth (1953) p. 53, Schmalenbach (1916) p. 39. Overall on the development Luttermann (2003) Einf BilanzR recitals 67-95.

[264] It seems an ironical twist in the history of common law that the Law Lords treated the core of the case as a question of statutory interpretation.

[265] Justice Hugh Williams, High Court of New Zealand, in Rickett and Grantham (1998), foreword. On the triumph of the company legal form 1856-1914: Ireland (1983). Cf. Gower (2021), from 2-001 (chapter 2).

[266] See, e.g., *Pioneer Concrete Services Ltd v Yelnah Pty Ltd* [1987] 5 ACLC 467. Austin, Corporate groups, in Rickett and Grantham (1998) pp. 71-89. Cf. on global enterprise and atomistic law Conard (1993). See on valuation below 8.4.2 (*lex aestimatio*). On cash pooling below 4.7.3 with Luttermann and Geißler (2012); cf. BGH, 28.06.2022 (II ZR 112/21), <openJur 2022, 14696>.

general, the classical dualism, the tension between corporate shareholders and creditors, is integrated.

This static view and inclusion curtails the situation structurally, thus leading to inadequate results, namely – in an uncontrolled way – easily to excessive shifts of risks and wealth (assets, *Vermögenstransfers*). This means massive advantages (profits) are created systematically in the course of valuation (accounting, financial reporting) – as widely with so-called "shareholder value" – unilaterally at the expense of massive disadvantages (esp. losses in value, *Wertverlusten*) for other investors (so-called "debtholders") or actors. Basically, that is not legitimate, neither internally according to the different categories of investors nor externally for further cooperation partners of the corporation, so-called "stakeholders" (e.g., employees, business partners, suppliers, community). The static framework should be reasonably resolved for the good governance of the corporation. What is therefore imperative is a reasonable, structurally comprehensive order of assets (*Vermögensordnung*, see 1.6, 3.3.4 and chapter 8), responsibility and liability in the corporation as an independent legal entity (see 3.6.2 and chapters 6, 7).

Basically, the financing function of the corporation (as a permanent financial instrument, *Finanzfunktion*)[267] provides the adequate measure within the constitution of liberty, id est the sustainable finance of the human corporation. This has to be realised in minds and markets. Generally through the law, namely accounting law (financial reporting, auditing). Fundamentally through valuation as a reasonable order of assets, therefore also for a share in profit and loss of the corporation (liability order). Legally, accounting law is aimed at the relevant life and economic circumstances, id est it sustainably captures the actual circumstances (facts not fictions).[268] We have already shown that by attributing assets to the corporation via contracts and accounting law, these become legally independent with regard to the shareholders as well as with regard to third parties. With the corporation as a legal subject, different property spheres (*Vermögenssphären*) come into existence. This at the same time determines the assets (positions) relevant for questions of liability in the framework of accounting law and the community of venture (*Wagnisgemeinschaft*, see 2.6.2). Not one-sidedly oriented towards the protection of "creditors", but generally balanced for those bearing an entrepreneurial risk. What is effective is to build investor confidence based on sustainable financial reporting and auditing (see Fig. 1.2).[269]

The relevant assets (*Vermögen*) are the so-called liable capital of the corporation (*Haftkapital*, see Fig. 3.3). In the life circumstances of corporate financing, there is the following crystallisation: What is interesting from a business perspective and

[267] See above 1.3.2; also 1.5.1, 2.6.3 and 3.5.3, below 3.7.

[268] See above 3.2.2 and 3.5.5.

[269] Luttermann (2003) Einf BilanzR recitals 26-43 (with recitals 19-25): a capital market concept (investor protection law), cf. recitals 90-95 (German law). See 1.5.2 on the concept of trust and control, substance and individual responsibility. Cf. above 3.5.3 on corporate finance and relational contract law with Macneil (1978), McDaniel (1986) and (1988). Overall Luttermann (1998), esp. pp. 21-23 and 160-162 (reasonable risk bearing), pp. 311-330 (investor protection and corporate governance), and pp. 471-485 (capital market legal structures).

paramount for the law is how many recoverable assets (*Haftungsmasse*) are available to the corporation for running balancing losses (payments due). This is legally the crucial point as generally proven by the law of insolvency (see 3.4.1) an this is where the privileged status of the corporation ends (3.4.4). Remember, in particular it is the shareholders who are responsible for corporate financing. That is the reason why a share in the success of the corporation is methodologically an excellent criterion for corporate law. Since the Roman-canonical law this is considered as essential for a shareholder (*socius*). However, third parties (non-shareholders, bondholders) traditionally may participate in profit and loss of a corporation in the context of the law of obligations. Agreed through a general legal transaction, it is about investors' participation in losses on the basis of contract law (liability). Investment is to be understood as a contractually agreed risk-reward-constellation based on reasonable information (i.e. financial reporting, key information documents, see 8.3.3).[270]

Practice implements this in manifold hybrid financial instruments facilitating positions of participation (*Beteiligungspositionen*), particularly with regard to profits, as shown with the trust indenture (3.6.3), within the framework of the law of obligations (*Schuldrecht*) instead of company law (*Gesellschaftsrecht*). This seems irritating in the dual concept of "equity capital" and "debt capital" in accounting and taxation. If we break through the encrusted patterns of thought, this much becomes clear: The liability function provides the measure. It overlays formal equity (*Eigenkapital*) and debt capital (*Fremdkapital*). In terms of business and law, what counts is first and last the liable capital (*Haftkapital*) a corporation has at its disposal. This comprises the capital assets under corporation law (*gesellschaftsrechtliches Kapitalvermögen*) and the hybrid (debt, third party) capital assets, which are also liable (altogether *Haftkapital*, liable capital). This is to be represented in the accounts. In this way, the deadlocked debate on the equity base (*Eigenkapitalausstattung*) and the protection of the "capital" of the corporation – similar to core capital and supplementary capital of credit institutions – might be mitigated. As a sound example for hybrid instruments, we may point to participation right capital (in Germany: *Genußrechtkapital*).[271]

As an overall concept of good governance, id est sustainable finance and financial reporting (accounting, auditing) for the human corporation, the "liable capital" (*Haftkapital*) provides a sound basis and more entrepreneurial flexibility in line with the concept of trust.[272] Corporations may thereby tailor their financial circumstances and increase their rating (*Bonität*). Based soundly in valuation law (*Bewertungsrecht*), the liable capital concept offers a structurally adequate order – literally: contractually. This is what our constitution of liberty thrives on with private

[270] German: *vertragliche Chance-Risiko-Konstellation*, see Luttermann (1998) pp. 145-162, basically on "common purpose" (see 3.7) and capital investment.

[271] See below 6.4.3 (*Genußscheine*). Fundamentally Luttermann (1998).

[272] See above 1.5.2 and chapters 4 to 7. Luttermann (1998), esp. from p. 530 and pp. 548-549, Luttermann (2001a) pp. 2436-2437. Luttermann (2003) Einf BilanzR recitals 107-122 (liability and liquidity) and 123-133 (limits of accounting).

entrepreneurship (*Privatautonomie*). All in all, in the financing of corporations, individual security (*creditor self-help*) may work systematically through certain stipulations for providing capital.[273] This must be accompanied by a reasonable valuation law, which is given meaning through civil law (i.e. human corporation),[274] preventing overregulation. In the final instance, it is piercing the corporate veil (*Durchgriffshaftung*) that overall provides protection against abuse in the case of a corporation (legal person) as the bearer of an enterprise, as is the case internationally.[275]

## 3.7 On the Common Purpose: Corporative Structures and Networks (AI, DAO etc.)

Capital and liability are the expression of the financing function that coins the corporation (see 1.5.1). This points to evolutionary steps of entrepreneurial organisation (contract, legal construction), which mark perspectives for further investigation, theory and practice. If the investors of an enterprise or project (*Kapitalgeber* – lenders of capital) are conceived of as a community of chance and risk, id est of venture (*Wagnisgemeinschaft*, see 1.3.3), sitting in the same boat, the seating order is of interest as the legal basis of the community (*Gemeinschaft*). It is a common purpose (*gemeinsamer Zweck*, see 2.1) that works here sustainably, supporting the enterprise and the investors (see 1.5.2: concept of trust). The common purpose is traditionally – as in more modern corporate and network structures – regarded as the impetus of the cooperation, determining its order as the vital law of the association (*Verband*).[276] Practically, it is about a community of purpose (*Zweckgemeinschaft*), about entrepreneurial chance and risk, id est thus in the last instance about participation in the result of the enterprise (gain, loss).

Research shows a promising development of the corporation as bearer of the enterprise, at the same time company and legal entity (legal person). Usually the *animus societatis contrahendae* stands for a "real" company, expressing as "common" (from Latin *communis*) the relation of law and obligation of an individual person (citizen – *Bürger*) to the whole (the community), in the conceptual core and vice versa; also something of "the most familiar type", familiar (*vertraut*) resp. well-known (*wohlbekannt*, Latin *familiaris*), commonality (*Gemeinsamkeit*) for familiarity (Latin *familiaritas*), in a comprehensive sense creating community

---

[273] See above 3.6.4 and Luttermann (1998), from p. 291. Luttermann, Wicher (2005) on corporate bonds (*Unternehmensanleihen*).

[274] See in detail chapters 4 and 5. Luttermann (2003) Einf BilanzR recitals 48-51, Großfeld and Luttermann (2005) recitals 25, 203. Chapter 7 on the duties of corporate directors.

[275] See 3.2.3 and 3.4.1. On the Anglo-American legal system Davies (2002), from p. 68 (creditor self-help), from p. 36 (corporate personality, piercing the corporate veil).

[276] See immediately following on DAOs. Overall Luttermann (1998) pp. 145-162.

(Gemeinschaft, Latin *universalitas*):[277] common is what everyone contributes to and from which all common needs (*gemeinschaftliche Bedürfnisse*) are financed, in particular also in a capitalist way, id est in an economic sense a common treasury (*gemeinsame Kasse*). This is accompanied by, e.g., the – reciprocal – obligations to stand up for each other (*Einstandspflichten*, liability) and more than anything else, regular information, id est the disclosure of the real financial circumstances: financial reporting (accounting).

A development of the digital age is the decentralised autonomous organisation (DAO), also called a decentralised autonomous corporation (DAC). In general, DAOs are described as "digitally native vehicles for organizing a network of humans toward a common goal",[278] id est providing resources (blockchain technology, knowledge) for their endeavour (peer to peer network). The common purpose here also unites those involved, who it was possible to include worldwide through the technological organisation (smart contracts, voting rights). This characterises the DAO as a decentralised, state-independently conceived construct (cf. Wyoming DAO LLC as a legal status),[279] and highlights new ways for governance (network structures), finance (cryptocurrency, crowdfunding), reporting and documentation (global ledger, DLT).[280] A fascinating area of the law, from the legal nature of the organisation to abuse, where promises of security may fail technically (cf. quantum computing) as well as at the human level.[281] Complementarily, transnationally viable entrepreneurial structures may develop, manifold competencies optimised together, beyond traditional patterns (global enterprise, cf. MNE).[282] In any case,

[277] See already above 1.3.3 and Grimm, Deutsches Wörterbuch, 3169-70 (*Gemein*), 3195 and 3263-64 (*Gemeinsame* up to *Gemeinsamkeit*); cf. Brown (1993) p. 453 (common: "shared alike by all the persons or things in question, or by all humankind").

[278] Owocki, Brezina (2025) p. 5. Cf. Chohan (2024), Han, Lee, Li (2025) and an evolving resource: https://www.thedaobook.io/ (accessed: 22.08.2025). McGurk, Reichenbach (2024), esp. chapter 3 (on "the token economy").

[279] Limited Liability Company (LLC) as a "legal wrapper", i.e. under state law, see Grant, Kirby, and Hawkins (2024); similar "Decentralized Organisations" (DOs, Tennessee Code Ann. §48-250-101 through 48-250-115). Utah Decentralized Autonomous Organizations Act (Code Ann. §48-5-101–406): legal personality for DAOs (LLD). Cf. Metjahic (2018) 1567: a "general partnership", also under California law in *Sarcuni v. bZx DAO*, No. 22-618 (S.D. Cal. Mar. 27, 2023), resp. *In re bZeroX, LLC*, CFTC No. 22-31 (Sept. 22, 2022) an "unincorporated association".

[280] Distributed Ledger Technology (DLT), see below 4.11.2. McGurk, Reichenbach (2024), esp. chapter 14 (on dispute resolution and remedies, smart contracts). See below 8.4 with 1.6.2 (state-coined order) and 4.8, 4.10.3 (multijurisdictional approach) with 9.1 (rationality – *Vernünftigkeit*, Greek *phrónesis*).

[281] Generally 3.5.6 (global ledger) with 4.8.4, 4.10.2 and 8.3.2 as well as in 9.6 (quantum computing); also, e.g., Lee and Fricotté (2025), He (2023), Morrison, Mazey, Wingreen (2020), Minn (2019). On "The DAO"-hack (Ethereum blockchain, hard fork) Minaev (2023). Grant, Kirby, and Hawkins (2024) 87-88.

[282] See above 1.3, below 6.5.1, 9.4 and 8.2 on development: "the voices of separate nations", Conard (1993) p. 707; on valuation 8.4.2. Cf. a multinational enterprise (MNE): a group of companies (*Konzern*), i.e. subsidiary undertakings under common control of a parent undertaking; in Germany § 290 HGB and Art. 22 Directive 2013/24/EU (see 4.7). Overall OECD-UNSD

it is sustainably about personal responsibility, rationality, intelligence and energy (see 6.8.5, chapters 7 and 9).

In legal practice, the boundaries – classically – conceived for a society (Latin *societas*) become blurred between company law investors (partner, equity capital – *Gesellschaftsrecht*) and law of obligations investors (creditor, debt capital – *Schuldrecht*, cf. 3.6.3: hybrid financial instruments). However, financial reporting (accounting, auditing) remains fundamental for the relations of the persons involved, internally and externally. What is more: the significance that substantial information gained through the extended admission of family-external members as associates (Latin *socii*) into the community (company, see 1.3.3, 2.3.3), is vital for the modern corporation to develop in the direction of comprehensive sustainability (human corporation), id est ecological and juridical verifiability (*Nachprüfbarkeit*).[283] The development of the economic organisation and legal formation of the stand-alone corporation with separate assets (capital) happens in culturally multi-layered processes. In an overview, there are phenomena (cooperation, corporative structures, cf. chapter 8) that can be marked in the development of business and undertakings over centuries as follows:[284]

(1) **Family business** (*Familienunternehmen*), only natural persons (*natürliche Personen*, humans – *Menschen*), cooperative organisation (*genossenschaftliche Organisation*);[285]
(2) **Project undertaking**, project- and capital-focused (*kapitalintensives Projektunternehmen*);[286]
(3) **Large family enterprise**, permanent, family-run (*familiengeführtes Großunternehmen*), more or less – silent – participation of others (*Fremden*);[287]
(4) **Company** (association, cooperative, partnership) with non-family members (*Personengesellschaft mit Fremden*);
(5) **Corporation**, in the modern form of a stock corporation (company limited by shares – *Kapitalgesellschaft*),[288] esp. a publicly held corporation (*börsennotierte*

multinational enterprise information platform: https://unstats.un.org/unsd/business-stat/mne-platform/ (accessed: 22.08.2025).

[283] See above 1.2 with 3.5, 3.6, 2.6.2 and chapters 4 (esp. 4.1, 4.11.4), 5 (esp. 5.2.4) and 8 (esp. 8.3.3). Luttermann (2023) recitals 32-39 (ecological sustainability), recitals 40-44 (juridical sustainability).

[284] Of course, various developments have an impact, sometimes in parallel and sometimes overlapping. See 2.3.3, 3.8 (basic patterns). Altogether 8.3 and chapter 9.

[285] See 3.8, on family business 1.3.3, 2.3.3. Cf. family or clan (*Sippe*) as a company or a larger group (e.g., in Scotland as a community), developing a territory: Lynch (2011), overall for the development in German history Gierke (1868 et seq.).

[286] Private (e.g. *commenda*) and governmental (the Roman *societates publicanorum*) see 2.3.3. Cf. modern project company, special purpose vehicle (SPV) or similar. See financial structures below 6.8.5.

[287] Silent partners (*stille Gesellschafter*) as with Jakob Fugger, family and others, see 3.8.

[288] Often as part of a group comprising several companies under uniform management (control), located in different countries (*lex societatis*): MNE, see above footnote 281, below 6.5.1 and 8.4.2.

*Aktiengesellschaft*), as a legal person (*juristische Person*), responsibly led by corporate directors with other people's money (human corporation);[289]
(6) **AM-Corporation** as a corporation, significantly influenced by institutional asset managers (AM – *Vermögensverwalter*);[290]
(7) **AI-Corporation** as a corporation, characterised by artificial intelligence (AI – *Künstliche Intelligenz*): leading to a so-called *"electronic person"* (ePerson – *elektronische Person*),[291] a creation of the law, of human being at all?
(8) **Global Special Purpose Partnership** (GSPP, *Globale Zweckpartnerschaft*), contract sui generis, natural persons as members of a permanently – digitally – organised transnational network structure with limited liability for a common purpose;[292]
(9) **Universal Corporation**.

## 3.8 Comparative Perspectives and Basic Patterns

As we can see, the modern corporation touches virtually every area of life. Remember the corporation itself is deemed a fiction, a virtual reality (see 3.4.1). It is about the relationship of humans and so-called "robots" (artificial intelligence, AI: see 9.6 with 6.8.5). Images appear in our heads, like in Fritz Lang's early silent movie Metropolis (1927) with the invention of a machine-man (*"Maschinenmensch"*):[293] a new take on the old theme "man and machine", which philosophically belongs to technology (Ancient Greek τέχνη – *téchne*, see 3.9) as well as vitalising the political economy and our present in economy and society.[294] Already, AI is silently working widely on capital markets and in corporations algorithmically like BlackRock's

[289] See chapter 2 and, e.g., below 7.3.1 (on the necessary human responsibility).

[290] Private corporations or funds, sovereign wealth funds, see above 3.5.6, 2.5.3, below 6.2.3, 6.5.1 (common ownership) and 7.8.3. Cf. corporate group (*Konzern*).

[291] See below 3.8 and 6.8.5 with 9.6, 9.7. European Parliament, Civil law rules on robotics, 16.02.2017 (2015/2103(INL)), recital 59 f): "creating a specific legal status for robots in the long run, so that at least the most sophisticated autonomous robots could be established as having the status of electronic persons responsible for making good any damage they may cause, and possibly applying electronic personality to cases where robots make autonomous decisions or otherwise interact with third parties independently". On civil liability for AI European Parliament, 20.10.2020 (2020/2014(INL)), OJ C 404, 06.10.2021, pp. 107-128. Cf. Bertolini (2020), Eidenmüller, Wagner (2021), from pp. 95, 106-112; Yalman (2024).

[292] Cf. foregoing "decentralised autonomous organisations" (DAOs), civil law and cooperative structures. Note overall financial contribution, financial reporting and valuation (see chapters 4, 5) as well as globally chapters 8 and 9.

[293] Front page of *Die Filmwoche*, Berlin, 12.01.1927, announcing Metropolis, reprint in Heinzlmeier (1990) p. 34. On generative AI above 3.5.6 (data), below 9.6.

[294] Cf. the *Maschinenfragment* of Karl Marx (1857/58), about machines as productive forces, and René Descartes (1648) about man (French *l'Homme*) and the machine of his body (*de la Machine de son Corps*). Cf. Regulation (EU) 2023/1230 on machinery, 14.06.2023, OJ L 165, 29.06.2023, pp. 1-102.

"Aladdin", as powerful opinion forces "embedded in code":[295] Wall Street's epic "numbers game" in corporate finance and valuation (financial reporting),[296] creating and shifting "shareholder value" with mathematically stilted models, theories and instruments (leverage, derivatives, quantitative easing), entering spectacular levels globally.

The images may change over time, but on the markets – as seen with Mozart – what counts is the "more beautiful" presentation (picture) of the corporation within the financial statements (disclosure).[297] In general, a warning sounds from contemporary pop poetry: "Don't pay the ferryman, until he gets you to the other side."[298] This applies in particular to comparative law. Overall, it is about basic patterns (*Grundmuster*). This is illustrated by milestones in the development of corporative structures (see 3.7). They convey cultural-historical impressions and point to the general problem of historical continuity, to "constant questions of the law"[299] in general. For the regulation of certain circumstances of life, the same basic patterns occur again and again in law, even in different legal cultures. Purchase (*Kauf*), rent (*Miete*), loan (*Darlehen*), to name a few civil law forms of contract, are determined by logical structures limiting the respective range of variation of possible legal regulations.[300] This also applies to companies, for capital contribution (investment) in own or third-party commercial transactions.

The possible solutions for the financing of enterprises and the concomitant division of risk (loss) and chance (gain) of entrepreneurial action are limited. The interests of those involved cannot be clothed in any number of legal forms. The family (from Latin *familia*) in its natural community generally forms the point of departure and reference: "a group of people living as one household", id est "a group as an organisational unit of society" being "significantly connected by common features".[301] The family as a life community (*Lebensgemeinschaft*) of its members, also working comprehensively at the economic level (e.g., family living, family planning, family income and credit): a family business (*Familienunternehmen*).[302] This leads to the phenomenon of the large family-run enterprise,[303] in German Renaissance, e.g., that of the famous Fugger family with world-spanning business transactions, also with and decisive for popes and monarchs; id est with political

---

[295] See Cathy O'Neil below 6.6.3, on "Aladdin" 3.5.5. See also 9.5 and 9.6.

[296] See above 3.2.1, 3.5.3, and overall chapter 4.

[297] On Mozart at the outset above 3.1 and overall chapter 4.

[298] Chris de Burgh, Don't pay the ferryman, on the album "The Getaway", 1982.

[299] German original: *Dauerfragen des Rechts.*

[300] Luttermann (1998) pp. 36-37. See Luttermann (1999b), (2009) on Islamic finance, and (2017) on Chinese foreign investment law, gold trade notes. See above 1.6.3.

[301] Brown (1993) p. 913 (family).

[302] More sharply formulated: the family/clan as a company (*Familie/Sippe als ein Unternehmen*); cf. above 3.7, number (1).

[303] See above 3.7 (3).

influence right up to financing the election of the Spanish Habsburg emperor Karl V. in 1519 – the monarch on whose empire "the sun never sets".[304]

Later, the chartered company develops as an incorporated association with investors, e.g., the East India Compagnies in several nations of Europe (Britain, the Netherlands, France), partly share-based, doing overseas trade with India and China. The idea of an independent monetary association gained ground and the money itself "became an entrepreneur".[305] In the Netherlands the publicly held corporation is officially called *Naamloze Vennootschap* (N.V.), id est an enterprise without a name (cf. in France: *Société Anonyme*, S.A.). This is reminiscent of power and cultural diversity, the linguistic references (*Sprachenbezüge*) for the conceptual formation of the law – the creation of a legal person alongside the human being (natural person, see 7.3.1). In a comparative view, there are references to Roman *societas* (partnership) and *universitas* (corporation).[306] Both vehicles, basic patterns of global economic and political interests and philosophical ideas,[307] formed in many ways by humans and the environment in their own time. Language designates essential relations, making basic patterns apparent (see 3.7). From a human perspective, the development with the corporation illustrates a depersonalisation, including corporations (legal person) without a single human being as shareholder.

A human corporation? – The course of history is open, of course. Ingenuity can bring about something new. Perspective is treated as a cultural technique of view and representation:[308] the picture of the corporation (information).[309] In times of digitisation, AI is urging:[310] the last instance? – Phenomenally, the fundamental entrepreneurial issue for any person (human, entity), whether along with corporate or cooperative structures, is financing (see 1.3.2). In company with other people (investors),[311] it is always – globally for value creation with corporations and capital markets – about "other people's money" (see 3.3.2). It is always about good governance, about sustainable finance, valuation and financial reporting under the

---

[304] Holy Roman Emperor, Archduke of Austria, King of Spain etc., who also ruled in the Americas, as far as they belonged to the Spanish crown. Overall Pölnitz (1949), see on Fugger above 2.3.3.

[305] Klein (1904) p. 5, German original: *"Unter den Problemen (...) entsprang eines von besonderer Tragweite dem originellen Versuche, Erwerbsunternehmungen ausschließlich aus Geldbeiträgen zu bilden, das Geld selbst zum Unternehmer zu machen. Bis dahin war das Rückgrat aller Unternehmungsformen die Person. (...). Die Niederländer haben (...) im 17. Jahrhundert (...) den Gedanken einer selbständigen Geldvereinigung gefaßt."* Cf. the much older Roman *societates publicanorum*, above 2.3.3.

[306] See, e.g., Tierney and Toddington (2005), Jongh (2014).

[307] On the history of political pluralism, esp. with Thomas Hobbes and Otto von Gierke: Runciman (1997).

[308] Belting (2011) pp. 8-11. On questions of valuation chapter 5 (esp. 5.3.4).

[309] See above 3.1 and 2.6.2 on financial reporting as information (from Latin *forma* for "form, picture", and *informare* for "to shape, brief", i.e. vividly expressed to "put someone in the picture").

[310] See 3.7, esp. (5) to (7). On depersonalisation Rathenau above 3.5.4; cf. overall chapters 6 (esp. 6.8.5) and 7.

[311] Id est non-family members in the traditional view, see above 3.7, number (4).

imperative of truth (see chapter 4). And of course this is only possible with personal responsibility and accountability, what else: If one is sure, the human being is indispensable (see chapters 6 and 7). In order to establish sustainable business activity, we should finally establish the corporation on a sustainable basis.

## 3.9 Human Corporation: Further Investigation

This needs to be carried out sustainably through true financial reporting and auditing with the human corporation (real disclosure). Capital market financing and sound valuation centers around the corporation's visible image: its competitively better situation of assets (liabilities), financial position and profit (instead of loss) documented in the financial statements as the picture of the corporation attracts investors, raises valuations (ratings) and lowers risk interests, id est the capital costs for the enterprise. Just as, according to Aristotle, skillful craftsmanship (*Sachkundigkeit*, Ancient Greek *téchne*) works through a practical sense of the good (Ancient Greek *phrónesis*),[312] the common idea of humanity is clear: A good economy and society is created, sensibly in harmony with the environment and human rights for general prosperity. The transformation process must be designed in such a way that the continuity that creates harmony among people (legal peace) can be maintained in the dialogue of cultures.[313]

What remains fundamentally responsible is human beings, id est the corporate directors of the corporation plus its auditors, and the reference of all of them to facts, the *"tatsächlichen Verhältnisse"* (actual facts). Good is not achieved mathematically, but – by way of lively communication – through reason (sanity, *Vernünftigkeit*, cf. *phrónesis, noûs*) and humanity,[314] which as jurisprudence (Latin *prudential* prudence) sustainably establish a culture of responsibility (*Verantwortungskultur*): Law as practised ethics for a human corporation and economy as a sustainable way of life (see 2.2.2 and 9.1).[315] For this, we will show "financial reporting as verified information for investors" under the imperative of truth (*Bilanzwahrheit*, see chapter 4) and develop company valuation with a civil-procedural concept "as a legal act of sustainable value creation" (see chapter 5). This leads to "global climate change for people, investment, and capital markets (see chapter 6), in a deeper perspective with "the imperative of personal responsibility and valuation in law and practice" providing a goal-oriented template on good corporate governance (see chapter 7).

---

[312] See, e.g. Gadamer (1998) pp. 6-7 (29: *Sachkundigkeit* – Greek *téchne*); cf. above 3.8, also see 1.1, 1.2.

[313] Luttermann (1999b).

[314] See Gadamer (1998) pp. 9, 20, from 41, 61-62; also below 4.12.3 and chapter 9.

[315] With Schweitzer (1923) pp. 93 and 352. Cf. Gadamer (1998) ibid., Smith (1759/1790$^6$) and Phelps (2007).

Overall, we can see further now for the human corporation, as required for a sustainable world and peace. So let us emphasise this once again: The goal is, as said initially, to incorporate substance for a better world, id est a human corporation for a good economy as a sustainable economy (see chapter 1). Basically and practically, the overall issue is an adequate international law as a company financing law (*Unternehmensfinanzrecht*): a sustainable law of corporate finance, valuation and reporting, establishing an order of assets in a transnational perspective (*globale Vermögensordnung*).[316] Humans, their economy and environment have to be reconciled. To this purpose, sustainable finance and financial reporting for corporate prosperity is highlighted *de lege lata* and *ferenda* (see chapter 8). In order to found the human corporation in practice in a sustainable way, this leads to the Nicomachean question of complementarity (see chapter 9). Let us thus continue our journey along the clear course with confidence.

## References


Ackerman, T. C., Jr., & Sterrett, J. K. (1976). California's new approach to dividends and reacquisitions of shares. *UCLA Law Review, 23*, 1052–1093.

Aliber, R. Z., Kindleberger, C. P., & McCauley, R. N. (2023). *Manias, panics and crashes: A history of financial crises* (8th ed.). Palgrave Macmillan.

Ballantine, H. W., & Hills, G. S. (1935). Corporate capital and restrictions upon dividends under modern corporation laws. *California Law Review, 23*, 229–263.

Balz, M., & Landfermann, H.-G. (1995). *Die neuen Insolvenzgesetze*. IDW-Verlag.

Barth, K. (1953). *Die Entwicklung des deutschen Bilanzrechts und die ihm zugrundeliegenden Bilanzauffassungen handelsrechtlich und steuerrechtlich* (Vol. 1). Selbstverlag.

Bedts, R. F. de (1964). *The New Deal's SEC: The formative years*. Columbia University Press.

Belting, H. (2011). *Florence and Baghdad: Renaissance art and Arab science*. The Belknap Press of Harvard University.

Berle, A. A., Jr. (1928). *Studies in the law of corporation finance*. William S. Hein & Co.

Berle, A. A., Jr. (1938). Accounting and the law. *The Journal of Accountancy, 65*, 368–378.

Berle, A. A., Jr. (1959). *Power without Property*. Harcourt, Brace & World.

Berle, A. A., Jr., & Fisher, F. S., Jr. (1932). Elements of the law of business accounting. *Columbia Law Review, 32*, 573–622.

Berle, A. A., Jr., & Means, G. C. (1932, 1967). *The modern corporation and private property* (2nd ed.). Harcourt, Brace & World, 1967.

Bernstein, P. L. (1993). *Capital ideas: The improbable origins of modern Wall Street*. Free Press.

Bertolini, A. (2020). *Artificial Intelligence and civil liability*. European Parliament, Policy Department for Citizens' Rights and Constitutional Affairs, PE 621.926. https://www.europarl.europa.eu/RegData/etudes/STUD/2020/621926/IPOL_STU(2020)621926_EN.pdf (accessed: 22.08.2025).

Bierce, A. (1911). *The devil's dictionary*, first published by Doubleday, Page & Co. (in 1906, partly) and by Arthur F. Bird (in 1907 as: *The cynic's word book*).

Blackstone, W. (1766). *Commentaries on the laws of England, book the second (of the rights of things)*. Clarendon Press.


[316] Luttermann (2015a) and (2015b). See on the denotation of "asset" (*Vermögen*) below 8.1 (footnote 3).

Booth, R. A. (2000). A Chronology of the Evolution of the MBCA. *The Business Lawyer, 56*, 63–67.

Brandeis, L. D. (1914). *Other people's money and how the bankers use it*. Frederick A. Stokes Company Publishers.

Brealey, R. A., Myers, S. C., Allen, F., & Edmans, A. (2025). *Principles of corporate finance* (15th ed.). McGraw Hill.

Brown, L. (Ed.). (1993). *The new shorter Oxford English dictionary on historical principles* (2 Vols.). Clarendon Press.

Buxbaum, R. M., & Hopt, K. J. (1988). Legal harmonization. In M. Cappelletti, M. Seccombe, & J. Weiler (Eds.), *Interpretation through law* (Vol. 4). de Gruyter.

Chandler, A. D. (1977). *The visible hand: The managerial revolution in American business*. Harvard University Press.

Chatov, R. (1975). *Corporate financial reporting: Public or private control*. Free Press.

Chohan, U. W. (2024). *Decentralized autonomous organizations (DAOs): Their present and future* (March 8, 2024). https://ssrn.com/abstract=3082055 (accessed: 22.08.2025).

Choper, J. H., Coffee, J. C., & Gilson, R. R. (1995). *Cases and materials on corporations* (4th ed.). Wolters Kluwer.

Cicero, M. T. (44 BC). De officiis (German *Vom pflichtgemäßen Handeln*, English translation: Walter Miller. Harvard University Press, 1913).

Clark, W. H., Jr. (2011). The relationship of the Model Business Corporation Act to other entity laws. *Law and Contemporary Problems, 74*, 57–77.

Clark, G. L., Dixon, A. D., & Monk, A. H. B. (2013). The ethics of global investment: Norway's government pension fund, chapter 5. In G. L. Clark et al. (Eds.), *Sovereign wealth funds: Legitimacy, governance, and global power*. Princeton University Press.

Coffee, J. C. (2001). The rise of dispersed ownership: The roles of law and the state in the separation of ownership and control. *Yale Law Journal, 111*, 1–81.

Coffee, J. C., Gilson, R. J., & Quinn, B. J. M. (2022). *Cases and materials on corporations* (9th ed.). Wolters Kluwer.

Coffee J. C., & Klein, W. A. (1991). *Bondholder coercion: The problem of constrained choice in debt under offers and recapitalization*. The Center for Law and Economic Studies, Columbia University School of Law, Working Paper No. 53.

Commentaries. (1971). *Commentaries on model debenture indenture provisions 1965*, ed. by American Bar Foundation, corporate debt financing project: model debenture indenture provisions all registered issues 1967 and certain negotiable provisions.

Conard, A. F. (1993). Global Enterprise and atomistic law. *The Journal of Corporation Law, 18*, 707–712.

Conaway Stilson, A. E. (1995). Reexamining the fiduciary paradigm at corporate insolvency and dissolution: Defining director's duties to creditors. *Delaware Journal of Corporate Law, 20*, 1–122.

Davies, P. L. (2002). *Introduction to company law*. Oxford University Press.

Deitz, A. J. S., McDonald, J. A., Graebner, R., & Togawa Mercer, S. (2019). Indented: Recent court decisions on New York law-governed indentures and their impact. *Butterworths Journal of International Banking and Financial Law, 34*, 245–248.

Descartes, R. (1677). *L'Homme de René Descartes*. Girard (with the Traité de la Lumière), as Traité de l'Homme later being published (both) under the title Le Monde (The world).

De Spiegeleer, J., Van Hulle, C., & Schoutens, W. (2014). *The handbook of hybrid securities*. Wiley.

Du, K. (2022). Accounting in an age of big data. *The Journal of Finance and Data Science, 8*, A1–A2.

Easterbrook, F. H., & Fischel, D. R. (1991). *The economic structure of corporate law*. Harvard University Press.

Edmans, A., Levit, D., & Reilly, D. (2019). Governance under common ownership. *The Review of Financial Studies, 32*, 2673–2719.

Ehmke, D. C. (2018). *Bond debt governance: A comparative analysis of different solutions to financial distress of corporate bond debtors*. Nomos.

Eidenmüller, H., & Wagner, G. (2021). *Law by algorithm*. Mohr Siebeck.

Eisenberg, M. (1974). The Model Business Corporation Act and the "Model Business Corporation Act Annotated". *The Business Lawyer, 29*, 1407–1431.

Eisenberg, M. (1976). *The structure of the corporation: A legal analysis*. BeardBooks.

Fischel, D. R. (1989). The economics of lender liability. *Yale Law Journal, 99*, 131–154.

Fletcher, W. M. (1995). *Cyclopedia of the law of private corporations* (permanent ed. (cumm. suppl.)). Thomson/West.

Friedman, L. M. (1985). *A history of American law* (2nd ed.). Simon & Schuster.

Gadamer, H.-G. (1998). ed. and translated, *Aristoteles: Nikomachische Ethik VI*. Vittorio Klostermann.

Galbraith, J. K. (1994). *A short history of financial euphoria*. Viking Penguin.

Gallardo, E. (2011). *California changes law to streamline standards for distributions and dividends*. https://corpgov.law.harvard.edu/2011/09/29/california-changes-law-to-streamline-standards-for-distributions-and-dividends/ (accessed: 22.08.2025).

Gardiner, G. H. (1931). Corporate bonds, mortgages, collateral trusts and debenture indentures. In A. A. Ballantine et al. (Eds.), *Some legal phases of corporate financing, reorganization and regulation*. Macmillan.

Gierke, O. F. von (1868 et seq.). *Das deutsche Genossenschaftsrecht*. Weidmann (German law of cooperatives, 4 Vols., until 1913).

Giovagnoli, R., & Lowe, R. (Eds.). (2020). *The logic of social practices*. Springer.

Goldstein, E., & Hamilton, R. W. (1983). The Revised Model Business Corporation Act. *Business Lawyer, 38*, 1019–1029.

Gorris, J. M., Hamermesh, L. A., & Strine, L. E. (2011). Delaware corporate law and the Model Business Corporation Act. *Law and Contemporary Problems, 74*, 107–120.

Gower. (2021). *Principles of modern company law*, by P. L. Davies, S. Worthington, & C. Hare (11th ed.). Thomson Reuters.

Grant, D. M., Kirby, E. M., & Hawkins, S. R. (2024). Decentralized autonomous organizations: To statutorily organize or not? *Wyoming Law Review, 24*, 59–88.

Grimm, J., & Grimm, W. (1854 et seq.). *Deutsches Wörterbuch*. Hirzel.

Großfeld, B. (1968). *Aktiengesellschaft Unternehmenskonzentration und Kleinaktionär*. Mohr Siebeck.

Großfeld, B. (2019). *Schritte über Grenzen: Rechtsvergleichende Kulturerfahrung*. Lit Verlag.

Großfeld, B., & Luttermann, C. (2005). *Bilanzrecht: Die Rechnungslegung in Jahresabschluß und Konzernabschluß nach Handelsrect und Steuerrecht, Europarecht und IAS/IFRS* (4th ed.). CF Müller.

Hackney, W. P. (1957). The financial provisions of the Model Business Corporation Act. *Harvard Law Review, 70*, 1357–1405.

Halbhuber, H. (2017). Debt restructurings and the Trust Indenture Act. *American Bankruptcy Institute Law Review, 25*, 1–44.

Hamilton, R. W. (1984). *Corporation finance: Cases and materials*. West Publishing Co.

Hamilton, R. W. (1987). *The law of corporations* (2nd ed. and 4th ed., 1996). West Publishing Co.

Han, J., Lee, J., & Li, T. (2025). A review of DAO governance: Recent literature and emerging trends. *Journal of Corporate Finance, 91*, Article 102734 (April 2025).

Hanks, J. J., Jr. (2011). Legal capital and the Model Business Corporation Act: An essay for Bayless Manning. *Law and Contemporary Problems, 74*, 211–230.

Hansen, J. W. (1936). Hybrid securities: A study of securities which combine characteristics of both stock and bonds. *New York University Law Quarterly Review, 13*, 407–438.

Hayek, F. A. von (1960). *The constitution of liberty*. University of Chicago Press.

He, V. F., & Puranam, P. (2023). Some challenges for the "new DAOism": A comment on Klima DAO. *Journal of Organization Design, 12*, 293–295.

Healy, R. E. (1938). The next step in accounting. *The Accounting Review, 13*, 1–9.

Heinzlmeier, A. (1990). *Fritz Lang*. Verlagsunion Erich Pabel.
Hembrecht, I. (Ed.). (2013). *China Investment Corporation: China's key sovereign wealth fund & Chinese investment issues*. Nova Science Publishers.
Hills, G. S. (1935). Model Corporation Act. *Harvard Law Review, 48*, 1334–1380.
Holmes, O. W. (1881). *The Common Law*. Little, Brown, and Company, here: ed. by M. DeWolfe Howe, Belknap Press of Harvard University Press 1963 (Back Bay Books).
Huppertz, H. (1930). *Convertible Bonds als Aktienwandelobligationen und andere „Mischformen" als Mittel der Kapitalbeschaffung der Aktiengesellschaft der Vereinigten Staaten von Amerika*. Verlag Spaeth & Linde.
Ireland, P. (1983). The triumph of the company legal form, 1856-1914. In J. Adams (Ed.), *Essays for Clive M. Schmitthoff* (pp. 29–58). Professional Books.
Isaacs, N. (1923). Business security and legal security. *Harvard Law Review, 37*, 201–213.
Jongh, M. de. (2014). *Tussen societas en universitas: de beursvennootschap en haar aandeelhouders in historisch perspectief*. Doctoral thesis, Erasmus University Rotterdam (Between Societas and Universitas: the listed company and its shareholders in historical perspective).
Karmel, R. S. (1991). Is it time for a Federal corporation law? *Brooklyn Law Review, 57*, 55–96.
Keynes, J. M. (1919). *The economic consequences of the peace*. Harcourt.
Klein, F. (1904). *Die neueren Entwicklungen in Verfassung und Recht der Aktiengesellschaft*. Manzsche Buchhandlung.
Knight, F. (1921). *Risk, uncertainty and profit*. Houghton Mifflin Company. (here: Chicago 1971 with an introduction by Stigler).
Landau, R. I. (1992). *Corporate trust administration and management* (4th ed.). Columbia University Press.
Landau, R. I., & Peluso, R. I. (2015). *Corporate trust administration and management* (7th ed.). Infinity Publishing.
Larcom, R. C. (1937). *Delaware Corporation*. Johns Hopkins Press.
Lastra, R. M., Fearnley, T., & Satragno, L. (2022). Sovereign wealth funds and ethical investment: The case of Norway, chapter 11. In M. R. Dahlan, R. M. Lastra, & G. Rochette (Eds.), *Research Handbook on energy, law and ethics*. Elgar.
Lee, J., & Fricotté, A. (2025). DAO token transferability: Property, contract, and technology. *European Journal of Risk Regulation, 16*, 1–17. https://doi.org/10.1017/err.2024.93 (accessed: 22.08.205)
Leffson, U. (1987). *Die Grundsätze ordnungsmäßiger Buchführung* (7th ed.). IDW-Verlag.
Levitt, A. (1998). *The "numbers game"*, 28.09.1998. https://www.sec.gov/news/speech/speecharchive/1998/spch220.txt (accessed: 22.08.2025).
Li, H. (2009). China Investment Corporation: A perspective on accountability. *The International Lawyer, 43*, 1495–1513.
Lim, E. (2014). Of 'landmark' or 'leading' cases: Salomon' challenge. *Journal of Law and Society, 41*, 523–550.
Lipson, J. C., & Hamermesh, L. A. (2020). *Model Business Corporation Act Annotated* (5th ed.) – Front Matter, Temple University Legal Studies Research Paper 2020-26.
Lipton, A. (2025). The legitimation of shareholder primacy. *Journal of Corporation Law* (forthcoming, also: European Corporate Governance Institute, Law Working No. 826/2025). https://papers.ssrn.com/sol3/papers.cfm?abstract_id=5120765 (accessed: 22.08.2025).
Lipton, P. (2014). The mythology of Salmon's case and the law dealing with tort liabilities of corporate groups: An historical perspective. *Monash University Law Review, 40*, 452–487.
Lomax, D. F., & Gutmann, P. T. G. (1981). *The Euromarkets and international financial policies*. Palgrave Macmillan.
Lubben, S. J. (2022). Protecting Ma and Pa: Bond workouts and the Trust Indenture Act in the 21st century. *Cardozo Law Review, 44*, 81–143.
Luttermann, C. (1998). *Unternehmen, Kapital und Genußrechte: Eine Studie über Grundlagen der Unternehmensfinanzierung und zum internationalen Kapitalmarktrecht*. Mohr Siebeck.

Luttermann, C. (1999a). *Bilanzrecht in den USA und internationale Konzernrechnungslegung*. Mohr Siebeck.
Luttermann, C. (1999b). Dialog der Kulturen: Vergleichendes Handels- und Kapitalmarktrecht im Sprachspiegel. In U. Hübner & W. F. Ebke (Eds.), *Festschrift for Bernhard Großfeld* (pp. 771–789). Verlag Recht und Wirtschaft.
Luttermann, C. (2000). Bewertungsrecht im Internetzeitalter: Über Finanzkommunikation, Börsenkurs, Wahrscheinlichkeit und "virtuelle" Aktiengesellschaft. *Die Aktiengesellschaft (AG), 45*, 459–469.
Luttermann, C. (2001a). Unternehmensfinanzierung, Geschäftsleiterpflicht und Haftkapital bei Kapitalgesellschaften. *Der Betriebs-Berater (BB), 50*, 2433–2437.
Luttermann, C. (2001b). Aktienverkaufoptionsanleihen ("reverse convertible notes"), standardisierte Information und Kapitalmarktdemokratie. *Zeitschrift für Wirtschaftsrecht (ZIP), 2001*, 1901–1906.
Luttermann, C. (2003). In B. Kropff & J. Semler (Eds.), *Münchener Kommentar zum Aktiengesetz* (Vol. 5/1, 2nd ed.). CH Beck Verlag.
Luttermann, C. (2008). Über Vertragsverhältnisse und Bewertungsrecht: Geld, Zeitwert und internationaler Goldstandard. *Finanz-Betrieb (FB), 9*, 193–204.
Luttermann, C. (2009). Islamic Finance: Ein Dialog über Recht, Weltwirtschaft und Religionen. *Juristenzeitung (JZ), 64*, 706–715.
Luttermann, C. (2013). Neue Bilanzrichtlinie: Europäisches Bewertungsrecht in prozessualer Praxis. *Neue Zeitschrift für Gesellschaftsrecht (NZG), 16*, 1128–1133.
Luttermann, C. (2015a). Corporate law and the *Vermoegensordnung* (order of assets). *European Business Law Review (EBLR), 26*, 31–48.
Luttermann, C. (2015b). Über Idee und Methodik eines internationalen Investitionsschutzes (Vermögensordnung) durch Privatrecht und Völkerrecht. *Zeitschrift für Europarecht, Internationales Privatrecht und Rechtsvergleichung (ZfRV), 56*, 274–282.
Luttermann, C. (2017). VR China: Neues Foreign Investment Law and Gold Trade Notes. *Recht der Internationalen Wirtschaft (RIW), 63*, 255–263.
Luttermann, C. (2023). Unternehmensbewertung im Spannungsfeld von Rechts- und Wirtschaftswissenschaft. In K. Petersen, C. Zwirner, & G. Zimney (Eds.), *Handbuch Unternehmensbewertung* (3rd ed., pp. 163–202). Bundesanzeiger Verlag.
Luttermann, C., & Geißler, S. (2012). Haftungsfragen transnationaler Konzernfinanzierung (cash pooling) und das Bilanzstatut der Gesellschaft. *Praxis des Internationalen Privat- und Verfahrensrechts (IPRax), 32*, 55–62.
Luttermann, C., & Luttermann, K. (2021). Towards peace in Europe: On legal linguistics, prosperity and European identity – the European Reference Language System for the European Union. *International Journal of Legal Discourse, 6*, 7–41.
Luttermann, C., & Wicher, C. (2005). Rechtsordnung für Unternehmensanleihen: Vertragsrecht, Hybridformen und Standardisierung. *Zeitschrift für Wirtschaftsrecht (ZIP), 24*, 1529–1535.
Luttermann, L. (2022). Klimawandel und Business Judgement: Nachhaltige Finanzierung als unternehmerisches Sorgfaltskonzept. *Recht der Internationalen Wirtschaft (RIW), 68*, 809–820.
Luttermann, L. (2023). Nachhaltigkeitsberichterstattung in den USA, Unternehmensbewertung und Compliance. *Recht der Internationalen Wirtschaft (RIW), 69*, 483–495.
Luttermann, L. (2024). Unternehmensführung: Nachhaltige Finanzinformation (U.S. SEC Climate Rules/EU), Wertschöpfung und Bankenfinanzierung. *Recht der Internationalen Wirtschaft (RIW), 70*, 410–422.
Luttermann, L. (2025). Nachhaltige Wirtschaftsaktivitäten: Eine europäische Eröffnungsbilanz aus Finanzdaten der Bankenregulierung. *Recht der Internationalen Wirtschaft (RIW), 71*, 26–43.
Lynch, M. (Ed.). (2011). *Oxford companion to Scottish history*. Oxford University Press.
Macneil, I. R. (1978). Contracts: Adjustment of long-term economic relations under classical, neoclassical and relational contract law. *Northwestern University Law Review, 72*, 854–905.
Manning, B., & Hanks, J. J., Jr. (1990). *Legal capital* (3rd ed.). Foundation Press.
Manning, B., & Hanks, J. J., Jr. (2013). *Legal capital* (4th ed.). Foundation Press.

Marsh, H., Jr., & Finkle, R. R. (1995). *Marsh's California corporation law* (3rd ed. 1990 (supp. 1995)). Wolters Kluwer.

Marx, K. (1857/58). Fragment über Maschinen. In K. Marx (Ed.), *Grundrisse der Kritik der politischen Ökonomie, Marx-Engels-Werke (MEW)* (2nd ed., Vol. 42, pp. 590–609). Dietz Verlag, 2005.

McCormick, E. T. (1948). *Understanding the Securities Act and the SEC.* American Book Company.

McDaniel, M. W. (1986). Bondholders and corporate governance. *Business Lawyer, 41*, 413–460.

McDaniel, M. W. (1988). Bondholders and stockholders. *Journal of Corporation Law, 13*, 205–315.

McGurk, B., & Reichenbach, S. (2024). *Financial services law and distributed ledger technology: Regulating cryptoassets and decentralised finance.* Edward Elgar Publishing.

Mestmäcker, E.-J. (2007). A legal theory without law: Posner v. Hayek on economic analysis of law, Mohr Siebeck.

Metjahic, L. (2018). Deconstructing the Dao: The need for legal recognition and the application of securities laws to decentralized organizations. *Cardozo Law Review, 39*, 1553–1567.

Milhaupt, C. J., & Pistor, K. (2008). *Law and capitalism: What corporate crisis reveal about legal systems and economic development around the world.* The University of Chicago Press.

Miller, J. (2023). *Larry Fink's BlackRock: How BlackRock loves us, watches us, and destroys us.* Miller.

Minaev, A. (2023). *The DAO hack: Understanding the infamous attack.* https://cryptodose.net/learn/the-dao-hack/ (accessed: 22.08.2025).

Minn, K. T. (2019). Towards enhanced oversight of "self-governing" decentralized autonomous organizations: Case study of the DAO and its shortcomings. *New York University Journal of Intellectual Property and Entertainment Law, 9*, 139–178.

Morrison, R., Mazey, N. C. H. L., & Wingreen, S. C. (2020). The DAO controversy: The case for a new species of corporate governance? *Frontiers Blockchain, 3*, 25. https://www.frontiersin.org/journals/blockchain/articles/10.3389/fbloc.2020.00025/full (accessed: 22.08.2025).

Nicholas, P., Jr. (2004). The agency that kept going: The late New Deal SEC and shareholder democracy. *Journal of Policy History, 16*, 212–238.

Nilsen, H. R., Sjåfjell, B., & Richardson, B. J. (2019). The Norwegian Government Pension Fund Global: Risk based versus ethical investments. *Vierteljahrshefte zur Wirtschaftsforschung, 88*, 65–78.

Norris, W. J. (2016). *Chinese economic statecraft.* Cornell University Press.

Owocki, K., & Brezina, J. "Puncar". (2025). *How to DAO: Mastering the future of internet coordination*, Portfolio Penguin Random House.

Payne, J. (1997). Lifting the corporate veil: A reassessment of the fraud exception. *The Cambridge Law Journal, 56*, 284–290.

Phelps, E. (2007). Macroeconomics for a modern economy. *The American Economic Review, 97*, 543–561.

Phillipson, R. (1992). *Linguistic imperialism.* Oxford University Press.

Pollock, F., & Maitland, F. W. (1982). *The history of English law* (special ed., Vol. 1). Legal Classics Library.

Pöhls, M. (1842). *Das Recht der Actiengesellschaften mit besonderer Rücksicht auf Eisenbahngesellschaften.* Hoffmann and Campe.

Pölnitz, G. von (1949). *Jakob Fugger: Kaiser, Kirche und Kapital in der oberdeutschen Renaissance.* Mohr Siebeck.

Prins, N. (2014). *All the Presidents' bankers: The hidden alliances that drive American power.* Nation Books.

Rathenau, W. (1917). *Vom Aktienwesen: eine geschäftliche Betrachtung.* S. Fischer (On the nature of stocks).

Rathenau, W. (1918). *Von Kommenden Dingen.* S. Fischer (translation by E. and C. Paul: Rathenau, *In days to come*, 1921).

Renaud, A. (1863). *Das Recht der Actiengesellschaften*. Tauchnitz.
Rickett, C. E. F., & Grantham, R. B. (Eds.). (1998). *Corporate personality in the 20$^{th}$ century*. Hart Publishing.
Roberts, R., & Kynaston, D. (2002). *City state: A contemporary history of the City of London and how money triumphed*. Profile Books.
Røste, O. B. (2021). *Norway's sovereign wealth fund: Sustainable investment of natural resource revenues*. Springer.
Runciman, D. (1997). *Pluralism and the personality of the state*. Cambridge University Press.
Savigny, F. C. von. (1840). *System des heutigen römischen Rechts* (Vol. II). Veit.
Schmalenbach, E. (1916). Über das allgemeine Bilanzrecht. *Zeitschrift für handelswissenschaftliche Forschung (ZfhF), 11*, 1–52.
Schumpeter, J. A. (1947/2018). *Kapitalismus, Sozialismus und Demokratie* (9th ed., 2018). A. Francke Verlag (*Capitalism, socialism and democracy*, 5$^{th}$ ed. 1976, George Allen & Unwin Ltd).
Schweitzer, A. (1923). *Kultur und Ethik (Kulturphilosophie I and II)*. CH Beck Verlag, 1990.
Seavoy, R. E. (1982). *The origins of the American business corporation, 1784-1855*. Greenwood Press.
Shakespeare, W. (1600). *The merchant of Venice*. Thomas Heyes.
Shuster, G. W. (2006). The Trust Indenture Act and international debt restructurings. *American Bankruptcy Institute Law Review, 14*, 431–467.
Smith, A. (1759/1790$^{6}$). *The theory of moral sentiments, Edinburgh* (6th ed.). Penguin Books, 2009.
Smith, A. (1776/1789$^{5}$). *An inquiry into the nature and causes of the wealth of nations, London* (5th ed.). Bantam Classic Edition, 2003.
Smith, D. G. (2009). A federalism-based rationale for limited liability. *Alabama Law Review, 60*, 649–681.
Stiglitz, J. E. (2010). *Freefall: America, free markets, and the sinking of the world economy*. W. W. Norton & Company.
Strine, L. E., Jr. (2025). Ignorance is strength: Climate change, corporate governance, politics, and the English language. *Journal of Law and Political Economy, 5*, 170–220.
Strum, P. (1984). *Louis D. Brandeis: Justice for the people*. Harvard University Press.
Tierney, S., & Toddington, S. (2005). Societas, universitas and the third order of the political. *King's College Law Journal, 16*, 215–228.
Tooze, A. (2019). *Crashed: How a decade of financial crisis changed the world*. Penguin Books Great Britain.
Uhlman, R. E. (1938). The law of hybrid securities. *Washington University Law Quarterly, 23*, 182–207.
Vagts, D. F. (1966). Reforming the "modern" corporation: Perspectives from the German. *Harvard Law Review, 80*, 23–89.
Warren, C. (1911). *A history of the American Bar*. Little, Brown, and Company.
Weiner, J. L. (1928). Theory of Anglo-American dividend law: The English cases. *Columbia Law Review, 28*, 1046–1060.
Weiner, J. L. (1929). Theory of Anglo-American dividend law: American statutes and cases. *Columbia Law Review, 29*, 461–482.
Weiner, J. L., & Bonbright, J. C. (1930). Theory of Anglo-American dividend law: Surplus and profits. *Columbia Law Review, 30*, 330-358 and 954-985.
Wigglesworth, R. (2021). *Trillions: How a band of Wall Street renegades invented the index fund and changed finance forever*. Penguin Random House.
Williams, C. A. (2021). Fiduciary duties and corporate climate responsibility. *Vanderbilt Law Review, 74*, 1875–1916.
Wilson, W. (1913). *The new freedom: A call for the emancipation of the generous energies of a people*. Doubleday, Page & Co. (here: Gray Rabbit Publications, 2011).

Wilson Corley, K. M. (2024). *Garfield v. Allen*: The cat is out of the bag. *Tulsa Law Review, 59*, 169–192.

Wolfe, C. J. (2017). "An artificial being": John Marshall and corporate personhood. *Harvard Journal of Law and Public Policy, 40*, 201–235.

Yalman, B. (2024). Electronic personhood: A compact analysis of legal personality for artificial intelligence. *Ex/Ante, 2024*(1), 3–13.

# Part III
# Creation of Value (Facts, Facts, Facts)

# Chapter 4
# Financial Reporting: Verified Information for Investors (Accountability)

"But the disclosure must be real. (...) To be effective, knowledge of the facts must be brought home to the investor."*

*Louis D. Brandeis*

## Contents



*Brandeis, Other people's money and how the bankers use it, Stokes, New York 1914, p. 104.



C. Luttermann, *Human Corporation for Sustainable Development*,
https://doi.org/10.1007/978-3-032-07615-1_4

## 4.1 Real Financial Reporting

The law is an instrument of history, with the comparative perspective forming the basis in globalisation.[1] This clarifies life circumstances and insights for the sound development and implementation of the human corporation for a better world. We have examined the modern corporation in and through time, now here focused under "verified information for investors", id est real financial reporting (see Fig. 4.1). For while in other places, flags have been and still are opportunely changed, "full and real disclosure" (Brandeis)[2] is the fundamental basis, intended as the necessary balance, as becomes clear in sustainability: With such a basis, humankind, economy and the environment may be reconciled and promoted precisely through the reasonable use of the corporation (see chapters 1 to 3). Basically, it is about sensible rules which sustainably promote life in reason and peace, conceived in a holistic and practicable way (see chapter 9).

In the summer of 2007, when a precursor to this chapter was released,[3] the corporate world seemed in good shape to most people. Then came the so-called "financial crisis" (more precisely: world debt crisis, German *Weltschuldenkrise*) symbolically with the breakdown of Lehman Brothers Inc. (see 4.6.2) on 15 September 2008, regarded by many as a kind of natural disaster.[4] Since then, gigantic forces have been crippling companies, states and currencies; we are witnessing new orgies of debt ("quantitative easing" by the FED, ECB etc.). The crisis is man-made, and it demonstrates that the immoderate economic practice and theory of financial industry has failed; in spite of all this, the spectacle continues.[5] A pandemic (covid-19), the Russian war in the Ukraine, the Chinese-US rivalry, and President Trump's global tariff war exacerbate the situation. Deficits are becoming obvious, supply chains are breaking down, inflation and destitution are gaining ground. The world having fallen to pieces, a new order is required.

In this situation, there is an even greater challenge: climate change. The International Court of Justice, referring to scientific proof, speaks of "the urgent and existential threat posed by climate change" for both natural ecosystems and human

---

[1] After Großfeld (2019) pp. 2 and 6.

[2] See above the leitmotif of this chapter by Brandeis (1914), and 3.3.3.

[3] Luttermann in du Plessis, Großfeld, Luttermann et al. (2007) chapter 7.

[4] On the erosion of freedom, 23.06.2008: Luttermann (2008d). On the juridical analysis of the economy see, e.g., 1.6.2, 7.3.2 and 9.7. Luttermann (1998) pp. 465-485, Luttermann (2010a).

[5] See chapter 6 (globally on speculation) and chapter 7 (on individual responsibility). Basically for practicing valuation law see chapter 5 and Luttermann (2023a).

populations.[6] The hot breath of a new era, in which old authorities topple, clearing the vision.[7] What is essential through time, having been long neglected, impressively makes itself clear. Human rights and the environment as the simultaneously economic common basis gain ground in collective consciousness, in the reality of enterprises, projects and businesses, in our existence. We have designated this with the law as practised ethics for the human "in the midst of humans" as an entrepreneur in the principle of reasonableness.[8] It is about comprehensive sustainability, id est substance instead of the "numbers game" (good governance),[9] holistically real financial reporting for sustainable value creation.

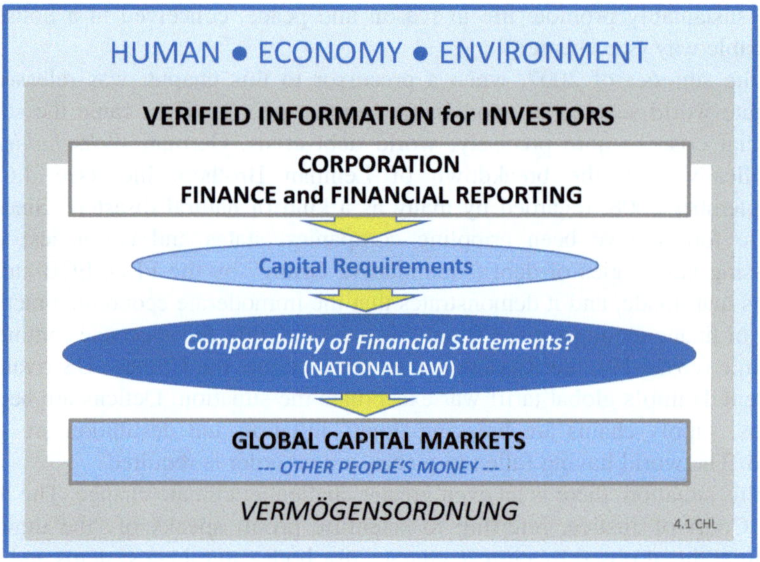


**Fig. 4.1** Corporate finance and financial reporting (accounting, auditing)

[6]ICJ, Advisory Opinion: Obligation of states in respect of climate change, 23.07.2025, (https://www.icj-cij.org/sites/default/files/case-related/187/187-20250723-adv-01-00-en.pdf, accessed: 22.08.2025) para. 73 with paras. 72-87.

[7]See Zweig (1934) pp. 24-29 (*Blick in die Zeit*). On sustainable finance Luttermann, L. (2022), (2024) and (2025).

[8]Luttermann (1998) pp. 139-144, Luttermann (2003a) Einf BilanzR recitals 128-130. Luttermann (2023a) recitals 1-47. See chapter 9 and now also the ICJ, Advisory Opinion, 23.07.2025, ibid., on that below 6.1.

[9]See Luttermann in du Plessis, Großfeld, Luttermann et al. (2007, 2012, 2017), chapter 7 (on "accounting", including auditing).

## 4.2 Sustainable Finance and Financial Reporting for the Good

### *4.2.1 Handling the Invisible: Images and Weltanschauungen*

Images are what touch us in particular. They motivate thinking and acting, they influence our being. This affects us, as corporations are presented through images in their annual financial statements (*Jahresabschlüssen*), id est in their accounts and disclosure (financial reporting). In a holistic sense of sustainability and the imperative of truth (*Wahrheitsgebot*, see 4.4.4), this is to be regarded as a structural element and crucial core of the law (see 3.1 with 2.6.3, 3.8). Though remaining an approximation, restricted in their own and a general knowledge perspective, images facilitate realisation. Abstraction is in effect perforated, we obtain an idea of other things and in particular an idea of what is essential in handling a corporation.[10] – How can we grasp what we cannot see?

That is, at the same time, the crux and the task we are given to solve – indeed with both, the corporation and the climate change. This is where they meet and where, if they are designed in a reasonable way, they may provide a common basis for the well-being of all of us. We will begin with the corporation, remembering: According to Friedrich Carl von Savigny, the corporation is a mere "fiction" of the law.[11] As a distinct legal person, the corporation (company) is "invisible, intangible, and existing only in contemplation of law" (John C. Marshall).[12] That is the case worldwide. No one has ever seen, for example, the Daimler AG (*Aktiengesellschaft*), the Alphabet Inc., the BHP Billiton Corp. or the Panasonic K.K. (Japanese *Kabushiki-gaisha*). Thus, corporate governance and the law associated with it deal with an artificial being, a creation of the – relevant national – law for business on globally coined markets. So how can we deal with something invisible?

Accounting (financial reporting) gives us the necessary and the only instrument to do so (see 3.2). By means of the financial statements, stating in words and numbers the corporation's assets and liabilities, financial position and performance, a picture of the corporation evolves. Such a picture is fundamentally the subject of company law and capital markets law, and it also includes the governance of the corporation. That makes accounting *the* documentary proof of good corporate governance. In the capital market concept, this refers to the investors: Financial reporting informs them about the real situation of assets, finances and revenue of the corporation. The investors are conceptually put in the picture (Lat. *in-forma*), as already shown (see 2.6.2); this is where we follow up with climate change and human rights for consolidation.

---

[10] Insightfully Jaspers (1932) pp. 28-29, see also pp. 45-48.

[11] See in more detail 4.4.1 (above, e.g. 3.5.5, 3.6.1, below 5.5.3) and Savigny (1840) pp. 85, 236 and 239.

[12] In *Dartmouth College v Woodward*, 17 U.S. (4 Wheat.) 518, 636 (1819).

### *4.2.2 Climate Change: Humankind, Environment, and Responsibility*

The climate change on our planet Earth is scientifically[13] recognised as man-made and an existential threat, along with the human rights situation. The International Court of Justice confirmed this and the following in his advisory opinion on July 23, 2025.[14] In the Paris Agreement of 2015, the United Nations set themselves the goal of world-wide climate protection (United Nations Framework Convention on Climate Change, UNFCCC).[15] In this, the states commit themselves to substantially reduce the emission of climate-damaging greenhouse gases (so-called decarbonisation), caused in particular by fossile fuels (coal, oil, gas). This marks a change of heart, a new era in the history of mankind. Mankind, economy and environment are to be reconciled (see chapters 1, 2). Everyone is called upon. We take responsibility. This is an imperative act of reason.

The Paris Agreement as a treaty of international law (*Völkerrecht*) provides a common framework of action. In the idea of justice, guided by "common but differentiated responsibilities and respective capabilities, in the light of different national circumstances", the aim is "equitable access to sustainable development" and to "eradicate poverty" – all in all "in accordance with best available science".[16] Sustainable economy, serving humans and the environment in a gentle way, is the global goal. Practically, it is about the sustainable, climate-compatible restructuring of the economy and its financing. The explicit demand is: "As part of a global effort, developed country Parties should continue to take the lead in mobilizing climate finance from a wide variety of sources, instruments and channels, (…)" (Art. 9 No. 3 Paris Agreement). This at the same time addresses the corporation as an instrument.

We have already shown that the corporation is predominantly a financial instrument (see 2.5). Designed in its structure after the model of the human being (see 7. 3.1), the corporation gathers investors as a capital provider (equity, debt) in the same boat for financing an enterprise or project. To this end, the corporate directors are

---

[13] See further Art. 18 with Art. 9, 10 Paris Agreement and The Intergovernmental Panel on Climate Change (IPCC, under: https://www.ipcc.ch/). Groundbreaking the climate scholars *Hasselmann* and *Manabe* (Nobel prize for physics 2021). From the perspective of valuation law Luttermann (2023a), esp. recitals 21-26, 44 and from 96.

[14] ICJ, Advisory Opinion: Obligation of states in respect of climate change, 23.07.2025, (https://www.icj-cij.org/sites/default/files/case-related/187/187-20250723-adv-01-00-en.pdf, accessed: 22.08.2025), on this see above 1.2, below 6.1.

[15] The Paris Agreement under https://unfccc.int/process-and-meetings/the-paris-agreement/the-paris-agreement (accessed: 22.08.2025), *Deutsches Zustimmungsgesetz* 28.9.2016, BGBl. II 2016, 1082. See already chapters 1 and 2.

[16] See preamble as well as Art. 2 and 4 Paris Agreement. Confirming ICJ, Advisory Opinion, 23.07.2025 (https://www.icj-cij.org/sites/default/files/case-related/187/187-20250723-adv-01-00-en.pdf, accessed: 22.08.2025), e.g. paras. 136, 224, 283-286 and 347. Cf. above 1.2, 1.4.2, below 6.1.1, 8.2.1.

accountable in the well-known capital market concept.[17] The Paris Agreement in general marks a new point of reference. In enhancing the implementation of the UNFCCC and its objective, it "aims to strengthen the global response to the threat of climate change, in the context of sustainable development and efforts to eradicate poverty", explicitly through:

> "Making finance flows consistent with a pathway towards low greenhouse gas emissions and climate-resilient development." (Art. 2 No. 1(c) Paris Agreement).

The term "finance flows" in the sense of the Paris Agreement is to be understood comprehensively. It is about the practical steering function (*Lenkfunktion*, see 1. 5.3): Mindful of their regulatory power, the parties practically address the global financial markets on which capital is traded, because climate risks are (potentially) financial risks – including for corporations. It is this that places the institutional steering function of financial market regulation, which we had early on highlighted with accounting and appraisal for good corporate governance,[18] in precisely this exceptional dimension of sustainability (verifiability), in the context of climate protection and human rights. An epochal process. Holistically conceived for a responsible community, this is the basis for a global order of assets (*globale Vermögensordnung*), which remains to be developed (see chapter 8).

### *4.2.3 The European Green Deal*

The change of mind is gaining ground (see 1.2),[19] in the treaty states of the Paris Agreement there is political action. The European Union is leading the way, its internal markets traditionally being oriented towards human rights and the environment as values (Art. 2 and Art. 3 section 3 TEU). The Union has approved the Paris Agreement under the UNFCCC,[20] through its regulations establishing a comprehensive kind of sustainability for humans and climate protection. As European law, and at the same time in the sense of verifiability also constitutionally, this applies to the valuation of companies (financial reporting, auditing) in an elementary way, the economy and society as a whole in the largest internal market (*Binnenmarkt*) in the world. In 2019, the European Parliament symbolically declared a climate and

[17] On business judgement Luttermann, L. (2022).

[18] See chapter 5 and Luttermann in du Plessis, Großfeld, Luttermann et al. (2007) chapter 7. Pioneering for the transformation economy Luttermann, L. (2024) and (2025) with data from EU banking regulation: a European opening balance (*Eröffnungsbilanz*) for 2023 on sustainable business activities.

[19] ICJ, Advisory Opinion, 23.07.2025, ibid., on request of the General Assembly of the United Nations (resolution 77/276), supported by around 130 states, see below 6.1.1.

[20] Council Decision (EU) 2016/1841 of 5 Oct 2016: https://eur-lex.europa.eu/legal-content/EN/TXT/HTML/?uri=CELEX:32016D1841&from=EN, accessed: 22.08.2025).

environmental emergency,[21] in order to emphasise the urgency for action for all actors.

To this end, the European Union presented its great plan for the implementation of the Paris Agreement in December 2019 through its Commission. This is the European Green Deal, the official name obviously reminiscent to U.S. President Franklin D. Roosevelt's famous New Deal of the 1930s (see 3.3.3) and even more comprehensive and ambitious with the revolutionary paradigm shift for the European Union to climate change and human rights (see 4.2.4); in 2025, the Clean Industrial Deal was added (see 1.4.2). The European Commission launched its European Green Deal simply as:

> "a roadmap for making the EU's economy sustainable by turning climate and environmental challenges into opportunities across all policy areas and making the transition just and inclusive for all."[22]

The political ambition is to become the world's first climate-neutral continent by 2050. In order to translate this remarkable objective into legislation, the Commission has since presented the new European climate law in numerous legal acts (esp. regulations, directives, see Art. 288 TFEU). Based on a comprehensive impact assessment for the economy, the society and the environment, the Union's binding target for 2030 has been increased towards at least 55% net emission reductions compared to the year 1990 (2030 Climate Target Plan). The goal of climate neutrality by 2050 is anchored in the European Climate Law (*Klimagesetz*), which – as a regulation under Article 288(2) TFEU: "binding in its entirety" – came into effect in all member states on July 19, 2021.[23] Consequently, trillions of euros have to be mobilised for sustainable investments, id est an overall transformation.

This is what the European Green Deal's Investment Plan (Sustainable Europe Investment Plan) and the so-called "Just Transition Mechanism" (JTM) are intended for. The EU Commission is undertaking a great effort. The Investment Plan, with a key role to be performed by the European Investment Bank (EIB), "will mobilise EU funding and create an enabling framework to facilitate and stimulate the public and private investments needed for the transition to a climate-neutral, green, competitive and inclusive economy"; regions particularly affected by the economic and social transformation are to receive special support (the JTM).[24] This applies to the whole internal market. What is required are responsible citizens, human beings as the

[21] European Parliament, 28.11.2019, Resolution on the climate and environmental emergency (2019/2930(RSP)).

[22] EU Commission, 11.12.2019, see – also in the text for the following data: https://ec.europa.eu/commission/presscorner/detail/en/ip_19_6691, accessed: 22.08.2025).

[23] Regulation (EU) 2021/1119 of the European Parliament and the Council from June 30 2021 on the creation of the framework for achieving climate neutrality and on the change of the regulations (EG) No 401/2009 and (EU) 2018/1999 (*Europäisches Klimagesetz*), OJ L 243, 09.07.2021, pp. 1–17.

[24] EU Commission, 14.01.2020 (https://ec.europa.eu/commission/presscorner/detail/en/ip_20_17, accessed: 22.08.2025).

entrepreneurs of their existence as a whole, although they are unfortunately still defamed as "consumers".[25] This appropriately designates the actual political task.

### *4.2.4 European Green Paradigm Shift: Sustainability*

We are experiencing a paradigm shift (see 4.2.3): the transition of the European Union to a modern, climate-resilient, resource-efficient and competitive economy. No net greenhouse gas emissions are to be released any more, and economic growth is to be disconnected from the use of resources by changing our patterns in production and consumption; this is accompanied by the human rights (Art. 2 TEU). It is about "sustainability": Sounding like a magic word, if it is conceived and practised comprehensively, this means the dawn of a new era (see 4.11.4 and chapter 1). Overall, it is about the so-called "socio-ecological" transformation of the economy. This affects the valuation of companies and projects, their management and financing in an elementary way in the sense of "sustainable business activity" (*nachhaltige Wirtschaftsaktivität*).

In order for the economy to be ecologically transformed and a sustainable system of financing to be created, the capital flow is to be directed to "sustainable" investments precisely through regulatory means, id est via the steering function (*Lenkfunktion*, see 4.2.2). The Regulation (EU) 2020/852 (so-called Sustainability Regulation) shows the way: In it, the Union commits the companies to disclose information specific to financial products to facilitate sustainable investment.[26] Financial reporting and auditing are recorded as a whole in financial terms and substance (real disclosure). What is thus clear is that the general foundations apply. The relevant factors are to be taken into account for the result, id est the figures of the annual financial statements, due to reasonable valuation law following the imperative of truth according to the "actual circumstances" (see German §§ 242, 264 and 317 HGB and generally valuation law).[27] The objective is a European valuation law, in particular for the corporation.

[25] See above 1.4.3. Critically Luttermann (2015d) 805, 809-10. Luttermann, C. and Luttermann, K. (2020) p. 218. Cf. Humboldt (1792) p. 16 and from 28.

[26] Regulation, 18.06.2020, on the establishment of a framework to facilitate sustainable investment, and amending Regulation (EU) 2019/2088, OJ EU of 22.06.2020, L 198/13. Overall Luttermann (2021). See EU Commission, Omnibus simplification packages, 26.02.2025, COM(2025)80 and COM(2025)81, to "reduce complexity of EU requirements for all businesses, notably SMEs and small mid-caps (SMCs)". On the transfer of wealth Luttermann (2015d) 805, from 809.

[27] Basically Luttermann (2003a) Einf BilanzR recitals from 1, Luttermann (2003a) § 243, 342 HGB recitals 7-25, and Luttermann (2003a) § 264 HGB recitals from 16. On valuation law Luttermann (2023b) recitals 22-38, on greenwashing below in 4.2.5. Cf. overall Task Force on Climate Related Financial Disclosure (current: www.fsb-tcfd.org). Luttermann (2012) on criminal law (*Vermögensbetreuungspflicht* – duty to look after assets). See overall chapter 5.

For determining the ecological sustainability of a business activity, six environmental objectives are named (Art. 9 Regulation (EU) 2020/852): (a) climate change mitigation; (b) climate change adaptation; (c) the sustainable use and protection of water and marine resources; (d) the transition to a circular economy; (e) pollution prevention and control; (f) the protection and restoration of biodiversity and ecosystems. From the point of view of European law – for the purposes of establishing the degree to which an investment is environmentally sustainable –, an economic activity shall qualify as environmentally sustainable where that economic activity meets specific criteria (Art. 3 EU Regulation 2020/852). The aim is to establish "a technically robust classification system at Union level to establish clarity on which activities qualify as 'green' or 'sustainable'."[28] – A monumental undertaking.

The objective is a classification system with a complete list of sustainable economic activities:[29] a casuistic relapse? – A "Platform on Sustainable Finance" (Art. 20 Regulation (EU) 2020/852; so-called Multi-Stakeholder-Platform)[30] will practically form – under regular control of the European Commission – the so-called "technical screening criteria". With the precautionary principle (*Vorsorgeprinzip*, cf. Art. 191 TFEU) they are to be guided by scientific results and technological developments[31] and should be integrated into the legal order; what has to be taken into consideration are the sustainability indicators of Regulation (EU) 2019/2088 on sustainability-related disclosures in the financial services sector. The general explanation is: "An economic activity should qualify as contributing substantially to one or more of the environmental objectives set out in this Regulation where it directly enables other activities to make a substantial contribution to one or more of those objectives."[32]

The valuation system with its valuation criteria should take into account environmental, social and economic externalities within a cost-benefit analysis (possibly life-cycle assessment, *Lebenszyklusbewertung*); they should "provide for sufficient legal clarity" (cf. 7.6) while being "practicable and easy to apply". They should be criteria "for which compliance can be verified within reasonable cost-of-compliance boundaries, thereby avoiding unnecessary administrative burden."[33] Accordingly, the Commission should take into overall account relevant Union law as well as the work, standards and current methodology of international organisations (e.g., OECD, UN-supported Principles for Responsible Investment, see 1.4.2). Thus, a wide field is designated.

---

[28] EU Sustainability Regulation 2020/852, recital 5.

[29] Delegated act, see Art. 10 to 15 Regulation (EU) 2020/852. Luttermann (2021) 191, 194. See on a general rule instead of casuistry above 3.5.5, below 7.8.1, and for financial reporting below 4.3.2, 4.4 to 4.6 and 4.8.4; overall in chapters 7 to 9.

[30] See: https://ec.europa.eu/info/business-economy-euro/banking-and-finance/sustainable-finance/overview-sustainable-finance/platform-sustainable-finance_en (accessed: 22.08.2025).

[31] Overall Art. 19 EU Sustainability Regulation 2020/852. Cf. German BVerfG, 24.03.2021, 1 BvR 2656 et al., ECLI:DE:BVerfG:2021:rs20210324.1bvr265618.

[32] EU Sustainability Regulation 2020/852, recital 39.

[33] EU Sustainability Regulation 2020/852, recitals 44 and 47.

### *4.2.5 Degree of Sustainability: Benchmarking and Greenwashing*

Questions of valuation, here in fact respectively the environmental "sustainability" of a specific business activity (see 1.6.2, 2.4.2, on "legal sustainability" see 4.11.4, 5.2.4), are known to be of a complex nature. They have to be answered in a scientifically comprehensive way. The so-called "technical valuation criteria" (*technische Bewertungskriterien*) stipulated in the valuation system appear as the building blocks of the valuation. They are to guarantee equal treatment of relevant business activities in a certain sector, if these contribute to one or more of the fixed environmental objectives (Art. 9 Regulation (EU) 2020/852, see 4.2.4) to the same degree. What also comes into consideration is the substantial reduction of negative effect during the economic lifetime of the funded economic activity environmentally harmful, in particular preventing carbon-intensive lock-in effects.[34]

Correspondingly, a degree of sustainability (*Nachhaltigkeitsgrad*) applies to valuation. Also with regard to sectors in a comparative view, e.g., of the sectoral average (benchmarking),[35] in an individual case "the degree to which an investment is environmentally sustainable" has to be determined (Art. 1 Regulation (EU) 2020/852). Thus, the world's first Green List (*Grüne Liste*) of sustainable business activities is intended to guarantee, in the sense of capital flow steering (see 4.2.4), "that investments are channelled towards economic activities that make the greatest positive impact on the environmental objectives":[36] through a common classification order (*Klassifizierungsordnung*) with uniform terminology for investors wanting to invest in projects (corporations) and business activities with substantial positive climate and environmental effects; such business activities should be prioritised with regard to valuation that "potentially contribute most to the environmental objectives" (so-called "positive effects").[37] This sounds vague and implies probabilities instead of reasonable certainty.[38]

The criteria of valuation are to guarantee targeted investments, so that the financing and valuation system can create a resource-efficient and competitively strong economy. What is remarkable is the problem of abuse, id est greenwashing. This is to be countered by sound scrutiny and clarification. First dimensions in the fierce political argument on the taxonomy of power generation through nuclear or gas power plants in the EU sustainability taxonomy as "sustainable" (green energy) are discernible. A wide, rocky field. Instead of abusive greenwashing, the scrutiny needs to be designed in a sustainable way on solid ground in individual cases: legally and in actual fact (law of evidence – *Beweisrecht*, see chapter 5), id est factually

---

[34]EU Sustainability Regulation 2020/852, recital 39.

[35]EU Sustainability Regulation 2020/852, recitals 39 and 45.

[36]EU Sustainability Regulation 2020/852, recital 48.

[37]See Art. 16 EU Sustainability Regulation 2020/852 and recitals 42 and 48.

[38]Cf. below 5.6.2, on reasonable certainty 7.4.2, 7.6.3 (with Adolf Berle) and 7.7.

guided by the scientific insights of the concrete economic situation according to the stipulations of the law.

## 4.3 Corporate Climate Change: Reflections and Roadmap

### *4.3.1 Squaring the Circle?*

We may put on record: The whole issue is fundamentally laid out with the Paris Agreement in the European Green Deal, while still appearing in need of clarification and politically dynamic. Groundbreaking, on request of the General Assembly of the United Nations, the International Court of Justice gives advice on environmental and human rights protection as international law.[39] The dimensions are indeed world-spanning, but the wheel does not need to be reinvented. For the necessary climate protection, which must be scientifically proven,[40] it is basically about a common human goal: justice and peace in an order of assets (*Vermögensordnung*), for reasonably the basis is peace under the law (*Rechtsfrieden*); in this, the human being acts as entrepreneur with a modern capital-economic practice (see chapter 8: global order of assets). Accordingly, what is required for the necessary balance of human beings, the economy and the environment is a new, more cooperative and substantially informed thinking and acting (see Fig. 4.4, chapter 9 on complementarity).

In general, a "climate change" is literally necessary by reason, in particular through rethinking, in fact a corporate climate change with the human corporation (see 8.2). This must be established in the law, generally in a valuation law, in order to be able to valuate the corporations (projects) in a sustainable way. Resources can be sensibly optimised with scientific excellence and human measure. The capital markets influence the governance, financing and valuation of the corporation (function of capital steering, see 4.2.4), whereas the field remains to be newly developed and worked on in legal comparison: sustainable, id est at the same time actually verifiable.[41] For legal practice, it must be taken into account that the qualification "sustainable", in colourful ("socio-ecological") terms, basically means a differentiation into "good" (*Gut*, positive) and "evil" (*Böse*, negative). Overall, it is reasonably the search for justice (*Gerechtigkeit*) – in the knowledge of one's own limitation. In a regulatory sense, this is about the human relationship of economy and the law, encompassing technology as an essential part and motor of the economy

[39] Overall ICJ, Advisory Opinion: Obligation of states in respect of climate change, 23.07.2025, (https://www.icj-cij.org/sites/default/files/case-related/187/187-20250723-adv-01-00-en.pdf, accessed: 22.08.2025), and on that in more detail see above 1.2, below 6.1.1.

[40] See below 4.2.5.

[41] From a regulatory perspective, see below 4.11.4 and 5.2.4. Note also EU Sustainability Regulation 2020/852, recital 35.

(man and machine, see 3.8, 6.2.3). This becomes particularly obvious with the accompanying digital transformation (see 9.6).

Thus the triad "human being (*Mensch*), economy (*Wirtschaft*) and environment (*Umwelt*)" opens up into global economy and geopolitics. For the international and European order, this also addresses so-called "social" functions and thus – besides economy and environment – social issues as the third dimension of sustainability.[42] This includes the universe of human rights, e.g., in particular the rights of employees (*Arbeitnehmerrechte*). In general, human rights, valid globally in the United Nations as international law, form the basis of valuation (cf. the Charter of Fundamental Rights of the European Union). What comes into the foreground is the "philosophy of human affairs" (Aristotle), the "life in the midst of life" (Albert Schweitzer) as the principle of reasonableness (see 1.1, 1.4.2). This leads to the Juridical Analysis of the Economy, anchored in civil law and international law, to the law as practised ethics – in the German original: *Das Recht als praktizierte Ethik.*[43] – The world is drawing together.

### 4.3.2 "California Dreaming" or Some Basic Perspectives

Climate change demands a change of thought for the humans on earth. Among nations, equality and responsibility are part of international law. The Paris Agreement of 2015 on climate protection legally binds[44] all treaty states to reduce climate-polluting gases through ambitious Nationally Determined Contributions (so-called decarbonisation). It is recognised that action is needed in the sense of justice and the common, but different responsibilities and capabilities, also through transfer of technology and finances (see 4.2.2). Indeed it is about the respective capabilities (*Fähigkeiten, Vermögen*), materially as well as practically, in order to protect the earth and humans. Overall, the human rights to life, health and a clean environment apply. Contrary interests move into the background. – A human dream? – A start has been made.

Reason demands appropriate thinking and acting. Jurisprudence as the means of a free business practice ordered sensibly with transparency and strong control. What remains remarkable in view of the environment-related standardisation and regulation, globally and in particular in the European Union, is this: Legally, powerful

[42]Explicitly EU Sustainability Regulation 2020/852, recital 2. On this Art. 2 No. 14, Art. 20 sec. 1 c) and sec. 2 j), Art. 26 sec. 2 b) EU Sustainability Regulation 2020/852. Overall Luttermann (2021). Cf. the Community Charter of Fundamental Social Rights of Workers (1989) and the European Social Charter (1961).

[43]See e.g., above 1.2, below 8.1, 9.1, 9.8. Fundamentally Luttermann (1998) pp. 139-144 and 465-485, Luttermann (2010a).

[44]See reaffirming this and in details: ICJ, Advisory Opinion: Obligation of states in respect of climate change, 23.07.2025, (https://www.icj-cij.org/sites/default/files/case-related/187/187-20250723-adv-01-00-en.pdf, accessed: 22.08.2025) para. 457, and reasons.

valuation structures evolve for assets, enterprises and the economy as a whole: climate risk as financial risk. This may lead. How far do our knowledge and power of cognition go? How is it for the investments wanted for research and development as well as for the use of new so-called "green" technology with impact analysis and degrees of risk (valuation, management, auditing), where investors are addressed? For the determination of sustainability, in European law "a business activity counts as ecologically sustainable", if it in fact fulfills four dimensions according to Article 3 EU Sustainability Regulation 2020/852. – A wide field, uncharted waters (*terra incognita*): new ground?

Historical insight holds, especially as the devastating world debt crisis with its causes and social dislocations still continues far and wide. Witnessing the events surrounding the collapse of the investment bank Lehmann Brothers., Inc. in 2008 as a visiting professor at UC Berkeley was a strange coincidence: in the Californian light, a dozen years earlier, I had researched basics and weaknesses in corporate finance and financial theory, valuation and the so-called "standard setting" for financial reporting ("U.S. GAAP"), which were now dramatically materialised worldwide.[45] Since then, it should be clear, that corporate finance, valuation and accounting (financial reporting, auditing: see 3.5.5, 4.9) is a core area of the law (*Bilanzrecht*), the documented proof of good corporate governance, at the same time procedurally as well as materially about the sustainable valuation of assets and companies in general (see 4.10.2 and chapter 5). Therefore, at the international level, the subject has to be further developed in legal comparison.[46] However, it is still, widely thought of not as a branch of the law, but rather as an economic domain for the production of so-called "profit".[47]

This is confirmed in practice, ultimately by the numerous accounting scandals that have been uncovered since the turn of the millennium, following Enron, WorldCom etc. right up until the present (e.g., BT Group, Kraft Heinz Co., NMC Health plc, Manitex International Inc., Wirecard AG).[48] – Who's next? – The world financial crisis, id est the world debt crisis (*Weltschuldenkrise*), the more so as it is still ongoing, shows dramatically how deficient and rotten the system and practice of the financing (i.e., the valuation and reporting) of companies is, especially in the stock markets (*Börsen*). Where the players, especially the "sophisticated" ones, lack the necessary sense of responsibility (ethos) and no referee blows his whistle, greed and abuse will reign.[49] Of course, auditors are essentially part of the game. The Financial Times reported that an industry tribunal fined KPMG its highest ever UK

[45] Publications in German, e.g., Luttermann (1998): a study on the basics of corporation finance and international capital markets law (incl. financial reporting) and Luttermann (1999a) with additional perspectives on group accounting (*Konzernrechnungslegung*). See overall also chapter 6.

[46] See below 4.4.1 and chapters 8 and 9. Basically Luttermann (1999e).

[47] Luttermann (1997). Basically Luttermann (2003a) and (2004), Luttermann (2006). Similarly on the "numbers game" Levitt (1998), see below 4.6.1.

[48] See esp. on Wirecard below 4.9.4 and overall chapters 6 and 7.

[49] See Luttermann (2010a) and below chapter 6.

fine (2022: £14.4mn) "for deliberately misleading the UK regulator during inspections of its audits" of collapsed multinational construction company Carillion plc; the Financial Conduct Authority (FCA) insisted: "Stop complaining about audit fines and improve your work".[50] – It is about an ongoing struggle (see 4.6.4, 4.9).

While such players accumulate large profits – or better: sham gains – in a short time into their private purse, gigantic losses are, in the final instance, socialised through government support: at the expense of the citizens (tax-payers, savers) as the real "lender of last resort"; a gigantic transfer of wealth (assets) worldwide that has to be recognised and solved as a whole (see 4.8). Britain's National Audit Office resumed on the FCA, regulating 50,000 financial services firms and financial markets in the UK: "The FCA is attempting a significant amount of change, on a number of fronts, all at the same time. This brings risks."[51] – Of course, representatives of the law and other couleur are also involved. The phalanx of actors, if players like in Mozart's Magic Flute (see 3.1) or others in the great theater of life, seems almost limitless. This recalls common characteristics in courts and theaters, and imitates Shakespeare's attitude towards drama, as described by Peter Ackroyd: "In dreams nothing is real, nothing is burdened with responsibility, nothing has meaning".[52] But here, it is about means of "rational intelligence",[53] the constitution of liberty (see 1.4.1), isn't it?

Markets of a civil society are based on faithful accounting (financial reporting, see Fig. 4.3): *Bilanzwahrheit* ("a true and fair view") for private entrepreneurship and the community (*res publica*). It stands for individual responsibility (see chapter 7) without which there is no enduring freedom nor prosperity. This is emphasised by the Paris Agreement of 2015 as the framework of international law: It is intended to improve the global reaction to the threat by climate changes, together with sustainable development also for the abolishment of poverty, in a coordinated way.[54] Holistic thinking is the guiding principle of the legal analysis of the economy, which comprises the environment and technology:[55] A sound framework for the promotion of sustainable investments for humans and the environment demands systematic, interdisciplinary development, no fragmentary work (casuistics).[56]

---

[50] Sir Jon Thompson, FCA chief executive, reports, 03.08.2022 by FT (Michael O'Dwyer, https://www.ft.com › content › ac6cce71-aaf2-485b-b8b9-bbe701dd7414, accessed: 22.08.2025). See also below 4.6.4 (on FCA) and chapter 7. Note overall Vagts (2009), Eisenberg (2005) on the adequate regulation of financial information (p. 177: "independent outside auditor"), on the juridical analysis of the economy see below 7.3.2.

[51] National Audit Office, Report: Value for Money, 08.12.2023: https://www.nao.org.uk/reports/financial-services-regulation-adapting-to-change/ (accessed: 14.7.2025).

[52] Ackroyd (2007) p. 240.

[53] Ibid.

[54] See above in 1.4.2, 2.1 and 2.2.

[55] See, e.g., 1.6.2, 7.3.2 and 7.4. Fundamentally Luttermann (1998) pp. 465-485 and Luttermann (2010a).

[56] See above 3.5.5 and 4.2.4. Luttermann (2021) 191, 195-196.

### 4.3.3 Progress: Let There Be More Light

The global climate change thus requires sharpening one's view even more. So we continue our journey through the world of corporations, now to highlight the basics of real financial reporting (*Rechnungslegung*, accountability), id est verified information for investors; this holistically includes the audit (*Prüfung*), which is holistically related to financial reporting (*Rechnungslegung*). The focus is comparatively on the European Union with Germany and the international legal environment (esp. U.S. GAAP/IFRS). Corporate governance, finance and valuation, id est financial reporting (accounting, auditing), due to its evolution, is largely coined interculturally (transnationally). This remains necessary in order to shape it for the good,[57] the more so as the concept stood the test of time and is even corroborated through the epochal turn of the economy towards humans and the environment – truly sustainable.[58]

Let there be more light. This denotes creation and science[59] as well as our objective, to establish the human corporation through sustainable finance and financial reporting (auditing), id est based on facts instead of fictions (real disclosure, see 3.3.3). In this comprehensive sense, the legal concept of "accounting as the documentary proof of good corporate governance" was developed[60] and is reaffirmed here. The approach includes the substantive civil-procedural concept of company valuation as a legal act of sustainable value creation (see chapter 5). It stands for individual responsibility and freedom. The unity of these two, inseparable for lasting peace and wealth overall, forms the foundation of economic practice as in thinking and regulation: global climate change for people, investment and capital markets (see chapter 6), complemented by the imperative of personal responsibility and valuation in law and practice (compliance, see chapter 7).

Human corporation is about the future of the planet Earth for us and for generations to come (see chapter 1). In the face of legions of accounting scandals and the ongoing world debt crisis, which are destructively continuing the "history of financial euphoria" (Galbraith), this work is the expression of necessity. Through the basic ethical values embodied in this legal concept, we may gain a future of entrepreneurial freedom, which forms the foundation for general prosperity (civil society). This is guided by the recognition that any legal order is a *Vermögensordnung* (order of assets),[61] which is to be conceived at a global level and established for fair competition and the common good, with private law and

---

[57] See overall chapters 1, 2 and 3.

[58] See 4.2.3, 4.6, 4.10 and 4.11.4. Overall chapters 8, 9 and Luttermann (2003a) as well as (2023a) recitals 17-47.

[59] Cf. Genesis 1.3, the motto of the University of California at Berkeley.

[60] First presented in English in the first edition of du Plessis, Großfeld, Luttermann et al., German corporate governance in international and european context (2007) 177-204 (chapter 7). Basically Luttermann (1998) and (2003a).

[61] See chapter 8 (with footnote 3 on the denotation of "asset", *Vermögen*) and Luttermann (2015a).

international law.[62] We must, in corporate governance in particular, reunite freedom and responsibility for a human corporation. This is a task that applies to and makes demands on everyone. Basically, the human corporation is about a good economy (see 8.3).

This holds true, the more we understand the call for humanity. People, their economy and the environment must be reconciled. We learn about human rights and climate change in their significance for life and prosperity, in a common environment, indeed globally as a community of fate (*Schicksalsgemeinschaft*). One which takes its future into its hands, reasonably, in order to master the challenges. Entrepreneurially, to stay in our image, as a venture community (*Wagnisgemeinschaft*).[63] With the corporation, reasonably understood and made use of in its financing function (see chapters 1 to 3), an essential element of a sustainable solution. This cooperatively leads to climate partnership for a global *Vermögensordnung* (see chapter 8) in complementarity (see chapter 9). Therefore, we continue with a key question of good corporate governance: What is financial reporting all about?

## 4.4 Financial Reporting: Accounting Law (*Bilanzrecht*)[64]

### *4.4.1 Accountability*

Accounting is simply a means of reporting about "other people's money". This phrase, well known as the title of Louis D. Brandeis' book from 1914 about misuses of corporations and markets,[65] is still at the core of today's corporate governance standards. Since ancient times,[66] accounting has been the figural expression of accountability (financial reporting, see Fig. 4.2). "Account" (from Latin *accomp[u]tare*) means to give a counting, a reckoning of something (e.g. money). In German, such an action is called *Rechenschaft geben* ("to give account") or *Rechnung legen* ("to render account").[67] The noun is *Rechnungslegung* ("accounting"), which is semantically equivalent to "financial reporting", from Old French *raport* and Latin *reportare* (see 2.4.2).

It should be noted at the outset that it is those responsible for directing and managing the business of the corporation (corporate directors) who are collectively

---

62 Basically Luttermann (2015c). See continuative chapters 8 and 9.

63 Synonymously: risk community, cf. above 3.5.4.

64 See Luttermann (2003a), Großfeld and Luttermann (2005).

65 On other people's money and how the bankers use it, Brandeis (1914), see already above, e.g. 3.3.3.

66 Mattessich (1995) pp. 15–40, Luttermann (1996b).

67 The basic description in German civil law is § 666 *Bürgerliches Gesetzbuch* (BGB): *"Der Beauftragte ist verpflichtet, dem Auftraggeber die erforderlichen Nachrichten zu geben, auf Verlangen über den Stand des Geschäfts Auskunft zu erteilen und nach der Ausführung des Auftrags Rechenschaft abzulegen."*

**Fig. 4.2** Accountability of corporate directors

responsible for the financial statements (accounts) of a corporation. The decisive European Accounting Law Directive (2013/34/EU)[68] explicitly states in Article 33 under the heading "Responsibility and liability for drawing up and publishing the financial statements and the management report":

> "1. Member States [like Germany, the author] shall ensure that the members of the administrative, management and supervisory bodies of an undertaking, acting within the competences assigned to them by national law, have collective responsibility for ensuring that:
> (a) the annual financial statements, the management report and, when provided separately, the corporate governance statement; and
> (b) the consolidated financial statements, the consolidated management reports and, when provided separately the consolidated corporate governance statement,
>
> are drawn up and published in accordance with the requirements of this Directive and, where applicable, with the international accounting standards adopted in accordance with Regulation (EC) No 1606/2002.
>
> 2. Member States shall ensure that their laws, regulations and administrative provisions on liability, at least towards the undertaking, apply to the members of the administrative, management and supervisory bodies of the undertakings for breach of the duties referred to in paragraph 1."

[68] Directive 2013/34/EU, 26.06.2013, on the annual financial statements, consolidated financial statements and related reports of certain types of undertakings, amending Directive 2006/43/EC and repealing Council Directives 78/660/EEC and 83/349/EEC, OJ of 29.6.2013, L 182/19, as amended (16.12.2022). See on the – corresponding – old law in du Plessis, Großfeld, Luttermann et al. (2012) p. 279. About sanctions see 4.9.7. Directive 2013/34/EU amended, including by the Directive (EU) 2024/1306, 29.04.2024.

The joint responsibility of the members of the administrative, management and supervisory bodies for drawing up and publishing annual or consolidated financial statements and management reports is termed the "minimum requirement" (*Mindestanforderung*): The member states may go further and introduce "direct responsibility to shareholders or even other stakeholders". In any case the bodies mentioned act within the competencies assigned to them by the national law of the respective member state.[69] European law thus affirms the responsibility of the executives of a company ("undertaking" – *Unternehmen*, consider 4.7).

This is to be seen within the context of German company law, in particular with regard to personal responsibility and duty of care of the board members (see 4.4, chapter 7). Germany adheres to a two-tier board system for the *Aktiengesellschaft* (AG, publicly held corporation):[70] a supervisory board (*Aufsichtsrat*) and a management board (*Vorstand*). The legal representatives of the *Aktiengesellschaft* are the members of the management board. They have to comply with the German Act on Public Limited Companies of 1965 (*Aktiengesetz* 1965, AktG) and with the German Commercial Code (*Handelsgesetzbuch*, HGB). They are responsible for the bookkeeping (*Buchführung*; § 91 *AktG*) as well as for the annual accounts/financial statements (*Jahresabschluss*) and the consolidated accounts/consolidated financial statements (*Konzernabschluss*) pursuant to the legal requirements (§§ 264 and 290, 315e HGB). In the course of the scandal of the Wirecard AG, the legislator considerably increased the demands for accounting control and auditing (also with regard to criminal law),[71] to ensure the accuracy of the financial reporting of companies.[72] In order to restore stability and public trust in the markets, the imperative is to tell the truth (see Fig. 4.2 with 4.4.4).

As part of that duty, the members of the management board have to sign the annual financial statements and the consolidated financial statements (§§ 245, 298 (1) HGB).[73] This signature serves as approval for the financial statements and the consolidated statements and is the step required to make them available to others, in other words, authorising them to be made known publicly – with the probative force of a private document (*Privaturkunde*) under German civil procedure law (§ 416 *Zivilprozessordnung* – ZPO; see also 5.5.1 and 5.6.2). The signature may be electronic under current German law.[74] The signing of the documents is a significant

[69] Overall: Directive 2013/34/EU, recital 40. See 4.4 and chapter 7.

[70] See also in practical terms, e.g., below 4.6 (valuation for corporate directors, esp. 4.6.5), 4.7 (company groups) and 4.9 (auditing, control and sanctions). On strategic governance and audit committee 4.12. Basically Luttermann (2003b) and (2001).

[71] See 4.9.5 on the FISG (law for reinforcing the integrity of the financial markets). Basically Luttermann (2012).

[72] Explanatory memorandum, draft law of the Federal Government (*Begründung, Gesetzentwurf der Bundesregierung*), Deutscher Bundestag (German Parliament), Drucksache 19/26966, p. 1 (in A.). See below 4.9.

[73] See also below 5.5.1 and 6.8.2. Overall Luttermann (2003a) § 245 HGB recitals 1-55.

[74] Originally the German *Signaturgesetz*, out of force due to law of 18.07.2017 (BGBl. I p. 2745) with effect from 29.07.2017, replacing: Regulation (EU) No. 910/2014 with German eIDAS-

step as the directors have to give the legally required "picture" (*Bild*) of the corporation, that is, a sustainable statement of the previous business year's corporate governance as a legal act (*Rechtsakt*, i.e.: the documentary proof of – hopefully always – good corporate governance, see 4.9 for safeguarding: auditing, control and sanctions).

As part of the annual financial report, an issuer's statement (*Erklärung*) is required by the persons responsible for the financial statements. The issuer's statement must state that the financial statements give "a true and fair view" (*ein getreues Bild,* i.e. *Bilanzwahrheit* the imperative of truth, see 4.4.4) of the corporation's financial position (so-called *Bilanzeid*).[75] Apart from that, the financial statements can form the basis of a civil claim or government sanctions against the corporation if they do not give "a true and fair view" of the corporation's financial position.[76] The financial statements enable markets and investors to evaluate the corporation, including its shares, bonds and credit standing (rating) generally.[77]

## 4.4.2 A Complete Set of Financial Statements

For a company (*Kapitalgesellschaft*), as a permanent financial instrument in business created by law (see basically 2.5), financial statements are part of its corporate DNA. Principally, there is a complete set of financial statements comprising a balance sheet (*Bilanz*), a profit and loss account (*Gewinn- und Verlustrechnung*, also known as an income statement), and notes (*Anhang* – explanatory supplement). These documents constitute a composite whole (§ 264 (1)(1) *Handelsgesetzbuch* – HGB). An annual review (*Lagebericht*, also known as a directors' financial review) under § 289 of the HGB is also required (§ 264(1)(1) HGB). According to Chapter 5 (Art. 19 and 20) of the Accounting Law Directive 2013/34/EU, it is termed the "management report" in the English version; the so-called "sustainability reporting" of all "public-interest entities" (ex-Art. 19a) has since been reformed.[78]

In the sense of accountability the issue is overall transparency through the disclosure of periodic and ongoing information, which must materially provide "a true and fair view" (§§ 264(2)(1), 289(1) HGB).[79] Capital-market oriented companies (§

---

*Durchführungsgesetz* and *Vertrauensdienstegesetz* (VDG). For electronic disclosure see www.unternehmensregister.de (current, § 325 HGB).

[75] See § 264(2)(3) and § 289(1)(5) HGB, § 114(2) No. 3 and § 115(2) No. 3 WpHG (*Finanzbericht*); note also below 4.9.5. Cf. IAS 1.16 statement of compliance (*Übereinstimmungserklärung*).

[76] See below 4.5 and note 4.8.6–4.8.7.

[77] See below 4.6.1. Luttermann (2011b) p. 330.

[78] See below 4.4.8 and 4.7.1, cf. 4.4.3, 4.8.6.

[79] See 4.4.1 and 4.5. Cf. Art. 1(1) Directive 2004/109/EC, 15.12.2004, on the harmonisation of transparency requirements in relation to information about issuers whose securities are admitted to trading on a regulated market, OJ 31.12.2004, L 390/38, amended, including by Directive (EU) 2023/2864, 13.12.2023.

264d HGB: *kapitalmarktorientierte Kapitalgesellschaften*), for whom it is not mandatory to draw up consolidated accounts (*Konzernabschluss*), have to set up the following extra statements: a cash flow statement (*Kapitalflussrechnung*) and a statement of changes in equity (*Eigenkapitalspiegel*). These documents, together with the balance sheet, the profit and loss account, and the notes, constitute a composite whole (§ 264(1)(2) first half-sentence HGB). Optionally, they may be accompanied by a segment report (*Segmentberichterstattung*, § 264(1)(2), second half-sentence HGB). Large companies – according to rules "on disclosure of non-financial information" – have to publish reports on the social and environmental impacts of their activities (*Nachhaltigkeitsreport*).[80] However, it should be noted: Relevant processes and data generally relate to entrepreneurial financing and, as far as they have a material effect, they belong – predominantly – in the financial statements.[81]

Stock-market corporations as well as corporations that have only issued other securities as shares (bonds, debentures, notes) for trading in an organised market (§ 2(11) *Wertpapierhandelsgesetz* – WpHG) and whose issued shares are traded via a multilateral trading system on their own accord (§ 2(8)(1) No. 8 WpHG) have to include a corporate governance statement (*Erklärung zur Unternehmensführung*) in their management report (§ 289f HGB, Art. 20 Accounting Law Directive 2013/34/EU).[82] Information about environmental concerns (*Umweltbelange*), employee concerns (*Arbeitnehmerbelange*), social concerns (*Sozialbelange*), respect for human rights (*Achtung der Menschenrechte*) and combating corruption and bribery (*Bekämpfung von Korruption und Bestechung*) must be provided in a non-financial statement (*nichtfinanzielle Erklärung*, §§ 289b, 289c HGB). Overall, it is obviously about documentation (see 4.4.8). Under the imperative of truth (*Wahrheitsgebot*, see 3.3.4), the information must be verifiable, id est be in fact truly sustainable.

### *4.4.3 European Law and "IFRS"*

This sustainability is, of course, necessary in particular for a corporation (juridical person) and legally conceived in a procedural way (see 4.10.2, chapter 5) in the European economic hemisphere. German accounting law for corporations is an integral part of the law of the European Union.[83] The member states are bound by

[80] Corporate Sustainability Reporting Directive (CSRD): Directive (EU) 2022/2464 of 14.12.2022, amending Regulation (EU) No 537/2014, Directive 2004/109/EC, Directive 2006/43/EC and Directive 2013/34/EU, as regards corporate sustainability reporting, OJ EU 16.12.2022, L 322/15. See on European Sustainability Reporting Standards (ESRS) EU Commission delegated Regulation (EU) 2023/2772 of 31 July 2023, OJ EU 22.12.2023, L.

[81] See below 4.5.3 and 4.6.5. Basically Luttermann, L. (2022) pp. 810 (I.), 813-815 (IV.).

[82] See for statements on consolidated accounts (*Konzernerklärung*) §§ 315b to 315d HGB.

[83] See below 4.4.6. Großfeld and Luttermann (2005) recitals 7–26.

given standards of the Union laws. Directives (*Richtlinien*) and regulations (*Verordnungen*) are the instruments (see Art. 288 TFEU). Both are directed towards achieving the aims of the Treaty of Rome (1957), complemented especially by the Treaty of Maastricht (1992): to establish a common internal European Union market (internal market, *Binnenmarkt*) with the free movement of persons, goods and services, and capital.[84] That includes the harmonisation of company law and financial reporting (accounting) within the member states.

In order to attain harmonisation focused on freedom of establishment (*Niederlassungsfreiheit*),[85] the European Council has acted by means of directives;[86] some have since been subjected to a reform.[87] Since then there has been an elementary legal basis, the Directive 2013/34/EU of 26 June 2013 on the annual financial statements, consolidated financial statements and related reports of certain types of undertakings (Accounting Law Directive).[88] Their aims are: "facilitating cross-border investment and improving Union-wide comparability and public confidence in financial statements and reports through enhanced and consistent specific disclosures".[89] That is a reaction to enduring practices of far-reaching accounting irregularities and catastrophic conditions in the balances revealed by the world debt crisis. Good corporate disclosure, accompanied by good audits, is elementary here (see 4.9). In order to reach this aim, the national provisions are coordinated "concerning the presentation and content of annual financial statements and management reports, the measurement bases used therein and their publication in respect of certain types of undertakings with limited liability".[90]

As the legal explication (*ratio legis*) goes on to say, this is particularly important in order to protect the shareholders, members and third parties in such companies (types of undertakings) that provide no safeguards to third parties beyond the amounts of their net assets (companies with limited liability, *Kapitalgesellschaften*) which operate in more than one member state.[91] The provisions for determination and valuation in financial reporting (valuation law) and the disclosure obligation are set as a correlate for the privilege of entrepreneurial action in a – basically – liability-restricting legal form (see § 1(1)(2) AktG). The accounting legislation of the Union, thus the directive emphasises, "needs to strike an appropriate balance between the interests of the addressees of financial statements and the interest of undertakings in

---

[84] Treaty on the European Union, Art. 3 No. 3. Treaty on the Functioning of the European Union (TFEU) Art. 26.

[85] TFEU Art. 50(2)(g) and 54 (ex-EC Treaty, Art. 44(2)(g) and 48).

[86] Legal basis: TFEU Art. 288(3); ex-EC Treaty Art. 249(3).

[87] On the preparation of the reform already in the 2nd ed (2012) p. 281 (footnote 27); there are also references on the earlier legal foundations.

[88] Amending Directive 2006/43/EC of the European Parliament and of the Council and repealing Council Directives 78/660/EEC and 83/349/EEC, OJ of 29.6.2013, L 182/19. Overview on that law: Luttermann (2013). See also below 4.5.5 and 4.9.3.

[89] Directive 2013/34/EU, recital 55.

[90] Directive 2013/34/EU, recital 3.

[91] Ibid.

not being unduly burdened with reporting requirements".[92] The guiding idea is overall the main goal (*die Hauptzielsetzung*) of European law: Accounting as a legal act under the principle of "a true and fair view" (*Bilanzwahrheit*, see 4.4.4).

According to global financial markets, the European Union is applying international accounting standards. Accounting Law Regulation (EC) 1606/2002[93] prepares the Union for the so-called "International Accounting Standards" (IAS), renamed as "International Financial Reporting Standards" (IFRS). It may reinforce the freedom of movement of capital in the internal market and help to enable EU companies to compete on an equal footing for financial resources worldwide. IFRS should, providing that they ensure a high degree of quality, transparency and comparability for financial reporting in the Union,[94] be made obligatory for all publicly-traded EU companies. The regulation aims to protect investors, to maintain confidence in the financial markets in the "post-Enron era", and to contribute to the efficient and cost-effective functioning of the capital markets and the internal market. We can put on record that under the Accounting Law Regulation (EC) 1606/2002 generally "international accounting standards" can be adopted (not only the so-called "IFRS/IAS") if they fulfill the legal standards (see 4.4.4); this also applies to international sustainability disclosure standards (see 4.8.8).

In 2014, the Commission had the goal to harmonise financial reporting of listed companies through accounting law regulation, evaluated from the perspective of stakeholders under the criteria effectiveness, efficiency, relevance, coherence and EU added value. It came to the conclusion: "The key findings showed that the objectives of the Regulation have been met".[95] This seems a questionable assessment in view of the narrow data basis and overwhelming shortcomings in practice – in the past and in the meantime also up to the present, proven by numerous accounting scandals such as Wirecard AG and the ongoing regulatory debate (see 4.4.2). It is significant that the Commission itself has already suggested grave improvements, e.g. for the quality of the "IFRS", the IFRS Foundation's funding and decision-making process (incl. the Monitoring Board, see 4.4.4), a simplification of legislation and coherence, an endorsement process (EFRAG, ESMA) and governance arrangements (matters of public interest, principle of prudence; cf. 4.11.4, 3. 3.4). This confirms the following essential point.

---

[92] Directive 2013/34/EU, recital 4. See generally on the privilege of limited liability for corporations above 3.4.1, 3.4.4 and 3.6.4.

[93] On the application of international accounting standards see (2002) OJ L 243/1 (also called: "IAS Regulation". Legal basis for the regulation (*Verordnung*) is Art. 288(2) TFEU (ex-Art. 249(2) of the EC Treaty). See Großfeld and Luttermann (2005) recitals 146–68.

[94] In detail below 4.4.5.

[95] EU Commission, Evaluation of Regulation (EC) No 1606/2002, COM(2015) 301 final, 18.06.2015, p. 10 (No 4.); on this: Commission Staff Working Document, SWD(2015) 120 final. Cf. European Parliament, Report on IAS, IFRS, EFRAG, and PIOB (A8-0172/2016: https://www.europarl.europa.eu/doceo/document/A-8-2016-0172_EN.html, accessed: 14.7.2025).

### 4.4.4 The Imperative of Truth (General Rule) and Conflict of Laws

The principle of a true and fair view (*Grundsatz der Bilanzwahrheit* – the imperative of truth, see 4.4) has to take precedence in every case, including that over aspects of efficiency. The European Union is permitted to adopt international standards of financial reporting only if they are in line with the legal requirements of the Accounting Law Regulation (EC) 1606/2002 Article 3(2). This regulation says that the "international accounting standards can only be adopted if:

- they are not contrary to the principle set out in Article 2(3) of Directive 78/660/EEC and in Article 16(3) of Directive 83/349/EEC [now: Art. 4(3) and – for consolidated financial statements – in conjunction with Art. 24(1) of Directive 2013/34/EU][96] and are conducive to the European public good and,
- they meet the criteria of understandability, relevance, reliability and comparability required of the financial information needed for making economic decisions and assessing the stewardship of management."

Article 4(3) of Accounting Law Directive 2013/34/EU lays down for the European Union the principle of a true and fair view (i.e., the imperative of truth – *Bilanzwahrheit*) as "the primary objective" of financial reporting (accounting, *Hauptziel*, see 4.6.3). This is confirmed by reform legislation: In full knowledge of established case law of the European Court of Justice the general rule of accounting was taken over unchanged into the Directive 2013/34/EU (see overall 4.5.2 and Fig. 4.4). This is the legal measure of all accounting according to European law, that is, including financial statements according to the so-called "IFRS", which have been adopted in the European Union. The principle of "a true and fair view" (*Grundsatz der Bilanzwahrheit und Bilanzklarheit*)[97] and "the European public good" (*das europäische öffentliche Interesse*) form the basis of European accounting law (cf. 4.10.1).

This marks its significance. As the epitome of the law of financial reporting and auditing, id est the law of valuation (see chapter 5), the complete internal market of the European Union is encompassed as a legal area. The phrase "European public good" is described as "the idea of a shared commitment to the pursuit of a common sense of what is good for a self-recognised collective".[98] This means that in the

---

[96] According to Accounting Law Directive 2013/34/EU, Art. 52: (1) Directives 78/660/EEC and 83/349/EEC are repealed. (2) References to the repealed directives shall be construed as references to this directive and shall be read in accordance with the correlation table in Annex VII.

[97] On clarity (*Klarheit*) above 4.5.5 and 4.8.2; also in practical terms, e.g., 4.5.3, 4.6.4 and 4.6.5, 4.12.1. Basically on the imperative of truth (*Bilanzwahrheit* and *Bilanzklarheit*) as the general rule of accounting and auditing Luttermann (2003a) §§ 243, 342 HGB recitals 7-10, 11-25 (*Bilanzwahrheit*) and 73-80 (*Bilanzklarheit*). Overall Luttermann (2003a) annotation of § 264 HGB.

[98] Walker (2020) p. 2.

multilingual setting of the Union it is about the common values and goals (Art. 2, 3 TEU), namely justice, peace and prosperity:[99] legally transmitted in the sense of "a true and fair view" (*Bilanzwahrheit*), essential in practicing financial reporting and auditing. This is shown by the Commission of the European Union in its critique of the amendment for the IFRS Foundation Due Process Handbook (2019 ED): it "does not fully meet the expectation expressed by the European Commission as a member of the Monitoring Board as it may not sufficiently bridge the gap between the limited scope of the IASB's impact assessment and the endorsement criteria of the European Public Good set out in [Accounting Law Regulation (EC) 1606/2002 Art. 3(2)]".[100] This at the same time corroborates fundamental deficits of the "IFRS" (see 4.4.5).

Overall, the following needs to be clarified: The general rule internationally is thus a conflict of laws (*Kollisionsnorm*).[101] It works like the *ordre public* in the national domain of International Private Law (e.g., see in Germany Art. 6 *Einführungsgesetz zum Bürgerlichen Gesetzbuch,* EGBGB). Correspondingly, in the Accounting Law Regulation (EC) 1606/2002, the term "the European public good" is laid down. Applied correctly, the *Kollisionsnorm* should provide protection from international (foreign) accounting regulations running counter to the European legal order ("the European public good", Art. 3(2) of Accounting Law Regulation (EC) 1606/2002), which is ethically founded and mandatory. This also applies to the excessive transfer of wealth (assets) through so-called "international standards" of valuation and accounting, such as the "IFRS" (see below 4.8, esp. 4.8.6).

### 4.4.5 IASB/IFRS: Lack of Legitimacy and of Quality

The objections to IASB are elementary, just as the accompanying deficits of the "IFRS". This criticism continues, as do the deficiencies, which are by now legion, and it is also adduced here, in view of its significance for necessary reforms.[102] The European Parliament has commented unequivocally on the IASB as a standard setter and on the "IFRS". Remember, in its report of 5 February 2008, it demands, with a view to the IASB and its supervision body, the IASCF,[103] "that governance and

[99] Luttermann, C. and Luttermann, K. (2021).

[100] EU Commission, Report to the EU Parliament and the Council on the activities of the IFRS-Foundation, EFRAG and PIOB in 2018, 29.10.2019 (COM 2019) 549 final, pp. 4-5. Accordingly EU Commission, Fitness Check on the EU framework for public reporting companies, SWD(2021) 81 final, 21.04.2021, p. 7. Cf. in general, e.g., EU Commission, Report to the EU Parliament and the Council on the activities of the IFRS Foundation, EFRAG and PIOB in 2023, 13.11.2024, COM (2024) 528 final. Cf. Bensadon and Praquin (2016), Palea (2018).

[101] Seminally Luttermann (2010d) 346, 354.

[102] See also, e.g., below 4.11 with chapters 8 and 9.

[103] International Accounting Standards Committee Foundation, renamed: "IFRS Foundation", a not-for-profit corporation under the General Corporation Law of the State of Delaware (USA).

accountability must be improved".[104] The Parliament also decrees "that the IASCF is a private self-regulatory body which has been given the role of lawmaker in the European Union by virtue of Regulation (EC) No 1606/2002". That is not covered by European Law. It seems all the more questionable as the report presented to the Parliament, here provided in its English version, goes on to emphasise:

> "[the EP] acknowledges some concerns about the fact that the IASCF/IASB may lack transparency and accountability as a consequence of not being under the control of any democratically elected government, the EU institutions not having established the accompanying procedures and practices as regards consultation and democratic decision-making that are usual in their own legislative procedures."[105]

The (original) German version of the report, presented by the German rapporteur Alexander Radwan, is sharper in its essence. The European Parliament has adopted this into its resolution, which states: "Parliament underlines that the IASCF/IASB lack transparency, legitimacy, accountability and are not under the control of any democratically elected parliament or government."[106] However, deficiencies still remain,[107] structurally basic and encompassing the whole: What about democratically required legitimacy, transparency, accountability and control? – This should be remembered when talking about the so-called "IFRS" in general and in particular in the domain of the European Union (see 4.8).

In the European Parliament, great deficits of the "IFRS" with regard to democracy, financial market stability and common interest orientation are still addressed: What is demanded is a stronger participation of the parliament in the process of standard setting; the criticism also covers the complexity of the "IFRS" and the performance hitherto of the privately organised European Financial Reporting Advisory Group (EFRAG), prominently involved in the process of standard setting. Research suggests that "a single voice for Europe is not likely to be attained".[108] This is part of the discourse on the position and function of the European Union in the framework of international financial, monetary and regulatory institutions.[109] This is corroborated – before Brexit and still valid in its meaning – by the British Parliamentary Commission on Banking Standards. This marks the "IFRS" in the Report "Changing Banking for Good" as inconsistent with the mandate of truth and ineffectual for regulation purposes. The prominently staffed Commission

[104] European Parliament (EP), A6–0032/2008 (Radwan Report) No 8.

[105] EP, A6–0032/2008 (Radwan Report) No 2.

[106] EP non-legislative resolution (INI/2006/2248: 24/04/2008, see: www.europarl.europa.eu/sides/getDoc.do?type=TA&reference=P6-TA-2008-0183&language=EN, accessed: 22.08.2025).

[107] See also 4.4.4 with 4.8.6 and 4.8.7 (comparative law, linguistics), 4.10 (legal protection) and 4.12 (world monopoly). Cf. the IASB/IFRS Foundation on governance enhancements, current: www.ifrs.org. De Luca, Prather-Kinsey (2018).

[108] In search of a single voice Mourik and Walton (2018).

[109] Basically: ECON, Report on the EU role in the framework of international financial, monetary and regulatory institutions and bodies (2015/2060 (INI)), 17.03.2016 (so-called "Goulard Report"). Cf. Crawford, Ferguson, Power, and Helliar Power (2014).

recommends: "to create a separate set of accounts for regulators according to specified, prudent principles set by the regulator."[110] A clear verdict.

What is of particular importance is the European Securities and Markets Authority (ESMA), whose guidelines are to promote the consistent application of "IFRS" and extend the convergence of enforcement practices across the European Union.[111] The topic is increasingly addressed. For example, in the name of the (former) EU-Commissioner Michel Barnier, the Maystadt Report investigated the following question: Should IFRS-Standards be more "European"?[112] – There is worldwide research, as numerous publications demonstrate.[113] This shows the influence of the G20 on the "IFRS", institutional and also personal involvement in the realm of the "IFRS" as well as grievous deficiencies in "due process" (of law, cf. *Rechtsstaatsprinzip*).[114] Even the EU-Commission sees the necessity for reform in the interest of the European public.[115]

Special attention should be given to the intention of establishing a world monopoly of the valuation of companies (assets) with the "IFRS": beyond democratic legitimation and control through the digitalisation of financial communication (see 4.12, 8.3). This is all the more true under the mandate of sustainability. On the occasion of the UN World Climate Conference 2021, the IFRS Foundation Trustees, the private repository of the so-called "IFRS" announced the implementation of an "International Sustainability Standards Board" (ISSB), in order to launch relevant publicity rules: the original and actual business model of the private organisation, "a world valuation monopoly" is to be expanded and completed.[116] The problems are manifold.

---

[110] Fifth Report, 19.06.2013: https://publications.parliament.uk/pa/jt201314/jtselect/jtpcbs/27/27ii.pdf, p. 463 (No 1039, accessed: 22.08.2025). See also below in 4.5.4.

[111] ESMA, Guidelines on enforcement of financial information, 2014/1293. Cf. ESMA, Guidelines on Alternative Performance Measures, 2015/1415. Homepage: www.esma.europa.eu.

[112] Philippe Maystadt, Should IFRS-Standards be more "European"? – Mission to reinforce the EU's contribution to the development of international accounting standards, October 2013. Cf. EU Commission, Fitness Check on the EU framework for public reporting companies, SWD(2021) 81 final, 21.04.2021, pp. 4-7 (key findings).

[113] Basically below 4.5.3. Cf. Amisi (2013), Bamber and McMeeking (2016), Crawford, Helliar, and Power (2016), Sanada (2012). Raffournier (2014) 281, 294-298.

[114] Wingard, Bosman, and Amisi (2016). See also below 4.10.3. Cf. on multi-functionaries ("shadow elite") in 6.5.3.

[115] EU-Commission, Report on IFRS-Foundation, EFRAG and PIOB in 2018, 29.10.2019 (COM 2019) 549 final, pp. 4-5. Cf. EU Commission, Report to the EU Parliament and the Council on the activities of the IFRS Foundation, EFRAG and PIOB in 2023, 13.11.2024, COM(2024) 528 final.

[116] Two more lobby organisations are included as of June 2022: the so-called Climate Disclosure Standards Board (CDSB) and the so-called Value Reporting Foundation (VRF with Integrated Reporting Framework and SASB Standards); see generally: https://www.ifrs.org/news-and-events/news/2021/11/ifrs-foundation-announces-issb-consolidation-with-cdsb-vrf-publication-of-prototypes/, accessed, 22.08.2025). See below 4.11.

### 4.4.6 German and European Law (“IFRS”)

Germany, as a member state of the European Union, is subject to European law, which is governed by the principle of conferral (*Grundsatz der begrenzten Einzelermächtigung*) in accordance with the principles of subsidiarity (*Prinzip der Subsidiarität*) and proportionality (*Prinzip der Verhältnismäßigkeit*).[117] This law must be observed, transposed and enforced (see 4.9.3, 4.10.3). The Accounting Law Regulation (EC) 1606/2002 is binding in its entirety and directly applicable in all member states.[118]

Therefore, consolidated accounts of publicly-traded companies for each financial year starting on or after 1 January 2005 are to be prepared in conformity with the “IFRS” adopted by the European Community.[119] Meanwhile, the European Community has adopted most of the so-called “International Financial Reporting Standards” (International Accounting Standards).[120] The treatment of financial instruments (IAS 39 – recognition and measurement) shows some omissions, where some rules of “IAS/IFRS” have not been adopted in the European Union.[121] Remember: The accounting of financial instruments according to “IAS/IFRS” and U.S. “GAAP” (so-called “toxic assets”) is among the fundamental problems of the financial industry (world debt crisis etc.) and demands a solution.[122]

The member states have options in relation to annual accounts (annual financial statements, also separate financial statements, *Einzelabschluss*), and whether or not the standards should apply to non-publicly traded companies. They may permit or require companies to prepare their annual and/or consolidated accounts in conformity with the adopted “IFRS”.[123] The German legislature has partly adopted those options in relation to companies.[124] Note, however, that a German company

[117] See TEU Art. 5(1) with (2) to (4), and Accounting Law Directive 2013/34/EU, recital 1.

[118] TFEU Art. 288(2)(2) (ex-EC Treaty, Art 249).

[119] Accounting Law Regulation (EC) 1606/2002 Art. 4; § 315e HGB. Effective (April 2011): Commission Reg (EU) No 149/2011 of 18 February 2011 amending Reg (EC) No 1126/2008 adopting certain international accounting standards in accordance with Reg (EC) 1606/2002, OJ L 46, 19.02.2011, p. 1. Cf. Pereira and do Céu Gaspar Alves (2017).

[120] Overview: Commission Regulation (EU) 2023/1803 of 13.08.2023 adopting certain international accounting standards in accordance with Regulation (EC) No 1606/2002, OJ EU 26.09.2023, L 237/1.

[121] IAS 39 (2004) recitals 9b, 35 and 81A: fair value option and hedge accounting. See Commission Reg (EC) No 1864/2005 of 15.11.2005 (resolving the fair value option carve-out). IAS Regulation, implementing and delegated acts, see: https://finance.ec.europa.eu/regulation-and-supervision/financial-services-legislation/implementing-and-delegated-acts/international-accounting-standards-regulation_en (accessed: 22.08.2025).

[122] See 4.6.1 and 4.6.3. Cf. IFRS 9 (Financial Instruments), effective date in the EU: 01.01.2018, Accounting Regulatory Committee (ARC, 27.06.2016). Cf. Commission Regs (EU) No 1374/2013 (IAS 36) and 1375/2013 (IAS 39) of 19.12.2013.

[123] Accounting Law Regulation (EC) 1606/2002 Art 5. On implementation: https://www.iasplus.com/en/publications/europe/implementation-of-ias-regulation (accessed: 22.08.2025).

[124] § 315e(3) and § 325(2a) HGB.

with limited liability has to provide its legally prescribed annual accounts (*Jahresabschluss*) in accordance with the *Handelsgesetzbuch* (HGB), the German Commercial Code (§§ 264–289 HGB). These and other paragraphs of the HGB transpose the Fourth Council Directive 78/660/EC on the annual accounts of certain types of companies. The company is free to conduct extra reporting according to "IAS/IFRS", that is, a – costly – second set of financial statements.

This regulation preserves the traditional link between commercial law (*Handelsrecht*) and tax law (*Steuerrecht*): generally, the commercial accounts (*Handelsbilanz*) are authoritative (*maßgeblich*) for the tax accounts (*Steuerbilanz*).[125] So the legislature has fixed the key role of the annual accounts – the basis of trading profits – for the taxation and the corporate law of a company.[126] Accordingly, the ECJ has delivered preliminary rulings (*Vorabentscheidungen*), requested, among others, by a German tax court.[127] Overall, a comprehensive treatment of the fundamental significance of the principle of true financial reporting (*Bilanzwahrheit*) as the measure of proof – at the same time also for taxation according to performance capacity (*Leistungsfähigkeit*);[128] this is procedurally and materially borne by the concept of the order of assets (*Vermögensordnung*) that is elementary for any legal order (see 4.10.2).

### 4.4.7 Regulatory Interactions

The Accounting Law Regulation (EC) 1606/2002 is directly applicable to the company drawing up accounts, while Accounting Law Directives apply to companies through their transposition into the national (in this case German) law.[129] In relation to the consolidated accounts (*Konzernabschlüssen*) of listed German companies, this means that in addition to the process of adoption and practice under Article 3(2) of Accounting Law Regulation (EC) 1606/2002 (see 4.4.3–4.5.3), there is an interaction of the German national law (HGB) and the Accounting Law Regulation to the extent that both deal with the same subject matter.

The EU Commission[130] explained that no transposed provision of the Accounting Directives may restrict or hinder a company's compliance or choice under adopted "IASs/IFRSs", further to the Accounting Law Regulation (EC) 1606/2002. So, in

---

[125] § 5(1) *Einkommensteuergesetz* (German Income Tax Code) with § 8(1) *Körperschaftsteuergesetz* (German Corporation Tax Code).

[126] *Deutscher Bundestag* to the *Bilanzrechtsreformgesetz, Bundestags-Drucksache* 15/3419, 24.06.2004, 23–24 (argumentation of the bill).

[127] ECJ, 14.09.1999 (C–275/97 – *DE + ES Bauunternehmung GmbH*, DE) ECR I–5331; ECJ, 07.01.2003 (C–306/99 – *BIAO*, FR) ECR I–1. See Großfeld and Luttermann (2005) recitals 300, 313–316.

[128] Luttermann (2010d).

[129] TFEU Art. 288(2) and (3); ex-EC Treaty, Art. 249(2) and (3).

[130] Comments concerning certain Articles of the Regulation (EC) 1606/2002 (Nov 2003) 10–12.

Germany, a company applies endorsed "IASs/IFRSs" to its consolidated accounts irrespective of any contrary, conflicting or restricting requirements in the national law (e.g. §§ 290–315 HGB). Matters that are outside the scope of the Accounting Law Regulation (EC) 1606/2002, like publication (*Offenlegung*), and audit (*Prüfung*), are subject to national rules by means of the Accounting Directives.[131] member states must ensure that no additional element of national law is contrary to, conflicting with or restricting a company's compliance with the adopted "IFRSs", further to Accounting Law Regulation (EC) 1606/2002 (see 4.4.4, 4.5).

This interaction is the same for unlisted companies that use the option of drawing up accounts according to the adopted "IFRSs"; the relevant rule in Germany for consolidated accounts is § 315e(3) HGB. Drawing up their annual accounts, these companies in Germany must continue to comply with the national accounting requirements derived from the Accounting Directives (e.g. the *Handelsgesetzbuch*, see discussion above in 4.4.1). They then take precedence over any "IASs/ IFRSs". The company is free, however, to draw up a – costly – extra set of annual financial statements to comply with "IFRS" (see 4.4.6).

### *4.4.8 Corporate Governance Statement (Management Report)*

Companies with their registered office in the European Union, whose securities are traded on a "regulated market" of any member state (cf. Directive 2004/39/EC Art. 4(1) point (14), Directive 2014/65/EU Art. 1(1)), are obliged to disclose an annual corporate governance statement (*Erklärung zur Unternehmensführung*) in their management report (*Lagebericht*) as a specific section.[132] One of the main objectives is to strengthen public confidence in financial statements and reports. The management report "shall include a fair review of the development and performance of the undertaking's business and of its position, together with a description of the principal risks and uncertainties that it faces" (Directive 2013/34/EU Art. 19(1)).[133] Information to be provided additionally in terms of sustainability reporting (*Nachhaltigkeitsberichterstattung*, e.g. environmental, social: Directive 2013/34/EU Art. 19a, see §§ 289b, 289c HGB and 4.4.2) leads to the question of whether

[131] See particularly in Germany §§ 315e and 316–335c HGB.

[132] Accounting Law Directive 2013/34/EU Art. 20(1). Cf. previously: Directive 2006/46/EC (2006) OJ L 224/1, Art. 1.7 (Amendment to Directive 78/660/EC, Art. 46a).

[133] On this Directive 2014/95/EU, 22.10.2014, amending Directive 2013/34/EU as regards disclosure of non-financial and diversity information by certain large undertakings and groups, OJ L 330, 15.11.2014, 1. About liability see below 4.9.6.

something that affects the corporation is *not* "financially" relevant at all. In any case, it should be noted that climate risk is in principle a financial risk.[134]

The management report shall include a corporate governance statement (*Erklärung zur Unternehmensführung*, Directive 2013/34/EU Art. 20). That statement shall be included as a specific section of the management report and shall contain, as a minimum, specific information. Among those duties are:

- A reference – where applicable – to (i) the corporate governance code to which the undertaking (company) is subject and (ii) which the undertaking (company) may have voluntarily decided to apply; (iii) all relevant information about the corporate governance practices applied over and above the requirements of national law (Art. 20(1)(a)).
- The extent to which an undertaking (company), in accordance with national law, departs from a corporate governance code referred to under points (a)(i) or (ii), an explanation by the undertaking (company) as to which parts of the corporate governance code (in accordance with national law) it departs from and the reasons for doing so. Where the company has decided not to refer to any provisions of a corporate governance code (see (a)(i) or (ii)), it shall explain its reasons for not doing so (Art. 20(1)(b)).
- A description of the main features of the undertaking's (company's) internal control and risk management systems in relation to the financial reporting process (Art. 20(1)(c)).
- The composition and operation of the administrative, management and supervisory bodies and their committees (Art. 20(1)(f)).[135]

The member states are free to permit that the information required be set out in a separate report published together with the management report or a document publicly available on the undertaking's (company's) website (Directive 2013/34/EU Art. 20(2)).[136] The regulation aims at promoting harmonised, credible financial reporting processes across the European Union. In accounting matters, therefore, it focuses on the members of the company body that are responsible for the preparation of the company's financial reports and the management report (see 4.4.8). Overall the "duty to ensure that the information included in a company's annual accounts

---

[134] See below 4.5.7 (completeness) and basically Luttermann, L. (2022). Cf. Accounting Law Directive 2013/34/EU Art. 19a(3): "references to, and additional explanations of amounts reported in the annual financial statements". Commission Delegated Regulation (EU) 2023/2772 of 31 July 2023 supplementing Directive 2013/34/EU of the European Parliament and of the Council as regards sustainability reporting standards, OJ L EU 22.12.2023. On the financial function of the corporation, e.g., above 1.3.2, 1.4.1 and 2.5.

[135] See Art. 20 Accounting Law Directive 2013/34/EU (cf. Directive 78/660/EC, new Art. 46a(f)) with Directive 2014/95/EU, also on description of the diversity policy applied for administrative, management and supervisory bodies (Art. 20(1)(g)).

[136] For sanctions, see below 4.9.7. Regarding non-financial key performance indicators (e.g., information relating to environmental and employee matters), see Accounting Law Directive 2013/34/EU, Art. 19(1)(3).

and annual reports gives a true and fair view", emphasised earlier already,[137] still applies. So again, we see accounting (financial reporting) and individual responsibility as the epitome of good corporate governance.

## 4.5 Financial Statements: "A True and Fair View"

### *4.5.1 International Focus and Comparative Law*

International financial markets generally call for "international standards" for financial statements. However, it should be noted at the outset that the imaginary concept of "accounting as the international language of finance"[138] is a dangerous phantom. This is comparable to the slating of the "Continental" or "German" style of accounting as "inscrutable",[139] "arcane" or "murky"[140] and to the crushed myth of "U.S. GAAP" (so-called "Generally Accepted Accounting Principles", cf. Pax Americana) as the "investors' best protection".[141] In practice, there are different cultures at work, different languages within so-called "international standards"; we will take a more detailed look at this later (see 4.8.6 to 4.8.7). Nevertheless, there is a common measure of sustainability:[142] the general rule (*Generalnorm*), named the principle of "a true and fair view" (*ein getreues Bild, Bilanzwahrheit*), as will be shown below (see 4.5.2). It should be emphasised again that the European reform legislation has confirmed this principle as the core of the law for financial reporting (accounting) and auditing (the *ratio legis*, see 4.4.4).[143]

Firstly, after the fall of Enron Corp. and other scandals of manipulated accounts worldwide (WorldCom, Xerox, AIG, Nortel Networks, Ahold, Bankgesellschaft Berlin, Parmalat, SK Group/South Korea, Satyam/India etc.), the number of which – only the cases uncovered – has long been legion and is still increasing[144]

---

[137] Directive 2006/46/EC, see recital 4 in the preamble. Cf. Accounting Law Directive 2013/34/EU, Art. 19(1)(1) with Art. 20(1)(1); see also, ibid., recitals 26 and 42.

[138] See on cultural and legal diversity, multilingualism below 4.4.6, 4.8.7 and, e.g., Bormann (1996), Großfeld and Luttermann (2005) recitals 169–72.

[139] Wall Street Journal Europe, 15.03.1995, 1.

[140] Wall Street Journal Europe, 22.02.2000, 4.

[141] See also 4.8, 4.9 and 6.2.1. For the USA see also 8.3.1 with Vagts (2009) p. 686. Basically Luttermann (1999a).

[142] See 4.11.4 and, e.g., on Rathenau, Berle and Means in 3.5.4–3.5.5. Cf. below 6.7, 6.8 and chapters 8, 9.

[143] Accounting Law Directive 2013/34/EU, Art. 4(3), 19(1), 24(1) and recitals 9, 26, 42, 43.

[144] More recently, e.g., Wirecard (Germany), FTE Networks and VMware (USA), Noble Group Ltd. (Singapore), Etihad Etisalat Co. (Saudi Arabia), Penn West Petroleum Ltd. (Canada), Tesco (UK), Toshiba (Japan), Zhengzhou Siwei (China). Cf. Cornerstone Research, Accounting Class Action Filings and Settlements, 2022 (www.cornerstone.com). SEC Enforcement Division's Financial Reporting and Audit (FRAud) Group: https://www.sec.gov/spotlight/financial-reporting-and-

**Fig. 4.3** Faithful accounting as good corporate governance

everyone should be aware that accounting is not about "the numbers". It is about giving a reasonable picture of the corporation by means of its financial statements. The number is the sign of the completed limitation.[145] It is the names of the items and the notes on those (*Bilanzposten*) that give meaning to the numbers. Hence, it is "words *and* numbers" that have to be carefully considered by the responsible board members and their auditors and, of course, by the investors. The world debt crisis since the autumn of 2007 confirms without doubt that the issue is not abstract figures. Rather, the issue is the actual circumstances (facts, *die tatsächlichen Verhältnisse*, see 4.5.3), which have a massive impact on the living conditions (*Lebensverhältnisse*) of people and the order of economy and society as a whole.

Since words and the law itself exist in a living language, cultural aspects are essential for reporting in international markets. The "words and numbers" in financial statements are the result of a wide variety of different influences. They derive from the active parties' views of chances, risks and uncertainties, and the environment. We can thus say that altogether they stem from the individual *Weltanschauung* (view of the world). However, nationally-based rules of law (*Rechtsnormen*, e.g., company law, insolvency law, tax law) are still the often prevailing forces (see 4.8.6) in the realm of corporate governance with financial reporting as an act of communication (information, see 2.6.2). Hence, comparative law (*Rechtsvergleichung*) is the key to a common basis as shown by the multilingualism of the law of the

audit-task-force.shtml (accessed: 22.08.2025). Amiram, Bozanic, Cox, Dupont, Karpoff, and Sloan (2018).

[145] Spengler (1990) p. 77.

European Union, a community of law (*Rechtsgemeinschaft*), and the need for translations within international environments.[146] A common understanding is based on the imperative of truth (see 4.5.2), which applies comprehensively in the sense of sustainability (see 4.4.7, 4.11.4).

### 4.5.2 European Court of Justice (ECJ)

Within the European Union, the decisions of the European Court of Justice take precedence over national law as far as European law is concerned (cf. Art. 19 TEU). The Court has jurisdiction to deliver preliminary rulings concerning, among other things, the Treaty on the Functioning of the European Union (TFEU) and the validity and interpretation of Acts of the institutions of the Community.[147] That includes the directives and regulations concerning accounting and auditing.[148] Any court of a member state where such a question is raised may request the European Court of Justice to give a ruling thereon; if there is no judicial remedy under national law, that national court shall bring the matter before the European Court of Justice.[149] The Court's rulings on accounting matters use a fixed point of reference: the principle of "a true and fair view". According to Article 4(3)(1) of Accounting Law Directive 2013/34/EU (formerly: Art. 2(3) and (5) of Directive 78/660/EC),[150] the annual financial statements (accounts) shall give "a true and fair view of the undertaking's [company's] assets, liabilities, financial position and profit or loss".

[146] See below 4.8.7 and Luttermann (1999a). Großfeld and Luttermann (2005) recitals 86–110. On reforms Luttermann, C. and Luttermann, K. (2020), Luttermann, K. (2011). Basically on "a true and fair view" Luttermann (2003a) § 264 HGB recitals 16-30 (general rule), 31-105 (comparative law) and 106-169 (practical legal principles). Cf. Aldeia (2019) on Portugal and Spain, overall Nobes and Parker (2020).

[147] TFEU Art. 267(1)(a) and (b), ex-EC Treaty Art. 234(1)(a) and (b).

[148] See above 4.4.3, below 4.5.2, 4.9.1 and 4.10.1.

[149] TFEU Art. 267(2) and (3), ex-EC Treaty Art. 234(2) and (3).

[150] Cf. ECJ, 18.06.2015 (C-508/13 – *Estland*, ET) ECLI:EU:C:2015:403. About the scope of the directive ECJ, 05.10.2023 (C-279/22 – *Nemzeti Adó*, HU) ECLI:EU:C:2023:734. See also Directive 78/660/EC, fourth recital in the preamble. This is also the case for the application of IFRS in the European Union according to Art. 3(2) of the Accounting Law Regulation (EC) 1606/2002; see above 4.4.4.

The Court of Justice has firmly established that compliance with that principle "is the primary objective of the Directive" (*Hauptzielsetzung,* French *objectif primordial*).[151] This legislation has been confirmed by the Court in more recent decisions.[152] In order reflect that general provision, the German legislature has transposed Article 2(3) of Directive 78/660/EC (now: Directive 2013/34/EU, Art. 4(3)(1)) into § 264(2)(1) HGB: *"ein den tatsächlichen Verhältnissen entsprechendes Bild"* (see 4.5.6); in the German rulings of the European Court of Justice, this is literally called "*Bilanzwahrheit*"! So too, the lawmakers of the other member states have adopted this in their national provisions. The meaning of "a true and fair view" (ratio legis) is firmly embedded by way of national terminology in several jurisdictions, for example *"ein getreues Bild"* (Austria),[153] *"une image fidéle"* (France), *"een getrouw beeld"* (The Netherlands), *"una imagen fiel"* (Spain).[154] The interpretation in the member states has to be made in conformity with the European law; that is, in the multilingual Community of the European Union by means of the comparative method (*rechtsvergleichende Methode*).[155]

We have to keep records, as the European Court of Justice requires: financial statements (annual or consolidated accounts) must give "a true and fair" record. To give "a true and fair view" is the legal measure of practice in accounting and auditing. It governs the interpretation of every accounting rule and controls every accounting practice. Financial statements must be clear (*klar*) in form, and true (*wahr*) in their contents. Facing that high standard, the biblical question may arise: "What is truth?" (John, 18, 38). – Surely, it is not about something mystic or supernatural. Accounting is a human discipline with true and fair accounting as the ethical standard.[156] "Truth" (*Wahrheit*) is a human dimension, with nothing mythological or divine about it, and hence accounting is naturally limited (see 4.5.3).[157] With that in mind, the phrase "a true and fair view", like its synonyms in other languages, is a pan-European term. Fundamentally, it is the idea and *ratio*

---

[151] ECJ, 27.06.1996 (C–234/94 – *Tomberger*, DE) ECR I–3133, recital 17; ECJ, 14.09.1999 (C–275/97 – *DE + ES Bauunternehmung GmbH,* DE) ECR I–5331, recital 26; ECJ, 07.01.2003 (C–306/99 – *BIAO*, FR) ECR I–1, recitals 72–76.

[152] ECJ, 03.10.2013 (C-322/12 – *Gimle SA*, FR) ECLI:EU:C:2013:632, recital 30; ECJ, 06.03.2014 (C-510/12 – *Bloomsbury NV*, NL) ECLI:EU:C:2014:154, recital 18. ECJ, 15.06.2017 (C-444/16 – *Immo Chiaradia SPRL*, FR) ECLI:EU:C:2017:465, recital 40; ECJ, 21.09.2018 (C-640/18 – *Wagram Invest SA*, FR) ECLI:EU:C:2020:293, recital 32.

[153] For details of the relationship to the German text, see Luttermann (2003a) § 264 HGB, recitals 34–36 and 83–105 (ECJ rulings).

[154] ECJ, 27.06.1996 (C–234/94 – *Tomberger*, DE) ECR I–3133, recital 17; ECJ, 14.09.1999 (C–275/97 – *DE + ES Bauunternehmung GmbH,* DE) ECR I–5331, recital 26; ECJ, 07.01.2003 (C–306/99 – *BIAO*, FR) ECR I–1, recitals 72–76. Cf. ECJ, 05.10.2023 (C-279/22 – *Nemzeti Adó*, HU) ECLI:EU:C:2023:734, recitals 6, 46 (area of application).

[155] See for example ECJ, 17.12.1998 (236/97 – *Codan*, DA) ECR I-8679; thereon Luttermann (1999d). See already above 4.5.1 and overall Luttermann (2003a) § 264 HGB recitals 16-169.

[156] See below 4.6.3–4.6.5.

[157] See below 4.5.6, 4.6.5 (with physics, Bohr), and basically Luttermann (2003a) § 264 HGB recitals 19–21 and 121–128.

*legis*, the aim and the measure of accounting and auditing (financial reporting), nationally and internationally.[158]

### 4.5.3 Guidance: Facts and Materiality

In practice, the responsible accountant has to apply the general rule of "a true and fair view" (Directive 2013/34/EU, Art. 4(3))[159] in the light of the rulings of the ECJ (see 4.5.2). The European Judges have determined that the principle of "a true and fair view" (*Bilanzwahrheit*) "requires, first, that the annual accounts of companies should reflect the activities and transactions which they are supposed to describe and, secondly, that the accounting information be given in the form judged to be the soundest and most appropriate for satisfying third parties' needs for information, without harming the interests of the company".[160] The same applies to consolidated accounts.[161] Basically, what applies for practice is the following: It is all about facts, about "a true and fair view" (more precisely: *die "tatsächlichen Verhältnisse"*, see 4.6.5, 4.10.2); for this, systematically the complementary relationship between the general rule (§ 264(2)(1) HGB) and other rules of accounting (also so-called "principles", see 4.6.4 and Fig. 4.4) holds.[162] Overall, it is about "sustainability" (*Nachhaltigkeit*) in its very meaning of verifiability (*Nachprüfbarkeit*), id est a documentary proof (see 4.11.4).

Accordingly, it is to be understood that "items in the profit and loss account and balance sheet shall be accounted for and presented having regard to the substance of the transaction or arrangement concerned" (Directive 2013/34/EU, Art. 6(1)(h)). This principle aims at the economic reality, id est the actual circumstances of the company (substance over form).[163] Overall, the principle of materiality (*Wesentlichkeit*) is guiding: the requirements set out in this Directive "need not be complied with when the effect of complying with them is immaterial" (Directive 2013/34/EU, Art. 6(1)(j)).[164] The principle emphasised there is already embodied for the person obliged to provide a financial report with the imperative of truth (*Wahrheitsgebot*) as the measure of diligence.[165] With the "actual circumstances"

---

[158] See ibid., from p. 787 (recitals 83–105); Parker and Nobes (1994).

[159] Previously: Directive 78/660/EC Art. 2(3). In Germany: § 264(2)(1) HGB.

[160] ECJ, 14.09.1999 (C–275/97 – *DE + ES Bauunternehmung GmbH*, DE) ECR I–5331, recitals 26 and 27; ECJ, 07.01.2003 (C–306/99 – *BIAO*, FR) ECR I–1, recital 72.

[161] Accounting Law Directive 2013/14/EU Art. 4 (ex-Directive 83/349/EC Art. 16(3)), § 297(2)(2) HGB.

[162] Globally on complementarity (i.e. a mutual complent – *Komplementarität*) see chapter 9.

[163] See Accounting Law Directive 2013/34/EU Art. 6(1)(h), Art. 43(4) and recital 16.

[164] See also Art 2 No 16 and recital 17. Luttermann (2008b).

[165] See 4.6.5, 5.6 and 6.4; c.f., § 264(1) and (2)(1) HGB, § 276 BGB. On "audit materiality" see 4.9.1.

(facts), this of course systematically comprises the aspect coming to the fore with the so-called global climate change for the financial position of the corporation, also dealt with in particular as *environmental due diligence* and *human rights due diligence*.[166] In any case, it is from this perspective as well that the relevant circumstances are also to be included in financial reporting and auditing in the sense of materiality (see 4.5.3, 4.5.5 and Fig. 4.6).

Overall, in short: Conceptually, adequate presentation is required, id est reasonableness (*Angemessenheit*, see 1.1). This concerns the significance of a process for the recipient horizon (*Empfängerhorizont*, see 4.5.6): It is not pedantry that is required, but rather concentrating on what is essential; in this process, several smaller, in themselves insignificant events may build up to a significant whole regarding their effect. This applies to recognition, measurement, presentation, disclosure and consolidation. A procedurally designed legal concept provides a comprehensive basis (see 4.6.4, 4.10.2 and chapter 5). In the light of this, the focus is clearly on legal aspects. There is, however, an old and widespread conception among accountants who feel entitled to decide of their own accord about the measure and rules of accounting. This conception, though still fostered by members of the accounting profession along with distorting kinds of "dynamic concepts" of accounting[167] for obvious business reasons, is fundamentally misleading; this seems skewed also in the discourse about a "double materiality".[168] To put it colloquially, one may say that it's a story of asking the fox to look after the geese. – One that will never end?

So it seems if we look at the times of the so-called "modern corporation" since Berle, Means and Rathenau, which we have already explored (in chapters 2 and 3, see also 4.6). Hence, we can affirm: the measure is *not* what accountants and auditors or their profession may deem to be a general standard. By means of the principles of a constitutional state, the measure is what is legally necessary and fixed (see 4.5.5). Accordingly, at the end of the day, the constitutionally independent judges (*Gericht*) have ultimately to decide under the law about the practice of "a true and fair view".[169] For all of the European Union, the judges of the European Court of Justice are called upon to determine the common meaning. Further guidance in theory and practice – for reasonable people and generations to come – is provided below.[170]

[166] See chapter 1 (esp. 1.1. to 1.3, 1.6.1) and below 4.5.7, 7.7.3. Cf. in European law the Corporate Sustainability Due Diligence Directive (EU) 2024/1760, 13.06.2024, OJ L, 05.07.2024. With a corporate due diligence concept (Sustainable Business Finance Navigator) Luttermann, L. (2022) and (2024).

[167] Cf. above 4.4.5. See, e.g., Nobes (2006) 81, 85, referring to Mary Arden, The true and fair requirement, Counsel's Opinion (Foreword to: Accounting Standards Board, Accounting Standards, London 1993).

[168] Cf., e.g., Baumüller and Sopp (2022).

[169] On German accounting principles (*Grundsätze ordnungsmäßiger Buchführung*—GoB) see *Bundesfinanzhof* (I 208/63) *Bundessteuerblatt* (BStBl) III 1967, 607. Luttermann (1996b) pp. 595, 613.

[170] See below, esp. 4.6.3–4.6.5, 4.10.2 and chapter 5 (valuation).

### 4.5.4 *"IFRS", Company Law, and Tax Law*

The measure of "a true and fair view" applies to the process of the endorsement of "IFRS" into European law as well as to the application of the adopted "IFRS" within the European Union, and consequently to the financial statements of German-listed companies. It must be repeated[171] that the application of international accounting standards ("IAS/IFRS") is regulated by Accounting Law Regulation (EC) 1606/2002. According to Article 3(2), an international accounting standard can only be adopted by the European Community if it is not contrary to the "true and fair" principle set out in Article 4(3) of Directive 2013/34/EU for annual accounts and in Article 4(3) with Article 24(1) of Directive 2013/34/EU for consolidated accounts (see above 4.4.4).

Attention must be paid to the legal standing of "IFRSs" within the European Union and in Germany. The adoption of international accounting standards is regulated by Articles 3(1) and 6 of Accounting Law Regulation (EC) 1606/2002. At the end of the explanation of the process for adopting these standards, Article 3(4) of Accounting Law Regulation (EC) 1606/2002 states: "Adopted international accounting standards shall be published in full in each of the official languages of the Community [Union], as a Commission Regulation, in the Official Journal of the European Communities [Union]." By means of that procedure, the "IFRSs" adopted and published in the 24 (23) official languages of the European Union (state of 2025) are part of European law. This means that the English language monopoly no longer stands, all the more so since the status of English is legally controversial after Brexit.[172] The said "IFRS", as well as the European accounting regulations and directives, are subject to the authority and rulings of the European Court of Justice (see 4.5.2).[173]

So at best, it is about so-called "European IFRS". However, the "IFRS" even in Great Britain, the English mother conuntry, do not conform to the regulatory requirements, as already elaborated above (see 4.4.5). The IFRS "brought shame" on the auditing profession, Lord Lawson emphasised in the House of Lords: "The true and fair have effectively gone and the importance of prudence has given way to box-ticking."[174] Practice, however, even after Brexit, seems unchanged, still widely marked by the old spirit (see 4.5.3). This is impressively proven by the accounting and auditing sector's UK watchdog, the Financial Conduct Authority (FCA) and its

[171] See above 4.4.4 with 4.4.5 to 4.4.7 and below 4.8.6.

[172] Luttermann, C. and Luttermann, K. (2021).

[173] Luttermann (2003a) Einf BilanzR recitals 163, 329 and 250–251.

[174] Financial Services Bill, 23.10.2013, Column 1012 (https://publications.parliament.uk/pa/ld201314/ldhansrd/text/131023-0001.htm, accessed: 22.08.2025). See already the Cadbury Report, below 7.2.1. Cf. Großfeld and Luttermann (2005) recitals 148-172.

failed predecessor, the Financial Reporting Council, imposing record financial sanctions on the industry in order to improve the sector's work (see 4.3.2).[175] Basically, it is about cause and effect. The House of Lords has focussed: "Who watches the watchdogs? Improving the performance, independence and accountability of UK regulators".[176] Period.

That is hardly surprising. Looking at it in a more detailed way, e.g., Lord Sikka fundamentally remarked that "IFRS" has "no clear concept of capital maintenance" while other peers in the House of Lords specifically criticised IFRS 17 (insurance contracts) and IAS 19 (employee benefits) heavily under the mandate of "true and fair" accounting.[177] Can it be more explicit? – Both standards (IFRS 17, IAS 19) have, however, been adopted by the European Union – each of them by recommendation of the EFRAG. The European Union's "IFRS 17" (EU-IFRS 17) comes with an optional exemption from applying the annual cohort requirements relating to the recognition of the profit in the contract, the contractual service margin, in profit or loss. The reasoning: "annual cohort requirement as a unit of account for groups of insurance and investment contracts does not always reflect the business model, nor the legal and contractual features of intergenerationally-mutualised and cash flow matched contracts referred to", while "those contracts represent more than 70% of the total life insurance liabilities in the Union".[178]

Regulation in the best interest of whom? – EFRAG itself remained discordant on whether the grouping into annual cohorts "meets the technical endorsement criteria, or is conducive to the European public good"[179] under Article 3(2) of Regulation (EC) No 1606/2002 (see 4.4.4). – It should be noted that this EU regulation concerns not only the so-called "IFRS" of the IASB (London) or the now accompanying "IFRS Sustainability Disclosure Standards" ("IFRS S"): According to the Accounting Law Regulation (EC) 1606/2002, the European Union can generally accept "international standards" if these standards fulfill the legal stipulations. The idea is that in the case of a conflict of international laws this leads to peaceful cooperation in order to counteract excessive external influence (see basically 4.4.4). This principle

---

175 See August 3, 2022 by FT (https://www.ft.com/content/ac6cce71-aaf2-485b-b8b9-bbe701dd7414, accessed: 22.08.2025).

176 House of Lords, Industry and Regulators Committee, 1st report of session 2023-24, HL Paper 56, 08.02.2024 (https://committees.parliament.uk/publications/43211/documents/215050/default/, accessed: 22.08.2025). Also on "watchdogs" below 4.9.1, 7.2.1 (Cadbury Report).

177 Stephen Bouvier, Accounting standards come under fire from UK lawmakers, 10.05.2021 (https://www.ipe.com/news/accounting-standards-come-under-fire-from-uk-lawmakers/10052688.article, accessed: 22.08.2025).

178 See Commission Regulation (EU) 2021/2036 of 19.11.2021, OJ EU 23.11.2021, L 416/3, recital 10.

179 See Commission Regulation (EU) 2021/2036 of 19.11.2021, OJ EU 23.11.2021, L 416/3, recital 8 with the reference: "This is in line with the views expressed by stakeholders on EFRAG's endorsement advice and the views of Member State experts in the Accounting Regulatory Committee". Cf. EFRAG Endorsement Letter, 31.3.2021 (current: <www.efrag.org>). Critically EU Commission, Fitness Check on the EU framework for public reporting companies, SWD(2021) 81 final, 21.04.2021, p. 7.

is increasingly gaining in significance in view of global developments (climate change litigation and regulation). What is at stake is prosperity, good leadership, financing and valuation of a corporation, which remains to be developed.[180]

International accounting standards also influence the relationship between company law and tax law. We will deal with that later (see 4.7.2), but the key point has to be emphasised. The said principle of "a true and fair view", id est the imperative of truth (*Bilanzwahrheit*), is *the* common measure of accounting. There are widespread attempts to differentiate purposes and sub-purposes of accounting, especially in relation to tax accounts, on the one hand, and commercial accounts, on the other. These differentiations are will-o'-the-wisps. It is fundamental that company law and tax law concern a single corporation (legal entity – *Rechtssubjekt*). Jurisprudence has to deal with and show that single corporation as the invisible entity[181] in a reasonable way. Regardless of "purposes", this is always achieved by means of the said principle of "a true and fair view" (*Bilanzwahrheit*).[182] This was examined more closely in chapter 3 (see also 4.4.4).

## 4.5.5 Rules of Accounting

Accounting is about valuation (see 4.6) and information (see 4.4.1); at the same time, financial reporting and auditing in their legal sense are the measure for the valuation of companies (assets) in general (see chapter 5). Rules of accounting, all originating under the imperative of truth in the general rule of "a true and fair view" (*Bilanzwahrheit*, see 4.5.1), guide the practice of financial reporting and auditing. Article 3(2) of Accounting Law Regulation (EC) 1606/2002 designates[183] four criteria for the adoption of "international accounting standards" (not necessarily the "IFRS",[184] but in accordance with the IASB Conceptual Framework for Financial Reporting [2010, IASB CF., rev. 2018, formerly: IASB Framework, IASB F.][185]): (a) understandability (IASB CF.QC30–32, IASB F.25, *Verständlichkeit*), (b) relevance (IASB CF.QC6–11, IASB F.26–30, *Relevanz*), (c) reliability (IASB F.31–38, *Verläßlichkeit*),[186] and (d) comparability (IASB CF.QC20–25 – IASB

[180] See above 4.2 and 4.3 with 4.4.3; basically in chapters 1, 2, 8 and 9. Cf., e.g., Palea (2018), Bensadon and Praquin (2016).

[181] See above 4.2.1 and 4.4.6, below 4.7.2.

[182] Luttermann (2003a) Einf BilanzR recitals 282, 343, see also, ibid., recitals 299, 414 and 11–15; Großfeld and Luttermann (2005) recitals 314, 62. Luttermann (2010d).

[183] For the actual wording, see above 4.4.4. On the reform of the CF: Exposure Draft ED/2015/3 (May 2015). On the development: www.ifrs.org and www.iasplus.com/en/projects/major/cf-iasb (both accessed: 22.08.2025)

[184] See above 4.5.4 (with 4.4.4).

[185] Framework as published by the EU Commission in November 2003 (IASB F.).

[186] See IASB F.46. Not explicitly adopted in the IASB Conceptual Framework for Financial Reporting (2010); see, e.g., QC12–16 (faithful representation).

F.39–42, *Vergleichbarkeit*). Similarly, the FASB designs its Conceptual Framework as "a body of interrelated objectives and fundamentals" of financial reporting.[187]

In that context, overall considerations are given in IAS 1.15–46 (Presentation of Financial Statements, 2007, in the meantime amended several times). They are fundamentally far-reaching, corresponding with rules (*Einzelregeln*), especially Article 6 of the Accounting Law Directive 2013/34/EU (formerly: Art. 31 of the Fourth Directive (EEC) 78/660), and hence the German *Handelsgesetzbuch* (HGB).[188] Foremost is "clarity" (*Klarheit, Bilanzklarheit*, § 243(2) HGB)[189] as the stylistic (formal) companion of "a true and fair view" (fair presentation, *Bilanzwahrheit*: § 264(2)(1) HGB): the accountant shall give reliable information in plain words and fair presentation,[190] with no marketing puffs. Among the considerations are also: going concern (*Unternehmensfortführung*: § 252(1) No 2 HGB);[191] accrual basis of accounting (*Periodenabgrenzung*: §§ 242(1)(1), 252 (1) HGB);[192] and comparability (comparative information, *Vergleichbarkeit*), including consistency of presentation (*Stetigkeit*: § 252(1) No 1 HGB).[193] Aggregation (*Gebot der Einzelbewertung*: § 252(1) No 3 HGB)[194] and offsetting (*Verrechnungsverbot*: § 246(2) HGB)[195] are only allowed for immaterial amounts or items (see on materiality 4.5.3).[196]

Both aspects point to the overall concept of materiality (*Wesentlichkeit*). It is a practical guideline for faithful (*getreues*) reporting in the sense of providing "a true and fair view".[197] A vivid description is given in IAS 1.7 with IAS 8.5 (Accounting Policies, Changes in Accounting Estimates and Errors, 2003; cf. CF QC11, IASB F.30):

> [Material] "Omissions or misstatements of items are material if they could, individually or collectively, influence the economic decisions that users make on the basis of the financial statements. Materiality depends on the size and nature of the omission or misstatement judged in the surrounding circumstances. The size or nature of the item, or a combination of both, could be the determining factor."

This definition of material had been revised (Amendments to IAS 1 and IAS 8, 31 October 2018, see IAS 1.7 and IAS 8.5: "Material"), including three additional

---

187 See currently the Conceptual Framework: https://www.fasb.org; cf. IASB CF (rev. 2018).

188 For a discussion of the qualitative characteristics of accounts, see Großfeld and Luttermann (2005) recitals 317–337.

189 Accounting Law Directive 2013/34/EU Art. 4(2): "the annual financial statements shall be drawn up clearly" (formerly: Directive 78/660/EC Art 2(2)). Cf. below 7.6.3.

190 IASB CF.QC 30–32 and 12–16. Formerly: IASB F.25 and 46, IAS 1.13–22 (2003).

191 Accounting Law Directive 2013/34/EU Art. 6(1)(a). Cf. IASB F.23.

192 Accounting Law Directive 2013/34/EU Art. 6(1)(d). Cf. IASB F.22.

193 Accounting Law Directive 2013/34/EU Art. 6(1)(e). Cf. IASB F.39-42.

194 Accounting Law Directive 2013/34/EU Art. 6(1)(f).

195 Accounting Law Directive 2013/34/EU Art. 6(1)(g).

196 See §§ 256, 240 HGB; c.f., Accounting Law Directive 2013/34/EU Art. 6(1)(h) and (j).

197 Accounting Law Directive 2013/34/EU Art. 6(1)(j) and Art. 4(3) (Germany: § 264(2)(1) HGB).

aspects (obscuring, could reasonably be expected to influence, primary users). It reads like this (which is further explained there):

> "Information is material if omitting, misstating or obscuring it could reasonably be expected to influence decisions that the primary users of general purpose financial statements make on the basis of those financial statements, which provide financial information about a specific reporting entity."

This vast area will be discussed in greater detail. It should already be emphasised here: Materiality is all about facts, all the "actual circumstances" (*die "tatsächlichen Verhältnisse"*, see 4.5.7, 4.6) that bring up "a true and fair view" of the corporation. Hence, the financial statements have to document financially a true picture of all the relevant material aspects of the corporation in terms of "sustainability", id est in its very meaning of verifiability (*Nachprüfbarkeit*, see 4.11.4). Aspects (issues) that cannot have any material financial impact will generally be immaterial (see already 4.5.3).

### *4.5.6 Expectation Gaps and Procedural Law*

According to the IASB, the qualitative characteristics of the IFRS "identify the types of information that are likely to be most useful",[198] id est the qualitative characteristics of useful financial information (see CF, rev. 2018). Still,[199] this is a broad description that has to be refined. The IASB determines the relation "likely to be most useful to the existing and potential investors, lenders and other creditors". That is more specific than what is found in the Preface to IFRS,[200] but it remains vague.[201] The financial statements should provide information about "the financial position, financial performance and cash flows of an entity that is useful" to those users "in

---

[198] IASB CF (2010) QC1; cf. IASB F.24-46 (2003). Currently: www.ifrs.org.

[199] See IASB F.5 (1989/2001): qualitative characteristics are intended to "determine the usefulness of information in financial statements". The "Introduction" of the IASB Conceptual Framework (CF, 2010) under the heading "Scope" simply speaks of: "(b) the qualitative characteristics of useful financial information". See also aspects of the CF (OB1: "useful financial information"), OB2: "The objective of general purpose financial reporting is to provide financial information about the reporting entity that is useful to existing and potential investors, lenders and other creditors in making decisions about providing resources to the entity. Those decisions involve buying, selling or holding equity and debt instruments, and providing or settling loans and other forms of credit." Cf. Staubus (1999).

[200] IFRS Preface 10 (2010): Financial statements "are directed towards the common information needs of a wide range of users, for example, shareholders, creditors, employees and the public at large".

[201] IASB Conceptual Framework (2010) QC1 (cf. OB2). See on reasonable certainty and meaningless rules below 4.6.3. Note basically also 7.6.3.

making economic decisions".[202] What is in factual terms "the future economic benefit embodied in an asset"[203]? This is accompanied by guesswork under the veil of mathematical logic, models and formulas. The all-embracing term "decision usefulness" tends to be meaningless.[204] We have to consider the object and the limits of accounting.[205]

The accountant has to report faithfully (*getreu*), according to the governing measure of "a true and fair view" (*Bilanzwahrheit*, see 4.4.4). Linked in a peculiar way, this is also now hinted at in the IASB: "If financial information is to be useful, it must be relevant and faithfully represent what it purports to represent".[206] The reference point "useful", however, remains misleading. Financial reporting is not about "usefulness". The law determines as the objective that the accountant is to render an account that demonstrates good corporate governance of other people's money (duty of care), id est according to the law (see 4.4.1). Financial statements have to "show the results of management's stewardship of the resources entrusted to it".[207] In form and content, reporting is directed at the so-called recipient horizon (*Empfängerhorizont*). German courts, when deciding cases in the area of corporations and capital markets law, often employ the standard of an "average informed" (*durchschnittlich informierten*) and "reasonable, intelligent" (*verständigen*) investor (in other words: *"verständiger Durchschnittsanleger"*).[208] These are the legal standards commonly used for "the average consumer" and "the ordinary man" (*Leitbild des Normalverbrauchers*).[209]

Basically, the role of the law in this area is to determine the limits of accounting according to its actual possibilities (see 4.5.3). The German version of Article 4(3) of the Accounting Law Directive 2013/34/EU states that the accounts shall give *"ein den tatsächlichen Verhältnissen entsprechendes Bild"* of the company (§ 264(2)(1) HGB).[210] Translated literally, this means "a picture in accordance with the factual realities". That view, supported by the mathematical approach to accounting (the said focus on the numbers), can be misleading, resulting in the creation of expectation gaps on the side of the readers of the accounts (*Erwartungslücken*). A "fact" (*Tatsache*) is an event of the past or the present that is accessible to proof. But

[202] IAS 1.9 (2003) sentence 2. IASB Conceptual Framework (2010) QC1: "for making decisions about the reporting entity on the basis of information in its financial report (financial information)".

[203] See IASB, CF 4.8. Cf. below 4.10.2 and 5.5.

[204] On meaningless rules below in 4.6.3 and 7.6.3 to 7.6.6.

[205] Luttermann (2003a) Einf BilanzR recitals 123–133; for further information about the "decision-usefulness concept" see Ballwieser (2004). Empirical research: EFRAG/ICAS, Professional investors and the decision usefulness of financial reporting (March 2016).

[206] IASB Conceptual Framework (2010) QC4 and QC12-16.

[207] IAS 1.9 (2003) sentence 3.

[208] BGH, 02.10.2003 (I ZR 252/01) ZIP 2004, 184, 186 (regarding an investment, misleading sales promotion); see also 4.5 and 7.4.2. Compare to IASB Conceptual Framework (2010) QC 32.

[209] BGH, 16.12.2004 (I ZR 222/02) WRP 2005, 480, 483; Großfeld and Luttermann (2005) recitals 97–99, 255–268 (*Empfängerhorizont*).

[210] See above 4.4.1 and 4.5.2.

we should keep in mind that accounting is a valuation under the principle of a going concern.[211] Hence, accounting embraces the uncertain dimension of the future and cannot be treated as something merely statistical. The procedural concept provides – in the sense of sustainability (*Nachhaltigkeit*) – the practical guideline (see 4.6.4, 4.10.2, 4.11.4 and chapter 5).

### *4.5.7 Completeness: No "Off-Balance Sheet"*

A true and fair view requires that in the final accounts (financial statements), the circumstances of the company regarding assets, liabilities, financial position and profit or loss be presented in totality (§§ 264(2)(1) HGB), id est in completeness (*Vollständigkeit*, § 246(1)(1) HGB: all assets [*sämtliche Vermögensgegenstände*] and liabilities [*Schulden*]). Under the overall imperative of truth ("a true and fair view" – *Bilanzwahrheit*) this means comprehensively for the actual circumstances of the corporation as a whole. In particular the concomitant financial risks shall be recognised and measured on a prudent basis (*Vorsichtsprinzip*, Accounting Law Directive 2013/34/EU Art. 6(1)(c)): "all liabilities arising in the course of the financial year concerned" (ii) and "all negative value adjustments shall be recognised, whether the result of the financial year is a profit or a loss" (iii). This means that "all foreseeable risks and losses" that have arisen up to the balance sheet date must be taken into account (§ 252(1) No (4) HGB: *"alle vorhersehbaren Risiken und Verluste"*).

This is a matter of course for faithful information, measurement (see 4.6.3) and the required capital maintenance (cf. 3.6.4), both with regard to material issues (see 4.5.3, 4.5.5). It is exactly what makes accounting (financial reporting and auditing) an expression of careful corporate governance, id est good governance (compliance). At the same time, this gains particular importance through the requirement of sustainability, both in civil-procedure (see 5.5.2) and transformation of the economy. Climate risks must be included and disclosed as financial risks (costs, see 4.2.2). The apparently widespread practice of treating business and risks outside of balance sheet and reporting, id est by not accounting for all relevant financial issues (e.g. climate risk, see 4.4.8 and 4.3), is adverse to this demand. Such lack of information is characteristic of deficient accounting in the financial statements. The imperative of truth demands overall transparency in a true and fair view (real disclosure, e.g. due diligence concerning environment, human rights).[212] It also comprises in particular circumstances of the *Konzern* (group of affiliated companies), as becomes clear from the overall perspective (e.g., Panama Papers, see 4.7.3).

---

[211] See § 252(1) No 2 HGB and Accounting Law Directive 2013/34/EU Art. 6(1)(a).

[212] Specifically e.g. on payments according to Accounting Law Directive 2013/34/EU Art. 48(2). Cf. above 3.3.3, below 7.7.3 (sustainable disclosure).

This is practiced within a system and internationally, in order to obfuscate the financial circumstances and especially the degree of debt (leverage) or the situation of the risk of the corporation. This is well-known, as the case of the Enron Corporation illustrated around the turn of the millennium (see also Lehman Brothers Inc.: 4.6.2). Contract constructions with particular effect here are those with special purpose vehicles, also called special purpose entities (SPEs, *Zweckgesellschaften*). The Powers Report[213] documents: "Many of the most significant transactions apparently were designed to accomplish favorable financial statement results, not to achieve *bona fide* economic objectives or to transfer risk." It goes on to remark: "Some transactions were designed so that, had they followed applicable accounting rules, Enron could have kept assets and liabilities (especially debt) off of its balance sheet; but the transactions did not follow those rules." Enron conducted asset sales and hedges, but in reality, it did not transfer the concomitant risk to the SPEs. This went undetected – or at least undisclosed – for a long time.

Among the strategies used for accounting manipulation (the "numbers game") with shifts and concealment of risks and profit[214] are hybrid financial instruments (hybrid debt),[215] synthetic leasing and securitisations (derivatives). Formally, it is even possible to generate tax-deductible running costs at the same time.[216] A remedy against this, generally and common internationally, is the economic view of a "contractual" equity capital according to trade and tax law (substance over form). The Accounting Law Directive 2013/34/EU[217] strengthens this position. A sound basis is the liable capital of a corporation (*Haftkapital*, see 3.6) as a legal concept of accounting (*Rechtskonzept der Rechnungslegung*) for limited liability (legal person, limited partner or other contractual liability).[218] The SEC adopted final rules for disclosure of aggregate contractual obligations and of off-balance sheet arrangements (to be set apart in a designated section of Management's Discussion and Analysis of Financial Conditions and Results of Operations, MD&A) – including the statutory safe harbor protections to forward-looking information.[219]

---

[213] Powers, Troubh, and Winokur (2002) at p. 4. See also *Newby v Enron Corporation*, 2002 WL 31854963 (S.D. Tex. Dec. 20, 2002). Cf. Abrams (2012).

[214] On the scope e.g. below in 4.6.2 (Lehman Brothers Inc.) as well as also SEC fraud charges on ITT Educational Services Inc. (concealing mounting failures in two off-balance-sheet student loan programs): www.sec.gov/news/pressrelease/2015-86.html (accessed: 22.08.2025) and Form 8K File No. 001-13144 (CIK: 0000922475, 08.06.2016, in: EDGAR, under www.sec.gov).

[215] See on objective disadvantage of hybrid "creditors" in Germany, e.g., BGH, 02.12.2021 (IX ZR 110/20) NZG 2022, 458, <openJur 2022, 2596> (so-called *Genußrecht* – profit participation right).

[216] Maydew (2005). On "Enron" Luttermann, *Handelsblatt*, 30.01.2002, p. 10.

[217] See Accounting Law Directive 2013/34/EU Art. 6(1)(h) and recital 16; cf. above 4.5.3.

[218] Basically Luttermann (1998) from p. 330, p. 421 et seq. and p. 528 et seq.; Luttermann (2001) and Luttermann (2009c).

[219] Sections 27A of the Securities Act and 21E of the Securities Exchange Act. Final Rules under S 401(a) of the Sarbanes-Oxley Act of 2002, see: www.sarbanes-oxley-101.com/SOX-401.htm (accessed: 22.08.2025).

In principle, it is generally about the appropriate presentation of the corporation within its financial statements. The European law[220] explicitly demands information on type, purpose and financial consequences of essential procedures beyond the accounts (material off-balance sheet arrangements, cf. 4.5.7, 4.6.2). An obligation to report and auditing duty (audit materiality) already existed;[221] also internationally for the complete financial report as well as for individual account balances, types of business transactions and questions of publication (ISA 320.7). In short, the demand for completeness explicitly requires comprehensive information (§§ 246(1), 251 HGB and, e.g., §§ 284, 285 No 3, § 289 HGB). The imperative of truth (*Bilanzwahrheit*, § 264(2)(1) HGB), which sustains and characterises the whole of financial reporting and auditing (§ 317(1)(3) HGB, see 4.4.4), is the reason of this obligation for the accountant (*Rechnungsleger*, corporate director: see 4.4, 3.3) and the auditor (*Wirtschaftsprüfer*, see 4.9) in general (see 4.6.1, 4.6.5).

## 4.6 Valuation

### *4.6.1 Financing and the "Numbers Game"*

Valuation is the essence of corporate accounting and financing, id est, the epitome of running a business (corporation, project) successfully. Though not commonly realised, it is also a key matter of jurisprudence, society and law. Members of the management board are responsible for the corporation's finances since they have to lead the corporation.[222] If insolvency (*Zahlungsunfähigkeit*) or over-indebtedness (*Überschuldung*) occurs, they legally have to call for bankruptcy – resp. restructuring – procedures (*Insolvenzverfahren*).[223] And the information provided to shareholders must include heavy losses according to the stated capital (*Grundkapital*) on the balance sheet (§ 92 AktG, see generally 3.4.3). These examples, of course, have some special significance that relates to the overall picture of the corporation and its financing function in terms of sustainability (value creation, *Wertschöpfung*).

[220] Cf. inter alia Directive 2006/46/EC, 14.06.2006, OJ L 224/1 and Accounting Law Directive 2013/34/EU Art. 19, 20 and 41; see above 4.4.8. This also applies to the rules of Directive 86/635/EC, 08.12.1986 on the annual accounts and consolidated accounts of banks and other financial institutions and the rules of Directive 91/674/EC, 19.12.1991, on the annual accounts and consolidated accounts of insurance undertakings, both updated.

[221] Luttermann (2003a) § 264 HGB recitals 207–213; Großfeld and Luttermann (2005) recitals 266–267, 335–337, 1413 (group) and 1780 et seq. (auditing).

[222] § 76(1) AktG. Original text: "*Der Vorstand hat unter eigener Verantwortung die Gesellschaft zu leiten.*" See below 6.1 and 6.4.

[223] §§ 17–19 *Insolvenzordnung* (InsO – German Code of Insolvency), see above 3.4.1. Luttermann and Geißler (2013).

Financing, accounting and valuation (i.e., financial reporting) are generally interlinked. This is elementary for any company and comprises the practice of good corporate governance (duty of care, compliance); accordingly, this also concerns auditing (see 4.9) as well as questions of the valuation of companies (assets) and shares in many circumstances (*Lebensverhältnisse*, on this whole complex see in more detail chapter 5). On capital markets, especially stock exchanges, participants are focused on "the numbers". In financial reporting, meeting or missing the so-called "consensus estimates" of shady committed or qualified "analysts" (whatever that term means!) immediately causes sharp rises and falls in a corporation's shares (rsp. bonds) and hence its valuation. Corporate directors therefore try to meet or even beat the "consensus estimates". In 1998, Arthur Levitt, then SEC Chairman, in a speech entitled "The 'Numbers Game'", criticised the manipulation of figures that is commonly referred to as "earnings management" (or in fact also: fraud).[224]

Corporate managers, auditors, and analysts are still playing that numbers game, as shown by uncovered manipulations of financial statements by major companies like the American International Group (AIG) and General Electric.[225] The rising numbers (cf. 4.5.1) of discovered cases may be due less to higher numbers of manipulations (criminal energy); instead, they are probably a sign of an increased sensibility for the problem as well as higher intensity and better quality of control (see 4.9). Accounting manipulation, earnings management is a worldwide game – even before Berle and Means (see 3.3). A wide variety of techniques is used as part of this game, including things like "big bath" restructuring charges, "magic accounting" in acquisitions and mergers, off-balance-sheet finance and so on. Such window dressing, downplayed as "creative accounting", is the gateway to fraud (*Betrug*) and dishonesty, or, in German criminal law, *Untreue* (breach of trust). This is confirmed by German cases and court rulings.[226]

---

[224] See with details below 7.6.1, and overall Levitt (1998), speech at NYU Center for Law and Business, on that Luttermann (1999a) p. 4-5. For examples see Großfeld and Luttermann (2005), e.g., recitals 89–90, 647, 757–758, 1530–1532, 1661–1663.

[225] See, e.g., SEC, Press Release, 09.12.2020: https://www.sec.gov/news/press-release/2020-312 (accessed: 22.08.2025). Cf. Moneywatch, General Electric accused of fraud "bigger than Enron" by Madoff whistleblower, 16.08.2019 (https://www.cbsnews.com/news/general-electric-accounting-fraud-bigger-than-enron-alleged-by-madoff-whistleblower/); Andrew Edgecliffe-Johnson, Gary Silverman, James Fontanella-Khan, GE closes a defining chapter in US corporate history, Financial Times, 10.11.2021 (https://www.ft.com/content/1ca38b2c-a9ce-4450-b156-a17a24e33976, accessed: 22.08.2025). Heese, Jonas, and David Lane, "GEnron"? Markopolos versus General Electric (A), Harvard Business School Case 121-005, January 2021 (Rev. May 2021).

[226] See salient the case of Wirecard AG, e.g., 4.9.4. Some more examples are: Balsam AG, Bankgesellschaft Berlin AG, Flowtex AG, Comroad AG. See also, for example, BGH, 16.12.2004 (1 StR 420/03) wistra 2005, 139 (§ 400(1) No. 1 AktG); BGH 21.08.1996 (4 StR 364/96) wistra 1996, 348 (§ 331 No 4 HGB, § 266 StGB); *Oberlandesgericht Frankfurt* 19.06.2002 (2 Ws 36/02, § 400(1) No 1 AktG) wistra 2003, 196; *Finanzgericht München* 15.06.1998 (7 K 499/96) EFG 1998, 1481. In more detail Luttermann (2012). See below 4.10.2.

### *4.6.2 The Fall of Lehman Brothers Inc.*

The case of the investment bank Lehman Brothers Inc., whose bankruptcy on 15 September 2008 (see 4.1) deepened the world debt crisis (*Weltschuldenkrise*), highlights the gigantic dimension of accounting manipulations around the globe. To make it clear: It is about the participation in prosperity (*Wohlstand*) worldwide, about its tremendous shift due to the valuation games (see 4.6.1 and chapter 5). The Court report of March 2010 on the case documented devastating details in nine volumes of 2,200 pages before the New York Bankruptcy Court.[227] According to this report, the top managers concealed the circumstances of the corporation and the corporate group systematically in the accounts. German law explicitly penalises such behaviour (see, e.g., § 331 HGB, § 400 AktG); enforcement is needed worldwide (see 4.9, 4.10 and 6.5).

According to the court report, at Lehman Brothers Inc., short-term lending was central. Securities that Lehman held were "sold" under the contractual condition that the seller (dealer) buy them back from the buyers (other banks) at a certain date and for a certain price (so-called "repo transaction", more fittingly: bogus transactions). The short-term repurchase agreement (nickname: "Repo 105") was classified as a "sale" and Lehman used the cash to – temporarily – pay down the corporation's debt. These financial transactions (in fact: accounting fraud), which were launched with a deadline with the help of British lawyers, but were otherwise economically useless, removed some 49 billion U.S. dollars from the Lehman balances (off-balance sheet, cf. 4.5.7). This masked the precarious financial situation of the bank, in particular the extreme rate of outside capital (*Fremdkapital*, leverage). It is reported that insiders warned against this practice, and the auditors (in this case, Ernst & Young LLP) knew about it. The seven banks involved also included the Deutsche Bank AG.[228]

The case of Lehman Brothers Inc. does not reveal a new trick. This and similar practices going beyond the accounts and fair presentation (*Bilanzwahrheit*) are widespread. We have already referred to the special purpose vehicles that attracted special attention not only in the U.S., but around the world at the turn of the millennium with the accounting scandals of Enron & Co.[229] The game seems to have been carried on happily. Sequels are obviously running. The SEC is conducting

[227] Report of Anton A. Valukas, *In re Lehman Brothers Holdings Inc., et al.*, Bankruptcy Court S.D. N.Y., Chapter 11 Case No. 08–13555 (03–11–2010).

[228] See article by Craig Spector and Michael Corkery, The Wall Street Journal, 15.03.2010, pp. 16–17 as well as 22.03.2010, 16–17. For further background information, see Jennifer Hughes, Accounting: Fooled again, Financial Times, 19.03.2010, p. 7. See also below 6.6.

[229] See above 4.5.7 and Claus Luttermann, *Handelsblatt*, 30.01.2002, p. 10 (on the case of Enron Corp.). On the financial industry, see chapter 6.

such accounting fraud actions (e.g., Bank of America, Diamond Foods, CVS Caremark, JDA Software).[230] In addition, The Wall Street Journal ran the following headline: "Enterprise Tech Companies Hold Billions in Off-Balance Sheet Debt" (e.g., IBM, Microsoft, Oracle); the issue is the practice of financial reporting about leasing transactions, which masks the true degree of leverage.[231] It remains a wide field.

### *4.6.3 The Legal Focus of Accounting Practice*

This development and court rulings against "creative accounting"[232] underscore the importance of the duty to provide "a true and fair view" (*Bilanzwahrheit*). As the ethical basis of accounting, this principle should guide any accounting decision as well as auditing (see 4.9). Of course, "valuation" appears to be a subjective concept. International comparisons highlight different concepts and perceptions of risk and uncertainties being at work here. Fundamentally, differences in alternative accounting systems can be perceived, at least since the listing of the then Daimler-Benz AG[233] 1994 at the New York Stock Exchange: the same company is shown differently in its financial statements according to the German *Handelsgesetzbuch* (European law) versus the U.S. "GAAP" (delisting 2010).[234]

Such differences, of course, also appear in terms of the practice – and the transitional processes – for sustainable business activity (sustainability, see 2.4.2). They must be borne in mind when discussing so-called "international" standards of accounting. At the core is the concept that accounting is basically valuation. It follows that the standards of accounting, id est of financial reporting and auditing, are standards of valuation (see in detail chapter 5). Different types of cultural influences (*Weltanschauungen*) work as powerful forces in this area (see 4.5.1). But, as will be revealed further, cross-culturally essential private and political

---

[230] See also Pareteum Corp., Kraft Heinz Co., and basically SEC on measures of a company's cooperation in order to settle accounting fraud cases: www.sec.gov/litigation/investreport/34-44969.htm (accessed: 22.08.2025) on more data: SEC, Division of Enforcement, Annual Report (www.sec.gov).

[231] See 6.8.5 on finance structures and the AI megahype. On public companies FASB, 25.02.2016: Accounting Standards Update (ASU) 2016-02, Leases (Topic 842), for not-for profit companies from 2022/23; cf. IFRS 16 (Leases, 2016). Rachael King, 22.03.2016: total impact for all companies $2 trillion (http://blogs.wsj.com/cio/2016/03/22/enterprise-tech-companies-hold-billions-in-off-balance-sheet-debt, accessed: 22.08.2025). Cf. Albrecht, Albrecht, and Albrecht, Zimbelman (2025); Zhang, Chen, and Jin (2020). See also above 4.5.7.

[232] See, e.g., *Flynn v. Bass Bros. Flynn v. Bass Bros. Enterprises, Inc.*, 744 F.2d 978, 986 (3rd Cir 1984), above 4.6.2, and below 4.9-4.10, 5.6, 7.6.1. Luttermann (1999a). On accounting fraud SEC, Strategic Plan, Fiscal Years 2018-2022, and rsp. for 2022-2026, focused primarily to "protect the investing public against fraud, manipulation, and misconduct", see above 4.5.7 and 4.6.1-4.6.3.

[233] Renamed in: DaimlerChrysler AG (1998) and Mercedes-Benz Group AG (2022).

[234] For some comparative "numbers", see Luttermann (1998) p. 25.

interests in the race for a share of limited resources (profit) are even more powerfully at work. Reasonably, the common good must be heeded. The European Court of Justice, authoritative for Germany as a member state of the European Union, is setting the stage in this regard. When valuing items, the Judges have determined that prudence (*Vorsicht*) must always be observed. However, the amount of provisions (*Rückstellungen*) for liabilities and losses, for example, "must not exceed what is needed"[235] (cf. 4.5.2 and chapter 5, esp. 5.6.2 and 5.6.3 with Fig. 5.3).

Based on the true facts of the case, id est on sustainability in terms of verifiability (*Nachprüfbarkeit*, see 4.11.4) the accountant has to fix a reasonable amount for every item in the – financially and hence legally relevant – figures of the financial statements (*Zahlenwerk*). He or she has to observe the existing rules, e.g. on a historical cost basis, recognition of acquisition and production cost (*Anschaffungs- und Herstellungskosten*, § 255(1)–(3) HGB). This is also true for accounting on the basis of "fair value" (*beizulegender Zeitwert*, § 255(4) HGB, see 4.8.3 and 7.5.2). For necessary estimates, the accountant is guided by connecting facts (see 5.5.3) and the principle of benchmarking (*Vergleichsinformation*); in other words, looking at similar transactions or at competitors in the particular area of business. In essence, the requirement is always to objectify materially (*im Wesentlichen*) as much as possible. Necessary predictions are to be made in accordance with the acknowledged rules of probability[236] (calculus, *Wahrscheinlichkeitsrechnung*).

This underlines the importance of the general norm of accounting (see 4.4.4), of course also for the globally increasing movement of so-called "green" sustainability (*Nachhaltigkeit*, see 4.2.5). It is always about giving "a true and fair view" (see 4.5 and 4.11.4). In practice, this measure is the guide used to determine how to account for the company's assets, liabilities, financial position and profit or loss (with the principle of materiality, see 4.5.3). By no means is it, as some commentators would suggest, "effectively meaningless as a restriction"[237] or "so vague that other arguments would be more pertinent".[238] Such wording and acting, of course, demonstrate a substantial lack of understanding of basic legal concepts and principles as procedural measures for the implementation in practice (see 4.6.4): It is only from this that the legal protection becomes necessary for all concerned, which also works to the advantage of carefully acting corporate directors and the auditors (*Rechtsschutz*).[239]

In the proper view of law as systematic regulation it is reasonably about the relationship between rules in the sense of complementarity (see 4.6.4). The

---

[235] ECJ, 07.01.2003 (C–306/99 – *BIAO*, FR) ECR I–1, recital 75, regarding Art 31(1)(c) and 42(1) of the Fourth Directive 78/660/EC; cf., e.g., Accounting Law Directive 2013/34/EU Art. 6(5).

[236] Basically Luttermann (1998) pp. 229-237 (with modern game theory); see also below 9.6 (AI, engineering) and 5.6 (judicial practice).

[237] Alexander (2006) 65, 70. See on that Wüstemann and Kierzek (2006) 92, 101–102.

[238] Nobes (2006) 81, 84.

[239] See below 4.9, 4.10 and, e.g., with a sound concept of entrepreneurial diligence Luttermann, L. (2022) and (2024).

European Court of Justice has shown the interplay of the general rule (*Generalnorm*, i.e. the imperative of truth, see 4.4.4 with Fig. 4.4, 4.5.2) and other rules of accounting (other so-called "principles", rules, see 4.5.5), for example, in the case of *DE+ES Bauunternehmung GmbH* about global provisions (*Pauschalrückstellungen*) for a number of potential liabilities.[240] The Court rejected a result that would not only be incompatible with the rule of making valuations on a prudent basis, but also "with the principle of the 'true and fair view', compliance with which is the primary objective of the Directive [78/660/EEC]";[241] identical now effective: Accounting Law Directive 2013/34/EU (see 4.4.4).

### 4.6.4 The Procedural Law of Faithful Accounting

The rulings of the European Court of Justice document the complementary relationship (*Komplementärverhältnis*) between the general rule (*Generalnorm*), named "the principle of 'the true and fair view'" (cf. Accounting Law Directive 2013/34/EU Art. 4(3)(1), § 264(2)(1) *HGB*), and the other rules of accounting (*Einzelregeln*).[242] "Complementary" comes from the noun "complement" (from Latin *complementum*), that means completeness or fullness; that is, a thing which, when added, completes or makes up a whole[243] (see chapter 9). The general rule, stating the objective and rationale of accounting (*ratio legis*), influences the other rules, giving the keynote for reasonable treatment of single items. The general rule is embodied systematically and becomes even clearer in terms of practical guidance, if considered with the other rules in their totality. Both categories in their interaction enrich and complement each other.

This shows a natural principle: What is more or less one-sided will tend towards equalisation, id est equilibrium (*Gleichgewicht*, cf. basic thermodynamics). The law, engendered by and oriented towards life itself, participates in this as a reasonable structural framework. It must be noted, however, that this should not be misinterpreted as some kind of arbitrariness (*Willkür*). The legal measure is "a true

240 Directive 78/660/EC Art. 2(3) and (5), Art. 20(1), Art. 31(1)(c); cf. Accounting Law Directive 2013/34/EU Art. 4(3) and (4), Art. 12(12)(1), Art. 6(5). See German law: §§ 264(2)(1), 249(2), 252(1) No 3 HGB.

241 See above 4.5.2 and with more details ECJ, 14.09.1999 (C–275/97 – *DE + ES Bauunternehmung GmbH*, DE) ECR I–5331, recitals 24–40 (26); thereon Luttermann (1999c).

242 Also so-called "principles", see 4.6.3. In more detail Großfeld and Luttermann (2005) recital 230.

243 Brown (1993) p. 460 (complenentary). Cf. at least simplistic (misleading): *"Lex specialis derogat legi generali"*. Basically Luttermann (2003a) § 264 HGB recitals 16-21, 42-169 as a practical guide on the general rule of the German and European law of financial reporting (accounting, auditing), the imperative of truth (*Bilanzwahrheit*, see above 4.4.4), with esp. recitals 136-140 on the complementarity of the general rule and special rules; also Luttermann (2003a) Einf BilanzR recitals 126-130 (ethical foundation, i.e. juridical analysis of the economy). See below 7. 3.2 with 9.7 and 9.9.

**Fig. 4.4** The procedural law and practice of faithful accounting

and fair view", id est the imperative of truth (*Gebot der Bilanzwahrheit*) as the *ratio legis* ultimately linked with the concept of materiality (*Wesentlichkeit*, cf., Art. 6(1)(j) Accounting Law Directive 2013/34/EU).[244] Overall this is methodologically a procedure that is oriented towards the legal order as an order of assets (*Vermögensordnung*); this must also be established internationally (see 4.10). In focusing on a particular case, the European Court of Justice evaluates whether a separate valuation of potential liabilities is necessary, using the standard of "a true and fair view" (*Bilanzwahrheit*) as the measure.[245]

The procedural law also gives a substantial clue as to what "a true and fair view" for single items is (see Fig. 4.4). The German Code of Civil Procedure (*Zivilprozeßordnung,* ZPO) is representative for handling the questions at issue. This Code, applying also to disputes about matters of financial reporting (accounting and auditing), generally requires true statements before the court (§ 138(1) ZPO). The judges have to decide out of free conviction (*freier Überzeugung*) if they consider a factual assertion (*tatsächliche Behauptung*) to be true (§ 286(1) ZPO). Estimates, as

[244] See above 4.5.3 and below 4.8.4 and 4.9.1.

[245] ECJ, 14.09.1999 (C–275/97 – *DE + ES Bauunternehmung GmbH*, DE) ECR I–5331 (ECLI:EU:C:1999:406), recitals 28–40; see in the authentic text (recital 26) in the German language (Art. 41 Rules of Procedure of the Court of Justice): *"Eine andere Auslegung [wäre] mit dem Grundsatz der Bilanzwahrheit unvereinbar, dessen Beachtung die Hauptzielsetzung der Richtlinie darstellt"* (cf. recital 26 in English: "Any other interpretation [...] would be incompatible [...] with the principle of the 'true and fair view', compliance with which is the primary objective of the Directive"); thereon Luttermann (1999c).

far as they are necessary, have to be reasonable (§ 287 ZPO, see 5.5.3). So, as a rule, the accountant must objectify as far as possible. *If* a factual assertion is "true", this can be decisive for the individual case. Concerning that judicial core question of what is "true", the German *Bundesgerichtshof* (BGH, the highest civil court) wrote about the judge's conviction *mutatis mutandis*: what is required is a level of certitude that silences doubts without fully ruling them out.[246]

### 4.6.5 Conclusion for Corporate Directors and Auditors

We now can determine the legal measure for the practice of corporate directors, their accountants, and auditors. Their duty to give (rsp., audit) an account requires careful valuation for a true, faithful picture of the corporation. According to the meaning of "truth" explained above (and note again that *Bilanzwahrheit* is a semantic equivalent of "a true and fair view", as the European Court of Justice confirms in its decisions, see 4.5.2), it is not about metaphysics or philosophical questions (cf.: "What is truth?", John 18, 38). In the realm of law, id est in terms of human affairs (*menschlichen Angelegenheiten*), it is always and accordingly in financial reporting on other people's money (accounting, auditing) – legally embedded systematically in the procedural concept (see 4.6.4, 4.10.2) – about facts and materiality (see Figs. 4.4 and 4.6 with 4.5.3).

If we look at physics (the epitome of so-called "exact science"), this is described in a scientifically comparable way. Pioneered by Nils Bohr's idea, which essentially states: Physics does not say how nature (the world) is, but only what we can say about it.[247] Anton Zeilinger even goes one step further saying: "What can be said about nature, in principle, also defines what can exist"; adding that "we can observe reality, we can make measurements," but that it is not the case that we "can say anything about the essence of reality".[248] Well, that is about *the* question "that I may detect the inmost force / which binds the world, and guides its course" as Johann Wolfgang Goethe, jurist and student of nature, put it[249] in the literary masterpiece *Faust* (monologue in the night!), the human tragedy. But the realisation remains: It is

---

[246] BGH, 14.12.1993 (VI ZR 221/92) NJW–RR 1994, 567, 568, German original: *"Es genügt vielmehr ein für das praktische Leben brauchbarer Grad von Gewißheit, der den Zweifeln Schweigen gebietet, ohne sie völlig auszuschließen."* Equally German Bundesverfassungsgericht (BVerfG, Federal Constitutional Court) 18.01.2001 (1 BvR 1273/96) NJW 2001, 1639, 1640. On more details for valuation chapter 5 (esp. 5.6.5).

[247] Bohr at the 1927 Volta Conference in Como (according to Hermens, 2013): "It is wrong to think that the task of physics is to find out how nature is. Physics concerns what we can say about nature." Cf. Petersen (1963) pp. 8, 12 (there without proof).

[248] Zeilinger, interview with Manuel Ansede, 14.06.2023, El País Science (https://english.elpais.com).

[249] German original Goethe (1808), *Nacht* (night): *"Daß ich erkenne, was die Welt im Innersten zusammenhält"*.

always about proof, a sufficient factual basis, id est sustainability (*Nachhaltigkeit*) in terms of verifiability (*Beweis*).

This human insight is at the same time the measure for accounting and auditing (financial reporting). Accordingly, the responsible accountant (*Rechnungsleger*, i.e., corporate director) has to relate what in actual fact can be said about the relevant circumstances of the company (see 4.5.3, on estimates: 5.5.3, 5.6.2 and 5.6.3 with Fig. 5.3). The auditor has to check correspondingly. The measure of accounting and auditing ("a true and fair view") is that no one has to state how the world – the corporation – is. But responsible accountants (corporate directors) legally have to state – in terms of sustainability as verifiability (*Nachprüfbarkeit*) – what can be said about the world (knowledge), the corporation; id est in fact about the assets, liabilities, financial position and profit or loss of the company (see 4.4 and, e.g., under European law in Germany § 264(2) and § 317(1)(3) HGB).[250]

That needs to be achieved in a clear way within the financial statements of the company (*Jahresabschluß*), id est essentially in the financially relevant figures (*Zahlenwerken*), documenting factually in words and numbers, a true and fair picture of the corporation (real disclosure, see 4.2.1, 4.4, 4.5 and chapter 3). Diligence (*Sorgfalt*) and prudence (*Vorsicht*) are required. This also applies to the inclusion of future developments, insofar as these are necessary (cf. going concern, reserves, provisions etc.) and sustainable. Overall, the imperative of truth (*Bilanzwahrheit*) provides guidance. This holds globally for financial reporting and auditing, id est for good corporate governance (compliance) of the human corporation.[251] We will further treat practical questions of valuation in chapter 5 (esp. in 5.5 and 5.6).

## 4.7 Accounting and Company Groups (*Konzerne*)

### *4.7.1 Consolidated Financial Statements*[252]

The above-named characteristics also apply to consolidated financial statements (*Konzernabschlüsse*) of the companies of a group (*Konzern*). The accounts shall be drawn up clearly (§ 297(2)(1) HGB) and they shall give "a true and fair view" (*Bilanzwahrheit*, § 297(2)(2) HGB): *"ein den tatsächlichen Verhältnissen entsprechendes Bild"*, id est a picture of the assets and liabilities, financial position and performance of the group according to the actual circumstances. This measure has also to be observed when the consolidated financial statements are drawn up in terms of "IFRSs" (or other "standards"). Article 3(2) of Accounting Law Regulation

[250] See Luttermann (2003a) § 264 recitals 19–21 and 121–28. See procedurally below 4.10.2, 5.6.2, and 5.6.3, 8.3.3.

[251] Luttermann (2004).

[252] See Großfeld Luttermann (2005) recitals 1229–1447 (general rules), recitals 1448–1560 (HGB/European Law) and recitals 1561–1730 (IAS/IFRS).

(EC) 1606/2002 refers to Articles 4(3) and 24(1) (in conjunction with Art. 52(2)) of the Accounting Law Directive 2013/34/EU,[253] see above 4.4.3).

Commonly, corporate directors, accountants and investors have to pay attention to the special issues and quality of consolidated accounts. In Germany, consolidated financial statements were legally established by § 329 AktG in 1965.[254] Foreign affiliated companies were not required to comply because of the precariousness of addressing unfamiliar conditions abroad. Basically, of course, the same problem still exists. Valuation is often a difficult task in familiar surroundings, and it is all the more difficult in regard to foreign patterns of time, geography, culture and language, public and private order, as well as accompanying standards of value. This at the same time corroborates the core aspects for the treatment of the situation of the group (concern, *Konzern*) in accounting and auditing:

(1) In the concern, the mandate of "a true and fair view" (*Bilanzwahrheit*) also applies as a general norm of accounting and auditing (see 4.5).
(2) Accordingly, the actual circumstances in the concern have to be represented, id est conclusively in the very sense of sustainability (*Nachhaltigkeit*, see 4.5.3 and 4.11.4).
(3) In particular in an international dimension, the concern opens further possibilities of manipulation, deception and fraud in dealing with other people's money (see 4.7.2).

Since 1985, the German Law (§ 290 HGB) requires that every parent company (*Mutterunternehmen*) with a subsidiary (*Tochterunternehmen*) draw up consolidated accounts and a consolidated annual report (*Konzernlagebericht*) in accordance with the European Law (formerly: Seventh Directive (EEC) 83/349). The Accounting Law Directive 2013/34/EU continues the legal situation according to Chapter 6 (Art. 21-29). The parent company shall be consolidated with all of its subsidiaries, regardless of where the registered offices of the subsidiaries are situated (§ 294(1) HGB: so-called *Weltabschluss,* world financial statement). The assets, liabilities, financial positions and profits or losses of the undertakings (*Unternehmen*) shall be shown as if the parent and its subsidiaries were "a single undertaking" (*"als ob [sie] ein einziges Unternehmen wären"*, § 297(3)(1) HGB).[255] In complying with that fictional requirement, the accountant has to decide as to how far adjustments are to be made resulting from the particular characteristics (*Eigenart*) of the consolidation (§ 298(1) HGB).[256]

A complete set of consolidated accounts comprises a consolidated balance sheet (*Konzernbilanz*), a consolidated profit and loss account (*Konzern-Gewinn- und*

[253] Ex-Art. 16(3) of the Seventh Directive 83/349/EC.

[254] On the historical development Luttermann (2003a) Einf BilanzR recitals 103-106.

[255] Based on Art. 24(7) Accounting Law Directive 2013/34/EU (ex-Art. 26(1) Seventh Directive 83/349/EC).

[256] See especially Art. 24(1) and (10)-(14) Accounting Law Directive 2013/34/EU (ex-Art. 17 and 29 of the Seventh Directive 83/349/EC). On "fictions" below 7.3.1.

*Verlustrechnung*), the notes on the accounts (*Konzernanhang*), a cash flow statement (*Kapitalflußrechnung*), and a consolidated account of changes in equity (*Eigenkapitalspiegel*). Those documents – together with the consolidated annual report (management report, *Konzernlagebericht*: §§ 290(1), 315 HGB) – are mandatory (§ 297(1)(1) HGB); the management report comprises a consolidated corporate governance statement (acc. to §§ 315(1), 315d HGB, cf. 4.4.2). A larger parent company also has to include "non-financial information" on the social and environmental impacts (acc. to §§ 315b, 315c and §§ 289c-e HGB, *nichtfinanzielle Konzernerklärung*).[257] Segment reporting (*Segmentberichterstattung*) may be added (§ 297(1)(2) HGB). The consolidation procedures for the parent company and its subsidiaries as "a single undertaking" (§ 297(3)(1) HGB)[258] are made up of four elements: the "equity of the group" (*Kapitalkonsolidierung*), intragroup balances (*Schuldenkonsolidierung*), intragroup transactions (*Zwischenergebnisse*), and intragroup income and expenses (*Ertrags- und Aufwandskonsolidierung*).[259]

Consolidated accounts of publicly-traded companies (stocks, bonds) governed by the law of a member state of the European Union (such as Germany) are to be prepared in conformity with the "IFRSs" adopted as European law.[260] Some companies, such as those whose securities are (or were) listed on the New York Stock Exchange,[261] have (or had) to apply the "IFRSs" only for each financial year starting on or after 1 January 2007.[262] European Law endorsed IFRS 10 (Consolidated Financial Statements) in an amended version with an effective date of October 10, 2023.[263] Accordingly, and due to the concept of "control",[264] the accountant has to present financial information about the group as "a single economic entity".[265]

---

[257] See above 4.4.2, below 4.7 and Corporate Sustainability Reporting Directive (CSRD): Directive (EU) 2022/2464 of 14.12.2022, amending Regulation (EU) No 537/2014, Directive 2004/109/EC, Directive 2006/43/EC and Directive 2013/34/EU, as regards corporate sustainability reporting, OJ EU 16.12.2022, L 322/15. See on European Sustainability Reporting Standards (ESRS) EU Commission delegated Regulation (EU) 2023/2772 of 31 July 2023, OJ EU 22.12.2023, L.

[258] Art. 24(7) Accounting Law Directive 2013/34/EU (Seventh Dir 83/349/EC Art. 26(1)).

[259] See Commission Regulation (EU) 2023/1803 of 13.08.2023 adopting certain international accounting standards in accordance with Regulation (EC) No 1606/2002, OJ EU 26.09.2023, L 237/1. Basically above 4.4.3, 4.4.5 to 4.4.7, 4.5.4, 4.5.5 and Accounting Law Directive 2013/34/EU Art. 24(2), (5) and (7). Cf. for details Großfeld and Luttermann (2005) recitals 1448–1560.

[260] See § 315e HGB. Based on Art. 4 of Accounting Law Reg (EC) 1606/2002.

[261] For example: Daimler AG (delisting: 07.06.2010), Deutsche Bank AG, Fresenius Medical Care AG, Deutsche Telekom AG (delisting: 21.06.2010), Siemens AG (delisting: 15.05.2014), and SAP SE. See on details Bessler (2012). While, e.g. VIA optronics AG delist 2024, see for the opposite Amy Lewin, JPMorgan: Why list in Europe if you can list in the US?, 09.08.2024 (under: https://sifted.eu).

[262] Details in Art. 57 of the *Einführungsgesetz zum* (Introductory Act to the) HGB (EGHGB), based on Art. 9 of Regulation (EC) 1606/2002.

[263] Commission Regulation (EU) No 1254/2012, OJ EU, 29.12.2012, L 360/1.

[264] IFRS 10.5-9 (cf. formerly: IAS 27.12–21 (2003)). Likewise with the concept of "control" consolidation pursuant to § 290 (2) HGB.

[265] IFRS 10.5-9 (cf. IAS 27.4 and – formerly – 22 (2003)).

To be legally precise, we should say "a single enterprise",[266] or – even better – "as if they [the group members] were a single undertaking";[267] otherwise further judicially unintended obligations may ensue (see 4.6.2).

### 4.7.2 *Liability: Separate Legal Entity and International Taxation*

Consolidated financial statements are of increasing practical, albeit legally limited importance under a globalised perspective. Participants of capital markets are often focused on these since many companies are subsidiaries or a parent of a group of affiliated companies (*verbundene Unternehmen*, cf. §§ 291-393 AktG). These form power structures with huge accumulations of assets as well as massive scope for accounting maneuvers and manipulations, shaping the financial statements of group members (so-called *Verschiebebahnhöfe*, marshalling yards).[268] In terms of valuation, too, the whole seems to be more than the sum of its pieces. Hence, investors like to see the "whole thing" (cf. MNE, 3.6.2). That can, however, result in a dangerous blurring of other aspects, especially the essential feature of liability. This needs to be considered in greater detail.

A company with limited liability as a separate legal person is structured, of course, simply to limit liability (§ 1(1)(2) AktG, see 2.4.3). Consolidated accounts ignore that. By means of the law in the consolidated financial statements, the assets, liabilities, financial positions and profits or losses of the companies included in a consolidation shall be shown as if those companies were "a single undertaking" (enterprise).[269] Limitations on liability may suffer harm from the "single undertaking" (enterprise) approach which may lead to a liability incurred by one company becoming a liability of the group (*Konzernhaftung*).[270] This may also gain ground with the requirements (e.g., duty of care, duty of loyalty, *Sorgfaltspflichten*), which business leaders (corporate directors) are increasingly confronted with in corporate governance and compliance (esp. climate change litigation, see 8.5). Moreover, from regarding a group of affiliated companies as "a single economic entity",[271] it may be only a small step to unitary taxation of a "unitary business" (*Einheitsunternehmen*), particularly in an international arena.[272] A marked perspective is provided in

[266] IAS 27.6 and 15 (2000).

[267] Art. 24(7) Accounting Law Directive 2013/34/34/EU (ex-Art. 26(1) Seventh Directive 83/349/EC).

[268] See transfer prices (*Verrechnungspreise*) in multinational enterprises (*Konzern* – group), e.g., Levey and Wrappe (2019), Monsenego (2022). Cf. below chapter 8.

[269] Ibid. Cf. § 297(3)(1) HGB: "*ein einziges Unternehmen*".

[270] See Rieckers (2004).

[271] IAS 27.4 and 22 (2003). Cf. IFRS 10.1 and IN1-12 (2011).

[272] Luttermann (1996a) 935, 947.

multinational companies (MCNs)/ multinational enterprises (MNEs) by corporate tax planning with strategies of Base Erosion and Profit Shifting (BEPS), id est "exploiting gaps and mismatches in tax rules", esp. in times of digitisation.[273] A global, still challenging field of consideration.

The concept of the separate legal entity (*Juristische Person*) is not infinite; see, for example – though very rare – cases of "piercing the corporate veil" (the so-called *Durchgriffshaftung*).[274] But it is a fundamental and far-reaching concept for the Western order of business and society. In Germany, a group of affiliated companies is not a taxable person (*Steuersubjekt*).[275] Therefore, the concept of "unitary taxation", with many years' standing in the U.S., actually seems to be only a thread, if a business is taxable in the U.S.[276] But as discussed, changes may occur. The "unitary business" approach is part of the discussions about a harmonised tax system for the European Union.[277] This concerns tax competition between the member states. This is shown by a questionably low tax rate for corporations (e.g. in Bulgaria, Cyprus, Latvia, Lithuania) and in particular the realities in Ireland (see, e.g., the case of Apple Inc.),[278] as well as the unsound practices of the Tax offices in Luxemburg under Jean-Claude Juncker (Prime Minister and Finance Minister in personal union, thereafter President of the EU-Commission, see so-called "Lux Leaks").[279]

The circumstances work in a complex way and touch the nerve of the existence of a nation (*Staat*: financing, budget authority). This also illustrates how elementary the subject matter of valuation, accounting and auditing dealt with here in fact

---

[273] See OECD, Inclusive Framework on Base Erosion and Profit Shifting (BEPS): https://www.oecd.org/tax/beps/ (accessed: 22.08.2025) and Report, Tax challenges arising from digitalisation, 2020. Council Directive (EU) 2016/1164 of 12 July 2016 laying down rules against tax avoidance practices that directly affect the functioning of the internal market, OJ L 193, 19.07.2016, pp. 1–14; Council Directive (EU) 2017/952 of 29 May 2017 amending Directive (EU) 2016/1164 as regards hybrid mismatches with third countries OJ L 144, 07.06.2017, pp. 1–11.

[274] Also called "lifting the corporate veil", see above 2.4.3 and for the German law as well below 4.7.3. Rickett and Grantham (1998).

[275] See § 1 *Einkommensteuergesetz* (German Income Tax Code) and § 1(1) *Körperschaftsteuergesetz* (German Corporation Tax Code).

[276] See overall Luttermann (1994) and Luttermann (1996a).

[277] See, e.g., Palanský and Schultz (2024), Dias and Viegas (2021), Kuhr (2013), Weiner (2005). Overview by the EP, Direct taxation: personal and company taxation, fact sheet 05/2024, and updated: https://www.europarl.europa.eu/committees/en/fisc/about.

[278] See ECJ, 10.09.2024 (C-465/20 P – *Commission v. Ireland, Apple et al.*, EN) ECLI:EU:C:2024:724. Cf. Wang (2018), Alex Barker and Arthur Beesley, Brussels' €13bn tax bill clears way for further crackdowns on Apple, Financial Times, 31.08.2016, 1. See above 2.3.2: Google monopolises via digital technologies.

[279] On this: www.icij.org/project/luxembourg-leaks/luxembourg-leaks-stories-around-world, accessed: 22.08.2025). Lachapelle (2022) according to "public interest".

is. Measures against tax dumping and a common consolidated corporate tax basis are discussed (CCCTB).[280] Centralism is threatening to gain ground. Internationally the issue is fairness and transparency with the OECD (BEPS project, country-by-country reporting)[281] and, foremost, individual integrity (cf. Panama Papers (2016), Paradise Papers (2017), Pandora Papers (2021) and see 6.2.3).[282] For the record: So far, in Germany, like in most countries, it is quite rightly not consolidated financial statements, but the annual results of the financial statements of the single company (*Jahresabschluß*, §§ 242, 264 HGB) that are the legal basis for tax purposes and the distribution of profits.

### 4.7.3 Cash Pooling and Liability (Separate Legal Persons)

In the realm of corporate finance, in relation to cash pooling between affiliated companies, the German Federal Court of Justice (*Bundesgerichtshof*, BGH) has ruled that the executive director (*Geschäftsführer*) of a private limited company (*Gesellschaft mit beschränkter Haftung*, GmbH) is under a legal duty to run the business of the company with the degree of skill, care and diligence required of a decent business person.[283] Thus, if the subsidiary is a company with limited liability, the executive director is obliged to ignore any directives or instructions from the parent company if such directives or instructions would not be in the best interests of his company (the subsidiary), particularly if such directives or instructions would threaten the continued existence of the subsidiary (cf. bankruptcy).[284]

The Federal Court of Justice (*Bundesgerichtshof*, BGH) basically confirms this with its subsequent jurisdiction.[285] The company and its legal relationships are documented in the accounts (financial statements), id est the annual financial statements (*Jahresabschluß*) as separate financial statements (*Einzelabschluß*, see §§ 242, 264 HGB). The accounts establish the company, assign a certain amount of

[280] See Council Directive (EU) 2016/1164 of 12 July 2016 laying down rules against tax avoidance practices that directly affect the functioning of the internal market, OJ L 193 19.7.2016, p. 1. Cf. Bayet-Report (COM(2016)0026 (2016/0011(CNS)), EU Parliament, Proposal for a Council Directive (withdrawn: EP, Legislative train 12.2024).

[281] Dias and Viegas (2021). See the U.S. exit from OECD global tax, e.g.: www.lemonde.fr/en/economy/article/2025/06/28/trump-forces-the-rest-of-the-world-to-exempt-us-companies-from-global-tax-on-multinationals_6742805_19.html, accessed: 22.08.2025).

[282] Overall Luttermann (2016b). Cf. EU Commission, Proposal for a Directive amending Directive 2013/34/EU as regards disclosure of income tax information by certain undertakings and branches, 12.04.2016 COM(2016) 198 final.

[283] See §§ 43(1) and 35(1) *GmbHG* read together. See also below 6.4.

[284] BGH, 17.09.2001 (II ZR 178/99 — *Bremer Vulkan*) BGHZ 149, 10 (I.1.). See Luttermann (2001). Under criminal law BGH, 13.05.2004 (5 StR 73/03) BGHSt 49, 147.

[285] Seminally BGH, 16.07.2007 (II ZR 3/04 — *Trihotel*) BGHZ 173, 246. On this Luttermann (2008a), BGH, 15.09.2014 (II ZR 442/13) <https://openjur.de/u/771965.html>. See also BGH, 21.10.2021 (IX ZR 265/20) BGHZ 231, 328.

assets to it and thereby demarcate it from other spheres of competence (property, see 1.4.1, 2.4.3). This perspective is necessary in view of the separate legal personality, which means limited liability. At the same time, this corresponds to the general, probably international view of the company (corporation) as an artificial being: in legal transactions, it only becomes conceivable and tangible through accounting (financial reporting, see 4.2.1). The *Bundesgerichtshof* emphasised this, for example, for a private limited company (GmbH) in the light of thin capitalisation (*materielle Unterkapitalisierung*) and in the stage of liquidation (*Abwicklung, Liquidation*).[286] This points to insolvency law, which also has to be observed here, and the discussion about an international regulation for the insolvency of affiliates (*verbundene Unternehmen*, see 4.8.8).

This seems to illustrate clearly that there are fundamental exceptions to the common "single entity" approach. Looking at the complete picture, it needs to be said that the "single entity" approach to consolidated financial statements ("a single undertaking") is the exception. For the record: The standard by means of the law is still the corporation (company) as a separate legal person. This confirms the significance of (separate) financial reporting for each legal person (see 4.2.1). This will remain the standard until some other concept has proven to be superior in reasonably regulating business and society. The seeds of the concept of the *Vermögensordnung* (order of assets; see 4.8.1, 4.10.2) are already inherent in the imperative of individual responsibility and the structure of separate (legal) persons.

## 4.8 Accounting, International Allocation of Assets, and Reform

### *4.8.1 Legal Order and Competition*

In the framework of company financing (*Unternehmensfinanzierung*, corporate finance), accounting law (*Bilanzrecht*) demands that the accounts be arranged according to assets (*Vermögen, Aktiva*) and liabilities (*Verbindlichkeiten, Passiva*). With the globalisation of the financial markets, the plight has international dimensions, as the case of Lehman Brothers Inc. and the world debt crisis show (see 4.6.2 and chapter 6). Let us reiterate: the corporation, invisible due to its character as a legal person (*Rechtssubjekt*), becomes tangible only as the bearer of assets (contractual partner) in the accounts (see 4.2). This makes its valuation as a legal domain elementary (*Bewertungsrecht*). If someone is able to present a better picture in the

[286]BGH, 28.04.2008 (II ZR 264/06 — *Gamma*) BGHZ 176, 204 (NZG 2008, 547) and BGH, 09.02.2009 (II ZR 292/07 — *Sanitary*) BGHZ 179, 344 (NZG 2009, 545). Cf., e.g., BGH, 19.11.2019 (II ZR 233/18) openJur 2020, 1196 and BGH, 06.11.2018 (II ZR 199/17) BGHZ 220, 179 and BGH, 21.10.2021 (IX ZR 265/20), BGHZ 231, 328. *Differenzhaftung* (liability for the difference) rejected for mergers involving limited liability companies in return for capital increase (*Kapitalerhöhung*): BGH, 06.112018 (II ZR 199/17), BGHZ 220, 179.

**Fig. 4.5** The multijurisdictional approach on global capital markets

accounts, he will, e.g., enjoy better creditworthiness (*Bonität*, rating) and is able to finance himself under the terms of competition on capital markets through lower risk interest rate (*Risikozins*).

This is a notable advantage: As a rule, competitors have to compensate for the disadvantage that they encounter on the financing side on the side of product or service, that is, through – better – quality of products or services. Accounting law (financial reporting and auditing) thus constitutes an extremely forceful instrument for directing global capital flow (investment).[287] It is used massively in the course of climate change regulation, in order to redirect investments in "environmentally sustainable economic activities" (see 1.5.3, 8.2.3). Wherever the flows of capital go, products and services are developed and produced, leading to employment and prosperity (i.e. wealth, *Wohlstand*) – the economic basis for lasting peace (see chapters 1, 2 and 9). In the strong competition regarding services and products, disadvantages in the financing of a company are difficult to recoup. The concepts and regulations of accounting law shape the content of the accounts. Accounting law (valuation) is thus about the legal order of entrepreneurial profits and losses, about contractual and property rights, risk transfer and questions of liability.

Internationally, accounting law (valuation, financial reporting) is the core of fair competition and the legal order as an order of assets (*Vermögensordnung*), the

[287] Großfeld and Luttermann (2005) recital 91. In detail Luttermann (2009a). Christensen, Lee, and Walker (2009). Cf. in terms of transnational transfer of wealth above 1.3 (Fig. 1.1) and below 6.2 (Fig. 6.1), on regulation as a powerful steering tool (*Lenkinstrument*) for capital flows see 1.5.3, 8. 2.2.

financing of companies and – in the last instance – of the wealth of nations and humans.[288] This applies all the more in the light of global developments in business and regulation in view of climate change, where the overall issue is sustainability (see chapter 8). – So who sets the standards? – In the world debt crisis, we are experiencing – ongoing – gigantic shifts of profit and property (assets, toxic assets) under U.S. "GAAP" and "IFRS". This leads us to the following question: Who checks and ensures that the standards are reasonable and that they are in fact uniformly applied? In actual fact, there is a "battle of the law".[289] Let us examine some central aspects of sustainable solutions and imminent reforms.

## *4.8.2 Reform in Germany (BilMoG, BilRUG, and Beyond)*

Germany has carried out, and will continue to do so, reforms of financial reporting where the parliament considers this to be necessary (see 4.8.2, 4.9.2). First, with the *Bilanzrechtsmodernisierungsgesetz* (BilMoG, Accounting Law Modernisation Act),[290] that provided also for the implementation of the Directive 2006/46/EC;[291] it was followed by the *Bilanzrichtlinie-Umsetzungsgesetz* (*BilRUG, Accounting Law Directive Transposition Act*)[292] for the implementation of the Directive 2013/34/EU. Through those Acts, numerous accounting law norms were changed within the German law, especially in the *Handelsgesetzbuch* (HGB, Code of Commercial Law, see 4.8.3). This was accompanied by the European reform of the legal requirements for the annual audits.[293] These reforms are a reaction to international developments, which had hitherto been influenced by Anglo-American – neoclassical – theories and practices according to U.S. "GAAP" and "IFRS".

The aim of the reform of the HGB, at least up to the major legislative actions mentioned, is deregulation (cf. 4.8.2). The focus is on small and medium-sized entities, but the reform also provides alleviations in accounting for companies (corporations, e.g. AG, GmbH). These goals of the BilMoG are confirmed by the legislator of the BilRUG: Harmonisation at the European level, aiming at unifying accounting at the individual and the concern level, is meant to reduce the bureau-

---

[288] Luttermann (2015a). See also below 4.10.2 and chapters 1, 2 and 8.

[289] Cf. the clairvoyant writing "*Der Kampf ums Recht*" of Ihering (1872).

[290] Of 25.05.2009, *Bundesgesetzblatt* (BGBl) I 1102 came into effect on 29.05.2009. See below 4.8.3.

[291] Of 14.06.2006, OJ L 224/1 (*Abänderungsrichtlinie*). Directive 2006/43/EC, 17.05.2006 is also implemented by this (*Abschlußprüferrichtlinie*). See below 4.9.2.

[292] Of 17.07.2015, BGBl I 1245.

[293] E.g., *Abschlussprüfungsreformgesetz* of 10.05.2016, BGBl I 2016; Regulation (EU) No 537/2014, 16.04.2014, on specific requirements regarding statutory audit of public-interest entities and repealing Commission Decision 2005/909/EC, OJ L 158/77. See below 4.9.2.

cratic burden for small and medium-sized companies; at the same time responsible entrepreneurship is to be promoted.[294] The principles of materiality (*Wesentlichkeit*, Art. 6(1)(j)) and of substance over form (*wirtschaftliche Betrachtungsweise*, Art. (1) (h)) are regarded as essential innovations of the Accounting Law Directive 2013/34/EU. However, they already hold in German law under consideration of the general norm (Art. 4(3)(1) of Accounting Law Directive 2013/34/EU, §§ 264(2)(1), 317(1) HGB, see 4.4.4).[295] What has predominantly been changed by the BilRUG is what has to be stated in the notes (*Anhang*, cf. §§ 284, 285 HGB) and in the management report (*Lagebericht*, cf. § 289 HGB).[296]

Financial reporting and auditing remain a regulatory focus. Remarkable changes were brought about by more recent stipulations of European law (e.g., Corporate Sustainability Reporting Directive, CSRD,[297] with European Sustainability Reporting Standards, ESRS,[298] by the European Financial Reporting Advisory Group, EFRAG, in accordance with Art. 19a, 29a Directive 2013/34/EU; the *Aktionärsrechterichtlinie*[299]), also in the course of digitisation.[300] What has as great effect as regards corporate reporting are technological innovations and, of course, the "green" paradigm shift to the environment and human rights (sustainability, *Nachhaltigkeit*). Sustainable business activity (*nachhaltige Wirtschaftstätigkeit*) requires fundamental financial and

[294] Deutscher Bundestag, *Gesetzentwurf BilRUG*, 20.02.2015, BT-Drs. 18/4050, p. 1.

[295] Cf. principles of orderly bookkeeping (*Grundsätze ordnungsmäßiger Buchführung – GoB*) Thus the explicit reasoning *Begründung zum BilRUG*, ibid., p. 41-42. Cf. above 4.5.3.

[296] Ibid., *Bundestags-Drucksache* 18/4050, 42-45 (synopsis); Deutscher Bundestag, *Rechtsausschuss zum* BilRUG, 17.06.2015, *Bundestags-Drucksache* 18/5256; cf. legal basis: Accounting Law Directive 2013/34/EU Art. 15 to 20. Generally on the reform from a practical perspective, see, e.g., Russ, Janßen, Götze (2015).

[297] Directive (EU) 2022/2464, amended by Directive (EU) 2025/794, 14.04.2025, OJ L 794, 16.04.2025, p. 1. Cf. Directive 2014/95/EU: *Umsetzungsgesetz zur Stärkung der nichtfinanziellen Berichterstattung der Unternehmen in ihren Lage- und Konzernlageberichten (CSR-Richtlinie-Umsetzungsgesetz,* CSR-RUG*)* of 11.04.2017, BGBl. I 802. See Directive (EU) 2024/1306 of 29.04.2024 amending Directive 2013/34/EU as regards the time limits for the adoption of sustainability reporting standards for certain sectors and for certain third-country undertakings, OJ L, 2024/1306, 8.5.2024. Cf. Proposal for amending Directive 2013/34/EU et al. of 21.04.2021 (COM/2021/189 final).

[298] Commission Delegated Regulation (EU) 2023/2772, 31.07.2023, supplementing Directive 2013/34 as regards sustainability reporting standards, OJ L, 22.12.2023. On sustainability reporting below 4.4.2 and 4.7.1. See EU Commission, Omnibus simplification packages, e.g., 26.02.2025, COM(2025)80 and COM(2025)81, to "reduce complexity of EU requirements for all businesses, notably SMEs and small mid-caps (SMCs)".

[299] Directive (EU) 2017/828 amending Directive 2007/36/EC as regards the encouragement of long-term shareholder engagement: *Gesetz zur Umsetzung der zweiten Aktionärsrechterichtlinie* (ARUG II) of 12.12.2019, BGBl. I 2637.

[300] See, e.g., Directive (EU) 2013/50 on transparency requirements: *Gesetz zur weiteren Umsetzung der Transparenzrichtlinie-Änderungsrichtlinie zum einheitlichen elektronischen Format für Jahresfinanzberichte* (ESEF, see 4.11.2) of 12.08.2020, BGBl. I 1874. Directive (EU) 2019/1151: *Gesetz zur Umsetzung der Digitalisierungsrichtlinie* (DiRUG) of 05.07.2021, BGBl. I 3338.

organisational transformation, leading through sustainable financial reporting (valuation law, see 4.2 and chapter 5). – Let us note here: With the reforms, the German legislator confirms the European-influenced accounting law, which comprises accounting and auditing; this remains to be taken into consideration more strongly (see 4.9 and 4.12).

However, the basis for a comprehensively conceived and practiced valuation is established: the indicator for a just order of assets (*Vermögensordnung*) as a legal order, also internationally (see 4.8.1, 4.10.2). With a view to the "IFRS", the German legislator of the Accounting Law Modernisation Act (BilMoG) writes: The modernisation of accounting law is to make the proven commercial accounting law into a "full, but more cost-effective and easier alternative" in relation to international standards.[301] The cornerstones and the practical guidelines of the HGB-accounting law remain untouched by this. This is confirmed by the legislator of the BilRUG. Therefore, the HGB-accounts remain the basis for the valuation of the payments to the stakeholders (dividends) and other participants. The HGB-accounts also remain the foundation for fiscal profit assessment (§ 5(1) EStG, § 8(1) KStG, see 4.4.6).

The systematically established commercial law system with the general rule of "a true and fair view" including clarity (*Bilanzwahrheit* and *Bilanzklarheit*, §§ 264, 243 HGB) and the principles of orderly bookkeeping (*Grundsätze ordnungsmäßiger Buchführung*, GoB) remain in effect; we have already shown practical guidance (e.g. 4.5.3, 4.6.4). This includes in particular the principle of prudence (or so-called conservatism, *Vorsichtsprinzip*), the principle of realisation (*Realisationsprinzip*, § 252(1) No 4 HGB), the going concern principle (*Prinzip der Unternehmensfortführung*, § 252(1) No 2 HGB) and the accrual basis of accounting (*Periodenabgrenzung, Stichtagsprinzip*, S 252(1) No 3 HGB).

### 4.8.3 The BilMoG: Some of the Rule Changes

Main changes also remain decisive for practice in German law under the BilRUG (see 4.8.2) as already described according to the BilMoG; therefore, possibly in the light of further changes, the following applies. The weighting of certain rules has been changed[302] in order to strengthen the informative function of financial reporting in terms of commercial law (HGB, cf. basically on communication

[301] Explanation of the draft law of the German Federal government for the Accounting Law Modernisation Act (*Bilanzrechtsmodernisierungsgesetz*, BilMoG) of 30.07.2008, *Bundestags-Drucksache* 16/10067, 1. On the draft Luttermann (2008c).

[302] Generally on the reform from a practical perspective, see, e.g., Kessler, Leinen, and Strickmann (2009).

4.12.3). It should be emphasised that now the goodwill or company value also counts as a temporarily available asset for the accounts; this is possible through a legal fiction (§ 246(1)(4) HGB: *"gilt als"*, shall be deemed as). The interpretation of the term "asset" (*Vermögensgegenstand*)[303] remains unchanged. This remains to be assessed anew in view of more recent developments and requirements in the course of "sustainable economic activity" (*Nachhaltigkeit*, see 4.12.1).

The prohibition on recognising internally generated intangible non-current assets (*selbst geschaffene immaterielle Vermögensgegenstände des Anlagevermögens*) has been partially lifted[304] (§ 248(2)(1) HGB). There is now a choice (*Wahlrecht*).[305] The production costs from the development phase (which are an asset in the sense of § 246(1) HGB) may be activated; the production costs from the research phase cannot be activated (§ 255(2) and (2a) HGB), for the character of research as an asset is, as a rule, too uncertain without affirmation through the market (e.g., licence contract as a so-called third-party business). That confirms: It is still and foremost about substance, not a numbers game. To be clear right from the outset, the responsible corporate directors and auditors have to handle this carefully within the financial reports strictly in terms of sustainability as verifiability (*Nachprüfbarkeit*, see 4.1, 4.11.4 with 4.10).

The motivation of the legislator for this substantial change in the German law stems from insights of the knowledge society (*Wissensgesellschaft*). "Intangibles", particularly patents, are gaining extraordinary importance in many domains (e.g., in the domains of medicine and genetic engineering, biotechnology, chemistry and synthetic biology, nanotechnology, mechanical engineering, AI).[306] The reform legislation brings this fact to the attention of the auditors to a much greater degree than formerly. At the same time, new, innovative entrepreneurs and companies (corporations) of small and medium size (start-ups) are to be given the opportunity of presenting themselves in an attractive way.[307] In the light of the uncertainty and concomitant possibilities for manipulation (research and development costs, capitalisation practices), this remains a critical field internationally.[308] This is the reason for the prohibition to pay corresponding profits (§ 268(8) HGB so-called payout block, *Ausschüttungssperre*). This is to guarantee that substance (capital) remains in the corporation. A practical building block for sustainable finance and financial reporting (human corporation).

---

[303] See Großfeld and Luttermann (2005) recitals 355–357 and 359–361.

[304] Cf. still the earlier § 248(2) HGB old version.

[305] This corresponds to Annex III(C)(I)(1) of the Accounting Law Directive 2013/34/EU (cf. Council Dir 78/660/EEC) Art. 9. Compare IAS 38 (Intangible Assets).

[306] See overall below 9.5 and 9.6, above 3.7 (developmental history).

[307] See 4.2.1 and 4.6.1. Cf. statistical evidence: European Commission, How do companies "perceive" their intangibles? (2014/2016). IDW S 5 (Principles for the evaluation of intangible assets).

[308] See, e.g., Garanina (2016); Triki-Damak and Halioui (2013).

What the reform also introduced is a valuation with "fair value" (*beizulegender Zeitwert*). This value corresponds to the market price (§ 255(4)(1) HGB). If there is no active market for the determination of the market price (so-called "mark-to-market"), the "fair value" is to be determined with the help of generally recognised valuation methods (§ 255(4)(2) HGB, "mark-to-model" – *beigelegter Zeitwert*, see 7.5.2). If that is also impossible, the acquisition and production costs are to be continued (§ 255(4)(3)–(4), § 253(4) HGB). This change is contentious;[309] it seems like a concession to the spirit of the outdated Anglo-American valuation patterns (the "numbers game", gateway for manipulation and fraud).[310] This applies in particular to the accounting of financial instruments in financial institutions. Here, a deduction for risk has to be made (§ 340e(4) HGB). It remains questionable whether that is sufficient in the light of the world debt crisis ("toxic assets").[311] The measures of sustainability fundamentally speak against this (see 5.2.4).

## *4.8.4 German and European Rule of Law (SMEs)*

The development in Germany is a signal for the state and perspectives of financial reporting internationally, the more so in times of a challenging "climate change" worldwide. German legislature wants to provide the practical domain with "a full, but more cost-effective and easier alternative" with the reform of the Code of Commercial Law (HGB) in comparison to the "IFRS".[312] This wording sounds inconsistent, however, as HGB and "IFRS" are not on a par (*gleichwertig*). Therefore, it must be emphasised that German legislature in fact says that financial reporting in terms of the HGB-commercial law remains the basis of profit payments due to the lack of "alternative possibilities".[313] This position is confirmed by the more recent BilRUG for the implementation of the Accounting Law Directive 2013/34/EU: It supports in particular the smaller and medium-sized companies, which form the backbone of the German economy (so-called *Mittelstand*, see 4.8.2 and 4.8.4).

---

309 On this, e.g., IDW RS-HFA 9; Schildbach (2010); Wolz, Kümpel, and Oldewurte (2012). See below 7.5.2. In legal comparison, Luttermann (2003a) § 264 HGB recitals 42–82; Luttermann (2009a).

310 See Levitt (1998) and above 4.6.1 with chapter 6. Cf., e.g., Guermazi (2022).

311 See above 4.4.6, 4.7.1 and chapter 5. Cf. Kranz (2010).

312 *Bundestags-Drucksache* 16/10067, p. 32 (and 1), on the BilMoG.

313 Ibid.

This at the same time characterises the legal situation in the European Union, as was already shown for the clearly regulated and limited adoption of the "IAS/IFRS" (Accounting Law Regulation (EC) 1606/2002, see 4.4.4). There are concomitant practical problems. The IASB, the London-based private standard setter, is proactively working on the "IFRS".[314] Corresponding to the output from the IASB of new, amended or revised "IFRS", the procedure of adoption within the EU is working (see 4.4.3); hence, this is almost a never-ending story. This is illustrated by the ongoing discussion to extend the "IFRS" as mandatory for annual accounts and other companies. In 2008, the IASB published its "IFRS for small and medium-sized entities" (IFRS for SMEs), which is controversial in Germany and the EU.[315] There are hundreds of thousands of such companies not only in Germany but in Austria, the Netherlands and other European countries, too: They are the epitome of entrepreneurship and represent 99% of all businesses in the Union.[316]

That is the expression of our time-proven culture: The law is fixed systematically (legal system, *Gesetzesrecht*) instead of by case (case law system, *Fallrecht*);[317] and it is conceived rather from the smaller entrepreneurial units (bottom-up), e.g. the merchant (*Kaufmann*, § 1 HGB) or the family-like partnership (*Handelsgesellschaft*, § 105 HGB), instead of being broken down to these units from the large capital-market oriented companies (top-down). Accordingly, in Germany – at least for accounting under the German, European-influenced HGB – bureaucratic burdens have been reduced (e.g. attachments, additional documents to be provided), also through higher threshold levels for the classification as a medium-sized company (*mittelgrosses Unternehmen*, cf. §§ 267, 267a HGB).[318] No patchwork (so-called "rules-based approach", cf. 3.5.5) can sustainably support a true and fair view (*Bilanzwahrheit*) in accounting and auditing; it is systematic regulation and practice from the basis up which can do this (so-called "principles-based approach", see 4.6.4).

At this point, it is still not clear where the journey is heading and to what extent it will change the national laws of the member states. Digital developments may have a great impact, for decentral, network-like structures (e.g., distributed ledger technology) as well as for a global monopolisation (e.g., "XBRL/IFRS", see 4.11). The discourse on "sustainability" has to be conducted in a pioneering way, counterbalancing in both dimensions (see 5.2.4, 8.4.3). In Germany, the sensible relationship in accounting between tax law and company law is at stake (see 4.4.6). This much is clear: German legislation explicitly preserves "the advantages of the

---

[314] See https://www.ifrs.org/projects/work-plan/ (updated).

[315] On the current status: https://www.ifrs.org/issued-standards/ifrs-for-smes/. Cf. Quagli and Paoloni (2012). Basically on IAS/IFRS for SMEs see Ebke, Luttermann, and Siegel (2007).

[316] For more information: https://single-market-economy.ec.europa.eu/smes_en (updated). Note also below 4.11.3.

[317] See on casuistry (*Kasuistik*) above 4.2.4 and overall 3.5.5, 7.8.1.

[318] Deutscher Bundestag, Gesetzentwurf Bilanzrichtlinie-Umsetzungsgesetz – BilRUG, 20.02.2015, *Bundestags-Drucksache* 18/4050, 2 and 41.

decisiveness of financial reporting in terms of commercial law for fiscal profit, ascertainment of profits" and "the cornerstones of financial reporting in terms of commercial law just as (...) the system of the principles of proper bookkeeping".[319]

This clearly refutes the IASB and "IFRS". This also applies to the "IFRS for Small and Medium Sized Entities" ("IFRS for SMEs"). In the light of its complexity and the density of regulations, it says in legal terminology that the "IFRS for SMEs" is not suitable for meeting the needs of small and medium-sized entities for a financial report that is informative, while being limited to the necessities.[320] The essential argument – with the basically insufficient conception of so-called "standard setting" of the IASB (see, e.g., 4.4.5 and 4.9.7) – is still the following: the "IFRS for SMEs" are materially deficient. This applies likewise to the "full IFRS", which is also corroborated by European institutions.[321] Conceptually, the principle of prudence (*Vorsichtsprinzip*) takes a back seat in the "IFRS" (still similar to its patron, the so-called "U.S. GAAP"),[322] while it dominates in European and German accounting law.

This is fatal, as the world debt crisis since the fall of Lehman Brothers Inc. (see 4.6.2) has borne witness to on a global scale. It contradicts the European general rule of a true and fair view (*Bilanzwahrheit*, see 4.4.4 and 4.5.2), that is imperative for financial reporting and auditing (value creation, *Wertschöpfung*, see Fig. 4.4) – all the more in terms of the overall meaning of "sustainability" (*Nachhaltigkeit*) as verifiability (*Nachprüfbarkeit*, see 4.11.4): real financial reporting as verified information. – Is there any better concept?

### *4.8.5 Fair Competition?*

At the same time, this shows the competitive dimension in a European and a global dimension – also for transformation. With accounting law, the setting of standards for financial reporting, the international issue is the ordering of assets (*Vermögen*) and participation in prosperity, as has been shown. This is all the more true since, with global climate change, the common good and common goals are here at stake. To this end, fair competition is necessary in a legal order. What is required are cooperative approaches (see 4.8.8),[323] in any case no one-sidedness. German

---

[319] Translated from: *Gesetz zur Modernisierung des Bilanzrechts* (BilMoG — Draft), *Bundestags-Drucksache* 16/100667, p. 32. On this Luttermann (2008c). Specifically on accounting in family firms Reuther and Fink (2010).

[320] *Bundestags-Drucksache* 16/10067, 33, on the draft of the IFRS for SMEs (February 2007). Seminally see Luttermann (2007a).

[321] See above 4.4.5, below 4.8.8; cf. 4.4.4.

[322] Together with principles of realisation and of imparity in the accounting of "profit", see Art. 6(1) (c) of the Accounting Law Directive 2013/34/EU (Regulation 78/660/EEC Art. 31(1) lit. c) and § 252(1) No 4 HGB.

[323] Overall see chapters 8 (esp. 8.4) and 9.

legislation has rightly pointed this out. In the light of the neglect of the principle of prudence (*Vorsichtsprinzip*), it says that not only does the transition to the "IFRS" not produce any additional benefit, as compared to accounting according to German commercial law (HGB), but on the contrary, there is even the danger that due to the degree of detail of the "IFRS", competition-relevant data may have to be disclosed by German companies.[324]

This may be tolerable for corporations oriented towards the capital markets as well as for diversified large corporations operating internationally. However, according to legislation, it may threaten the existence of small and medium-sized companies.[325] The following must be borne in mind: even in the U.S., the rules of mandatory disclosure of the Securities and Exchange Commission (SEC) apply only to public corporations with upwards of 500 shareholders. In the U.S., there is no systematic regulation of medium-sized companies; this is also true of the convergence project for the harmonisation of accounting standards between the Financial Accounting Standards Board (FASB) in the U.S. and the IASB in London. Although both sides continuously declare that a single set of globally accepted accounting standards is the aim, actual convergence remains open in spite of numerous common projects of IASB and FASB.[326] The SECs Electronic Data Gathering, Analysis, and Retrieval (EDGAR) system supports "IFRS" taxonomies. But general harmonisation is still lacking, both conceptually and methodologically, especially as no uniform application can be provided (see 4.8.6).

Obviously, the SEC strategically relies on the FASB "to promote high-quality accounting standards" for "the needs of investors", does not refer to the IASB ("IFRS") anywhere in its strategy plan and "will consider, among other things, whether a single set of high-quality global accounting standards is achievable".[327] Overall, the regulation of financial reporting, valuation and auditing proves to be an eminently political field, in which an institutional change (here: "IFRS" adoption) is difficult.[328] This applies all the more as it shows the basic attitude. Although praised by media (propaganda with so-called "Generally Accepted Accounting Principles", U.S. "GAAP") as a global stronghold of transparency and protection of investors, the U.S. and its federal states have hardly any general, uniformly valid duties of

---

[324] BilMoG, *Bundestags-Drucksache* 16/10067, p. 33.

[325] Ibid.

[326] See IFRS: https://www.ifrs.org/news-and-events/updates/iasb/2024/iasb-update-june-2024/ (accessed: 22.08.2025). Cf., e.g., Murphy, O'Connell, and Ó hÓgartaigh (2013), Sanko and Koldovskyi (2017), Lucchese and Di Carlo (2020), Rey, Maglio, and Rapone (2020), Lin, Pownall, Sawani, and Wang (2024); in the practice of a major auditing firm: Deloitte, U.S. GAAP and IFRS standards: understanding the differences, Dec. 2020.

[327] SEC, Strategic Plan, Fiscal Years 2014-2018: Protecting investors, maintaining fair, orderly, and efficient markets, and facilitating capital formation, 13-14. Cf. SEC, Strategic Plan, Fiscal Years 2018-2022, and rsp. for 2022-2026, focused primarily to "protect the investing public against fraud, manipulation, and misconduct".

[328] Becker, Daske, Pelger, Zeff (2022).

disclosure for corporations.[329] Politically, it is about its own interest as a global leading power, internationally propagating, even enforcing transparency, while itself showing up as the "biggest tax-haven on earth": as has been proven by research and real transparency, e.g. like the Pandora Papers (2021).[330]

In contrast, European law, which has hitherto been interpreted in a particularly strict fashion in Germany with the company register (*Unternehmensregister*, § 325 HGB), opens up corporations located in Germany for worldwide inspection via the internet.[331] Competitors around the globe, while themselves remaining anonymous, are easily able to acquire information about the financial situation of a German (European) competitor. The problem is exacerbated by uniform computer language as well as various regulation (XBRL, see 4.11.2). This is a massive distortion of the markets. Fair competition still demands an adequate reform. Remember, the financing of any company, the human corporation as a publicly efficient tool as such is basically always about other people's money (see 4.4.1 and 3.3). – Is there another concept for achieving good corporate governance (human corporation), id est a "good economy"?

### *4.8.6 Comparative Law: Regional "IFRS"*

Of course, in a global dimension, cultural and geographical peculiarities (*Weltanschauungen*) must be taken into account. Notwithstanding, the IASB, with its so-called "IFRS", intends a "global language of finance", which is to cover 95% of all companies.[332] They declare: IFRS "have become the de facto global standard for financial reporting".[333] – One size fits all? – The world-spanning claim of the IASB sounds fantastic. However, it is not only specific accounting rules such as religion-based "Islamic Finance" that make it fail.[334] Independent research reveals diversity worldwide, in important markets "IFRS" are not allowed for regulated

[329] Siegel (2007), see also Vagts (2009). In terms of sustainability reporting (*Nachhaltigkeitsberichterstattung*) on the SEC below in 6.7.2, Luttermann, L. (2023) and (2024). Overall critically, e.g., Levitt (1998), Luttermann (1999a) and Stiglitz (2010), esp. from p. 147. See also chapter 6.

[330] Noked and Marcone (2022), Luttermann (2016b). Cf. Financial Secrecy Index 2022 et seq., current: https://fsi.taxjustice.net/.

[331] See Schön (2009) and Stark (2007).

[332] IASB: About the IFRS for SMEs (https://www.ifrs.org/) and Tweedie, Chairman IASB (Toronto, 25.04.2008): "IFRSs as a common financial reporting language throughout the world". Cf. below 4.11.3.

[333] IFRS Foundation, The Global Financial Reporting Language (May 2016).

[334] Luttermann (2009b). Cf. Mohammed, Fahmi, Ahmad (2015).

reporting or they are only of restricted scope.[335] Discrepancies are evident in the valuation circumstances in the U.S., for instance with the convergence project between IASB and FASB (see 4.8.5). Legal comparison reveals a multi-faceted picture in the wider surroundings as well.

Australia, for instance (cf. similarly also the Oceanic neighbor state New Zealand),[336] maintains differences in regard to global standards of valuation that are substantial even for the Anglo-American culture. In Australia, the "IFRS" were introduced as "Australian Equivalents to IFRS" (AIFRS) only under the reservation of the national corporate law.[337] The aim is the promotion of the Australian economy in the worldwide competition in the capital markets, as stated by the Financial Reporting Council: "to promote the adoption of international best practice accounting standards in the Australian accounting standard setting processes if doing so would be in the best interests of both the private and public sector in the Australian economy" (Sec 225(2)(g) ASIC Act 2001).[338] "International standards" (so-called "IFRS") may be changed by "Australian application paragraphs", which are added by parliament or the executive power. Even if extensive harmonisation of the Australian requirements regarding "IFRS" is demanded, what does the practical implementation look like? Research examines practice under the Australian version of "IFRS" and identifies material non-compliance among Australian companies.[339]

This marks off a wide field that remains to be investigated. The mentioned non-compliance may raise questions about accounting and audit quality in Australia and may even suggest poor regulatory oversight.[340] Basically, one should be clear about the legal framework. The Australian Accounting Standards Board (AASB) has to observe "the interests of Australian corporations", which raise capital in major international financial centres (Sec 227(2) ASIC Act 2001). What counts is "the national interest" (*ordre public*, cf. above 4.4.4): "The text of the international

---

[335] See, e.g., above 4.4.5 and 4.5.4. Also to be considered is voluntary adaption, see Nobes (2015); on Canada, Japan and Switzerland Nobes and Zeff (2016); on "global IFRS adoption" Song and Trimble (2022). Cf., e.g., Asian-Oceanian Standard-Setters Group (AOSSG), Financial Reporting by Islamic Financial Institutions, March 2015, and results of a follow-up survey, AOSSG, Nov 2023 (https://www.aossg.org/images/about-us/member%20organisation/Updated_review_of_IFIs_FS_website_publication.pdf, accessed: 22.08.2025). Mulyany and Ariffin (2018), Calder (2020).

[336] See External Reporting Board (XRB): New Zealand Equivalents to IFRS (*NZ IFRS*) and the new Accounting Standards Framework (www.xrb.govt.nz). On the adoption of NZ IFRS (2007-2014): www.treasury.govt.nz/publications/guidance/reporting/nzifrs, accessed:22.08.2025).

[337] See on company law and accounting law in Australia Luttermann (2007b). Cf. Haswell and Lanfield-Smith (2008). For developments: www.aasb.gov.au (updated) and Chen, Lu, Shan and Taylor (2025).

[338] Australian Securities and Investments Commission Act 2001 (as registered: 20.09.2022); see also Sec. 224(b) and (c) ASIC Act 2001.

[339] Wang (2019).

[340] Ibid, 679. Cf. Chen, Lu, Shan and Taylor (2025), esp. pp. 2, 5 and 35-36: lack of "evidence-based policy" instead of "policy-based evidence".

accounting standard may be modified to the extent necessary to take account of the Australian legal or institutional environment" (Sec 227(4) ASIC Act 2001). The AASB can set its own, primary standards. Basically in this case, as in the European Union, national accounting norms stand as conflict of laws (*Kollisionsrecht*), intended to prevent excessive international influence (see 4.8.8).

China, in a perhaps still ongoing transformation process, has been propagating "IAS/IFRS", also modified in Hong Kong (HK Financial Reporting Standards): The internet giant Alibaba Group Holding Ltd. avoided this regulation in 2014 and staged its stock market launch in New York (according to US "GAAP").[341] The Ministry of Finance of China and the IFRS Foundation in 2015 confirm in a joint statement the goal of full convergence:[342] This is an ambitious project in view of the practice of accounting manipulation, weak institutional infrastructure and massive differences between "IFRS" and China GAAP; foreign-invested enterprises in China are required to prepare financial reports using Chinese Accounting Standards (CAS), in particular the Accounting Standards for Business Enterprises (ASBE).[343] The question remains, however, whether the legal adoption is in fact anything more than lip service, paid for admission to the world markets.[344] This may be especially attractive for developing countries, e.g. for Nigeria: "IFRS" as a product with "network effects".[345] However, this does not improve the quality of financial information.

Japan seems strange, in particular with regard to "IFRS". They appear at the stock market exchange in Tokyo (TSE) voluntarily as an accounting framework besides Japanese GAAP, US GAAP and more recently with Japan's Modified International Standards (JMIF): Accounting standards comprising "IFRSs" and the ASBJ modifications.[346] Japan thus still views the "IFRS" with reservations, seeking to preserve their traditional character in accounting as well: "IFRS must accurately reflect the

[341] Overall Luttermann (2014). Cf. SEC probes Alibaba accounting practices: www.wsj.com/articles/alibaba-discloses-sec-probe-of-its-accounting-practices-1464195695 (accessed: 30.06.2025).

[342] Of 18.11.2015 (Beijing Joint Statement). Cf. Moser (2014), Xie, Zhang and Zhai (2022). On 19.06.2023 the IFRS Foundation opens an ISSB office in Beijing. On manipulation, e.g.: Tingting An, Case study on accounting fraud of U.S.-listed Chinese companies, MIT thesis 2014; Francine McKenna, 20.06.2016: www.marketwatch.com/story/after-china-fraud-boom-nasdaq-steps-up-scrutiny-of-shady-listings-2016-06-20 (accessed: 22.08.2025). Wang, J. and Wang, D. (2022).

[343] DeFond, Gao, Li, and Xia (2019), Zhang and Ye (2020). Cf. Wang and Campbell (2012), Faiyyaz and Malik (2022). Note the foreign investment law: Luttermann (2015b); on developments under: www.mof.gov.cn (updated). Basically Luttermann and Hartwig (2004).

[344] On a significant increase in exports "after converging with IFRS": Xie, Zhang and Zhai (2022). Overall literature review Jiannan and Huaying (2024).

[345] Odia and Ogiedu (2013). For India, e.g.: Pal (2015); Latha and Sridar (2022).

[346] For up-to-date information: https://www.asb.or.jp/en/. Cf. Accounting Standards Board of Japan (ASBJ), 25.07.2016: www.asb.or.jp/asb/asb_e/endorsement/jmis/20160725.jsp. (accessed: 18.07.2025).

economic reality of businesses and trade practices in Japan".[347] As in Europe, the demand is for "improved accountability [and governance]" of the IASB.[348] The Financial Services Agency (FSA) of Japan designates "IFRSs" for voluntary use by companies, but the core line remains: "the time has not yet arrived to make a decision on mandatory application of IFRS in Japan".[349] Japanese listed firms can voluntarily use IFRS (since 2010) and IFRS-aligned sustainability disclosure standards are introduced (2025).[350] Most of all, there is an awareness in Japan also that, economically, accounting law is about the essence of a global order of assets and fair competition (see 4.8.1).

### *4.8.7 Limits, Linguistic Diversity, and European "IFRS"*

Indeed, around the world, under the appealing label "IFRS", variants are developing that are regionally shaped by specific regulation, legislation, and court decisions (see 4.8.6). It is about sovereign decisions, which – guided by the rule of law (*Grundsatz der Rechtsstaatlichkeit*) – originate in the respective jurisdiction and refer to it. The IASB cannot offer this.[351] With its "IFRS", for all its palatefulness ("global language of finance"), it takes a wide reach without corresponding regulatory competence. In spite of this, the IFRS Foundation with the "International Sustainability Standards Board" (ISSB) additionally wants developing standards that can "provide a common language for sustainability information, to enable comparable and consistent sustainability disclosures across global capital markets".[352] As mentioned earlier, specific relations and limitations are in effect legally all over the world, in particular cultural and geographical peculiarities (see 4.9.6).

This is also the case in the European Union. The legal situation is clear for adopted IFRS: with their publication in the Official Journal (OJ) they become European law, which is guaranteed by the European Court of Justice (see 4.5.2).[353] Overall, the legal stipulations apply that are valid for the adoption of

[347] Japan Financial Services Agency (JFSA), Application of IFRS in Japan (13.02.2009), 7 et seq., and Regulatory Notices (March 2010). On the European Union see above 4.4.5.

[348] JFSA, Application of IFRS in Japan (13.02.2009), 7 et seq, and Regulatory Notices (March 2010).

[349] JFSA, Report of the Business Accounting Council on the use of IFRS in Japan, 20.06.2013, p. 4 (www.fsa.go.jp/en/news/2013/20130621-1.html, accessed: 22.08.2025). Gu (2021). On current status: www.fsa.go.jp/en (updated).

[350] On voluntary adaption Gu (2021), cf. on mandatory adaption Tsunogaya (2016).

[351] See above 4.4 and 4.5. Cf. on the failure of global adaption De Luca and Prather-Kinsey (2018).

[352] See IFRS on a "comprehensive global baseline" of sustainability disclosures for the capital markets: https://www.ifrs.org/use-around-the-world/why-a-global-baseline-for-capital-markets/ (accessed: 22.08.2025).

[353] TFEU Art. 3 No 3(4). On languages and the law in the EU see Luttermann, K. (2014), Luttermann, C. and Luttermann, K. (2020).

so-called "international accounting standards", id est in particular: They cannot be contrary to the principle of "a true and fair view" (*Bilanzwahrheit*), but must be conducive to the "European public good" (*Europäisches öffentliches Interesse*). This means that the European Union as a legal community must be protected from a foreign regime regarding international private law (see 4.4.4). The European Court of Justice has the final word in the interpretation and practice of the adopted "IFRS" (EU-IFRS, cf. Art. 267 TFEU). The European language regime must be observed in this context. In the canon of the 24 official languages of the Union, a decision by the Court is only authentic the respective language of the case (Art. 41 Rules of Procedure of ECJ, Art. 342 TFEU). If this is German, e.g., the German version is authentic; if the case is conducted in Italian, only the Italian version of the judgment is authentic.

The translations that this system requires for accounting law terminology contain seeds of conflict. This was demonstrated at an early stage: In a Europe with many official languages (*Amtssprachen*), the translation of the norms (legal language) can and is easily used and abused for legal politics. This comprises questionable implementation of legal acts, designed for legal unification in the internal market (regulations, Art. 288(2) TFEU) or legal harmonisation (directives, Art. 288(3) TFEU). This is demonstrated by the European accounting directives: Different language versions (translations) of the general norm for financial reporting and auditing lead to different liability situations for accountants and auditors in individual member states.[354] Such a legal gradient may be practically exploited through so-called "language shopping", id est choosing a favorable language version.[355] It should be emphasised once again that directives and regulations, in contrast to the rulings by the European Court of Justice as just shown, are considered authentic in each of the 24 official languages (Art. 55 TEU, Art. 358 TFEU).

This includes the "IFRS" adopted in the Union (so-called EU-"IFRS", see 4.4.3). They have to be published in each official language in the Official Journal of the European Union and are therefore authentic in 24 language versions.[356] It has not been widely investigated how legal practice in the member states, as well as at the supranational level, deals with this situation. In any case, the monopoly of the English language that is often propagated by the IASB is broken in this way. In the best case, the European law and its languages will lead to European "IFRS".[357] They have their own characteristics, whereas other languages and cultures may promote other values in accounting. With the exit of the UK ("Brexit"), English

[354] See Luttermann (1999b). Luttermann (2003a) Einf BilanzR recitals 142-151 and § 264 HGB recitals 42-169. Cf. above 4.5.2.

[355] See Luttermann, C. and Luttermann, K. (2021), Luttermann, C. and Luttermann, K. (2020) pp. 130-136. Basically for the ECJ on languages Chapter 8 of the Rules of Procedure of ECJ (Art. 36 to 42), Art. 342 TFEU.

[356] Basically Art. 55 TEU, Art. 358 TFEU. Cf. empirically Baskerville and Evans (2011). See also Luttermann and Wiese-Ptak (2015).

[357] See 4.4.4, 4.5.1 and 4.5.2. Luttermann (2002).

may not have lost its status as an official language in the Union,[358] but it will probably become weaker.

### 4.8.8 European Law and Multijurisdictional Approach

European accounting law is authoritative in Germany and, in case of conflict of laws (*Kollisionsrecht*), in the EU as a whole in relation to international standards ("IFRS", see 4.4.4). This must be borne in mind with regard to further reforms, legal comparison and convergence internationally, also with regard to IFRS Sustainability Disclosure Standards ("IFRS S"). The same applies to a lack of substance and uniformity of the "IFRS". The European Financial Reporting Advisory Group (EFRAG)[359] regards the "IFRS for SMEs" in particular as incompatible with the European accounting directives. Although EFRAG has claimed possible interpretational freedom in favour of "IFRS", there remain numerous accounting treatments that are mandatory in the "IFRS", but which are inadmissible according to European law.[360] Overall, reasons and discussion endure as described (see 4.4.5 and 4.11.3).

Let's take a look back: Corporate governance is about accounting as a means of financing a company most efficiently. Therefore, the free flow of capital (Art. 63 TFEU) is one of the advantages of the European Union establishing an internal market (*Binnenmarkt*) among the member states and their companies. European capital markets should also be more easily used by third country issuers. Legislation of the European Union[361] concerns information contained in prospectuses to be published when securities are offered to the public or admitted to trading in accordance with "IFRS". Efforts for the convergence of the standards for the publicity of

[358] See for a critical view on this and overall on legal linguistics Luttermann, C. and Luttermann, K. (2021).

[359] EFRAG was set up in 2001 to assist the EC-Commission in the endorsement of IFRS (www.efrag.org). See also EC-Commission Summary Reports on: Review of the Accounting Directives (October 2009) and The IFRS for SMEs (May 2010); Study on the Accounting Regime of Limited Liability Micro Companies (June 2019).

[360] Cf., e.g., 4.5.4 (Lord Sikka); Endorsement Status Report, current: www.efrag.org/Endorsement. Report of 28.05.2010 (www.accountancyage.com/aa/news/1808000/ifrs-smes-incompatible-eu-directives-efrag, accessed: 22.08.2025). Cf. Mourik and Walton (2018).

[361] See Directive 2003/71/EC, OJ L 345, 31.12.2003, 64, repealed (end of validity: 20.07.2019) by Regulation (EU) 2017/1129, OJ L 168, 30.06.2017, 12-82. Cf. Institute of Chartered Accountants in England and Wales (ICAEW), The effects of mandatory IFRS adoption in the EU: a review of empirical research, 2015/2018.

corporations are intended to facilitate the capital flow also beyond the borders of the internal market. A draft by the European Commission[362] proposed as early as 2004 that it should be accepted that the historical information required in a prospectus is prepared in accordance with the Generally Accepted Accounting Principles (GAAP) of either Canada, Japan or the USA. The Committee of European Securities Regulators (CESR) recommended[363] that the European Commission accept US GAAP, Japanese GAAP, Canadian GAAP and South Korean GAAP as equivalent to "IFRS" adopted by the Union pursuant to the Accounting Law Regulation 1606/2002.

The European Union has proceeded along this path, propelled by the catastrophic development of the world debt crisis with the fall of the investment bank Lehman Brothers Inc. in the USA (see 4.6.2, 6.6). Fundamentally it has to be emphasised for further developments: The internationally-proven concept of reciprocal recognition promises to be the most fruitful procedure. Diversity is part of the international legal order. The world debt crisis bears witness to the transition to the global trade of corporations. As accounting, auditing and also insolvencies[364] show, the classical national state is, however, forced to take action where transnational coordination is lacking. Thus, e.g., the European Union prompted a discussion "on the conditions for integrating the IASCF/IASB into the system of international governance" (IMF, OECD, World Bank etc.).[365] The concept of a multijurisdictional system must be developed as an international sound and sustainable system of a *Vermögensordnung* (a legal order of assets) to this end (see 4.10.2 and chapter 8).

The European Union, in practical terms, has established a mechanism for determining the equivalence of the financial reporting standards of third countries with those of the Union (Commission Reg (EC) No 1569/2007).[366] Accordingly, this regulation exempts third country issuers from the obligation to restate historical financial information that was drawn up according to national accounting standards

[362] EC Commission, Draft Commission Reg, amending Commission Reg (EC) 809/2004 of 29 Apr 2004 implementing Directive 2003/71/EC of the EP and of the Council as regards information contained in prospectuses as well as the format, incorporation by reference and publication of such prospectuses and dissemination of advertisements, Working Document ESC/23/2006–rev3. Commission Delegated Reg (EU) 2016/301, 30.11.2015, supplementing Directive 203/71/EC and amending Reg (EC) No 809/204, OJ L 58, 04.03.2016, 13. On the implementation of financial services legislation OJ C 284 E 21.11.2002, 115 (Lamfalussy report).

[363] CESR, Advice on the equivalence of Chinese, Japanese and US GAAPs (CESR/07-761, Dec 2007) and on Canadian and South Korean GAAPs (CESR/08-293, May 2011).

[364] See UNCITRAL, Practice Guide on Cross-Border Insolvency Co-operation (2009). For the European Union: Regulation (EU) 2015/848 of 20 May 2015, OJ L 141, 19-72 (amended, e.g.: Regulation (EU) 2023/2844).

[365] European Parliament (EP), non-legislative resolution (INI/2006/2248: 24/04/2008). Cf. Palea (2018) on IFRS in the EU.

[366] Of 21.12.2007 establishing a mechanism for the determination of equivalence of accounting standards applied by third country issuers of securities pursuant to Directive 2003/71/EC and 2004/109/EC, OJ L 340, 22.12.2007, 66 (updated); e.g., Commission Implementing Decision (EU) 2015/1612 of 23.9.2015 (with IFRS), OJ L 249, 25.09.2015, 26. Overall EU Commission: https://finance.ec.europa.eu/eu-and-world/equivalence-non-eu-financial-frameworks_en (accessed: 22.08.2025).

(multijurisdictional approach, see 4.8.8 and Fig. 4.5). The Commission recognised US "GAAP" and Japanese "GAAP" as equivalent to the "IFRS"[367] and published a report in 2010[368] that treats the convergence of "IFRS", introduced into the Union in 2005 (see 4.4.3), with the "GAAP" of third countries (e.g., Canada, China, India, South Korea). Those who use other standards have to prove that they are of equivalent quality and that the financial statements have been filed with "a competent authority". This is an important step towards harmonising the international context for companies. The EU–U.S. Joint Financial Regulatory Forum is leading the way for broader cooperation, meanwhile focusing on seven topics:[369]

(1) market developments and financial stability,
(2) operational resilience and digital finance,
(3) the sharing and financial reporting of financial data,
(4) anti-money laundering and countering the financing of terrorism,
(5) sustainable finance,
(6) banking and insurance, and
(7) capital markets.

With climate change, it is in particular the implications of sustainable finance (valuation) that come into the foreground for the reasonable regulation of corporate governance.[370] Of course, mutual recognition is necessary, especially in the case of the USA for accepting European accounting law to enter into their capital markets.[371] In fact, the question of harmonisation remains to be clarified by way of legal comparison. Globalisation is founded on regionally strong structures.[372] In Europe, the principle of subsidiarity is decisive (Art. 5 TEU), to be implemented in a European accounting law upheld by the European Court of Justice. – On a global

[367] EU Commission, 22.04.2008, Report on convergence between IFRS and third country national GAAP and on the progress towards the elimination of reconciliation requirements that apply to Community issuers under the rules of these third countries.

[368] EU Commission, 04.06.2010, Report to the European Securities Committee and to the European Parliament on convergence between IFRS and third country national GAAPs: COM(2010)292 final.

[369] Joint Statement, 10.12.2024: https://finance.ec.europa.eu/publications/joint-statement-eu-us-joint-financial-regulatory-forum-december-2024_en (accessed: 22.08.2025). Cf. Joint Statement, 20.07.2022: (1) market developments and current assessment of financial stability risks, (2) sustainable finance, (3) multilateral and bilateral engagement in banking and insurance, (4) regulatory and supervisory cooperation in capital markets, (5) financial innovation, and (6) anti-money laundering and countering the financing of terrorism (https://home.treasury.gov/news/press-releases/jy0882 (accessed: 22.08.2025).

[370] With a concept of sustainable due diligence and value creation Luttermann, L. (2022) and (2024): Sustainable Business Finance Navigator (SBFN).

[371] See 4.8.5 and Luttermann (1999a) pp. 134–136 (calling for an "International Court of Accounting").

[372] Luttermann (1997) and (2010c). On form and function Gilson (2001). Cf. Cross and Prentice (2007) pp. 202-208: competitive regulation (superior securities law). Comparatively on "international accounting" Nobes and Parker (2020).

scale, where are comparable structures, e.g. an International Court of Accounting[373]? – Standard setting, suitable for sustainable financial reporting and auditing (valuation), includes strong enforcement and judicial relief (*Rechtsschutz*). The best rules are merely "words, words, words" (Shakespeare), if they are not secured procedurally (see 4.9.7, 4.10).

## 4.9 Auditing, Control, and Sanctions

### *4.9.1 On Watchdogs and Materiality*

The annual accounts (financial statements, management report) of a company with limited liability are subject to a statutory audit (§ 316(1) HGB), so are the consolidated financial statements and management reports (§ 316(2) HGB).[374] An independent auditor (*Abschlussprüfer*, certified public accountant) is to conduct the audit, providing the statutory rules and additional terms of the memorandum of association (*Gesellschaftsvertrag*) or of the articles of incorporation (*Satzung*) have been observed; that includes the bookkeeping (see Fig. 4.6).[375] Just as for accounting, the measure to be applied is the general provision of "a true and fair view" (i.e., *Bilanzwahrheit*): The auditor is to carry out the audit in a conscientious manner in order to identify material errors (*Unrichtigkeiten*) and violations (*Verstöße*) according to the measure of "a true and fair view" and in accordance with the rules applying to audits of corporations (so-called principle of audit materiality).[376]

The auditor gives an account of the audit and findings in an audit report (*Prüfungsbericht*, § 321 HGB). In his conclusion, the auditor then provides an audit opinion (*Bestätigungsvermerk*). Different categories have been in international use since 2005: the audit opinion is unrestricted in the absence of objections, or restricted in the case of objections (§ 322(2) HGB). If those objections are material (*wesentlich*) or if it is not possible to give an opinion based on the examination, the

[373] Basically above 3.5, esp. 3.5.5. See Luttermann (1997) 485, 504 and (1999a) pp. 134-136 (reprint).

[374] See Großfeld and Luttermann (2005) recitals 1767–1797.

[375] See §§ 317(1)(1) and 238–241a HGB; see also § 91(1) AktG.

[376] See § 317(1)(3) HGB (see 4.5.3 and 4.10.3) with reference to § 264(2) HGB (see 4.4.4 and 4.5 for "a true and fair view", *Bilanzwahrheit*). On the selection of the auditor (§ 319 HGB): BGH, 21.01.2010 (Xa ZR 175/07) NZG 2010, 310. On the effectiveness of the appointment: BGH, 28.04.2022 (IX ZR 69/21) <openJur 2022, 12162>. On remuneration and insolvency: BGH, 28.04.2022 (IX ZR 68/21) <openJur 2022, 11892>.

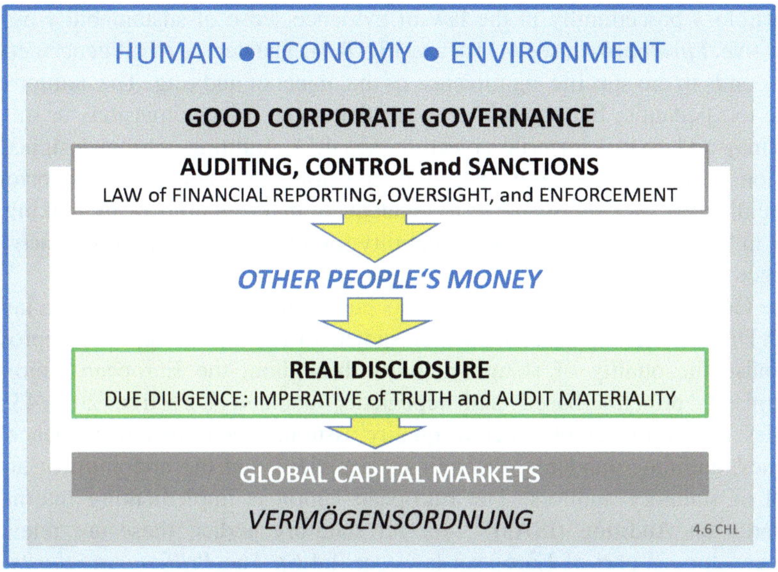


**Fig. 4.6** Auditing the reporting of other people's money for real disclosure

auditor shall refuse to give an audit opinion. Materiality (*Wesentlichkeit*), referring to the measure of "a true and fair view",[377] has to be specified in the light of the circumstances of the particular case. The German Bundesgerichtshof (BGH), for example, ruled that a profit-reducing accounting fault of 44,186 DM (*Deutsche Mark*) is a "vanishingly small item" (*"ein verschwindend geringer Posten"*) when considered in relation to 32.75 million DM consolidated profit.[378] The more recent case of the Wirecard AG shows a completely different extreme: at around 1.9 billion euros, the balance sheet manipulation amounted to almost a third of the audited balance sheet total (*Bilanzsumme*, see 4.9.4).

Taken as a whole, the financial statements must be sustainably reasonable (*angemessen*). For this, the mandate of "a true and fair view" (*Bilanzwahrheit*) provides the legal measure as due diligence (*Sorgfaltspflicht*); of course, this includes issues of financial reporting driven by climate change like in general valuation (e.g. financial risks, environmental and human rights).[379] This is to be practiced by the auditor in an individual case when auditing the financial statements

---

[377] See German §§ 264(2)(1) and 297(2)(2) HGB. On materiality, see above 4.5.3 and Luttermann (2008b), on reform 4.9.2, 4.9.5 and basically Luttermann (2017).

[378] BGH, 18.06.2001 (II ZR 212/99) BGHZ 148, 123, 128–129 (MLP AG). Cf. BGH, 15.12.2005 (III ZR 424/04) <openJur 2011, 11887>; BGH, 12.03.2020 (VII ZR 236/19) <openJur 2020, 5531>. On manipulation and "red flags" Luttermann (2006).

[379] See below 4.9.2, overall chapters 1, 2 and 5. Basically ICJ, Advisory Opinion: Obligation of states in respect of climate change, 23.07.2025 (https://www.icj-cij.org/sites/default/files/case-related/187/187-20250723-adv-01-00-en.pdf, accessed: 22.08.2025). See below 6.1.

as a whole – procedurally in the law of evidence sense of sustainability as verifiability (*Nachprüfbarbeit*, see 4.11.4 and Fig. 4.7). The degree of diligence necessary corresponds to the specific significance of the object of auditing. The auditor should not be too pedantic, but should be aware that some minor omissions or misstated items may add up to a material objection (see 4.5). Auditing is to be designed in an occasion-related way, possibly graded. In any case, the auditor must not perform his task negligently (*nachlässig*), e.g. by inadequate investigations or by making statements in "the dark"; otherwise even liability for a particularly serious breach of due diligence may be considered.[380]

The German law of the statutory audits (auditors) is based on European law. The Eighth Directive (EEC) 84/253 has been subject to a reform designed to improve and harmonise the quality of statutory audits throughout the European Union. The modernised, principle-based and repeatedly updated Directive 2006/43/EC[381] includes: public oversight, external quality assurance, auditor independence, code of ethics, auditing standards, disciplinary sanctions and the appointment and dismissal of statutory auditors. The European Union is implementing International Standards on Auditing (ISAs)[382] for all statutory audits; these are relevant in Germany, too, as part of European law (see 4.4.6). The *Prüfungsstandards* (audit standards) of the *Institut der Wirtschaftsprüfer* (IDW), the private professional organisation of auditors in Germany, have already been adjusted to implement the ISAs. They are not legal norms (*Rechtsnormen*).

## 4.9.2 Basics, Reforms, and Lessons from the Crisis

International standards of auditing have been legally entrenched in Germany in the German Code of Commercial Law (HGB) through the Accounting Law Modernisation Act of 2009 (BilMoG).[383] According to this Act, the independent auditor is obliged to apply the international standards that have been adopted by the European Commission (§ 317(5) HGB). By this Act, European law has been implemented, in

[380] BGH, 12.03.2020 (VII ZR 236/19) <openJur 2020, 5531> recital 41. See more closely below 4.10 and chapters 5 and 7.

[381] On statutory audits of annual accounts and consolidated accounts, amending Directive 78/660/EC and Directive 83/349/EC and repealing Directive 84/253/EC (2006) OJ L 157/87. Directive 2006/43/EC amended, e.g., by Accounting Law Directive 2013/34/EU (see 4.4.3), Directive 2014/56/EU and, more recently, by Directive 2022/2464/EU (see 4.9.2); on the European single access point (ESAP) Directive 2023/2864/EU.

[382] Introduced by the International Auditing and Assurance Standards Board (IAASB, www.iaasb.org). Literature synthesis by Haapamäki and Sihvonen (2019).

[383] *Gesetz zur Modernisierung des Bilanzrechts*, 25.05.2009, BGBl I 1102, see above 4.8.2.

particular Directive 2006/43/EC on Statutory Audits (*Abschlußprüferrichtlinie*).[384] From this, further modifications[385] ensue, such as duties of the independent auditor to inform the supervisory board or the audit committee (§ 171 AktG) and to declare his or her independence in written form (§ 321(4a) HGB). The rules on rotation and times-out ("cooling off")[386] have changed European law: audit partners responsible for carrying out a statutory audit ("key audit partners") shall "cease their participation in the statutory audit of the audited entity not later than seven years from the date of their appointment".[387]

European law for auditors and statutory audits has been drastically reformed in the wake of the world debt crisis. At the core remains the Directive 2006/43/EC, which "lays down the conditions for the approval and registration of persons that carry out statutory audits, the rules on independence, objectivity and professional ethics applying to those persons, and the framework for their public oversight". The Directive has been revised for further harmonisation "in order to allow for greater transparency and predictability of the requirements applying to [persons carrying out statutory audits] and to enhance their independence and objectivity in the performance of their tasks."[388] The goal is the establishment of minimum standards (*Mindestanforderungen*) for the quality of auditing within the European Union. Basically, the aim is to establish trust among market players on a sustainable basis through true financial information (see altogether chapter 6). European legislation says decisively:[389]

> "Statutory auditors and audit firms are entrusted by law to conduct statutory audits of public-interest entities with a view to enhancing the degree of confidence of the public in the annual and consolidated financial statements of such entities. The public-interest function of statutory audit means that a broad community of people and institutions rely on the quality of a statutory auditor's or an audit firm's work. Good audit quality contributes to the orderly functioning of markets by enhancing the integrity and efficiency of financial statements. Thus, statutory auditors fulfil a particularly important societal role."

The European Union underscores the "green" paradigm change laid out with the United Nations in the Paris Agreement (see 1.4.2), the comprehensive transformation of corporations and capital markets in the context of the European Green Deal

---

[384] OJ L 157, 09.06.2006, 87. Amended by Directive 2008/30/EC, OJ L 81, 20.03.2008, 53.

[385] Overview in *Bundestags-Drucksache* 16/10067, 39–41. Merkt (2009). See also above 4.9.1.

[386] Cf. ex-§ 319a(1) No 4 HGB, but note: § 319a repealed by Art. 11 FISG of 03.06.2021 (BGBl I S. 1534) with effect from 01.07.2021. See further below 4.9.3 and 4.9.5.

[387] Art. 17(7)(1) of the Regulation (EU) No 537/2014, 16.04.2014, on specific requirements regarding the statutory audit of public-interest entities and repealing Commission Decision 2005/909/EC, OJ L 158, 27.05.2014, 77 (Amendment: OJ L 170, 11.06.2014, 66), see that Art. 17 for details on the duration of the audit engagement.

[388] Directive 2014/56/EU, 16.04.2014, amending Directive 2006/43/EC on statutory audits of annual accounts and consolidated accounts, OJ L 158, 27.05.2014, 196, recital (1).

[389] Regulation (EU) No 537/2014, ibid, recital (1); equally: Directive 2014/56/EU, ibid, recital (2).

(see 2.1, 4.2).[390] In view of the insight "that many undertakings do not disclose material information on all major sustainability-related topics, including climate-related information such as all GHG emissions, and factors that affect biodiversity."[391] For the financial reporting and auditing it is emphasised that "there is a clear need for a robust and affordable reporting framework that is accompanied by effective auditing practices to ensure the reliability of data and avoid greenwashing and double counting."[392] In the longer run, educated, well-advised or audited entrepreneurs should be able to recognise that sustainable business activities and financial reporting as verified information of investors pay off (see 1.5.2: concept of trust).

This designates the outstanding function and task of a legal system (see 4.9.4, 4.10) and any statutory auditors ("public watchdog", see 4.9.1), which is still unaltered. In the autumn of 2010, the European Commission already presented the "Green Paper: Lessons from the Crisis".[393] In this paper, which is guiding for the reforms, the Commission emphasised the eminent role of the auditors in the statutory audits, which are entrusted to them by the law: "This entrustment responds to the fulfilment of a societal role in offering an opinion on the truth and fairness of the financial statements of audited entities."[394] This confirms the core function of the general rule ("a true and fair view"), as explained above and confirmed through the reforms.[395] The Commission affirmed that the "independence of auditors should thus be the bedrock of the audit environment". It goes on to emphasise unequivocally: "It is time to probe into the true fulfilment of this societal mandate".[396] The Commission was concerned, among other things,[397] about a fundamental reform of

[390] Affirmative with basics ICJ, Advisory Opinion: Obligation of states in respect of climate change, 23.07.2025 (https://www.icj-cij.org/sites/default/files/case-related/187/187-20250723-adv-01-00-en.pdf, accessed: 22.08.2025). See on that below 6.1.

[391] Directive 2022/2464/EU, 14.12.2022, OJ L 322, 16.12.2022, p. 15–80, recital 13 (referring to a Commission report with "significant evidence"). See also EU Commission, Omnibus simplification package of 26.02.2025, COM(2025)80 and COM(2025)81, to "reduce complexity of EU requirements for all businesses, notably SMEs and small mid-caps (SMCs)".

[392] Ibid.

[393] 13.10.2010, COM(2010) 561 final. Cf. Commission, Green Paper on "Corporate Governance in financial institutions and remuneration policies", 02.06.2010, COM(2010) 284 final. Cf. already after the fall of Enron Corp., e.g. Seligman (2002), Macey and Sale (2003); see above 4.5.7 and below 6.5.1, 6.8.5. Luttermann (1999a).

[394] Green Paper COM(2010) 561 final, p. 3.

[395] See Accounting Law Directive 2013/34/EU, recital 43, highlighting the relevance of "a true and fair view" for an audit opinion; basically above 4.4.4 and 4.5.

[396] Green Paper COM(2010) 561 final, p. 3. Cf. § 321(4a) HGB: the auditor must confirm his independence (*Unabhängigkeit*) in the audit report (*Prüfungsbericht*).

[397] The Commission (COM(2010) 561 final, p. 5) strives for a debate in particular on: the role of the auditor and the independence of audit firms; the supervision of auditors; the configuration of the audit market; the creation of a single market for the provision of audit services; the simplification of rules for SMEs and Small and Medium Sized Practitioners (SMPs); and international co-operation for the supervision of global audit networks.

the audit sector, including a restructuring of the monopoly-like market structure ("big four" audit firms).[398]

Germany has implemented the European reforms, in particular in the form of: the *Bilanzrichtlinie-Umsetzungsgesetz* (BilRUG, see 4.8.2), the *Abschlussprüfungsreformgesetz* (AReG) for the implementation of the regulation (EU) No 537/2014,[399] and the *Abschlussprüferaufsichtsreformgesetz* (APAReG, see 4.9.3); earlier still, among others and following the model of the Sarbanes-Oxley-Act in the USA, the *Abschlußprüferaufsichtsgesetz* (Auditor Supervision Act) of 2004.[400] Still, the crisis was not prevented – either in Germany or in the other member states – with the approaches to a reform of the European law. As is the case all over the world, massive deficiencies have become obvious, particularly in the domain of auditing. And practice confirms the problems as an elementary as well as enduring, existential challenge – as the more recent accounting scandal of the Wirecard AG proves;[401] but let's follow the chronology for better comprehension.

### *4.9.3 Disclosure, Oversight, and Enforcement*

The annual accounts (financial statements), duly approved, and the annual report (management report), together with the statutory auditor's opinion, shall be published in accordance with the laws of the member state according to Article 30 of the Accounting Law Directive 2013/34/EU.[402] The same applies to consolidated accounts, especially in accordance with the adopted IAS/IFRS. In Germany, details are set forth in §§ 325–329 HGB. Some differences are allowed according to the size of the company.[403] Basically, the accounts – in German language (§§ 325(1), 244

[398] See further below 4.11 and 4.12. Cf. House of Lords, Auditors: Market concentration and their role, 15.03.2011 (https://publications.parliament.uk/pa/ld201011/ldselect/ldeconaf/119/11902.htm, accessed: 22.08.2025).

[399] Of 10.05.2016, BGBl. I 1142. Bundesregierung, *Gesetzentwurf* (Draft of the AReG), 11.01.2016, Bundestags-Drucksache 18/7219.

[400] BGBl I 3846. See also *Gesetz zur Einführung internationaler Rechnungslegungsstandards und zur Sicherung der Qualität der Abschlußprüfung (Bilanzrechtsreformgesetz)*, 08.12.2004, BGBl I 3166. General professional duties are regulated in particular in the *Wirtschaftsprüferordnung* (WPO).

[401] See 4.9.4 and chapter 6.

[402] Chapter 7 (Publication). Cf. former Directive 2009/101/EC, Chapter 2 (Disclosure, Art. 2 to 7), repealed 19.07.2017. For Germany's former law according to Art. 3 of Directive 68/151/EC see Großfeld and Luttermann (2005) recitals 1798–1803. *Gesetz über elektronische Handelsregister und Genossenschaftsregister sowie das Unternehmensregister (*EHUG*)*, 10.11.2006, BGBl I 2553 — electronically disclosed since 01.01.2007 (www.unternehmensregister.de).

[403] See §§ 326, 267 HGB. See BVerfG, 01.02.2011 (2 BvR 1236/10), (2011) BB 1136. Reform of § 325 HGB by law, 05.07.2021 (BGBl I 3338) with effect from 01.08.2022; for the application Art. 88 EGHGB.

HGB) – shall be submitted to the Commercial Register (*Handelsregister*, § 8 HGB) which is maintained electronically at the local court (*Amtsgericht*). Everyone is allowed to view these in order to gain information (§ 9(1) HGB).

European law[404] modifies professional law, liability (see 4.9.6) and supervisory law for auditors, in order to achieve the quality goals for statutory audits of public-interest entities (see 4.9.2). To this end, German legislation has reformed supervision of this professional set, id est auditors (*Abschlussprüfer*) and audit firms. Before the epic Wirecard scandal and its institutional reappraisal (see 4.9.5) the *Abschlussprüferaufsichtsreformgesetz* (APAReG)[405] had established the professionally independent *Abschlussprüferaufsichtsstelle* (APAS) at the *Bundesamt für Wirtschaft und Ausfuhrkontrolle* (Federal Office for Economic Affairs and Export Control) as from June 17, 2016.[406] The APAS has taken on the job of the former voluntary *Abschlussprüferaufsichtskommission* (APAK) and is to establish an appropriate public specialised supervision over the auditors (§ 66a WPO, *Abschlussprüferaufsicht*). This also involves that the APAS (1) randomly checks auditors and audit firms who conduct statutory audits, or (2) carries out concrete investigations based on a certain incident (e.g. "whistle-blowing");[407] the APAS is also (3) to participate in the European and international auditing boards for improving the quality of statutory audits.

Misuse and manipulation of corporate accounts had stimulated German legislature to introduce a two-tier enforcement system (ex-§§ 342b–342e HGB). The FREP (in German: Deutsche Prüfstelle für Rechnungslegung, DPR) had been established as a private law organisation, dominated and financed by market participants (companies, auditors etc.). The Panel was to examine, on concrete indication or spot-check, the financial reporting of companies.[408] As a legal requirement, incorrect

[404] Basic: Directive 2014/56/EU (see esp. Art. 30a–30f) and Regulation (EU) No 537/2014. On the relation of Directive, Regulation and German Law: *Bundesregierung, Gesetzentwurf* (Draft of the APAReG), 08.10.2015, *Bundestags-Drucksache* 18/6282, 55 (No 1).

[405] Of 31.03.2016, BGBl. I 518. *Bundesregierung, Gesetzentwurf* (Draft of the APAReG), 08.10.2015, *Bundestags-Drucksache* 18/6282.

[406] BAFA, see: www.bafa.de/bafa/de/apas (updated). APAS is the competent authority according to Art. 13(1)(3), Art. 14 and 17(8)(3), Art. 20(1) Regulation (EU) No 537/2014; see § 66-(2) *Wirtschaftsprüferordnung* (WPO).

[407] See Directive (EU) 2019/1937 (so-called Whistleblower Directive). Cf. Art. 26 of Regulation (EU) No 537/2014 and § 66a(6) WPO.

[408] See § 342b(2)–(5) HGB (superseded). Up-to-date information: www.frep.info/index_en.php. From jurisdiction, e.g., OLG Frankfurt/Main, 31.08.2010 (WpÜG 3/10) NZG 2010, 1433 (coercive payment — *Zwangsgeld*), and 31.05.2012 (WpÜG 2/12) ZIP 2012, 1662 (§§ 285 No 9(a) and 314(1) No 6(a) HGB), and 07.11.2013 (WpÜG 1/13) ZIP 2014, 79 (costs of the proceedings).

reporting identified in these examinations had to be reported to the *Bundesanstalt für Finanzdienstleistungsaufsicht* (BaFin, ex-§ 342b(6) HGB), the German regulatory authority for capital markets and services. Incorrect reporting was to be subject to further official proceedings, including sanctions and, upon reasonable suspicion, criminal prosecution. Errors discovered were published (ex-§ 37q(2) *Wertpapierhandelsgesetz*, WpHG).[409]

### *4.9.4 Meeting Reality: The Wirecard Debacle and the Icebergs*

Integrated into the iridescent history of the modern corporation, capital markets and financial regulation, this control structure lasted as was to be expected. Manipulation and fraud gained further ground in a frosty business climate, particularly in the fiasco of the Wirecard AG, the to date greatest accounting scandal in Germany. This ended a further sad chapter in 2021 (incl. the DPR, see 4.9.7) and once again induced efforts at reform. For the European Union, its Commission simply adjudged – with reference to "several recent failures of companies in Europe (e.g. Wirecard, Carillion)" as follows:[410] "the three pillars that underpin the quality and reliability of corporate reporting by listed companies have not fully played their intended role; without a new EU intervention, it is likely that problems will persist." For better comprehension, let us first take a look at some relevant life circumstances, id est reality (facts).

The Wirecard AG, once listed at the Frankfurt Stock Exchange (Germany), has fallen apart as the epicenter of an international financial drama. It was in the limelight as a "rising star" of a new, digital business world and, in particular since September 2018, as a component of the German DAX stock index, which represents the development of the value of significant companies in Germany. Wirecard globally handled cash flows as a payment service provider between dealers and credit card companies (banks), early on criticised for business practices that were aggressive and also intransparent with regard to accounting, with remarkable profitability and in the end with around 6,000 employees. Treated as a seminal technology company of a cashless new world ("billion tech darling"), the firm enjoyed political attention and promotion to the apex: A "who is who" with Ministers and the German Chancellor, stating in the Parliamentary Committee of Inquiry (*Untersuchungsausschuss*) that the

[409] *Wertpapierhandelsgesetz*; e.g., the lack of a prognosis report (§§ 315(1)(5), 289(1)(4) HGB): OLG Frankfurt/Main, 24.11.2009 (WpÜG 11/09, 12/09) NZG 2010, 63. OLG Frankfurt/Main, 07.01.2016 (WpÜG 1/15) ZIP 2016 316 (procedural law). On access to courts: Hessischer VGH, 28.04.2010 (6 B 395/10) <openJur 2012, 32995>.

[410] EU Commission, Corporate reporting – improving its quality and enforcement, Call for evidence, Ref. Ares(2021)6964463 - 12/11/2021.

Wirecard Fall is a great setback for reputation[411] – a process that raised awareness of central deficits that had long been recognised as being in need of reform, some of which have still not been remedied.[412]

Insolvency came in August 2020. In the course of the admission of the Wirecard AG to the German DAX stock index, its business and accounting practices were scrutinised with increasing criticalness. A forensic investigation by auditor KPMG into allegations of accounting irregularities made by the Financial Times, carried through from October 2019 by order of Wirecard, confirmed in April 2020 that the existence of a billion euros accounted for in foreign bank accounts was not verifiable. In June 2020, after being postponed three times, statutory auditor EY (Ernst & Young) finally refused to sign off Wirecard's 2019 accounts, being unable to confirm the existence of 1.9 billion euros in cash balances on trust accounts, id est in effect: air bookings (*Luftbuchungen*) of about a quarter of Wirecard's balance sheet. The economic damage of this insolvency may be more than 30 billion euros.[413] The CEO came under charge of fraud, whereas the COO fled, entangled in the gray area of secret services and wanted on international arrest warrants, the head of the German Exchange Supervisory Authority (BaFin) was fired: sufficient material for a movie and numerous studies on the so-called "German Enron".[414]

Though the Wirecard story may seem as something special to the audience, experts know about the epic diversity of colourful costumes and images on the global stage (see 3.1). Where are they? – The field is wide and labelled: sustainable financial reporting, of course, including auditing and strict enforcement (sanctions, see 4.9.7). It is thus about the human corporation, its leadership, financing and valuation, about the constitution of entrepreneurial liberty and responsibility, about justice and peace, about prosperity as a whole (see chapters 8, 9). That is all. The European Commission, describing the political context while launching its public

[411] Deutscher Bundestag, *Bericht 3. Untersuchungsausschuss, Bundestags-Drucksache* 19/30900, 22.06.2021, 1602 and 1509-1602, esp. on accounting issues p. 193-223. Cf. Möllers (2021) and basically Luttermann (2017).

[412] Already concrete demands for fundamental reforms by Luttermann, e.g., (2003b), (2004) and (2017). See conceptually on the corporation and accounting law Luttermann (2003a) Einf BilanzR recitals 1-3, 26-43, 107-136 and overall in details Luttermann (2003a) § 264 HGB recitals 1-216.

[413] Overall final report Deutscher Bundestag, 3. Untersuchungsausschuss der 19. Wahlperiode (Wirecard), Bericht, 22.06.2021, Bundestag-Drucksache 19/30900. Cf. procedural in court BayObLG, 28.02.2025 (101 Kap 1/22) <openJur 2025, 10408>. See on criminal charges LG München I (4 KLs 402Js 108194/22), pending proceedings (since 08.12.2022), and below 4.9.7. LG München I, 05.05.2022 (5 HK O 15710/20) <openJur 2022, 10368> (invalidity of annual financial statements and appropriation of profits). On directors' and officers' liability for defaulted loans against three former directors of Wirecard AG (140 million euros in total): LG München I, 05.09.2024 (5 HK O 17452/21), NZG 2024, 1605 (juris no. NJRE001588978). Cf. LG Düsseldorf, 13.07.2023 (9a O 154/23) <openJur 2023, 7586> (Wirecard: manager's liability insurance).

[414] Ibid. See Jo, Hsu, Llanos-Popolizio, Vergara-Vega (2021). Investigative McCrum (2022). Cf. Harvard Business School Case Heese, Wang, and Labruyere (2021).

consultation on corporate reporting in the aftershocks of the fall of Wirecard, confirms:[415]

> "Corporate reporting by listed companies is the bedrock of capital markets as it gives investors the essential information they need to make sound investment decisions such as information about the financial situation of companies. Moreover, it enables stakeholders to hold companies accountable on, for instance, sustainability issues.
>
> In the EU member states, on average 59% of listed shares are held across borders. This initiative is important to achieve an efficient Capital Market Union (CMU), building on reliable information disclosed by companies in the whole Union.
>
> The quality and reliability of public reporting by listed companies rely on three main mutually reinforcing pillars: (i) corporate governance in these companies; (ii) statutory audit; and (iii) supervision and enforcement by public authorities."

For corporations, their good governance and financing, we have repeatedly shown the core function of financial reporting and valuation as a legal domain[416] with the comprehensive imperative of accounting truth (*Bilanzwahrheit*) internationally as well as their procedural implementation with regard to the players of the "numbers games" with magic flutes on the global markets – already years and decades ago.[417] The game goes on. Whether Enron, Lehman Brothers, or Wirecard: What is at work is "enrichment",[418] and icy greed always has a name, the tip of those icebergs floating on the global capital markets in a widely concealed dimension. Experts realise that the corporation as a financial construct without sustainable financial reporting and auditing, id est valuation in legal terms, remains "substantially meaningless".[419] Liberty requires personal responsibility. It is always the mindset that is decisive (see chapter 7).

### *4.9.5 Some Discernments and the German FISG*

Overall, it is about "a true and fair view" (*Bilanzwahrheit*) in financial reporting (valuation law) as the yardstick for the human corporation as well as reasonableness,

---

[415] EU Commission, Corporate reporting – improving its quality and enforcement, Call for evidence, Ref. Ares(2021)6964463 – 12/11/2021 (https://ec.europa.eu/info/law/better-regulation/have-your-say/initiatives/13128-Corporate-reporting-improving-its-quality-and-enforcement/public-consultation_en, accessed: 22.08.2025); also EU Commission, Report on Audit Market Monitoring, 28.01.2021 COM(2021) 29 final, pursuant to Art. 27 of Regulation (EU) No 537/2014. See above 4.9.2.

[416] Luttermann (1997), Luttermann (1999a), Luttermann (2003a) Einf BilanzR recitals 1-3, 107-122 and Luttermann (2003a) § 264 HGB recitals 119-168 (practical legal principles and references.

[417] See, e.g., with respective sources, in English: Luttermann, Accounting as the documentary proof of good corporate governance, chapter 7 in: du Plessis, Großfeld, Luttermann et al. (2007), 2d ed. (2012), 3rd ed. (2017); Luttermann (2015a). Previously already fundamentally in German, e.g., Luttermann (1998), (1999a), (2003a) and (2004).

[418] Overall see Galbraith (1994).

[419] See (also on) Berle and Means above in 3.5.3.

structurally and in the individual case (valuation). The sense for this holds and is indispensable – *conditio sine qua non* – also for reforms (like the German *FISG*), id est here for the auditors and supervisors. The attitude counts. In any case, implementation depends on the people responsible, especially on the professional training of accountants and auditors,[420] which is still deficient. If the whole field of financial reporting, id est corporate finance, valuation and auditing is not holistically conceived, taught and practiced as an eminent domain of the law for the corporation and financial markets (corporate groups), for good corporate governance and general prosperity, what will remain is doctoring at the symptoms instead of curing the causes of the disease (see 4.12 and chapter 6).

Reality speaks for itself. According to documents seen by Reuters, the news agency reports that the "German government examined the possibility of bailing out Wirecard just three days before it collapsed".[421] Another story, but the basic tunes seems familiar. We remember the epic case of the investment bank Lehman Brothers Inc. in the USA, which globally marked the – continuing – world debt crisis (*Weltschuldenkrise*, so-called "financial crisis").[422] There, a US administration with Henry M. Paulson, its minister of finance (2006–2009) as well as former Chairman and CEO of the investment bank Goldman Sachs Inc. (1999–2006), a direct competitor of Lehman Brothers, orchestrated the downfall: after the financial industry[423] (not only) at Lehman Brothers had for years – under regulation and supervision of the state (SEC, Fed etc.) as well as cooperation of auditors – amassed huge debts in the accounts ("toxic assets"), the government did not fill that "capital hole".[424]

Questions remain. Henry Paulson was considered the "Wall Street Bailout King":[425] After the investment bank Bear Stearns Inc., also a direct competitor of Lehman Brothers Inc., had already been rescued in May 2008 under his regime, hundreds of billions of dollars (taxpayer money!) flowed to numerous banks at home and abroad through government rescue programs.[426] The global damage, in particular from deficient regulation, supervision and auditing (i.e. financial reporting!), remains without a number. This basic pattern is documented vividly for the complete

---

[420] On this Luttermann (2017), Member of the Reform Commission appointed by the German Federal Ministry of Economics, Berlin.

[421] Reuters, Timeline: The rise and fall of Wirecard, a German tech champion, 16.03.2021: www.reuters.com/article/us-germany-wirecard-inquiry-timeline-idUSKBN2B811J (accessed: 22.08.2025).

[422] Also on the world-changing dimension Tooze (2018). See in details chapter 6.

[423] See above 4.1, 4.4.6, and 4.6.2, below, e.g., 4.11.1 and chapter 6 (esp. 6.6, 6.7, and 6.8.5).

[424] On the event see Henry Paulson (2013) p. 196 (171-249).

[425] CBS – Mysteries of history, calculated risk: U.S. Treasury Secretary Henry Paulson the Wall Street bailout king, 2010: <www.youtube.com/watch?v=eq-fVzuZAec>. Cf. Gretchen Morgenson, Don Van Natta Jr., Paulson's Calls to Goldman Tested Ethis, 08.08.2009: www.nytimes.com/2009/08/09/business/09paulson.html (accessed: 22.08.2025). Cf.

[426] Lucas (2019): a total of $498 billions fair value bailout costs in the US. Cf. US Treasury for TARP as of 30.09.2023: $443.5 billions https://home.treasury.gov/data/troubled-asset-relief-program (accessed: 22.08.2025).

disaster by the U.S. Senator Carl Levin, Chairman of the Senate Permanent Subcommittee on Investigations, while investigating "the worst U.S. economic crisis since the 1930s, resulting in the foreclosure of millions of homes, the shuttering of businesses, and the loss of millions of American jobs":

> "Investment banks such as Goldman Sachs were not simply market-makers, they were self-interested promoters of risky and complicated financial schemes that helped trigger the crisis," said Sen. Levin. "They bundled toxic mortgages into complex financial instruments, got the credit rating agencies to label them as AAA securities, and sold them to investors, magnifying and spreading risk throughout the financial system, and all too often betting against the instruments they sold and profiting at the expense of their clients." The 2009 Goldman Sachs annual report stated that the firm "did not generate enormous net revenues by betting against residential related products." Levin said, "These e-mails show that, in fact, Goldman made a lot of money by betting against the mortgage market."[427]

That game runs via the accounts of the market players, marked by systematic manipulation (e.g., Ponzi scheme), deficient accounting and auditing rules and practices with in the last instance massive losses and skimming of excess profits through few main actors – in short: the "numbers game" with unilateral shift of wealth (*Vermögensverschiebung*, see 6.5.3, 1.4.3). Joseph Stiglitz describes the process as "the great American robbery" and "avarice triumphs over prudence", further stating: "As the U.S. government went about rescuing the banks, it should also have thought about accountability".[428] This is, of course, accompanied by a failure of the regulation, control and instrumental henchmen – wherever they may be. The same applies to the case of the Wirecard AG, in comparison played out on a provincial stage,[429] which on closer consideration corroborates the fundamental criticism in every respect. The explanation of the German supervisory reform in the *Gesetz zur Stärkung der Finanzmarktintegrität* (FISG) correspondingly names problem and goal:[430]

> The functioning of the German financial market is crucial for the German economy and the prosperity of the German Federal Republic. Manipulations of the accounts of capital market companies rock the faith in the German financial market and do it great damage. Recent

[427] U.S. Congress, Senate Subcommittee, on the role of investment banks, hearing 27.04.2010: https://www.hsgac.senate.gov/subcommittees/investigations/rep/senate-subcommittee-holds-fourth-hearing-on-wall-street-and-the-financial-crisis-the-role-of-investment-banks/, (accessed: 22.08.2025). Cf. Report of the Senate Subcommittee, Wall Street and the financial crisis: anatomy of a financial collapse, 13.04.2011: www.hsgac.senate.gov/imo/media/doc/PSI REPORT - Wall Street & the Financial Crisis-Anatomy of a Financial Collapse (FINAL 5-10-11).pdf (accessed: 22.08.2025).

[428] Stiglitz (2010) pp. 109 and 147 (109-183).

[429] See 4.9.4 and documents of failure: Böcking and Gros (2020); Langenbucher, Leuz, Krahnen, and Pelizzon (2020).

[430] Translation; see German original: Deutscher Bundestag, *Begründung, Gesetzentwurf der Bundesregierung, Drucksache* 19/26966, 24.02.2021, p. 1 (A.).

events have shown that in particular of accounting control (*Bilanzkontrolle*) must be strengthened and the final audit (*Abschlussprüfung*) must be further regulated, in order to secure the correctness (*Richtigkeit*) of the aucconting documents of companies. Need for improvement also exists, however, with regard to the surveillance structures and the powers of the *Bundesanstalt für Finanzdienstleistungsaufsicht* (BaFin, German Federal Financial Supervisory Authority) in the auditing of outsourcing on the side of the financial services companies.

The FISG is phrased accordingly. It is banking on an accounting control system that is influenced more strongly by the state. The BaFin, where the competences are bundled (the DPR, see 4.9.3, is history), may act directly against the capital market company in the case of suspicion. This is to make "for a real new beginning for the fight against accounting fraud".[431] The BaFin has a right to control in all capital market-oriented companies and may also inform the public earlier than before about its procedure in accounting control (§ 316a HGB).[432] The independence of the auditors is to be strengthened through an obligatory external rotation of auditors also for capital market companies after ten years,[433] extension of the separation of auditing and consulting in companies of public interest (§§ 316a, 319b HGB) as well as civil law liability of the auditor towards the company audited for violation of duty already in the case of negligence (*Fahrlässigkeit*, § 323 HGB).

These and further changes are to increase the quality of auditing. A wide programme, comprising a reasonable, effective control system and risk management system internally (§ 91(3) AktG)[434] and affecting in particular also the auditing committee in the stock company (*Prüfungsausschuss*, see 4.12.2). This is accompanied by an enforced accounting penal law (*Bilanzstrafrecht*), "in order to facilitate a sufficiently deterrent punishment":[435] of the people responsible in the company for taking a false balance sheet oath (*Bilanzeid*, § 331a HGB) as well as the auditors for providing a false audit opinion (*Bestätigungsvermerk*) for financial statements of companies of public interest (§ 332(2)(2) HGB, see 4.9.1). Overall, it is obviously about the attitude (*Haltung*) of the actors responsible and personal responsibility is emphasised – as has long been demanded (see chapter 7).

[431] Translation. German original Deutscher Bundestag, *Beschlussempfehlung des Finanzausschusses zum FISG, Drucksache* 19/29879, 19.05.2021, p. 131. Cf. on DPR above in 4.9.4. Cf. basically on private standard setting, e.g., Luttermann (2003a) Einf BilanzR recitals 152-163 (IAS/IFRS) and §§ 243, 342 HGB recitals 30-72 (DRSC).

[432] See specifically § 23(1)(3) ZAG, S 36(1)(3) *VAG* and S 28(1)(3) KWG.

[433] Ibid.

[434] See with a sound concept of financial due diligence Luttermann, L. (2022), (2023) and (2024): Sustainable Business Finance Navigator.

[435] Deutscher Bundestag, *Beschlussempfehlung des Finanzausschusses zum FISG, Drucksache* 19/29879, 19.05.2021, pp. 3, 118 and 128.

### 4.9.6 Liability in the European Context

Corroborated through recent practice and reform legislation, the following can be put on record: Liberty and responsibility (liability) are the two sides of corporate governance and financial reporting, id est accounting and auditing. Due to his eminent institutional function as an independent control instance ("public watch-dog", see 4.9.1), the statutory auditor is prominently involved in a system of liability (*Haftungssystem*) that also applies to himself. The member states of the EU "shall ensure that there are effective systems of investigations and sanctions to detect, correct and prevent inadequate execution of the statutory audit"; and they are obliged to set "effective, proportionate and dissuasive sanctions" for statutory auditors and audit firms, where statutory audits are not conducted in accordance with valid law (pursuant to Art. 30 Directive 2014/56/EU and Regulation (EU) No 537/2014).[436] Accordingly, in Germany the described system of supervision holds for auditors and others (see 4.9.3) as well as his personal responsibility and liability (§ 323 HGB).

The liability system essentially comprises personal liability of the executive corporate directors (e.g., § 76(1) AktG), it is about their actions: They sign responsible, in the sense of accountability, the annual (consolidated) financial statements to document that these accounts fulfill the legal requirements (§ 245 HGB, see 4.4.1). Pursuant to the European Commission (action plan), members of the administrative, management and supervisory bodies of a company with limited liability are collectively responsible towards the company for drawing up and publishing annual accounts (financial statements) and annual reports (management reports); it is analogous to members of a group drawing up consolidated accounts and consolidated reports.[437] Thus, member states are restricted from opting for a system of responsibility limited to individual board members. But member states remain free to set rules for imposing penalties on an individual board member by rulings of a court or other enforcement bodies (e.g. in Germany the *Bundesanstalt für Finanzdienstleistungsaufsicht*, BaFin, see 4.9.7).

The persons responsible are thus subject to the measures which European law and the law of the respective member state establish as a liability system. A public company (public interest entity) or other companies with limited liability will be liable for the acts of the members of the management and the supervisory boards if the members of the management board act as company organs. In other words, if they act as a company organ (*Gesellschaftsorgan*) and cause third parties to suffer damage by breach of contract, tort or other reasons, the public company is liable. This is based on the concept of liability of the company for the acts of its organs (*Organhaftung*).[438] In Germany, cases have come to public attention, in particular in

---

[436] See Art. 30 of Directive 2006/43/EC, amended by Directive 2008/30/EC, Directive 2013/34/EU and Directive 2014/56/EU.

[437] This holds according to Art. 33(1) of Accounting Law Directive 2013/34/EU also for accounts drawn up in accordance with Accounting Law Regulation (EC) No 1606/2002. Overall Luttermann (2013).

[438] Basically § 31 BGB (*Bürgerliches Gesetzbuch*).

connection with accusations of corruption against former members of the board of directors (e.g., Siemens AG).[439] In addition, there are increasingly cases in the wake of dealing with accounting manipulations as well as, in particular, excessive speculation deals of the corporate directors (see chapters 6 and 7).

The public company's liability for the acts of the members of the management and supervisory boards includes their acts associated with financial reporting. This is where the transgressions usually show up, for example in cases of corruption. The responsibility of members of the management and supervisory boards for financial statements (annual accounts, consolidated accounts) and management reports, including key "non-financial information",[440] needs further clarification. The Accounting Law Directive 2013/34/EU makes the following stipulation, based on the Action Plan of the European Commission,[441] in Article 33(1):

> "Member States [like Germany] shall ensure that the members of the administrative, management and supervisory bodies of an undertaking, acting within the competences assigned to them by national law, have collective responsibility for ensuring that the [annual/consolidated financial statements and management reports/corporate governance statements] are drawn up and published in accordance with the requirements of this Directive and, where applicable, with the international accounting standards adopted in accordance with Regulation (EC) No 1606/2002."

This regulation harmonises the liability laws (*Haftungsrecht*) in the internal market. The member states accordingly have to ensure that their laws, regulations and administrative provisions on liability, at least towards the undertaking, apply to the members of the administrative, management and supervisory bodies of the undertakings for breach of the duties referred to in (the above cited) paragraph 1 of Article 33 (Accounting Law Directive 2013/34/EU, Art. 33(2)). The requirements of sustainability (*Nachhaltigkeit*) and due diligence (*Sorgfaltspflicht*) must be observed. Overall, the issue is the duty to work diligently (see for corporate directors: 6.4). For statutory auditors and audit firms, European legislation says that they "should be liable for the financial damage caused by a lack of the care owed" because they are

---

[439] From jurisdiction, e.g., BGH, 16.02.2009 (II ZR 282/07) ZIP 2009, 717; cf. BGH, 14.05.2013 (II ZB 1/11) ZIP 2013, 1274. BGH, BGH, 06.09.2016 (1 StR 104/15) <openJur 2018, 1367>, BGH, 23.10.2018 (1 StR 234/17) <openJur 2019, 1983>. Cf. on GmbH: BGH, 12.01.2022 (1 StR 436/21) <openJur 2022, 10917>. See also above 4.9.4 (Wirecard AG), below 4.9.7 and 4.12.2.

[440] Directive 2014/95/EU, 22.10.2014, amending Directive 2013/34/EU as regards disclosure of non-financial and diversity information by certain large undertakings and groups, OJ L 330, 15.11.2014, 1. See on "non-financial reporting" EU-Commission Guidelines: https://finance.ec.europa.eu/publications/commission-guidelines-non-financial-reporting_en (accessed: 22.08.2025).

[441] See: Proposal for a Directive amending Directives 78/660/EC (concerning annual accounts of certain types of companies) and 83/349/EC (consolidated accounts), 27.10.2004 COM(2004) 725 final (2004/0250(COD)): "Member States shall ensure their laws, regulations and administrative provisions on liability apply to the members of the administrative, management and supervisory bodies referred to in [ex-Art. 50b (new Art. 50c) Dir 78/660/EC, ex-Art. 36a (new Art. 36b) Dir 83/349/EC]."

responsible for carrying out their work with due care.[442] This requires the concept of reasonableness.

### 4.9.7 Sanctions: Some Rules and Reasonableness

In practice, legal norms without strong enforcement (see 4.9.3) and tangible sanctions may easily remain no more than Shakespeare's "words, words, words". Responsible actors may, in the face of recent debacles, catch up (see 4.9.4, 4.9.5, on legal protection 4.10). Think about it, as we still note: Financial reporting and auditing are in general legal acts systematically related to legal norms (*Bilanzwahrheit*), no marketing events.[443] Basically, it is about other people's money (see 4.4.1). This is precisely why clear legal standards of financial reporting (accountability) are necessary (see 4.6.4). There must be no arbitrariness, as is even the case in the setting of so-called "standards" with the practice of the minority opinions in FASB and IASB. They can provide "authoritative support" and immunisation against liability in particular in weak court practice, in which judges rely merely on "expert opinions", thereby making themselves dependent.[444] Instead of this practice, the judges – as in all other areas of jurisdiction – are to valuate independently according to a legal standard (see § 286 ZPO in Germany and below 5.5.5 and 5.6.5).[445]

In Germany, some relevant sanctions are contained in §§ 331–335c HGB; some have been tightened in the course of the Wirecard scandal (see 4.9.4). It still applies in particular that any untrue or incorrect presentation (*unrichtige Darstellung*), such as the falsification or concealment of the company's financial position by a member of the management or the supervisory boards, can result in fines or imprisonment for

---

[442] Directive 2006/43/EC (amended by Directive 2008/30/EC, Directive 2013/34/EU and Directive 2014/56/EU) recital (19).

[443] Already in a lead article under that title (German: *"Rechnungslegung ist ein Rechtsakt, kein Marketing"*) for a wide audience Luttermann in Frankfurter Allgemeine Zeitung (FAZ) No. 48, 26.02.2007, p. 20. Cf. above 3.5.5.

[444] Luttermann (2015a) 31, 34-35 and already Luttermann (1998) pp. 419-421 and Luttermann (1999a) pp. 80-82, also called "dissenting opinions". Cf. Bradbury/Harrison (2015), Eisenberg (1976) pp. 188-195. See above 3.5.3, 3.5.5 and 7.5.2 (on the "discretionary power" of corporate directors).

[445] On the legal standard of *Bilanzwahrheit* ("a true and fair view") above 4.5 and procedurally under 4.10. Fundamentally Luttermann (2012) 251, 255-256.

up to three years for these members (§ 331 HGB).[446] False information given to the auditor is treated in the same way.[447] The same applies to the auditor if he gives a false report on the result of an examination, omits important circumstances in the examination report (§ 321 HGB) or gives the audit certificate (§ 322 HGB) wrongly (§ 332 HGB). For corporate directors, criminal liability is based on the duty that those who are responsible for giving statements (*Erklärungen*) have to state, to the best of their knowledge, that the financial statements give a true and fair view (*Bilanzeid*, § 264(2)(3) HGB).[448] This rule had been drafted on the model of the U.S. Sarbanes-Oxley Act of 2002, Section 302 (see below in 6.8.2).

The Accounting Law Directive 2013/34/EU, based on a suggestion by the European Commission[449] and without prejudice to the member states' sovereign criminal law (cf. Art. 5 TEU), emphasises the practical necessity for clear, deterrent sanction norms and their consistent enforcement. In principle, it states on penalties in Article 51 Accounting Law Directive 2013/34/EU:

> "Member States shall provide for penalties applicable to infringements of the national provisions adopted in accordance with this Directive and shall take all the measures necessary to ensure that those penalties are enforced. The penalties provided for shall be effective, proportionate and dissuasive."

Apart from criminal sanctions, a non-criminal fine (*Bußgeld*: § 334 HGB) or a fine (*Ordnungsgeld*: § 335 HGB) may be imposed in a case where accounting rules are violated. Simultaneous general statutory rules may apply, for example, concerning compensatory damages (*Schadensersatz*, e.g. § 331 No. 1 HGB with § 823(2) BGB,

---

[446] On the materiality of the infringement BGH, 16.05.2017 (StR 306/16) <openJur 2018, 3836> recital (40), cf. BGH, 15.08.2019 (5 StR 204/19) <openJur 2019, 31197>. See also § 400 AktG. More from jurisdiction e.g. BGH (BGH) 16.12.2004 (1 StR 420/03) BGHSt 49, 381 (Haffa/EM. TV); OLG Frankfurt/Main, 16.04.2014 (23 Kap 1/08) <openJur 2014, 19049> (Rev. BGH, II ZB 24/14); Kammergericht Berlin, 11.02.2010 (1 Ws 212/08) <openJur 2012, 12491>. OLG Celle, 30.09.2022 (13 Kap 1/16) <openJur 2022, 18730> (VW AG). On HSH Nordbank: BGH, 12.10.2016 (5 StR 134/15) <openJur 2018, 1332>; cf. LG Hamburg, 09.07.2014 (608 KLs 12/11) <openJur 2014, 27240>, and, 05.06.2019 (618 KLs 3/16): proceedings partly discontinued in exchange for fines (https://justiz.hamburg.de/pressemitteilungen/12673480/pressemitteilung-2019-06-06-olg-01/, accessed: 22.08.2025).

[447] See § 331 No 4 HGB. On this BGH, 21.08.1996 (4 StR 364/96) wistra 1996, 348; cf. BGH, 16.05.2017 (1 StR 306/16) <openJur 2018, 3836>.

[448] See § 331a HGB inserted by FISG 2021 (see above 4.9.5) and §§ 289(1)(5), 297(2)(4), 315(1)(5) HGB, *Transparenzrichtlinie-Umsetzungsgesetz,* BGBl 2007 I 10 (*Bundestags-Drucksache* 16/2498). But see Art. 4(2)(c), 5(2)(c) of Directive 2004/109/EC (amended inter al. by Directive 2013/50/EU) and already § 331 No 1 HGB; please note for civil liability § 93(2) AktG (see below 6.4).

[449] Proposal for a Directive amending Directives 78/660/EC and 83/349/EC, 27.10.2004 COM (2004) 725 final (2004/0250(COD)): "the Member States shall lay down the rules on penalties applicable to infringements of the national provisions adopted pursuant to [Dir 78/660/EC, rsp. 83/349/EC] and shall take all measures necessary to ensure that they are implemented. The penalties and measures provided for must be effective, proportionate and dissuasive." (cf. ex-Art. 60a Dir 78/660/EC and ex-Art. 48 Dir 83/349/EC). Cf. ECJ, 03.05.2005 (joined cases C-387/02 et al. – *Berlusconi*, IT) ECR I 3565.

the German Civil Code)[450] or criminal breach of trust (*Untreue*, § 266 StGB, the German Criminal Code).[451] This shows in particular that the corporate directors are responsible for the capital entrusted to them by the investors (so-called *Vermögensbetreuungspflicht*, asset care obligation) – id est, put succinctly: other people's money (see 4.4.1). Effective legal protection also includes liability (sanctioning), as it applies as a clear concept of civil law, basically ordered according to law of evidence, in financial reporting and auditing[452] (see 4.5.3 and chapter 5). This is actually recognised. In many cases, several offences come together, which overlays specific accounting offences.[453] In particular, the (criminal) breach of trust is gaining attention, especially in the reappraisal of the scandal of the Wirecard AG.[454] The trial acts as a signal far transcending the individual case.

The liability regime is integrated into the stipulations of the legal order, here in particular corporate law and capital market law[455] for financing and valuation of the corporation. Corporate governance and auditing are to be practiced accordingly. This guarantees that our legal community as an order of assets is not bogged down in economic excess.[456] This characterises the majority, as opposed to the hopefully increasingly small number of delinquents. It should be kept in mind, however, that a criminal charge is always *ultima ratio* (the last resort).[457] Overall, regarding sanctions under the rule of law (see 4.10), reasonableness is to be guaranteed: in the respective legal norms, proceeding "from the normal case of the decent person", as

---

[450] See 4.4. BGH, 21.03.2005 (II ZR 54/03) DStR 2005, 933, 936 (co-operative). Cf. personal liability of board members in cases of deficient ad-hoc-information BGH, 19.07.2004 (II ZR 402/02 et. al.) NJW 2004, 2664, 2668 and 2971 (*Infomatec AG*). On *Sittenwidrigkeit* (immorality, § 826 BGB) BGH, 25.05.2020 (VI ZR 252/19) <openJur 2020, 6141>.

[451] See, e.g., BGH, 27.01.2021 (3 StR 628/19) <openJur 2021, 35109> and BGH, 10.02.2022 (3 StR 329/21) <openJur 2022, 8539>. See also § 265b StGB (obtaining credit by false pretences – *Kreditbetrug*) and—in the case of insolvency—§§ 283, 283a StGB (bankruptcy – *Bankrott*), § 283b StGB (breach of the requirement to keep accounts – *Verletzung der Buchführungspflicht*).

[452] Fundamentally Luttermann (2012).

[453] See, e.g., BGH, 14.11.2019 (5 StR 76/19) <openJur 2019, 37936>.

[454] See, e.g., LG München I, 09.06.2022 (5 HK O 17659/21) <openJur 2022, 12054> (Ex-CEO on remand), OLG München, 20.09.2021 (13 W 1347/21) < openJur 2022, 1006> (shareholder damages in the event of criminal acts by the management board).

[455] Cf., e.g., BGH, 10.07.2018 (II ZB 24/14) <openJur 2018, 1001>; BGH, 12.03.2020 (VII ZR 236/19) <openJur 2020, 5531>. OLG München, 18.05.2022 (3 U 1342/22) <openJur 2022, 10780>, and 19.09.2022 (8 U 8302/21) <openJur 2022, 17794>.

[456] Luttermann (2012) 251, 257-258. Cf. BGH, 27.01.2021 (3 StR 628/19) <openJur 2021, 35109>; BGH, 05.05.2022 (III ZR 131/20) <openJur 2022, 12517>. See immediately below 4.10, also chapter 8.

[457] See BGH, 06.04.2000 (1 StR 280/99) ZIP 2000, 1210 with comment by Luttermann; also BGH, 13.05.2004 (5 StR 73/03) BGHSt 49, 147, and BGH, 13.12.2012 (5 StR 407/12) ZIP 2013, 313 (group of companies); BVerfG, 23.06.2010 (2 BvR 2559/08) BVerfGE 126, 170. Cf. BVerfG, 05.08.2020 (2 BvR 1985/19) <openJur 2020, 46548>. For more details about sanctions, see Luttermann (2003a) § 264 HGB recitals 19–21, 121–28, and 165–69.

well as in the application in individual cases. To this purpose, a regulatory framework building on individual responsibility is made.[458]

## 4.10 Legal Protection (*Rechtsschutz*)

### *4.10.1 European System*

A legal system (*Rechtsordnung*) requires a strong system and strong practice of legal protection (*Rechtsschutz*). Otherwise, the law remains a dead letter. This is an expression of sustainability (*Nachhaltigkeit*), foremost in the sense of verifiability (*Nachprüfbarkeit*): This is what the civil law concept of valuation refers to for the corporation as valuation law (*Bewertungsrecht*, see 4.10.2).[459] If there is a dispute about valuation-law questions among the parties involved (see 4.4.1), in the final instance it is independent judges who have to decide on the basis of facts, like in every civil case. This holds with the imperative of truth for financing, accounting and auditing of a company (group of companies), id est for valuation law as a whole (see chapter 5); on transnational markets under the rule of law it also applies internationally. In principle, it is about fairness in competition and transparency, about a legal order as an order of assets (*Vermögensordnung*, see 4.3.2, 4.11 and chapter 8).

Within the European Union, a system of legal protection has been institutionalised based on the national jurisdictions of the member states. In Germany, that is the jurisdiction of the Civil Procedure Law (*Zivilprozeßordnung*, ZPO) and of non-contentious proceedings (*Freiwillige Gerichtsbarkeit*). Financial reporting may also be subject to arbitration (*Schiedsgerichtsbarkeit*, § 1025 ZPO); in the case of foreign direct investment also internationally (§ 1061 ZPO). Where a question of European Law (e.g. concerning the Directives or Regulations, see 4.4.3) is raised before any court or tribunal of a member state (e.g. Germany), that court or tribunal may, if it considers that a decision on the question is necessary to enable it to give judgment, request the European Court of Justice to give a ruling thereon. If there is no judicial remedy against the court's decision under national law, that court shall bring the matter before the Court of Justice (TFEU Art. 267). In regard to that matter, the preliminary ruling of the Court of Justice is binding for all courts, government bodies, and so on, in the European Union.

The adopted "IASs/IFRSs", as a part of the European law under the strict regime of the Accounting Law Regulation 1606/2002 (see 4.4.3), are subject to that legal system.[460] So the following holds: This is an important means of safeguarding a high

---

[458] See hereinafter 4.10 and above 4.4.1, chapters 5, 7 and 9.8. Luttermann (2010b). Basically Luttermann (1998), esp. p. 552 with the quote from Max Hachenburg.

[459] See chapter 5 and Luttermann (2023a) recitals 40-44.

[460] See Großfeld and Luttermann (2005) recitals 168, 204–205, see also recitals 150–151 (European *ordre public*) and above 4.4.4.

level of quality and comparability in financial reporting in the internal market of the European Union (*Binnenmarkt*). Furthermore, by means of the principles of the Treaty on the European Union, "balanced economic growth and price stability, a highly competitive social market economy, aiming at full employment and social progress, and a high level of protection and improvement of the quality of the environment" is promoted throughout the Union "for the sustainable development of Europe" (Art. 3(2) TEU, see above 4.4.4: "European public good"). This leads to a harmonised legal order (*Rechtsharmonisierung*) and also to so-called European "IFRS" (regional "IFRS", cf. 4.8.6, Fig. 4.5). In this context, the principle of subsidiarity – at the same time as a kind of capacity building against centralism – has to be taken into consideration (Art. 5 TFEU, cf. below 8.5).

Since European Law is officially recorded in more than 20 official languages (see 4.8.7), the linguistic approach and comparative law are fundamental. The European Court of Justice's requirement of a uniform interpretation of all of the language versions is an onerous task for everyone in the member states. Even so, the law requires a comparison of the legal terminologies due to the *ratio legis* with all the rules of accounting in the process of implementation and practice.[461] It is about legal linguistics (*Rechtslinguistik*), further for the European Union as a multilingual legal community about a language law (*Sprachenrecht*, see Fig. 4.5)[462] and in general about peace.[463] The valuation of a corporation and its assets is a communicative process of the creation of value (*Wertschöpfung*) through financial communication[464] and good corporate governance: sustainable finance and financial reporting (see Fig. 4.8 with 5.3.4).

### *4.10.2 Procedural Concept of the Valuation of Companies (Assets)*

For the function of the human corporation as a financial instrument,[465] the following applies unconditionally: Accounting (financial reporting) is a legal act (*Rechtsakt*), not a marketing show; this also applies to auditing.[466] For justice to reign in practice, a strong and clear legal order is necessary, designed and enforced as an order of assets (*Vermögensordnung*).[467] As a concept of valuation, the financing, accounting

[461] See above 4.5.1–4.5.4 and 4.6.3–4.6.5.

[462] Basically Luttermann, C. and Luttermann, K. (2020).

[463] Luttermann, C. and Luttermann, K. (2021).

[464] See 4.12.3 and 8.3.3, Luttermann (2023a) recitals 91-95 (with further references).

[465] See above 2.5 and 3.7 (common purpose).

[466] See above 4.9.7 and chapter 3.

[467] Basic Luttermann (2015a). See above 4.8 and chapter 8; esp. the civil procedural significance of the signing of the accounts (§ 245 HGB, § 416 ZPO) below 5.5.1 and 5.6.2, above in 4.4.1, 4.6.4 and below 4.10.2.

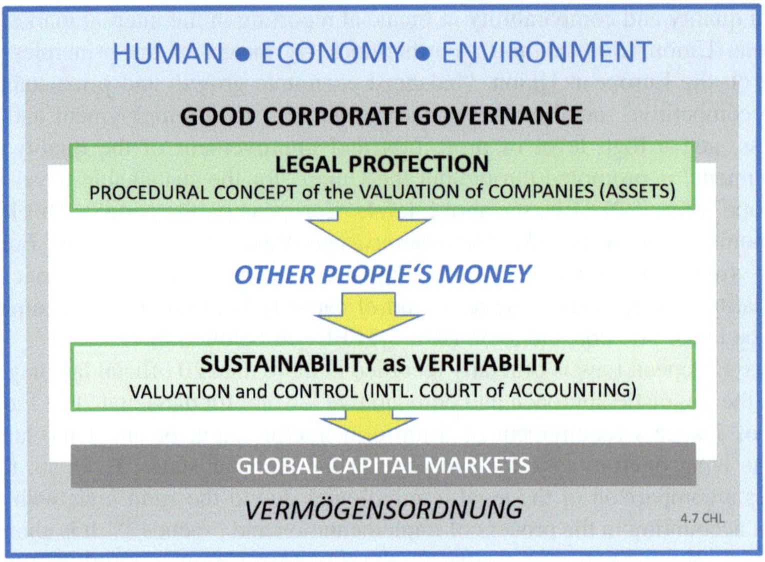


**Fig. 4.7** Legal protection and sustainability as verifiability

and auditing of a corporation are related, holistically oriented toward procedure law with the imperative of truth, materially and formally, in order to be able to guarantee reasonable legal protection for all persons involved. This shall be taken into focus again here with a true and fair view (*Bilanzwahrheit*), the guiding principle of European accounting law: "Annual financial statements should be prepared on a prudent basis and should give a true and fair view of an undertaking's assets and liabilities, financial position and profit or loss."[468]

As shown (in 4.6.5) and explicitly implemented in German law, we are dealing with a human category (human corporation, not something mythical or irrational): The directors, obliged to provide financial reports, have to give a picture corresponding to the factual realities of the company (§ 264(2)(1) HGB, see 4.4 and chapter 9). The general norm for corporate directors, for corporate finance and financial reporting and auditing (§ 317(1)(3) HGB) is aimed at the representation of the economic substance, the substance (reality, materiality) of the circumstances – facts instead of mumbo jumbo (hope values, *Hoffnungswerte*). That has to be practiced in the sense of finding the truth: It is about the processes open to proof (*Beweis*, § 286(1) ZPO), id est in the sense of the civil procedure law (*Beweisrecht*) about verifiability (sustainability, *Nachhaltigkeit*).[469] With the present and the past, this also comprises estimates directed towards future circumstances (§ 287 ZPO): Without a sufficient factual basis, corporate directors evade the law through

[468] Accounting Law Directive 2013/34/EU, recital 9 and Art. 4(3), version in English. Cf. German version, ibid, and transformation in German law § 264(2)(1) HGB.

[469] See for more details, e.g., above 4.5.3, 4.6.4 and 4.6.5, below 4.11.4; overall chapters 5 and 7. Luttermann (2023a) recitals 40-44.

untenable prognoses ("out of the blue", see 5.5, 5.6). By thus avoiding the legal order, they cannot claim any legal protection either (see 5.6.2, Fig. 5.3); they are subject to sanctions (see 4.9.7).

Accordingly, the imperative of truth (*Bilanzwahrheit*) is the measure of proof in practice, related to the systematic regulation of accounting and auditing through European law and German legislation. This holds overall and to an unlimited degree also for standards designed privately in other ways, in particular the so-called "IFRS". Otherwise they will take us back to – long-gone – times where practice counted as *the* legal yardstick in business dealings. – Doesn't that sound like setting the fox to keep the geese? – Experience shows that instead of business circles, it is *independent* people (institutions) which must lay down the law, pronounce judgment and impose sanctions. This is confirmed by European legislation[470] and the European Court of Justice (see 4.5.2). With the member states of the European Union, they establish a transnational system of a legal order of assets (*Vermögensordnung*).[471]

### *4.10.3 International Court of Accounting*

We are living in times of technological, economic and sociopolitical changes. The world is being regauged. The European Model is a blueprint for the international harmonised development of accounting and auditing (i.e., financial reporting) as the documentary proof of good corporate governance. The global spread and implications of so-called "IFRSs" beyond the European Union should always be borne in mind.[472] The influences of different jurisdictions worldwide have the potential to result in more or less obvious changes to practices and "realities of laws" under the overall label "IFRS"; and this is exactly what is happening – more or less and in different ways (cf. "European IFRS", "Chinese IFRS", "AIFRS" etc., see 4.8.6). The legal order must be designed reasonably, id est sustainable (*nachhaltig*, see 4.10.2).

An international court for accounting matters (*Internationales Bilanzgericht*, see Fig. 4.7)[473] could establish and safeguard a reasonably harmonised practice of international standards of financial reporting (cf. questionable IFRS, ISA, IVS etc.); in addition, with climate change there are, among others, so-called "International Sustainability Standards" ("IFRS S", see overall 4.11.1). – What about the law? Remember Aristotle:[474] there is no difference between not using the laws

---

470 Cf. systematically Accounting Law Directive 2013/34/EU, among other things also recital 22: "Estimation involves judgements based on the latest available reliable information", i.e. systematically in the sense of the measure of proof mentioned the "evidence considered".

471 Cf. already Luttermann (2000a) on the basis of European accounting law (financial reporting, auditing) and the European Court of Justice in *Centros*: ECJ, 09.03.1999 (C-212/97 – *Centros*, DA) ECLI:EU:C:1999:126.

472 See esp. 4.8.6–4.8.8, 4.11 and 4.13.

473 See proposal by Luttermann (1999a) pp. 134–136.

474 Rhetoric, book I, chapter 15. See also below chapter 9.

and their not being enacted. This type of development seems to be the inevitable result of globalisation and internationalisation of financial reporting (accounting and auditing standards) or, to put it differently, the convergence of accounting standards that were, not so long ago, perceived as quite different. We must go further in our thinking. In particular in view of the global climate change, which is moving humans and the environment into focus. We should see the human corporation as the core instrument of a sustainable economy for global climate partners in a complementary global order of assets (see chapters 8 and 9).

It has to be made immediately clear: This is intended as a non-centralised political system, that is, light-years away from autocracy and the "one size fits all" well-known from American advertisements. It breathes the supranational spirit of the European motto *unity in diversity*:[475] a fair system for human affairs.[476] In this context the principle of subsidiarity has to be observed (see 4.11.3) for a strong multijurisdictional system of an international order of assets (*Vermögensordnung*), which protects foreign investors through private and international law.[477] This leads us to essential conclusions for the handling of accounting and auditing matters, id est the corporation itself (see 4.12). First, however, an important development, still gone virtually unnoticed, needs to be highlighted.

## 4.11 Perspectives of a World Monopoly: "IFRS/S" and XBRL

### *4.11.1 Sustainability: Information and the Claim to Monopoly*

The driving force in this process is the IASB (London) and its sphere, greatly influenced by the globally operating actors of the so-called financial industry managing big money.[478] The aim propagated by the IASB is to develop, "in the public interest", a "single set of high quality, understandable, enforceable and globally accepted financial reporting standards": And this "upon clearly articulated principles", as the IASB emphasised – still valid according to reason and practice – in view of its own lack of a concept.[479] The IASB itself made the following statement regarding its conceptual framework project: "Our Framework needs

[475] As the guiding principle of the European Union. Cf. the motto of the federally designed United States of America (USA) *"e pluribus unum"*. Andreas Follesdal, Federalism, in Zalta (2018).

[476] Cf. Aristotle, Politics, book I, chapter 2.

[477] Fundamentally on international investment protection Luttermann (2015c).

[478] Prominently the "big four" audit companies (Deloitte, EY, KPMG and PwC) and the large circle of financial players, e.g, investment funds and banks, insurance companies and other institutions.

[479] IFRS Foundation, Constitution 2a (2010). Cf. Preface to IFRS 6a. The Wall Street Journal, 03.02.2010, 12, about IASB-Chairman Tweedie: "'The ayatollah of accounting' strongly defends his principles". See also on the ongoing lack of legitimacy above 4.4.5. Cf. overall Bensadon and Praquin (2016).

updating (...) it does not have a measurement concept – it has a list of measurement choices."[480] – Anything new? (see, e.g., 4.4.4). Financial reporting and auditing is then to provide comparable information worldwide: the king's standard!

In some places, this may still sound good. However, the key question remains: *what* king's standard and *what* "standard" anyway? The IASB wants to develop a conceptual framework "that is rooted in fundamental economic concepts rather than one based on a collection of arbitrary conventions",[481] "a more complete, clear and updated set of concepts".[482] Which "economic concepts" are meant remains unclear in the face of the worldwide catastrophic economy, which is decisively influenced by some Anglo-American theories and practices.[483] The IASB continues its own mission, and accordingly, the conceptual framework (rev. 2018) seems quite questionable with gaps and inconsistencies to the standards (IFRS).[484] It is still emphasised: "The Conceptual Framework is not a Standard. Nothing in the Conceptual Framework overrides any Standard or any requirement in a Standard."[485] – So, just one question: Where is the measure? – Without that, "standard setting" remains a nice try, casuistry, a worthless endeavour. Sustainably, a legal concept is needed that shows the way (see 4.4).[486]

The "IFRS" are definitely not principle-based (see 4.11.4), but merely a topic-related accumulation of so-called "standards", largely a patchwork. As shown, the European Union bases itself upon this quicksand. Since 2005, companies oriented towards the capital market have had to set up consolidated financial accounts according to the "IFRS" (cf. § 315e HGB). This act of desperation is about to be extended to medium-sized companies (e.g., German GmbHs, Dutch BVs) through the "IFRS for Small and Medium Sized Entities" (IFRS for SMEs). In this way, the IASB wants to cover 95% of all enterprises worldwide: a world monopoly for the valuation of property, for the formulation of accounting rules as a standard for the national, European and international competition of companies.[487] The "IFRS" actors reach out even more rigorously with the foundation of the International

[480] IFRS, Conceptual Framework for Financial Reporting, Project Summary and Feedback Statement (September 2010), 2.

[481] Ibid.

[482] As of 2016 (accessed: 08.08.2016, no longer avialable). Cf. on CF 2018 (https://www.ifrs.org/issued-standards/list-of-standards/conceptual-framework/, accessed: 22.08.2025): "to ensure that the Standards are conceptually consistent and that similar transactions are treated the same way, so as to provide useful information for investors, lenders and other creditors." See above 4.5.6 on "decision usefulness" and below 4.11.4 ("useful", citing: CF (2018) 1.2 and SP1.2).

[483] See on further development chapters 6, 8 and 9.

[484] Cf., e.g., Pelger (2020); Evans, Lusher, and Day (2022); Shkulipa (2021).

[485] IFRS, Conceptual Framework for Financial Reporting, rev. 2018, SP1.2.

[486] See, for more details, e.g. 4.2, 4.3 and 4.5; for the rational also 3.2 and 3.3, on a general rule instead of casuistry above 3.5.5, below 7.8.1.

[487] See above 4.8.6. Critically on the world monopoly of the IASB as an uncontrolled power also already Luttermann, IASB: *Eine unkontrollierte Macht*, Handelsblatt, 16.07.2009, 6; Luttermann (2011a) and Luttermann (2023a) recitals 78-85. Cf. On IFRS monopoly and the pied piper of financial reporting Sunder (2011).

Sustainability Standards Board (ISSB) and the "IFRS Sustainability Standards" ("IFRS S", both abbreviated here as: "IFRS/S"), what is promoted is:

> "International investors with global investment portfolios are increasingly calling for high quality, transparent, reliable and comparable reporting by companies on climate and other environmental, social and governance (ESG) matters. (…) The intention is for the ISSB to deliver a comprehensive global baseline of sustainability-related disclosure standards that provide investors and other capital market participants with information about companies' sustainability-related risks and opportunities to help them make informed decisions."[488]

This "green" sustainability, orchestrated by the IFRS Foundation into a global coronation mass (see 4.11.4), confirms: it is really about a huge claim, it is about the whole, the dimension of which has hitherto largely been misjudged. Including the small and medium-sized companies, it encompasses the backbone of the economic and social order, and free entrepreneurship as a whole – including the smaller and medium-sized auditors (certified public accountants). The dimension is enormous, for in financing, accounting and auditing of companies we are dealing with accountability, id est valuation as – true – information (see 4.4.1 to 4.4.4). In this age of an information society valuation counts as a "production factor" (*Produktionsfaktor*) besides the classic threesome of land, labor and capital – by any means: Worldwide digital financial communication is the new royal road.[489]

## *4.11.2 XBRL: The Financial Reporting Revolution*

The IASB (IFRS Foundation, see 4.11.4) is conducting the revolution[490] silently on a technological basis via the internet; and be aware that also here advanced artificial intelligence is on the increase (AI, see 9.6 to 9.8). The digital era of communication is conquering the financial markets (corporate finance, see 6.8.5) and thereby the accounting and auditing of companies, id est establishing a worldwide kingdom of valuation (*Unternehmensbewertung*): digital data transfer as a business, a business area with a key global function – both in economic and legal terms. The magical formula from actors in the U.S. is eXtensible Business Reporting Language (XBRL). This computer language is without competition as the standard for electronic data transfer worldwide. The American Institute of Certified Public Accountants (AICPA), the lobby of the auditors, has been promoting the project since 1998.

---

[488] Announcement on the creation of the ISSB: 03.11.2021, see on current information: https://www.ifrs.org/groups/international-sustainability-standards-board/ (accessed: 22.08.2025).

[489] See 4.12.3 (with 3.7), 7.4.1, 8.3.3 (valuation as a communicative process), and already Luttermann (2023a) recitals from 78, esp. 91-100, Luttermann and Pöschk (2014). Cf. also below 8.3.1 and chapter 6.

[490] See below 4.12.3 with 4.13, above 4.8.5, and on this topic from an intercultural perspective Luttermann, C. and Luttermann, K. (2007).

With XBRL, business-oriented data processing for auditing was developed, the prototype of a world protocol (*Weltprotokoll*).[491]

This is in fact quite ingeniously conceived and in its comprehensiveness an instrument of power (business model): By way of digitisation, this world protocol is quietly capturing bookkeeping, accounting and the auditing of companies – in practice the epitome of corporate finance, valuation (rating) and communication – worldwide. This has tremendous impact on the corporation, initially in particular in its elementary financial function (see 2.5), on the entire corporate governance (compliance), globally on the capital markets and, last but not least, on society and individual investments (wealth) – the order of assets (*Vermögensordnung*, see chapter 8). XBRL defines the structure of documents, classifies relevant business relations and generates accounts according to defined categories, so-called "taxonomies" (*Klassifizierung*, classification). Such presentation hierarchies reflect specific ordering systems (e.g., "U.S. GAAP", German HGB). XBRL can be used with different programs, displayed in any web browser via Inline XBRL (iXBRL), and read by humans and machines (AI). In this way, contents remain untouched. Auditors and other actors can access the data for their own analysis of the balance sheets and for purposes of auditing (valuation).

That sounds like good news. The digital financial world, e.g., with the help of financial services (FinTech), blockchain, distributed ledger-technologie (DLT) and more to come, seizes the markets and companies in a digital eco-system.[492] At that, European guidelines provide the basis with the mandates of informational truth, essentiality and verifiability, which is to be implemented economically-technologically. To this end, asset values must be digitally recorded and be transferable (so-called tokenisation), and DLT must be employed along the supply chain. This leads to triple – instead of, as hitherto, double-entry bookkeeping (*Buchführung*, worldwide ledger) and revolutionises accounting and auditing processes with adjusted so-called "smart contracts" for reinforced control: establishing trust with transactions on the blockchain in order to participate in value creation (*Wertschöpfung*).[493] Is it good news, a new kind of corporate finance and valuation, of financial reporting and governance?

The development is highly dynamic. Just look at how artificial intelligence (AI) is conquering the corporate world and our lives (see 3.7, 9.6 with 6.8.5). Living and working in a time of disrupting digital business may be seen as "the era of the chief

[491] Tim Bray et al. (eds.), Extensible Markup Language (XML) 1.0 (Fifth Edition, www.w3.org/TR/REC-xml, accessed: 22.08.2025). Banzal (2020).

[492] Teigland, Siri, Larsson, Puertas, and Ingram Bogusz (2020).

[493] To the overview Vukovic, Maiti, and Grigorieva (2022). On technology and forms of networking (AI, DLT, DAOs etc.) above 3.7 and below, esp. 9.5 to 9.7. On the development of bookkeeping and accounting law Luttermann (1996b).

digital officer" with "digital functionality [bringing] greater transparency" that "helps us validate trust with every signal, every transaction".[494] However, abuse – on new levels – in finances, valuation and accounting remain in the corporation with human greed, e.g., in crowdfunding and crypto exchanges (see 4.11.4, chapter 6). In any case, it is in particular the economic-technological interface, providing more scope to the fiction and practice of the corporation, which must be apprehended in a legally reasonable way.[495] The European Securities and Markets Authority (ESMA) establishes the European Single Electronic Format (ESEF) in harmonisation of transparency requirements,[496] an electronic reporting format in which issuers on European Union regulated markets are to prepare their annual financial reports (AFRs) since January 1, 2020 using XBRL; and it should be noted: The taxonomy to be used for ESEF is an extension of the "IFRS", prepared and updated annually by the IFRS Foundation.[497]

The technical form, however, can only provide what its creators have designed. Overall, it is about the content of the AFRs, also in company-specific extensions, in the last instance about interpretation, responsibility, verifiability and of course about due diligence (liability). At the same time, the form creates pressure for a uniform accounting world, in order to achieve compatibility for data transfer with subsidiaries (daughter companies), service providers and investors, regulators. Correspondingly, the taxonomy defines which data and contents an XBRL instance (*Instanz*) captures. All in all, the standard of accounting and auditing can thus be materially changed beyond democratic legitimisation (see 4.4.5, 4.5.4). Technology paves the way to a world monopoly for "IFRS" (the IASB) for the valuation of companies (assets: see chapter 8; note, e.g., the so-called "Goldman Sachs Algorithm" in 6.9). – Who controls this power?[498]

### 4.11.3 "IFRS for SMEs" as a Trojan Horse and Subsidiarity

The silent revolution has been going on long since in our midst, with clear signs and critical references in prominent places.[499] In Germany, both the official commercial

---

[494] Wang (2015) pp. 69-88, 170.

[495] Basically above 3.7 and chapter 9.

[496] Directive 2013/50/EU of Oct 22, 2013 on the harmonisation of transparency requirements, OJ EU, Nov 6, 2013 L 294/13, recital 26.

[497] See below 4.11.4 and more on ESEF under www.esma.europa.eu, esp. ESMA, ESEF Reporting Manual: Preparation of Annual Financial Reports in ESEF format (ESMA32-60-254rev). Brands, Holtzblatt, and Koskentalo (2022).

[498] Leading article for a wider audience Luttermann, *IASB: Eine unkontrollierte Macht*, Handelsblatt, 16.07.2009, p. 6.

[499] Ibid. See also Luttermann (2011b) and Luttermann, editorial (*Die erste Seite: Die Monopolfrage* – The monopoly question, for Otto Sandrock on his 80th birthday), in: 56 Recht der Internationalen Wirtschaft (RIW) 2010 (vol. 3) p. I.

register (*Handelsregister*) and the official company register (*Unternehmensregister*) are among the institutions using XBRL. Corporations are obliged to disclose their final accounts electronically (§ 325 HGB). From 2012 on, those subject to taxation have had to convey their accounts according to the XBRL/HGB taxonomy.[500] The IASB has already integrated "full IFRS" for entities that participate in public capital markets and "IFRS for SMEs" in its taxonomy (2010 onward). This practically makes the "full IFRS" a dictate for the far more numerous entities not publicly accountable for their accounts. – Overall, it is about opinion "embedded in code" (Cathy O'Neil),[501] form shapes the content (see 4.11.2, 1.5.3).

We remember: The "IFRS Taxonomy", whose updates appear with the publication of new or amended "IFRS", is "developed through a formal system of due process": this ensures, the IASB emphasised,[502] "transparency and compliance with best practice" – not a word, however, is spoken about being oriented towards a set of principles (cf. 4.11.1). The "due process" practice and the narrative are continued. For the IFRS Taxonomy Consultative Group (ITCG) the following explicitly applies: "The aim of using a single, high quality, easily enforceable and globally accepted IFRS Taxonomy to mark up digital reports is to facilitate the efficient dissemination, processing and accessing of IFRS financial statements."[503] Members of the ITCG "review in depth the IFRS Taxonomy and ensure that it meets expected market standards and best practices from both a data content and architectural perspective."[504] – Well, focusing on "expected market standards" and the like may work in a fairytale (see 4.9.2, 3.1), but for sustainable regulation and practice?

Also to remember: In the IASB, the so-called "due process" is in fact questionable,[505] particularly in regard to "IFRS for SMEs". Deficiencies have been made out and the IASB itself has said that the final title "IFRS for SMEs" does not necessarily describe the scope of the standard;[506] a grandiose self-assessment and recommendation. The regulation and practice of financial reporting for private companies (SMEs) even with regard to consolidated financial statements of privately held

[500] See § 5b *Einkommensteuergesetz* (EStG) and Federal Ministry of Finance (*Bundesministerium der Finanzen*), 28.09.2011, IV C 6 - S 2133-b/11/10009. Cf. Hoffmann, Gösele, Küpper (2013).

[501] See above 3.8 and below in 6.6.3.

[502] Explicitly, quoted following Claus Luttermann in: Du Plessis, Großfeld, Luttermann (2017) p. 392 (7.10.3); cf. Amendments to IFRS for SMEs (May 2015) and Second Comprehensive Review of the Standard (Exposure Draft Sept 2022). On the 2025 IFRS for SMEs Accounting Standard: https://www.ifrs.org/issued-standards/ifrs-for-smes/, accessed: 22.08.2025).

[503] See IFRS as of 2022 (accessed: 05.12.2022). Cf. IFRS (www.ifrs.org/groups/ifrs-taxonomy-consultative-group/, accessed: 22.08.2025): "The IFRS digital taxonomies help facilitate the digitalisation of general purpose financial reports prepared in accordance with IFRS Standards. By digitalising financial reports using the IFRS digital taxonomies, information in those reports becomes machine-readable, allowing users to extract, compare and analyse information efficiently."

[504] Ibid (2022), and cf. (2025): to "ensure that the taxonomies meet expected market standards and best practices from both a data content and architectural perspective".

[505] See, e.g., above 4.4.4, 4.4.5 and 4.5.4.

[506] See Ram and Newberry (2013) and above 4.4.5 and 4.8.4. Cf. also Devi and Samujh (2015). With special focus on Fiji: Chand, Patel, and White (2015).

groups, in a global dimension appears confusing and full of variants: voluntary adoption of full IFRS, by allowing or requiring the use of (an adapted version of) "IFRS for SMEs", or sticking to national or European "GAAP".[507] This criticism thus points to a broad, multifariously differentiated spectrum, and it still continues, also with regard to "due process".[508] This, as well as the focus on "best practice" emphasised by the IASB (IFRS Foundation), underlines the fundamental criticism of this so-called "standard-setting" – particularly in the "public interest" (see 4.11.4).[509]

Beside the XBRL/IFRS taxonomy, which is oriented towards the relatively few large publicly-owned firms, id est corporations on so-called "big boards" (securities exchanges, *Börsen*), other specific taxonomies (e.g., the German HGB, for Japanese "GAAP" or the "AIFRS") may soon be regarded as inefficient, at least with regard to costs.[510] Thus, the further development of accounting (financial reporting) and auditing will be subject to a new episode of the Ancient Greek story of the Trojan Horse. The question is:[511] One may wonder how long specific taxonomies (like XBRL for HGB) will remain, that is, specific standards of accounting (cf. the so-called "Microsoft syndrome"). In other words: when will the switch from the technical-factual different taxonomies (for German HGB, EU-IFRS, AIFRS, U.S. "GAAP" etc.) to the economically powerful uniform "XBRL/IFRS" taxonomy take place? – In regulatory reporting, this has in fact already taken place with the European Single Electronic Format running on the basis of the IFRS/iXBRL taxonomy (ESEF, effective since January 1, 2020, see 4.11.2).

The world should be gauged with one measure. However, as shown, the so-called "IFRSs" are a flawed "measure" (*Messlatte*), if one at all, in themselves and internationally anyway. Although digitisation (and AI) cannot remedy the inherent shortcomings of "IFRS", it may gloss over these all too well. Rule of law (*Rechtsstaatlichkeit*) requires watchfulness in particular where technological development becomes redefining with at first sight elegant – here: digital – but questionable "solutions" (note: substance over form!). Where has the practically proven principle of subsidiarity gone that the European Union is pledged to (Art. 5 TEU)? – The Accounting Law Directive 2013/34/EU is based on the "think small first" principle in order to avoid disproportionate and costly administrative burdens on SMEs,[512] id est, it is "bottom up" instead of – as for the "IFRS/U.S. GAAP" – "top down" from the big players. Who protects this entrepreneurial basis?

---

[507] Gassen (2017).

[508] See below 4.11.4. In the literature, e.g., on Spain Bautista-Mesa, Muñoz-Tomás, Horno-Bueno (2019); on Brazil Gonçalves, Freitas de Moura, and Motoki (2022). Benhayoun and Marghich (2017).

[509] See esp. 4.10.2 and 4.4.5. See also chapter 9.

[510] Cf. Hellman, Nilsson, Tylaite, Vural (2022).

[511] Claus Luttermann in: Du Plessis, Großfeld, Luttermann (2017) p. 392 (7.10.3).

[512] Accounting Law Directive 2013/34/EU, recital 10. See also internationally above 4.8.4 and 4.8.8 (multijurisdictional approach).

### 4.11.4 In the Public Interest: Sustainability as Verifiability

Still, we are witnessing how the model of the so-called U.S. "GAAP", with its patterns of corporate finance, valuation and reporting (leverage, "shareholder-fair value" etc.)[513] has not only failed to avert the world debt crisis: It is this unsound but powerful business model of the financial industry (Wall Street and City of London type, see 3.3.2, 7.2.1) that is being spread forcefully around the globe (the Pax Americana),[514] creating a world monopoly of the valuation of corporations (assets, liabilities). We have to realise that the drama of financial crises has changed the world[515] and is ongoing at high speed with politics, the evolution of technologies and disrupting businesses (see, e.g., 1.5.3, 3.7). The process of transformation of economies and societies is just starting on an even larger scale with worldwide shifts and upheavals, the global climate change, generative AI etc. (see 6.8.5, 9.6) and us all, being more or less inevitably participants, too.

With the idiosyncratic force of global capital markets and corporations the so-called "IFRS" propagated by the IFRS Foundation and their off-spring, the so-called "International Sustainability Standards" ("IFRS S"), are central. The expressed goal: reporting required by the now two standard-setting bodies IASB ("IFRS") and ISSB ("IFRS S") should be integrated.[516] What is remarkable is that the IFRS Foundation itself is a non-profit corporation incorporated in the federal state of Delaware (USA), claiming to act "in the public interest".[517] This sounds strange, especially since that small US state is regarded as a "loophole" by tax and fraud experts,[518] enjoying questionable reputation: "Delaware's race to the bottom stains its reputation as the epicenter of all things corporate."[519] The business orientation is marked: "Delaware's carefully calibrated positioning in the charter market has largely eliminated meaningful competition among the [US] states for the quality of corporate law."[520] Recall U.S. President Joe Biden's primary residence in

---

[513] See above 4.8 and chapter 9.

[514] See above 2.3.2, below 6.2.1 (cf. already Luttermann in Du Plessis (2017) pp. 433-434) and Luttermann (1999a). Cf. Kavame Eroglu (2017).

[515] Tooze (2018).

[516] Via the "Integrated Reporting and Connectivity Council", see in more detail: www.ifrs.org (updated).

[517] Cf. on Delaware above 4.4.2 and 2.4.1.

[518] David Morris, What's the matter with Delaware? How Joe Biden's home State became a global tax avoidance hub, 15.11.2022 (https://www.coindesk.com/opinion/2022/11/15/delaware-corporate-taxes, accessed: 22.08.2025), representing 45% of US GDP and two-thirds of Fortune 500 corporations and "effectively anonymous registration for shell companies that can be used to hide investment holdings from real estate to equities to, at least in theory, crypto." (e.g., the FTX-scandal in Nov. 2022). Cf. Dave Taylor, Johns Hopkins Undergraduate Law Review, 15.10.2018 (https://jhulr.org/2018/10/15/the-siphon-state-the-9-5-billion-reason-why-corporations-love-delaware/, accessed: 22.08.2025).

[519] Nguyen (2021) 717, 750. See also above 2.4.1 and 3.4.2.

[520] Anderson (2018) 657, 658. Cf. above 2.4.1.

Greenville, Delaware, an upscale suburb of Wilmington, a world-renowned tax haven and the company address of the IFRS Foundation.[521]

In "the public interest" is a significant claim. Does that not rather demand trustworthiness? Correspondingly, lack of legitimation and quality is tangible in particular with Delaware as the "de facto capital of corporate America": This is shown by Hal Weitzman of the University of Chicago Booth School of Business, who attests in various facets,[522] how Delaware, due to its tremendous clout, is effectively writing the corporate code for the entire United States and "the rules for much of the world". However, centralist power within the USA (the so-called "federal Cesar")[523] fundamentally contradicts the spirit of the U.S. Constitution of liberty and at least outside of the USA is not tolerable. The settlement of the IFRS Foundation in Delaware (USA) lies in the logic of its silent power structure, which works globally via the London-based IASB (ISSB)[524] and the so-called "IFRS/S". And this is true although they are practically non-recognised in the USA as such. This together with their connection to Delaware is quite rightly causing irritation in other countries. Selling to the world what you don't think is good (enough) for yourself?

The whole thing does in fact seem strange, well overlaid medially. What is propagated as "IFRS/IFRS S" by the privately organised, self-appointed standardiser IFRS Foundation (IASB/ISSB) are simply the rules of a foreign power. With the application of the "IFRS/S" it is thus about core questions of conflict of laws (*Kollisionsrecht*) that are of globally fundamental economic significance, as shown:[525] The rules of financial reporting and auditing influence the valuation (*Bewertung*), financing and governance of a corporation and via the capital markets globally drive capital flows; accordingly, a solid, sustainable basis is needed for this in legal terms (*lex aestimatio*, see 2.1, 8.4.2). But contrary to what is advertised, the IFRS Foundation ("IFRS/S") does not in fact provide "a set of high-quality, understandable, enforceable and globally accepted accounting standards".[526] The reality reveals a manifold spectrum and "standards" (delivered immediately with minority

---

[521] According to company-information service (www.gov.uk), company no. FC023235, overseas company address: 1209 Orange Street Wilmington, New Castle County, Delaware 19801, United States. One of more than two million legal entities incorporated in Delaware (2023 Annual Report), out of a population of about one million (2020 Census). Cf. with U.S. President Barack Obama, 05.04.2016: https://www.washingtonpost.com/news/wonk/wp/2016/04/05/how-the-u-s-became-one-of-the-worlds-biggest-tax-havens/ (accessed: 22.08.2025).

[522] See total Weitzman (2022). Cf. for IFRS/S above 4.11.1.

[523] Berle (1938) p. 369 called the (then) new SEC a "synthetic czar in the accounting field". Overall, with references, Luttermann (1998) pp. 372-375, 427-440 on standard setting as politics and realities; cf. Belkaoui (1985) pp. 9-11 ("politicalization of accounting"). Cf. above chapter 3 (esp. 3.3.3, 3.5.4) and below 7.6.

[524] See on the "City of London" above 3.3.2 and below 6.2.1, 6.2.2 and 7.2.1.

[525] See above, esp. 4.2, 4.5.4 and 4.8.8.

[526] See IFRS Foundation, e.g.: www.ifrs.org/news-and-events/news/2020/08/what-is-the-due-process-and-why-does-it-matter/ and www.ifrs.org/use-around-the-world/why-global-accounting-standards/ (both accessed: 22.08.2025).

opinions, i.e. options) lacking in substance and measure.[527] The so-called "Conceptual Framework" ranking itself *second* to any "standard" (i.e. "IFRS/S"), claims as its purpose:[528]

> "The objective of general purpose financial reporting is to provide financial information about the reporting entity that is useful to existing and potential investors, lenders and other creditors in making decisions relating to providing resources to the entity."

Is that what matters "in the public interest"? – As demonstrated, financial reporting is the epitome of accountability in relation to the truth (*Bilanzwahrheit*). In a procedural concept of a search for truth, id est based on facts (substance), also for necessary prognoses on the basis of the connecting facts (*Anknüpfungstatsachen*, see 5.6.2). Mere hope values as in neoclassical practice ("creating shareholder value") are to be avoided, in order to prevent illegitimate transfer of assets. Sustainability as a task of the law means verifiability according to the rules of evidence for legal protection (see 4.10 and Fig. 4.7). Otherwise, the "modern corporation" (human corporation) in its financial function and instruments is substantially meaningless (see 3.5.3). Old financial industry takes a different path with "IFRS/IFRS S" (briefly: "IFRS/S"). And again, the paramount question remains: Who legitimates and controls this vast, global-reaching power?

## 4.12 Strategic Governance and Audit Committee

### *4.12.1 Sustainable Corporate Finance and Investment*

Accounting and auditing are a legal duties, no marketing show. The responsible corporate directors, their accountants and auditors, however, should see financial reporting much more as an entrepreneurial opportunity. Giving "a true and fair view" of the company every fiscal year in the accounts/financial statements means a safeguard against sanctions and liability claims (see 4.10.2): the best evidence of sound business practice, opening up potential investment opportunities. It is about substance, which as a sustainable economic activity can bear ups and also downs – as long as the balance of life is maintained. Telling the investors the whole story clearly ("the good, the bad, and the ugly")[529] creates confidence (*Vertrauen*) in the light of substance and sustainability, even in a year of minor success. Such corporate governance is necessary for the sustainable development of a company in the longer

[527] Critically already above, e.g. in 4.9.7.

[528] See Conceptual Framework (2018) 1.2 and SP1.2.

[529] German: *"Das Gute, das Schlechte und das Häßliche"*. See above 4.5, esp. 4.5.1 (with Fig. 4.3): "a true and fair view", i.e. the imperative of truth (*Bilanzwahrheit* and *Bilanzklarheit*, see 4.4.4). Basically on individual responsibility and the concept of trust above 1.5.2 and chapter 7 (esp. 7.7.3), on "real disclosure" above 3.3.3.

term and for the integrity of capital markets worldwide.[530] Sustainability is what counts for prosperity.

True and fair accounts are simultaneously *the* documentary proof for corporate directors and responsible accountants (see 4.4.1). The accounts/financial statements can prove whether corporate directors have carried out their duties (compliance), that is, whether they have provided good corporate governance. And if they have done so, there is no reason to hide. So again: tell the true story clearly (imperative of truth, see 4.4.4). In this way, accounting protects against unrealistic expectations and claims – against the evil "numbers game".[531] Therefore, the strategic formula for far-sighted fair corporate governance is protection and confidence through true information. Economists may call that a typical "win–win situation". On the other hand, shady areas and marketing puffs in the accounts/financial statements should always set off an alarm signal at first sight (red flags), especially for the members of the supervisory board and the external auditor. That alarm signal should trigger deeper and more penetrating investigation into the actual financial position of the corporation by those auditing or supervising the business of the corporation and acting as watchdogs, that is, foremost the members of the supervisory board and the external auditor.[532]

Overall, it is about personal responsibility: that is the necessary basis of a freely organised community (*Vermögensordnung*) under the rule of law, guaranteeing everyone's individual liberty as an entrepreneur in fair competition (see further chapter 7). That is why corporate governance must recognise accounting matters as vital. A human corporation in its core function as a permanent financial instrument is represented in the documented valuation, id est sustainable financial reporting (accounting). Accountable means being responsible *to* persons (investors etc.) and *for* things (investments, assets etc.).[533] Responsibility (duty of care) should in general be demanded as the measure (due diligence). Of course, it is about the autonomy of the individual: true responsibility is fundamentally sovereign, not tolerating an employee mentality and informed by personal integrity.[534] For good corporate governance and a good economy as a whole, everyone must keep this in mind and practice it.

[530] Großfeld and Luttermann (2005) recitals 86–96.

[531] See above 4.6.1 and 4.8.1, 4.10–4.11. Also Luttermann (2003a) Einf BilanzR recitals 123–133 and on § 264 HGB recitals 119–169.

[532] See below 4.12.2, above 4.9; cf. Crumbley and Fenton (2021), Young (2006).

[533] Cf. Old French *acomptable*, Brown (1993) p. 15 (accountable).

[534] See below 6.4, 6.7-6.9, and chapter 7 with the motto by Elias Canetti. On the erosion of freedom Luttermann (2008d). See further below 4.12.2.

### 4.12.2 *Human Corporate Supervisory Boards and Advisors*

The human corporation is an ingenious financial instrument for doing good (i.e. human corporation). For this, freedom to conduct a business is fundamentally tied to personal responsibility, legally expressed in due diligence (duty of care, *Sorgfaltspflicht*).[535] Reasonably established, this provides the basis for good management, financing and valuation (financial reporting) of the corporation, id est for sustainable, entrepreneurially value-creating decisions in general: in view of worldwide climate change, in particular for the respect of human rights (human rights due diligence) and the protection of the environment (environmental due diligence) as a whole; sensible in the application of modern technology and science. Accordingly, business operation must be designed sustainably, promoted through systematically structured research and counselling.[536]

What is indicative is the dual organisation of the corporation that is traditional in Germany: the executive or management board (*Vorstand*) with its role of managing the corporation under its own responsibility (§ 76(1) AktG), and the supervisory board (*Aufsichtsrat*) with the task of monitoring the management (§ 111(1) AktG), partly with mandatory participation of employee representatives at supervisory board level (supervisory codetermination, so-called *mitbestimmter Aufsichtsrat*) and an “all-inclusive stakeholder focus” as a *leitmotif* for corporate governance. That two-tier board system, in contrast to a unitary board system, in its multipartite management structure characterises a clear differentiation of persons (corporate directors) in their respective function, that is basically their competencies. As a theoretical model, this structurally provides a sound control system, a kind of balancing of powers, which may serve sustainability well in practice.

This does not mean preferring one approach over another in a narrow-minded way or playing them off against one another. Rather, it is about building overall the best possible regulatory system from basic elements. The failing in particular of the Wirecard AG (2020), listed at the Frankfurt Stock Exchange, again proves that any system in the last instance depends on the persons responsible for being implemented sustainably well. And this case lays bare and also confirms constructional weak points. The German legislator has reacted with stricter stipulations for bigger, id est “publicly relevant” corporations, with (in translation) the following reasoning:

---

[535] See above 4.12.1 with 4.4.1, 4.7.2 and overall chapter 7. See also in European law the Corporate Sustainability Due Diligence Directive (EU) 2024/1760, 13.06.2024, OJ L, 05.07.2024.

[536] See, e.g., the Sustainable Business Finance Navigator by Luttermann, L. (2022), (2023) and (2024).

> Through legal obligations for listed joint stock corporations to establish an adequate and effective internal control system as well as a corresponding risk management system and through the obligatory establishment of an audit committee in supervisory boards of publicly relevant corporations, the company-internal control systems are fortified and the structures of responsibilities improved.[537]

This strengthening of corporate governance as "the regulatory framework for the management and supervision of companies"[538] fortifies – finally – the supervisory board. For "publicly relevant companies" (*Unternehmen von öffentlichem Interesse*, § 316a HGB), an audit committee is to be established (see § 107(4) and (3)(2) AktG) that fulfills the requirements according to § 100(5) AktG (see below). The obligation to establish an audit committee (*Prüfungsausschuss*) is based on its high significance for the accounting process (if necessary, including bookkeeping, § 91(1) AktG)[539] and auditing (i.e. financial reporting), thus the legislator: The establishment of an audit committee "serves the effectiveness and efficiency of the work of the supervisory board" and meanwhile is said to have become reality in most companies with larger supervisory boards ("best practice"). Now, every member of the audit committee has a claim to information – besides the obligation of the executive board to inform (§ 90(1) AktG) – directly towards all central units of the first management level beneath the executive board (§ 107(4)(4) AktG) with regard to tasks relating to the audit committee (§ 107(3)(2) AktG).

The high significance of a corporate audit committee with experts of financial reporting and auditing (i.e. financing, valuation) brings to mind my early (2003) recommendations,[540] that pursuant to the significance of good corporate governance, an audit committee with independent experts should be established. European Law demands that for each public-interest entity (see Art. 41(1) of Directive 2006/34/EC). Conventionally, this is a committee of the board of directors that is charged with matters relating to financial reporting and auditing. The European Commission (following 2005) gave a recommendation that includes the role and operation of the audit committee with respect to the internal policies adopted by the company and to the external auditor engaged by the company. The committee members "should,

[537] Original in German: Deutscher Bundestag, *Begründung, Finanzmarktintegritätsstärkungsgesetz – FISG, Gesetzentwurf der Bundesregierung, Drucksache* 19/26966, 24.02.2021, p. 2 (B.) and 55 (A.I.). See above 4.9.4 (on Wirecard) and 4.9.5 (on the reaction of the legislator).

[538] Ibid on FISG, accompanied by amendments to the Stock Exchange Act (*Börsengesetz*) to improve the quality of admission of companies to the qualified market segments of the stock exchange.

[539] See also §§ 238, 239 HGB with §§ 242, 243 and 264 HGB.

[540] Fundamentally in German Luttermann (2003b); also Luttermann in Du Plessis, Großfeld, Luttermann et al., German Corporate Governance in International and European Context (Springer, New York): 1st ed. (2007) p. 203, 2nd ed. (2012) pp. 325–326, and 3rd ed. (2017) p. 394.

collectively, have a recent and relevant background in and experience of finance and accounting for listed companies appropriate to the company's activities".[541]

For this reason, each company (in Germany, the EU) should establish an audit committee as a committee of the supervisory board (or advisory council – *Beirat*), in its own best interest, by means of the law or on a voluntary basis.[542] It is essential that independent financial experts (*Bilanzexperten*) are appointed to that committee.[543] In 2009, legislation in Germany made at least one such member mandatory (§ 100(5) AktG);[544] the FISG of 2021 makes a second expert mandatory.[545] Basically, the advice applies to every corporation. The European Commission[546] recommends for company leaders in general: "A director should be considered to be independent only if he is free of any business, family or other relationships with the company, its controlling shareholder or the management of either, that creates a conflict of interest such as to impair his judgement." Foremost and ultimately, independence is the essence of the one's inner attitude (*innere Haltung*, see chapter 7).

### 4.12.3 Communication: Information as Creation of Value

Good governance is to be communicatively shaped with financial reporting for the human corporation as a strategic task for its directors (see 8.3.3). With information, id est financial reporting and auditing, it builds on substance in terms of sustainability (see Fig. 4.8).[547] Guided under the imperative of truth (*Wahrheitsgebot*) by

541 Commission Recommendation 15.02.2005 on the role of non-executive or supervisory directors of listed companies and on the committees of the (supervisory) board (EC) 2005/162, OJ L 52, 25.02.2005, section III (11.2.) and Annex 1 (4.).

542 See § 161 AktG (§ 314(1) No 8 HGB) and German Corporate Governance Codex (CGC, 2022) *Grundsatz* 14 (audit committee) and *Grundsatz* 15 (personal qualification); cf. CGC (2017) 5.3.2 and 7.2.1. See already Luttermann (2003b).

543 Luttermann (2003b).

544 See generally § 324 HGB. On this, e.g., *Oberlandesgericht München*, 28.04.2010 (23 U 5517/09) ZIP 2010, 1082. Basically Directive 2006/43/EC Art. 41; *Bundesregierung*, *Gesetzentwurf*, 30.07.2008, *Bundestags-Drucksache* 16/10067, 101-2. Bahreini (2012).

545 See § 105(5) AktG: One expert must have expertise in the domain of financial reporting (*Rechnungslegung*), one must have expertise in the domain of auditing (*Abschlussprüfung*). This means that one member with expertise in both domains is not sufficient, as the German Bundestag explicitly says, see Deutscher Bundestag, *Begründung*, *Finanzmarktintegritätsstärkungsgesetz* – FISG, *Gesetzentwurf der Bundesregierung*, *Drucksache* 19/26966, 24.02.2021, pp. 115-116 (§ 100).

546 Recommendation of Feb 15, 2005 on the role of non-executive or supervisory directors of listed companies and on the committees of the (supervisory) board (EC) 2005/162, OJ L 52, 25.02.2005, section III (13.1). See in more detail below in 6.3.3.

547 See above 4.11.1 (right at the end), 4.12.1 and chapters 5 and 7.

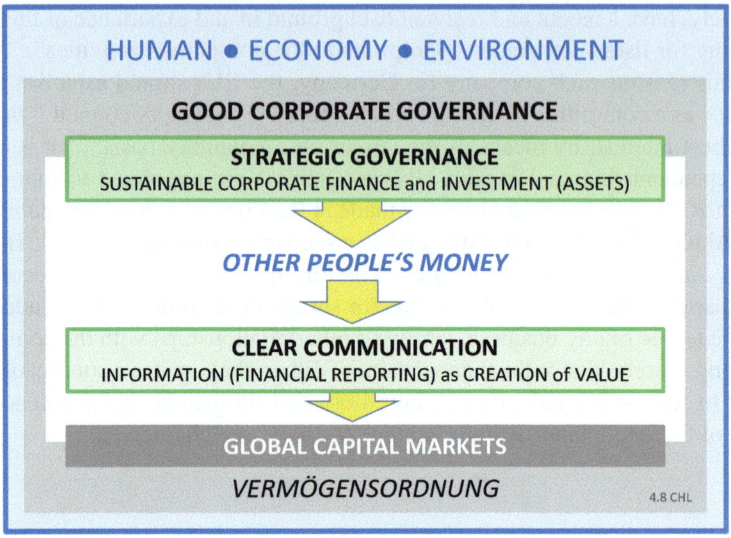


**Fig. 4.8** Information (communication) as creation of value

independent personalities who are responsibly active in a sustainable way in clear company-internal structures (executive board, supervisory board, advisory council, see chapter 7). And who then simply do what the financial concept of the corporation is legally laid out for: report clearly on their business dealings and material projects, provide correct account of the corporation in its dealings with other people's money, as already said – the good, the bad and the ugly. Communicatively, sustainable entrepreneurial creation of value (i.e. substance) is a legal act.

Actually, humans themselves create value. In the context of the community (*Gemeinwesen*) as a legal and economic order, humanity itself is "the ultimate source of value".[548] It adds – truly carried out with facts (substance) under the imperative of truth (see 4.4.4, 4.6.4) – value through language (information), that is, trust through clear communication,[549] and provides reason for sound financial communication (value creation, *Wertschöpfung*). Of course, not in the way it happens worldwide with unbalanced, uncontrolled creating only the so-called "shareholder value"[550]

[548] Korsgaard (2008) p. 85, cf. pp. 147-148. See below 5.3.4. Cf. Schweitzer's leitmotif (above, preface of this book): The foundation of law is humanity (*Humanität*).

[549] See 2.5.3, 2.6.2, 4.4.5 and 4.11.1; on the concept of trust above 1.5.2 (with Fig. 1.2), on the process of pricing 5.3.3 and valuation 5.3.4. Basically on information above 2.6.2. Cf. Gadamer (1998) 62.

[550] Rappaport (1998), critical review by Luttermann (2000b). Luttermann (2007c). Cf., e.g., Mulford and Comiskey (2005). On profit shifting and the audit committee Delis, Delis, Karavitis, Klassen (2023). Interdisciplinary in depth Großfeld (2010), from p. 178 and from p. 216.

with sham and soft information (hope values) in the still ongoing "numbers game". Such patterns of valuation soak through the capital markets globally with the debt economy doctrine (leveraging). Alluringly expressed in the style of scientificity in manipulated valuations and accounts, the whole thing simply aims at the production of "profit" (i.e. sham gains) that only count for a relatively small number of people in real terms. Thus, financing and investment proliferate into the effective, uncontrollable game with expectations. A gigantic transfer of wealth (assets).

Instead, it is sustainable information (facts) that count in financial reporting and auditing of the human corporation. In the valuation of companies, what is expedient for science and practice is this: The law and the economy, designed appropriately and recorded in a transparent way on the basis of facts (imperative of truth – *Bilanzwahrheit*) are a communicative process to success – increasingly making use of digital technology (see 4.11). Overall, for low-conflict communication, id est communication in human affairs that is as legally secure as possible, it is about clear language (*klare Sprache*).[551] This is how we create and convey human values (*Werte*) and creation of value (*Wertschöpfung*). In particular and in general, this facilitates the necessary basis of trust (legal protection) in freedom through responsibility (see chapter 7). It is on this basis that entrepreneurial progress is peacefully achieved. Clear language and communication carry the economy and the law with humanity as the basis of all valuation.[552]

## 4.13 Accountability: The Future of Information

Accounting, deriving from accountability (*Rechenschaft*) and together with auditing (i.e. financial reporting), is globally the embodiment of verified information. It means responsibility (*Verantwortlichkeit*) for good corporate governance. But theory and practice (regulation, auditing, legal enforcement) show grave deficiencies in the world debt crisis and daily business life. As a remedying measure, emphasis should be placed on the basic idea that corporate directors have a legal duty to inform the investors about their investment (money).[553] The information must give "a true and fair view" (*ein getreues Bild*) of the company, including prudent forecasts (*Prognosen*),[554] based on facts (*tatsächlichen Verhältnissen*). Soft information should be avoided so as not to slide from accounting into meaningless forms and

[551] See, e.g., above 4.7.3 and below 7.6.3. Basically Luttermann, C. and Luttermann, K. (2021).

[552] On law as practised ethics here overall (esp. 1.1, 1.6.1, 2.2.2 and chapter 9).

[553] See above 4.4.1, also 2.6.3 and 3.3 with 7.6.3.

[554] Based on connecting facts (*Anknüpfungstatsachen*), see below 5.5.3, 5.6.2.

fortune-telling (*Wahrsagerei*). For accounting, id est sustainable financial reporting, the general measure of "true and fair" (*Bilanzwahrheit*, imperative of truth) is the maxim on which to act.

This is in the vested interest of the corporate directors and their auditors. With true and fair accounting and auditing, they can gain lasting trust and avoid liability, having the documentary proof of good corporate governance (due diligence, compliance). The corporation becomes tangible in legal relations only in its picture of financial reporting (*Bilanzbild*). It comes into being, lives and decays according to certain valuation rules (*Bewertungsrecht*): They must be set independently and be controlled rigorously; this also holds internationally (e.g. for so-called "IFRS"). The foundation of true and fair accounting is firmly embedded for German and European companies with limited liability and imprinted by the European law and its Court of Justice (see 4.4.4). Harmonisation (not achievement of "uniformity") of the accounting law in the sense of the proven multijurisdictional approach and the decisive conflict of laws (*Kollisionsrecht*)[555] is the bridge to solid common standards of good corporate governance and valuation (*lex aestimatio*, see 2.1, 8.4.2).

Global markets deal with present and future wealth (*Wohlstand*). In international competition, political catchphrases abound. A prominent one is "hidden reserves" as described in "German accounting", although in the U.S., while also widely practised, this is downplayed as "cookie jar reserves". Comparative work can unmask such tricks and strengthen the common idea of true and fair accounting.[556] At the core, worldwide, is the integrity of the individuals acting on capital markets (see chapters 6 and 7). This is what needs to be nurtured instead of a disastrous economy, pushing us over the brink. A common idea of corporate finance and accounting, id est of valuation and information[557] (see chapter 5), should be jointly developed. What is required is a sustainable order of assets (*Vermögensordnung*)[558] as a legal order (*Rechtsordnung*), to be established worldwide for the protection of the people's investments and fair competition with private and international law (rule of law).[559]

Real financial reporting requires common standards, the process of evaluation is key here (see chapter 5). Cultural differences may fade into the background in the longer term. The concept of liberty that the human corporation carries is based on diversity, the principle of subsidiarity and cooperation.[560] Experience tells us that we should curtail any power and promote fair competition. Misuse and fraud cannot be

---

[555] See above 4.8.8, 4.11.4. According to the European Union Luttermann (2000a).

[556] See Levitt (1998) and already Brandeis (above 3.3.3, 3.5.4) and Berle (below 8.3.2). For more examples, see Luttermann (2003a) § 264 HGB recitals 62–82.

[557] See above 2.6.1 and 2.6.3 as well as below 7.6.3.

[558] See above 4.9.2, 4.11.4, and chapter 8. Luttermann (2015a).

[559] Luttermann (2015c) and, esp. on the international rule of law Luttermann (2016a).

[560] See on climate partners Luttermann (2022) and ICJ, Advisory Opinion, 23.07.2025, (https://www.icj-cij.org/sites/default/files/case-related/187/187-20250723-adv-01-00-en.pdf, accessed: 22.08.2025), para. 140 with paras. 301-308, on that below 6.1. On the principle of subsidiarity in European law (Art. 5 TEU) see above 4.11.3. On a global *Vermögensordnung* (order of assets) see chapter 8.

fully eliminated, but we must sanction them rigorously when they occur. However, we should not make accounting and auditing too hazardous for responsible individuals.[561] Rather, financial reporting must be based on facts only, id est "the disclosure must be real".[562] Jurisprudence drafts legal rules based on the idea of the decent individual. And therefore, again: Sustainability is what counts for the human corporation and the prosperity of us all worldwide.

## References


Abrams, C. (2012). FASB's failure to regulate off-balance sheet special purpose entities and the downfall of securitization. *Asper Review of International Business and Trade Law, 12*, 39–74.

Ackroyd, P. (2007). *Shakespeare: The biography*. Vintage Books.

Albrecht, W. S., Albrecht, C. O., Albrecht, C. C., & Zimbelman, M. F. (2025). *Fraud examination* (7th ed.). Cengage Learning.

Aldeia, S. (2019). The "true and fair view" concept in business and tax law: The Portuguese and Spanish case studies. *Academy of Accounting and Financial Studies Journal, 23*(2).

Alexander, D. (2006). Legal certainty, European-ness and Realpolitik. *Accounting in Europe, 3*, 65–80.

Amiram, D., Bozanic, Z., Cox, J. D., Dupont, Q., Karpoff, J. M., & Sloan, R. (2018). Financial reporting fraud and other forms of misconduct: A multidisciplinary review of the literature. *Review of Accounting Studies, 23*, 732–783.

Amisi, B. (2013). *The legitimacy of IFRS: An assessment of the due process of standard-setting*. University of South Africa.

Anderson, R. (2018). The Delaware trap: An empirical analysis of incorporation decisions. *Southern California Law Review, 91*, 657–710.

Arden, M. (1993). *The true and fair requirement, counsel's opinion*. Foreword to Accounting Standards Board, Accounting Standards.

Bahreini, D. (2012). *Der unabhängige Finanzexperte i.S.v. § 105 Abs. 5 AktG*. Duncker & Humblot.

Ballwieser, W. (2004). The limitations of financial reporting. In C. Leuz, D. Pfaff, & A. Hopwood (Eds.), *The economics and politics of accounting* (pp. 58–77). Oxford University Press.

Bamber, M., & McMeeking, K. (2016). An examination of international accounting standard-setting due process and the implications for legitimacy. *The British Account Review, 48*, 59–73.

Banzal, S. (2020). *XML basics*. Mercury Learning and Information.

Baskerville, R., & Evans, L. (2011). *The darkening glass: Issues for translation of IFRS*. https://ssrn.com/abstract=1910446 (accessed: 22.08.2025).

Baumüller, J., & Sopp, K. (2022). Double materiality and the shift from non-financial to European stustainability reporting: Review, outlook and implications. *Journal of Applied Accounting Research, 23*, 8–28.


[561] Cf. Judge Learned Hand in *Dabney v Chase National Bank*, 196 F.2d 668, 675 (2nd Cir. 1952). See chapters 7 and 9.

[562] Brandeis (1914) p. 104.

Bautista-Mesa, R., Muñoz-Tomás, J. M., & Horno-Bueno, M. P. (2019). Does the IASB know the needs of SMEs? A comparative analysis between the IFRS for SMEs and full IFRS due processes. *Spanish Accounting Review, 22*, 203–217.

Becker, K., Daske, H., Pelger, C., & Zeff, S. A. (2022). IFRS adoption in the US: An analysis of the role of the SEC's Chairs. *Journal of Accounting and Public Policy, 41*, 107016.

Belkaoui, A. (1985). *Public policy and the practice and problems of accounting*. Quorum Books.

Benhayoun, I., & Marghich, A. (2017). IFRS for SMEs: A structured literature review. *International Journal of Accounting and Financial Reporting, 7*, 538–561.

Bensadon, D., & Praquin, N. (Eds.). (2016). *IFRS in a global world*. Springer.

Berle, A. A., Jr. (1938). Accounting and the law. *The Journal of Accountancy, 65*, 368–378.

Bessler, W. (2012). The listing and delisting of German firms on NYSE and NASDAQ: Were there any benefits? *Journal of International Financial Markets, 22*, 1024–1053.

Böcking, H.-J., & Gros, M. (2020). *Gutachten für BaFin (§ 342b(4) HGB)*, 11.10.2020. www.accounting.uni-frankfurt.de/fileadmin/user_upload/dateien_abteilungen/abt_rec/LS_Boecking/Dokumente/Rechtsgutachten_BaFin_Boecking_Gros_20201011_inkl_2Anhaenge_und_2Anlagen.pdf (accessed: 22.08.2025).

Bormann, M. (1996). Internationale Harmonisierung der Rechnungslegung. *Recht der Internationalen Wirtschaft (RIW), 42*, 35–40.

Bradbury, M. E., & Harrison, J. A. (2015). The FASB's dissenting opinions. *Accounting Horizons, 29*, 363–375.

Brandeis, L. D. (1914). *Other people's money and how the bankers use it*. Frederick A. Stokes Company Publishers.

Brands, K., Holtzblatt, M., & Koskentalo, E. (2022). The European Union's ESEF iXBRL mandate: Finland's experience as an early adopter. *Journal of Emerging Technologies in Accounting, 19*, 271–278.

Bräuer, M. (2011). Die Pflicht zur Offenlegung der Rechnungslegung: Plädoyer für die Beibehaltung auch für Klein(st)unternehmen. *Neue Zeitschrift für Gesellschaftsrecht (NZG), 14*, 53–56.

Brown, L. (Ed.). (1993). *The new shorter Oxford English dictionary on historical principles* (2 Vols.). Clarendon Press.

Calder, R. (2020). Sharīʿah-compliant or Sharīʿah-based? The changing ethical discourse of Islamic finance. *Arab Law Quarterly, 34*, 1–24.

Chand, P., Patel, A., & White, M. (2015). Adopting IFRSs for SMEs. *Australian Accounting Review, 25*, 139–154.

Chen, Y., Lu, M., Shan, Y., & Taylor, S. L. (2025). *Twenty years of mandatory IFRS in Australia: Evidence, gaps and future insights (January 14, 2025)*. AASB Research Centre Working Paper No. 25-01. https://ssrn.com/abstract=5096241 (accessed: 22.08.2025).

Christensen, H. B., Lee, E., & Walker, M. (2009). Do IFRS reconciliations convey information? The effect of debt contracting. *Journal of Accounting Research, 47*, 1167–1199.

Crawford, L., John, F., Power, D., & Helliar, C. (2014). Control over accounting standards within the European Union: The political controversy surrounding the adoption of IFRS 8. *Critical Perspectives on Accounting, 25*, 304–318.

Crawford, L., Helliar, C., & Power, D. (2016). The temporal nature of legitimation: The case of IFRS 8. *Accounting in Europe, 13*, 43–64.

Cross, F. B., & Prentice, R. A. (2007). *Law and corporate finance*. Edward Elgar.

Crumbley, D. L., & Fenton, E. D. (2021). *Forensic and investigative accounting* (10th ed.). CCH Inc.

DeFond, M., Gao, X., Li, O. Z., & Xia, L. (2019). IFRS adoption in China and foreign institutional investments. *China Journal of Accounting Research, 12*, 1–32.

Delis, F., Delis, M. D., Karavitis, P. I., & Klassen, K. J. (2023). Corporate governance and profit shifting: The role of the audit committee. *European Accounting Review, 32*, 809–839.

De Luca, F., & Prather-Kinsey, J. (2018). Legitimacy theory may explain the failure of global adoption of IFRS: The case of Europe and the U.S. *The Journal of Management and Governance, 22*, 501–534.

Devi, S. S., & Samujh, R. H. (2015). The political economy of convergence: The case of IFRS for SMEs. *Australian Accounting Review, 25*, 124–138.

Dias, A., & Viegas, M. (2021). Country-by-country reporting: A step towards unitary taxation? *Intereconomics, 56*, 167–173.

du Plessis, J. J., Großfeld, B., Luttermann, C., Saenger, I., & Sandrock, O. (2007). *German corporate governance in international and European context*. Springer Verlag.

du Plessis, J. J., Großfeld, B., Luttermann, C., Saenger, I., Sandrock, O., & Casper, M. (2012). *German corporate governance in international and European context* (2nd ed.). Springer Verlag.

du Plessis, J. J., Großfeld, B., Luttermann, C., Saenger, I., Sandrock, O., & Casper, M. (2017). *German corporate governance in international and European context* (3rd ed.). Springer Verlag.

Ebke, W. F., Luttermann, C., & Siegel, S. (Eds.). (2007). *Internationale Rechnungslegungsstandards für börsenunabhängige Unternehmen?* Nomos Verlag.

Eisenberg, M. (1976). *The structure of the corporation: A legal analysis*. BeardBooks.

Eisenberg, M. (2005). The architecture of American corporate law: Facilitation and regulation. *Berkeley Business Law Journal, 2*, 167–184.

Evans, G., Lusher, J., & Day, S. (2022). Completeness of the qualitative characteristics using Foucauldian critical discourse analysis and content analysis paradigms: Towards a revised conceptual framework. *Journal of Financial Reporting and Accounting, 20*, 334–351.

Faiyyaz, A. G., & Malik, A. (2022). Adoption of International Financial Reporting Standards: A literature review. *American Journal of Economics and Business Innovations, 3*, 36–43.

Gadamer, H.-G. (Ed.). (1998). *Aristoteles, Nikomachische Ethik VI*. Vittorio Klostermann.

Galbraith, J. K. (1994). *A short history of financial euphoria*. Viking Penguin.

Garanina, T. (2016). Earnings management and R&D costs capitalization: Evidence from Russian and German markets. *Investment, Management and Financial Innovation, 13*, 77–85.

Gassen, J. (2017). The effect of IFRS for SMEs on the financial reporting environment of private firms: An exploratory interview study. *Accounting and Business Research, 47*, 540–563.

Gilson, R. J. (2001). Globalizing corporate governance: Convergence of form or function. *American Journal of Comparative Law, 49*, 329–357.

Goethe, J. W. von (1808). *Faust: Eine Tragödie, Erster Teil*. JG Cotta'sche Buchhandlung.

Gonçalves, F. J. A., Freitas de Moura, A. A., & Motoki, F. Y. S. (2022). What influences the implementation of IFRS for SMEs? The Brazilian case. *Accounting & Finance, 62*, 2947–2992.

Großfeld, B. (2010). *Dreaming law: Comparative legal semiotics*. German Law Publishers.

Großfeld, B. (2019). *Schritte über Grenzen: Rechtsvergleichende Kulturerfahrung*. LIT Verlag.

Großfeld, B., & Luttermann, C. (2005). *Bilanzrecht (Accounting Law): Die Rechnungslegung in Jahresabschluß und Konzernabschluß nach Handelsrecht und Steuerrecht, Europarecht und IAS/IFRS* (4th ed.). CF Müller Verlag.

Gu, J. (2021). Voluntary IFRS adoption and accounting quality: Evidence from Japan. *Economic Research, 34*, 1985–2012.

Guermazi, W. (2022). International financial reporting standards adoption in the European Union and earnings conservatism: A review of empirical research. *International Journal of Disclosure and Governance, 20*, 200–211.

Haapamäki, E., & Sihvonen, J. (2019). Research on international standards on auditing: Literature synthesis and opportunities for future research. *Journal of International Accounting, Auditing and Taxation, 35*, 37–56.
Haswell, S., & Lanfield-Smith, I. (2008). Fifty-seven serious defects in 'Australian' IFRS. *Australian Accounting Review, 18*, 46–62.
Heese, J., Wang, C. C. Y., & Labruyere, T. (2021). *Wirecard: The downfall of a German fintech star*. Harvard Business School Case 121-058, March 2021 (revised April 2021).
Hellman, N., Nilsson, H., Tylaite, M., & Vural, D. (2022). The impact of an IFRS for SMEs-based standard on financial reporting properties and cost of debt financing: Evidence from Swedish private firms. *European Accounting Review, 31*, 1175–1205.
Hermens, R. (2013). Speakable in quantum mechanics. *Synthese, 190*, 2365.
Hoffmann, R., Gösele, S., & Küpper, U. (2013). *Die elektronische Steuerbilanz*. BoD.
Humboldt, W. von (1792). *Ideen zu einem Versuch, die Grenzen der Wirksamkeit des Staats zu bestimmen* (2010 edition). Reclam.
Ihering, R. von (1872). *Der Kampf ums Recht*. Manz.
Jaspers, K. (1932). *Die geistige Situation der Zeit* (8th imprint 1979 (of the 5th ed. 1932)). de Gruyter.
Jiannan, Y., & Huaying, Y. (2024). IFRS in China: A systematic literature review. *American International Journal of Business Management, 7*, 261–265.
Jo, H., Hsu, A., Llanos-Popolizio, R., & Vergara-Vega, J. (2021). Corporate governance and financial fraud of Wirecard. *European Journal of Business and Management Research, 6*, 96–106.
Kavame Eroglu, Z. G. (2017). The political economy of international standard setting in financial reporting: How the United States led the adoption of IFRS across the world. *Northwestern Journal of International Law and Business, 37*, 459–516.
Kessler, H., Leinen, M., & Strickmann, M. (Eds.). (2009). *Handbuch Bilanzrechtsmodernisierungsgesetz*. Haufe.
Korsgaard, C. M. (2008). The dependence of value on humanity. In J. Raz (Ed.), *The practice of value* (pp. 63–85). Clarendon Press.
Kranz, A. (2010). *Die Fair Value-Bewertung von Finanzinstrumenten (HGB/IFRS): Eine kritische Analyse unter Berücksichtigung ausgewählter Aspekte der Finanzkrise*. Akademische Verlagsgemeinschaft.
Kuhr, J. (2013). *Grundsätze Europäischer Unternehmensbesteuerung*. Springer Gabler.
Lachapelle, A. (2022). Comment on ECtHR, decision Halet v. Luxembourg ("Lux Leaks" case): Does the criterion of "public interest" always imply checking whether the disclosed information is also "contributing to a public debate on a matter of general interest"? *Tijdschrift voor fiscaal recht, 621*, 425–433.
Langenbucher, K., Leuz, C., Krahnen, J. P., & Pelizzon, L. (2020). *What are the wider supervisory implications of the Wirecard case?* SAFE White Paper, No. 74.
Latha, C., & Sridar, P. (2022). The Impact of IFRS Adoption on Developing Countries: A Case Study of India. *Journal of Contemporary Issues in Business and Government, 28*, 774–783.
Levitt, A. (1998). *The "numbers game"*, 28.09.1998. https://www.sec.gov/news/speech/speecharchive/1998/spch220.txt (accessed: 22.08.2025).
Levey, M. M., & Wrappe, S. C. (2019). *Transfer pricing: Rules, compliance and controversy* (5th ed.). Wolters Kluwer.
Lin, S., Pownall, G., Sawani, A., & Wang, C. (2024). The effect of the FASB-IASB convergence project on the rules- and principles-based nature of US GAAP and IFRS. *Review of Accounting Studies*. https://doi.org/10.1007/s11142-024-09851-7 (accessed: 22.08.2025).
Lucas, D. J. (2019). Measuring the cost of bailouts. *Annual Review of Financial Economics, 11*, 85–108.

Lucchese, M., & Di Carlo, F. (2020). Inventories accounting under US-GAAP and IFRS standards: The differences that hinder the full convergence. *International Journal of Business and Management, 15*, 180–195.

Luttermann, C. (1994). Unitary Taxation und U.S. Supreme Court: Die Entscheidung Barclays Bank PLC/Colgate-Palmolive Company v. Franchise Tax Board of California. *Internationales Steuerrecht (IStR), 3*, 489–493.

Luttermann, C. (1996a). Besteuerung multinationaler Konzerne in den Vereinigten Staaten von Amerika. *Recht der Internationalen Wirtschaft (RIW), 42*, 935–948.

Luttermann, C. (1996b). Über Buchführung und Bilanzrecht: 502 Jahre nach Erscheinen der Summa de arithmetica, geometria, proportioni et proportionalita von Luca Paciuolo. In J. Baetge, D. Börner, K.-H. Forster, & L. Schruff (Eds.), *Festschrift for Rainer Ludewig* (pp. 595–626). IDW Verlag.

Luttermann, C. (1997). Zum Rechtsgebiet der internationalen Konzernrechnungslegung. In K.-H. Forster, B. Grunewald, M. Lutter, & J. Semler (Eds.), *Festschrift for Bruno Kropff* (pp. 485–506). IDW Verlag.

Luttermann, C. (1998). *Unternehmen, Kapital und Genußrechte: Eine Studie über Grundlagen der Unternehmensfinanzierung und zum internationalen Kapitalmarktrecht*. Mohr Siebeck.

Luttermann, C. (1999a). *Bilanzrecht in den USA und internationale Konzernrechnungslegung*. Mohr Siebeck.

Luttermann, C. (1999b). Die bilanzrechtliche Generalnorm im europäischen Sprachenspiel: Eine Verlaufsstudie zur Rechtspolitik. In R. de Groot & R. Schulze (Eds.), *Recht und Übersetzen* (pp. 115–123). Nomos Verlag.

Luttermann, C. (1999c). Pauschalrückstellung für potentielle Gewährleistungsverbindlichkeiten. *Neue Zeitschrift für Gesellschaftsrecht (NZG), 2*, 1039–1040.

Luttermann, C. (1999d). Rechtssprachenvergleich in der Europäischen Union: Ein Lehrbuchfall. *Zeitschrift für Europäisches Wirtschaftsrecht (EuZW), 10*, 401–404.

Luttermann, C. (1999e). Dialog der Kulturen: Vergleichendes Handels- und Kapitalmarktrecht im Sprachspiegel. In U. Hübner & W. F. Ebke (Eds.), *Festschrift for Bernhard Großfeld* (pp. 771–789). Verlag Recht und Wirtschaft.

Luttermann, C. (2000a). Mit dem Europäischen Gerichtshof (Centros) zum Internationalen Unternehmens- und Kapitalmarktrecht: Kollisionsrecht in den Zeiten des Internet. *Zeitschrift für Europäisches Privatrecht (ZEuP), 8*, 907–921.

Luttermann, C. (2000b). Review of Alfred Rappaport, Creating Shareholder value (2nd ed.). *Die Aktiengesellschaft (AG), 45*, 2000, 143.

Luttermann, C. (2001). Unternehmensfinanzierung, Geschäftsleiterpflicht und Haftkapital bei Kapitalgesellschaften. *Betriebs-Berater (BB), 56*, 2433–2437.

Luttermann, C. (2002). Wirtschaftsprüfer, Internationale Rechnungslegung in der Europäischen Union und Sprachenfrage. *Zeitschrift für Vergleichende Rechtswissenschaft (ZVglRWiss), 101*, 158–174.

Luttermann, C. (2003a). In B. Kropff & J. Semler (Eds.), *Münchener Kommentar zum Aktiengesetz* (Vol. 5/1, 2nd ed.). CH Beck Verlag.

Luttermann, C. (2003b). Unabhängige Bilanzexperten in Aufsichtsrat und Beirat. *Der Betriebs-Berater (BB), 58*, 745–750.

Luttermann, C. (2004). Bilanzwahrheit international: Die Rechtsanbindung von Rechnungslegung und Wirtschaftsprüfung. *Zeitschrift für Vergleichende Rechtswissenschaft (ZVglRWiss), 101*, 18–30.

Luttermann, C. (2006). Unternehmenskontrolle und Bilanzmanipulation nach anglo-amerikanischen Mustern (IAS/IFRS und U.S. "GAAP"). *Die Wirtschaftsprüfung (WPg), 59*, 778–786.

Luttermann, C. (2007a). Die Rechtsordnung der Rechnungslegung. In W. F. Ebke, C. Luttermann, & S. Siegel (Eds.), *Internationale Rechnungslegungsstandards für börsenunabhängige Unternehmen?* (pp. 47–65). Nomos Verlag.

Luttermann, C. (2007b). Gesellschafts- und Bilanzrechtsrefonn in Australien: Perspektiven regionaler "IFRS" und Europäisches Bilanzrecht. *Recht der Internationalen Wirtschaft (RIW), 53*, 825–831.

Luttermann, C. (2007c). Zur Rechtspraxis internationaler Unternehmensbewertung bei der Publikums-Aktiengesellschaft. *Neue Zeitschrift für Gesellschaftsrecht (NZG), 10*, 611–618.

Luttermann, C. (2008a). Juristische Person, Konzern und Existenzvernichtungshaftung. *Juristische Arbeitsblätter (JA), 40*, 833–838.

Luttermann, C. (2008b). Wesentlichkeit (Materiality) als Haftungsvermeidung in den USA. *Recht der Internationalen Wirtschaft (RIW), 54*, 577–583.

Luttermann, C. (2008c). Zum Gesetz zur Modernisierung des Bilanzrechts. *Zeitschrift für Wirtschaftsrecht (ZIP), 29*, 1605–1614.

Luttermann, C. (2008d). Die Erosion der Freiheit. *Frankfurter Allgemeine Zeitung*, 23.06.2008, p. 22.

Luttermann, C. (2009a). "Fair Value": Mythos, Methoden und Maß international. *Recht der Internationalen Wirtschaft (RIW), 55*, 1–11.

Luttermann, C. (2009b). Islamic Finance: Ein Dialog über Recht, Weltwirtschaft und Religionen. *Juristenzeitung (JZ), 64*, 706–715.

Luttermann, C. (2009c). Vermögensordnung, Kommanditistenhaftung und Scheingewinn (§ 172 HGB). *Neue Zeitschrift für Gesellschaftsrecht (NZG), 12*, 1140–1141.

Luttermann, C. (2010a). Juristische Analyse von Ökonomie, Staat und Gesellschaft. *Zeitschrift für Rechtspolitik (ZRP), 43*, 1–4.

Luttermann, C. (2010b). Das Bilanzstatut: Über Abkoppelungspraxis und Schadensersatz von Vorständen, Aufsichtsräten und Abschlußprüfern bei Bilanztatbeständen. *Die Aktiengesellschaft (AG), 55*, 341–350.

Luttermann, C. (2010c). Europäisches Bilanzrecht für mittelständische Gesellschaften: IFRS (for SMEs) als Reformkonzept? *Recht der Internationalen Wirtschaft (RIW), 56*, 417–424.

Luttermann, C. (2010d). Bilanzregeln und Finanzkrise: Die Besteuerung nach Leistungsfähigkeit und Bilanzwahrheit als Beweismaß. *Steuer und Wirtschaft (StuW), 87*, 346–355.

Luttermann, C. (2011a). Europäische Gesellschaften zwischen Weltmonopol (IFRS/XBRL) und Freiheitsverfassung. *Juristenzeitung (JZ), 66*, 965–972.

Luttermann, C. (2011b). Kopernikanische Wende zum Wahrheitsgebot oder eine europäische Ratingagentur nach US-Mustern? *Europäisches Wirtschafts- und Steuerrecht (EWS), 22*, 330–333.

Luttermann, C. (2012). Wirtschaftsstrafrecht: Zur prozessualen Lösung von Bewertungsfragen bei Vermögensdelikten als Freiheitsbasis. *Zeitschrift für Wirtschafts- und Steuerstrafrecht (wistra), 32*, 251–258.

Luttermann, C. (2013). Neue Bilanzrichtlinie: Europäisches Bewertungsrecht in prozessualer Praxis. *Neue Zeitschrift für Gesellschaftsrecht (NZG), 16*, 1128–1133.

Luttermann, C. (2014). Alibabas Wunderwelt: Perspektiven chinesischer Kapitalmarkt- und Gesellschaftsrechtspraxis. *Recht der Internationalen Wirtschaft (RIW), 60*, 777–784.

Luttermann, C. (2015a). Corporate law and the *Vermoegensordnung* (order of assets). *European Business Law Review (EBLR), 26*, 31–48.

Luttermann, C. (2015b). Rechtsreform für ausländische Investoren in China. *Internationales Steuer- und Wirtschaftsrecht (IWB), 20*, 185–192.

Luttermann, C. (2015c). Über Idee und Methodik eines internationalen Investitionsschutzes (Vermögensordnung) durch Privatrecht und Völkerrecht. *Zeitschrift für Europarecht, Internationales Privatrecht und Rechtsvergleichung (ZfRV), 56*, 274–282.

Luttermann, C. (2015d). Kapitalmarktrechtliche Information bei Finanzprodukten (PRIIP), Privatautonomie und Vermögensordnung. *Zeitschrift für Wirtschaftsrecht (ZIP), 36*, 805–814.

Luttermann, C. (2016a). German and Russian direct investment under the rule of international law. *Zeitschrift für internationales Wirtschaftsrecht (IWRZ), 2*, 90–95.

Luttermann, C. (2016b). Ist Panama überall: Mit Briefkastenfirmen über Hongkong, USA, EU zu Transparenzgebot und internationalem Steuerrecht? *Recht der Internationalen Wirtschaft (RIW), 62*, 397–405.

Luttermann, C. (2017). Wirtschaftsprüferausbildung, zivilprozessuales Bewertungskonzept und Zukunft des Berufsstandes. *Der Betrieb (DB), 71*, 137–144.

Luttermann, C. (2019). Die herrschende Meinung und Bewertungsrecht für Unternehmer. In W. A. Tönnes (Ed.), *Festschrift for Bernhard Großfeld* (pp. 245–256). C.F. Müller.

Luttermann, C. (2021). Grüner Paradigmenwechsel für Unternehmensfinanzierung, Vermögensanlage und Bewertungsrecht. *Recht der Internationalen Wirtschaft (RIW), 67*, 191–200.

Luttermann, C. (2022). Klimapartner einer kooperativen Weltvermögensordnung. *Recht der Internationalen Wirtschaft (RIW), 10*(October), p. I (editorial, *Die erste Seite*: https://online.ruw.de/suche/pdf/riw/riw-10-2022-i-d3f3bdcf9c541ac4fde57cadb3ca5968.pdf, accessed: 22.08.2025).

Luttermann, C. (2023a). Unternehmensbewertung im Spannungsfeld von Rechts- und Wirtschaftswissenschaft. In K. Petersen, C. Zwirner, & G. Zimney (Eds.), *Handbuch Unternehmensbewertung* (3rd ed., pp. 163–202). Bundesanzeiger Verlag.

Luttermann, C. (2023b). Juristische Anforderungen an eine ordnungsmäßige Unternehmensbewertung und an ein Bewertungsgutachten. In K. Petersen, C. Zwirner, & G. Zimney (Eds.), *Handbuch Unternehmensbewertung* (3rd ed., pp. 653–682). Bundesanzeiger Verlag.

Luttermann, C., & Geißler, S. (2013). Rechtsbasis und Praxis einer Kultur der Unternehmenssanierung. *Zeitschrift für das gesamte Insolvenzrecht (ZinsO), 18*, 1381–1386.

Luttermann, C., & Hartwig, T. (2004). Unternehmensformen und Bilanzrecht in der VR China für ausländische Investoren. *Recht der Internationalen Wirtschaft (RIW), 50*, 506–513.

Luttermann, C., & Luttermann, K. (2004). Ein Sprachenrecht für die Europäische Union. *Juristenzeitung (JZ), 59*, 1002–1010.

Luttermann, C., & Luttermann, K. (2007). IFRS, Kultur und Internet: Eine 'Weltsprache' der Rechnungslegung? *Recht der Internationalen Wirtschaft (RIW), 53*, 434–440.

Luttermann, C., & Luttermann, K. (2020). *Sprachenrecht für die Europäische Union*. Verlag Mohr Siebeck.

Luttermann, C., & Luttermann, K. (2021). Towards peace in Europe: On legal linguistics, prosperity and European identity – the European Reference Language System for the European Union. *International Journal of Legal Discourse, 6*, 7–41.

Luttermann, C., & Pöschk, M. (2014). Digitale Finanzkommunikation (XBRL/IFRS) für die Rechts- und Wirtschaftspraxis. *Wirtschaftswissenschaftliches Studium (WiSt), 43*, 663–668.

Luttermann, C., & Wiese-Ptak, P. (2015). Europäisches und polnisches Bilanzrecht: Grundlagen, System und Praxis nach der Richtlinie 2013/34/EU. *Osteuropa-Recht (OR), 61*, 461–473.

Luttermann, K. (2011). Cultures in dialogue: Institutional and individual challenges for EU institutions and EU citizens from the perspective of legal linguistics. *Journal of Language and Communication Studies, 46*, 25–38.

Luttermann, K. (2014). Languages in dialogue for European identity. In V. Gutsehe & R. Nate (Eds.), *Cultural identities in Europe: Nations and regions, migration and minorities* (pp. 69–88). Königshausen & Neumann.
Luttermann, L. (2022). Klimawandel und Business Judgement: Nachhaltige Finanzierung als unternehmerisches Sorgfaltskonzept. *Recht der Internationalen Wirtschaft (RIW), 68*, 809–820.
Luttermann, L. (2023). Nachhaltigkeitsberichterstattung in den USA, Unternehmensbewertung und Compliance. *Recht der Internationalen Wirtschaft (RIW), 69*, 483–495.
Luttermann, L. (2024). Unternehmensführung: Nachhaltige Finanzinformation (U.S. SEC Climate Rules/EU), Wertschöpfung und Bankenfinanzierung. *Recht der Internationalen Wirtschaft (RIW), 70*, 410–422.
Luttermann, L. (2025). Nachhaltige Wirtschaftsaktivitäten: Eine europäische Eröffnungsbilanz aus Finanzdaten der Bankenregulierung. *Recht der Internationalen Wirtschaft (RIW), 71*, 26–43.
Macey, J., & Sale, H. A. (2003). Observations on the role of commodification independence, and governance in the accounting industry. *Villanova Law Review, 48*, 1167–1187.
Mattessich, R. (1995). *Critique of accounting: Examination of the foundations and normative structure of an applied discipline*. Quorum Books.
Maydew, E. (2005). Discussion of firms' off-balance sheet and hybrid debt financing: Evidence from their book-tax reporting differences. *Journal Accounting Research, 43*, 283–290.
McCrum, D. (2022). *Money men: A hot startup, a billion dollar fraud, a fight for the truth*. Bantam Press.
Merkt, H. (2009). *ISA and their adoption in the EU: Legal aspects and unsettled questions, Essays in honor of Eddy Wymeersch*. Cambridge University Press.
Mohammed, N. F., Fahmi, F. M., & Ahmad, A. E. (2015). The influence of AAOIFI accounting standards in reporting financial institutions in Malaysia. *Procedia Economics and Finance, 31*, 418–424.
Möllers, T. M. J. (2021). The Wirecard accounting scandal in Germany, and how the financial industry failed to spot it. *The International Lawyer, 54*, 325–360.
Monsenego, J. (2022). *Introduction to transfer pricing* (2nd ed.). Kluwer.
Moser, R. (2014). IFRS and convergence in China and the USA. *Journal of Technology Management in China, 9*, 56–66.
Mulford, C. W., & Comiskey, E. E. (2005). *Creative cash flow reporting: Uncovering sustainable financial performance*, 2005.
Mulyany, R., & Ariffin, N. M. (2018). Islamic finance and the convergence towards IFRS: The State of research development. *Journal of Accounting Research Organization and Economics, 1*, 85–97.
Murphy, T., O'Connell, V., & Ó hÓgartaigh, C. (2013). Discourses surrounding the evolution of the IASB/FASB Conceptual Framework: What they reveal about the 'living law' of accounting. *Accounting, Organizations and Society, 38*, 72–79.
Mourik, C. van, & Walton, P. (2018). The European IFRS endorsement process: In search of a single voice. *Accounting in Europe, 15*, 1–32.
Nguyen, X.-T. (2021). Promoting corporate irresponsibility? Delaware as the intellectual property holding state. *The Journal of Corporation Law, 46*, 717–750.
Nobes, C. W. (2006). Revenue recognition and EU endorsement of IFRS. *Accounting in Europe, 3*, 81–89.
Nobes, C. W. (2015). International differences in IFRS adotions and IFRS practices. In S. Jones (Ed.), *The Routledge companion to accounting theory* (chapter 8).
Nobes, C. W., & Parker, R. H. (2020). *Comparative international accounting* (14th. ed.). Pearson.
Nobes, C. W., & Zeff, S. (2016). Have Canada, Japan and Switzerland adopted IFRS? *Australian Accounting Review, 78*, 284–290.

Noked, N., & Marcone, Z. (2022). International response to the U.S. Tax Haven. *Yale Journal of International Law, 48*, 177–222.

Odia, J. O., & Ogiedu, K. O. (2013). IFRS adoption: Issues, challenges and lessons for Nigeria and other adopters. *Mediterranean Journal of Social Sciences, 4*, 389–399.

Pal, S. (2015). *Differences between IND AS and IFRS: Can full convergence ever occur between the two?* CMC Senior Theses, Paper 1089.

Palanský, M., & Schultz, A. (2024). *EU-wide unitary taxation: A path to a fair corporate tax system*, February 15, 2024. https://ssrn.com/abstract=4811958 (accessed: 22.08.2025).

Palea, V. (2018). Financial reporting for sustainable development: Critical insights into IFRS implementation in the European Union. *Accounting Forum, 42*, 248–260.

Parker, R. H., & Nobes, C. W. (1994). *An international view of true and fair accounting*. Routledge.

Paulson, H. M. Jr. (2013). *On the Brink: Inside the race to stop the collapse of the global financial system* (updated ed.). Grand Central Publishing.

Pelger, C. (2020). The return of stewardship, reliability and prudence: A commentary on the IASB's New Conceptual Framework. *Accounting in Europe, 17*, 33–51.

Pereira, A., & do Céu Gaspar Alves, M. (2017). Earnings management and European regulation 1606/2002: Evidence from non-financial Portuguese companies listed in Euronext. *Revista de Contabilidad, 20*, 107–117.

Petersen, A. (1963). The philosophy of Niels Bohr. *Bulletin of the Atomic Scientists, 19*, 8–14.

Powers, W. C., Troubh, R. S., & Winokur, H. S. (2002). *Report of investigation by the special investigative committee of the board of directors of Enron Corp.* 2002 WL 198018.

Quagli, A., & Paoloni, P. (2012). How is the IFRS for SME accepted in the European context? An analysis of the homogeneity among European countries, users and preparers in the European commission questionnaire. *Advances in Accounting, 28*, 147–156.

Raffournier, B. (2014). The application of IFRS across different institutional environments. In: C. van Mourik & P. Walton (Eds.), *The Routledge companion to accounting, reporting and regulation* (pp. 281–298).

Ram, R., & Newberry, S. (2013). IFRS for SMEs: The IASB due process. *Australian Accounting Review, 23*, 3–17.

Rappaport, A. (1998). *Creating shareholder value: A guide for managers and investors* (2nd ed.; 1st ed. 1986). Free Press.

Reuther, F., & Fink, C. (2010). Besonderheiten der Bilanzierung in Familienunternehmen. *Betriebs-Berater (BB), 65*, 363–367.

Rey, A., Maglio, R., & Rapone, V. (2020). Lobbying during IASB and FASB convergence due process: Evidence from the IFRS 16 project on leases. *Journal of International Accounting, Auditing and Taxation, C, 41*. https://doi.org/10.1016/j.intaccaudtax.2020.100348

Rickett, C. E. F., & Grantham, R. B. (Eds.). (1998). *Corporate personality in the 20th century*. Hart Publishing.

Rieckers, O. (2004). *Konzernvertrauen und Konzernrecht*. CH Beck Verlag.

Russ, W., Janßen, C., & Götze, T. (Eds.). (2015). *BilRUG: Auswirkungen auf das deutsche Bilanzrecht*. IDW Verlag.

Sanada, M. (2012). *Legitimacy of global accounting standards: A new analytical framework*. http://papers.ssrn.com/sol3/papers.cfm?abstract_id=1990796 (accessed: 22.08.2025).

Sanko, H., & Koldovskyi, A. (2017). Comparative analysis of IFRS and US GAAP. *Financial Markets, Institutions and Risks, 1*(1), 14–22. https://doi.org/10.21272/fmir.1(1).14-21.2017 (accessed: 22.08.2025).

Savigny, F. C. von (1840). *System des heutigen römischen Rechts* (Vol. II). Veit.

Schildbach, T. (2010). Fair Value: Leitstern für Wege ins Abseits. *Deutsches Steuerrecht (DStR), 48*, 69–75.

Schön, W. (Ed.). (2009). *Rechnungslegung und Wettbewerbsschutz im deutschen und europäischen Recht*. Springer.

Seligman, J. (2002). No one can serve two masters: Corporate and securities law after Enron. *Washington University Law Quarterly, 80*, 449–517.

Shkulipa, L. (2021). Grouping of major changes in conceptual framework of financial reporting and analysis of new challenges. *Studia Universitatis Economics Series, 31*(2). https://doi.org/10.2478/sues-2021-0007 (accessed: 22.08.2025).

Siegel, S. (2007). Accounting for non-listed companies under United States laws, regulations, andaccounting and auditing standards. In W. F. Ebke, C. Luttermann, & S. Siegel (Eds.), *Internationale Rechnungslegungsstandards für börsenunabhängige Unternehmen?* (pp. 95–111). Nomos Verlag.

Song, X., & Trimble, M. (2022). The historical and current status of global IFRS adoption: Obstacles and opportunities for researchers. *The International Journal of Accounting, 57*, 1–37.

Spengler, O. (1990). *Der Untergang des Abendlandes: Umrisse einer Morphologie der Weltgeschichte*. CH Beck Verlag (reprint of the 33-47 ed 1918).

Stark, C. (2007). *Gesellschaftsrechtliche Publizität und Schutz personenbezogener Daten*. Nomos Verlag.

Staubus, G. J. (1999). *The decision-usefulness theory of accounting: A limited history*. Garland Publishing.

Stiglitz, J. E. (2010). *Freefall: America, free markets, and the sinking of the world economy*. W. W. Norton & Company.

Sunder, S. (2011). IFRS monopoly: The pied piper of financial reporting. *Accounting and Business Research, 41*, 291–306.

Teigland, R., Siri, S., Larsson, A., Puertas, A. M., & Ingram Bogusz, C. (Eds.). (2020). *The rise and development of FinTech: Accounts of disruption from Sweden and beyond*. Routledge.

Tooze, A. (2018). *Crashed: How a decade of financial crises changed the world*. Penguin Books.

Triki-Damak, S., & Halioui, K. (2013). Accounting treatment of R&D expenditures and earnings management: An empirical study on French listed companies. *Global Business Economic Research Journal, 2*, 50–71.

Tsunogaya, N. (2016). Issues affecting decisions on mandatory adoption of International Financial Reporting Standards (IFRS) in Japan. *Accounting, Auditing & Accountability Journal, 29*, 828–860.

Vagts, D. F. (2009). The financial meltdown and its international implications. *American Journal of International Law, 103*, 684–690.

Vukovic, D. B., Maiti, M., & Grigorieva, E. M. (Eds.). (2022). *Digitalization and the future of financial services: Innovation and impact of digital finance*. Springer Nature.

Walker, N. (2020). *The European Public Good and European Public Goods*. University of Edinburgh, Research Paper Series No 2020/20.

Wang, B. (2018). After the European Commission ordered Apple to pay back taxes to Ireland: Ireland's future in the new global tax environment. *Indiana Journal of Global Legal Studies, 25*, 539–564.

Wang, J., & Wang, D. (2022). Corporate fraud and accounting firm involvement: Evidence from China. *Journal of Risk and Financial Management, 15*(4), 1–16.

Wang, R. 'Ray'. (2015). *Disrupting digital business: Create an authentic experience in the peer-to-peer economy*. Harvard Business Review Press.

Wang, X. (2019). Compliance over time by Australian firms with IFRS disclosure requirements. *Australian Accounting Review, 29*, 679–691.

Wang, Y., & Campbell, M. (2012). Earnings management comparison: IFRS vs. China GAAP. *International Management Review, 6*, 5–11.

Weiner, J. M. (2005). *Formulary apportionment and group taxation in the European Union: Insights from the United States and Canada.* Working Paper, EU-Commission, March 2005 (Doc. TAXUD/2005/2601—EN).

Weitzman, H. (2022). *What's the matter with Delaware? How the first State has favored the rich, powerful, and criminal – and how it costs us all.* Princeton University Press.

Wingard, C., Bosman, J., & Amisi, B. (2016). The legitimacy of IFRS: An assessment of the influences on the due process of standards setting. *Meditari Accountancy Research, 24*, 134–156.

Wolz, M., Kümpel, K., & Oldewurte, C. (2012). Der Fair Value in den IFRS: Das Problem einer systeminhärenten Sackgasse. *Praxis der internationalen Rechnungslegung (PiR), 8*, 103–109.

Wüstemann, J., & Kierzek, S. (2006). True and fair view revisited: A reply to Alexander and Nobes. *Accounting in Europe, 3*, 91–116.

Xie, L., Zhang, M., & Zhai, S. (2022). IFRS convergence and international trade: Evidence from China. *Accounting and Business Research, 52*, 838–864.

Young, M. R. (Ed.). (2006). *Accounting irregularities and financial fraud: A corporate governance guide* (3rd ed.). CCH Inc.

Zalta, E. N. (Ed.). (2018). *The Stanford Encyclopedia of Philosophy*. https://plato.stanford.edu/archives/sum2018/entries/federalism/ (accessed: 22.08.2025).

Zhang, Q., Chen, S., & Jin, Y. (2020). The impact of off-balance-sheet regulations on bank risk-taking: Evidence from China. *Research in International Business and Finance, 54*, 101297.

Zhang, W., & Ye, J. (2020). China's convergence with IFRS: analysis of dual-listed companies. *Abacus, 56*, 104–139.

Zweig, S. (1934). *Triumph und Tragik des Erasmus von Rotterdam*. Fischer Verlag, 1992.

# Chapter 5
# Company Valuation as a Legal Act of Sustainable Value Creation

> "Eine Waage, die nicht zittert, kann nicht wägen."*
>
> *Erwin Chargaff*

## Contents



---

*Chargaff, *Das Feuer des Heraklit: Skizzen aus einem Leben vor der Natur* (Heraclitean fire), 1979, p. 241, translated: A scale that does not tremble cannot weigh. See on this also below 7.9.



C. Luttermann, *Human Corporation for Sustainable Development*,
https://doi.org/10.1007/978-3-032-07615-1_5

## 5.1 Creating Value Sustainably

If you want to deceive people, the main thing is to make plausible the absurd, writes Johann Wolfgang von Goethe:[1] Was the highly gifted poet, naturalist and jurist also thinking of economic processes? – His words sound timeless like a wake-up call against the abuses in capital markets and for the human corporation. A return to substance and personal responsibility, to the unity of liberty (*Freiheit*, private autonomy) and responsibility (*Verantwortung*, liability) particularly in corporate governance of the "modern corporation" is a global need.[2] Both must be established in a carefully balanced way for sustainable value creation (*Wertschöpfung*) through humanity – all the more so in our time of climate change in need of environmental and human rights protection, holistically (e.g. climate risk as a financial risk).[3]

We have already shown for financial reporting and auditing (corporation finance, *Unternehmensfinanzierung*) that an evidence-based valuation of assets (company valuation, *Unternehmensbewertung*) is the material basis for responsibly governing and financing a corporation: a legal act of sustainable value creation and a proof of good corporate governance (*gute Unternehmensführung*).[4] In the following, we will continue with this general substantive-evidential concept of valuation (*Bewertung*) for a sustainable *Vermögensordnung* (order of assets).[5] The guidelines show legal core aspects for a disciplined, proper valuation of companies (shares, bonds, hybrids) – for the "modern corporation" as a human corporation. This is necessary on many occasions (see 5.3.2) and in general to establish a sustainable order globally.

The International Court of Justice speaks of climate change as "a common concern of humankind".[6] Economy, corporation and valuation have a fundamental

---

[1]Goethe (1833) recital 318. German original: *"Wer die Menschen betrügen will, muß vor allen Dingen das Absurde plausibel machen"*. Cf. Rathenau above 3.5.4 (quote, at the very end) with Berle and Means in 3.5.5. Overall see chapter 6.

[2]See, e.g., above 2.4.2, in more detail chapter 3 as well as chapters 6 and 7.

[3]See, e.g., above 2.6.3 (No. (3)), and overall, esp. below 5.2.4 and chapters 1 and 2.

[4]See chapter 4 and chapter 1.

[5]Fundamentally Luttermann (2015a), Luttermann in du Plessis, Großfeld, Luttermann et al., chapter 8, and in German: Luttermann (2000), (2003), (2023a) and (2023b) with further references. See also Luttermann (1999b) and (2019).

[6]ICJ, Advisory Opinion, 23.07.2025 (https://www.icj-cij.org/sites/default/files/case-related/187/187-20250723-adv-01-00-en.pdf, accessed: 27.08.2025), para. 364; see chapters 1, 2 and 6 (esp. 6.1).

impact, literally in all walks of life: potentially for a better world. A comprehensive concept is required on an international scale, as in practice vague valuation patterns (plausibilities) prevail arbitrarily. Immoderation is widespread (haphazard prognoses, hope values etc.), worlds of make-believe are produced. And this is true although the capital markets are dealing with “other people’s money”.[7] The numbers game, playing with mathematical formulas and models, seem like “accounting hocus-pocus”, reaching out from Wall Street (resp. City of London) and the market-listed corporations around the globe and thus shaping the valuation of companies with its number mysticism (manipulation).[8]

However, valuation issues (appraisal of assets and companies, *die Bewertung von Vermögensgegenständen und Unternehmen*) are legal issues (*Rechtsangelegenheiten*),[9] precisely because other interests, id est other people’s money is involved (see 3.3.3). The valuation of companies and shares (assets, *Eigen- und Fremkapital*, i.e. equity, debt and hybrid financial instruments) is a legal domain. The objective is the protection of people and assets (interests) involved, a kind of valuation that is adequate for each individual case and the interests involved precisely because it is generally established as a rule of law (*Rechtsgebiet*) with sound principles and judicial protection (*Rechtsschutz*).

To this purpose, we will sustainably develop the basic idea of the order of assets (*Vermögensordnung*, see 5.2) in the context of corporate finance and governance (5.3); an example is the in theory and practice prominent cash compensation of minority shareholders (5.4). This is then followed, conceived as protection against fantasy valuations (i.e. unreasonable wealth transfer, see 5.2), by binding legal standards for a proper valuation (5.5) with core aspects for legal practice and protection (5.6) as well as comments on legal comparison globally (5.7).

## 5.2 Sustainable Valuation of Companies as a Legal Domain

### *5.2.1* Vermögensordnung*: The Order of Assets*[10]

In the constitution of liberty, our economic and legal order is an order of assets (*Vermögensordnung*): Specific assets are each attributed to a legal subject (natural person or juridical person, e.g. a corporation) and are dealt with in business, id est contractually as stipulated in mutual attraction. The function of a free market

[7] Louis D. Brandeis, see above 3.3 and 4.4.1.

[8] See above 4.6, and chapter 6; cf. basically the leitmotif of chapter 1. Practically Levitt (1998) and Jones (2011).

[9] Großfeld, Egger, Tönnes (2020), Fleischer and Hüttemann (2024). Cf. Matschke, Brösel, Toll (2024, Business Valuation: 2021), Brealey and Myers (2003), Koller, Goedhart, Wessels (2020).

[10] Basics Luttermann (2015a), (2023a), (2023b) and (2012a). On the denotation of “asset” (*Vermögen*) see below 8.1 (footnote 3).

economy is that people bind themselves contractually (i.e. *vertraglich*) – quite in their own interests (self-love), both intending "only his own gain" (Adam Smith).[11] Peace and prosperity are built on this. For the material basis, this fundamentally includes numerous issues of valuation in legal relations (see 5.3.2). We can see this for corporations regarding their financing. This is founded on forms of financing classically ordered by the law: under corporate law, assets (equity, i.e. shares or stocks – *Gesellschaftsrecht*) and creditor positions under the law of obligations (debt, i.e. loans, bonds, hybrids – *Schuldrecht*).[12]

This is shown in the accounts (financial reporting) of the corporation (see for the presentation of the balance sheet: § 266 HGB; cf. Art. 10 Accounting Law Directive 2013/34/EU[13]). On the liabilities side of the balance sheet (*Passivseite*), they tell us who invested capital on what legal basis. Conceptually, capital of the shareholders (owner's equity, *Eigenkapital*) and capital of the creditors (debt capital, *Fremdkapital*) constitute the capital structure of the corporation, its financing. The passivised capital (financial means) turns into activated capital through investments (asset side of the balance sheet, *Aktivseite*). The law says: For liabilities of a corporation, "it is only the corporation assets that are liable to the creditors" (§ 1(2) AktG, § 13(2) GmbHG). This means there are different spheres of assets, namely the sphere of the shareholders (natural persons, juridical persons) and that of the corporation – as the capital recipient – itself as a separate legal entity (juridical person – *juristische Person*). The assets spheres (*Vermögenssphären*) thus also denote the order of liability (*Haftungsordnung*, cf. 3.6 on "liable capital").

Overall, the material nucleus of any order of assets (*Vermögensordnung*) is the following: *What* is valued as "assets" (cf. §§ 246–251 HGB) *in what way* (cf. §§ 252–256a HGB) is determined by the law, id est specifically valuation law (*Bewertungsrecht*, accounting law). This is to prevent the assets situation – here: of the corporation – being represented as *too* good (i.e. too valuable) or *too* bad (i.e. too worthless); at the same time, it prevents illegitimate transfer of assets (valuables, i.e. shifting of wealth) between, e.g., majority and minority shareholders or between shareholders and bondholders.[14] This is, in the last instance, also proved by insolvency law: The assets attributed to the failed corporation (debtor) are included in the insolvency estate (*Insolvenzmasse*; see in Germany § 35 *Insolvenzordnung* – InsO), in order to be able to satisfy the asset demands of the creditors as far as possible.[15]

---

[11] Smith (1776/1789[5]) p. 572.

[12] Overall, also on perspectives of development, chapter 3.

[13] Alternatively determining two layouts set out in annexes III and IV.

[14] See 5.2.3 and 5.4; also above 1.4.1, 2.3.2 and 3.5 as well as below 6.2, 6.5.3 and 6.6.4 (transfer of wealth). In Germany, e.g., BGH, 02.12.2021 (IX ZR 110/20) NZG 2022, 458, <openJur 2022, 2596> (objective disadvantage of creditors, here: profit participation right – *Genußrecht*); see also following footnote.

[15] Ibid., recital 13 (on § 129(1) InsO); also BGH, 22.07.2021 (IX ZR 26/20) WM 2021, 1646, <openJur 2021, 34119> recital 14; BGH, 07.04.2022 (IX ZR 107/20) NJW-RR 2022, 844, <openJur 2022, 9476>.

### 5.2.2 Valuation Law: Juridical Analysis of the Economy

In the valuation of corporations (rsp. shares, assets and liabilities), legal experts and economists, of course, meet, id est, it is a field of tension between law and economics. Fundamentally, the aim is legal certainty (*Rechtssicherheit*), id est the solution and, at best, the avoidance of conflicts (peace under law, *Rechtsfrieden*).[16] Reasonably in general and for a *Vermögensordnung* (order of assets), the ethical penetration of the economic domain, the law is primary (see Fig. 5.3). This is disregarded by simple ideas of an "economic analysis of the law" – falsely on a world-wide scale promoted and adopted as a "legal theory", while actually eliminating the law.[17] Let us take a look at relevant life circumstances (*Lebensverhältnisse*): People act in a market-based way through supply and demand. They negotiate the valuation of the contractual object consensual (*einvernehmlich*) at the agreed price.

It is responsible decisions made by people, not the planning dirigism of central organs that constitute free communities (*freie Gemeinwesen*). Private autonomy, id est freedom of contract (*Vertragsfreiheit*), and "competition as a discovery procedure" (Friedrich August von *Hayek*), id est fair competition of performance, prevent market-radical practices. They build on a canon of values (legal principles); without the coordinating function of the market mechanism, the so-called "invisible hand" (orig. of Jupiter, the ancient Roman deity) reaches into the void. That is why *Adam Smith*, the moral philosopher erroneously seen as a mere market liberal,[18] regarded humanistic core virtues such as decency, measure, sense of community and sense of duty as forming a common basis of action (common sense).[19] A market economy needs this basis: an ordering frame as a so-called free space (*"einen freien Raum"*, Friedrich Carl von Savigny),[20] providing man and his – economic and other – activities with freedom and security for individual development.

This also includes the valuation of companies (shares) as a core element of market economy; it is remarkable in particular that, in climate change, the transformation of the economy is being shaped in the direction of sustainable business on an epoch-

---

[16] On reasonable certainty see below 7.6.3.

[17] See below 7.3.2 and 7.4.1, 8.2.2. Luttermann (1998), esp. pp. 465-485 and Luttermann (2010a), Mestmäcker (2007).

[18] See for an efficient market economy, instead of the epigones, on Milton Friedman, who reinforced the primacy of the law, below 7.3.3 and above 2.6.1.

[19] Adam Smith (1790, 1st ed. 1759) on the "theory of moral sentiments"; this is what his second, better-known work, the "Wealth of Nations" (1776), is based on. Cf. above 4.12.3, below 5.3.4 with Korsgaard (2008). Smith (1723–1790) was unfortunately not able to "endeavour" and "to execute this great work to my own satisfaction" – a long-planned book (third main work) on the theory of jurisprudence: "an account of the general principles of law and government", Smith (1759/1790[6]) advertisement and p. 403; but see transcripts of his lectures on jurisprudence, Smith (1762/1982). Brealey and Myers (2003) p. 3: "Finance is about money and markets, but it is also about people."

[20] See above 2.2.2; cf. also below 7.3.

making scale (see 5.2.4). Here as everywhere, freedom may be used in a regular way or be abused. We have been witnessing this with massive dislocations in the world debt crisis since 2008. With their insubstantial financial instruments and chain securitisations (CDSs, CDOs, so-called "toxic assets"), careless actors show:[21] Where players lack ethos and no referee blows the whistle, there is chaos (see 6.6). In spite of all interdisciplinarity, experience teaches us: It is not the actors (market players) or "what is common in commerce" that determine the legal principles and rules, but what is legally required must be the measure for reasonable solutions.

### *5.2.3 European Law and International Law Perspectives*

The international conditions need to be established in this way as well. The European Union sets the respective signs. It is in accounting law (*Bilanzrecht*), the core of valuation law for corporations and their shares (assets),[22] that the European legislator has anchored the ethical dimension. For in the Accounting Law Directive 2013/34/EU – as has been the case long since – the objective of "improving Union-wide comparability and public confidence in financial statements and reports"[23] is underlined. Authoritatively, the legislator confirms the ethical precept to "give a true and fair view" (*Bilanzwahrheit*, the imperative of truth) as the general norm (i.e. the measure) of the overall accounts (valuation, appraisal of companies).[24] The European Court of Justice emphasises this as the "primary objective" (i.e., the *ratio legis*), while regarding the principle of making valuations on a prudent basis as "of particular importance".[25]

The legal, ethical foundation and pervasion of the valuation of corporations (shares, assets and liabilities) can take effect internationally. This goes back to Adam Smith, who saw ethics and legal science as the moral basis of economics.[26] In view of the present circumstances in a conciliatory way in an Anglo-American and Continental dimension, at the same time also as a bridge in particular to Asia, where, e.g., Confucianism is rooted, influencing economic structures and procedures – possibly even more so in the near future, especially in China and far beyond. The

[21] On this U.S. Senate, Subcommittee on Investigations: Wall Street and the Financial Crisis: Anatomy of a Collapse (13.4.2011). Luttermann (2008b). On financial engineering (CDO) see below 6.6.4 (with Fig. 6.2).

[22] See below 5.5, above 4.4 to 4.6 and 4.10.2.

[23] Recital 55, Directive 2013/34/EU on the annual financial statements, consolidated financial statements and related reports of certain types of undertakings, OJ L 182, 29.06.2013, 19-76.

[24] See Art. 4(3) Accounting Law Directive 2013/34/EU, and in detail above 4.4.4 and 4.9.2.

[25] ECJ, 03.10.2013 (C-322/12 – *Gimle SA*, FR) ECLI:EU:C:2013:632, recitals 30, 32 on Article 31(1)(c) Directive 78/660/EEC. See on this also ECJ, 23.04.2020 (C-640/18 – *Wagram Invest SA*, FR) ECLI:EU:C:2020:293, and below 5.5.4.

[26] Smith, Adam (1790). See also chapters 8 (esp. 8.1) and 9.

traditional Confucian system is built on justice, on progress through economic development, aiming at the practical harmony of economy and ethics:[27] Virtuousness – espcially in the so-called "elites" – not as an end in itself, but rather as the epitome of a general prosperity that is accompanied by justice, thereby permanently establishing a peaceful community (see chapters 1, 8 and 9).

In general, translated into our time, these are very relevant perspectives; not least for a transnational order of groups of companies (*Konzerne*) and insolvency order, for international investment protection. On the contrary, the common ethical perspective is valid globally, as it has by now become clear that with climate change, it is all about the protection of the foundations of human life (see 5.2.4). In short: overall for a globally negotiated multijurisdictional system of an order of assets (*Vermögensordnung*).[28] This affects virtually all areas of life, economy and society and, with that, all legal domains (such as contract law, corporation law, *Gesellschafts- und Konzernrecht*, capital market law, insolvency law, but also tax law, commercial criminal law). Hitherto they have widely been treated and practiced separately, nationally as well as internationally. Accounting and valuation law, however, can form the common substance and structure, providing the general humus for a holistically conceived order.

Valuations mark legal key areas: For the best of entrepreneurs, markets and societies, they should not be left to immoderation (arbitrariness). This is evidenced by political Keynesianism, degenerated for decades (debt economy, *Schuldenwirtschaft*)[29] and the – ongoing – world debt crisis with careless actors in the global financial industry. And to be crystal-clear: this is no matter of what nationality the actors are, but of what mindset they are. Again and again, massive revaluations are undertaken, in particular with financial instruments and unilateral profit distributions (*Gewinnausschüttungen*),[30] id est transfer of wealth: Is that fair ("fair value")?[31] – What is required is a valuation law (*Bewertungsrecht*) that establishes adequate valuation of a corporation procedurally with financing and accounting (financial reporting) sustainably over the lifetime of a corporation.

### 5.2.4 Sustainability: The Corporate Paradigm Revisited

The modern corporation as a human corporation is sustainably designed in its financing function and valuation legally through financial reporting and auditing

[27] Impressively Huan-Chang (1911).

[28] See above 4.8, also chapters 8 and 9.

[29] Cf. Luttermann (2011a) p. 217 (*"Barbarische Politik"*). See also 5.7 and 6.7.

[30] See, e.g., BGH, 02.12.2021 (IX ZR 110/20) NZG 2022, 458, <openJur 2022, 2596> (objective disadvantage of creditors, here: profit participation right – *Genußrecht*). Basically on this Luttermann (1998).

[31] See above 5.2.1, below 6.6 and 7.5 to 7.7. Overall Luttermann (2009).

(law of valuation – German *Bewertungsrecht*).[32] Sustainability (*Nachhaltigkeit*) is "the quality of being sustainable", derived from the verb *to sustain* (Old French *so (u)stenir*, from Latin *sustinere*), which means "support as valid, correct, just", id est: "be adequate as a ground or basis for; substantiate, corroborate".[33] This points to the content (i.e., facts, instead of so-called "soft information") which has to be argued and proven concretely in any valuation (cf. 8.3), "sustainable" thus also comprising "able to be upheld or defended".[34] In a natural sense – especially in agriculture –, sustainable yield (*nachhaltiger Ertrag*) is only achieved if the soil is kept in good shape (so-called "ecological sustainability").[35] We can therefore generally state that sustainability is regarded as imperative to maintain and support life or an institution, to bear and to keep going for a long period.[36]

This denotes "sustainability" (*Nachhaltigkeit*) in its "dual" character as the paradigm of the human corporation. In general, for the corporation, its investors and the environment, it is thus about concrete substance – instead of shortsighted speculation, vague hopes and numbers games: indeed legally in any economic, financial process to be recorded in valuation law (due diligence). Facts are required. It is this what the civil-procedural, evidence-based concept of valuation presented here stands for by law – both practically and theoretically as valuation law (*Bewertungsrecht*, see Fig. 5.3). Sustainability thus basically means verifiability (*Nachprüfbarkeit*, so-called "legal sustainability", see 4.11.4). This concurs with sustainability as an idea, an action motive and a goal in the relation of humans and the environment, in particular for the protection of natural resources, as it now appears in regulations: as a sustainable economic activity (on the EU Green Deal see 1.4.2, cf. 6.7.2). This is also a question of valuation, which in turn is shaped and needs to be determined by valuation law (on reasonable certainty: 7.6.3).

In this respect, sustainability is associated with a paradigm shift. This appears to be another, more modern meaning of the term "sustainability" (*Nachhaltigkeit*). Holistically, due to the paradigm shift, the economy is to be transformed "green" through "sustainable economic activity" (*nachhaltige Wirtschaftstätigkeit*) in a "socio-ecological" way (see 2.2). This concerns the parameters and the duty of care of those responsible. Thus, in valuation, it is in particular human rights protection (human rights due diligence) and environmental protection (environmental due diligence) that come to the fore as the value basis. In this, relevant valuation rules hold, fundamentally the regulation (EU) 2020/852 on the establishment of a

---

[32] See chapter 4 with above 2.5 and, e.g., 3.2.2.

[33] Altogether: Brown (1993) p. 3163 (sustain).

[34] Ibid.

[35] Grimm (1889) column 69 (*Nachhaltig*), in German: *"Nachhaltiger Ertrag wird nur erzielt, wenn der Boden in gutem Stand erhalten wird"*.

[36] Cf. Middle English: Brown (1993) p. 3163 (sustain).

framework to facilitate sustainable investment (cf. taxonomy on sustainability);[37] this concerns the global dimension.[38] It is meant to direct capital flows into sustainable business activity. A tremendous instrument, in practice the separation of "good" (*Gut*) and "evil" (*Böse*),[39] which harbours the dangers of centralism: Who takes control?

In any case, sustainability and the human corporation must be understood in its very character. Sustainability is intrinsic to the corporation: in the sense of a permanent form for business (*Unternehmensträger*) that must be financed and governed sustainably (see 2.4.3). In this practice, financial reporting and auditing serve as proof in dealing with other people's money, id est sustainability as a synonym for verifiability (see 4.11.4). The corporation is not intended as an object of short-term speculation, but as a stable financial instrument of entrepreneurial capabilities, id est sustainable economic activity. The "dual" character can therefore manifest itself as one. What remains essential are facts and the relation to facts, which, scientifically driven, carry the valuation. Truth becomes clear in its elementary overall significance, as shown: What is required is sustainable valuation as a legal act for verified information,[40] id est sustainable value creation (*nachhaltige Wertschöpfung*).

## 5.3 Human Corporate Governance and Valuation Law

### *5.3.1 Financing and Valuation of Corporations*

Valuation is thus obviously a legal act. It is linked to the financing of the corporation in an elementary way.[41] It accompanies the directors of the corporation (management board *Vorstände*, supervisory board *Aufsichtsräte*) as a key task of corporate governance through all its phases of existence: from the foundation (capital raising *Prinizip der Kapitalaufbringung*, e.g., §§ 26, 27, 33, 46 AktG) over the development of the enterprise (capital maintenance *Prinzip der Kapitalerhaltung*, e.g., §§ 57, 71-71e AktG) with transactions (Mergers & Acquisitions) and restructuring to redevelopment as well as the liquidation of the corporation (§§ 271-274 AktG). The

[37] OJ L 156, 09.06.2022, pp. 159–159; on this Luttermann (2021). See above 4.2 and 4.11. Cf. United Nations, Sustainable Development Goals (SDGs): https://sdgs.un.org/goals (accessed: 27.08.2025).

[38] Cf. overall ICJ, Advisory Opinion, 23.07.2025 (https://www.icj-cij.org/sites/default/files/case-related/187/187-20250723-adv-01-00-en.pdf, accessed: 27.08.2025), on that, e.g., above 1.2, below 6.1. See also 6.8.5 with regard to AI and investment (corporate finance, valuation).

[39] Overall chapters 1 and 2. Cf. basically on resonableness chapter 9 (esp. 9.9).

[40] See above 4.12.3 on communication (information as creation of value) with Fig. 4.8, and below 5.3.4 on the source of value (humanity).

[41] Luttermann (2000). See above, esp. chapters 1 to 3. On personal responsibility and practice of valuation see chapter 7.

proper valuation of assets belongs here; this commonly involves legal norms. This is all the more true as the mandate of sustainability relates to the corporation as a whole with its financing (see 5.2.4). The accompanying valuation acts, the determination of "sustainable economic activity" (Art. 4 of Regulation (EU) 852/2020), are original legal acts.[42] They are a significant element of good corporate governance (duty of care).[43]

But how does valuation take place? More precisely in legal terms: How *should* valuation be carried out? – This question is the inevitable companion of any chief executive and chairman any time in the business and transactions of the corporation. For it is – according to the German law – his duty to file for insolvency without culpable procrastination in case of insolvency (§ 15a(1)(1) InsO). This includes over-indebtedness, that is, when the property of the corporation no longer covers its liabilities (application deadline: no later than six weeks after the occurrence of over-indebtedness, §§ 15a(1)(2), 19 InsO), as well as the – prospective – inability to pay (application deadline: no later than three weeks after the occurrence of illiquidity (default), § 15a(1)(2) and §§ 17, 18 InsO).[44] The threat is personal liability (§§ 64 GmbHG, §§ 92, 93 AktG) and punishment according to criminal law (§ 15a (4) and (5) InsO). Valuations are also significant for the question of the liability of the directors and chief executives (*Geschäftsführer*) on the grounds of an existence-destroying intervention into the property of the corporation (so-called *Existenzvernichtungshaftung* – existence destruction liability, see § 826 BGB)[45] and under criminal sanction (*Vermögensbetreuungspflicht* – asset care obligation, see § 266 StGB);[46] likewise in corporate group relationships (*Konzernverhältnissen*, e.g., so-called cash pooling).[47]

With regard to existence-destroying intervention, the German Federal Supreme Court[48] has set down the following example: This is (only) the case if the assets (*Vermögensgegenstände*) are transferred under value. – The overall issue thus concerns questions of valuation (values), sustainable financing (liquidity) and the

---

[42] Overall on Regulation (EU) 852/2020 see Luttermann (2021).

[43] Basically Luttermann, L. (2022) and (2024) with an innovative concept of due diligence for corporate directors (Sustainable Business Finance Navigator).

[44] See already above 3.4.1.

[45] *Bundesgerichtshof* (BGH) 20.07.2009 (II ZR 273/07) BGHZ 182, 103, <openJur 2011, 2899>; Luttermann (2008a). BGH, 16.07.2007 (II ZR 3/04 – *Trihotel*) BGHZ 173, 246, <openJur 2011, 7477>; BGH, 24.07.2012 (II ZR 177/11) NJW 2012, 3231, <openJur 2012, 71996>.

[46] See, e.g., BGH, 26.11.2015 (3 StR 17/15) BGHSt 61, 48, <openJur 2016, 6879>, BGH 17.12.2020 (3 StR 403/19) < https://www.hrr-strafrecht.de/hrr/3/19/3-403-19.php>; cf. BGH, 19.05.2021 (1 StR 496/20) NJW 2022, 341, < https://datenbank.nwb.de/Dokument/870103/> (both accessed: 27.08.2025). See on the case of the Wirecard AG in 4.9.4 and 4.9.5. Generally Luttermann (2012b).

[47] See above 4.7.3 and Luttermann and Geißler (2012). Cf. BGH, 28.06.2020 (II ZR 112/21) <openJur 2022, 14696>.

[48] BGH, 23.04.2012 (II ZR 252/10) BGHZ 193, 96 (Leitsatz; <openJur 2012, 68535>. Cf., e.g., BGH, 06.11.2018 (II ZR 199/17) <openJur 2019, 98>.

assets of the corporation (order of assets, *Vermögensordnung*).[49] Legally, this also applies to the directors of the supervisory board (*Aufsichtsräte*) and the auditors of the corporation, the representatives of the responsible authorities of the regulators (e.g., the *Bundesanstalt für Finanzdienstleistungsaufsicht*, BaFin) as well as the – current or potential – investors, employees and business partners of the corporation; practically also the work of analysts and other interested parties. This underscores sustainability, which is designed holistically: It demands reasonable valuation on the basis of facts and science (see 5.2.4). Let us take a look at relevant life conditions and legal norms.

### *5.3.2 Valuation: Occasions and Legal Foundations*

Occasions for the valuation of corporations and/or – some of – its assets (appraisal of business) are manifold; for the foundation of a corporation in particular as non-cash contributions (*Sacheinlagen*, §§ 5(4), 9 *GmbHG*, §§ 27, 36a AktG). Later, valuation has to take place when capital is increased (*Kapitalerhöhungen*, § 56 GmbHG and § 183 AktG): The payment to be made is not to be "inadequately low" (§ 255(2)(1) AktG). Valuations occur in case of compensation for damages (*Schadensersatz*, e.g., in the case of interventions in commercial operations, §§ 823, 249 BGB); also for cash compensation of retiring partners (§ 728 BGB). They may also be occasioned contractually (mergers & acquisitions), besides, e.g., deficit-conditioned diminution of the buying price (§ 459 BGB), in the whole domain of business transactions. Now in general, aspects of sustainability need to be taken into special consideration: In the economy of transformation, reappraisal advances to the new normal practically worldwide. We will take a look at classical examples by reference to the German law.

Valuation has to be legally formed in the case of mergers (*Verschmelzungen*, §§ 9, 12 UmwG). Practically, we see this with cash compensation of departing shareholders such as in the case of form-changing conversion (*formwechselnde Umwandlung*, § 207 UmwG), and merger by absorption (*Aufnahme*, §§ 29, 30 UmwG) or formation of a new company (*Neugründung*, § 36 UmwG). In the case of a takeover the bidder is obliged to offer the shareholders of the target company a "fair equivalent" (§ 31(1) WpÜG) or they have to pay "adequate" – id est always reasonable (*angemessene*) – compensation in the case of exclusion (§ 39a WpÜG). Respective protection for minority shareholders through compensation (*Wertersatz*) may be taken into consideration at the stock market in the case of delisting of a corporation. The legislator has determined an obligatory public purchase offer, after

[49] Luttermann (2015a) and (2012a). Globally Luttermann (2015b).

the Federal Supreme Court[50] had ruled adversely, while emphasising the comprehensive order for protection (see now: § 39(3) BörsG, § 31 WpÜG and §§ 3-7 WpÜG-Angebotsverordnung).[51] The cash compensations for minority shareholders in affiliation agreements (*Unternehmensverträgen*, §§ 291, 292 AktG) are specifically regulated.[52]

A valuation of companies (shares) may be conditioned by family law, e.g. in the case of gain adjustment between spouses (§ 1373 BGB), where initial assets (*Anfangsvermögen*, § 1374 BGB) and final assets (*Endvermögen*, § 1375 BGB) have to be determined with regard to their value (§ 1376 BGB). Inheritance law requires determination of value for the renouncement of inheritance (§ 1943 BGB), the dissolution of the community of heirs (*Erbengemeinschaft*, §§ 2032, 2042 BGB) and the legal portion (*Pflichtteil*, §§ 2303, 2311 BGB). Tax law requires valuations also regarding the share value (*Anteilswerte*) of the working assets of the company (*Betriebsvermögen*, § 6 EStG) as well as inheritance and gift tax (§ 12 ErbStG); this is regulated by valuation law (*Bewertungsgesetz*, BewG).[53] Valuation issues also accompany foreign direct investments in the case of transnational settlement claim (e.g., compensation).[54] On the whole, a world apparently to be regauged.[55]

### 5.3.3 *Valuation Law for Entrepreneurs (***Unternehmer***)*

Accounting, auditing and their legal norms establish the constitution of the company (the entrepreneur), of the human corporation. Accounting law is the nucleus and the essence (*Wesensgehalt*) of a general valuation law. In Germany, legislation emphasises this for elementary questions of valuation in insolvency law by explicit reference to the norms of the German Commercial Code (*Handelsgesetzbuch*, HGB) for the annual accounts (in the case of capital reduction, *Kapitalherabsetzung*,

[50] BGH, 08.10.2013 (II ZB 26/12 – *Frosta*) NJW 2014, 146, <openJur 2013, 42881>, following the BVerfG (*Bundesverfassungsgericht*) 11.07.2012 (1 BvR 3142/07, 1569/08 – *MVS Zeppelin AG and Lindner KGaA*) <lexetius.com/2012,2761>; to this BVerfG, 05.11.2015 (1 BvR 1667/15) <openJur 2019, 43017>. A different stance has been taken by the BGH, 25.11.2002 (II ZR 133/01 – *Macrotron*) BGHZ 153, 47 (NJW 2003, 1032, <openJur 2010, 9212>), and BGH, 28.06.2011 (II ZB 2/10) ZIP 2011, 1708, <openJur 2011, 94428>; on this Luttermann (2011b). Cf. BGH, 29.09.2015 (II ZB 23/14) BGHZ 207, 114, <openJur 2016, 126>.

[51] Explicating reasoning on the *Gesetz zur Umsetzung der geänderten Transparenzrichtlinie* (2013/50/EU), *Bundestags-Drucksache* 18/6220 (30.09.2015), 83-86.

[52] See in the following under 5.4.

[53] Of 16.10.1934, as amended on 02.11.2015, BGBl I 1834.

[54] Luttermann (2015b). Cf. overall chapter 4, esp. 4.7 (company groups), 4.8 (international allocation of assets) as well as 4.11 (private world monopoly of valuation: "IFRS/ISS, XBRL"), and below 8.4.2 on the traditional view of handling corporations (*lex societatis*), resp. investments (assets, *lex rei sitae*), with a transnational measure of valuation (*lex aestimatio*).

[55] See chapters 1, 2 (the "green" paradigm shift), chapters 6, 7 (individual responsibility), and overall on global perspectives chapters 8, 9.

see 4.6.4). Therefore we see: Where legal protection is required, the valuation of corporations and share ownership (assets) cannot make do with the arbitrary mathematical use of models, expectations and arithmetic operations (the "numbers game").[56] As a legal domain, the company valuation (appraisal of business, *Unternehmensbewertung*) is a legal act, in order to determine the business foundation and the business results for the entrepreneurs (shareholders, *Anteilseigner*) and their business partners in a sustainable, id est, a verifiable way (see 5.2.4).

The general issue is to establish the order of assets (*Vermögensordnung*) as the basis of our economy and society in the sense of a legal order (*Rechtsordnung*). The primary status of the law secures entrepreneurial freedom, constitutionally guaranteed (in Germany: Art. 2(1) and Art. 14 *Grundgesetz*, GG). This freedom is labelled as private autonomy (*Privatautonomie*) with the freedom of contract (*Vertragsfreiheit*). This provides the actors of the valuation of a company with the necessary legal basis, at the same time serving to avoid – as far as possible – conflict and liability (conflict resolution). This is still often not seen, but it becomes clear in the case of cash compensation (see 5.4). In the constitution of liberty, the following applies: Through the law, people individually gain a "secure, free space" (Friedrich Carl von Savigny)[57] in their community as market actors for their legal transactions, id est their entrepreneurial actions in the shape of contracts. This remains to be taken into particular consideration, where due to climate change valuation has to take place anew and private autonomy is at stake (see 5.3.2).

Let us recall the basic idea: Legislation limits its own influence to setting the framework. For debt obligations, this includes the regulation of extreme cases such as usury (*Sittenwidrigkeit*, violation of moral principles, § 138 BGB, e.g., surety of a fortuneless relative).[58] Material valuation in the sense of contractual justice, however, is regarded as the general responsibility of the market actors themselves. Their valuations may be personally influenced and motivated by manifold factors. The contractual partners negotiate the price (according to Roman law: *do ut des*). They agree in contract, thereby setting "something", a thing or a service (i.e. an asset, *Vermögensgegenstand*), in a relation of value to an equivalent (commonly a currency, e.g. euro or US-dollar, as exchange value, so-called value relation, *Wertrelation*). This characterises the process of pricing in general: a communicative process where information serves as creation of value (see 4.12.3).

---

[56] See esp. above 4.6.1 and chapter 6.

[57] See above 2.2.2, cf. 3.6.5. Luttermann (2015a).

[58] See BVerfG, 06.12.2005 (1 BvR 1905/02) BVerfGE 115, 51, <openJur 2010, 3167>; BGH, 16.06.2009 (XI ZR 539/07) NJW 2009, 2671, <openJur 2011, 2795>. Cf., e.g., BGH, 15.11.2016 (XI ZR 32/16) NJW-RR 2017, 241, <openJur 2018, 1514>. On duty of loyalty (*Treuepflicht*) among associates BGH, 12.04.2016 (II ZR 275/14) NJW 2016, 2739, <openJur 2016, 7127> (*Media-Saturn Holding GmbH*).

### *5.3.4 Valuation of Companies (Source of Value)*

In principle, as shown there, this also applies to the valuation of companies and assets (appraisal of business, *Unternehmensbewertung*). It is therefore reasonable to base this on the data of commercial book-keeping (*Buchführung*), accounting (financial reporting) and auditing, which in regard to accounting law (e.g. German HGB) is regulated as valuation law (*Bewertungsrecht*). Where the parties (creditors and debtors) are not able to come to an agreement contractually, it is the legal order that provides regulation (e.g. in insolvency law §§ 222, 254, 254a InsO: insolvency plan).[59] The omnipresent question of the so-called "fair price" (Latin *iustum pretium*) was already manifoldly debated in Ancient Greek philosophy, because the issue all round is about justice for peace, especially in the economy (from Ancient Greek *oikos*).[60] The basic idea has remained the same ever since: law and economy need to be set as one.[61] Particularly at the international or global level, different cultures of valuation can have an impact (on complementarity see chapter 9).

What can be said, in any case, is that no thing has an objective value (in itself, *an sich*);[62] however, it does or should have substance, which has to be fundamentally recognised (so-called asset, see 5.6.1).[63] Basically, we shape value (or worthlessness) ourselves, humanity in practice being "the ultimate source of value" (see Fig. 5.1).[64] But humans have been removed from the equation. Reasonableness (Greek *phrónesis*) knows that basically it is in fact about more substance (precious metals, energy).[65] Jurisdiction therefore relies on the contractual agreement between private parties for a free society, id est on reason as the guiding principle in thought and deed in a sound framework of order for self-responsibility (*Eigenverantwortung*) and fair market-based conditions, as set out above (see 5.2, 5.3.3). The reticence of German legislation is thus wise (cf. practised ethics, 9.1).[66] This shows in practice: According to civil law, a contract may therefore – insofar as there is no false information – not be contested on the grounds of errors regarding a value or a

---

[59] See BGH, 07.05.2015 (IX ZB 75/14) ZIP 2015, 1346, <openJur 2015, 11126>. On the *GmbH*: BGH, 08.04.2020 (II ZB 3/19) ZIP 2020, 1124, <openJur 2020, 5804>; BGH, 09.11.2021 (II ZB 1/21) ZIP 2022, 122, <openJur 2022, 656>.

[60] Meaning the family and/or the family's house and belongings (*Besitztümer*) as a comprehensive household and economic community, see above 3.7: (1) family business. Overall see chapter 9.

[61] See *Prolog auf Aegina* (Prolog on Aegina, Greece) in Luttermann, C. and Luttermann, K. (2020) pp. 1-4, with references to Socrates, Aristotle, Xenophon of Athens and others.

[62] Cf. Großfeld and Luttermann (2005) recital 426 (HGB/tax law), recitals 942-949 (IFRS).

[63] Note also esp. 6.6.2 (gold standard), 4.5.6 (expectation gaps), 4.6 and 5.6 (guideline for valuation). On the denotation of "asset" (*Vermögen*) see 8.1 (footnote 3).

[64] Korsgaard (2008) p. 85. See above 4.12.3, esp. with 4.6.5 and chapters 8 and 9. Cf. Belting (2011) pp. 9-10 and above 3.8. On depersonalisation in 3.5.4 and 3.7, 8.3.2.

[65] See 5.2.2 to 5.2.4 and 5.6 on judicial practice. Basically above 1.6.2, below 8.1 (with Phelps), 6.6.2 and 9.1, 9.8-9.9 (on reasonableness, *phrónesis*). Overall Luttermann (2008c).

[66] Luttermann (1998), esp. pp. 139-143 (on reasonableness), and Luttermann (2013).

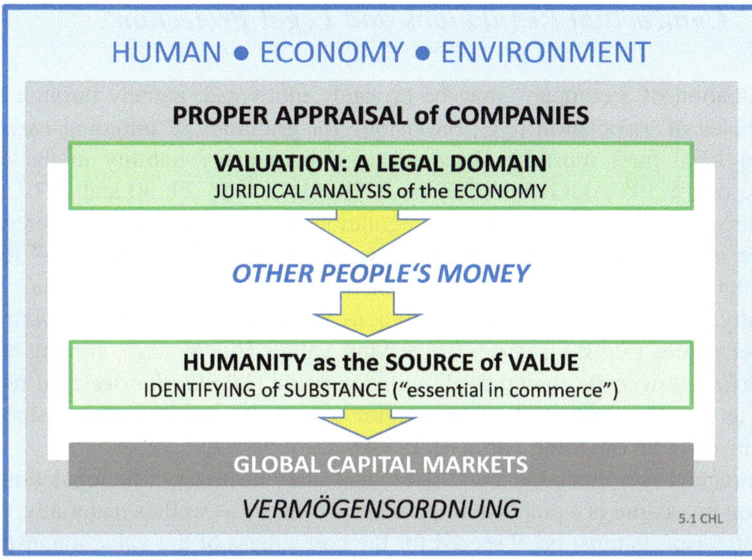


**Fig. 5.1** Humanity, valuation and the law

market price. What does constitute the right to challenge is an error on those characteristics (*Eigenschaften*) of a person or an object that are regarded as "essential in commerce" (*als im Geschäftsverkehr wesentlich*, § 119(2) BGB), the so-called value-creating factors (*wertbildende Faktoren*, see also 8.3.3) in a contractual relationship.[67]

Depending on the individual case, this may concern, e.g., the technical condition and the age of an object (vehicle, machine, antiques etc.), the location and development potential (e.g., contamination) of a site, the turnover of a gain-oriented business, the validity of a licence contract in a property right, the bankruptcy of a contract partner, the authenticity of a work of art. With regard to the law of evidence, the issue is always facts, id est truth (factual basis, see 5.5). In practice, that is the information (from Latin [*in-*]*formare*) that literally puts one in the picture and makes possible reasonable valuation. Information is "knowledge or facts communicated about a particular subject",[68] id est of an asset, liability etc. (business valuation). As a legal act (*Rechtsakt*), it needs to be as reliable as is necessary in terms of facts (truth) and materiality (see 4.5.3, 4.13). This leads us right into the practice of the appraisal of companies (valuation law).

---

[67] See, e.g., BGH, 08.06.1988 (VIII ZR 135/87) NJW 1988, 2597 (authorship painting), BGH, 09.10.1980 (VII ZR 332/79) BGHZ 78, 216 (year of production, https://lorenz.userweb.mwn.de/urteile/bghz78_216.htm); BGH, 19.12.2002 (III ZR 41/02) NJW-RR 2003, 374 (land value), <openJur 2010, 8956>). On the buildability of a plot of land: *Reichsgericht* (RG), 31.05.1905 (Rep. V. 596/04) RGZ 61, 84, 86, BGH, 10.03.1978 (V ZR 69/76) NJW 1978, 1429.

[68] Cf. The New Shorter Oxford English Dictionary, 1993, p. 1364 (information): A formal (written) "statement of the facts of a civil claim". See above, e.g., 4.3.2, 4.5.3 and 4.11.3.

### *5.3.5 Contractual Regulations and Legal Protection*

The valuation of a company may be privately motivated, namely through bylaws and articles of association (e.g., provisions for gratuities of outgoing partners).[69] Binding legal facts must be observed (e.g. redundancy liability in the case of squeeze-out, § 305 AktG and §§ 327a, 327b AktG,[70] §§ 29, 30 and 207 UmwG). The European Union adds specific regulation to sustainability "for determining whether an economic activity qualifies as environmentally sustainable" (cf. Art. 1 Regulation (EU) 2020/852, see so-called "technical valuation criteria": 4.2.5). Generally, valuation is based on regulations such as market values (*Marktwerte*), net asset values (*Substanzwerte*) or carrying values (*Buchwerte*), earning-capacity values (*Ertragswerte*) or even the liquidation value (*Liquidationswert*); it regularly serves as a value bottom line (minimum value) for the company value to be determined for an outgoing partner (cf. 5.4).

Contractual specifications are possible and often necessary; the regulation of the valuation procedure is a practical imperative. Formally as well as materially, general protection aspects must be observed for the correctness of the valuation, especially a – systematically and in fact still – excessive transfer of assets (wealth) must be prevented. This applies in particular in view of the valuation practice conducted unilaterally for shareholders – to the detriment of other financers (or interests, cf. stakeholders, savers in times of crisis)[71] – of "creating shareholder value" (i.e. leverage, see 5.2.1, 4.11.4). The more recent discourse on sustainability shows that holistically also the stakeholders should be taken into the picture (see 4.2, 4.12.2).[72] Protection aspects involve, in particular, minimum values (*Mindest-werte*, bottom lines) as indicated. Surcharges (*Preisaufschläge*, so-called "good-will") are generally without problems, because they are given voluntarily. However, the "interests of third parties" that have to be protected (e.g. of the minority shareholders) need to be observed. The buying price may be unreasonably high (cf. § 138 BGB, see 5.3.3).

The valuation reason (*Bewertungsanlass*) may thus provide a special measure for the resolution of a case. This ranges from the link between trade law and tax law (§ 5(1) EStG, § 8 KStG, so-called *Maßgeblichkeit* – decisiveness) up to insolvency

[69] Cf. OLG Nürnberg, 20.12.2012 (12 U 49/13) ZIP 2014, 171 (Russian-roulette-clause). OLG Koblenz, 20.02.2009 (10 U 57/05) <openJur 2015, 22383>).

[70] E.g., OLG Frankfurt am Main, 29.01.2016 (21 W 70/15; see: <www.lareda.hessen.de>), and OLG Stuttgart, 05.11.2014 (20 W 4/12) <openJur 2014, 457> (§ 305 AktG). OLG Karlsruhe, 22.06.2015 (12a W 5/15) ZIP 2015, 1874 (§ 327b AktG).

[71] See, e.g., below chapter 6, esp. 6.6 on bailouts in the world debt crisis, and 6.7 on macroeconomics of human corporation ("Too-big-too-fail"?).

[72] Basically Luttermann (1998) already for all so-called "debtors" (bondholders, hybrid financiers, i.e. financial instruments (bonds, debentures etc.) with typical "equity"-features like income participation). See above, e.g., 3.6 and 3.7.

circumstances (§ 19 InsO), e.g., also in the case of the swap of claims (*Forderungen*) into shareholder or membership rights (Debt-Equity-Swap, § 254(4) InsO).[73] Depending on the individual case, procedural help in questions of valuation generally may come from an arbitrator's award (§§ 317–319 BGB) as well as formally from an arbitration court (*Schiedsgericht*, §§ 1025-1066 ZPO). International jurisdiction has to be observed in each case, e.g. in the case of compensation claims of an investor.[74] This applies in particular, also in a legal-comparative perspective where relations of climate change (sustainability, see 5.2.4) occur with regard to valuation law.

## 5.4 Cash Compensation of Minority Shareholders (Partners)

### *5.4.1 Conditions of Valuation Law*

What is important in corporate practice is cash compensation of minority partners (*Barabfindung*). This is the case in affiliation agreements about control (*Beherrschung*) and transfer of profits (*Gewinnabführung*) and is regulated in German law in §§ 291, 293b and e, § 305 AktG (see also §§ 327a, 327b AktG, squeeze-out). Legal protection is provided by a judicial procedure, the so-called *Spruchverfahren* (SpruchG)[75] as a part of non-contentious jurisdiction (*Freiwillige Gerichtsbarkeit*). Cash compensation is also relevant for the limited liability companies (GmbH). Here, we also find questions of valuation regarding the acquisition of own company shares or their recovery (§§ 33, 34 GmbHG). We will take a closer look at cash compensation in (listed) corporations (*Aktiengesellschaft*, AG), id est, the modern corporation, as this highlights the economic and legal foundations of company relations and their valuation. This provides orientation and decisive approaches to a solution for the practice of valuation law.

In the contract of domination and transfer of profits (*Beherrschungs- und Gewinnabführungsvertrag*, §§ 291 AktG), the law guarantees minority shareholders

[73] OLG Karlsruhe, 30.09.2015 (7 AktG 1/15) <openJur 2015, 19315>. BGH, 17.09.2014 (IX ZB 26/14) ZIP 2014, 2040. On taxability BFH, 3.12.2019 (VIII R 43/18) <openJur 2021, 36748>.

[74] BGH 24.06.2014 (VI ZR 347/12) <lexetius.com/2014,2880>. Cf. BGH, 09.02.2017 (IX ZR 66/16) <openJur 2018, 2035>.

[75] *Spruchverfahrensgesetz* of 12.06.2003, as amended on 11.12.2023, BGBl 2023 I No. 354. Court costs (*Gerichtskosten*) are only to be imposed on the applicants in exceptional cases (e.g. abuse of rights – *Rechtsmissbrauch*), § 15(1) SpruchG, see: BGH, 31.01.2024 (II ZB 5/22) ZIP 2024, 1070 recital 82. Cf. on this BGH, 18.03.2025 (II ZB 7/24) ZIP 2025, 1154, ECLI:DE:BGH:2025:180325BIIZB7.24.0 (mergers of cooperatives). See Wertheimer (1998) how courts in the USA determine fair value (shareholders' appraisal remedy).

an appropriate adjustment payment (*angemessene Ausgleichszahlung*, § 304 AktG)[76] as well as an appropriate cash compensation (*angemessene Barabfindung*, § 305 AktG, i.e. cash settlement). The so-called "outside shareholder" (i.e., those shareholders who are not party to the affiliation agreement) can demand from the other party in the contract that he receive an "adequate compensation" (*angemessene Abfindung*) for his shares, set down in the domination and transfer of profits contract (§ 305(1) AktG). As in company law in general, the legislator has not determined any method of valuation.[77] What counts is the merger value ratio (*Verschmelzungswertrelation*): The compensation in shares is regarded as adequate if it corresponds to the exchange ratio (*Umtauschverhältnis*) in the fusion of the companies involved (§ 305(3)(1) AktG).[78] Adequate cash compensation must take into consideration the circumstances of the corporation at the time of the decision-making by the shareholders' meeting regarding the contract (§ 305(3)(2) AktG).

What can be stated for practice is this: The share value (*Anteilswert* – equities) liable for compensation of the shares held by the minority shareholder is related to the value of the corporation. According to the legal premises, corporations entering into an affiliation agreement are to be valuated; namely in relation to "the circumstances of the corporation" on the reference date (*Stichtag*).[79] This systematically corresponds to the general norm of accounting law (§ 264(2)(1) HGB, see on this 5.5.1). Legislation thus determines company valuation as a legal task, embedded in the procedural framework of truth (*Wahrheit*) and measure of proof (*Beweismaß*, i.e. facts, see 4.6). On the whole, this shows and underscores for practice the financial function of the human corporation: Under the imperative of truth and sustainability, it is based on accounting and auditing, id est, sustainable financial reporting (see chapter 4).

---

[76] Cf. e.g., BGH, 19.04.2011 (II ZR 244/09) NZG 2011, 780, and BGH, 19.04.2011 (II ZR 237/09) BGHZ 189, 261, <openJur 2011, 92241>; on this BVerfG, 05.12.2012 (1 BvR 1577/11) <openJur 2013, 41952>. BGH, 12.01.2016 (II ZB 25/14) <openJur 2016, 5477>; BGH, 15.09.2020 (II ZB 6/20) BGHZ 227, 137, <openJur 2020, 76150>. Cf. above in 5.2.1.

[77] See, e.g., BGH, 15.09.2020 (II ZB 6/20) BGHZ 227, 137, <openJur 2020, 76150>, with further evidence in recital 26. BGH, 21.02.2023 (II ZB 12/21), BGHZ 236, 180, <openJur 2023, 4380>, BVerfG, 16.05.2012 (1 BvR 96/09 et al.) <openJur 2012, 133672>.

[78] Also § 320b(1)(4) AktG. Luttermann (2001). Cf. according to tax law Luttermann (2010c). See also BFH, 10.05.2016 (IX R 13/15) <openJur 2016, 13387> and (for GmbH) BFH, 02.07.2019 (IX R 13/18) BFHE 265, 333 <openJur 2020, 82286>.

[79] See, e.g., BGH, 15.09.2020 (II ZB 6/20) BGHZ 227, 137, <openJur 2020, 76150> recital 34. Cf. § 305(3)(2) AktG: "*Die angemessene Barabfindung muß die Verhältnisse der Gesellschaft im Zeitpunkt der Beschlußfassung ihrer Hauptversammlung über den Vertrag berücksichtigen.*"; analogously § 327b(1)(1) AktG.

### 5.4.2 Corporation and Jurisdiction

Basically, the issue is the legal protection of the share ownership (*Anteilseigentum*) embodied in the share, id est, the private benefit (*Privatnützigkeit*) and the power of disposition (*Verfügungsbefugnis*) regarding property regulated by company law, guaranteed by constitutional law (Art. 14 *Grundgesetz*, GG in Germany). These share ownerships impart both the membership status within the corporation (*Mitgliedschaftsrechte*) as well as the proprietary claims of the shareholder (*Vermögensrechte*).[80] However, the legal task of compensating the outgoing minority shareholders in a proprietarily adequate way remained fundamentally unsolved. *Rechtshonoratioren* (legal notables) for generations avoided the legal treatment of valuation issues. Climate change accentuates aspects of valuation, crucially with human rights and environment protection, within the legal order – where they have always been located and now inescapably remain: It is about legal imperatives (*Rechtsgebote*, see chapters 1 and 4).

In practice, legal protection was weak in cases of valuation, over the decades a legal vacuum developed regarding valuation. In Germany, a guiding decision by the Federal Supreme Court of Justice[81] from 1967 was influential in this respect, having refuted the stock market price (*Börsenkurs*) as the basis for the company law according to questions of valuation. The judges, caught in the error of an objectively available value ("house number"), searched for "the true value" (German original: *"den wahren Wert"*) of the shares as something mythical. Subsequently, judges at German civil courts widely confined themselves to determining valuation according to economically driven methods of earning-capacity value (*Ertragswertmethoden*) as the measures. This legal vacuum was practically filled by economists as "experts" with mathematically stilted valuation opinions.[82] With this factual change of paradigm, practice at court developed a "total dependence on expert opinions". [83] Actually, it is then not the judges who decide, but rather economic experts (e.g., certified public accountants). – Where is the necessary legal protection (*Rechtsschutz*)?

---

[80]BVerfG, 20.12.2010 (1 BvR 2323/07) ZIP 2011, 170, <openJur 2013, 25915>; confirmed by: BVerfG, 24.05.2012 (1 BvR 3221/10) ZIP 2012, 3020, <openJur 2013, 26198>.

[81]BGH (*Bundesgerichtshof*), 30.03.1967 (II ZR 141/64) AG 1967, 264.

[82]Cf. BGH, 12.01.2016 (II ZB 25/14) BGHZ 208, 265, <openJur 2016, 5477>, BGH, 15.09.2020 (II ZB 6/20) BGHZ 227, 137, <openJur 2020, 76150>. Earlier evidence in *Hüffer* (1997) § 305, recital 19; cf. critically already Luttermann on OLG Celle (9 W 128/97) EWiR 1998, 821, and on OLG Düsseldorf (19 W 3/93 AktE) EWiR 1998, 677.

[83]Emmerich and Sonnenschein (1997) p. 293; Ammon (1998). Practical guidance below 5.6.

Juridical analysis of the economy[84] teaches us: That does not work in practice (see chapter 6). It took a long time, needed fresh thinking, until the German Federal Constitutional Court made a correction. Following one literature source[85] in 1999 in the case DAT/Altana,[86] the judges ruled that it was "incompatible" with Article 14(1) GG not to take into consideration the stock market price in determining adjustment payments or compensations (...) according to §§ 304, 305, 320b [AktG] when fixing adequate compensation; the stock market price need not always be decisive by itself: Exceeding it would be uncritical constitutionally, but remaining below it could also be constitutionally founded (e.g., in the case of narrow markets, manipulation of markets). The protection of Article 14(1) GG, thus the judges in permament jurisdiction,[87] captures the substance of this share ownership in its membership law and property law arrangement. The stock market price (*Börsenkurs*) is basically regarded as the minimum value of the company share (stock). According to the actual circumstances (§ 305(3)(2) AktG), this may in fact have a higher value.

The civil courts have since followed this principle in determining legally required "adequate compensation": The basis is the stock market price of the share, generally to be determined based on an average rate weighted according to the turnover within a three-month reference period before the announcement of a structural measure (e.g., the affiliation agreement).[88] This goes in the right direction, the reference period should, however, be longer (at least a year), making it factually (empirically) more reliable.[89] According to the Federal Supreme Court,[90] the development of the market rates may make an adaptation imperative under specific circumstances. This illustrates how living conditions and economic expertise may be captured in a legally sensible way – in the concept of justice with the imperatives of truth and sustainability, here: for sustainable economic activity of the human corporation (see 5.2).

---

[84] See below Fig. 5.3. Basically on the topic of reasonable compensation (fair valuation) of minority shareholders Luttermann (1999b). See overall on juridical analysis, e.g., above 5.2.2, 1.6.2, below 7.3.2 and chapter 9.

[85] BVerfG, 27.04.1999 (1 BvR 1613/94) BVerfGE 100, 289, 308 with Luttermann (1999b). On this procedure Heigel (2007) p. 73.

[86] See previous footnote. Cf. BVerfG, 07.08.1962 (1 BvL 16/60) BVerfGE 14, 263, 283, <openJur 2011, 118107>; BVerfG, 06.12.2016 (1 BvR 2821/11 et al.) BVerfGE 143, 246, <lexetius.com/2016,3662>.

[87] BVerfG, 05.12.2012 (1 BvR 1577/11 – Wella AG), III.1.a: ZIP 2013, 260, <openJur 2013, 41952>; also, e.g., OLG Düsseldorf, 18.03.2024 (I-26 W 13/20 AktE) <openJur 2024, 8537> recital 40.

[88] BGH, 19.07.2010 (II ZB 18/09 – *Stollwerck AG*) BGHZ 186, 229, NZG 2011, 939 (1. headnote), <openJur 2010, 11922>; BGH, 29.09.2015 (II ZB 23/14) BGHZ 207, 114, <openJur 2016, 126>, BGH, 31.01.2024 (II ZB 5/22) <openJur 2024, 4211>. Cf. critical Luttermann on BGH (II ZB 2/10) EWiR 2011, 619.

[89] Luttermann (1999b) 45, 51: longer reference period for adequacy and against abuse.

[90] BGH, 28.06.2011 (II ZB 10/10) <openJur 2011, 94726>. See detailed information on judicial review BGH, 31.01.2024 (II ZB 5/22) ZIP 2024, 1070, <openJur 2024, 4211>, from recital 25.

### 5.4.3 General Protection System

Overall, a more effective legal protection (*Rechtsschutz*) against the abuse of economic power is developing. This must also encompass the taxation of the squeeze-out of corporate shareholders;[91] and, of course, the measures of sustainability (see 5.2.4). Let us take a look at the complete context. Valuation law (*Bewertungsrecht*) is supported by civil law. Affiliation agreements between companies intervene in organisational structures, for through the contract of domination, one corporation subjects itself to the direction of another corporation; as a rule, it transfers its profits to the controlling corporation (§ 291 AktG). This concerns the constitiutional guarantee of property (*Eigentumsgarantie*, Art. 14 GG) of the minority shareholders.

This "dispossession" (*Enteignung*) was already taken into consideration by legislation in its civil legal concept. It is based on the minority shareholders outside of the contract of domination themselves having claims: adjustment payments (according to § 304 AktG) and cash compensation (according to § 305 AktG). For the domination and transfer of profits contracts (*Beherrschungs- und Gewinnabführungsverträge*) are contracts to the detriment of third parties (*Verträge zu Lasten Dritter*), id est to the detriment of outside shareholders as the affected minority (so-called *"außenstehende Aktionäre"*). Here and in general, that is, also for capital investors (in the case of hybrid financial instruments such as income bonds, preferred debentures, see 5.4.5), an unjustified transfer of assets (values, wealth) should be prevented, id est: The company assets (*Vermögen*) must not be transferred without adequate compensation.[92]

It should be noted that the asset position (*Vermögensposition*) regarding the law on stock companies is embedded in the framework of the corporation as such. This also applies to the content of the asset position. The Federal Constitutional Court emphasises that the shareholder is to be compensated for the loss caused by the structural measure (e.g. §§ 319-320b AktG):[93] His position is genuinely burdened with the possibility, in the final instance through the decision of the majority (i.e., in a legally ordered procedure against compensation), of being withdrawn (squeeze-out). The shareholder accepts this in buying the shares. That means he acquires a genuinely restricted position as a shareholder of the corporation (asset position), which, however, is necessarily protected by valuation law (see 5.4.1).

---

[91] Questionable: BFH, 13.10.2010 (I R 79/09) BFHE 231, 529, <openJur 2011, 88911>; FG Düsseldorf, 11.08.2009 (6 K 3742/06 K, G) EFG 2010, 133. With a different view: Luttermann (2010c). Cf., e.g., BFH 31.05.2017 (I R 37/15) BFHE 258, 484, <openJur 2020, 83015>.

[92] Basically Luttermann (1998) pp. 536-539. Corr. BGH, 28.05.2013 (II ZR 67/12) BGHZ 197, 284, <openJur 2013, 32852>. BGH, 29.04.2014 (II ZR 395/12) <openJur 2014, 11118>. Cf. BFH, 12.3.2014 (I R 87/12) BFHE 244, 567, <openJur 2014, 16560>.

[93] BVerfG, 29.11.2006 (1 BvR 704/03) NJW 2007, 828, 829, <openJur 2011, 118984>; see Luttermann (2007b). Cf. BVerfG, 26.04.2011 (1 BvR 2658/10) <openJur 2012, 133638>.

### 5.4.4 *Entrepreneurial Freedom and Protection of Third Parties*

First let us look at the situation of conflict: The parties of the affiliation agreement (§ 291 AktG) burden the minority shareholders of the controlled company (*abhängiges Unternehmen*) by intervening in existing shareholder rights (contractual rights) and asset relations with the control and transfer of profits agreed upon. Such one-sided interventions violate private autonomy, id est, the universal right of every person to fashion his living conditions (*Lebensverhältnisse*), namely his legal situation, in any way he wants (contractual freedom, *Vertragsfreiheit*). That is why such interventions are generally forbidden by German law.[94] However, in legal fact the minority shareholders of the grouped company cannot prevent the affiliation agreement.

At the same time, the shareholder majority in the corporation may devaluate the asset position of the minority shareholders, right up to complete withdrawal through squeeze-out (§§ 327a, 327b AktG, see 5.4.3). The majority may also act in other massive ways: The controlling company has the directing power with regard to the *Konzernrecht* (law of corporate groups, § 308 AktG), determines company politics, executes accounting law discretion (*Bilanzermessen*), can direct so-called "hidden reserves" (*stille Rücklagen*), profits and losses within the group of companies. The majority can thus undermine the existential basis of the controlled corporation, namely the substance (assets) through the affiliation agreement. This concerns the share value (resp. the value of debt items, e.g., loans, debentures, bonds as well as hybrid financial instruments, see 5.4.4) of the now – as a result of the affiliation agreements – dependent corporation, indicated at the markets by the lower share price (resp., bond price).

However, the German Stock Corporation Act condones the affiliation agreement that is causal, because it works to the disadvantage of the minority, saying: "Payments of the corporation due to a domination or transfer of profits contract do not count as a violation against §§ 57, 58 and 60" (see § 291(3) AktG). The strict binding of assets according to the Stock Corporation Act is thus loosened to a large extent. This does not mean that the legal order, in particular the – overall guiding – concept of justice, is forfeited. The motive for the derogation regarding the law of shareholders is that the legislator intends to provide the majority shareholders of a corporation with entrepreneurial flexibility – but not for free (see 5.4.5). Holistically, valuation law comes into play here, quite sensibly for the financing of the human corporation and the legal order as a sustainable order of assets (*Vermögensordnung*, see chapter 8).

---

[94] See generally BGH, 12.10.2011 (VIII ZR 50/11) <openJur 2011, 117396> recital 18. Cf., e.g., also BGH, 22.04.2010 (I ZR 74/08) BeckRS 2010, 24954 recital 36; BGH, 20.10.2010 (XII ZR 25/09) NJW 2011, 61 recital 19; BGH, 27.01.2016 (XII ZR 33/15) BGHZ 208, 357, <lexetius.com/2016,325> recital 50.

### 5.4.5 Valuation Law Consequences

Legislation solves a situation of conflict here (*Rechtsstreit*, see 5.4.4). Ultimately, the minority shareholders of the corporation should not be able to obstruct the majority, for whom private autonomy (*Privatautonomie*) with the freedom of contract (*Vertragsfreiheit*, see 5.3.3) also applies. However, the legislator definitely wants to balance the conflict parties with regard to property rights (equities, claims to profit participation, transfer of wealth),[95] id est reimburse the minority shareholders affected by the affiliation agreement (squeeze-out, see 5.4.3) through cash payment. The legislative motives regarding the Stock Companies Act emphasise that the law cannot make the outside minority shareholders accept the fundamental change in their associate status without a right to compensation.[96] In principle, this applies accordingly to all affected ownership positions (e.g. claims to profit participation, *Gewinnbeteiligung*).

However, in the practice of company valuation, the procedure usually leads to a loss for them: For who will buy (without a discount!) the minority shares (income bonds etc.) of a controlled corporation? – Therefore, the following applies: Majority shareholders may make the affiliation agreement; in return, minority shareholders not involved receive adjustment payments (*Ausgleichszahlungen*, i.e. steady financial compensation, § 304 AktG) respectively a cash compensation (*Barabfindung*, i.e. exit with one-time financial compensation, § 305 AktG). This means that a legal obligatory relation (*gesetzliches Schuldverhältnis*)[97] holds between the minority shareholders of the – now – controlled corporation and its majority shareholder, for which the latter lays the foundation with the closing of the intercompany agreement (*Unternehmensvertrag*) and which he has to substantiate basically in amounts of money by a cash compensation (*Barabfindung*) directly in the affiliation agreement (§ 305(1) and (2) AktG). This idea can serve as a general rule for a comprehensive protection concept that covers all financiers of the corporation.

The legal regulation thus balances out the power within the corporation with regard to the shareholders' property rights (assets – *Vermögen*). The shareholder majority can act as entrepreneurs within the organisational framework of the corporation, whereas the outside minority shareholders are protected by adjustment payments and cash compensation. However, this only holds insofar as the cash payments are in fact "adequate" (i.e. reasonable, *angemessen*) – in case of conflict investigated and confirmed or adjusted by a court, id est independent judges. This is the inalienable legal protection (*Rechtsschutz*) and underlines the fact that the determination of the compensation as a question of valuation is genuinely (*genuin*) a legal matter (*Rechtsfrage*). Compensation (valuation) is therefore fully subject to

[95] Note in principle above 5.2.1 (order of assets – *Vermögensordnung*). Overall with transnational perspectives see chapters 1 and 8.

[96] Reasoning on § 305(1) AktG, printed in Bruno Kropff, Aktiengesetz (IDW, Düsseldorf 1965) pp. 165, 397.

[97] Luttermann (2006a), so already Luttermann (1997) 1181, 1183-84.

legal examination on application according to the law of judicial procedure (§ 305(5)(2) AktG).[98]

## 5.5 Legal Objectives for Proper Valuation

### *5.5.1 Imperative of Truth: Factual Basis (Sustainability)*

Valuation law is, as shown, systematically embedded in the general order of the economy and the law – the order of assets (*Vermögensordnung*, see 5.2.1). Valuation law creates a framework of order for the determination of asset values (valuation, *Bewertung*), which is fundamentally related to the imperative of truth (*Wahrheitsgebot*) in civil proceedings (see 5.6) along with sustainability (see 5.2.4). That means we are basically dealing with facts, in the valuation of companies with their actual circumstances (see Fig. 5.2). This is fixed by the general norm of accounting law: In the annual accounts, a "view that corresponds to the actual circumstances" of the corporation is to be conveyed (§§ 264(2)(1), 243(1) HGB: principle of "a true and fair view", *Bilanzwahrheit*, cf. Art. 4(3)(1) Directive 2013/34/EU: "shall give a true and fair view").[99]

That is financial reporting as verified information for investors[100] and forms the general basis for the valuation of companies. Jurisprudence here follows natural observation, for the issue is always one and the same company. The determination (*Feststellung*) of the annual accounts, for the corporation according to §§ 172, 173 AktG, constitutes their validity (§ 416 *Zivilprozessordnung*. ZPO).[101] The imperative of truth is the epitome of the ideal of justice as the core of any legal order. Legally, a relation to truth (*Wahrheitsbezug*) is always a factual relation (*Faktenbezug*). In particular, the basis should be the present (*Gegenwart*) and the past (*Vergangenheit*). The third time dimension "future" (*Zukunft*), in contrast, opens up the horizon of arbitrary

---

[98] See above 5.4.1. Cf. BGH, 12.03.2001 (II ZB 15/00) BGHZ 147, 108, <openJur 2010, 5114>; BGH, 09.10.2006 (II ZR 46/05) BGHZ 169, 221 <openJur 2011, 11057>; see also, e.g., BGH, 21.02.2023 (II ZB 12/21) BGHZ 236, 180 <openJur 2023, 4380>, BGH, 31.01.2024 (II ZB 5/22) <openJur 2024, 4211>. For the GmbH: BGH, BGH, 08.01.2019 (II ZR 364/18) BGHZ 220, 354 <openJur 2019, 2503>, BGH, 26.01.2021 (II ZR 391/18) <openJur 2021, 6046>. Cf. on hybrid financial instruments (here: *Genußrechte*) BGH, 01.10.2020 (IX ZR 247/19) <openJur 2020, 75694>. Overall 5.5.3, 4.6.4 and below 7.7.3.

[99] In detail Luttermann (2003) § 264 HGB recitals 16-169 and Luttermann (2003) §§ 243, 342 HGB recitals 7-10, Luttermann (2010b) 346-355.

[100] See chapter 4 (the "documentary proof of good corporate governance").

[101] BGH, 02.03.2009 (II ZR 264/07) NZG 659, 661, <openJur 2011, 3690>. Cf. BGH, 18.07.2013 (IX ZR 198/10) <openJur 2013, 32091>. See also § 245 HGB: in 5.6.2 and in 4.4.1. Determination of the balance sheet as an acknowledgment of debt (*Schuldanerkenntnis*), tax cases: BFH, 10.05.2016 (IX R 13/15) <openJur 2016, 13387>, BFH, 02.07.2019 (IX R 13/18) BFHE 265, 333 <openJur 2020, 82286>; cf. BFH, 10.11.2022 (IV R 8/19) BFHE 278, 487 <openJur 2023, 1004> (at least indicative significance).

guesswork, painfully observable in the disaster economy with the untenable valuations according to "IFRS" (U.S. "GAAP", ISA, IVS); the likewise so-called "standards" on disclosures about sustainability-related financial information are joining that circle ("IFRS S", see 1.5.3). There, as already highlighted with Goethe at the beginning of this chapter, we are largely dealing with vague, hypothetical valuations (*Scheinwerte, Hoffnungswerte*, altogether so-called "toxic assets", *toxische Vermögenswerte*, see 5.5.3).[102] Connecting facts (*Anknüpfungstatsachen*) must be observed (see 5.5.2, 5.5.3).

The factual relation naturally and legally draws a necessary line against such hope values, such flight into the future with the inalienable imperative of truth (*Wahrheitsgebot*). The paradigm of sustainability does not open up any room for manoeuvres, but rather expressly affirms the requirement for – if necessary, scientifically and "objectively"[103] – substantiated information and evaluation, id est verification (law of evidence, *Beweisrecht*, see 5.2.4 and chapter 4). Properly viewed, the reference to facts based on accounting law (*Bilanzrecht*) and civil procedure law (*Zivilprozessrecht*) is fundamental for the law of valuation

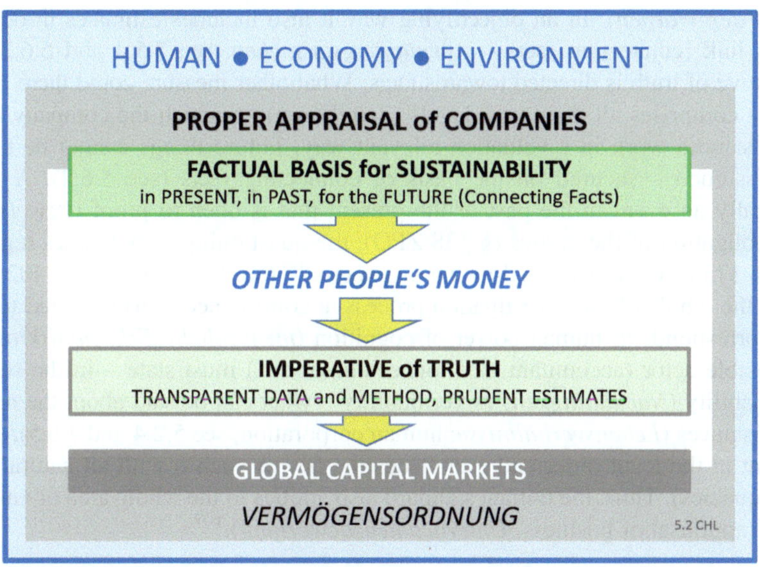


**Fig. 5.2** Truth and fact base for sustainable valuation

[102] See below 5.6.1, also above 4.5.6, 4.9.5, 4.10.2 and below 7.7.3.

[103] See for aspects of climate change (due diligence standard of conduct) ICJ, Advisory Opinion: Obligations of states in respect of climate change, 23.07.2025 (https://www.icj-cij.org/sites/default/files/case-related/187/187-20250723-adv-01-00-en.pdf, accessed: 27.08.2025), para. 300 with paras. 280-299, e.g.: appropriate measures, scientific and technological information, relevant international rules, risk assessment and environmental impact, precautionary approach. On the relevance for peoples and individuals (corporations) see below 6.1 (esp. 6.1.3).

(*Bewertungsrecht*) as such: the rampart against inadequate valuation and the accompanying arbitrary shift of assets (values); with regard to the conflict of laws (*Kollisionsrecht*), the protection necessarily takes effect also in transnational circumstances.[104] This is uniformly demanded by the imperative of truth and, where the issue is in fact the same company, independent of the occasion of valuation (see 5.3.2).

### 5.5.2 Valuation Concept by Civil Procedure Law

This is the materially substantial concept of the valuation of companies (shares, financial instruments), sustainably shaped by civil procedure law (*Zivilprozessrecht*), which forms a sound evidentiary basis (see 5.2.4). The valuation process with its contents and methodology as well as the result as a whole is subject to the control of judges, id est it is embedded in civil procedure law (civil law).[105] What is decisive – in the German as well as the European legal order and, with the idea of justice under the rule of law, at the same time also universally reasonable – is the imperative of truth (*Gebot der Warheit*). In an objectifying way it also includes estimates through the factual link (connecting facts – *Anknüpfungstatsachen*, see 5.5.4 and 5.6.2). The imperative of truth is directed towards facts: What other measure could there be?

That comprises all three time levels (*Zeitebenen*) on which the company and its circumstances work in a valuation-relevant way. Future things cannot be proven, only assumed – secured on the basis of connecting facts (see 5.6.2). A fact is practically an event in the past or the present that is open to proof (*Beweis*). The truth obligation of the parties (§ 138 ZPO), the questioning of witnesses regarding facts (§ 373 ZPO), as well as drawing on experts[106] (*Sachverständige*, §§ 402 to 414 ZPO): the whole of the investigation process at court is necessarily related to facts. This corresponds to human power of cognition (*menschliche Erkenntniskraft*): the responsible actor (accountant, auditor, evaluator etc.) must state – in the sense of sustainability (*Nachhaltigkeit*) as verifiability – what can be said about the relevant circumstances (*Lebensverhältnisse*: human corporation, see 5.2.4 and 4.6.5). That is relevant in the legal order and establishes the law as such – with all natural limits (inadequacies). Thus, the human standard also applies to the whole area of valuation issues (appraisal of business, *Unternehmensbewertung*).[107]

[104] In more detail on this Luttermann (2015b). See above 5.4.3 and 4.4.4 and 4.8.

[105] Accordingly in cases concerning expropriation law (*Enteignungsrecht*, Art. 14, 15 GG – German *Grundgesetz*) procedurally also in the administrative court (*Verwaltungsgericht*). See also in practical terms above 4.6.4 and 4.6.5 for corporate directors and auditors.

[106] In more detail on expert opinions (*Sachverständigengutachten*) on valuation Luttermann (2023b), esp. recitals 22-36 and 45-55. Cf. Weil, Frank, and Evans (2017).

[107] See with reference to physics above 4.6.5, and below 5.6. Overall chapter 9.

This is what the search for a decision is based on, which in the case of dissent among the parties involved takes place before court (adjudication). The judge has to decide and to reason whether and why he regards "a factual statement as true or not true" (§ 286(1) *ZPO*, see in more detail 5.6.5). That is the measure of proof (*Beweismaß*), which holds, in the sense of a fair valuation, for the adequacy of company valuation (appraisal of business). Overall, this comprises all aspects of valuation, in particular under the dually characterised paradigm of sustainability (see 5.2.4): By consistently building on facts and science, we separate arbitrariness (*Willkür*) from the law. From this follows the determination of the adequate value of assets (see, e.g., § 305(3)(2) AktG: *"die angemessene Barabfindung"*, the adequate cash compensation).[108]

### 5.5.3 *Accounts: Estimates and Analysis of the Past*

Of course, companies are designed for the present and the future. The law of evidence comprises this time dimension in the shape of prognostications (estimates, cf. cash compensation of retiring partners: § 728(1)(1) and (2) BGB, cf. ex-§ 738(2) BGB). In company valuation, these follow the going-concern premise (§ 252(1) no. 2 HGB, Art. 6 no. 1(a) of Accounting Law Directive 2013/34/EU). They include necessary estimates about future circumstances, regarding the trade accounts, e.g., for accruals (*Rückstellungen* – § 249(1)(1) HGB) and in general taking into account the principle of prudence (*Vorsichtsprinzip*, § 252(1) no. 4 HGB, see 5.5.4). Basically, full evidence applies (*Vollbeweis*, § 286(1) ZPO). What may be taken into consideration is relief of evidence (*Beweiserleichterung*, § 287 ZPO).[109] However, this does not mean discharge from the imperative of truth nor from the reference to facts that any estimate must be based on in a verifiable manner (connecting facts, *Anknüpfungstatsachen*, see 5.6.2).

This leads to discipline in the practice of company valuation (assets, appraisal of business), where it is widely opinions (*Werturteile* – value judgements) that come to the fore: Investors, thus the assumption, will only pay for future surplus (*künftigen Überschuss*, net incomes). So the aim is a so-called "future success value" (*Zukunftserfolgswert*) which, based on the company concept and "with all realistic future expectations", is to represent the objectified value of the company (discounted: cash value at the deadline).[110] This often requires prognostications.

---

[108] Fundamentally on "value" (*Wert*) and "price" (*Preis*) see Luttermann (2023a) recitals 1-3.

[109] Generally, e.g., BGH, 01.04.2021 (I ZR 9/18) MDR 201, 895, <openJur 2021, 34754> recital 53. Violation of the laws of reasoning (*Verstoß gegen Denkgesetze*): BGH, 23.09.2021 (I ZB 20/21) <openJur 2021, 44088> recital 70.

[110] Germany, private *Institut der Wirtschaftsprüfer* (IDW – Institute of Certified Public Accountants) Standard: IDW S 1 (2008) recital 29. Cf. below 5.6.1 and overall IDW *Grundsätze zur Durchführung von Unternehmensbewertungen* (IDW ES 1 *neue Fassung* – Principles for the performance of business valuations, new version 2025). Note on the private IDW below in 5.5.5.

These are "the key problem of any company valuation".[111] Prognostications easily (mis)lead, as the world debt crisis shows in manifold ways,[112] into the foggy realms of fortune-telling: the results are arbitrarily subjective, excessively blown-up values of hope (*Hoffnungswerte*, see 5.6.1 and also for guidance in 4.6.3, 4.10.2). The difficulty comprises the valuation of "sustainable economic activity" overall right up to abuse (greenwashing, see 4.2.5).

It is against illegitimate arbitrariness that the norms of commercial law (resp. EU regulation) are effective: As shown above, based on the principle of "a true and fair view" (*Bilanzwahrheit*, §§ 243, 264 HGB), the separate financial statement of the corporation is drawn up formally and materially as a legal act (see 4.4.1). It is only this fact that makes the corporation and its enterprise (assets, *Vermögensgegenstände*) tangible as the contractual actor (partner) in legal and economic affairs (see 4.2). It is only this that makes it possible for the human corporation to promote the common good sustainbly through individual entrepreneurship (the "invisible hand", see 5.2.2 and 7.3.3). This needs to be taken heed of: Accounting law with the going-concern premise goes further than the analysis of the past. It does look into the future, but in a strictly ordered way (i.e. verifiably). European legislation confirms this in its Directive 2013/34/EU, elaborating on the question of estimates (reasonableness):

> "Estimates should be based on a prudent judgement of the management of the undertaking and calculated on an objective basis, supplemented by experience of similar transactions and, in some cases, even reports from independent experts. The evidence considered should include any additional evidence provided by events after the balance-sheet date."[113]

This fits into the civil-procedural concept presented here for the valuation of companies (assets) and provides further guidance for practice (on the evidential proceedings at court see also 5.6.2). Overall, this provides the necessary factual basis (so-called connecting facts, *Anknüpfungstatsachen*) for realistic, verifiable estimates and thereby systematically a standard for proper valuation; a connecting fact may be seen as a "starting point" (*Anhaltspunkt, Anknüpfungspunkt*) – for adequate further investigations and conclusions.[114] Overall, this comprises the valuation aspects of sustainability, in general and with scientific underscoring as well as where – environmentally – a "degree" of sustainability (*Nachhaltigkeitsgrad*) is to be evaluated (cf. Art. 1 No. 1 Regulation (EU) 2020/852; also above 5.5.1). Basically, as in practice, the issue is facts, facts, facts (see 5.6.2 and 4.6.3 to 4.6.5, 7.7.3).

---

[111] So IDW S 1, recital 68.

[112] Cf. Luttermann (2023a) recitals 17-23.

[113] Directive 2013/34/EU on the annual financial statements, consolidated financial statements and related reports of certain types of undertakings, OJ L 182, 29.06.2013, 19, recital 22.

[114] See, e.g., BGH, 01.04.2021 (I ZR 9/18) MDR 201, 895, <openJur 2021, 34754> recitals 50, 53 and 56; BGH, 24.01.2022 (Via ZR 100/21) NJW-RR 2022, 1033, <openJur 2022, 5837> recital 28. On more judicial practice below 5.6.5.

### 5.5.4 *Insolvency Law (Reorganisation) and the Principle of Prudence*

This denotes *the* basis of valuation for legal and business affairs. Legislation confirms this with its reform of insolvency law, aiming primarily not at divestiture (*Zerschlagung*) but at reorganisation (*Sanierung*), financial recovery and continuation of companies. If the capital of a corporation is decreased, value decrease and other losses must be explicitly determined and explained according to the norms of the HGB[115] (i.e. according to European law). All in all, it can be said that the basis of valuation is facts, conclusive documents (e.g., annual accounts, bookkeeping); this also applies to estimates (so-called connecting facts, see 5.6.2). The accounting approach (so-called *bilanzielle Betrachtungsweise*, balance sheet perspective), conceived and practiced procedurally as shown, holds for company law and the law of corporate groups (*Konzernrecht*) as well as for "living" enterprises in general (principle of going concern, § 252(1) no. 2 HGB).[116]

With regard to valuation law, the concept includes the principle of prudence according to commercial law and European accounting law (§ 252(1) No. 4 HGB, Art. 6 no. 1(c) Accounting Law Directive 2013/34/EU). For a corporation and its enterprise, that is to be continued live within time. For the organs responsible (corporate directors) this means: They act under uncertainty and have to take precautions, id est exercise prudence (*Vorsicht*). This is generally true; for example, insolvency (§ 17(2)(1) InsO) can be determined on the basis of budget plans.[117] The European Court of Justice emphasises the principle of making valuations on a prudent basis (*Vorsichtsprinzip*) as being "of particular importance" and "taking account of all elements" (profits made, charges, income, liabilities and losses) – of course with "observance of the requirement of a true and fair view".[118] Prudence is thus a legal requirement. Reservations are justifiable, if prudence is excessive. It is not permitted in the general sense of abuse, here with a legal basis on which, e.g., profit distribution and liability are based.[119]

This includes an international view. Practices that we would call "hidden reserves" (*stille Rücklagen*) are wrapped up and designated more prettily in other

[115] Reasoning, *Entwurf eines Gesetzes zur weiteren Erleichterung der Sanierung von Unternehmen* (E-ESUG), *Bundestags-Drucksache* 17/5712, 04.05.2011, 32. ESUG of 07.12.2011, BGBl. 2011 I 2582. See Luttermann and Geißler (2013).

[116] E.g., BGH, 31.05.2011 (II ZR 141/09 – *Telekom*) BGHZ 190, 7, <openJur 2011, 94343>; BGH, 01.12.2008 (II ZR 102/07 – *MPS*) BGHZ 179, 71, <openJur 2011, 3976>. Cf. BGH, 15.12.2020 (XI ZB 24/16) BGHZ 227, 137, <openJur 2021, 6414>.

[117] BGH, 28.06.2020 (II ZR 112/21) <openJur 2022, 14696> (cash-pool-system, liquidity balance – *Liquiditätsbilanz*). On "prudence" specifically for criminal proceedings BGH, 04.10.2018 (3 StR 251/18) <openJur 2018, 1067>; cf. Luttermann (2012b).

[118] ECJ, 03.10.2013 (C-322/12 – *Gimle SA*, FR) ECLI:EU:C:2013:632, recitals 30-33, on Article 31(1)(c) Directive 78/660/EEC. Cf. Art. 6(1)(c) Directive 2013/34/EU.

[119] Besides accounts-based covenants e.g. legally the balance-sheet profit (§ 58(4) AktG) and the limitation of liability (§ 13(2) GmbHG, § 1(1)(2) AktG).

places, e.g. in the USA, with the harmless term of "cookie jar reserves".[120] In some places, pretty words may have an effect. Overall, however, the principle of prudence is subject to the obligation of adequacy (prohibition of excess, *Übermaßverbot*) under the imperative of truth: Classic boundaries blurring through hybrid forms of financing, protection of creditors and associates are in principle equal in a protection system based on accounting law.[121] In a holistic perspective, this includes substance-related valuation (so-called "fair value", see 5.6.1). With regard to valuation law, it is always factual information on all material aspects (see 4.5.3) that is required.

### 5.5.5 Legal Protection and Valuation Methods

For the practice of company directors and actors of the valuation of a company (shares, bonds) that concerns the interests of third parties, the following applies: Company valuation is a legal act, not fortune telling (*Wahrsagerei*, see 5.3.2); this also applies to the work of a competent examiner that is contractually stipulated or generally regulated by the law (e.g., § 293b AktG: *"sachverständiger Prüfer"*). As far as the manner of valuation is not legally regulated, the jurisdiction of the Federal Court of Justice as the highest civil court in Germany rules: In the case of an argument between the parties of a court case, it is the task of the trial judge (*Tatrichter*) to select and apply an adequate manner of valuation in a way that is specific to the facts of the individual case.[122] This is a clear precept that is binding to all persons concerned and at the same time a benchmark for good practice. In relation, economic positions in theory and practice (e.g., models, formulas of valuation) take a back-seat.[123] They are subject to judicial review (*Rechtsprüfung*).

For effective legal protection, it is materially true that the valuation is oriented towards determining the "full, true" value (*den "vollen, wirklichen" Wert*) of the

[120] See above 5.4.3 (at the end) and Luttermann (2003) § 264 HGB recitals 76-78.

[121] Luttermann (2003) Einf BilanzR recitals 26-43.

[122] BGH, 29.09.2015 (II ZB 23/14) BGHZ 207, 114, <openJur 2016, 126> recital 42 with 20-22, BGH, 21.032.2023 (II ZB 12/21) BGHZ 236, 180, <openJur 2023, 4380> recital 22. Also, e.g., BGH, 15.09.2020 (II ZB 6/20) BGHZ 227, 137, <openJur 2020, 76150> recital 26; BGH, 17.11.2010 (XII ZR 170/09) <openJur 2011, 13374>, FamRZ 2011, 183, 1, headnote, following the BGH, 12.07.1995 (XII ZR 109/94) BGHZ 130, 298, 303; BGH, 17.07.2002 (XII ZR 218/00) FamRZ 2003, 153, 154. This means it is not a precept by the GG: BVerfG, 26.04.2011 (1 BvR 2658/10) BB 2011, 1518 (with remark Hartwin Bungert), <openJur 2012, 133638>. Cf. Wertheimer (1998) 613, 712 emphasises "that courts determine fair value in a manner consistent with the purposes of the remedy".

[123] See Luttermann (2023a). Cf. BGH, 15.09.2020 (II ZB 6/20) BGHZ 227, 137, <openJur 2020, 76150> recital 26 with 20, and in more detail: OLG München, 09.04.2021 (31 Wx 2/19 et al.) <www.gesetze-bayern.de/Content/Document/Y-300-Z-BECKRS-B-2021-N-9687?hl=true> recital 44 (accessed: 27.08.2025). Basically on market value BGH, 21.02.2023 (II ZB 12/21) BGHZ 236, 180 <openJur 2023, 4380>.

company share (financial instrument) as explained.[124] Despite this, the judges aim at economic or business valuation theory and practice as a point of reference “by way of an estimation”: The question of the most suitable valuation method is “no legal question, but part of fact determination” (*Tatsachenfeststellung*).[125] This seems to miss the legal point: The method shapes the result of the valuation, which is not to be at the discretion of the circles involved (so-called *“beteiligte Verkehrskreise”*, e.g., auditors). The legal standard (norm) must be fixed independently, as shown here (see 5.6). The judges, however, then also speak of it being a legal question (*Rechtsfrage*) whether a valuation method selected by the trial judge (*Tatrichter*) or a calculation procedure chosen within the valuation method contradicts the legal goals of valuation.[126] The German Ferderal Constitutional Court provides a general constitutional measure,[127] correspondingly:

> “Minority shareholders do not have a constitutional right that the ‘true’ value of the share in the corporation always be determined by drawing on every conceivable method of company valuation and the compensation to be calculated according to the principle of the ‘most favourable’. (…) What is required constitutionally are merely the selection of a method that is adequate and significant in the given case and the judicial verifiability of its application.”

This underlines the described procedural concept. Valuation in principle is about qualities (substance), which are regularly expressed in quantities (numbers). However, this must not be mathematically reduced, not by methods and practices of valuation either, as if with their help a “precise” (exact) company value could be fixed for a certain cutoff date (*Stichtag*). Each method (practice) is based on its own (idiosyncratic) assumptions, models, formulas, id est on value judgements (*Werturteile*). They come logically – apparently unavoidably – in a mathematical guise. It is precisely these abstractions that judges need to break through, uncovering the assumptions, circumstances and valuations effective behind them (Latin *Cui bono?*), in order to be able to find out as to what degree they correspond to the existing legal standards, id est the law (see 7.6 and 7.7). Judges have to judge (*beurteilen*), not to calculate (*berechnen*, Latin *judex non calculat*),[128] in order to determine an adquate compensation (*Abfindung*, see §§ 305, 327, 328 AktG).

Certain codes of regulation may provide orientation, such as the “Standard: Principles for carrying out company valuations” (IDW S 1) privately trimmed by the *Institut der Wirtschaftsprüfer* (Düsseldorf/Germany). Auditors accordingly

---

[124] BVerfG, 27.04.1999 (1 BvR 1613/94) BVerfGE 100, 289, 306, <openJur 2011, 118597>. See on this also above 5.3.5, cf. below 5.6.5.

[125] BGH, 29.09.2015 (II ZB 23/14) BGHZ 207, 114, <openJur 2016, 126> (on § 327f AktG); BGH, 15.9.2020 (II ZB 6/20) BGHZ 227, 137, <openJur 2020, 76150> recital 19. Also BGH, 21.02.2023 (II ZB 12/21) <openJur 2023, 4380> recital 22; BGH, 31.01.2024 (II ZB 5/22) <openJur 2024, 4211> recital 27. Note below 5.6.

[126] BGH, 21.032.2023 (II ZB 12/21) BGHZ 236, 180, <openJur 2023, 4380> recital 22. See also preceding footnote and on constitutional law the following one. Cf. for Austria: OGH (Austrian High Court), 27.02.2013 (6 Ob 25/12p) GES 2013, 131.

[127] BVerfG, 16.05.2012 (1 BvR 96/09) BVerfGK 19, 388, ZIP 2012, 1408, <lexetius.com/2012 ,3603> recital 18. On this BGH, 12.01.2016 (II ZB 25/14) BGHZ 208, 265, <openJur 2016, 5477>.

[128] Digesten Justinians 49, 8, 1 § 1 (Macer), cf. Germany § 319 ZPO. Luttermann (2023b) recitals 14-16. See below 9.9; also 5.3.4, 5.6.5 and above 4.9.5, 4.10.2.

valuate companies, without, however, diminishing self-responsibility (liability). Such "standards" are non-committal and fully subject to court investigation:[129] They do not bind the expert either; he must execute his duty of care (*Sorgfaltspflicht*) himself according to the legal precepts (e.g., § 317 HGB, see 4.9). This is corroborated by the case of the Wirecard AG and the legislator of the FISG (see 4.9.5) in the sense of the imperative of truth and sustainability (see 4.2), which apply in valuation in general. For in order to guarantee adequate legal protection, in the valuation of companies (shares) as a legal event, the following holds: It is not the parties involved that determine the legally required standard themselves, it is independent organs who do this (legislator, judges, see 5.6.2).

## 5.6 Judicial Practice (*Rechtsschutz*): Core Aspects and Consequences

### *5.6.1 Substance-Oriented Valuation (Fair Value)*

Some core aspects and consequences shall be presented here in more detail for practical work, in particular with the human corporation. First the obligation for substance-oriented valuation, in the sense of "fair value", a term that unfortunately haunts theory and practice of capital markets and corporate governance as a catchword in falsifying ways. – Who is interested in substanceless corporations? – Market competition eliminates them where state subsidies do not hinder.[130] Proper company valuation materially demands substance that provides a factually adequate, fair valuation of companies (shares, financial instruments, see 5.3.4). That is the fundamental idea of *fair value*.[131] However, that term is discredited, its sense of a sound *Vermögensordnung*, an order of assets and currency as a legal order (*Rechtsordnung*) being submerged. Reflecting sustainability in its authoritative character (see 5.2.4) opens up sources from which general prosperity may be created.

In the realm of "IFRS, IFRS S"/U.S. "GAAP" (IVS, ISS, ISA), we find mainly arbitrary, mathematically designed model values (*Modellwerte*) floating around under the label of "fair value", due to a lack of market values: Things appear volatile in valuation (price), where instead of steady value standards (e.g., a fine ounce of gold, energy), there is the rule only of paper currencies (*fiat money*), face values (*Nennwerte*) and inflation (zero or negative interest, quantitative easing). In

[129] On this BGH, 29.09.2015 (II ZB 23/14) BGHZ 207, 114, <openJur 2016, 126>; OLG Karlsruhe, 23.07.2015 (12a W 4/15) <openJur 2015, 19254>; see also limited BGH, 15.09.2020 (II ZB 6/20) BGHZ 227, 137, < openJur 2020, 76150>. Basically above, esp. 5.5.2, and below 5.6. Cf. Matschke, Brösel, Toll (2024), from p. 829.

[130] Like, e.g., the rescue of private banks in the financial crisis since 2007, see below 6.7.

[131] Fundamentally Luttermann (2009). See below 7.5–7.7 (on "fair value" and good corporate governance), also 4.10.2, 6.7.2 and chapter 9. How courts determine fair value, see Wertheimer (1998).

valuations, the quicksand of merely projected "asset values" is heaped on top, often expressing mere hopes (see 5.5.3). Accordingly, even the key term "asset" (*Vermögenswert*) comes with tremendous perspectives of hope, e.g.: as a resource "from which future economic benefits are expected to flow to the entity".[132] This practice of allegedly "fair" valuation gives the problem a dramatically sharper edge: Valuations pushed up without reference to reality (facts!) and lacking in substance during an economic boom induce excessive pay-outs (*Ausschüttungen*: dividends, boni), id est the loss of real substance; in a phase of downward swing, the valuations then melt down – "assets", financial power, liquidity of a corporation diminish (cf. against this § 268(8) HGB: payout block, see 4.8.3).

This is a procyclic trap and at the same time an invitation to abuse by financial acrobats ("numbers game"). – Is that "fair"? – In financial industries' neo-classical financial theories and practices synthetic-hypothetical valuations are thus created without reference to facts. There is a system to this arbitrariness,[133] spreading globally even after the financial crisis. There were in fact early, fundamental warnings, also by U.S. judges: "presentations of future earnings, appraised asset valuations and other hypothetical data are to be discouraged".[134] That means no fortune-telling, no typs of oracles or crystal balls, no mathematically modeled dreamworlds but instead facts and the truth – id est sustainability in terms of verifiability. The matter is simple. Nothing true may be known about the future, wrote Friedrich Schiller (1759–1805), Goethe's congenial companion: "The art of seers is a vain nothing, they are deceptors or themselves deceived".[135] – This is a reasonable warning, indeed, it applies internationally.

---

[132] IAS 38.8(b) (2014), there "[refer: paragraph 17]" for "future economic benefit"; see also IFRS Accounting Standards 2025 with IASB CF4.3 to 4.25 (2018): "the potential to produce economic benefits" (4.4 and 4.14) "even if the probability (…) is low" (4.15). Cf. on assets, e.g., IASC F.53 (2001): "The future economic benefit embodied in an asset is the potential to contribute (…) to the enterprise", and F.89: "An asset is recognised in the balance sheet when it is probable that future economic benefits will flow to the enterprise" (according to F.55). See also above 4.4.6 and below 7. 5.2. Cf. on market value (*Börsenwert*) Luttermann (1999b), Luttermann (2023a), recitals 48-67 and affirmative BGH, 21.02.2023 (II ZB 12/21) BGHZ 236, 180, <openJur 2023, 4380>, BGH, 31.01.2024 (II ZB 5/22) <openJur 2024, 4211>. Basically on the measure of value Luttermann (2008c).

[133] See for a general view chapter 6 and already Luttermann (2006b). Critically on valuation theory Hering, Olbrich, Rollberg (2010). Cf., e.g., Kaaya (2015), Mechelli and Cimini (2021), Palea (2018). Overall Bensadon and Praquin (2016).

[134] *Flynn v. Bass Bros. Flynn v. Bass Bros. Enterprises, Inc.*, 744 F.2d 978, 986 (3rd Cir 1984). Altogether Luttermann (1999a), Luttermann (2006b) and (2007b).

[135] Schiller (1803), act four, appearence four (Princess Isabella). Cf. Blaise Pascal (Pensées, 1669/ 1670, 172): The past and the present are our means, the future alone is our end. So we never live, but we hope to live; and, as we are always preparing to be happy, it is inevitable we should never be so. Seneca (Epistulae morales, [liber XVI] 98): "*Calamitosus est animus futuri anxious.*", according to Montaigne, Essais, 1595, first book (III, English: Unhappy the mind that is anxious about things to come). Cf. Luttermann (1998), from p. 210, esp. on probability theory and value theory pp. 229-233 (about Pascal: 230-231), leading to modern game theory. See chapter 9 (esp. 9.5–9.7).

### 5.6.2 Estimated Values: Basis and Limits of Discretion

In the valuation of companies (shares, financial instruments) as an act of the law, arbitrariness (*Beliebigkeit*) is generally legally inacceptable.[136] We have already seen that regarding valuation, estimates are also subject to the imperative of truth (*Gebot der Wahrheit*) and therefore reference to facts must be made clear also when exercising discretionary power (see 5.5.3). All this is supported and secured – due to the concept of civil procedure – by sustainable action (see 5.2.4). For practice this means: Estimates are actually only permissible where complete transparency about all "decisive circumstances presents difficulties" out of all proportion to significance of the litigious claim (§ 287(2) ZPO). This is often easily stated in company valuations (procedural economicalness, *Prozessökonomie*). However, in the face of considerable asset values that are usually contested, this should be closely checked in each individual case – of course, in the authoritative dimension of truth and materiality (see 4.5.3).

In any case, it is the judge only, not the expert (*Sachverständiger*), who may execute judicial discretionary power (*richterliches Ermessen*). This is also important with a view to time-consuming and costly expert opinions and necessarily comprises the valuation methods to be used (e.g., for risk markup commonly a capital asset pricing model, CAPM).[137] Expert opinions as well as the experts themselves are fully subject to the imperative of truth. The judge himself is limited in his discretionary power. As far as the estimate is permissible according to German law § 287 ZPO (see 5.5.3),[138] he is obliged to make use of all ways available to him to gain insight, and he has to make the "actual foundations of his estimate and its analysis" explicit in his decision in an objectively verifiable way.[139] It is not sufficient to refer to abstract, general criteria for his judgement.[140] For foundations for his estimate (so-called connecting facts, *Anknüpfungstatsachen*), he should make particular use of conclusive business documents; e.g., the accounts and the profit and loss calculations of the corporations' – audited – financial reporting as well as – digitally kept – inventories and books (§§ 238-240 HGB, see on § 245 HGB: above in 4.4.1).

---

[136] See above 4.10.2 and below 7.6.3 on reasonable certainty.

[137] See 5.5.5. See for an exemplary critique LG München I, 31.07.2015 (5 HK O 16371/13 – *MAN SE*) BeckRS 2015, 13240 (ZIP 2015, 2124), B.II.1.b.(2), also LG München I, 08.02.2017 (SHK 7347/15) <openJur 2021, 6875>, from recital 117. Cf. OLG München, 17.07.2014 (31 Wx 407/13) ZIP 2014, 1589; OLG Düsseldorf, 28.08.2014 (I-26 W 9/12) <openJur 2014, 22517> (about IDW-Standards: ZIP 2014, 2388). On empirical determination of the market risk premium: OLG Karlsruhe, 23.07.2015 (12a W 4/15) <openJur 2015, 19254>; to calculate the beta factor: OLG Karlsruhe, 13.05.2013 (12 W 77/08 (13)) <openJur 2013, 34634> (*ABB AG*; BB 2013, 2544).

[138] Cf. BGH, 01.04.2021 (I ZR 9/18) MDR 201, 895, <openJur 2021, 34754> recital 65.

[139] BGH, 17.11.2010 (XII ZR 170/09) <openJur 2011, 13374>, FamRZ 2011, 183, 2. headnote and recital 34, BGH, 02.02.2011 (XII ZR 185/08) BGHZ 188, 249, <openJur 2011, 94711>; cf. BGH, 10.04.2025 (III ZR 431/23) <juris.de> no. NJRE001607107 (review due to violation of laws of thought – *Verstoß gegen Denkgesetze*).

[140] BGH, 16.06.1992 (VI ZR 264/91) VersR 1992, 1410-1411. Cf. BGH, 08.12.1987 (VI ZR 53/87) BGHZ 102, 322, BGH, 17.10.2001 (IV ZR 205/00) NJW-RR 2002, 166, <openJur 2010, 5598>.

The foundation of the estimate must be presented and proved by the party bearing the burden of producing evidence (*Darlegungslast*) and the burden of proof (*Beweislast*). This may be done by presenting conclusive documents (e.g., attested annual financial statement). The basis of the estimate must comprise all measurement factors essential for the valuation of the company (share, financial instrument).[141] On this basis of facts, necessary estimates are to be made – of course, sustainably and with prudence. Any estimate should be as close to reality as possible[142] (see 4.10.2). Rounding must not falsify the results. Probabilities should be recognised according to the law of evidence (*Beweisrecht*), but must not lead to a haphazard estimate.[143] In any case, facts must form the material basis from which adequate judgement and reasoning follow (see 5.5.3). With this, it is possible to implement what practical reason in general and its legal order demand for adequate conflict resolution in an individual case.

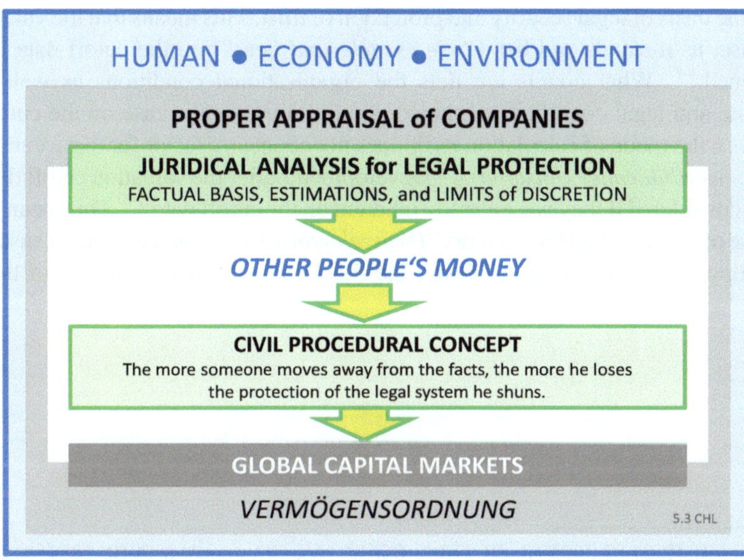


**Fig. 5.3** Juridical analysis of the economy and protection through the civil procedural concept

[141] See also below 5.6.3.

[142] BGH, 16.06.1992 (VI ZR 264/91) VersR 1992, 1410-1411.

[143] Cf. § 294 ZPO (prima facie evidence – *Glaubhaftmachung*) and § 286(1) ZPO (full proof – *Vollbeweis*). Fundamentally on probability calculation and value theory Luttermann (1998) pp. 229-233.

### 5.6.3 Guideline for Implementation and Examination

We may therefore set down for the practical design and examination of the valuation of a company or its assets (financial instruments, appraisal of business): Careful analysis of the past and the present of the company are in focus (see 5.5.3). It is "the central point of departure" also for prognostications, in particular for "attainable" surpluses (*erzielbare Überschüsse*);[144] thus, the future may be included with prudence. But with the imperative of truth and reference to facts there are material limits within civil law (esp. civil procedure law, see also 4.10.2): This is the basis of any valuation, which also includes all forecasts (*Prognosen*) and estimates (*Schätzungen*, see 5.5.2). This includes essential aspects being substantiated and expressed sustainably. The trial judge himself is obliged to state the factual foundation of his estimate and its analysis in a manner that is objectively verifiable.[145] It is about an "objective basis" in the circumstances given on the valuation cutoff date[146] (see 5.6.5).

Valuation is principally tied to a cutoff date (cutoff date principle, *Stichtagsprinzip*). This is the basis of legal security and protection of trust. This means that the value of the enterprise, as it stands and lies (*"wie es steht und liegt"*) on the cutoff date is to be determined:[147] What counts are thus the organisational conditions as well as the economic and legal conditions of the corporation that are the case on the cutoff date (*Stichtag*); the mode of calculation itself does not count as a factor for the accumulation of value (*wertbildender Umstand*).[148] Developments after the valuation cutoff date may only be considered if they were already inherent on the cutoff date.[149] This means that in the sense of the so-called "root theory" (*Wurzeltheorie*) it is practically about sustainable connecting facts (*Anknüpfungspunkte*, see 5.5.3). For the determination of the asset

[144] On this BGH, 21.07.2003 (II ZB 17/01) BGHZ 156, 57, <openJur 2010, 10341>. See also BGH, 29.09.2015 (II ZB 23/14) BGHZ 207, 114, <openJur 2016, 126>, BGH, 12.01.2016 (II ZB 25/14) BGHZ 208, 265, <openJur 2016, 5477>, BGH, 21.02.2023 (II ZB 12/21) BGHZ 236, 180, <openJur 2023, 4380>, BGH, 31.01.2024 (II ZB 5/22), ZIP 2024, 1070, <openJur 2024, 4211>.

[145] BGH, 04.07.2013 (III ZR 52/12) NJW-RR 2014, 492, <openJur 2013, 31338> recital 93.

[146] BGH, 20.01.2022 (III ZR 194/19) NJW-RR 2022, 411, <openJur 2022, 4100> recital 28. See Luttermann (2023b) recital 14.

[147] See on the whole issue (with further references) BGH, 29.09.2015 (II ZB 23/14) BGHZ 207, 114, <openJur 2016, 126> esp. recital 48. Cf. BGH, 21.07.2003 (II ZB 17/01) BGHZ 156, 57, NJW 2003, 3272, 3273, <openJur 2010, 10341> recital 23.

[148] See BGH, previous footnote: <openJur 2016, 126> recitals 47-51.

[149] BGH, 08.11.2017 (XII ZR 108/16) NJW 2018, 61, <openJur 2018, 4049> recital 42, BGH, 05.12.2018 (XII ZR 116/17) MDR 2019, 294, <openJur 2019, 200> recital 36.

value (*Vermögenswert*) over the net asset value (*Substanzwert*) on the cutoff date the transferable part of the goodwill value (*ideeller Geschäftswert*) on the cutoff date is also considered.[150] As a rule, the data from the financial statements of the last three to five years may form the basis of the valuation.[151]

Of course, for necessary estimates as well as generally for reference to the future it can always be said: The further away the target of prognostications lies (the more complex they are), the more they divert from facts, that is from the present (past, substance analysis), the vaguer the enterprise becomes, with legal relevance disappearing. Such untenable valuations do not deserve the quality mark of the law, which is precisely what the actors of such estimates or prognostications (valuations) are attempting to evade (see Fig. 5.3 with 5.2.4, 8.3.3). The presentation and the judgement are therefore based on adequacy, factually and scientifically secured, specifically in terms of time, space, and transparency, sustainable in the imperative of truth (see 5.6.4). This materially legal concept designed according to civil procedure law disciplines company valuation and protects those affected. As a whole, this is a human deed of applied reason, which may work towards general prosperity (creation of real value).[152]

### *5.6.4 Due Diligence (Liability) and Appraisal Report*

In valuation law (*Bewertungsrecht*), the imperative of truth characterises proper company valuation, as shown along with sustainability as verifiability (see 5.2.4). At the same time, this denotes the diligence required in commercial intercourse (*"die im Verkehr erforderliche Sorgfalt"*, see in German law, e.g., § 276(2) BGB and § 347 HGB; cf. § 93(1)(1) AktG, §§ 43(1), 64(2) GmbHG, see below 6.4). This due diligence is generally to be exercised by corporate directors and also by the appraiser (*Gutachter*, see § 410 ZPO: swearing-in). It is also the basis of liability. Liability is modifiable within the legal boundaries (e.g. § 276(3) BGB). The – financial – expert

[150] See on valuation of a medical office BGH, 22.11.2017 (XII ZB 230/17) NZG 2018, 396, <openJur 2018, 4220> recital 13 (with further references). See affirmatively BGH, 25.09.2024 (XII ZB 508/23) NJW 2025, 60, <openJur 2024, 10498> recital 27.

[151] BGH, 22.11.2017 (XII ZB 230/17), ibid., previous footnote.

[152] See chapter 4 (4.1: real financial reporting), and for further development chapters 8 and 9.

must not act carelessly, e.g. investigating negligently in the sense of a lack of conscience (§ 826 BGB, e.g., haphazard data).[153] In the case of a flawed expert opinion a third party may be drawn into the domain of protection with regard to liability law.[154] In a sustainable perspective individual consideration as a working field expands to the complete picture (the whole, *zum Ganzen*).

Climate change with the issue of sustainability emphasises and extends in particular entrepreneurial due diligence (*Sorgfaltspflichten*) through regulation and jurisdiction. This reaches the human corporation globally via the capital markets in their elementary financing function as well the economy and society as a whole (see 9.1). What gains particular prominence are human rights (human rights due diligence) and environmental protection (environmental due diligence), while both also merge into one (e.g., working conditions, drinking water). This materialises into manifold due diligence for those who are entrepreneurially responsible, e.g., in supply chains (see the German Supply Chain Due Diligence Act of 2021)[155] and also leads to questions of liability. The "green" paradigm shift opens up a field for all actors, accordingly especially for the financing and valuation of corporations. Their good management, oriented towards sustainable economic activity, is served by a concept of diligence for entrepreneurial decision making.[156] Moderate requirements are imperative in the sense of sustainability (see 5.2.4). What should be taken particular note of are, e.g., advisory or audit contracts, explanations (*Erklärungen*) and audit certificates (*Testat*) by auditors.[157]

Valuation (creation of value) and corporate management (supervision, consulting, surveying) must be conceived and designed holistically, in particular for the human corporation (see 5.3.4). What remains in general is: Deficiencies of an appraisal report (*Bewertungsgutachten*)[158] must be judged according to the

[153] See, e.g., BGH, 26.06.2001 (X ZR 231/99) NJW 2001, 3115, <openJur 2010, 8451> recital 31, BGH, 15.12.2020 (XI ZB 24/16) BGHZ 228, 133, <openJur 2021, 6414>. In the valuation of real estate and buildings: BGH, 24.09.1991 (VI ZR 293/90) NJW 1991, 3282, 3283; cf. BGH, 20.05.2003 (VI ZR 312/02) NJW 2003, 2825. On valuation report BGH, 10.10.2013 (III ZR 345/12) BGHZ 198, 265, <openJur 2013, 41589>, BGH, 25.06.2020 (III ZR 119/19) NJW 2020, 2471, <openJur 2020, 32195>. Intentional delay of insolvency: BGH, 27.07.2021 (II ZR 164/20) NJW 2021, 3330, <openJur 2021, 34121>.

[154] BGH, 14.06.2012 (IX ZR 145/11) BGHZ 193, 297, <lexetius.com/2012,2653>. Cf. BGH, 14.11.2000 (X ZR 203/98) NJW 2001, 514, BGH, 20.04.2004 (X ZR 250/02) BGHZ 159, 1, <openJur 2012, 56786>. BGH, 29.06.2023 (IX ZR 56/22) NJW 2023, 2775 <openJur 2023, 7996>. See no restriction necessary in the case BGH, 05.03.2015 (IX ZR 133/14) BGHZ 204, 231, <openJur 2015, 6275>.

[155] *Gesetz über die unternehmerischen Sorgfaltspflichten in Lieferketten* (so-called *Lieferkettensorgfaltspflichtengesetz, LkSG*), 16.07.2021, BGBl I 2021, 2959. Of course, it must not escalate bureaucratically. Cf. above 4.2.4, 4.2.5 and 5.3.5.

[156] Luttermann, L. (2022) and (2024). See above 4.12.

[157] BGH, 21.11.2018 (VII ZR 3/18) <openJur 2019, 2285> (for investment products), BGH, 12.03.2020 (VII ZR 236/19) NJW-RR 2020, 1049, <openJur 2020, 5531> (immoral damage).

[158] Objections to an expert opinion also possible (only) in the second instance: BGH, 10.04.2025 (III ZR 431/23) <juris.de> no. NJRE001607107.

imperative of truth and should therefore be avoided. The aspects mentioned above provide guidance here (see also 5.6.5). The concept of materiality (*Wesentlichkeit*), shaped by accounting law (see 4.5.3) and forming the general basis of valuation law (see 5.5), should be adhered to in practice.[159] The significance of an error (e.g., determination of certain calculation factors) must always be weighted within the whole picture. An error falsifying the final result is always significant (*wesentlich*). If other errors that have an opposite effect of approximately the same amount offset this error, it is regarded as negligible.[160] But note: In general, it is the situation in each individual case (*Einzelfall*) that counts.

### 5.6.5 Judicial Practice in the Law of Evidence

Valuation and thus any appraisal report must be conceived with regard to their legal recognition in civil law proceedings through the trial judge (*Tatrichter*, see 5.5.5). Basically it is true that facts constitute the basis of a proper valuation of companies (shares, financial instruments) under the imperative of truth (*Wahrheit*) and clarity (*Klarheit*), id est in practical implementation: sustainability as verifiability (see 5.2.4). This basis must be provided by the expert (*Sachverständiger*).[161] The judge determines the topic of proof (*Beweisthema*, § 284 ZPO) and then in the final instance acknowledges the result of the evidentiary hearing (*Beweisaufnahme*, i.e., expert appraisal): He judges the facts from a legal point of view, orders the facts (actual circumstances) significant for the valuation of the company (share) according to the relevant legal norms, gives an overall appraisal and his verdict (see 5.5.5).

The determination of the adequate value of the corporation is the very own task of the judge,[162] not to be delegated under the stipulations of civil proceedings, and must be consistently fulfilled; in litigation cases (e.g., SpruchG), the principle of official investigation (*Amtsermittlung*) comes into consideration. The trial judge has to determine the facts and select and employ the suitable mode of valuation.[163] Overall,

[159] See for guidance above 5.6.3 and 5.6.4 as well as 4.5.3, 4.5.7 and 4.6.5. Basically Großfeld and Luttermann (2005) recitals 335-337, 1780.

[160] BGH, 14.07.1986 (II ZR 249/85) NJW-RR 1987, 21, 22. Cf. BGH, 01.10.1997 (XII ZR 269/95) WM 1998, 628 (manifest inequity).

[161] On objections to an expert opinion of the court-appointed expert (*Gerichtsgutachten*) BGH, 10.04.2025 (III ZR 431/23) <juris.de> no. NJRE001607107.

[162] See BGH, 31.01.2024 (II ZB 5/22) ZIP 2024, 1070, <openJur 2024, 4211> recital 63 (in detail 63-70): The court (*Beschwerdegericht*, court of appeal) does not need to seek expert advice when reviewing the compensation of minority shareholders. BGH, 21.02.2023 (II ZB 12/21) BGHZ 236, 180, <openJur 2023, 4380>, from recital 27.

[163] BGH, 04.07.2013 (III ZR 52/12) NJW-RR 2014, 492, <openJur 2013, 31338> recital 93, BGH, 21.02.2023 (II ZB 12/21) BGHZ 236, 180, <openJur 2023, 4380>, from recital 27.

complacencies are to be avoided. The expert should only be heard for assistance,[164] if need be as a consultant (*Fachberater*, § 144(1)(1) ZPO),[165] through concrete order for evidence (*Beweisbeschluss*, § 359 ZPO).[166] The trial judge (*Tatrichter, erkennender Richter*) is to present the actual basis of his valuation or estimate along with the analysis (§§ 286, 287 ZPO) in an objectively verifiable way, making use of administrative and evaluative discretionary powers on his own.[167] By general standards, the valuation by the trial judge, thus the German Federal Supreme Court, can only be examined as to whether it violates laws of thought (*Denkgesetze*) or experiential propositions (*Erfahrungssätze*) or is otherwise based on legally erroneous considerations (*rechtsfehlerhafte Erwägungen*).[168] Whether the valuation method selected by the trial judge or a mode of calculation selected within it contradict the legal valuation objectives is a legal question (*Rechtsfrage*).[169]

Accordingly, for the valuation in the individual case, the following applies: The court (i.e. the judge, bench) decides according to its own free conviction (*Überzeugung*) and gives reasons why it deems an actual claim to be true or not true (§ 286(1) ZPO). It is not absolute, unalterable certainty or near-certain probability that is required. The Federal Supreme Court (*Bundesgerichtshof*), the highest German civil court, specifies this – according to human nature (limits, see 4.5.6) and the spirit of the law – in the following way (trans.): A degree of certainty useful for

[164] BGH, 04.07.2013 (III ZB 52/12), ibid., recitals 93 and 124.

[165] Cf. Deutscher Bundestag, *Begründung* BReg, 09.10.2019, Bundestags-Drucksache 19/13828, pp. 18-19: *Das Gericht kann einen Sachverständigen als Fachberater hinzuziehen, um sich damit "die erforderliche Sachkunde zum richtigen Verständnis des Parteivorbringens und zur Erfassung des Sachverhalts zu verschaffen"*.

[166] See Luttermann (2023b) recitals 53-54.

[167] BGH, 04.07.2013 (III ZR 52/12) NJW-RR 2014, 492, <openJur 2013, 31338> recitals 93 and 124 (with reference to German law § 319(1)(2) BGB).

[168] BGH, 04.07.2013 (III ZR 52/12) NJW-RR 2014, 492, <openJur 2013, 31338> recital 93. Cf. BGH, 05.12.2018 (XII ZR 116/17) MDR 2019, 294, <openJur 2019, 200> recital 27, BGH, 23.09.2021 (I ZB 20/21) NJW 2022, 393, <openJur 2021, 44088> recital 70. BGH, 10.04.2025 (III ZR 431/23) <juris.de> no. NJRE001607107.

[169] BGH, 15.09.2020 (II ZB 6/20) ECLI:DE:BGH:2020:150920BIIZB6.20.0, recital 13.

practical life that silences doubts would be sufficient,[170] doubts need not be completely excluded;[171] this reaffirms case law as a legal obligation in general, also according to European law.[172] This is materially the demand that the expert (valuator) and his appraisal report have to fulfill with conclusive evidence. To a limited extent, relief measures may take effect depending on the individual case[173] (see 5.5.3). Overall, questions of valuation present themselves as a legal domain just as verifiability shows itself as sustainability (and vice versa, see 5.2.4).

## 5.7 Sustainable Global Perspectives

The valuation of a company (or a share, bond), the appraisal of business (assets) as an object of a legal relationship is a legal act (*Rechtsakt*). This characterises the valuation of companies (*Unternehmensbewertung*) as a legal domain internationally. The issue is assets and liabilities (financial instruments), protection from unlawful transfers of wealth (assets, see 5.2.1), the basis of entrepreneurial freedom and fair competition, financing and liability of the corporation. All in all, the issue, therefore, is a good order of assets as a legal concept internationally. The human corporation with its financial function (see chapter 3) is fundamental for establishing a sustainable economy for the prosperity of humans and the environment (human corporation, see chapters 2, 8). Valuation issues are essential in that process of transformation as well as generally (appraisal, revaluation). They accompany corporate directors and corporate governance in manifold ways over the life span of a corporation – as the epitome of responsible, good entrepreneurship (*Verantwortungskultur*).[174]

What has become tangible with the world debt crisis, in which huge speculative losses caused privately by the "numbers game", id est valuation games,[175] are socialised (see chapter 6), is the following: The essential unity of freedom (private autonomy) and responsibility (liability) has been disrupted. For the unity of freedom

---

[170] BGH, 28.01.2003 (VI ZR 139/02) VersR 2003, 474, 475, confirmed in BGH, 04.11.2003 (VI ZR 28/03) VersR 2004, 118, BGH, 08.07.2008 (VI ZR 274/07) <lexetius.com/2008,1875> recital 11, BGH, 16.04.2013 (VI ZR 44/12) NJW 2014, 71, <openJur 2013, 22510> recital 13, BGH, 01.10.2019 (VI ZR 164/18) NJW 2020, 1072, <openJur 2019, 34209> recitals 13-14. See above 4. 6.4 (with the original quote in German). In the VW AG proceedings (so-called "diesel scandal"): BGH, 29.07.2021 (VI ZR 1118/20) BGHZ 231, 1, <openJur 2021, 34114> recital 23.

[171] BVerfG, 18.01.2001 (1 BvR 1273/96) NJW 2001, 1639, 1640, BGH, 17.2.1970 (III ZR 139/67) BGHZ 53, 245, 255-56; established jurisdiction, e.g., BGH, 12.02.2008 (VI ZR 221/06) NJW 2008, 1381, BGH, 01.10.2019 (VI ZR 164/18) NJW 2020, 1072, <openJur 2019, 34209> recitals 13-14, BGH, 29.07.2021 (VI ZR 1118/20) BGHZ 231, 1, <openJur 2021, 34114> recital 23.

[172] Cf. BVerfG, 04.03.2021 (2 BvR 1161/19) ECLI:DE:BVerfG:2021:rk20210304.2bvr116119, recital 55 and ECJ, 06.10.1982 (C-283/81 – *CILFIT*, IT) EU:C:1982:335, recital 14.

[173] On the minor burden of proof under § 287 ZPO, e.g.: BGH, 23.06.2020 (VI ZR 435/19) VersR 2021, 1497 recital 13, <openJur 2020, 32203> recital 18.

[174] See above 1.1, 1.3.1 and 2.2.2, below Part IV (Integrity, with chapters 6, 7) and chapter 9.

[175] See above 4.5.1 (with 2.4.2), below esp. 6.6.2, 6.8.1 and 9.8.

and responsibility (see chapter 7), necessary globally for the sustainable transformation of economy and corporate business, a legally effective basis is required. This is real financial reporting (accounting law as, e.g., harmonised at the European level, see chapter 4) as the basis for a general valuation law: ethically founded with fairness and conceived more broadly as the material core of a responsibly designed *Vermögensordnung* (order of assets, see chapter 8).[176] The primate of the law holds, in particular under the rule of law transnationally also for an international investment law.[177] This is where manifold relations come into play, with valuation practice and jurisdiction also being questionable positions.[178] This has to be clarified in legal comparison, in the final instance in a global system of legal protection (*internationaler Rechtsschutz*).[179]

Climate change inevitably underscores this challenge. The green paradigm change is comprehensive (see chapter 1): for the protection of humans and the environment, jurisprudence and regulation, which records corporate financial reports; relevant sustainable information, audited data on emissions and supply chains etc. is required (cf. assurance services, see 5.6.4). Global goals shape a global community and joint solutions. In the European Union, e.g., the European Court of Justice does its work and carries the principle of mutual trust "accorded by the Member States to their respective legal systems and judicial institutions";[180] this is supported by the principle of subsidiarity (Art. 5(3) TEU), which has to be taken into consideration (see 4.11.3). Otherwise national and international law (*Völkerrecht*) is applicable.[181] The imperative of fidelity (*Treuegebot*), of "fair and equitable treatment" is universal, for without fidelity no human intercourse is possible (Aristotle): the culture of responsibility.[182] This can sustain valuations, the human corporation and cooperative structures among climate partners (see chapters 8 and 9).

Accordingly, valuation relations (*Bewertungsverhältnisse*) are subject to the primate of the law: The law of financial reporting (accounting, auditing) and valuation (*Bewertungsrecht*) is elementary for good corporate governance. In the

[176] Luttermann (2015a), see above 4.8 to 4.12 and overall chapters 8 and 9. Basically Luttermann (2012a).

[177] E.g., Luttermann (2016).

[178] E.g., discounted cash flow (DCF) methods, cf. Mulford, Comiskey (2005), Jennergren (2023), *Ramcell, Inc. v. Alltel Corp.*, C.A. No. 2019-0601-PAF (Del. Ch. July 1, 2022), *HBK Master Fund v. Pivotal Software, Inc.*, C.A. No. 2020-0165-KSJM (Del. Ch. Aug. 14, 2023); Gleißner, Kamarás (2023): simulation-based valuation.

[179] See above 4.10. Comparative juridical analysis, e.g.: Luttermann (2003) § 264 HGB recitals 16-169. Takahashi, Fleischer, Baum (2013).

[180] ECJ, 13.05.2015 (C-536/13 – *Gazprom OAO*, LT) ECLI:EU:C:2015:316, recital 37 (arbitration).

[181] ECJ, 20.06.2022 (C-700/20 – *London Steam-Ship Owners'Mutual Insurance Association Limited*, EN) ECLI:EU:C:2022:488, recital 45.

[182] See above 1.1, 1.3.1. Altogether Luttermann (2015b) 274, 279-281.

final instance, what counts is control by independent judges (legal protection). For numbers (formulas) do not prove anything. We need to break through their abstractness for an adequate order of assets (*Vermögensordnung*, see chapter 8), grasping actual life conditions. In any case, a proper valuation is based on the evidence of facts (substance). The further an appraiser (valuator, accountant, auditor etc.) departs from this (prognostic horison), the less the legal order will offer to him protection (from liability etc.).[183] The civil procedural concept provides a systematic and material standard for this with the imperative of truth and sustainability. It is by this that we separate arbitrariness from the law.[184] This is how we substantially establish a better, sustainable world for ourselves and future generations.

## References


Ammon, L. (1998). Rechtsprechungsübersicht zum aktienrechtlichen Spruchverfahren. *Praxis der Freiwilligen Gerichtsbarkeit (FGPrax), 4*, 121–124.

Belting, H. (2011). *Florence and Baghdad: Renaissance art and Arab science*. The Belknap Press of Harvard University.

Bensadon, D., & Praquin, N. (Eds.). (2016). *IFRS in a global world*. Springer.

Brealey, R. A., & Myers, S. C. (2003). *Capital investment and valuation*. McGraw Hill.

Brown, L. (Ed.). (1993). *The new shorter Oxford English dictionary on historical principles* (2 Vols.). Clarendon Press.

du Plessis, J. J., Großfeld, B., Luttermann, C., Saenger, I., Sandrock, O., & Casper, M. (2017). *German corporate governace in international and European context* (3rd ed.). Springer Verlag.

Emmerich, V., & Sonnenschein, J. (1997). *Konzernrecht* (5th ed.). CH Beck Verlag.

Fleischer, H., & Hüttemann, R. (Eds.). (2024). *Rechtshandbuch Unternehmensbewertung* (3rd ed.). CH Beck Verlag.

Gleißner, W., & Kamarás, E. (2023). *Company valuation using the DCF method and CAPM: You shouldn't trust the result.* https://ssrn.com/abstract=4396512 (accessed: 27.08.2025).

Goethe, J. W. von (1833). *Maxime und Refektionen*. Hamburg edition (14th ed. 2005, Vol. XII).

Grimm, J., & Grimm, W.. (1889). *Deutsches Wörterbuch* (Vol. 13), here: dtv München 1991.

Großfeld, B., Egger, U., & Tönnes, W. A. (2020). *Recht der Unternehmensbewertung* (9th ed.). RWS Verlag.

Großfeld, B., & Luttermann, C. (2005). *Bilanzrecht (Accounting Law): Die Rechnungslegung in Jahresabschluß und Konzernabschluß nach Handelsrecht und Steuerrecht, Europarecht und IAS/IFRS* (4th ed.). CF Müller Verlag.

Heigel, L. M. (2007). *Unternehmensbewertung zwischen Recht und Markt*. Peter Lang.

Hering, T., Olbrich, M., & Rollberg, R. (2010). Zur angelsächsischen Bewertungstheorie als Mitursache der Finanzkrise. In F. Keuper & F. Neumann (Eds.), *Corporate governance, risk management and compliance* (pp. 29–43). SpringerGabler.

Huan-Chang, C. (1911). *The economic principles of Confucius and his school* (2 Vols.). Columbia University New York.

Jennergren, L. P. (2023). *Which purpose of firm valuation in litigation?* The HQ example. https://ssrn.com/abstract=4569283 (accessed: 27.08.2025).


[183] See above 5.6.2 with Fig. 5.3 and chapter 4.

[184] See above 4.10.2. Basically Luttermann (2004) and (2007a).

Jones, M. J. (Ed.). (2011). *Creative accounting, fraud and international accounting scandals*. Wiley & Sons.

Kaaya, I. D. (2015). The international financial reporting standards (IFRS) and value relevance: A review of empirical evidence. *Journal of Finance and Accounting, 3*, 37–46.

Koller, T., Goedhart, M., & Wessels, D. (2020). *Valuation: Measuring and managing the value of companies* (7th ed.). Wiley & Sons.

Korsgaard, C. M. (2008). In J. Raz (Ed.), *The practice of value* (pp. 63–85). Clarendon Press.

Levitt, A. (1998). *The "numbers game"*, speech of 28 Sept 1998 at NYU Center for Law and Business. https://www.sec.gov/news/speech/speecharchive/1998/spch220.txt (accessed: 27.08.2025).

Luttermann, C. (1997). Der Abfindungsanspruch außenstehender Aktionäre. *Juristenzeitung (JZ), 52*, 1181–1184.

Luttermann, C. (1998). *Unternehmen, Kapital und Genußrechte: Eine Studie über Grundlagen der Unternehmensfinanzierung und zum internationalen Kapitalmarktrecht*. Mohr Siebeck.

Luttermann, C. (1999a). *Bilanzrecht in den USA und internationale Konzernrechnungslegung*. Mohr Siebeck.

Luttermann, C. (1999b). Zum Börsenkurs als gesellschaftsrechtliche Bewertungsgrundlage. *Zeitschrift für Wirtschaftsrecht (ZIP), 20*, 45–52.

Luttermann, C. (2000). Bewertungsrecht im Internetzeitalter: Über Finanzkommunikation, Börsenkurs, Wahrscheinlichkeit und "virtuelle Aktiengesellschaft". *Die Aktiengesellschaft (AG), 45*, 459–469.

Luttermann, C. (2001). Der "durchschnittliche" Börsenkurs bei Barabfindung von Aktionären und Verschmelzungswertrelation. *Zeitschrift für Wirtschaftsrecht (ZIP), 22*, 869–872.

Luttermann, C. (2003). In B. Kropff & J. Semler (Eds.), *Münchener Kommentar zum Aktiengesetz* (Vol. 5/1, 2nd ed.). CH Beck Verlag.

Luttermann, C. (2004). Bilanzwahrheit international: Die Rechtsanbindung von Rechnungslegung und Wirtschaftsprüfung. *Zeitschrift für vergleichende Rechtswissenschaft (ZVglRWiss), 103*, 18–30.

Luttermann, C. (2006a). Rechtsnatur und Praxis des Abfindungsanspruchs (§ 305 AktG) als gesetzliches Schuldverhältnis. *Neue Zeitschrift für Gesellschaftsrecht (NZG), 9*, 816–819.

Luttermann, C. (2006b). Unternehmenskontrolle und Bilanzmanipulation nach anglo-amerikanischen Mustern (IAS/IFRS und U.S. "GAAP"). *Die Wirtschaftsprüfung (WPg), 59*, 778–786.

Luttermann, C. (2007a). Normenklarheit im Steuerrecht und "unbestimmte" Rechtsbegriffe? *Finanz-Rundschau (FR), 89*, 18–23.

Luttermann, C. (2007b). Zur Rechtspraxis internationaler Unternehmensbewertung bei der Publikums-Aktiengesellschaft. *Neue Zeitschrift für Gesellschaftsrecht (NZG), 10*, 611–618.

Luttermann, C. (2008a). Juristische Person, Konzern und Existenzvernichtungshaftung. *Juristische Arbeitsblätter (JA), 40*, 833–838.

Luttermann, C. (2008b). Kreditversicherung (Credit Default Swaps): Vertrag, Restrukturierung und Regulierung (Hedge-Fonds, Rating, Schattenbanken). *Recht der Internationalen Wirtschaft (RIW), 54*, 737–743.

Luttermann, C. (2008c). Über Vertragsverhältnisse und Bewertungsrecht: Geld, Zeitwert und internationaler Goldstandard. *Finanz-Betrieb (FB), 9*, 193–204.

Luttermann, C. (2009). "Fair Value": Mythos, Methoden und Maß international. *Recht der Internationalen Wirtschaft (RIW), 55*, 1–11.

Luttermann, C. (2010a). Juristische Analyse von Ökonomie, Staat und Gesellschaft. *Zeitschrift für Rechtspolitik (ZRP), 43*, 1–4.

Luttermann, C. (2010b). Bilanzregeln und Finanzkrise: Die Besteuerung nach Leistungsfähigkeit und Bilanzwahrheit als Beweismaß. *Steuer und Wirtschaft (StuW), 87/40*, 346–355.

Luttermann, C. (2010c). Die Besteuerung bei aktienrechtlichen Zwangsausschlüssen. *Finanz-Rundschau (FR), 92*, 193–200.

Luttermann, C. (2011a). Die Finanzaufsicht des Vatikans, Zentralbanken und Reform internationaler Währungsunordnung. *Recht der Internationalen Wirtschaft (RIW), 57*, 214–220.

Luttermann, C. (2011b). AG: Beherrschungs- und Gewinnabführungsvertrag, Abfindung, Referenzzeitraum, Vermögensverschiebung. *Entscheidungen zum Wirtschaftsrecht (EWiR), 26*, 619–620.

Luttermann, C. (2012a). Internationale Vermögensordnung, Insolvenzrecht und Schulden(transfer)-systeme. *Zeitschrift für Wirtschaftsrecht (ZIP), 33*, 305–313.

Luttermann, C. (2012b). Wirtschaftsstrafrecht: Zur prozessualen Lösung von Bewertungsfragen bei Vermögensdelikten als Freiheitsbasis. *Zeitschrift für Wirtschafts- und Steuerstrafrecht (wistra), 31*, 251–258.

Luttermann, C. (2013). Recht als praktizierte Ethik und unternehmerische Verantwortungskultur. In E. Weber (Ed.), *Albert Schweitzer – Hundert Jahre Menschlichkeit: Spital Lambarene (1913–2013)* (pp. 74–76). Deutscher Hilfsverein für das Albert-Schweitzer-Spital in Lambarene e.V.

Luttermann, C. (2015a). Corporate law and the *Vermoegensordnung* (order of assets). *European Business Law Review (EBLR), 26*, 31–48.

Luttermann, C. (2015b). Über Idee und Methodik eines internationalen Investitionsschutzes (Vermögensordnung) durch Privatrecht und Völkerrecht. *Zeitschrift für Europarecht, Internationales Privatrecht und Rechtsvergleichung (ZfRV), 56*, 274–282.

Luttermann, C. (2016). German and Russian direct investment under the rule of international law. *Zeitschrift für Internationales Wirtschaftsrecht (IWRZ), 1*, 90–95.

Luttermann, C. (2017). Reform der Wirtschaftsprüferausbildung, zivilprozessuales Bewertungskonzept und Zukunft des Berufsstandes. *Der Betrieb (DB), 71*, 137–144.

Luttermann, C. (2019). Die herrschende Meinung und Bewertungsrecht für Unternehmer. In W. A. Tönnes (Ed.), *Festschrift for Bernhard Großfeld* (pp. 245–256). C.F. Müller.

Luttermann, C. (2021). Grüner Paradigmenwechsel für Unternehmensfinanzierung, Vermögensanlage und Bewertungsrecht. *Recht der Internationalen Wirtschaft (RIW), 67*, 191–200.

Luttermann, C. (2023a). Unternehmensbewertung im Spannungsfeld von Rechts- und Wirtschaftswissenschaft. In K. Petersen, C. Zwirner, & G. Zimney (Eds.), *Handbuch Unternehmensbewertung* (3rd ed., pp. 163–202). Bundesanzeiger Verlag.

Luttermann, C. (2023b). Juristische Anforderungen an eine ordnungsmäßige Unternehmensbewertung und an ein Bewertungsgutachten. In K. Petersen, C. Zwirner, & G. Zimney (Eds.), *Handbuch Unternehmensbewertung* (3rd ed., pp. 653–682). Bundesanzeiger Verlag.

Luttermann, C., & Geißler, S. (2012). Haftungsfragen transnationaler Konzernfinanzierung (cash pooling) und das Bilanzstatut der Gesellschaft. *Praxis des Internationalen Privat- und Verfahrensrechts (IPRax), 32*, 55–62.

Luttermann, C., & Geißler, S. (2013). Rechtsbasis und Praxis einer Kultur der Unternehmenssanierung. *Zeitschrift für das gesamte Insolvenzrecht (ZinsO), 16*, 1381–1386.

Luttermann, C., & Luttermann, K. (2020). *Sprachenrecht für die Europäische Union.* Mohr Siebeck.

Luttermann, L. (2022). Klimawandel und Business Judgement: Nachhaltige Finanzierung als unternehmerisches Sorgfaltskonzept. *Recht der Internationalen Wirtschaft (RIW), 68*, 809–820.

Luttermann, L. (2024). Unternehmensführung: Nachhaltige Finanzinformation (U.S. SEC Climate Rules/EU), Wertschöpfung und Bankenfinanzierung. *Recht der Internationalen Wirtschaft (RIW), 70*, 410–422.

Matschke, M. J., Brösel, G., & Toll, C. (2024). *Unternehmensbewertung: Funktionen, Methoden, Grundsätze* (5th ed.). SpringerGabler.

Mechelli, A., & Cimini, R. (2021). The effect of corporate governance and investor protection environments on the value relevance of new accounting standards: the case of IFRS 9 and IAS 39. *Journal of Management and Governance, 25*, 1241–1266.

Mestmäcker, E.-J. (2007). *A legal theory without law: Posner v. Hayek on economic analysis of law*. Mohr Siebeck.

Mulford, C. W., & Comiskey, E. E. (2005). *Creative cash flow reporting*. Wiley & Sons.

Palea, V. (2018). Financial reporting for sustainable development: Critical insights into IFRS implementation in the European Union. *Accounting Forum, 42*, 248–260.

Schiller, F. (1803). *Die Braut von Messina oder die feindlichen Brüder.* J. G. Cotta'sche Buchhandlung.

Smith, A. (1759/1790[6]). *The theory of moral sentiments* (6th ed.). Penguin Books, 2009.

Smith, A. (1762/1982). In Meek, Raphael and Stein (Eds.), *Lectures on jurisprudence* (Report of 1762-3 and Report of 1766). Liberty Fund.

Smith, A. (1776/1789[5]). *An inquiry into the nature and causes of the wealth of nations* (5th ed.). Bantam Classic Edition, 2003.

Takahashi, E., Fleischer, H., & Baum, H. (2013). Unternehmensbewertung im Recht der Aktiengesellschaft: Ein japanisch-deutscher Rechtsvergleich. *Zeitschrift für Japanisches Rechts (ZJapanR/J.Japan.L), 36*, 1–52.

Weil, R. L., Frank, P. B., & Evans, E. A. (2017). *Litigation services handbook: The role of the financial expert* (6th ed.). Wiley.

Wertheimer, B. T. (1998). The shareholders' appraisal remedy and how courts determine fair value. *Duke Law Journal, 47*, 613–715.

# Part IV
# Good Economy Through Integrity

# Chapter 6
# Global Climate Change for People, Investment, and Capital Markets

"But one thing is certain: there will be another of these (great speculative) episodes and yet more beyond."*

*John Kenneth Galbraith*

## Contents



**Galbraith*, A short history of financial euphoria, 1994, p. 110.



C. Luttermann, *Human Corporation for Sustainable Development*,
https://doi.org/10.1007/978-3-032-07615-1_6

## 6.1 Global Climate Change

### *6.1.1 United Nations, People, and Environment*

The International Court of Justice (ICJ, The Hague), on request of the General Assembly of the United Nations, delivered an advisory opinion on "Obligations of States in respect of Climate Change" on July 23, 2025.[1] It is a milestone in global awareness-raising, ten years after the Paris Agreement of 2015 (see 1.4.2). The Court highlights "the customary duty to prevent significant harm to the environment".[2] This duty requires States to "use all the means at [their] disposal in order to avoid activities which take place in [their] territory (…), causing significant damage to the environment of another State",[3] i.e. transboundary environmental harm, especially by anthropogenic emissions of greenhouse gases (GHG, see 1.4.2).

This principle, according to the Court, "also applies to the climate system, which is an integral and vitally important part of the environment and which must be protected for present and future generations." (intergenerational equity, trustees for humanity).[4] This establishes the imperative of intertemporal justice (*Gebot der Generationengerechtigkeit*) in the general sense worldwide for humankind. In doing so, the Court speaks of "the urgent and existential threat posed by climate change", referring to the "relevant scientific background" and designates the

[1] ICJ, Advisory Opinion, 23.07.2025 (https://www.icj-cij.org/sites/default/files/case-related/187/187-20250723-adv-01-00-en.pdf, accessed: 25.08.2025), jurisdiction in accordance with Art. 96 UN Charter and Art. 65 ICJ Statute ("legal question"). Request for an advisory opinion by the UN General Assembly, resolution 77/276 of 29.03.2023.

[2] ICJ, Advisory Opinion, 23.07.2025, ibid., paras. 134 and 172.

[3] ICJ, Advisory Opinion, 23.07.2025, ibid., para. 272, citing *Pulp Mills on the River Uruguay (Argentina v. Uruguay)*, Judgment, I.C.J. Reports 2010 (I), p. 56, para. 101.

[4] ICJ, Advisory Opinion, 23.07.2025, ibid., para. 273 with paras. 73-74, and para. 156; see below 6.1.3. Cf. German BVerfG, 29.04.2021 (1 BvR 2656), ECLI:DE:BVerfG:2021:rs20210324.1bvr265618, on this above 1.4.2.

consequences of climate change "severe and far-reaching; they affect both natural ecosystems and human populations."[5] The case in the forum of the United Nations, initiated by students, was carried out by the island nation of Vanuatu, which is particularly threatened by climate change, with the support of around 130 states. The obligations (duties) and remedies apply worldwide (see 6.1.3 and 1.2, Fig. 6.3). The Court especially addresses:

> "the obligation of prevention under customary international law in the context of 'protection of the climate system and other parts of the environment from anthropogenic emissions of greenhouse gases'. The main elements of this duty are (a) the environmental harm to be prevented and (b) due diligence as the required standard of conduct."[6]

In all of our world, it is about the community of destiny that we have already described with the term climate partners (*Klimapartner*).[7] This makes the transnational dimension tangible as a shared task. The Court, in view of the related practice of states according to customary international law,[8] "considers that the duty of States to co-operate for the protection of the environment is a rule whose customary character has been established".[9] It is important to realise: We are climate partners in a cooperative global *Vermögensordnung* (see chapters 8 and 9).[10] This includes the corporate world with all its people and markets.

### *6.1.2 The Human Factor in a Corporate World*

Human community is built on personal responsibility in the constitution of freedom (i.e. culture of responsibility, see chapters 1, 2 and 7). This applies to all people and their institutions (state, market, corporate world). It shapes the human corporation as conditio sine qua non, a human corporation – instead of depersonalisation – and its environment (see 6.1.3). The responsibility, the management of the large corporations (*Aktiengesellschaften, börsennotiert*) has long since been in the hands of the directors: thus wrote Walther Rathenau, German foreign minister in the Weimar Republic and sophisticated industrialist in 1917 on contemporary practice,[11] thereby capturing the core, set down legally in the nature of the (publicly held) corporation.

---

[5]See ICJ, Advisory Opinion, 23.07.2025, ibid., para. 73 with paras. 72-87.

[6]ICJ, Advisory Opinion, 23.07.2025, ibid., para. 273. On legal consequences see below 6.1.3.

[7]Luttermann (2022).

[8]UN General Assembly, 24.10.1970, Declaration on Principles of International Law concerning Friendly Relations and Co-operation among States in accordance with the Charter of the United Nations, A/RES/2625(XXV).

[9]ICJ, Advisory Opinion, 23.07.2025, ibid., para. 140, also paras. 301-308.

[10]Luttermann (2022), German original: *"Klimapartner einer kooperativen Weltvermögensordnung"*. See also above 1.2.

[11]Rathenau (1917) p. 13. On Walther Rathenau also in chapter 3, esp. 3.5.4.

This is characteristic of an institution that humans have created as a reproduction (*Nachbildung*) of their own nature (see 7.3.1); we refer to it as the human factor (see 6.6.2). This is authoritative for the law of the corporation, for the legal circumstances and leads the way for the human corporation as the epitome of a powerful permanent financial instrument. We can say: the universal instrument for establishing sustainable economic activity (see 6.7) and prosperity around the world that is common to us all (see chapter 8). For this, the following is essentially valid: The directors, id est in particular the executive directors, constitute the powerhouse of the corporation and, due to their decisions, they are personally responsible for good corporate governance and compliance (see chapter 7). What does this mean for practice, particularly in the face of global complexity?

Let us take an example. The German law on stock companies says in § 76-(1) *Aktiengesetz* (AktG): The management board (executive board – *Vorstand*) in the two-tier system is to direct the corporation according to its own responsibility. It is an indispensable organ of the global model of the modern corporation, the stock corporation (*Aktiengesellschaft*, AG), which as a legal person is unable to act in itself. That is why only a natural, fully legally competent person may become a member of the board of executive directors (*Vorstände*, § 76(3) AktG).[12] Legally, the board may consist of one or more persons; if the capital stock is more than three million euros, it must in principle – unless the articles of incorporation stipulate otherwise – comprise at least two persons (§ 76(2) AktG). The board is entitled to manage the business (§ 77(1) AktG), id est to legally act for the corporation.

The board has the liberty (discretion) to make its decisions according to its own responsibility (not subject to directives) in the interest and for the well-being of the corporation (see 6.4); in so doing, the board is subject to the power of control of the supervisory board (*Aufsichtsrat*, § 111(1) AktG).[13] Thus, corporate governance (compliance)[14] is comprehensively designed, in particular through the green paradigm change (see 6.1.1, 6.7.2 and chapter 1). It is normative with regard to the directors (members of the supervisory board, *Aufsichtsräte*) who act on the basis of personal responsibility. This is emphasised by obligations of the organisation (§§ 76(1) and 91(2) AktG), by the obligation to sign the financial report (§ 245 HGB) as well as civil and criminal law sanctions (liability).[15]

Control of large companies, in Germany formerly executed by strong banks (so-called "house banks" – *Hausbanken*) in the real economy, is now widely characterised by the forces of global capital markets. This is why the focus should be on their basis and practices (corporate finance, investment, speculation) and on

---

[12] Basically on fiction and reality below 7.3.1.

[13] BGH (German *Bundesgerichtshof*), 7.3.1994 (II ZR 52/93) BGHZ 125, 239, 246, <www.jurion.de/Urteile/BGH/1994-03-07/II-ZR-52_93> recital 19.

[14] See details esp. in 6.4 and 6.5.3 (duty of care), and 6.8 (global aspects).

[15] With regard to criminal law, e.g., § 400 AktG and § 331 HGB, § 266 StGB, see Luttermann (2012). On § 245 HGB below 6.8.2 and above 4.9.6, comprehensively Luttermann (2003a) § 245 HGB. Pitkowitz (2014).

personal responsibility, which is already legally valid and therefore must in fact be executed with regard to personal liability. Overall, for the modern corporation as a human corporation it is about sustainability through sound finance, valuation and reporting (see chapters 3 to 5).

### *6.1.3 People as Trustees (Climate Partners)*

The individual as a person (*Mensch*) has a key function, practically making the difference between "good" and "evil". Humans shape the constitution of liberty, necessarily on a scientific basis "best available science"),[16] the law as practised ethics, especially in their environment (see 9.9, Fig. 6.3). This applies, too, in the face of climate change as a global, common challenge of humankind, also where the legal responsibility of states is concerned. They are not an end in themselves and, like any corporation (legal entity), are responsibly represented by people (natural persons). It is about the legal consequences with respect to "peoples and individuals".[17] The International Court of Justice in its landmark opinion notes on climate change that:

> "States have obligations under international human rights law to respect, protect and ensure the enjoyment of human rights of individuals and peoples. Human rights are focused on the protection of individuals and peoples and are not limited to specific fields of activity."[18]

Of course, human rights are equal and inalienable rights, they are basically the expression of the inherent dignity of every human being (*Menschenwürde*) and they are universally declared.[19] Discussing "the right to a clean, healthy and sustainable environment as a human right" and "the adverse effects of climate change on the enjoyment of human rights", the Court concludes that:

> "States must therefore take their obligations under international human rights law into account when implementing their obligations under the climate change treaties and other relevant environmental treaties and under customary international law, just as they must take their obligations under the climate change treaties and other relevant environmental treaties and under customary international law into account when implementing their human rights obligations."[20]

[16]See ICJ, Advisory Opinion, 23.07.2025, ibid., paras. 280-289, 347, also, e.g., paras. 136-137, 214, 254 and 347 with 158, 180, and 293-294 (precautionary principle); also above 1.2 and, e.g., 1.4.2, 4.2.2 and chapter 9.

[17]ICJ, Advisory Opinion, 23.07.2025, ibid., para. 111. Cf. chapters 1 and 2.

[18]ICJ, Advisory Opinion, 23.07.2025, ibid., para. 371.

[19]Preamble, Universal Declaration of Human Rights, 10.12.1948, UN General Assembly resolution 217 A. See also chapter 1. Luttermann (2013).

[20]ICJ, Advisory Opinion, 23.07.2025, ibid., para. 404, the two preceding quotes in para. 371, and overall paras. 371 to 404.

This has far-reaching effects, affecting states[21] and corporations (legal persons) as well as everyone (natural person) as a responsible actor; it is about the human corporation and the true nature of sustainability (see 8.4.3). Accordingly, trusteeship is also established.[22] Corporate directors count as trustees, acting with other people's money,[23] as is the case in the concept of trust for investment (see 1.5.2). The corporation in their financial function and global capital markets participate in the transition through due diligence with regard to human rights and the environment, in terms of fiduciary duty[24] and liability law (cf. climate change litigation, on the rights of Nature see 1.4.2). Subsequently,[25] we look at capital markets and greed, which for the human corporation is yesterday's world.

## 6.2 Politics of Corporate Financial Oligarchy

### *6.2.1 Pax Americana ("America First")*

"America first" is well known as a slogan by U.S. President Donald Trump. Generally, it stands for a policy of national reflection and non-interference abroad, originally coined 1915 by U.S. President Woodrow Wilson, the "godfather of American internationalism himself", against the United States entering the world war.[26] After winning two world wars and with the end of the British Empire, the USA emerged as the dominant world power (Pax Americana, see 2.3.2): with a neoclassical economy and corporate capitalism at its core, as demonstrated by "shareholder value" and "economic analysis of law" (see 6.7.3). – How about human values and substance for sustainable corporate business in a good economy, banking on trust?

Corporate governance, running a corporate business, means that the issue everywhere is modern corporate finance, money (capital) as the basis and substance of entrepreneurial action: Other people's money, as Louis D. Brandeis phrased it 1914 (see 3.3.3). That is why capital is defined as "money plus trust" (*Geld plus Vertrauen*), and why the corporate directors are personally responsible (see 2.7, 3.3 and 3.6).[27] They are accountable to the investors who have entrusted them with

---

[21] On legal consequences (e.g. reparation, restitution, compensation) arising from wrongful acts: ICJ, Advisory Opinion, 23.07.2025, ibid., paras. 444-455.

[22] See ICJ, Advisory Opinion, 23.07.2025, ibid., para 156, on that above 6.1.1. See Fig. 6.3. On the rights of Nature see above 1.4.2.

[23] See above 3.3.3 (U.S. President F.D. Roosevelt, Brandeis), 3.4.4 (trust fund theory), and 3.6.3 (corporate trust indenture). Overall chapters 4 and 7.

[24] Fundamentally on fiduciary duties and corporate climate responsibility Williams (2021).

[25] Cf. Luttermann in du Plessis, Großfeld, Luttermann et al. (2017) chapter 9 (banking on trust).

[26] Leffler and Hitchcock (2018) p. 33 (citation), and overall. Cf. President Trump's America First Priorities, 20.01.2025 (https://www.whitehouse.gov/briefings-statements/2025/01/president-trumps-america-first-priorities/, accessed: 25.08.2025). Overall above 2.3.2 (big business in the world).

[27] Cf. also above 3.4.4 and *Garfield v. Allen, 277 A.3d 296* (Del. Ch. 2022).

their money about the transactions executed with this money (accountability, see chapter 4). This brings the financial markets into focus for any corporation as well as its directors. In particular, where green paradigm change is meant to direct capital globally into so-called "sustainable economic activities": the socio-ecological transformation of the economy (see 6.1, and chapter 1).

The world has to be regauged. A financial world, for which a Copernican turn towards the imperative of truth (*Gebot der Wahrheit*) is long overdue,[28] globally characterised by interests and forces from the Pax Americana (see 2.3.2). Private actors widely shape and dominate practice, accompanied and promoted by public representatives (institutions). The U.S. Congress traditionally emphasises the significance of the competitive power of the domestic markets for national economy and security.[29] Basically, the issue is: "Promoting global preeminence of the American Securities Markets".[30] This is generally still true. Even in the face of the world debt crisis, driven by the financial industry (Wall Street, City of London, see 7.2) and already breaking out in the subprime mortgage markets and credit markets, the U.S. Chamber of Commerce defined the core aim as "the continued global leadership of America's capital markets".[31]

However, it is precisely the U.S. business environment that is eroding with a failing political system: America's political system is recognised as "broken" and its "dysfunction" as "the single most important challenge to U.S. economic progress".[32] The Capitol riot, a mob storming the U.S. Congress on January 6, 2021, set the torch.[33] – Remember: The USA, as Larry Summers critically warned regarding the reform of the global economic architecture, act as "the underwriter of the global economic system".[34] This is a system significantly managed by the privately-run

[28] Luttermann (2011) and, in terms of transforming the economy sustainably, Luttermann (2023) recitals 24-47, 78-85 and 96-100. See below 6.7.2, 6.9 and chapter 7.

[29] See, e.g., Senate, Committee on Banking, Housing, and Urban Affairs, 101st Cong. 1st Session, Report 101-155, The Securities Acts Amendments of 1989, Oct. 2, 1989, p. 13.

[30] See Report pursuant to Sec 509(5) of the National Markets Improvement Act of 1996, October 1997: www.sec.gov/news/studies/acctgsp.htm (accessed: 25.08.2025). Cf. above 6.2.1, see also 6.7.2, 1.4.2 and 2.1, 2.3.2.

[31] U.S. Chamber of Commerce, Strengthening U.S. capital markets, March 2008, 2. Cf. Goldman Sachs Group, Inc., American preeminence in a rattled world (January 2019) and, from its investment strategy group, America powers on (January 2024). On limits for extraterritorial effect of U.S. securities law *Morrison v. National Australia Bank*, 561 U.S. 247 (2010) and below 6.5.3.

[32] Porter/Rivkin/Desai/Raman (2016). Overall Stiglitz (2010), Tooze (2019) and Wedel (2009). Cf. fundamentally Applebaum (2024) on "Autocracy, Inc.".

[33] Cf. again U.S. President Donald Trump, above 6.2.1, and Daniel Day, 29.04.2025: https://edition.cnn.com/politics/fact-check-trump-false-claims-debunked (accessed: 25.08.2025). Cf. Applebaum (2024), from p. 193.

[34] Summers, Time US leadership woke up to new economic era, 05.04.2015: www.ft.com/intl/cms/s/2/a0a01306-d887-11e4-ba53-00144feab7de.html (accessed: 25.08.2025). Cf. Aliber, Kindleberger, McCauley (2023), esp. from p. 321 (chapter 13). Lessons from the crisis: Tirole in Dewatripont, Rochet, Tirole (2010) pp. 47-77.

"Federal Reserve System" (Fed), which has functions of a central bank: "an independent entity within government".[35]

Remember, shortly before U.S. President Woodrow Wilson installed this powerhouse of international finance in 1913, he made a clear-sighted comment, writing: "A great industrial nation is controlled by its system of credit."[36] Through the Pax Americana, this has long since been the case worldwide: Corporate finance and governance, id est valuation and financial reporting (see chapter 3), is characterised via global capital markets with corporate anonymity through structures, theories and practices of investment banking, financial engineering, leveraging etc. à la "Wall Street": Pax Americana as a "global market order" (cf. "order of assets" *Vermögensordnung*, see 6.5.3 and Fig. 6.1). Joseph Stiglitz describes the banking system in view of the 2008 financial meltdown as: "The Great American Robbery"[37] (see 6.4.3).

### 6.2.2 Casino Wall Street for the Greater Good?

In view of the greater good, the challenges of our time (see 6.1), the global "robbery", as Joseph Stiglitz describes it, is an anachronism. It acts as a continuation of the history of financial euphoria that John Kenneth Galbraith (1993) told us about; let us examine this more closely. The cover of Time Magazine two weeks after the fall of Lehman Brothers Holdings Inc. on September 15, 2008, captures the rude reality neatly: "How Wall Street sold out America: They had a party. Now you're going to pay".[38] This is what we as citizens (tax-payers, savers) – in a muddy composite of never-ending crises – are experiencing around the globe through state actions such as unlimited debt and glut of money (*fiat money*) with zero interest or even negative interest rates (so-called "quantitative easing" – QE) and inflation.

We are to pay the price for the excesses of the global financial industry (see 6.6), as we encounter it in the form of corporatism as small financial oligarchy (see 6.2.3), of course with European participation. "Bundesbank burns through more than €20bn to cover huge losses", it says in 2024, wiping out the reserves with more losses to come: The Eurozone banking system has also piled up mountains of trash by buying trillions in bonds (toxic assets, monetisation).[39] It is a vicious game that,

[35] Fed: www.federalreserve.gov/faqs/about_14986.htm (accessed: 25.08.2025). Meanwhile, following *Seila Law LLC v. Consumer Financial Protection Bureau*, 591 U. S. 197 (2020), at 222, n. 8, affirming *Trump v. Wilcox*, 605 U.S. ___ (2025), 145 S. Ct. 1415, 1415 (2025) (per curiam): "The Federal Reserve is a uniquely structured, quasi-private entity that follows in the distinct historical tradition of the First and Second Banks of the United States."

[36] Wilson (1913) p. 175. See the (longer) quotation in the time context above 3.3.2.

[37] Stiglitz (2010) p. 109. Overall Luttermann (2010b).

[38] Time Magazine, September 2008. On Lehman Brothers Holdings Inc. see in 6.6.3 and in more detail above 4.6.2.

[39] Headline cited: Financial Times, 23.02.2024 (www.ft.com). See also, e.g., NZZ, 23.02.2024: *"Milliardenverluste: Die EZB und die Bundesbank erhalten die Rechnung für ihre ultraexpansive Geldpolitik"* (www.nzz.ch).

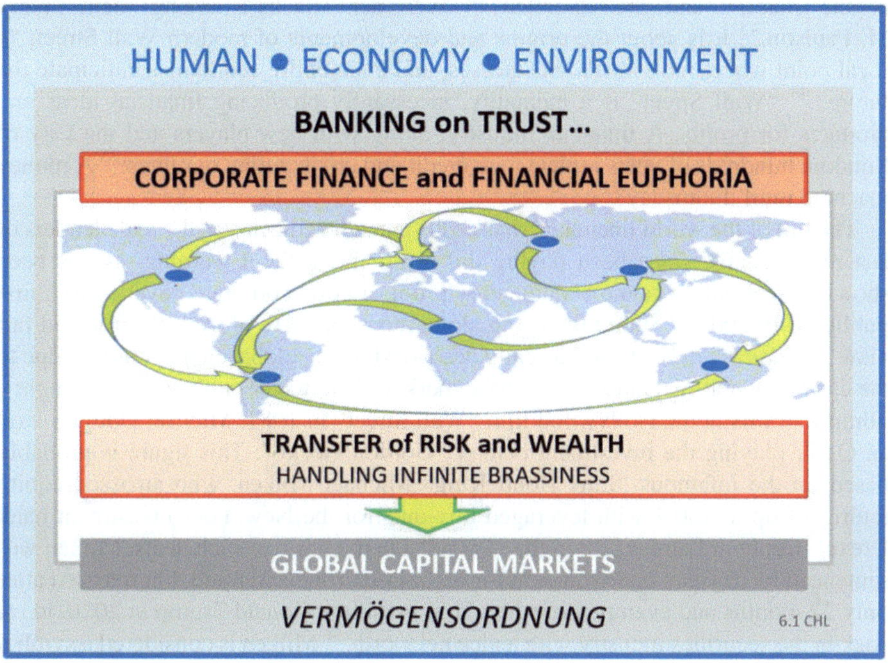


**Fig. 6.1** Corporations, capital markets, and financial euphoria

without fundamental reforms, will continue to disintegrate societies (see 6.4.3). Companies (corporations) of the real world economy are also massively affected. This explicitly includes the reluctance of government officials especially to provide financial assistance to Lehman Brothers Holdings Inc. and handling the financial crisis in general ("too big to fail", see 6.2.3 and 6.7.1), as has been written:

> "The mindlessness of the responses of the US Treasury and Federal Reserve officials to the implications of the surges in property prices is staggering. The taxpayers of America should consider a class-action lawsuit to claw back their salaries and their honorary degrees. Good luck."[40]

History took a different course. It is a game of self-appointed "masters of the universe", in the style of the LTCM-debacle (see 2.3.2) – only on the factually global scale with "money illusion"[41] for the masses: the wonderful process of enrichment for the lucky few.[42] One main actor was, besides Secretary of the US Treasury Henry M. Paulson (Ex-chairman and CEO Goldman Sachs, see 6.6.3), Ben Bernanke as chairman of the Federal Reserve (2006–2014), who received the Nobel Memorial Prize in Economics in 2022 for "research on banks and financial crises" – what luck (see 6.7.1). Janine Wedel talks about the new system of powerful players

---

[40] Aliber and Kindleberger (2015) p. 339.

[41] Ibid., p. 59.

[42] An instructive view is provided by Galbraith (1994).

in the shadow and the so-called "Government Sachs", among them Henry M. Paulson.[43] It is about the origins and developments of modern Wall Street: "a focal point where individuals, businesses, and even entire economies anticipate the future".[44] "Wall Street" is a mentality, incessantly producing financial ideas and products for profits. A financial industry, along with new players and the City of London, hundreds of years replete with credit and crisis, ruling our lives:[45] A money machine until doomsday?

The bill of the world financial crisis (2008) that the citizens, as the real "lenders of last resort", have since been paying did not come without warning, as has been shown: "Accounting as the documentary proof of good corporate governance", first published in 2007.[46] Sound financing along the imperative of truth ("a true and fair view" – *Bilanzwahrheit*) was basically destroyed on the global capital markets due to the casino mentality that exists on these markets. The wider public already caught a glimpse of this in the Hollywood film "Wall Street" in 1987. Michael Douglas won an Oscar playing the investment banker "Gordon Gecko": This figure is probably based on the infamous "Junk Bond King" Michael Milken, who amassed equity returns of up to 100% with leveraged buy-outs for the New York investment bank Drexel Burnham Lambert LP in the 1980s.[47] On the basis of such deals, Milken was sentenced to 10 years imprisonment for organised crime and fraud, but released after only 22 months and even pardoned by U.S. President Donald Trump in 2020, id est back in the securities industry with a nice net worth.[48] Milken is considered a symbol of greed on New York Wall Street ("Casino Wall Street", see Fig. 6.1).

Soon, "Wall Street" with its neoclassical dogma of deregulation (see 6.3.2, 6.6.3) was everywhere. The practices and theory of company financing and the speculation with financial instruments spread around the globe: The financial industry also seized Germany and Europe with these methods. Investment bank abuses, high risk lending, inflated credit ratings – these are some keywords of "a devastating economic collapse" even in America.[49] A complex domain with fundamental links

[43] Wedel (2009), esp. pp. 7 and 204; see there also, e.g., pp. 117-121, 132, 139 and 145 on Larry Summers and Robert Rubin. Note below 6.6.3 and above 4.9.5 (deregulation). Cf. on Goldman Sachs' self-display on its "leading role" in the fall of the Berlin Wall: Roberts and Kynaston (2002) p. 201.

[44] Bernstein (1992) p. 6.

[45] Aliber, Kindleberger, McCauley (2023), esp. pp. 373-384. Kynaston (2012), Roberts and Kynaston (2002). See below 7.2.

[46] Luttermann in du Plessis/Großfeld et al. (2007) pp. 177–204 (cf. now chapter 4) with references published in German, overall Luttermann (1998) and (1999a).

[47] On this Luttermann (1998) pp. 261-262, 429.

[48] Seven billion dollars, estimated by Forbes The World's Billionaires: #474 Michael Milken (https://www.forbes.com/, as of 7/16/2025). Cf. 6.2.3.

[49] U.S. Senate, Permanent Subcommittee on Investigations, Wall Street and the financial crisis: anatomy of a financial collapse, April 13, 2011, p. 1. Cf. Stiglitz (2010) pp. 147-183, Aliber and Kindleberger (2015) pp. 313-339, Tirole, Lessons from the crisis, in Dewatripont, Rochet, Tirole (2010) pp. 11-47. Luttermann (2010b).

to corporate governance, with global phenomena which are increasingly forming, becoming obvious and needing to be taken note of. This can be shown here (of course not exhaustively) for the reader with specific aspects of corporate Germany within the context of European and international influences. These perspectives show[50] how important jurisprudence, moderate action by those responsible, and strict enforcement are, wherever careful action is lacking (see 6.4 and chapter 7).

### *6.2.3 Transparency is Key for Sustainability*

With sustainability, we are breaking new ground[51] in a strangely influenced world. The Financial Times described the financial year 2015 with the headline: "Bankers strain against shackles: The financial world is way off recovering from the crash of 2008".[52] It then went on to say that the regulatory focus had in fact switched from the banks, whose "buffering market making role" was moving to the insurance and asset management industries; some insurance companies (no reinsurance companies) are classed as "systematically important", with consequences for special capital buffers and oversight (regulation); ever-growing asset manager giants (BlackRock, Vanguard etc.), "have escaped the designation".[53] The global economy is ailing, particularly through too much borrowing (debt), fueled by unprecedented global disruptions (Covid-19 pandemic, war in Ukraine and global trade, inflation):[54] "Riding the Global Debt Rollercoaster" (IMF).[55]

In this context, we recall the Bank for International Settlements (BIS) comments made years ago: "The uneasy calm has given way to turbulence", there "was a growing perception in financial markets that central banks might be running out of effective policy options".[56] Warnings, highlights, alarm signals: The corporate world is being massively gripped by change, turmoil and manipulations,

---

[50] At the same time, of course, a kind of "blueprint" for abuse; cf. in contrast, e.g., 6.5.3 and 3.5.5 (casuistry), comprehensively chapters 7 and 9. In details on economic criminal law (*Wirtschaftsstrafrecht*) Luttermann (2012).

[51] See esp. above 4.2 and overall chapters 1 and 2.

[52] Financial Times, 9.12.2015 (www.ft.com/intl/reports/ft-year-in-finance, accessed: 25.08.2025). Cf. Shirin (2024), and currently: https://www.fsb.org.

[53] See the preceding footnote as well as below 6.5.1 and 6.7.2.

[54] See Rogoff (2022), Nemat, Rahat, Rossi and Salloum (2025). U.S. President Trump "upending global trade" with his 2025 "US trade war": Conteduca, Mancini, Borin (2025); cf. above 6.2.1: "America first".

[55] International Monetary Fund: www.imf.org/en/Blogs/Articles/2022/12/12/riding-the-global-debt-rollercoaster, accessed: 25.08.2025). Cf. OECD, General government debt, data under: https://data.oecd.org/gga/general-government-debt.htm. Prior data: Luttermann in du Plessis, Großfeld, Luttermann et al. (2017) 9.2.3. See below 6.8.5 on mountains of debt in the unprecedented AI megahype.

[56] BIS Quarterly Review March 2016 (www.bis.org/publ/qtrpdf/r_qt1603a.htm).

increasingly also understood as a risk in a financial world which around the globe is becoming more and more interconnected and confusing. Limited, urgently needed resources are being wasted (cf. chapters 1, 8 and 9). A former chief economist with Morgan Stanley wrote: "After the 2008 financial crisis, the US government and Federal Reserve spent trillions of dollars to bail out the people who created the crisis. Instead of facing bankruptcy and jail, these people have become richer than ever. Predictably, they have used their resources to rig the system further."[57] This corroborates the demand for sustainability (see 5.2.4).

It is about effective basic structures (rules) that prevent or contain personal failure as far as possible (see 6.5.3 and chapter 7). In this process, well-known human failings (e.g., manipulation), which may also be psychologically significant, need to be taken note of in particular in view of substantial financial incentives: the human factor, which is crucial in the distinction between "good" and "evil" (see chapters 4 and 5). Here on the capital markets and in corporate finance, where "money is the measure of capitalist achievement" and "the more money, the greater the achievement and the intelligence that supports it".[58] John Kenneth Galbraith already captured this individually and structurally at the end of the twentieth century in his short story of "financial euphoria" (see Fig. 6.1). He describes it this way:

> "we compulsively associate unusual intelligence with the leadership of the great financial institutions – the large banking, investment-banking, insurance, and brokerage houses. The larger the capital assets and income flow controlled, the deeper the presumed financial, economic, and social perception.
>
> In practice, the individual or individuals at the top of these institutions are often there because, as happens regularly in great organizations, theirs was mentally the most predictable and, in consequence, bureaucratically the least inimical of the contending talent. He, she, or they are then endowed with the authority that encourages acquiescence from their subordinates and applause from their acolytes and that excludes adverse opinion or criticism. They are thus admirably protected in what may be a serious commitment to error."[59]

Of course, there is more to it than just error, and correspondingly this also applies to government institutions (politics). Generally, self-service (fake, fraud, manipulation) is gaining ground, still, and this with more or less old patterns within the core strategy of profit maximisation in the evolution of new technologies (AI, Cyborgs, Bots, quantum computing, see 9.6 with 6.8.5). Financial engineering (see 6.6.4, esp. in the AI megahype 6.8.5) is changing the financial industry with humans and machines working together, disrupting digital business, in particular in the world of corporate finance with speculation of algorithmic trading (high-frequency trading). This is accompanied by computerised trading platforms (cf. 6.9: the Goldman Sachs Algorithm), dark pools, market gateways and distortions (flash crashs).[60]

---

[57] Xie (2016); cf. Zhu (2016). See Luttermann (2010a), (2010b) and (2011).

[58] Galbraith (1994) p. 14, and, p. 109, with the recommendation: "when a mood of excitement pervades a market or surrounds an investment prospect, (…), all sensible people should circle the wagons; it is the time for caution."

[59] Ibid., pp. 15-16.

[60] See below 6.6 and 6.8.5 (hyperspeculation, AI). Cf. Patterson (2012), Lewis (2014).

Financial technology companies spread with alternative financial channels, payment systems and services for regulatory reporting (Fintech, cf. 3.7).

Big old banks like JP Morgan Chase & Co. have become even larger in the course of the so-called "global financial crisis" (in fact: world debt crisis – *Weltschuldenkrise*). They are rising even in the face of criticism in the Federal Reserve System,[61] the divestiture of megabanks (Too-Big-to-Fail, Too-Big-to-Exist-Act) died in the U.S. Congress.[62] Obviously, concentration of assets is growing, especially with corporations in so-called "common ownership" (corporatism),[63] whereas state debts and inequality in the enduring world debt crisis and its offspring are rising dramatically on a global scale.

### 6.2.4 From Panama to Global Justice

In particular, however, intransparency prevails. There are reports of the increase of gigantic private assets since 2008, saying that only 1.2 percent of the adult world population have more than 47.8 percent of world assets at their disposal, whereas 2.8 billion adults have assets worth less than 10,000 US dollars.[64] A core problem are tax havens (*Steuerparadiese*); approximately more than twelve percent of the world's financial power is located there – largely tax-free.[65] The actual dimensions obscured are probably even greater, as shown by octopus-like financial architecture and multinational corporation structures (corporatism, see 6.2.2), shadow banks (financial engineering, gigantic derivate "assets"),[66] so-called "systemic risks" being inherent to financial institutions and markets,[67] and, in particular, the revelations of the Panama Papers (2016), Paradise Papers (2017), and Pandora Papers (2021) – the "rise of a global fourth estate".[68]

[61] Neel Kashkari, Governor Fed Bank of Minneapolis: https://www.minneapolisfed.org/speeches/2016/lessons-from-the-crisis-ending-too-big-to-fail, Justin Walton, 15.06.2025: https://www.investopedia.com/ask/answers/082115/why-do-some-people-claim-federal-reserve-unconstitutional.asp (both accessed: 25.08.2025). Cf. above 6.2.1 (footnote 31).

[62] S. 1206, 114th Congress (2015-2016), 05/06/2015, by (presidential candidate) Sen. Sanders (I-VT): www.govtrack.us/congress/bills/114/s1206; cf. 117th Congress, Committee House Financial Services, Hearing: Holding Megabanks Accountable, 21.09.2022: www.congress.gov/event/117th-congress/house-event/115151?s=1&r=6 (both accessed: 25.08.2025).

[63] See below 6.5.1 and Vitali/Glattfelder/Battiston (2011).

[64] Credit Suisse, Global wealth report 2022, p. 21. More recent data by the rescuer (aquirer) of the meanwhile failed Credite Suisse: UBS, Global wealth report (www.ubs.com).

[65] See Alstadsæter, Johannesen, and Zucman (2018) 89, 93. Cf. Zucman (2015) and Business Wire, 2023 Global offshore wealth management market report.

[66] Data of the BIS: https://data.bis.org/topics/OTC_DER (accessed: 25.08.2025). See below 6.6.4. Luttermann (2008b).

[67] See below 6.7.1. Generally Mishra (2019). See below 6.6.4. See current European Securities and Markets Authority – ESMA (www.esma.europa.eu), and annually: Financial Stability Board Global Monitoring Report on Non-Bank Financial Intermediation (www.fsb.org).

[68] Berglez and Gearing (2018).

Findings show: apart from political etiquette, ideologies and state formations, a certain type of people is united in their boundless striving for wealth (power). These elites, whether called "bankers", "statesmen" or something else, live in their own world on our planet.[69] Globally active, they need to be integrated in the sense of sustainability. A study of the New York Stock Exchange, the paragon of modern corporate finance, shows the technological revolution of security exchanges, flows of trading-related information and the perils of market fragmentation, leading silently to transfer of wealth from weak to powerful hands.[70] There are efforts to strengthen the regulation of beneficial ownership (dominium utile) and reduce anonymity in the establishment of shell companies (*Briefkastenfirmen*).[71]

All this underscores our focus on the personal responsibility of the actors and confirms the earlier finding that "new players" are dominant in town.[72] There may be nothing in names where well-known patterns are merely practiced under different designations. However, they show the way, identifying and personalising responsibility. In the face of the ongoing global debt crisis and the great lack of personal responsibility, this may pave the way for the necessary reform in order to rebuild trust in the corporate world and a sound economy for fair international competition (see 1.5.2). That lays the basis for a peaceful world and prosperity for individuals and nations. Basically, the issue is justice through an international order of assets (*Vermögensordnung*, see 6.2.3 and 5.2 with chapter 8).

## 6.3 Reflections on Corporations, Capital, and Control

### *6.3.1 Corporation Finance*

In practice, the point of departure is the financing of business: the corporation precisely exists in its function as a financial instrument permanently established by law (see 2.6.3).[73] Its initiators (founders, shareholders, partners) require capital and therefore: a company needs capital. For a corporation as a separate legal entity, this is at the same time the basis of liability and business. Economically, this means: money for the purpose of investment. The investors provide capital – via banks, exchanges, and the like – in order to attain a return through interest or other payments (return on

---

[69] On Panama Papers Luttermann (2016a). See, with current information and more references: International Consortium of Investigative Journalists (ICIJ, https://www.icij.org/investigations/paradise-papers/, accessed: 17.06.2025); Berglez and Gearing (2018); Bhuiyan (2022) on Pandora Papers. Luttermann (2011) and above 4.6.2, cf. Wedel (2009), Applebaum (2024) on "Autocracy, Inc.".

[70] Mattli (2019).

[71] On laws in the UK and the US according to ICIJ case studies Aristodemou (2024). Basically already Großfeld (1974), Luttermann (1993a) and (2016a).

[72] See below 6.5.1, 6.9 and chapter 7; already Luttermann in du Plessis/Großfeld et al. (2012) 8.4.1.

[73] Based on Luttermann (1998).

capital). It is "other people's money" (Louis D. Brandeis, see 3.3.2), the use and success of which the company directors have to account for (resp., to report on, i.e. financial reporting), as shown in chapter 4: Accounting and auditing as the documentary proof of good corporate governance.

Companies may finance themselves in different ways. To this end, the law provides contractual forms of financing, classically designed in a dual way: private property (equity, shares) for partners or shareholders (equity financed – *Eigenkapital*) and contractual arrangements (debt, bonds) for creditors (externally financed, i.e., leveraged – *Fremdkapital*). This is reflected in the balance sheets, as already seen for financial reporting.[74] Partly for tax reasons, hybrid financial instruments are popular. These instruments combine elements of "equity" and "debt" (e.g., perpetual debentures, income bonds, convertible bonds, profit participation certificates – *Hybridinstrumente*). From this range, which is open and permanently rearranged under private autonomy (see in chapter 3, esp. 3.6.3) by financial engineering (6.6.4, 6.8.5), the entrepreneurs and the investors make their choice based on the general freedom of contract (*Vertragsfreiheit*) and their own individual preferences.

In company financing (corporate finance), banks – or, in general, institutions in their banking functions (see 6.2.3) – play a major role all over the world: as shareholders or creditors of a corporation, as custodians of liquid funds, consultants, asset managers and financial services providers, or as intermediaries between the corporation and other financers on the capital markets. The issue is always more than "money for the purpose of investment" (capital). In practice, again, the "capital" is "money plus trust", which is built up through lasting good corporate governance (see 1.5, 4.13). This counts all the more in terms of "sustainability" (*Nachhaltigkeit*) within the holistic process of the socio-ecological transformation of the economy and, in practice, every corporation: an unparalleled and impressive yet powerful undertaking (see chapters 1 and 2). At the same time, investors gain certain forms of control (power) through various forms of financing.

### 6.3.2 Concepts and Practice of Control

Let us first take a look at the complete picture. Historically, there is a focus on differences in concepts of control in Germany (Continental Europe) and in common law jurisdictions.[75] Corporate law systems, based on Common law, emphasise the concept of "ownership" of the company by the shareholders: Conceptually, the shareholders control the company through their voting power as a personal right,

---

[74] See overall chapter 4 and above 5.2.1. Basically on corporation finance, disclosure and profit (liability) chapter 3.

[75] Overall with references Luttermann, du Plessis in du Plessis/Großfeld/Luttermann et al. (2012) 8.2.2 and 8.2.3 (pp. 832-833) and Luttermann, ibid., 3rd ed (2017) 9.4 (pp. 441-445).

which they exercise themselves (or by proxy) according to their own interests in the shareholders' meeting (*Hauptversammlung*) – the driver of "creating shareholder value" (see 6.2 and chapter 4). In Germany, by contrast, banks have traditionally played a decisive role in companies through their unique position as the enterprises' creditors or as owners of the equity interests.[76] The sheer number of such strong links shaped the concept (metaphor) of the so-called "Deutschland AG".

This was the basis of widespread criticism, in particular by actors of capital market practice, and countered by that of the banking establishment. Basically, here for generations the issue has been access to lucrative business fields, and this will remain so in the future. For a better understanding of law and practice in Germany, look at the control of a typical large German stock corporation and its management boards through the shareholders' meeting and the supervisory board until approximately the mid-1990s (cf. earlier articles).[77] This also marks the deregulation of the financial markets setting in globally at that time with US pre-eminence. The unleashed financial industry in "Wall Street" style then promoted the said world debt crisis (see 6.6), which we are all experiencing still. Even after the initial catastrophe, lobbyism is typical of the banking and financial sector.[78] An example is Jack Lew, initially an investment banker, then secretary of the U.S. Treasury (2013–2017): "From Wall Street failure to the pinnacle of finance in four short years".[79]

This "shadow elite"[80] shows the general significance, notably with the accompanying lobbyism. Due to its general social significance, it is particularly serious. This becomes obvious in the course of the world debt crisis, where the financial industry had the greatest impact. In particular for the large area of the real economy, it is therefore indispensable to take note of the influences of the financial industry, along with its institutions, that has long since established itself on a global scale. From a German perspective, the question is a better understanding of practice in the dual system of the stock corporation (*Aktiengesellschaft*, AG), and specifically the listed public stock corporation. A special focus is on the function of the management board (*Vorstand*) as well as control through the supervisory board (*Aufsichtsrat*, see 6.4), which are individually designed;[81] first, let us look at the personal requirement profile.

---

[76] Baums (1992).

[77] Luttermann in du Plessis/Großfeld/Luttermann/Saenger/Sandrock/Casper (2012) 8.3 (at pp. 334-338).

[78] Cf. on the practice of the "revolving doors" in the USA Luttermann (1999a) pp. 42–48, 99–100.

[79] The Wall Street Journal, 29.01.2013: Treasury Gets a Citibanker (www.wsj.com/articles/SB10001424127887324734904578243932620870510, accessed: 25.08.2025).

[80] See above 6.2.2 with Wedel (2009).

[81] Details du Plessis/Großfeld/Saenger/Sandrock in du Plessis/Großfeld/Luttermann et al. (2017) 1.4.

### 6.3.3 Personal Qualification and Independence

Personal qualification and independence (*Unabhängigkeit*) are the necessary basis for good corporate governance that is entrepreneurially sustainably successful (compliance, see 6.1). Basically, this applies to any member of the management and supervisory boards. Independence is an inner attitude, which, in the sense of a leadership personality with office and function, is based predominantly on expert competence.[82] This is shown by legislation, sharpened by the FISG 2020 (see 4.9.5), which obliges the members of the management board (*Vorstand*) who have been given this leadership job without instructions, to be executed on their own responsibility (§ 76 AktG), to execute the care of an orderly and conscientious business director in directing the business (§ 93(1)(1) AktG, see 6.4). For the members of the supervisory board (*Aufsichtsrat*), who, being personally responsible, have to meet certain requirements (§ 100 AktG), the imperative of independence (*Unabhängigkeit*)[83] is part of their control function: The members of the supervisory board (*Aufsichtsräte*) are to personally monitor the management by the executive directors (*Vorstände*, § 111 AktG).

Accordingly, conflicts of interests are to be avoided, as legally shown by the two-year cooling-off period (§ 100(2) no. 4 AktG), the prohibition of cross-over intertwinement (§ 100(2) no. 3 AktG) and in the case of business relationships (e.g., expert contract – *Beratervertrag*, § 114 AktG).[84] This includes not only exchange contracts, but all arbitrary or legal relationships conducted with the corporation by the member in the context of its own economic activities.[85] The statutes may demand personal requirements for the members of the supervisory board (§ 100(4) AktG). The law determines that, according to § 100(5) AktG, at least one member of the supervisory board must have competence (*Sachverstand*) in the area of accounting (*Rechnungslegung*) and one in the area of auditing (*Abschlussprüfung*, e.g., auditors, tax advisors, lawyers). Concretisation should be strict.[86] Regarding the independence required, legislation says that the fear of bias may be founded in an immediate or indirect business, financial or personal relation of the member of the supervisory

[82] For credit institutions and investment firms Art. 91 No. 1(1) Directive 2013/36/EU: "Members of the management body shall at all times be of sufficiently good repute and possess sufficient knowledge, skills and experience to perform their duties".

[83] Cf., e.g., BVerfG, 23.09.2002 (1 BvR 1717/00) NJW 2002, 419, <openJur 2012, 133297>.

[84] See, e.g. BGH, 29.06.2021 (II ZR 75/20) BGHZ 230, 203, <openJur 2021, 34352>.

[85] OLG Hamm, 28.05.2013 (27 W 35/13) ZIP 2013, 2008, <openJur 2013, 35472>. Cf. OLG Celle, 27.06.2018 (9 U 78/17) ZIP 2018, 1688 <openJur 2019, 38665>, depending on this: BGH (II ZR 273/18). OVG Sachsen, 03.07.2012 (4 B 211/12) ZIP 2012, 2111. On conflict of interests (liability) OLG Celle, 20.09.2022 (13 Kap 1/16) DB 2022, 2663, <openJur 2022, 18730> esp. recital 998.

[86] Already Luttermann (2003b). Cf. OLG München, 28.04.2010 (23 U 5517/09) ZIP 2010, 1082, <openJur 2012, 107791>, also Bahreini (2012). More details on accounting and auditing experts (*Bilanzrechtsexperten*) see above in chapter 4 (esp. 4.12). On the shareholders' right to information OLG Düsseldorf, 22.11.2012 (I-6 U 18/12) NZG 2013, 178, <openJur 2012, 131469>.

board with the management.[87] In the USA, so-called "independent directors" – whatever this may mean in practice – are gaining ground (see 6.7.3). Independence and expertise are composed holistically.

The § 100 AktG, reformed several times, is based on Article 39 Directive 2014/56/EU[88] (audit committee), where it says: "A majority of the members of the audit committee shall be independent of the audited entity." (fourth subparagraph of paragraph 1). This may be disregarded if – as according to the German AktG – all members of the audit committee are members of the administrative or supervisory body of the audited entity. German legislation reasons that the dual corporate governance in Germany already guarantees a generally high degree of independence through the institutional distinction between the supervisory board (audit committee, see 6.8.4, 4.12) and the management board.[89] The members of the supervisory board must all be familiar with the sector in which the corporation operates (§ 100(5) *AktG*). Further evidence of qualification and independence is provided by Article 39 No. 6 Directive 2014/56/EU (audit committee) as well as in general by the Commission Recommendation on the role of non-executive or supervisory directors of listed companies and on the committees of the (supervisory) board (2005/162/EC).[90]

## 6.4 Personal Responsibility (Germany, and Beyond)

### *6.4.1 Legal Foundations: Duty of Care*

The members of the management board have to employ the diligence of an orderly and conscientious managing director in managing the business (*"die Sorgfalt eines ordentlichen und gewissenhaften Geschäftsleiters"*: § 93(1)(1) AktG). That is the behavioural standard (*Sorgfaltspflicht*) any executive director has to comply with in his or her work; a violation of duty may be excluded according to § 93(1)(2) AktG (see 6.4.2). A member of the management board that violates his or her duties (e.g., the leadership task, § 76(1) AktG, special facts in § 93(3) AktG, regulation of bylaw – *Satzungsregelung*) is obliged to pay for ensuing damage to the corporation;

[87] German Federal Government, reasons given in the draft of the *Bilanzrechtsmodernisierungsgesetz* (BilMoG, 21.05.2008, *Bundestags-Drucksache*. 16/10067, 101).

[88] Of 16.04.2014, amending Directive 2006/43/EC on statutory audits of annual accounts and consolidated accounts, OJ EU (27.05.2014) L 158.

[89] German Federal Government, reasons given in the draft of the *Abschlussprüfungsreformgesetz* (AReG, *Bundestags-Drucksache* 18/7219, p. 56. AReG of 10.05.2016, BGBl. I 1142.

[90] 15.02.2005, OJ EU (25.2.2005) L 52/51. Cf. German Corporate Governance Code (as amended on 28. April 2022), esp. C. and D.2, D.3 (current version: www.dcgk.de/en/code//foreword.html). On developing best practice in the United Kingdom: HM Treasury, Audit and Risk Assurance Committee Handbook (www.gov.uk/government/publications/audit-committee-handbook).

the members of the board are liable as joint and several debtors (*Gesamtschuldner*, § 93(2)(1) AktG, §§ 249, 421 BGB). This liability regulation is binding for the compensation and the prevention of damages (general norm). It protects the limited assets of the corporation, which is liable to the corporation's creditors for the accounts payable (§ 1(1)(2) AktG; see also in 5.6.4).

The § 93 AktG also holds – with the exception of § 93(2)(3) AktG – for due diligence and responsibility of the members of the supervisory board (*Aufsichtsrat*, § 116 AktG). Specifically the special control function of the supervisory board is to be taken into consideration (§ 111(1) AktG).[91] This means that supervisory board members must exercise the diligence of a so-called decent and conscientious (*"ordentlichen und gewissenhaften"*) member of the supervisory board. For instance, they are explicitly liable if they fix "an inappropriate remuneration" for an executive director (§ 116, 87(1) AktG).[92] In order to be able to fulfil its legal function of control and counsel, the supervisory board has comprehensive right of information with regard to the management board (e.g., §§ 90, 111(2), 170 AktG); in the capacity as audit committee (member) also to the heads of the respective central sections of the corporation (*Zentralbereiche*, § 107(4)(4) AktG).[93] The management board, as the sole keeper of business secrets (*"Herr der Geschäftsgeheimnisse"*), may inform the supervisory board at an early stage about sensitive procedures, data and plans, for the supervisory board members are sworn to absolute confidentiality; in the case of a breach of this obligation they are made liable (§§ 116, 93(1)(3) AktG).[94]

The regulative framework in particular also comprises collisions of interests.[95] In the case of management board members, this specifically applies to the no-competition clause (§ 88 AktG) and to providing loans (§ 89 AktG). For members of the supervisory board, the circumstances may be more complex, as it is – still – generally part-time work (*"Nebentätigkeit"*) which must be professionalised for this very reason; this should be taken into account within the objective of duties (cf. 6.4.1). In any case, each member, by being appointed onto the management board (§ 84 AktG) or the supervisory board (§ 101 AktG), is subject to the

---

[91] See also below 6.5.2 (case of *IKB*).

[92] See, e.g., BGH, 28.04.2015 (II ZR 63/14) NJW-RR 2015, 988, <openJur 2015, 11014>. Cf. BGH, 15.01.2019 (II ZR 392/17) BGHZ 220, 377, <openJur 2019, 2336> (§ 112 AktG). In criminal cases BGH, 10.01.2023 (6 StR 133/22), NJW 2023, 1075, <openJur 2023, 2659> (*VW AG*).

[93] Extension inserted by the FISG of 2021, see above 4.9.5.

[94] BGH, 26.04.2016 (XI ZR 108/15) ZIP 2016, 1063, <openJur 2016, 6998>. Cf. on offences in connection with taxes BGH, 15.05.2018 (1 StR 159/17) NStZ-RR 2018, 368, <openJur 2018, 672>. Note on the duty of confidentiality BGH, 26.04.2016 (XI ZR 108/15) NJW 2016, 2569, <openJur 2016, 6998> (supervisory board); OLG Celle, 20.09.2022 (13 Kap 1/16) DB 2022, 2663, <openJur 2022, 18730> (management board).

[95] Cf., e.g., BGH, 09.03.2009 (II ZR 170/07) BGHZ 180, 105, <openJur 2011, 2383> (executive board dual mandate). OLG Celle, 20.09.2022 (13 Kap 1/16) DB 2022, 2663, <openJur 2022, 18730>.

organisational loyalty ties to the corporation (AG). – Overall, the regulations show that any member of a management or supervisory board is in the focus of corporate governance as a human being with his or her personal decisions (responsibility); this must also apply to cases of so-called "corporate misconduct" (see 6.5.3 and cf. 7.3.1).

## *6.4.2 Corporate Directors and Business Judgement*

The member of the management board is liable for any breach of duty (§ 93(1)(1) und (2)(1) AktG). This liability for his or her own culpable conduct does not apply if the member of the management board has fulfilled the legal measure of diligence. Legislation says in § 93(1)(2) AktG that it does not constitute a breach of duty if in making a certain decision the member of the management board could reasonably (*"vernünftigerweise"*) believe to be acting for the well-being of the company on the basis of adequate information.[96] This regulation refers to the obligations mentioned, according to the law and statutes (bylaws), in particular the duty to direct (*Leitungspflicht*, § 76(1) AktG), which have to be made concrete – also drawing on individual cases. The regulation is modelled on the Business Judgement Rule developed in the USA predominantly through the ruling of judges.[97] It signals that there is a certain scope for entrepreneurial decisions (safe harbour, *Schutzbereich*).

The member of the management board in general has a wide entrepreneurial decisional scope within the framework determined by the law and the statutes (bylaws, *unternehmerischer Entscheidungsspielraum*). However, it should be observed that in particular under the regulatory stipulations of sustainability, special duties of care (esp. human rights due diligence and environmental due diligence)[98] may hold, widely shaping corporate governance, finance and valuation; careful orientation is necessary for this (see 6.7). Within this framework, corresponding to the respective level of development, he or she may freely shape things according to duty, in principle without liability. The German Federal Supreme Court (*Bundesgerichtshof*, BGH) thus wrote that the management board is to be given wide scope for action in conducting business, as without this, entrepreneurial activity is simply not conceivable.[99] The judges elaborate on this fundamentally, here broadly translated:

---

[96] Original version in German: *"Eine Pflichtverletzung liegt nicht vor, wenn das Vorstandsmitglied bei einer unternehmerischen Entscheidung vernünftigerweise annehmen durfte, auf der Grundlage angemessener Information zum Wohle der Gesellschaft zu handeln."*

[97] See above 3.2.1 and 3.5.2. On the legal development in the USA Radin (2009).

[98] See in European law the Corporate Sustainability Due Diligence Directive (EU) 2024/1760, 13.06.2024, OJ L, 05.07.2024.

[99] Basic BGH, 21.04.1997 (Az. II ZR 175/95 – *ARAG/Garmenbeck*) BGHZ 135, 244. § 93(1)(2) AktG inserted by the *Gesetz zur Unternehmensintegrität und Modernisierung des Anfechtungsrechts* (UMAG), 22.09.2005, BGBl. I 2802; see German Federal Government, Reasoning E-UMAG, 07.01.2005, *Bundesrats-Drucksache* 3/05, pp. 18-21.

> Besides consciously taking business risks, this also includes the basic danger of misjudgements and erroneous evaluations, which any company leader, be he ever so responsible, is always subject to. If the supervisory board gains the impression that the management board lacks the necessary intuition for successfully directing the company, that is, the job of leading the company is not done well, this may be reason enough for replacing this person. From this, no obligation for compensation follows. This could only be considered if the limits within which entrepreneurial action based on a sense of responsibility, exclusively oriented towards the common good and founded on careful determination of the decisional basis, is clearly transgressed, entrepreneurial risk-taking has been irresponsibly overdrawn or the conduct of the management board has to be regarded as a violation of duty for other reasons.[100]

In the course of preventive monitoring (*präventive Überwachung*), the statutes (bylaws) or the supervisory board determine that the management board may conduct certain kinds of business (e.g., important measures regarding the property, finance and profit situation) only with the consent of the supervisory board (§ 111(4)(2) AktG).[101] Decisions of the management board that go against the law[102] or the statutes (bylaws) usually constitute breaches of duty (*Pflichtverstöße*). Proper entrepreneurial conduct excludes liability (§ 93(1)(2) AktG). Each member of the management board (executive corporate director – *Vorstand*) therefore has to demonstrate with facts and – if necessary – also prove that he or she has not violated his or her obligations – culpably (*schuldhaft*) – or that the damage would have occurred in the case of proper alternative action as well.[103]

The regulation applies only in the case of an "entrepreneurial decision" (*unternehmerische Entscheidung*: § 93(1)(2) AktG); its scope is also valid if no decision is made.[104] Not included in the scope of regulation are (only) obligations deriving from the law, the statutes (bylaws) and decisions of the shareholders' meeting (cf. §§ 93(4), 119 AktG) or the supervisory board (§ 111(4)(2) AktG), which factually do not leave the member of the management board any scope for judgement (so-called "bound decisions", *gebundene Entscheidungen*); this also applies to rules of procedure made for the management board by the supervisory board. Unaffected by the overall responsibility of the management board (collegial organ), diligence (culpability) and responsibility (liability) are to be valid for the individual members of the management board;[105] this is emphasised by the personal percentage excess in the D&O insurance (§ 93(2)(3) AktG).

---

[100] German original: BGH, 21.04.1997 (Az. II ZR 175/95 – *ARAG/Garmenbeck*) BGHZ 135, 244 (recital 22). Cf. below 6.5.2 (*IKB*). Pls. note on § 111(4)(2) AktG for the supervisory board: BGH, 10.07.2018 (II ZR 24/17) BGHZ 219, 193, <openJur 2018, 564> recital 55 (preventive control).

[101] See BGH, 10.07.2018 (II ZR 24/17) BGHZ 219, 193, <openJur 2018, 564>.

[102] Examples under 6.4.3.

[103] BGH, 15.01.2013 (II ZR 90/11) WM 2013, 456, <openJur 2013, 5641> and BGH, 04.11.2002 (II ZR 224/00) BGHZ 152, 280, at 284-285. Pls. note BGH, 08.07.2014 (II ZR 174/13) BGHZ 202, 26, <openJur 2014, 18972> (subject to approval by the annual general meeting).

[104] Overall Roth (2001).

[105] The regulations for members of the management board also apply for their deputies, § 94 AktG. Overall in terms of sustainability and financial due diligence Luttermann, L. (2022) and (2024).

### 6.4.3 Speculative Transactions

The personal responsibility (*Verantwortlichkeit*) of the members of management and supervisory boards (corporate directors) shows in company financing and in general in financial transactions essential for the corporation (see 6.5.1). This is illustrated by examples from jurisdiction in liability cases, initially from the problematic range of derivatives to interest rate hedging (see, e.g., 6.6.5). Depending on the object of the company, such interest rate swaps (*Zinstauschgeschäfte*) may only be allowed to a certain extent, e.g. with a mortgage bank (*Hypothekenbank*) according to the German mortgage bank law (*Hypothekenbankgesetz*).[106] A general prohibition is not assumed, in particular as interest swap deals are meant to secure interest, id est to function as auxiliary deals in financing the acquisition of real estate.[107]

That sounds good. However, one should remember the hazardous situation in particular in deals concerning mortgages for financing real estate in the USA, prior to the global "financial crisis" (2008), which stands for worldwide havoc on the financial markets with the mortgage banks Fannie Mae und Freddy Mac (subprime mortgage crisis): Long-term loans are given and financed with short-term periods, the risks being covered up through securitisations and derivatives, and disseminated globally (collateralised debt instruments – CDOs, see 6.6.4); interest rate hedging addresses the risk of rising interest rates. The U.S. Senate analyses these transactions as "high risk mortgage lending" reflecting "many of the trends affecting the U.S. financial system as a whole"[108] – and thereby the global financial world (Pax Americana, see 6.2.1). It was the concerted involvement of the banking system "in mortgage securitization that proved lethal", says Joseph Stiglitz:[109] Avarice triumphs over prudence with the well-known basic patterns of excessive risk-taking by banks, a rash of conflicts of interest, pervasive fraudulent behaviour, and of course the risky innovations of derivatives – all fuelled by cheap money (so-called QE: "quantitative easing", see 6.2.2).

---

[106] *Pfandbriefgesetz* (PfandBG – Mortgage Bond Act), 22.05.2005, BGBl. I 1373, amendments by Art. 8 of the Act of July 20, 2022, BGBl. I 1166. See, e.g., §§ 4(1a),(3), (3a) and (3b), 4b, 5(1)(2), 8, 10(2), and 28(1) No. 1 PfandBG.

[107] OLG Düsseldorf, 15.01.2015 (I-6 U 48/14, 6 U 48/14) ZIP 2016, 171 (final, BGH, 23.2.2016 – II ZR 49/15), with reference to BGH, 15.01.2013 (II ZR 90/11) WM 2013, 456. Note on duty to provide advice BGH, 22.03.2016 (XI ZR 425/14) NJW 2016, 2949, <openJur 2016, 5724>. On limitation of claims (*Verjährung*) BGH, 13.06.2023 (XI ZR 464/21) NJW 2023, 2714, <openJur 2023, 7516>.

[108] US Senate Permanent Subcommittee on Investigations. Wall Street and the financial crisis: anatomy of a financial collapse, April 13, 2011, 17 (17-26). See also below 6.5.2 and 6.6.1. Basically on the intelligent investor, i.e. investment versus speculation: Graham (2003).

[109] Stiglitz (2010) p. 7: "America's financial markets had failed to perform their essential societal functions of managing risk, allocating capital, and mobilizing savings while keeping transaction costs low. Instead, they had created risk, misallocated capital, and encouraged excessive indebtedness while imposing high transaction costs." – see resp. at p. 147 and pp. 169-176. Luttermann (2008b). See below 6.7.3.

This is an ongoing game, highly infectious for corporate finance and governance (see 6.8.5); a story basically repeating itself endlessly (see 6.9). Reality proves our assessment right yet again. The Washington Post, just after the 2023 banking crises with the collapse of major investment banks (First Republic Bank, Silicon Valley Bank, Credit Suisse AG etc.), wrote: "From the US to Europe and Hong Kong, commercial real estate has become the focus for investors trying to predict the next crisis after a decade of cheap borrowing came to an abrupt end."[110] While the financial system was initially stabilised by the orchestrated infusion of hundreds of billions in bailout money by Western central banks, the real estate crisis was further fuelled. In 2024, major real estate developers in China (Evergrande, Country Garden) collapsed.

Who will be next? – Is it any surprise that Credit Suisse, which was taken over by the UBS Group AG in 2023, had to admit to material weaknesses in its financial reporting? – Results of unbridled greed, reckless speculation and control failures over many years.

### 6.4.4 Focussing Law and Practice

From a legal viewpoint, this means that in practice entrepreneurially sensible business (*unternehmerisch sinnvolles Geschäft*) is to be determined: In the sense of § 93 AktG, making contracts in the way of interest swap deals constitutes a breach of duty if they are purely speculative deals. Basically – in particular also in terms of accounting (*bilanzielle Betrachtungsweise*), – it is about "other people's money", id est, the duty to look after assets (*Vermögensbetreuungspflicht*) by the persons responsible (*Entscheidungsträger*, managing directors) in a corporation or other institution (e.g., asset manager, city mayor).[111] The members of the management board act against their duty if they make interest swap deals without loan contracts being guaranteed at the same time that correspond to the interest swap deals regarding volume and period.[112] Consequently, each individual case must be carefully investigated with regard to its specifics (*Einzelfallbetrachtung*).

[110] Jack Sidders, 21.06.2023 (www.washingtonpost.com/business/2023/06/21/why-a-crisis-is-looming-in-commercial-real-estate-quicktake-lj5qetss/af3c32d2-103c-11ee-8d22-5f65b2e2f6ad_story.html, accessed: 25.08.2025). Cf. on the AI megahype below 6.8.5.

[111] See overall on the *Vermögensbetreuungspflicht* (asset care obligation) BGH, 16.07.2007 (II ZR 3/04 – *Trihotel*) BGHZ 173, 246, <openJur 2011, 7477> and above in 5.3.1 and 4.9.7. On speculative transactions, e.g., OLG Düsseldorf, 28.08.2020 (4 U 57/19) <openJur 2020, 47634>; cf. BGH, 23.04.2012 (II ZR 118/10) <openJur 2012, 69276> (prospectus liability). On financial derivatives and criminal law BGH, 19.09.2018 (1 StR 194/18) NJW 2019, 378, <openJur 2018, 6615> recital 27; BGH, 25.04.2019 (1 StR 427/18) NStZ 2020, 294, <openJur 2019, 31357>.

[112] Thus explicitly OLG Düsseldorf, 15.01.2015 (I-6 U 48/14, 6 U 48/14) ZIP 2016, 171 (final, BGH, 23.02.2016 – II ZR 49/15). OLG Düsseldorf, 13.12.2019 (4 U 23/18) <openJur 2020, 2699>.

The measures concern corporation finance (corporate governance) as a whole, namely the investors in hybrid forms of financing (§ 221 AktG, e.g., income bonds or debentures, participating notes; see 6.3.1). Their position is precarious[113] and has only partly been treated by jurisdiction. The German Federal Supreme Court rules that the liability of the corporation towards such investors, who give their capital to the corporation on the base of debt law (so-called bondholders, here: holders of participation certificates – *Genußscheinen*: § 221(3) AktG), does not correspond to the liability of the executive directors towards the corporation in the case of culpable business management according to § 93 AktG. The Federal Supreme Court sets "narrower" conditions – which is in fact somewhat questionable: The executive directors thus are not liable for all activities undertaken outside of the company objective.[114] In any case, financial reporting and valuation are the overall yardstick, right up to insolvency law.[115] Consequently, it should be taken into account for an adequate balance of interests that in a human corporation, providers of equity capital (*Eigenkapital*) and debt capital (*Fremdkapital*) form a community of venture (so-called *Wagnisgemeinschaft*).[116] This is proven by the increasing number of cases in which losses are shifted to main street creditors (so-called "bail-in")[117] and it even holds in European law for banks[118] (see, e.g., Cyprus, Italy, Portugal).[119]

For the question as to whether the company objective has been transgressed the circumstances have to be investigated according to the law and the statutes (bylaws, or decisions; see 6.4.2). The German Federal Supreme Court justifies its narrower view in favour of the executive directors with the necessity of interpreting the regulations of the statutes (bylaws). However, the judges see a liability of the corporation for an activity by the management board members (*Vorstände*) outside of the company objective that a sound businessman – who always regards the limits

---

[113] See above in 3.6.3 and 3.5.3. Basically, Luttermann (1998).

[114] BGH, 29.04.2014 (II ZR 395/12) ZIP 2014, 1166, <openJur 2014, 11118>. See on the distinction BGH, 21.07.2003 (II ZR 109/02) BGHZ 156, 38, <openJur 2012, 70835>; BGH, 21.11.2005 (II ZR 79/04) NJW-RR 2006, 471, <openJur 2011, 7859> (convertible bonds). Cf., e.g., BGH, 27.10.2005 (III ZR 71/05) NJW-RR 2006, 109, <openJur 2011, 12807>.

[115] See in chapters 4 and 5 (generally) and BGH, 07.04.2022 (IX ZR 107/20) NJW-RR 2022, 844, <openJur 2022, 9476>. Cf., e.g., BGH, 01.10.2020 (IX ZR 247/19) ZIP 2020, 2242, <openJur 2020, 75694>; BGH, 22.07.2021 (IX ZR 26/20) NJW-RR 2021, <openJur 2021, 34119>; BGH, 02.12.2021 (IX ZR 112/20) <openJur 2022, 21226>.

[116] Luttermann (1998) pp. 135-176 and 486-539.

[117] See above 6.6.1 and European Banking Authority (EBA), Guidelines on treatment of liabilities in bail-in (current under: www.eba.europa.eu). Cf. Maddaloni/Scardozzi (2022); Berger/Roman (2020).

[118] Directive 2014/59/EU establishing a framework for the recovery and resolution of credit institutions and investment firms, 15.05.2014, OJ EU, 12.06.2014, L 173/190; amendments, a.o., Directive (EU) 2019/2162. On recovery and resolution regime for banks *Deutsche Bundesbank Eurosystem* under: www.bundesbank.de.

[119] See in the case of Cyprus: ECJ, 20.09.2016 (C-8/15 P et al. – *Ledra Advertising/Commission and ECB*, EN) ECLI:EU:C:2016:701; ECJ, 16.12.2020 (C-597/18 P et al. – *Chrysostomides & Co.*, EN) ECLI:EU:C:2020:1028.

set by the company objective – would simply not undertake (so-called exceptional case of a qualified business activity constituting a breach of duty – *eine qualifiziert pflichtwidrige Geschäftstätigkeit*).[120] In this case, interest rate derivatives deals were concerned, and a similar decision was taken for losses from speculative trading "in the way of a roulette player" (*Roulettespieler*) on the crude oil option market.[121]

## 6.5 Multinational Developments and Management

### *6.5.1 The Wind of Change in Investment*

The world of business and financing and thus of corporate finance and governance are changing massively, as has been remarked earlier – globally in the so-called socio-ecological transformation of the economy (see chapter 1). International investment and multinational enterprises (MNEs) follow basic patterns that are quite well-known, but they are gaining ground and forming strange structures. MNEs, as described by the OECD, "usually comprise companies or other entities established in more than one country and so linked that they may co-ordinate their operations in various ways".[122] A world with its own rules of the game: This appears in a new light in particular since the Panama Papers and subsequent revelations (see 6.2.4), thanks to critical investigative journalists, with the real connections and dimensions slowly but hopefully steadily becoming clear: Decisive forces and structures (see 6.6 to 6.8), actors of power in our focus on personal responsibility (see 6.5.3 and chapter 7).

In Germany, the big companies and the business world as a whole are influenced by all this (see 6.2: Pax Americana). The dominant role of traditional banks is fading. New players are in town. Basically, that is a global phenomenon – it has been gaining ground fast since the turn of the century. We find a massive occurrence of investment banks and bank-like formations such as hedge funds and money managers, fintechs or structured investment vehicles (SIVs), so-called shadow banks (*Schattenbanken*). They are located beyond the classical forms of banks in – at least not explicitly – regulated areas, while at the same time basically doing classical banking business as well as financial deals with great leverage that seem innovative.[123] Such processes run outside of regulated structures (e.g., so-called "off-

[120] BGH, 29.04.2014 (II ZR 395/12) ZIP 2014, 1166, <http://lexetius.com/2014,1578> recitals 23, 47; BGH, 10.07.2018 (II ZR 24/14) NJW-RR 2019, 38, <openJur 2018, 1001>. Thus already BGH, 05.10.1992 (II ZR 172/91) BGHZ 119, 305, 331; on this Luttermann (1993b).

[121] BGH, 05.10.1992 (II ZR 172/91) BGHZ 119, 305. Cf. Luttermann (1998) pp. 86-134 and 486-539. Confirmed in BGH, 29.04.2014 (II ZR 395/12) ZIP 2014, 1166, <openJur 2014, 11118>.

[122] OECD Guidelines for Multinational Enterprises 2011 edition, part I, I.4 (www.oecd.org/daf/inv/mne/48004323.pdf). OECD Guidelines for MNEs (2023), I.4.: no "precise definition" of MNE required because "the *Guidelines* allow for a broad approach" (https://doi.org/10.1787/81f92357-en, both accessed: 25.08.2025). Basically Muchlinski (2021).

[123] In general see Luttermann (2008b). See above 5.5 and below 6.7.

balance sheet", cf. 4.5.7, 6.8.5), as we know since the Enron and Lehman scandals, and globally often in intransparent corporate group structures (off-shore), as illustrated by the Panama Papers (see 6.2.4). New generations of banks are emerging, although they are usually not called "banks", like on the internet and biotechnology revolutions, focusing on special sector industries. Their names are Microsoft, Alphabet, or Amgen, each of them controlling thousands of corporations globally in key high tech industries, forming our present and future.[124]

Actually, what counts is substance, not merely form. As Davies and Worthington put it earlier: "Globalisation has led multinational companies to acquire not only cross-border business activities, but also cross-border groups of investors".[125] This points to the structural phenomenon of so-called "common ownership", meanwhile associated with global asset managers (see 3.5.6). The power of pension funds (like CALPERS) and public pension reserve funds, with broad corporate portfolios, is huge; the present data only for the OECD show pension assets held with a volume of over $56 trillion (at the end of 2020), with a shift of investments from bonds towards equities, $51 trillion (2022).[126] What is emphasised is long-term financing for sustainable[127] and durable growth as a priority. This is accompanied by sovereign wealth funds (e.g., Norway Government Pension Fund)[128] and huge private asset managers (such as BlackRock, Vanguard, State Street); the numbers and floods of data can hardly be grasped any more.[129] They are progressively prepared to execute their power as shareholders and – comparatively unspectacular – even (more) as major bondholders within corporations. Martin C. Schmalz sums up:

> "The growth of intermediated asset management and consolidation in the asset management sector has led to more pronounced common-ownership links at the level at which corporate control is exercised. Recent empirical research has provided evidence consistent with the literature's prediction that common-ownership concentration (CoOCo) can affect product market outcomes. The resulting antitrust concerns have received worldwide attention. However, because CoOCo can change the objective function of a firm, the potential implications span all fields of economics that involve corporate conduct, including corporate governance, strategy, industrial organization, and financial economics."[130]

A truly broad, challenging field of research: the development of global financial structures (see 6.8.5). Sustainability as a paradigm shift may be enlightening and

---

[124] See 6.2.3 and 6.9. Already Luttermann (2003a) § 264 HGB recital 79.

[125] Davies and Worthington (2012) pp. 21-18, 771.

[126] OECD, Pension Markets in Focus 2021, 33. See for more recent data the annual OECD report "Pensions at a glance" (www.oecd.org).

[127] See 4.2, 4.3 and overall chapters 1 and 2. Luttermann (2023) recitals 1-47.

[128] See above 3.5.6, updated: https://www.swfinstitute.org/fund-rankings/sovereign-wealth-fund (accessed: 25.08.2025). Cf. Directive (EU) 2017/828, 17.05.2017 amending Directive 2007/36/EC as regards the encouragement of long-term shareholder engagement, OJ EU 20.05.2017 L 132/1.

[129] E.g., Boston Consulting Group, The $100 Trillion Machine www.bcg.com/publications/2021/global-asset-management-industry-report (accessed: 25.08.2025).

[130] Schmalz (2018). Cf. Backus/Conlon/Sinkinson, (2019), Klovers/Ginsburg in Charbit and Moretto (2021).

disciplining (see chapter 8). International capital markets, with a fast free-flow of private capital around the world, are changing the landscape all over the world and, of course, in Germany, too. Institutional investors (e.g. banks, insurance companies, pension funds) from other countries are investing extensively in corporations. Also, the vast range of private equity funds, including hedge funds, is acquiring impressive stakes in Corporate Germany. One example is the Deutsche Börse AG, the main operator of stock exchanges in Germany. Although a hostile takeover bid, led by Anglo-American hedge funds, failed, the number of Deutsche Börse AG's foreign shareholders was up to 85% in 2015 (90% already in 2005):[131] an international player with its base and international business in Germany, which has undertaken several attempts at transnational fusions, among others with the New York Stock Exchange (NYSE) and the London Stock Exchange (LSE).[132]

Additional data reveal the wind of change. To illustrate the point, one may focus on the development of the shareholder structure of some eminent German corporations; and the percentage of foreign shareholders in German corporations, as shown already.[133] The percentage of foreign investors in the corporations listed in the German Shares Index (Deutscher Aktienindex – DAX); on average in all the (formerly) thirty DAX corporations, the percentage had been 55% (2015); with meanwhile forty DAX members it is 51% (2024).[134] It should be noted – in terms of comparability – that a corporation in the USA is regarded as "foreign-controlled" (a subsidiary of a foreign-based corporation/multinational enterprise – MNE), if the MNE holds at least 10% of the shares; in turn, foreign direct investment (FDI) is assumed if a U.S. firm buys at least 10% of a foreign firm.[135]

### *6.5.2 Controlling German Banks: Mismanagement*

The wind of change will never stop blowing in the corporate world. More recent data confirm the massive change in the entrepreneurial culture in Germany and the large stock-listed corporations located here. The earlier dominance of the traditional banks, conceived as a classically inner circle characterised by reciprocal intertwining and control (cf. 6.8.4), has dissolved. Mismanagement, id est in particular personal

[131] Deutsches Aktieninstitut (DAI), DAI-Factbook 2006 (Oct 2006) 08.5–1, 2006. See Luttermann in du Plessis/Großfeld et al. (2012) p. 339 (8.4.1 with data).

[132] The merger between Deutsche Boerse and London Stock Exchange was prevented by European regulators, Reuters, 29.3.2017 (www.reuters.com/article/us-lse-m-a-deutsche-boerse-eu-idUSKBN1700XG, accessed: 25.08.2025).

[133] With data on the development Luttermann in du Plessis/Großfeld et al. (2012) p. 339 (8.4.1) and (2017) p. 447 (9.5.1). Cf. Julian Franks and Colin Mayer in: Chew and Gillan (2009) for the U.K., Germany and France.

[134] Data: EY, *"Wem gehört der DAX?"* 2024 (Juli 2024, www.ey.com), cf. for 2015 in Du Plessis/Großfeld/Luttermann et al. (2017) p. 447.

[135] Referring to U.S. statistics: Krugman/Obstfeld/Melitz (2023) p. 222.

responsibility (see chapter 7), shows up here. An even sharper shift has happened with regard to the German banks themselves. When referring to "German banks" and their control of Corporate Germany (the so-called "Deutschland AG"), we must in fact also ask: Who controls the "German banks"? This simple question has obviously not been in the mainstream discussion, nor even asked at all. The answer lies in a look at some statistics.

Take, for example, the former circle of four major private banks and others that were the centre of Corporate Germany: Deutsche Bank AG, Dresdner Bank AG, Commerzbank AG, HypoVereinsbank AG.[136] The Dresdner Bank AG was acquired in 2001 in a takeover by the Allianz AG, with 49.3% of foreign shareholders (and even 71% in 2008),[137] and again in 2008 by the Commerzbank AG (see more about this in 6.7.3). The HypoVereinsbank AG was bought by the Italian UniCredit Group (Milan/Italy) in 2005, is now its 100% member and since December 15, 2009 has been called "UniCredit Bank AG". Another main address of the "Deutschland AG", the regional state bank (*Landesbank*) WestLB AG in Düsseldorf, driven by actors as arrogant as incapable into international dimensions, was devolved in 2012 to the detriment of the German tax-payer, after gigantic bad speculations (*Fehlspekulationen*) in subprime markets in the USA (CDOs, ABSs).[138] The Hypo Real Estate Holding AG, also strongly involved there, was taken over by the state (see 6.6.1, 6.6.5).

The IKB Deutsche Industriebank AG (Düsseldorf) became famous in the world debt crisis. It was supposed to finance mid-tier businesses with state involvement (KfW Bankengruppe – Kreditanstalt für Wiederaufbau). The members of the management board invested in "off-balance sheets" activities (cf. 4.5.7) via structured investment vehicles in subprime-speculation transactions in the USA (asset-backed commercial papers, CDO). Because the market was already drying out, the other party allegedly asked:[139] "Who is the [buying] idiot?" The salesman Greg Lippmann, top global CDO trader of Deutsche Bank AG, is said to have answered: "Duesseldorf. Stupid Germans. They take the rating agencies seriously. They believe in the rules."[140] Lippmann termed "the industry's ongoing CDO marketing efforts" a Ponzi scheme "to dupe someone".[141] Human greed and stupidity remain constants.[142] The Court of Appeals (*Oberlandesgericht*) Düsseldorf suspected

[136] The merger of the former Bayerische Vereinsbank AG and the Bayerische Hypothekenbank AG (1998).

[137] Deutsches Aktieninstitut (DAI) Factbook 2006, 08.5–1, 2006 (DAI Factbook 2010).

[138] Successor bank: Portigon AG. Overall Trampusch, Linden, Schwan (2014).

[139] Steve Eisman from the Hedgefonds Front Point. On practice see below in 6.6.5.

[140] Citation: The Economist, The Bigger Fools, 22.04.2010 (www.economist.com/node/15955490, accessed: 25.08.2025) with reference to Lewis (2010). Lippmann was crown witness for the study of the US Senate (see the following footnote and 6.6.5). On the situation at the time, 10.08.2007: www.wsj.com/articles/SB118670471880693703 (accessed: 25.08.2025). Cf. Luttermann (1998) and (2011).

[141] US Senate Permanent Subcommittee on Investigations. Wall Street and the Financial Crisis: Anatomy of a Financial Collapse, April 13, 2011, at 10 (in detail, e.g.: 318-375). See below 6.6.5.

[142] Read the classic by Galbraith (1994).

improbity or significant breach of duty by the management and the supervisory board of the IKB (considerable violation of the company goal, §§ 93(1), 111(1) AktG: Investments in international credit portfolios) and opened a special audit (*Sonderprüfung,* § 142(2) AktG).[143]

The events in those times continuously illustrate the significance of a consistently legal review of human failings for the present and the future. In the course of the development, personal responsibility of the management and supervisory board members are concretised,[144] investor protection is improved,[145] the shareholder's right to information is strengthened (§ 131 AktG: *Auskunftsrecht*).[146] The whole field still remains to be systematically dealt with.[147]

At the turn from 2024 to 2025 there had been just two more or less "independent" major banks based in Germany: the Commerzbank AG with predominantly foreign shareholders, with the Italian UniCredit SE already striving for take-over.[148] The main bank as yet is the Deutsche Bank AG (based in Frankfurt am Main). But that former incarnation of Corporate Germany, in spite of poor business, still had 44% foreign shareholders in 2015[149] (51% in 2022, 48% in 2023)[150] and for a long time external chief operating officers, one from Great Britain, who has had to deal with a minefield of legal cases (provisions for 2015: 5.2 billion) around the globe, mainly from the era of his experienced predecessors from Switzerland (Josef Ackermann) and India/Great Britain (Anshu Jain).[151] Deutsche Bank is a leading international player on the global capital markets (see 6.6.5).

In view of the reality of global financing and value creation chains, indispensable for the socio-ecological transformation of the economy (see chapter 1), here as in a

---

[143] OLG Düsseldorf, 09.12.2009 (I-6 W 45/09) ZIP 2010, 28; BGH, 1.3.2010 (II ZB 1/10) ZIP 2010, 446. OLG Düsseldorf, 26.11.2015 (I-3 Wx 134/14) ZIP 2016, 1022. Cf. BGH, 15.09.2020 (II ZB 6/20) BGHZ 227,137, <openJur 2020, 76150>; above 5.3.1.

[144] LG München I, 10.12.2013 (5 HK O 1387/10) ZIP 2014, 570 (*Siemens/Neubürger*), OLG München (7 U 113/14, proceedings settled without decision); LAG Düsseldorf, 20.01.2015 (16 Sa 459/14) ZIP 2015, 829. See above 6.4 as well penally against Stefan Ortseifen (CEO, *IKB*): LG Düsseldorf, 14.7.2010 (14 KLs 130 Js 54/07) <openjur.de/u/144615.html>; BGH, 20.07.2011 (3 StR 506/10) ZIP 2011, 5, <openJur 2011, 94779>.

[145] BGH, 13.12.2011 (XI ZR 51/10 – *IKB*) BGHZ 192, 90, <openJur 2012, 52956>. OLG München, 15.12.2014 (KAP 3/10 – *Hypo Real Estate Holding AG*) *ZIP* 2015, 689 and BGH, 01.12.2015 (XI ZB 13/14) <lexetius.com/2015, 4182>.

[146] OLG Stuttgart, 29.02.2012 (20 W 5/11 – *Porsche Automobil Holding SE*) ZIP 2012, 970, on this: BGH, 06.11.2012 (II ZR 111/12) ZIP 2012, 2438. BGH, 14.01.2014 (II ZB 5/12) ZIP 2012, 970.

[147] On this Luttermann (2012).

[148] For current data: www.investor-relations.commerzbank.comO. Cf. on the involvement of the German taxpayers (world debt crisis) below 6.6.3.

[149] Compared with 53% (2010: Luttermann in du Plessis, Großfeld (2017) 9.5.2).

[150] After even 58% in 2021 (https://investor-relations.db.com/share/shareholder-structure).

[151] Cf. Financial Times, 13.08.2022 (www.ft.com/content/9cdf16a0-6681-4186-a73d-12275ac4c066) and The New York Times, 17.08.2022 (www.nytimes.com/2022/08/17/business/dealbook/anshu-jain-dead.html, both accessed: 25.08.2025).

global perspective the following holds: It is definitely a misnomer still to refer to "German banks", as such banks controlled by German managers, shareholders and the "Deutschland AG" as the point of reference have disappeared under the massive influence of the global capital markets. The numbers and circumstances send a strong message: Obviously, the former glory of German banks (i.e. actually: their people) controlling Corporate Germany has vanished – appropriately global: The major banks with traditional names that are still around now have to share the globalised playground with a variety of very strong international competitors (see 6.2.3). It is time to think rather in commonalities (*Gemeinsamkeiten*) and cooperative structures for solving globally pressing problems (see chapter 8), to be personally established (see chapter 9).

### *6.5.3 Personal Duties and Liability*

Decisive for this globalised playground – subject to the "green" paradigm shift – is the corporate financial oligarchy already mentioned (see 6.2), which is slowly being recognised. Legally, the issue is an order of assets (*Vermögensordnung*), id est adequate structures (rules) according to the concept of justice and the conduct of the persons responsible (here the corporate directors on the boards for management or supervision) according to these rules (duty of care – *Sorgfaltspflicht*, see 6.4 and chapter 7). That is, we are basically always dealing not with the abstract, but with people (*Menschen*) – it's all about them (see, e.g. 6.6.3). For the formation of the rules, the architecture of the market and corporate governance of a shadow elite is concerned: Professional prime movers wearing different hats (lobbyists, government insiders, elected officials, businessmen) and ordering the fields of domestic, foreign and international policy, the flow of power and money practically without or at least without appropriate control.[152]

The Pax Americana is shown by the U.S. Department of Justice (DOJ), which tightens civil and criminal law liability for company directors in the case of "corporate misconduct". According to what was initially an internal guideline (so-called "Yates Memorandum") for all kinds of investigations, U.S. attorneys must hold individuals who have broken the law personally responsible. In the aftermath of the financial crisis, this is meant with protecting the national economy and all the citizens, who depend "on effective enforcement of the civil and criminal laws that protect our financial system": To this end, the memorandum fixes six procedural key steps "to strengthen our pursuit of individual wrongdoing" and "to hold to account the individuals responsible for illegal corporate conduct" at all levels in corporate cases.[153] In particular, any cooperation credit for the corporation (still to be

[152] Wedel (2009), Mayer (2016). See also below 6.6.3 and chapters 7 to 9.

[153] U.S. Deputy Attorney General Sally Q. Yates, Individual Accountability for Corporate Wrongdoing, 09.09.2015 (www.justice.gov/dag/file/769036/download). On this Luttermann (2016a), Dervan (2016), Copeland (2017).

prosecuted) is provided on condition that "full cooperation" is given in clearing any misconduct of individuals; id est that all relevant information (also on managers, staff members) is laid open proactively to the authorities. The core principles of the Yates Memorandum meanwhile have been officially incorporated into the updated and renamed U.S. Justice Manual for U.S. Attorneys (2018).[154]

The concept that risks of personal liability rise drastically in corporations shows the practical connections and basically sounds adequate (see 6.1). However, it is remarkable that it is, in particular, European competitors who are in the focus of liability. BNP Paribas, Daimler, Deutsche Bank, Siemens, to name just a few: The DOJ is skimming off money on a massive scale, making use of the interest tool for asset transfer in the international order of assets (*Vermögensordnung*).[155] This remains to be clarified with the law of nations and international private law in the context of the disputed extra-territorial validity of U.S.-American law.[156] In fact, the system is reaching out anyway globally in a massive way over the international capital markets, in particular financing, valuation, financial reporting and auditing of the corporation – the Pax Americana of corporate governance (see 6.2.1). Volkswagen says its diesel fraud scandal has cost €31.3 billion.[157] Environmental enforcement has come to stay.

## 6.6 Global Finance and Hyperspeculation[158]

### *6.6.1 Financing of Infinite Brassiness*

Let us take a closer look at actors and practices. The financial industry shapes the real economy. With the financial management of companies (corporations), as the core function (see 2.2.1), this also applies fundamentally to their corporate governance. We are experiencing an economic world of catastrophes, geopolitically tectonic breaks, still in the clutches of the world debt crisis (see 6.2.3 and Fig. 6.1): the final match or finally time for real change? – Billions of investments (speculations)

[154] Source: https://www.justice.gov/jm/justice-manual (accessed: 25.08.2025).

[155] See on Deutsche Bank below 6.6.5. Luttermann (2015a) and (2015b).

[156] Sandrock (2016). Cf. among others (restrictively) *Morrison v. National Australia Bank Ltd.*, 561 U.S. 247 (2010); *Kiobel v. Royal Dutch Petroleum Co.*, 133 S.Ct. 1659 (2013); *European Community v. RJR Nabisco, Inc.*, 783 F.3d 123 (2nd Cir. 2015) and *RJR Nabisco, Inc. v. European Community*, 579 U.S. 325 (2016); more recent: *Smagin v. Yegiazaryan*, 37 F.4th 562, 567, 570 (9th Cir. 2022), upheld by the S.Ct.: *Yegiazaryan v. Smagin*, No. 22-381, 2023 WL 4110234, at *8 (U.S. June 22, 2023). See also below 6.6.5 (Deutsche Bank AG) and 6.7.1 (Apple Inc.).

[157] See Reuters, 17.03.2020 (www.reuters.com/article/us-volkswagen-results-diesel-idUSKBN2141JB, accessed: 25.08.2025). On the limitation of claims (*Verjährung*) BGH, 29.07.2021 (VI ZR 1118/20) BGHZ 231, 1, <openJur 2021, 34114>.

[158] Based on Luttermann (2010b) and (2008b). See below 6.8.5 on the megahype AI. Groundbreaking on "value investing", i.e. investment v. speculation, Graham (2003).

in dollars, euros, yens and other so-called "securities" (*Wertpapiere*, financial instruments) or crypto tools (tokens, currencies) etc. are burnt in many scenarios.[159] In surreal pictures, we see the Anglo-American guardians of allegedly "free" markets in Great Britain and the USA socialising losses of private speculators on a massive scale (quantitative easing, inflation, see 6.2.2), giving the kiss of life to bankrupt banks and mortgage financers (Fannie Mae, Freddie Mac, see 6.4.3): Dead men walking.

Worldwide, players and the involuntary audience (participants), the taxpayers, the average citizens and savers (*Sparer*) via compulsory expropriations (*Zwangsenteignungen*), id est in real terms also due to ongoing inflation (devaluation of the purchasing power of fiat money, *Kaufkraftverlust*), are experiencing a rough awakening. They see themselves, companies and states worldwide on the brink and are astounded at the way gigantic masses of bail-out and bail-in funds are toppling over the edge. Down into the fathomless abyss, in Germany, for example, embodied by the Hypo Real Estate Holding AG, IKB Deutsche Industriebank AG as well as the Federal State banks (Bayern LB, HSH Nordbank, West LB etc.).[160]

The European Union (EU), in particular the European Economic and Monetary Union (Art. 140 TFEU), have degenerated into a transfer union. The European Commission (EC) is acting with bureaucratic centralism, demanding its own taxing authority (*Steuerhoheit*) and the right to issue its own Eurobonds (budget law – *Verschuldungshoheit*, cf. Art. 125 TFEU, Art. 5 TEU); a questionable kind of new "central intelligence".[161] Factually, the European Central Bank – like the Federal Reserve System in the USA – is establishing uncontrolled money creation (i.e. fiat money, quantitative easing, cf. 6.6.2) and an unprecedented debt community (*Schuldengemeinschaft*) through monetarisation of state bonds and even secretly via the Agreement on Net-Financial Assets.[162] – Where is the democratic legitimation[163] for all of this? – Leading institutions (judges) differ on limits: The German

---

[159] See above 4.1 as well as 6.5.2, 6.6.4, and 6.8.5 (megahype AI).

[160] Cf. below 6.6.3 (Commerzbank AG). Reliable data are lacking, for Germany losses for the taxpayers from the rescue of banks are reported to amount to 50 bn. (24.12.2015: www.faz.net/aktuell/wirtschaft/wirtschaftspolitik/bankenrettungsbilanz-50-milliarden-euro-verlust-fuer-steuerzahler-13982985.html); cf. officially, also on the SoFFin (currently: https://www.fmsa.de/en/, both accessed: 25.08.2025).

[161] See Luttermann (2011) and Art. 5 TEU. On raising joint debt (European bonds, e.g., in order to finance defence) Enrico Colombatto, 22.01.2025: www.gisreportsonline.com/r/eurobonds (accessed: 25.08.2025), Favero and Missale (2010); ultimately also for the financing of Ukraine, largely regardeless of the circumstances (legal and economic situation, social realities, corruption, etc.), future generations, and a reasonable concept (peace plan) as a whole. See above 1.4.2 and on liberty and regulation below 8.2.3. Cf. in general on EU bonds Bletzinger, Greif and Schwaab (2022).

[162] Jeff Black (06.02.2016): www.bloomberg.com/news/articles/2016-02-06/after-17-years-ecb-reveals-547-billion-in-central-bank-assets (accessed: 25.08.2025). On the effect on the Deutsche Bundesbank (German central bank) below in 6.2.2.

[163] See Art. 5 EU Treaty: the principle of subsidiarity, see above 4.11.3. Cf. BVerfG, 21.06.2016 (2 BvR 2728/13 et al.) <https://lexetius.com/2016,1547>, BVerfG, 28.06.2016 (2 BvR 322/13) <http://lexetius.com/2016,1814>.

Constitutional Court (*Bundesverfassungsgericht*) opposes the European Court of Justice.[164]

The actual purpose of this drama, easily obscured in the wafts of mist with political din, is in fact dramatic, almost spooky. Due to banks, be it from the private or the public sector, being saved by taxpayers' money, the ethics of liberty and responsibility is ruptured: Careless action obviously does not lead to liability. Losses accrued in private autonomy are loaded off onto the "state", id est the taxpayer (*Steuerzahler* and *Sparer* – saver!) as the real "lender of last resort" in this drama – in fact, the end of private property and the modern corporation. Talk about "systemic" risks is meant to overlay this (see 6.7.1). This also applies to the further rounds of rescue for banks in Europe and in the final instance all around the globe, declared as "assistance" (bailout) "for Greece", "for Ireland", "for Portugal" etc. to the public. Cyprus joined that club, at the same time leading the rush to bail-ins, where the savings of the savers of insolvent banks are expropriated, as also in Spain and Italy:[165] The drama was unfolding further, instead of merely continuing. – What is next?

### 6.6.2 Excessiveness and Gold Standard

We are not talking about the consequences of inescapable natural catastrophes (see 4.1). It has always been and still is always people who are acting: the company managers responsible (executive directors, supervisory board members), the auditors, market supervisors, investors – no abstract "systems". Alan Greenspan, Chairman of the Federal Reserve from 1987 to 2006, seems to have conjectured "a collapsing financial asset bubble" already in 1996, which "threaten to impair the real economy, its production, jobs, and price stability", asking the presumably rhetorical question: "How do we know when irrational exuberance has unduly escalated asset values, which then become subject to unexpected and prolonged contractions (…)?"[166] – In spite of this, he, who himself emphasised the elementary significance of value-containing circumstances for liberty (gold as *the* "protector of property rights"),[167] fired the markets speculatively with fiat money ("boom-bust cycle"). – What person responsible took any notice of the warning signals?

---

[164] ECJ, 11.12.2018 (C-493/17 – *Weiss*, DE) ECLI:EU:C:2018:1000 and on ultra-vires-control BVerfG, 20.05.2020 (2 BvR 859/15 et al.) BVerfGE 154, 17, <openJur 2020, 5178>.

[165] On Cyprus: ECJ, 20.09.2016 (C-8/15 P – *Ledra Advertising/Commission and ECB*, EN) ECLI:EU:C:2016:701, ECJ, 16.12.2020 (C-597/18 P et al. – *Chrysostomides & Co.*, EN) ECLI:EU:C:2020:1028. On European law (BRRD) above 6.4.3.

[166] Greenspan (1996).

[167] Greenspan (1967) p. 101: "gold and economic freedom are inseparable", and Greenspan (2016) after the Brexit referendum. The U.S. Constitution, specifically Art. I, 10 restricts states from using anything other than gold and silver coin as legal tender for debt payments; this is increasingly reflected in the laws of U.S. states (e.g., Alaska, Arizona, Indiana, Kansas, Louisiana, South Carolina, Texas, West Virginia). See Utah (H.B. 306, precious metals amendments) pioneering a transactional gold bill. Brief history of the Gold Standard in the United States: https://www.congress.gov/crs-product/R41887 (accessed: 25.08.2025). Cf. Luttermann (2008a), below 7.3.3, 8.2.1 and 8.3.1.

This is like a blow in the face of the taxpayers (depositors). Along with justice, democracy and liberty have eroded.[168] Where has the sense of reason gone? Prudence and virtues from Adam Smith to Amartya Sen and beyond,[169] the foundation of a market economy and a society of free people – entrepreneurs like all of us (see chapters 1 and 2). We see how order is eroding: The law appears to be an empty form. Particularly valuation or objective and measurable standards, id est in accounting and auditing,[170] rules are being defined downwards, another "race to the bottom"? Right up to insolvency law, where in Germany at least on a temporary basis the insolvency fact of "excessive indebtedness" had been slackened (§ 19 InsO, see 3.4.1), in order to prevent collapses of companies on a massive scale. This again highlights the central legal function and great importance of accounting and valuation law, which was (and is) ignored in the "numbers game" of the players on the financial and capital markets:[171] Immoderate valuation of companies and financial instruments as the objects and instruments of speculators and excessive speculation.

Financial reporting (bookkeeping, accounting and auditing) is usually discounted as "technical stuff" – although this is where the heart of sound business with reasonable corporate finance beats (see chapters 3 and 4). But basically, the financial industry made a dramatic change on the capital markets, based on weak theories and valuation patterns (leveraging, shareholder value, rating, US "GAAP" etc.). A neoclassical econometrics of the "production of profit" (i.e., shareholder value) without bounds has gained ground. It pervades economic theory and practice, borne by the belief in a predictable future: A model-like mathematising guild (e.g., financial engineering, algorithmic trading, cyborg finance), which also conducts a regime of sham rationality with "economic analysis of the law".[172]

This provides a clear indication of reduction and deformation. This is proven by the ongoing global debt crisis ("financial crisis") and in particular by the global climate change, which is about humans, the economy and the environment as a whole. As the Paris Agreement of 2015 put it: "the principle of equity and common but differentiated responsibilities and respective capabilities, in the light of different national circumstances"'.[173] The International Court of Justice speaks of the duty of states "to co-operate for the protection of the environment" as a rule of customary international law in order to protect people (human rights law).[174] But neoclassical

[168] Luttermann (2008c). Depenheuer (2009).

[169] See Smith (1759/1790[6]), esp. pp. 401-403 and Sen (2009) pp. IX-XXIV, esp. p. XIII: "a climate of mutual trust has to be cultivated and fostered". On the concept of trust above 1.5.2, on the juridical analysis of the economy below 6.7.3 and chapter 9. Basically Luttermann (1998), esp. pp. 135-145 and 465-485, Luttermann (2010a).

[170] See chapters 4 and 5.

[171] See chapter 4. Urgently on the "numbers game" as chairman of the U.S. SEC Levitt (1998). Luttermann (1999a) pp. 3-5 and overall Luttermann (2011).

[172] See 6.2.3 and 6.9 ("Goldman Sachs Algorithm"), 6.8.5, 7.8, and 8.5. Basically Mestmäcker (2007), Luttermann (2010a) and (1998) pp. 465-485. Note on this 6.7.

[173] United Nations, Paris Agreement 2015, preamble, recital 3. See above 6.6.1 and overall chapter 1.

[174] See ICJ, Advisory Opinion, 23.07.2025 (https://www.icj-cij.org/sites/default/files/case-related/187/187-20250723-adv-01-00-en.pdf, accessed: 25.08.2025), paras. 140-142 with 371-404, also paras. 301-308. See above 6.1, below 6.7.2.

economic theory and its believers have failed because their constructs are not about people (see 6.7, 8.1). Before the first world economic crisis, the Great Depression of the 1930s, Frank Knight,[175] one of the founders of the Chicago school of economists, already saw "evil results of the failure to emphasize the theoretical character of economic speculation (...) in every field of practical economics".

Warnings such as this were lost in the wind. An economy without law (morals) and measure: no order of assets (*Vermögensordnung*).[176] Admittedly, around the turn of the millennium the highly speculative dot-com bubble had burst and many accounting scandals had been uncovered (e.g. Enron and WorldCom in the USA, Parmalat/Italy, SK Group/South Korea, Livedoor/Japan, Satyam/India). But the financial industry happily continued to celebrate its overindulgence of debts, securitisation and immoderate valuation.[177] In Germany, this was politically supported by the so-called *Finanzmarktfördergesetze* (financial market promotion laws) under the Federal government of Federal Chancellor Gerhard Schröder. This opened the door for the "securitization" of assets,[178] nowadays demonised also by politicians: Competition in the global marketplace as yet another "race to the bottom", abandoning the function of the law.

### *6.6.3 The Goldman Sachs Group, Inc. Case*

Some highlights may illustrate patterns of action. In addition to the case of Lehman Brothers, Inc. (see 4.6.2), mention may first be made of the investment bank Goldman Sachs Group, Inc., a key player of the global financial industry. Power structures (shadow elite, see 6.5.3) are here illustrated by two persons who, after leading Goldman Sachs changed to the office of the U.S. Secretary of Treasury, like Henry M. Paulson Jr. (2006–2009, prior: Chairman and CEO of Goldman 1999–2006). He orchestrated the acute financial crisis (*Weltschuldenkrise*) with the Troubled Asset Relief Program (TARP),[179] the salvage of Goldman Sachs and the demise of the competing investment banks Bear Stearns Companies, Inc. and Lehman Brothers Holdings, Inc.[180] A predecessor, Robert E. Rubin (member of

---

[175] Knight (1971) pp. 11–12.

[176] See above 5.2.2 and Luttermann (2009); also above 6.2.3 and 6.5.3.

[177] Informative Morris (2008). Comprehensive Aliber, Kindleberger, McCauley (2023).

[178] Kothari (2006), Zissu and Stone (2012).

[179] On the rescue measures U.S. Treasury (https://home.treasury.gov/data/troubled-asset-relief-program, www.nytimes.com/2009/03/16/business/16rescue.html, and www.nytimes.com/2011/12/04/business/secrets-of-the-bailout-now-revealed.html, all accessed: 25.08.2025). Berger and Roman (2020).

[180] On Lehman: www.nytimes.com/2014/09/30/business/revisiting-the-lehman-brothers-bailout-that-never-was.html, on Goldman: www.businessinsider.com/buffett-tells-country-tarp-gave-over-1-billion-to-goldman-sachs-2011-3?IR=T; cf. overall Henry Paulson (2010), www.nytimes.com/2009/08/09/business/09paulson.html (all accessed: 25.08.2025).

the board, Co-Chairman of Goldman 1990–92), was instrumental in the fatal deregulation of banks and financial markets as Secretary of the Treasury (1995–1999) and himself made a fortune in the financial crisis.[181]

The U.S. Securities and Exchange Commission (SEC) pressed charges against Goldman Sachs and their hedge funds manager Fabrice Tourre for securities fraud (*Wertpapierbetrug*). The reasoning essentially emphasises misleading statements and failures in the sales of financial instruments, namely so-called synthetic collateralized debt obligations (CDOs, here: Abacus 2007-AC1). This is no trivial offense. The SEC as the public watchdog of financial markets in the USA states: "Synthetic CDOs like ABACUS 2007-AC1 contributed to the recent financial crisis by magnifying losses associated with the downturn in the United States housing market."[182] The CDOs were structured intentionally by Goldman Sachs actors with reference portfolios of residential mortgage-backed securities (RMBS), valuated by rating agencies with "triple A" and sold to investors. There were targeted bets against the CDO. The SEC explained:

> "Undisclosed in the marketing materials and unbeknownst to investors, a large hedge fund, Paulson & Co. Inc. (Paulson), with economic interests directly adverse to investors in the ABACUS 2007-AC1 CDO played a significant role in the portfolio selection process. After participating in the selection of the reference portfolio, Paulson effectively shorted the RMBS portfolio it helped."[183]

Thereby, the fall of the so-called "securities" (in German: *Wertpapiere*, but in fact more paper than value, without any security at all) and large profits of the defendants (i.e., Goldman) were programmed, the buyers suffering all associated losses. For sure, computerisation is transforming financial markets (investment banking) and may in the actors' dealing rooms "rely upon a transactional, arm's-length model of business," – whatever that means, – "so that they need a reputation for competence and transparency, but not for their ability to sustain private, trust-based trade".[184] Well, then we can leave it all to technology in a brave new world (cf. 9.5 to 9.7). Who cares? – Just think: Every algorithm is an "opinion embedded in code",[185] id est indeed – along with the rising complexity in markets – a black box within computer programs.

---

[181] See, e.g., the abolition of the separation of credit banks and investment banks (Glass-Steagall Act of 1933). Already leading positions in Goldman from 1966-1990. After his time as Secretary of the Treasury among others with Citigroup Inc. (on this: www.nytimes.com/2009/01/10/business/10rubin.html?_r=2&hp, accessed: 25.08.2025) and financial counsellor of U.S. President Barack Obama.

[182] SEC, Litigation Release No. 21489, 16.04.2010: SEC v. Goldman, Sachs & Co. and Fabrice Tourre, 10 Civ. 3229 (BJ) (S.D.N.Y.), www.sec.gov/litigation/litreleases/2010/lr21489.htm (accessed: 25.08.2025).

[183] With Credit Default Swaps: see SEC (preceding footnote) as well as generally above 5.5.4. Note: founder of "Paulson & Co. Inc." is John A. Paulson (1994).

[184] Davidoff/Morrison/Wilhelm (2012) 529, at 551.

[185] See O'Neil (2016).

Goldman Sachs accepted the charges. With internal mails from hedge funds staff, the SEC showed that with the "Abacus 2007-AC1", the rating agencies, the CDO managers and the underwriters all acted in concert. This meant that the game on the RMBS market, which had in actual fact already been speculated into ruins, went on. A member of the Paulson staff, acting with Goldman, is cited as saying: The investors (those with real money) had neither the analytical tools nor an institutional framework for acting before the losses, which could have been anticipated from all available news sources, were actually realized.[186] This is not an individual case, but rather one piece of the puzzle of a global strategy, as a study by the US Senate proves (see 6.6.5). All in all, it is an evil game.

### 6.6.4 *Financial Engineering (CDOs and CDSs)*[187]

This evil game points to a greediness and striving for excessive profits, which has increasingly influenced capital markets, investors and banks – all the way to Bitcoin and the like: "worse than a Ponzi".[188] The Goldman case is only the tip of the iceberg. Collateralized Debt Obligations (CDOs, see Fig. 6.2) and Credit Default Swaps (CDSs) are symptomatic of the whole field: Financial engineering, continuous tinkering with what is generally called "financial instruments" (structured finance) with risk transfer in micro-economic structures (contracts, corporations) and macro-economic structures (markets) has massively changed the business world and corporate governance (see 6.7). Use is made of technical, quantitative methods, models and strategies (e.g., statistics, mathematical and computational finance).[189] Apart from the investment bankers, it is mainly the managers of hedge funds that stand for this in public. However, even so-called traditional banks such as the Deutsche Bank AG have taken this road (see 6.6.5). Let us for the moment remain with the structured finance products.

The credit default swap (CDS), subject also to CDO engineering (the "CDO machine", that right away), is located in the universe of structured financial instruments (derivatives). Basically, this is credit insurance. Credits and corporate bonds (debentures, notes)[190] may fail: The debtor is simply not able to fulfil his obligations

[186] See SEC v. Goldman, Sachs & Co. and Fabrice Tourre, 10 Civ. 3229 (BJ) (S.D.N.Y.), www.sec.gov/litigation/complaints/2010/comp-pr2010-59.pdf, no. 17.

[187] Overall Luttermann (2008b). Cf. above 3.6.3 and 3.6.4 (trust indenture). Basically on the ownership of securities (property interests, security entitlements) in the USA, see Uniform Commercial Code (UCC Art. 8: www.uniformlaws.org/acts/ucc), and, e.g., Facciolo (2000), Bjerre (2004), Talgo (2024). For global clearing and settlement across asset classes, see Depositary Trust and Clearing Corporation (www.dtcc.com).

[188] Aliber, Kindleberger, McCauley (2023), from p. 349.

[189] Kosowski and Neftci (2015), Chatterjee (2014). Beder and Marshall (2011). Critically already Taleb (2007).

[190] On the (traditional) terms above 3.6.3.

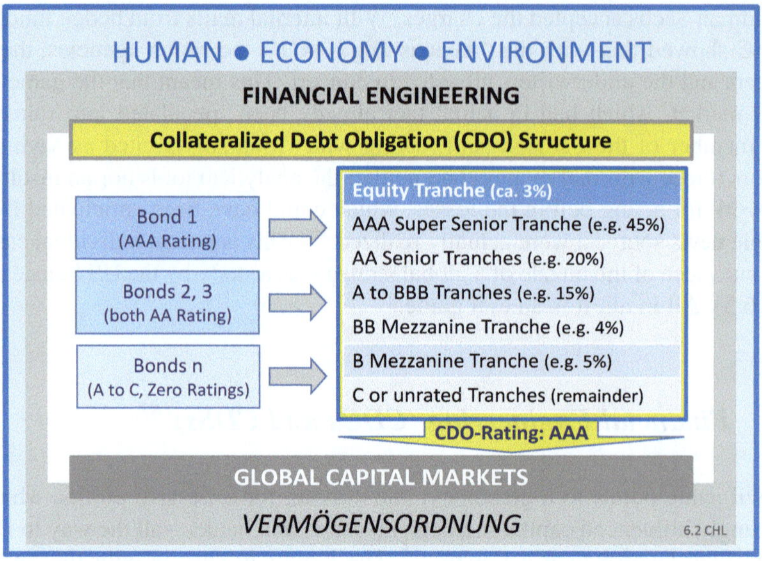


**Fig. 6.2** The structure of a "Collateralized Debt Obligation" (CDO, example) according to a rating system (cf. Moody's, Standard & Poor's, Fitch Ratings)

on time. The creditor can insure his demand. The initial situation is simple. In the contract of the (single-name) CDS there is the protection buyer (*Sicherungsnehmer*) and the protection seller (*Sicherungsgeber*). They agree for the duration of the contract (e.g., typically five years) that the protection seller provides something (settlement, see for Germany § 241 *Bürgerliches Gesetzbuch*, BGB) to the protection buyer in the case of the specific credit event (*Kreditereignis*). The credit event occurs with a third party, the reference entity (*Referenzschuldner*). This is usually a corporation, which has some kind of debt, e.g. in the form of a bond pending. The specific debt of the third party is the so-called credit asset (*Referenzaktivum*).

Examples of a specific credit event include: late payment, downgrading of rating (e.g. according to financial, environmental demands) or insolvency of the third party. The service of the protection seller is: (a) He pays a sum amounting to the nominal value of the CDS in cash to the protection buyer, who in exchange transfers the defaulting bond to the protection seller (physical settlement), or (b) the protection seller pays the protection buyer the difference between the nominal value of the CDS and the current value of the credit asset (cash settlement). The CDS thus transfers the failure risk between the counterparties from the protection buyer to the protection seller. For this, the latter receives regular bonus payments from the protection buyer during the term of the contract. In principle, the CDS is a sensible construction. However, its valuation is problematic: What value does it represent? This is related to the credit asset (e.g., a bond of the General Motors Company) and the rating of the counterparty, which, however, is usually unknown.

For practice creates any number of CDSs and structures them with the so-called Collateralized Debt Obligations (CDOs). These combine bonds or CDSs of different issuers, divided into risk classes (tranches, subject to change without disclosure, see Fig. 6.2).[191] According to their rating, they are valuated with – highly questionable – quantitative methods, and sold. Also included are synthetic, id est artificially created CDOs (within the "CDO machine" so-called CDO-squareds).[192] For the market does not actually contain enough bonds of (certain) corporations to cover the demand for CDOs. The parties of the CDO do not need to hold the credit asset or actually suffer a loss. This opens the door to speculation. Market participants bet on the failure of a creditor (short selling): With the assumed probability of the failure of the company (corporation) the value of the CDS rises. In this way, companies and even sovereign states (see, e.g., Greece, Ireland, Portugal) are made ready for attack – even by way of rumour: strategies of "make-believe" may knock out facts.

The amounts due are hardly conceivable. The Bank for International Settlements (BIS) has estimated the notional amount for the end of 2007 at 45 trillion US dollars and reported on resurging market presence (CDO)[193] in many colours (e.g., CLO).[194] The synthetic CDO structures are ready for transitional policies and games, fostering the economy with "green" activities and valuation. However, of course: "Buyers Beware".[195] If there is no active market, as was the case for many of these products in the crisis since 2008, the valuations (mark-to-model approach)[196] go completely haywire. The financial instruments then turn out to be what they mostly were right from the outset: "toxic assets". They are contained in the accounts of many companies and need to be written off. This fires crisis even more. Warren Buffet[197] talked about "financial weapons of mass destruction". The OTC

[191] The usual structure of the product had been described: Super-senior tranche (30-100%, cover system risks, valuated with "AAA"), one or more senior tranches (30-10%) or mezzanine tranches (10-3%) for losses ("AA" to "BB") and equity tranche (for first up to 3% losses [idiosyncratic risks], non-valuated – "toxic waste"), International Monetary Fund, Global financial stability report, April 2006, pp. 53–54, 62. Generally subject matter of freedom of contract. Cf. rules of valuation: FASB, FAS 157 – Fair value measurement (under: https://fasb.org).

[192] This means "CDOs from CDOs", i.e. in fact, "leverage on leverage"; also: leveraged super-senior products and CDOs with asset-backed securities (ABSs). Overall National Commission on the causes of the financial and economic crisis in the US, The financial crisis inquiry report, pursuant to Public Law 111-21, final report (official government ed., January 2011), esp. from p. 127 (the CDO machine). See also Deutsche Bank AG with CDO "Gemstone 7", as an example, below 6.6.5 and above 6.6.3 on the Goldman Sachs CDO "Abacus 2007-AC1".

[193] Antoniades/Tarashev (2014, www.bis.org). Data: International Swaps and Derivatives Association (www.isda.org); The Depository Trust and Clearing Corporation (www.dtcc.com).

[194] Collateralized Loan Obligation. See below 6.7.2 and Uzialko (2023).

[195] E.g., Alastair Marsh, 09.06.2022: www.bloomberg.com/news/articles/2022-06-09/does-this-cdo-come-in-green-with-esg-everywhere-buyers-beware (accessed: 25.08.2025).

[196] Cf., FASB, Statement of Financial Accounting Standards No. 157: Fair value measurements (cf. IASB, IFRS 13). On the downfall of Enron Corp. as an example for accounting fraud: Milhaupt and Pistor (2008) pp. 47-67.

[197] Berkshire Hathaway, Annual report to shareholders 2002. Cf. Tabassum and Yameen (2024).

[198] All risk categories, see: Bank for International Settlements, www.bis.org/statistics/dataportal/derivatives.htm (accessed: 25.08.2025).

derivatives notional amount is outstanding: 667 trillion US-dollars (2023), 729 trillion US-dollars (2024).[198]

### 6.6.5 The Case of Deutsche Bank AG

Classical financial business, financing real-economy industrial companies, seems to be fading. The financial industry with its profit-chasing products is enticing. Immoderate speculation has taken hold of the banking sector, in accordance with the investment banks and hedge funds, as the Deutsche Bank AG shows. Its hoard of derivatives contracts traded outside of the stock markets (e.g., CDSs, see Fig. 6.2) in 2014 amounted to the notional amount of 49.6 billion euros, in the financial report 1.75 billion euros are displayed: huge sums for risk management;[199] compare the German GDP in 2014: 2.915 billion euros.[200] Only JPMorgan Chase & Co. turned an even bigger derivative wheel globally. The International Monetary Fund saw the Deutsche Bank AG as "one of the most important net contributors to systemic risks in the global banking system".[201] The bank continues to cause market concerns and make headlines: "Deutsche Bank looks to escape a decade of scandal and strife",[202] but faces fines, including "for slow progress against money laundering".[203]

Although the façade may still lead one to believe something different: Deutsche Bank AG has long since changed from classic corporate governance, the sound as well as staid German model of the house bank (*Hausbank*),[204] to being a global player – a global, systematically important bank.[205] This was detectible at an early stage in what later became core markets of the crisis (subprime mortgages, CDO/CDS). The Deutsche Bank AG was among the great players worldwide, also in the fall of Lehman Brothers Holdings, Inc. (see 4.6.2). In 2008, it slid into an imbalance[206] and was sued by US authorities (May 2011). A study by the U.S. Congress already in April 2011 is very clear. The US Senate Permanent Subcommittee on Investigations calls the Deutsche Bank an investment bank (*sic*!) and – apart from Goldman Sachs – one of the leading triggers of the global financial

[198] All risk categories, see: Bank for International Settlements, www.bis.org/statistics/dataportal/derivatives.htm (accessed: 25.08.2025).

[199] See §§ 91(2), 93 and 111 AktG. On this below 6.8.2.

[200] *Statistisches Bundesamt* (www.destatis.de). Deutsche Bank AG, Annual Reports: https://investor-relations.db.com/reports-and-events/annual-reports/. See also 6.5.2.

[201] IMF, Country report No. 16/191: Germany stress testing the banking and insurance sectors, p. 5 (www.imf.org/external/pubs/ft/scr/2016/cr16191.pdf).

[202] Olaf Storbeck, Financial Times, 17.05.2022 (www.ft.com/content/06158598-daa0-4560-b072-a57bcbd7697c, accessed: 25.08.2025). See also below 7.2.1

[203] Pete Schroeder, Chris Prentice, 19.07.2023: www.reuters.com/business/finance/fed-fines-deutsche-bank-186-mln-insufficient-progress-addressing-anti-money-2023-07-19/ (accessed: 25.08.2025).

[204] See above 6.2.3 and below 6.7.3.

[205] According to the Financial Stability Board (FSB, for current data: www.fsb.org).

[206] On this already Luttermann (2008b) 741, 742.

crisis: "The investment banks that engineered, sold, traded, and profited mortgage related structured finance products were a major cause of the financial crisis".[207]

The gambling game of the Deutsche Bank AG was also about structured finance products, namely CDOs such as "Gemstone 7". Many of the residential mortgage backed securities (RMBS; see 6.6.3) combined in this were "likely to lose value" or were even dubbed by Greg Lippmann, the bank's top global CDO-trader, as "crap" and "pigs". Despite the poor quality of these underlying assets, the top three tranches of "Gemstone 7" received the top rating AAA by the two globally leading rating agencies Moody's Investor Service, Inc. and Standard & Poor's Financial Services LLC. The study by the U.S. Senate explains: Mr. Lippmann referred to the financial industry's ongoing CDO marketing efforts as a "CDO machine" or "Ponzi scheme", id est, a fraudulent system. Once, Mr. Lippmann, so the study says, was asked to buy a specific CDO security and answered that it "rarely trades", but he "would take it and try to dupe someone into buying it".[208] – Simply said: Greed eats up brains.

In the face of an already deteriorating market, the "Gemstone 7"-CDO was sold aggressively by the Deutsche Bank AG (volume: US$ 1.1 billion) and was in the last instance worthless. Investment banks sold structured finance products like these and similar ones massively around the globe; in 2006 und 2007 alone they amounted to around US$ 1 trillion CDO issuance. They earned fees in a range of US$ 5–10 million per CDO, the Deutsche Bank AG alone issuing 47 asset-back ed CDO from 2004 to 2008 (total securitisation: US$ 32.2 billion).[209] Both Deutsche Bank AG and Goldman Sachs, the U.S. Senate study reports, took substantial portions of the short side of CDO (RMBS), which they sold to their clients. This means they betted that the assets would lose value within the CDO or would not perform. Indeed, buyers, among them German Federal State banks, Hypo Real Estate Holding AG, IKB Deutsche Industriebank AG as well as, via funds, numerous private investors and in the last instance the taxpayers or the savers[210] lost hundreds of billions in US dollars. This much is to be said: The Deutsche Bank AG did not act as a bank, but in fact as a kind of casino. As a consequence, the U.S. Department of Justice presented the bank with a considerable sanction in the billions.[211]

The Deutsche Bank AG is considered a global player on the financial markets.[212] This makes demands on the corporate directors in particular in internal control and

---

[207] US Senate Permanent Subcommittee on Investigations, Wall Street and the financial crisis: anatomy of a financial collapse, April 13, 2011, pp. 7 and 11 (under the heading: "Investment Bank Abuses"). Cf. above 6.6.4.

[208] US Senate, ibid., p. 10. See above 6.5.2. On rating agencies Luttermann (2011).

[209] Data according to US Senate, ibid., pp. 333–335.

[210] Subsequent litigation, e.g., BGH, 13.12.2011 (XI ZR 51/10 – *IKB*) BGHZ 192, 90, <openJur 2012, 52956>; cf. above 6.6.3 and 6.5.2.

[211] $7.2bn. Cf. above 6.4.2 and – esp. on law of nations – in 6.5.3 (last paragraph).

[212] See, e.g., on the Deutsche Bank AG: BGH, 22.03.2011 (XI ZR 33/10) BGHZ 189, 13, <openJur 2011, 91599> (CMS Spread Ladder Swap). Cf. on the risk-related duty of disclosure: BGH, 20.01.2015 (XI ZR 316/13) NJW 2015, 1095, <openJur 2015, 5944>, BGH, 22.03.2016 (XI ZR 425/14) NJW 2016, 2949, <openJur 2016, 5724>, BGH, 07.02.2019 (III ZR 498/16) NJW 2019, 1137, <openJur 2019, 2231>, BGH, 16.05.2019 (III ZR 176/18) WM 2019, 1203, <openJur 2019, 28533>.

risk management (cf. §§ 91(2), 93, 111 AktG). Both have been and continue to be criticised in terms of financial burdens and transparency.[213] It is in this context that the idea of a "risk passport" (*Risikopass*) for each financial instrument is located, already published at the turn of the century and later enacted in law.[214] In 2010, Japan's Central Bank and Financial Services Agency ranked the Deutsche Bank AG – like the USA probably out of political motivation (cf. 6.5.3) – as "the world's most systemically financial institution" – even more than Goldman Sachs Group Inc. and JPMorgan Chase & Co.[215] The Financial Stability Board (FSB) lists the Deutsche Bank AG as a global systemically important bank.[216] Accordingly, the bank is also a particularly important player in the German area – but hardly in the sense of the old "Deutschland AG", as the macro-economic relations in particular demonstrate.

## 6.7 Macroeconomics of Human Corporation[217]

### *6.7.1 Real Economy and Systemic Risk: "Too-Big-to-Fail"?*

Banks and financial institutions in general have lost touch with the real economy (*Realwirtschaft*). This is a main cause of the world debt crisis and a tag to downplay, while the players of the financial industry are playing their own game. They are drifting off into a world of make-believe, doing financial engineering for endlessly new "financial instruments": abstract, often synthetic products, also with corporate bonds as underlying assets (structured finance products). The green wave, sweeping the globe with climate change, is also being processed: the link to sustainability can make a great difference (see 4.2). Derivatives Casinos like JP Morgan Chase, Deutsche Bank, UBS and Credit Suisse once each displayed more than $50bn in derivatives.[218] Instead of financing companies, that serves massive speculation,

[213] Proceedings by the German Bafin against Deutsche Bank are legion. Cf. Tom Sims, Marta Orosz, 04.01.2023: www.reuters.com/business/finance/deutsche-banks-rollercoaster-ride-towards-more-stability-2022-12-16/ (accessed: 25.08.2025).

[214] Originally with the idea of a so-called *Risikopass* (risk passport) for financial instruments Luttermann (2001) 1901, 1904-1905, enacted as the so-called key information documents (*Basisinformationsblatt*) for packaged retail and insurance-based investment products (PRIIPS) in Regulation (EU) No 1286/2014 of 26 November 2014, see Luttermann (2015c). See also below 8. 3.3.

[215] Bloomberg, Dec 28, 2010: Banks were ranked on the impact their failure would have on the global financial system (https://www.bloomberg.com). On "systemic risk" above 6.6.1.

[216] List of global systemically important banks: in bucket 2, as of Nov. 2024; cf. in bucket 3, as of Nov. 2015 (www.fsb.org).

[217] Based on Luttermann (2010a) and (2013), Luttermann (1998).

[218] According to: http://insideparadeplatz.ch/2016/02/10/50-980-000-000-000-die-derivat-bombe-mitten-im-herzen-vom-paradeplatz (accessed: 25.08.2025). Cf. above 6.6.5.

which entails covert transfer of risks. These are hardly understood any more even by the initiators, concealing their true nature of representing gigantic losses or debts.

This has fundamental consequences for the real economy and for us all. The community of a large number of small investors, savers and, in the final instance, taxpayers are expected to pick up the bill (bailout/-in, see 6.4.3). They are to bear the costs of failed investments for the squad of speculators, so-called "sophisticated investors", who underrated or consciously challenged the risk (loss). Those responsible obviously like to detract from causes and individual guilt: Banking on failure instead of banking on trust (see 1.5.2). For the socialisation of the gaming risks, a myth of "systematic risks" is woven. Some companies are even, according to supporting comments from the (then) U.S. Chairman of the Federal Reserve Bank Ben Bernanke,[219] "too-big-to-fail". His words are repeated by the protagonists of the private finance industry and politicians around the globe. In this practice, the proportion of the financial sector within the gross domestic product (GDP) has risen out of proportion, whereas, e.g., in the USA and Great Britain de-industrialisation is rampant.[220]

At the same time, influence and power of the financial industry have increased. Failure becomes tangible here: If indeed there are companies that are "too-big-to-fail", id est also "too-big-to-manage", the *Rechtshonoratioren* (legal honoraries) have failed systematically. For such a magnitude does not come into being over night or "out of the blue". Such firms are simply too big for them to be allowed to escape unscathed. With their implicit state guarantee, they distort competition to an unbearable degree. Why not establish or create "good banks" with shares for the citizens (as the real "lenders of last resort", see 6.2.2) that provide good returns on investments, instead of carrying on with the subsidisation of "bad banks"? Where is the economy with fair competition on free markets, when bankruptcy is eliminated for some players (see 6.6.1) and the biggest gamblers are supported, instead of promoting (see chapter 7) a culture of responsibility? Correcting these aberrations is essential for being sustainable and long overdue: Ending "too-big-to-fail", "too-big-to-regulate".[221] – Still sounds good, but: What is changing?

Inequalities are rising dramatically. Tax havens are at the core, since a large portion of the global financial assets is left untaxed: Apple Inc. paid only 0.005 per cent tax on its European profits via its Irish companies (2014) and has in turn for the time being received a 13-billion-euro tax bill due to illegal tax benefits.[222] Massive shifts and concentration of assets globally, while the OECD is tackling tax

[219] Speech: Financial reform to address systemic risk, 10.03.2009 (https://www.federalreserve.gov/newsevents/speech/bernanke20090310a.htm, accessed: 25.08.2025). Cf. above 6.2.2.

[220] See, e.g., Tomlinson (2016) and Di Berardino, D'Angelo, and Sarra (2025).

[221] Financial Stability Board (FSB), Progress and Next Steps Towards Ending "Too-Big-To-Fail" (02.09.2013: www.fsb.org/wp-content/uploads/r_130902.pdf). Cf. above 6.2.3 and Hellwig (2021), Ioannou, Iliopoulos, and Wójcik (2023).

[222] European Commission, 30.08.2016 (press release: http://europa.eu/rapid/press-release_IP-16-2923_en.htm, accessed: 25.08.2025; on this Philip Aldrick, America threatens tit-for-tat retaliation against Europeans, The Times, 31.08.2016, p. 9). See the result ECJ, 10.09.2024 (C-465/20 P – *Commission v. Ireland, Apple et al.*, EN) ECLI:EU:C:2024:724. Cf. above 6.5.3 and 6.2.4 (Panama Papers etc.).

avoidance[223] and debts are exploding, and megabanks have become even bigger (see 6.2.3). The Financial Stability Board sums up "some gaps", such as that "risks associated with credit intermediation may have shifted to non-bank finance" and "the resilience of non-bank financial intermediation".[224] Now, "too-big-to-regulate" is spreading with new technology (AI, see 6.8.5).[225] Early on, we spoke about the wind of change, about responsibility and sustainability: fundamental for the human corporation, finance (investment) and capital markets globally.[226] Will there be any sustainable consequences?

## 6.7.2 *Sustainability: The Practice of a Paradigm Shift*

Sustainability sounds new-fangled, but it remains, in its very character (see 5.2.4), the decisive factor of the human corporation: for the "socio-ecological transformation of the economy" in the sens of humanity (see chapter 1). The paradigm-shift needs to be conceived and practised holistically. We are thus at the beginning of a tough journey to real values (substance), to sustainable development instead of fast profits. Back to personal responsibility, as illustrated: financial reporting as verified information for investors.[227] This comprises, in each individual case of a "breach of duty" of a corporate director, of course the strict enforcement of personal responsibility (liability) according to the legal norms (see 6.4, 6.5.3). But that is still lacking. In practice, this means no less than a real paradigm shift is needed, a Copernican turn,[228] affecting powerful interests. Accordingly, the struggles are hard, and manifold signs are visible.

This has long since been the case, despite the facts on the table.[229] For instance, in 2010, the SEC made it easier for big shareholders to place their candidates for the board of directors on the company ballots (proxy ballots). The Business Round Table and the Chamber of Commerce contested this decision, to "preserve that traditional standard of corporate governance"; as the Wall Street Journal comments: "Around half of all Americans own stock directly or indirectly in a public company and want CEOs to make decisions based on long-term profitability, not anyone's

[223] On the OECD initiative "Base Erosion and Profit Shifting" (BEPS) see above 4.7.2.

[224] FSB, Evaluation of the effects of too-big-to-fail reforms: Final Report, 31.03.2021 (https://www.fsb.org/uploads/P010421-1.pdf). Cf. Hellwig (2021).

[225] See, e.g., Saad-Diniz and Puppe (2024). See also below 9.6.

[226] See 6.5.1 and 6.7.2 (already, e.g., Luttermann and Du Plessis in: Du Plessis, Großfeld, Luttermann et al. (2012) 8.4.1); see also above chapters 4 and 5.

[227] See above 5.6.1, chapter 4. On the transformation to sustainable business activities (financial due diligence) with data for 2023 from banking regulation Luttermann, L. (2024) and (2025): a European opening balance (*Eröffnungsbilanz*).

[228] So already explicitly Luttermann (2011), based on Luttermann (1998), with numerous pieces of evidence. See chapters 7 and 8.

[229] See, e.g., Luttermann (1998) and (1999a).

political agenda".[230] The United Kingdom's Independent Commission on Banking urged that the implicit government guarantee, which is encouraging too much risk taking, should be ended: "Banks ought to face market disciplines without any prospect of taxpayers' support".[231] This means that in case of failure, before the taxpayers are expected to pick up the bill, it is the shareholders and bondholders of the company who should bear the losses first. In the European Union, this role in financial institutions has already been legally allotted to the savers (*Sparer*, so-called "bail-in", see 6.4.3).

This order, in which losses are to be picked up, goes to the heart and fundamental purpose of a market economy with private property, private autonomy and fair competition. This highlights areas of conflict and approaches to a solution, consolidating the corporation in its eminent financing function – micro- and macroeconomically (see 2.5, 6.7): integral as a modern instrument (actor) of private entrepreneurship of humans in social community and the environment. Actually, this is self-evident in the sense of sustainability, conceived and practiced comprehensively. However, practice hitherto widely attests to the deficient reality of the corporate world with its neoclassical dogmatism of "maximising shareholder return" as the core problem (so-called "fair value", see 4.6.3). In more recent times, in autumn 2019, even some 200 chief executives from the Business Round Table (BRT) in the USA issued a remarkable "Statement on the Purpose of a Corporation":

> "While each of our individual companies serves its own corporate purpose, we share a fundamental commitment to all of our stakeholders. We commit to: Delivering value to our customers. (...) Investing in our employees. (...) Dealing fairly and ethically with our suppliers. (...) Supporting the communities in which we work. (...) and protect the environment by embracing sustainable practices across our businesses. Generating long-term value for shareholders, who provide the capital that allows companies to invest, grow and innovate. We are committed to transparency and effective engagement with shareholders. (...) Each of our stakeholders is essential. We commit to deliver value to all of them, for the future success of our companies, our communities and our country."[232]

Well, to remain clear: The country they commit to deliver to is the USA. An interesting statement from CEOs of corporations (e.g., Amazon, Apple, Fedex, MacDonald's, Microsoft, Visa), who practise business worldwide. And they proclaim: "to all of our stakeholders". That would be a break, as the New York Times put it, "with decades of long-held corporate orthodoxy": the Round table argues, "that companies should no longer advance only the interests of shareholders", promising "to protect the environment by embracing sustainable practices across

[230] The Wall Street Journal, 18.04.2011, 11 ("proxies vs. profits"). Cf. Hayden and Bodie (2012).

[231] ICB, Interim report: consultation on reform options (executive summary, April 2011), 2; cf. Final report, September 2011, Recommendations. Fikentscher (2009) and Möschel (2009).

[232] BRT, 19.08.2019: https://s3.amazonas.com/brt.org/BRT-StatementonthePurposeofaCorporationwithSignaturesJanuary2023.pdf (accessed: 25.08.2025).

our businesses".[233] Sounds bold, however, they should be judged by their deeds: Do they walk their talk? – The appraisals sound rather sceptical, the Guardian describes: "How a top US business lobby promised climate action – but worked to block efforts".[234] What seems to go with this is "window dressing", because "neither the law nor the incentive structure for CEOs has changed. (…) CEOs remain legally obliged – and can be expected – to prefer shareholder interests."[235] – Is that right?

In fact, the Business Round Table statement "did not represent a meaningful commitment (…) to bring about meaningful improvements in the treatment of stakeholders".[236] It turns out: Wall Street is alive, still[237] unbridled for profit production, risk and wealth transfer with financial engineering (see 6.2) and the old "numbers game" (see chapters 4, 5). Blossoming even more with green promises (greenwashing): Controlling against this there is the law (regulation, climate and human rights litigation), reasonably practised as sustainable financing of the corporation.

But just look what happened especially to the SEC climate disclosure rules (see 6.7.3)[238] and concerns for the loan market and the broader economy, id est risks of increased leveraged loans and collateralized loan obligations (CLOs). The SEC issued an Investor Bulletin on leveraged investment strategies attempting to magnify an investment's return (borrowing money, using options, or leveraged ETFs and the like).[239] Not exactly a sound signal to end the exaggerated ideology of "leverage".[240]

---

[233] David Gelles, David Yaffe-Bellany, Shareholder value is no longer everything, top CEOs say, New York Times, 19.08.2019: www.nytimes.com/2019/08/19/business/business-roundtable-ceos-corporations.html (accessed: 25.08.2025). Cf. further for corporate directors of a human corporation and sustainable investment esp. chapters 1, 8 and 9.

[234] Adam Lowenstein, 19.08.2022: www.theguardian.com/environment/2022/aug/19/top-us-business-lobby-group-climate-action-business-roundtable; cf. BRT view: www.businessroundtable.org/purposeanniversary and Alex Edmans, 07.09.2021: www.promarket.org/2021/09/07/business-roundtable-shareholder-capitalism-promise (all accessed: 25.08.2025). Empirically Tonti (2022) and El Ghoul, Guedhami, Jamshed (2025).

[235] Bainbridge (2021). Japanese law Watanabe (2020), cf. Harrison, Phillips, and Freeman (2020), Murray (2020). On "shareholder primacy" Lipton (2025).

[236] Bebchuk and Tallarita (2022) p. 55. Cf. with data Chirag Lala, Lenore Palladino, 19.08.2020: https://rooseveltinstitute.org/2020/08/19/shareholders-first-what-hasnt-changed-since-the-business-roundtables-2019-statement/ (accessed: 25.08.2025).

[237] See below 6.8.1 and for more data: SEC, Accounting and Auditing Enforcement Releases: www.sec.gov/divisions/enforce/friactions.htm (accessed: 25.08.2025).

[238] Also above 1.4.2 and, e.g., Cloud, Goldberg, Baker and Josefovits (2024), Morreale, Roisman and Arnold (2024). Luttermann, L. (2022), (2023) and (2024).

[239] SEC, Leveraged investment strategies: know the risks before using these advanced investment tools, Investor Bulletin, 10.06.2021. Cf. Uzialko (2023) and above 6.6.5 (on a "risik passport" – *Risikopass* for each financial instrument).

[240] See above 6.2.2, 6.3.1 and 3.3.3, 3.4.4, 3.6.2, below 6.9; basically in terms of "shareholder value", see 6.7.3, 6.8.1 and, e.g., 4.12.3, 5.3.5 and 7.1 with 7.4.3 and 7.8.2. Review of Alfred Rappaport, Shareholder Value, (2nd ed, Verlag Schäffer-Poeschel, Stuttgart 1999) by Luttermann: 45 Die Aktiengesellschaft (AG 2000) 143.

### 6.7.3 *Juridical Analysis of the Economy (Excessiveness)*[241]

Remember, corresponding to their responsibility for an adequate provision of capital, the decisive corporate directors and shareholders must finance the company (corporation) with more liable capital (i.e., in the classical sense in particular: "equity", cf. see 3.6) or do less high-risk business deals. This applies not only to financial institutions, but in principle to any company. And in terms of sustainability, id est a longer-term strategy, climate risks are proving to be significant financial risks. But under U.S. President Donald Trump, on March 27, 2025, the SEC officially declared that it has voted to "end its defense of the rules requiring disclosure of climate-related risks and greenhouse gas emissions".[242] – Why not a holistic approach?

Our findings highlight elementary structures and specific characters, like tips of a vast landscape of icebergs – one blends into the other. Wherever in the corporation and capital markets it is about personal responsibility (*persönliche Verantwortlichkeit*), this is legally integrated into the context (see 6.8, chapter 7). That, again, makes it clear that the dominating influence of individual shareholders – be it of a financial institution or whatever the player may be called – must be taken into account in each single case. However, in practice the issue in the publicly held corporations is in fact company financing in global competition. With financiers and financing patterns (hybrid financial instruments, derivatives, rating etc., see 6.3.1, 6.6.4) formed by the neoclassical capital market theories and the financial industry with the dogma of the "economic analysis of the law" (see 6.6.2, Fig. 6.3), this entire field is concerned with valuation and disclosure, with the picture of the company (corporation) in its accounts.[243]

Corporate finance and governance, conducted in the sense of "shareholder value" (leverage, see 6.7.2), shifts risks in a unilateral manner. Here, financial institutions exhibit especial creativity, as the example of the Commerzbank AG in Germany shows. The bank was close to bankruptcy in the world debt crisis through speculation losses and received 18.2 billion euros from the German government. According to the German *Handelsgesetzbuch* (HGB), interest should have been paid on this in years with balance sheet profit; for 2010, this would have been approximately 1.5 billion euros. However, due to high write-offs to the real estate subsidiary Eurohypo AG (asset-based finance), the Commerzbank AG showed 1.2 billion-euro losses according to the HGB (2011: 3.6 billion euros). Simultaneously, for the stock market it showed a profit of 1.4 billion euros for 2010 (2011: 638 million euros) in the

[241] Luttermann (2010a) and (2013), basically Luttermann (1998) pp. 465-485.

[242] SEC, 27.03.2025, press release 2025-58 (www.sec.gov/newsroom/press-releases/2025-58 accessed: 25.08.2025). See above 1.4.2, below 8.2.3 and 8.4.3.

[243] See above 3.1 and in detail chapter 4. Luttermann (1999a) and (2011).

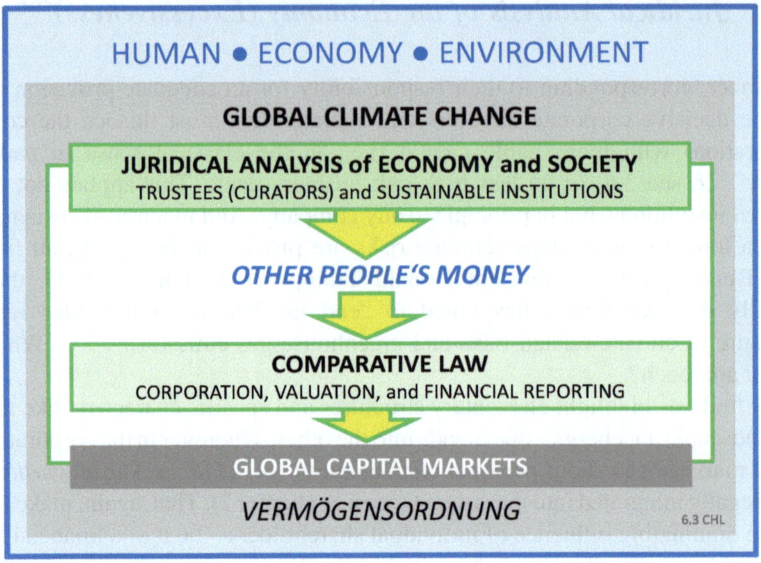


**Fig. 6.3** Juridical analysis of the economy and society for global climate change

accounts, according to the "International Financial Reporting Standards" (IFRS), and made bonus payments to leading staff members.[244] After flotation (increase of capital stock), one was surprised to read: "Commerzbank first-quarter profit jumps".[245] The German government in 2024 as the largest shareholder of Commerzbank AG, installed Jens Weidmann, a Chancellor Angela Merkel alumnus, as chairman of the bank's supervisory board.[246]

The evil game with numbers is causing further destruction of trust. The same can be said, e.g., of efforts by the Deutsche Bank AG and Barclays PLC to find a "US loophole" in order to avoid classification as a "bank-holding company" under the Dodd-Frank Act and "thicker capital cushions to absorb sudden losses in a crisis".[247] It is not about natural events (*Naturkatastrophen*), but about human deeds, to be attributed responsibly. Deutsche Bank AG, where CEO Josef Ackermann (counsel-

[244] Data under 23.02.2011 (according to https://www.handelsblatt.com/).

[245] The Wall Street Journal, 03.05.2011, 23.

[246] Currently: www.commerzbank.com; cf. above 6.5.2.

[247] The Wall Street Journal, 13.04.2011, 1 and 3.

lor of Chancellor Merkel, demanded greedy 25% of return on equity, saying he would be ashamed to accept state funds in the crisis, received material bailout-support by the Federal Reserve in the USA.[248] Transparency and honesty, id est real information (facts: "full and real disclosure", see 3.3.3),[249] create trust (see 1.5.2).

The debt orgy continues. This appears as a continuum that connects even opposing political positions. U.S. President Joe Biden celebrated the Inflation Reduction Act of 2022 with billions of dollars of subsidies, tax cuts, funds for a new clean energy economy. His successor, U.S. President Donald Trump is widely unwinding this, with corresponding expenses (government debt), while fossil fuels are now being propagandised ("Drill, baby, drill"), regardless of their environmental harm (GHG-emissions, see 1.4.2). Clear human values (measures) are imperative. The International Court of Justice has reaffirmed this for environmental and human rights (see 6.1). We will see how the transitions work (cf. Pax Americana, 6.2). It is a global task for all of us. In human communication, in business and in society worldwide, everything starts with clear language (see 4.12.3).[250]

The disaster economy discloses a lacking sense of values, of a fair balance (see 9.7-9.9). Only jurisprudence, being ethically founded, provides measure and form for the economy as a matter to be regulated. This is drowned out by the prophets of the model-like mathematical "economic analysis of the law", who base themselves on quantities instead of quality (see 6.6.2, 7.3.2). Life is differentiated and culturally varied on the global field of corporate finance. In principle, markets are based on moderation and fair players. Freedom of contract may be used according to the rules or it may be abused, as in the financial industry: Where players lack ethos and no referee blows his whistle, chaos will reign in place of the law.[251] John Locke wrote clear-sightedly: "Wherever law ends, tyranny begins."[252] This applies to all walks of life, but also for corporate activities.

[248] See above 6.4.3. Pam Martens, Russ Martens, 03.10.2016: https://wallstreetonparade.com/2016/10/germanys-deutsche-bank-again-in-trouble-received-a-u-s-bailout-twice-as-big-as-lehman-brothers/ (accessed: 25.08.2025); cf. James Felkerson, $29trn: A detailed look at the Fed's bailout by funding facility and recipient, 2011 (www.levyinstitute.org/pubs/wp_698.pdf). On Ackermann: Wilson, 01.12.2008, www.fnlondon.com/articles/ackermann-insists-return-in-investment-banking-still-possible-20081201, cf. DPA, 06.02.2023, https://finanzbusiness.de/nachrichten/banken/article14956369.ece (both accessed: 25.08.2025).

[249] On information and accountability above 4.12.3, 4.13. Cf. Freedom of Information Act (bailout data): *Bloomberg L.P. v. Board of Governors of the Federal Reserve System*, 601 F.3d 143 (2d Cir. 2010); on this John Berry, Bloomberg vs. Fed, 2012: www.international-economy.com/TIE_W12_Berry.pdf (accessed: 25.08.2025). On the Federal Reserve above 3.3.2.

[250] On business and financial communication, e.g., above 2.5.3, 2.6.2, below 7.6 and Luttermann (2023) recitals 91-95. Towards peace in Europe Luttermann, C. and Luttermann, K. (2021).

[251] See above 4.3.2 and Luttermann (2010a) 1, 2; basically Luttermann (1998) pp. 1, 465-485 and Luttermann (2003a) Einf BilanzR recitals 107-136.

[252] Locke (1689) chapter XVIII, sec. 202.

## 6.8 European, German, and Global Perspectives[253]

### *6.8.1 Financial Institutions and Beyond*

As a consequence of the world debt crisis with its epic excesses originating in the USA, the European Commission presented a Green Paper on Corporate governance in financial institutions and remuneration policies.[254] One of a number of analyses for the reform of the financial markets leading to their real "green" transformation. It contains basic statements for the European Union and international conditions, for the corporate governance of financial institutions and of listed companies in general. At the same time, the Green Paper highlights the basis of their relationship with each other. The key role of financial reporting and auditors (shown in chapter 4) is emphasised there, "as they provide assurance to the market that the financial statements (...) present a true and fair view,"[255] but only if they are prepared in accordance with acceptable standards and not in accordance with standards striving for "a race to the bottom". This is underscored by far-reaching reforms of financial reporting and auditing: sustainable financing and reporting for the good.[256]

It is particularly the effective strength of financial institutions and the suitability of their regulatory and supervisory systems to deal with financial innovation in a globalised world[257] that is questioned. As already said in the Larosiére Report, it is indisputable[258] "that boards of directors, like supervisory authorities (*Aufsichtsbehörden*), rarely comprehended either the nature and scale of the risks they were facing. In many cases, the shareholders did not properly perform their role as owners of the company." Corporate governance is not named as the direct cause of the crisis, but "the lack of effective control mechanisms contributed significantly to excessive risk-taking on the part of financial institutions."[259] As a consequence, the Capital Requirements Directive (2013/36/EU) has fixed rules for credit institutions and investment firms for better transparency (country-by-country reporting), an effective risk management (*Risikomanagement*, cf. German § 91(2) and (3) AktG) and the board composition – meanwhile being updated (see 6.8.4).[260] This is

---

[253] Luttermann (2003b).

[254] COM(2010) 284 final (02.06.2010). Cf. Directive (EU) 2017/828, 17.05.2017 amending Directive 2007/36/EC as regards the encouragement of long-term shareholder engagement, OJ EU 20.05.2017 L 132/1.

[255] COM(2010) 284 final, 3.7.

[256] See 4.2 and, e.g., Directive 2014/56/EU and Regulation (EU) No. 537/2014, overall chapters 3 and 4.

[257] COM(2010) 284 final, 1.

[258] COM(2010) 284 final, 1 with reference to: Report of the High-Level Group on Financial Supervision in the EU (February 25, 2009). Mr Jacques de Larosiére was chairman of the group.

[259] COM(2010) 284 final, 1.

[260] Consolidated text: http://data.europa.eu/eli/dir/2013/36/2022-01-01 (accessed: 25.08.2025). Cf. above 6.3.3 and below 6.8.2.

accompanied by a Regulation (EU, no. 575/2013) on prudential requirements as well as regulatory and implementing technical standards.[261]

Basically, the Green Paper and its consequences are an attestation of failure for all persons responsible (see chapter 7). This is all the more critical, as in particular for the climate-neutral restructuring of the economy the capital markets and its actors, id est the investors financing a corporation (equity, debt), have a decisive effect.[262] For our purpose, the role of shareholders is of particular importance. The increasing significance of the financial markets has "created new categories of shareholders" with "little interest in the long-term governance objectives of the business" in which they invest: short or even very short (quarterly or even shorter) investment horizons (see 6.6). This motivates excessive risk-taking (*Risikoexzess*) for the short-term production of (sham) profits[263] and excessive remuneration for executives and corporate directors, based on criteria (incentives) such as short-term share value or quarterly "profit".[264] This is in fact paid to the shareholders in Anglo-American practice on a quarterly basis. In the European Union, remuneration policies are legally addressed (e.g., Art. 92 to 96 Directive 2013/36/EU).[265]

Financial institutions as shareholders of other financial institutions and in particular of listed companies in general also participate in this. The financial industry fires the situation with its financial engineering and most recent digital technologies.[266] Thus, "the numbers game" is played and even intensified, finding its expression in reports according to U.S. "GAAP" and "IFRS"; it is tempting for executives "to cheat to meet Wall Street's expectations".[267] Thereby, industrial companies and the principles of the real world economy erode. Company law is entering the Digital Age (EU Digital Single Market Strategy),[268] which is strongly gaining ground with the right and the practice of reporting (IFRS/XBRL):[269] Digital finance communication strengthens financial reporting (see chapter 4) and the valuation of companies (see

[261] Consolidated text: http://data.europa.eu/eli/reg/2013/575/2024-01-01, European Banking Authority: www.eba.europa.eu/regulation-and-policy/single-rulebook/interactive-single-rulebook/100427 (both accessed: 25.08.2025).

[262] Cf. on Finnish companies data according to the Global Reporting Initiative (GRI) framework Hartikainen, Järvenpää, and Rautiainen (2021).

[263] See above 5.1 and 5.5.

[264] COM(2010) 284 final, 3.5. Cf. on "vesting equity" Edmans/Fang/Huang (2022). Mumu/Saona/Russel/Azad (2021).

[265] Reformed several times, e.g., Directive (EU) 2019/878 of 20.05.2019 and Directive (EU) 2021/338 of 16.02.2021.

[266] See above 6.2.3, 6.6.2 and 6.6.4.

[267] Linette Lopez, The great fraud reckoning, 31.01.2023, www.businessinsider.com/great-fraud-reckoning-expose-scam-companies-stock-market-chaos-2023-1?op=1: "corporate misery" (accessed: 25.08.2025); cf. already Levitt (1998), Luttermann (1999a) and (2011). See above 6.7.3, 5.5 and chapter 4.

[268] EU Commission, 06.05.2015 (COM(2015) 192 final), and Green Paper: Building a capital markets union, 18.02.2015 (COM/2015/063 final). Luttermann (2023) recitals 86-90.

[269] On the eXtensible Business Reporting Language (XBRL) above 4.11. Luttermann (2023) recitals 83-86. On AI below 9.6.

chapter 5) as an elementary field of company law and corporate governance overall. Of course, those managing and directing the corporation are again the point of focus.[270]

### 6.8.2 *Comparative Law: Corporate Directors (Boards)*

Diversity characterises corporate governance worldwide: This is illustrated by the persons (corporate directors) and legal foundations, especially the structures of the leading organs (boards of directors). Both elements work together, whereas the board structures are usually addressed, as here by the EU-Commission: "The financial crisis clearly shows that financial institutions' boards of directors did not fulfil their key role as a principal decision-making body. Consequently, boards of directors were unable to exercise effective control over senior management and to challenge the measures and strategic guidelines that were submitted to them for approval."[271] It is essential to note that the board structures can heavily influence the work (e.g., risk aversion, risk control) and the results of the corporate directors according to the valid law.

Content and enforcement of the directors' duties and responsibility are linked to this, and everything should be designed appropriately and sustainably.[272] Traditionally, the term "board of directors" focusses on a dualism: The unitary board system rooted in Common law and alongside this, the Continental European two-tier board system, shaped in particular in Germany, with a management board (*Vorstand*) and a supervisory board (*Aufsichtsrat*, see 6.1.2 and 6.8.4). Tradition and politics are, more or less openly, linked (overall see chapter 3). This is accompanied by a general critique of both types of boards, which may promote reasonable superordinate approaches. Regarding the members of the boards of directors the European Commission declares: "that their failure to identify, understand and ultimately control the risks to which their financial institutions were exposed is at the heart of the origins of the crisis."[273]

---

[270] On politicians, supervisory authorities, auditors etc. 5.6. Basically chapter 7. On digital financial communication above 4.11 and 4.12.3, Luttermann (2023) recitals 81-95, Luttermann and Pöschk (2014).

[271] COM(2010) 284 final, 3.3.

[272] E.g., on Germany's two-tier board system above 6.4 with §§ 90–93 AktG on directors' duties (e.g. bookkeeping, risk management, due diligence and business judgement) and §§ 243, 264 HGB (financial reporting); see Luttermann (2003a) Einf BilanzR recitals 60-193, as well as the commentaries on §§ 243,342 HGB and § 264 HGB. Cf. Directive (EU) 2017/828, 17.05.2017 amending Directive 2007/36/EC as regards the encouragement of long-term shareholder engagement, OJ EU 20.5.2017 L 132/1. On corporate sustainability reporting Directive (EU) 2022/2464, 14.12.2022, OJ EU 16.12.2022, L 322/15, and below chapter 8.

[273] COM(2010) 284 final, 3.3.

This comprises the duties of due diligence in the sense of institutional and personal responsibility of the executive and non-executive directors overall (duty of care – *Sorgfaltspflicht*, see 6.4.1). It should be added that the European Union itself contributed as one of the causes of the – ongoing – crisis, especially by its deficient regulation and control of financial reporting and auditing for financial institutions and listed companies in general.[274] The European Union lists reasons for the failure. A central point is the criticism that members of boards of directors do not make sufficient efforts to fulfil their duties (cf. 6.8.3, 6.8.4); the criticism includes[275] that (members of) boards of directors:

(1) do not have sufficiently diverse backgrounds (culturally, with regard to gender, educationally and socially),
(2) did not carry out a serious performance appraisal, neither individually nor for the whole board,
(3) were unable or unwilling to ensure an adequate risk management or risk appetite, and
(4) proved unable to recognise the systemic nature of certain risks, corporate governance issues were on the agenda (too) rarely.[276]

Such criticism applies to many companies (corporations) also beyond the financial sector, and basically to all corporate directors (board members – *Vorstand*, *Aufsichtsrat*) as a guideline (vade mecum – *Leitfaden*) for careful action (*sorgfältiges Handeln*, cf. German § 93 AktG, and above 6.4.2). What is decisive are the legal foundations. The – internationally necessary – legal comparison shows that in spite of global influences even in the European Union, where harmonisation is promoted in particular through capital market law (and by the ECJ, see *Centros*)[277] significant differences are effective especially in company law. This applies for the participation of employees (*Arbeitnehmer*) and election/nomination rights; in numerous European Union member states, there is a choice between one-tier and two-tier structures.[278]

### *6.8.3 Human Corporation Holistically*

Overall, the transnational dimension must be considered. This is already legally relevant in the European Union (as shown), but it gains significant importance globally. As the International Court of Justice explains generally (see 6.1), the duty of care includes the human rights due diligence (e.g., labor law and social law conditions) as well as environmental due diligence (e.g, to prevent significant

[274] See, e.g., above 4.1 and 4.4–4.5, 4.9.2. Cf. COM(2010) 284 final, 3.7 and 3.6.

[275] COM(2010) 284 final, 3.3, 3.4.

[276] Ibid.

[277] ECJ, 09.03.1999 (C-212/97 – *Centros*, DA) ECLI:EU:C:1999:126, on this Luttermann (2000).

[278] See Gerner-Beuerle/Paech/Schuster (2013) with Annex (Country reports).

harm to the environment). This affects the international law on the business activities of private actors (corporations), also serving as a legal framework for national legislation and for practice. Being innovative, the Sustainable Business Finance Navigator (SBFN) serves careful decision-making of corporate directors holistically.[279]

What should be taken note of is financing, valuation and financial reporting (auditing): This field connects company law and capital market law in a cross-section way and is thus in practice fundamental for good corporate governance. This has a lasting effect on directors (esp. presumably the so-called "independent" ones, see 6.8.4), investors (markets) and in particular on the relationship between financial institution/bank (as investor) and industrial company (corporation, as capital acquirer), because it builds up the most important entrepreneurial asset: trust (see 6.9, 2.7). This is accompanied by risk management (*Risikomanagement*, § 91(3) AktG, and *Überwachungssystem*, § 91 (2) AktG) as an integral part of financing, accounting and auditing (see §§ 264, 317 HGB). As always in corporate affairs it is about the human factor (see 6.1.2).

However, trust is lacking on the markets (see 1.5.2: intercultural concept of trust). In an exemplary fashion, the reform legislator therefore emphasises in the USA: "that CEOs and CFOs are responsible for the presentation of material in their company's financial reports" (cf. the case of Alibaba);[280] accordingly, they are required to make the statement (sanctioned with up to 20 years of prison) that the financial statements and disclosures "fairly present in all material respects" the financial conditions and the results of the operations of the company (so-called *Bilanzeid*, see 4.9.5).[281] This underscores the personal responsibility of the members of the boards of directors, which has long been anchored in German law: Every executive director (and his deputy, § 94 AktG) must sign and date the financial reports (§ 245 HGB); for the report period, this creates a document that counts as evidence also before court regarding the assets, liabilities, financial position and profit or loss of the company.[282]

The focus must be sharpened like here: It is not corporations that can act in a wrong way (so-called "corporate misconduct"), id est violate duties of diligence, but in actual fact only their responsibly acting directors.[283] This requires adequate qualifications, id est continuing education of the members of the board of directors of financial institutions as well as of listed companies in general – personally (see

---

[279] Luttermann, L. (2022), (2023) and (2024) pp. 410, 413-415 and 420-421. See also chapter 8.

[280] See above 6.2.3, 4.8.6 and Luttermann (2014).

[281] Secs 302, 906 Public Company Accounting Reform and Investor Protection Act of 2002 (Sarbanes-Oxley Act), 107th Cong.: Senate bill S. 2673, H.R. 3763. Citation: Committee on Banking, Housing, and Urban Affairs, Report to accompany S. 2673, 03.07.2002, under title III.B.

[282] See above 6.1 and 4.4.1. Luttermann (2003a) § 245 HGB recitals 452-469. Directive 2013/34/EU (annual and consolidated financial statements) and, e.g.: § 91 AktG (accountancy, risk management system of the corporation), § 289 HGB (directors' financial review), § 289a HGB (statement on corporate governance). Overall above 6.3.3, 6.4.

[283] On the origin of the corporation as a juridical person below 7.3.1. Cf. § 100(1) AktG.

6.3.3, 6.4) and in the sense of a strategic corporate governance plan (see 4.12). There is not so much a lack of substantive rules on directors' duties but rather a lack in their consistent execution (enforcement)[284] and of sustainable education and in particular in due professionalism (cf. duty of care, see 6.8.2).

### *6.8.4 Supervisory Board: Restriction of Mandates*

Holism means: together with the mentioned personal qualities of the members of the boards of directors, the restriction of the number of mandates for supervisory board members belong in this context. The European Commission sets the benchmark: "The basis for quality in a board of directors lies in its composition",[285] and it highlights the quality of appointment procedures. But how many mandates a person is allowed to exercise? – The diligent work demanded by law[286] (see 6.4) can, of course, not be carried out by one person in numerous mandates. In addition, the restriction of the number of permitted memberships in boards may, in principle, prevent excessive influence of individuals (and institutions). An indicatory example can be found in a historical practice that was the breeding ground for the proverbial "Deutschland AG" (Corporate Germany, see 5.2.3).

Hermann Josef Abs stands out as Speaker of the Board of the Deutsche Bank AG from 1957 to 1967, whom David Rockefeller, president of Chase Manhattan Bank, is said to have called "the leading banker of the world".[287] In fact, he was of dubious character. On the management board of the Deutsche Bank AG from 1938 onwards and sitting on more than 40 supervisory boards (banks, industrial groups) nationally and internationally, among them the vast chemical combine IG Farben AG, Abs took part in the criminal "Aryanisation" of Jewish property.[288] After the war, however, Abs made a successful transition. He positioned himself as a political counsellor and with the top position in the Deutsche Bank AG as well as, at some points, up to 30 mandates in supervisory boards,[289] Abs gained an exceptional amount of power. In order to restrict such power, the reform of the German law on stock companies in

---

[284] See above 6.5.3 (Yates Memorandum) and 4.9. Similarly Gerner-Beuerle/Paech/Schuster (2013) pp. 238-239.

[285] COM(2010) 284 final, 3.3. See basically above 6.3.3.

[286] Cf. Art. 91 No. 2 Directive 2013/36/EU for credit institutions and investment firms: "All members of the management body shall commit sufficient time to perform their functions in the institution".

[287] Time, 16.06.1967 (https://content.time.com/time/subscriber/article/0,33009,843981,00.html, accessed: 25.08.2025).

[288] At that time, the I.G. Farben AG (1925-2012) also conducted building projects for Auschwitz and its external camps with the help of forced labourers. Cf. in detail Gall (2005), Jehn, Kirschner, and Wurthmann (2022).

[289] Twenty (20!) of these at some point as chairman.

1965 limited the number of mandates in supervisory boards to 10 per person (so-called "Lex Abs").

Legislation names exclusion criteria for a supervisory board membership, among them the number of mandates, which as a rule should not exceed ten. This is still too many, even if the chair in a supervisory board counts as two mandates (§ 100(2) AktG).[290] European law says for prudential supervision, according to the number of directorships, one should take "into account individual circumstances and the nature, scale and complexity of the institution's activities"; it determines, that "members of the management body of an institution that is significant in terms of its size, internal organisation and the nature, the scope and the complexity of its activities", that only one executive directorship with two non-executive directorships or four non-executive directorships shall be held at the same time (Art. 91 no. 3 Directive 2013/36/EU).[291]

So, let us focus: The issues are personal requirements (competence, conflict of interests) and, basically, independence (*Unabhängigkeit*): the inner, responsible attitude (*Haltung*, *innere Einstellung*: integrity) of the person functioning as member of the supervisory board (see 6.3.3). However, wise self-restriction only rarely seems to be at work. This throws a characteristic light on the lucrative positions[292] of the multi-functionaries. They are, however, by no means a German peculiarity (cf. in Great Britain so-called "fat cats")[293] and are reminiscent of that modern-seeming type who likes wearing several hats (cf. so-called "shadow elite", 6.5.3). Manifestations of unbridled power (immoderateness – *Maßlosigkeit*). In view of the world debt crisis ("financial crisis"), the European Union observes that board members, "in particular non-executive directors, devoted neither sufficient resources nor time to the fulfilment of their duties".[294]

In fact, this is a reflection on all supervisory board members in a two-tier system, as very few of them serve on a full-time basis. Serving on several boards as shareholder representatives can, of course, be lucrative and add up to full-time employment, but it will put additional constraints on them to devote "sufficient resources (...) to the fulfilment of their duties".[295] Similar aspects may also hold for (non-executive) directors in the one-tier board system. In any case, there are reports on a shift in the composition of large public company boards from merely 20% "independent directors" (1950) to 75% (2005): as "a complementary institution to an

[290] Special characteristics need to be noted for foreign companies (groups). Cf. GCGC (April 2022), C.5: only two (July 2016, no 5.4.5: three) mandates instead of five mandates (June 2009). Already in favour of only four mandates by law: Luttermann (2003b).

[291] Status: Directive (EU) 2024/1619 of 31.05.2024.

[292] European Banking Authority, Remuneration data: www.eba.europa.eu/risk-analysis-and-data/remuneration-data (accessed: 25.08.2025); Beck, Friedl, and Schäfer (2020). OECD, Remuneration of Boards of Directors and Executive Management in State-Owned Enterprises, 2022.

[293] Owen Jones, 21.04.2016: www.theguardian.com/commentisfree/2016/apr/21/britain-corporate-fatcat-party-till-we-turn-music-off. Cf. with data Tonello and Tay (2021).

[294] COM(2010) 284 final, 3.3 (1st en-dash).

[295] Ibid.

economy of firms directed to maximize shareholder value",[296] id est in fact a one-sided transfer of wealth. "Independent" (*unabhängig*) thus sounds like a misnomer, which fits into the context of the currently predominant financial industry as described (see, e.g., 6.2, 6.5.3 and 6.7.3).

This illustrates the significance of a holistic view and treatment of corporations. It also highlights the global demand for scientific, legal and truly comparative investigation. The restriction of the number of the boards on which a person may sit is regarded as an effective means for improving the quality of the supervision: It is "the increasing complexity of the structure and activities" not only in financial institutions that speaks for implementing such a means.[297] In fact, it applies in general – as shown – to corporations, corporate finance and financial reporting, symbolically embodied in the "financial expert" and the audit committee (*Prüfungsausschuss*) of the supervisory board (*Aufsichtsrat*, see German § 100(5) AktG).[298] Basically, for adequate practice it is always about careful valuation and decision-making in the sense of sustainability for value creation (see 6.8.2).[299]

### *6.8.5 Smart Investors: Megahype AI, Financial Hybrids, and the Greater Good*

People create and preserve true values (see 5.3). Reasonableness (Greek *phrónesis*), sustainable business activity, climate change, environment and human rights illustrate that globally, for better or for worse (see 1.4, 1.7). The capital markets work like seismographs, "financial euphoria" repeatedly blossoming, in particular in technological progress. Symbolically, cryptocurrencies radiate like bitcoins with blockchain technology (DLT, see 1.5.3), innovative and highly volatile, right up the scandalous FTX cryptocurrency exchange of the founder Sam Bankman-Fried, who embezzled billions of dollars.[300] In general, in contradistinction to "speculator",

[296] Gordon (2007), cf. Ferrarini and Filippelli (2014) and above 6.3.3, below 7.4.2.

[297] COM(2010) 284 final, 5.1. See Luttermann (2003b) already demanding the further limitation of mandates and the improvement of the quality.

[298] On this see above 6.3.3 and 4.12, in general chapters 4 and 5.

[299] Luttermann, L. (2024), esp. pp. 413-415 and 420-421, with the Sustainable Business Finance Navigator (SBFN) for value creation through a financial due diligence concept (duty of care).

[300] Bankman-Fried for "multiple fraudulent schemes" sentenced to 25 years in prison: https://www.justice.gov/archives/opa/pr/samuel-bankman-fried-sentenced-25-years-his-orchestration-multiple-fraudulent-schemes (accessed: 24.11.2025).

it is about the "individual, nonprofessional investor".[301] Dante Alighieri affirms: "You were made not to live like beasts, but seek virtue and understanding".[302]

People as trustees individually (private autonomy) and on the whole (climate partners), this is what counts with measure and balance for the development of sustainable practise including all technologies in the course of the Copernican turn for the better:[303] the individual responsibility of the investor (human corporation, culture of responsibility – *Verantwortungskultur*, see 1.1). Artificial intelligence (AI) changes our lives, our way of thinking and acting (e.g., networks like DAO, see 3.7, 1.5.3), the future of life in the universe. AI may well encompass everything, humans and the Nature, society, the economy and the state, war and peace. How are democracy, the world of work and finance, human coexistence, interaction and cooperation influenced in the information age?

Corporations are "virtual cells" created by humans (see 7.3.1, 9.7), and they are booming in the high-tech industry (e.g., Alphabet/Google, Microsoft, Oracle). The Nvidia Corporation (Santa Clara, USA), developing graphics processing units (GPUs) and chipsets for computer and server, in October 2025 was the first corporation worldwide to exceed $5 trillion in market value (*Börsenwert*). – Speculative bubble? – Generative AI systems fuel the megahype; they are able to generate multiple types of outputs (data, e.g. text, picture, music, software code, drug discovery) – across all sectors (finance, marketing, healthcare, the media etc.). McKinsey talks about "$7 trillion in capital outlays needed by 2030" to scale AI data centres (see also, e.g., the so-called "Genesis Mission" by President Trump).[304] The global race for standards, markets and prosperity: milestones, leading to artificial general intelligence (AGI) and more, perhaps even to new entities (see 9.6).

Globally, investors on capital markets take part in this race. They finance the corporations and their infrastructure projects, the construction of gigantic data centers where AI is trained. The German Schwarz Group invests 11 billion euros in a gigafactory (100.000 GPUs) for Europe's digital sovereignty.[305] That means, participating in shaping the next generation of high-end-technology rather than be shaped by it, i.e. by other powers (see 4.11: monopoly of valuation). Meta Platforms, Inc. set up a complex finance structure for the Hyperion data centre (Louisiana) of

[301] Fundamentally, initially published in 1973: Graham (2003), p. 18 (and up to p. 34). Cf. above 6.6 and 6.4.3. Luttermann (2010b) and (2008a).

[302] Translation by Zweig, see Graham (2003), p. 536. Original Dante Alighieri, Commedia, Inferno, Canto XXVI, lines 119–120: "fatti non foste a viver come bruti, ma per seguir virtute e conocenza."

[303] See above 6.1 with 7.9 and overall esp. chapters 1, 2, and 7 to 9. Luttermann (1998), (2010a), and (2015a).

[304] McKinsey and Company, 28.04.2025, see: https://www.mckinsey.com/industries/technology-media-and-telecommunications/our-insights/the-cost-of-compute-a-7-trillion-dollar-race-to-scale-centers, and on the "Genesis Mission" President Trump, 24.11.2025, see: https://www.whitehouse.gov/presidential-actions/2025/11/launching-the-genesis-mission/ (accessed: 25.11.2025).

[305] Graphics processing units. On the project (ground-breaking ceremony: 17.11.2025): https://schwarz-digits.de/schwarz-digits-datacenter-luebbenau. See European High-Performance Computing Joint Undertaking: https://www.eurohpc-ju.europa.eu/index_en (both accessed: 24.11.2025).

$30 billion, comprising $3 billion of private-equity in a joint venture (Beignet Investor LLC), allocated to the alternative asset manager Blue Owl Capital (80% ownership in the data center) and to Meta (20%). Morgan Stanley issued $27.3 billion in debt by the largest-ever private bond offering with Pimco, LLC taking on $18 billon and BlackRock, Inc. about $3 billion.

Meta, as the leaseholder of Hyperion (with renewal every 4 years), has no long-term-liabilities, formally speaking, and will take most of the debt off its balance sheet. The Financial Times comments: "It's all wild and fascinating, if this sort of thing is your bag."[306] We are familiar with strange financial constructions, some operate fraudulently with financial engineering,[307] special purpose vehicles (SPV)[308] and "off-balance sheet" (see 4.5.7, 6.5.2). Meta guarantees Beignet's "long term income"[309] and appears as a financially strong corporation, but sells risks via financial products by Pimco, BlackRock, Blue Owl etc. to their investors. The Beignet bond, structured with armortisation, blurs the line between typical corporate bonds, project finance and private credit – some say, a "landmark transaction".[310] He colonises in the universe of hybrid financial instruments (see 6.3.1).

Investment prospects massively exceed previous dimensions, the flood of debt is rising extremely. OpenAI, Inc., known for the AI chatbot ChatGPT, runs $500 billion – not on its balance sheet and in close cooperation with competitors like Oracle, Microsoft, Arm, Nvidia – in the nationwide Stargate Project LLC, while similar actions take place elsewhere and Stargate UAE is building a pioneering compute capacity in Abu Dhabi.[311] A banking consortium is financing a Stargate flagship data center in Texas with a $38 billion credit.[312] Will Open AI, once

---

[306] 30.10.2025 (https://www.ft.com/content/d0344253-b0a2-4c6d-8b97-520243678afd, accessed 24.11.2025).

[307] Basically see above 6.6.4 and, e.g., also on marketable securitsation, 6.6.5 ("Gemstone 7"), and 6.6 ("Abacus 2007-AC1").

[308] Also under various names, see above 6.5.1: structured investment vehicles (SIV).

[309] According to the Financial Times, 30.10.2025 (https://www.ft.com/content/d0344253-b0a2-4c6d-8b97-520243678afd, accessed 24.11.2025) a "residual value guarantee" in case Meta "tries to squirrel out of the leases in the future" (end of the guarantee: May 2049; the Beignet bond, priced at par, comes with a coupon of 6.58%.

[310] See overall previous footnote, also citing Rosenbaum and Spear from JPMorgan Chase. Cf. already on corporate and project finance above 1.3, 1.5, and 1.6.2 with 2.5.2, 2.6.3, 3.6.3, and 3.7. Luttermann (2019).

[311] Overall Glover, 24.09.2025: https://builtin.com/articles/stargate-project; in China "DeepSeek-R1", a reasoning-first language model: https://deepseeksr1.com/r1/; on Stargate UAE: Gulf News, 22.05.2025: https://gulfnews.com/business/markets/new-gdrfadifc-agreement-to-simplify-investor-processes-1.500362020 (all accessed: 24.11.2025).

[312] Led by JPMorgan Chase and Mitsubishi UFJ Financial Group: The Wall Street Journal, 16.11.2025 (https://www.wsj.com/finance/investing/wall-street-ai-spending-bubble-810d270e, accessed: 24.11.2025).

founded as a nonprofit organisation, due to unforeseeable AI risks, remain "debt-free", and how about antitrust concerns[313]?

Worldwide things develop at a tearing pace. OpenAI once began with the aim to advance and share AI technologies "in the greater good".[314] In fact it is about humanity, even in the reconstruction of self-organising brain structures (neuromorphic computing, see 9.6). Big business is booming, AI uses up enormous resources (compute power), especially energy: transformation depends on and data centre electricity consumption is set globally to double by 2030,[315] driving up costs. AI may even reduce emissions overall. However, in terms of sustainability it is about real values, the human corporation and financing (valuation, financial reporting). Robert Shiller speaks of a "good society", and the "key to achieving our goals and enhancing human values", as he put it, is:

> "to maintain and continually improve a democratic financial system that takes account of the diversity of human motives and drives", redirecting "the inevitable human conflicts into a manageable arena".[316]

Naturally, that is a wide field. All the more so in times of climate change. Worldwide, this raises the existential question of planetary dimensions. The International Court of Justice emphasises that "above all, a lasting and satisfactory solution requires human will and wisdom – at the individual, social and political levels – to change our habits, comforts and current way of life in order to secure a future for ourselves and those who are yet to come"[317] (future generations). In the global context of, as we put it, "human (*Mensch*), economy (*Wirtschaft*), environment (*Umwelt*)": substance shapes an entrepreneurial culture of responsibility and complementarity in justice (see chapters 1, 8, and 9).

[313] See Singh (2025). On the Trump-endorsed plan, SCIAM, 22.01.2025: https://www.scientificamerican.com/article/heres-whats-in-stargate-the-usd500-billion-trump-endorsed-plan-to-power-u-s/ (accessed: 24.11.2025).

[314] See Sikka (CEO, Infosys Ltd. 2014–2017), 13.12.2015, just the day after the initiation of OpenAI: https://vishalsikka.blogspot.com/2015/12/openai-ai-for-all.html (accessed: 24.11.2025).

[315] To 945 TWh, see IEA, Energy and AI, 10.04.2025: https://www.iea.org/reports/energy-and-ai/; cf. IAEA, Power Reactor Information System: https://pris.iaea.org/PRIS/WorldStatistics/WorldTrendNuclearPowerCapacity.aspx (both accessed: 24.11.2025).

[316] Shiller (2012) pp. 239, 1–15. Cf. below 8.1, 8.2, and, on the true nature of sustainability see 8.4.3 with 3.5.6.

[317] ICJ, Advisory Opinion, 23.07.2025 (see following footnote), para. 456. Overall, see above 6.1 and chapters 1 and 2; on new minds and measures 8.2. Note elementary considerations above 1.4.2 on science and freedom.

## 6.9 Prospects for a Better World

Overall, it is about sustainability (see 4.11.4). The International Court of Justice reaffirms this with its landmark decision of 2025.[318] In 2012, the European Union already focused: "Good corporate governance is first and foremost the responsibility of the company concerned, and rules at European and national level are in place to ensure that certain standards are respected."[319] – We still see, as shown, massive deficits in business practice. Immoderateness reigns, fired by actors of the financial industry with crazy floods of debt (fiat money, quantitative easing). Judges at the German Constitutional Court stand up against this.[320] We need the Copernican turn to the imperative of truth (*Gebot der Wahrheit*), id est sustainability: focusing on facts and enforcement of personal responsibility (liability, see chapters 3 and 7).[321]

The actors and instruments of the financial industry along with macroeconomics take effect. However, this is a global characteristic: The real world economy and company financing in general are too lucrative for not to get involved; sweepingly in transforming the economy and corporations "socio-ecologically", id est reasonably. This leads to decisive influences, refined by the ability of supervisory boards to appoint the "right" person to a certain position (management board, chairperson) with specific contracts (§ 84 AktG). Accordingly, the German two-tier board system still is a clever invention in order to provide advice and to control power (see 6.1). What about personal responsibility? – The Financial Times[322] reported: "Goldman Sachs has begun quietly pushing a computer program that allows investors to trade in the $8.4tn US corporate bond market without ever having communication with a person at the investment bank" (the Goldman Sachs Algorithm, cf. 6.8.5). Perspectives of a world monopoly (see 4.11).

Where are we going? – The global problem, presumably as old as the human race, is, as Joseph Stiglitz put it clearly in 2010: "Avarice triumphs over prudence" (see 6.4.3). This is proven by history, much of which is a series of financial euphoria,

---

[318] See above 6.8.5 with ICJ, Advisory Opinion: Obligation of states in respect of climate change (see https://www.icj-cij.org/sites/default/files/case-related/187/187-20250723-adv-01-00-en.pdf, accessed: 25.08.2025). See on that above 6.1, and 6.7, 5.2.4 (sustainability).

[319] EU Commission, Action Plan: European company law and corporate governance - a modern legal framework for more engaged shareholders and sustainable companies (COM/2012/0740 final), under 1. (2nd paragraph); see Hopt (2015). On developments: https://commission.europa.eu/business-economy-euro/doing-business-eu/company-law-and-corporate-governance_en (accessed: 25.08.2025).

[320] See above 6.6.1: BVerfG, 20.05.2020 (2 BvR 859/15 et al.) BVerfGE 154, 17, <openJur 2020, 5178>.

[321] See also above 6.2.1, 6.5.3 and 6.7.2.

[322] 31.08.2016, p. 13: Robin Wigglesworth and Eric Platt, Goldman takes spoken word out of US bond trading.

which John Kenneth Galbraith[323] clear-sightedly and ironically described in 1990: "as ever, the rediscovered wonders of leverage, presently to be examined, and the parade of publicly celebrated genius". At every turn, as Erasmus of Rotterdam already knew, we meet people who are wonderfully blessed by imagination.[324] A global phenomenon with varieties, different names, sounds, and mechanisms (interests).[325] That is why legal comparison as comparison of cultures is necessary.

Globally, fair competition and far more cooperation for climate change[326] is required instead of using "economic instruments to promote and defend national interests" along with "unseen manipulation of markets and money" (Geoeconomics).[327] Financial institutions are global players, shunning the control classically organised by national states, which paradoxically, though, are held liable for them (see 6.7.1). This means that for the financial industry the dream of risk-free speculation has come true: Whereas taxpayers bear real losses, the players can really enjoy the (sham) gains. The basic issue is power and the balance of powers. In individual cases, this applies to the influence in the boardrooms of companies. In particular, however, it applies to the structural influence on whole industrial sectors and the financial markets, which are central to corporate governance (investment).

How about a reasonable, complementary practice of faculties (*Vermögen*).[328] Altogether, it is about our liberal constitution, which enforces sensible rules of freedom. The responsible players in economy and politics need to realise: "Banking on trust", instead of on failure, is the basis in Europe, the US and everywhere in the world, in order to prevent further catastrophes of the "corporate" world, to master the climate change, and to promote sustainable prosperity in freedom. To this end, sustainability in its legal sense (see 5.2.4, 6.1), has to be established comprehensively (see 1.5.2: a concept of trust, and chapters 7 to 9). Worldwide, autocrats, centralism and dehumanisation are massively gaining ground: Does freedom[329] have enough responsible friends?

---

[323] Galbraith (1994) p. 71, see also above 6.2.3. Continuing Luttermann (2023).

[324] Erasmus (1509/2003) p. 87.

[325] E.g., UK Stewardship Code, cf. Arsalidou (2012). See chapter 7.

[326] See 6.1 with chapters 1 and 2.

[327] On geoeconomics Blackwill and Harris (2017) p. 20, with reference, p. 33, to Jeremi Suri. Cf. above 6.2.1 and 2.3.2 (*Pax Americana*), 2.3.1 (*Pax Sinica*), and on Panama Papers etc. 6.2.4. Cf. overall Sen (2007).

[328] Encompassing abilities (*Fähigkeiten*), cf. on the denotation of "asset" (*Vermögen*) below 8.1 (footnote 3), and overall chapters 1, 8 and 9 (complementarity).

[329] On the erosion of freedom and individual responsibility Luttermann (2008c), 23.06.2008, about three months before the collapse of the investment bank Lehman Brothers Inc. at Wall Street, which is regarded as the starting point of the global financial crisis. Cf. Stiglitz (2010), Tooze (2019), Applebaum (2024), also Luttermann (2019). See Luttermann (2010a) and here on the juridical analysis of the economy, state and society, e.g., 1.6.2, 4.6-4.13, 6.7.3 and chapters 7, 9.

# References


Aliber, R. Z., & Kindleberger, C. P. (2015). *Manias, panics and crashes: A history of financial crises* (7th ed.). Palgrave Macmillan.

Aliber, R. Z., Kindleberger, C. P., & McCauley, R. N. (2023). *Manias, panics and crashes: A history of financial crises* (8th ed.). Palgrave Macmillan.

Alstadsæter, A., Johannesen, N., & Zucman, G. (2018). Who owns the wealth in tax havens? Macro evidence and implications for global inequality. *Journal of Public Economics, 162*, 89–100.

Antoniades, A., & Tarashev, N. (2014). Securitisations: Tranching concentrates uncertainty. *BIS Quarterly Review*, December 2014.

Applebaum, A. (2024). *Autocracy, Inc.: The dictators who want to run the world*. Random House.

Aristodemou, M. (2024). Are beneficial ownership laws important? Exploring the impact of Panama, FinCEN, and Pandora Papers on beneficial ownership laws in the UK and the US. *Journal of Economic Criminology, 5*, 100082.

Arsalidou, D. (2012). Shareholders and corporate scrutiny: The role of the UK stewardship code. *European Company and Financial Law Review, 9*, 342–379.

Backus, M., Conlon, C., & Sinkinson, M. (2019). *The common ownership hypothesis: Theory and evidence*. Brookings Institution.

Bahreini, D. (2012). *Der unabhängige Finanzexperte i.S.v. § 100 Abs. 5 AktG*. Duncker & Humblot.

Bainbridge, S. M. (2021). Making sense of the Business Roundtable's reversal on corporate purpose. *The Journal of Corporation Law, 46*, 285–319.

Baums, T. (1992). Corporate governance in Germany: The role of the banks. *American Journal of Comparative Law, 40*, 503–526.

Bebchuk, L. A., & Tallarita, R. (2022). *Will corporations deliver value to all stakeholders?* ECGI Working Paper Series in Law.

Beck, D., Friedl, G., & Schäfer, P. (2020). Executive compensation in Germany. *Journal of Business Economics, 90*, 787–824.

Beder, T. S., & Marshall, C. M. (2011). *Financial engineering: The evolution of a profession*. Wiley.

Berglez, P., & Gearing, A. (2018). The Panama and Paradise Papers: The rise of a global fourth estate. *International Journal of Communication, 12*, 4573–4592.

Berger, A. N., & Roman, R. A. (2020). *TARP and other bank bailouts and bail-ins around the world: Connecting Wall Street, main street, and the financial system*. Academic Press Elsevier.

Bernstein, P. L. (1992). *Capital ideas: The improbable origins of modern Wall Street*. The Free Press.

Bhuiyan, S. (2022). The Pandora Papers opens up Pandora's Box: Integrity in crisis. *Public Integrity, 25*, 245–256.

Bjerre, C. S. (2004). *The ABCs of the UCC – Article 8: Investment Securities* (2nd ed.). American Bar Association, ABA Section of Business Law.

Blackwill, R. D., & Harris, J. M. (2017). *War by other means: Geoeconomics and statecraft*. Harvard University Press.

Bletzinger, T., Greif, W., & Schwaab, B. (2022). *Can EU bonds serve as euro-denominated safe assets?* ECB Working Paper Series No 2712 (August 2022).

Chatterjee, R. (2014). *Practical methods of financial engineering and risk management: Tools for modern financial professionals*. Springer.

Chew, D., & Gillan, S. (Eds.). (2009). *Global Corporate Governance*. Columbia University Press.

Cloud, W., Goldberg, M. A., Baker, J., & Josefovits, M. D. (2024). The SEC's final climate disclosure rules: A retrospective review and summary of expected challenges. *The Journal of Federal Agency Action, 2*, 175–183.

Conteduca, F. P., Mancini, M., & Borin, A. (2025). *Roaring tariffs: The global impact of the 2025 US trade war*. https://cepr.org/voxeu/columns/roaring-tariffs-global-impact-2025-us-trade-war (accessed: 25.08.2025).

Copeland, K. B. (2017). The Yates Memo: Looking for "Individual Accountability" in all the wrong places. *Iowa Law Review, 102*, 1897–1926.
Davidoff, S. M., Morrison, A. D., & Wilhelm, W. J., Jr. (2012). The SEC v. Goldman Sachs: Reputation, trust, and fiduciary duties in investment banking. *The Journal of Corporation Law, 37*, 529–552.
Davies, P. L., & Worthington, S. (2012). *Gower and Davies' principles of modern company law* (9th ed.). Thomson Reuters.
Dervan, L. E. (2016). Corporate Criminal Liability, Moral Culpability, and the Yates Memo. *Stetson Law Review, 46*, 41–69.
Depenheuer, O. (Ed.). (2009). *Eigentumsverfassung und Finanzmarktkrise*. Springer Verlag.
Dewatripont, M., Rochet, J.-C., & Tirole, J. (2010). *Balancing the banks: Global lessons from the financial crisis*. Princeton University Press.
Di Berardino, C., D'Angelo, S., & Sarra, A. (2025). Can deindustrialisation be reversed? The role of outsourcing and foreign trade in the structural change of the main European economies (2010-2020). *Cambridge Journal of Economics, 49*, 731–753.
du Plessis, J. J., Großfeld, B., Luttermann, C., Saenger, I., & Sandrock, O. (2007). *German corporate governance in international and European context*. Springer Verlag.
du Plessis, J. J., Großfeld, B., Luttermann, C., Saenger, I., Sandrock, O., & Casper, M. (2012). *German corporate governance in international and European context* (2nd ed.). Springer Verlag.
du Plessis, J. J., Großfeld, B., Luttermann, C., Saenger, I., Sandrock, O., & Casper, M. (2017). *German corporate governance in international and European context* (3rd ed.). Springer Verlag.
Edmans, A., Fang, V. W., & Huang, A. H. (2022). The long-term consequences of short-term incentives. *Journal of Accounting, 60*, 1007–1046.
El Ghoul, S., Guedhami, O., & Jamshed, R. (2025). Redefining purpose: The effect of the 2019 Business Roundtable statement on corporate tax strategies. In *Business Ethics, the Environment & Responsibility*. https://doi.org/10.1111/beer.12804.
Erasmus of Rotterdam. (1509/2003), *Erasmi Roterodami, Laus stultitiae*, German ed., *Das Lob der Torheit*. Panorama Verlag.
Facciolo, F. J. (2000). Father knows best: Revised article 8 and the individual investor. *Florida State University Law Review, 27*, 615–714.
Favero, C. A., & Missale, A. (2010). EU Public debt management and Eurobonds (document requested by the European Parliament's Committee on Economic and Monetary Affairs, September 2010, IP/A/ECON/NT/2010-10: https://air.unimi.it/bitstream/2434/151705/2/download.do.pdf).
Ferrarini, G., & Filippelli, M. (2014). *Independent directors and controlling shareholders around the world*. European Corporate Governance Institute, Law Working Paper No. 258/2014.
Fikentscher, W. (2009). Finanzkrise, Wettbewerb und Regulierung. *Gewerblicher Rechtsschutz und Urheberrecht Internationaler Teil (GRUR Int), 58*, 635–646.
Galbraith, J. K. (1994). *A short history of financial euphoria*. Viking Penguin.
Gall, L. (2005). *Der Bankier Hermann Josef Abs* (3rd ed.). CH Beck Verlag.
Gerner-Beuerle, C., Paech, P., & Schuster, E. P. (2013). *Study on directors' duties and liability*. European Commission, DG Market.
Gordon, J. N. (2007). The rise of independent directors in the United States, 1950-2005: Of shareholder value and stock market rices. *Stanford Law Review, 59*, 1465–1568.
Graham, B. (2003). *The intelligent investor: the definitive book o value investing, updated with new commentary by J. Zweig, preface and appendix by W. E. Buffet*. HarperBusiness Essentials.
Greenspan, A. (1967). Gold and economic freedom. In A. Rand (Ed.), *Capitalism: The unknown ideal*. Signet (Penguin Group).
Greenspan, A. (1996). *The challenge of central banking in a democratic society*, 05.12.1996. www.federalreserve.gov/boarddocs/speeches/1996/19961205.htm (accessed: 24.08.2025).

Greenspan, A. (2016). *Greenspan warns a crisis is imminent, urges a return to the gold standard*, 28.06.2016. www.zerohedge.com/news/2016-06-27/greenspan-warns-crisis-imminent-he-urges-return-gold-standard (accessed: 24.08.2025).

Großfeld, B. (1974). *Basisgesellschaften im Internationalen Steuerrecht*. Mohr Siebeck.

Harrison, J. S., Phillips, R. A., & Freeman, R. E. (2020). On the Business Roundtable 'Statement on the purpose of a corporation'. *Journal of Management, 46*, 1223–1237.

Hartikainen, H., Järvenpää, M., & Rautiainen, A. (2021). Sustainability in executive remuneration: A missing link towards more sustainable firms? *Journal of Cleaner Production, 324*, 129224.

Hayden, G. M., & Bodie, M. T. (2012). The bizarre law & economics of *Business Roundtable v. SEC*. *Journal of Corporation Law, 38*, 1–45.

Hellwig, M. (2021). Twelve years after the financial crisis: Too-big-to-fail is still with us. *Journal of Financial Regulation, 7*, 175–187.

Hopt, K. J. (2015). Corporate governance in Europe. *New York University Journal of Law & Business, 12*, 139–213.

Ioannou, S., Iliopoulos, P., & Wójcik, D. (2023). Too-big-to-fail banking in Europe: An enduring challenge. *Review of Political Economy*. https://doi.org/10.1080/09538259.2023.2286482 (accessed: 24.08.2025)

Jehn, A. (2022). In A. Kirschner & N. Wurthmann (Eds.), *IG Farben zwischen Schuld und Profit: Abwicklung eines Weltkonzerns*. Historische Kommission für Hessen Verlag.

Klovers, K., & Ginsburg, D. (2021). Common ownership: Solutions in search of a problem. In N. Charbit & T. Moretto (Eds.), *Frédéric Jenny: Standing up for convergence and relevance in antitrust* (Liber Amicorum, Vol. II, pp. 261–285). Institute of Competition Law.

Knight, F. (1971). *Risk, uncertainty and profit, first publication 1921*. Chicago University.

Kosowski, R. L., & Neftci, S. N. (2015). *Principles of financial engineering* (3rd ed.). Elsevier.

Kothari, V. (2006). *Securitization: The financial instrument of the future*. John Wiley & Sons.

Krugman, P. R., Obstfeld, M., & Melitz, M. J. (2023). *International economics: Theory and policy* (12th Global ed.). Pearson.

Kynaston, D. (2012). *City of London: The History*. Vintage Books.

Leffler, M. P., & Hitchcock, W. (Eds.). (2018). *America first: The past and future of an idea* (pp. 33–51). Passport, (September 2018).

Levitt, A. (1998). *The "numbers game"*, speech of 28 Sept 1998 at NYU Center for Law and Business. https://www.sec.gov/news/speech/speecharchive/1998/spch220.txt (accessed: 25.08.2025).

Lewis, M. (2010). *The big short: Inside the doomsday machine*. Norton.

Lewis, M. (2014). *Flash boys: A Wall Street revolt*. Norton.

Lipton, A. (2025). The legitimation of shareholder primacy. *Journal of Corporation Law* (forthcoming, also: European Corporate Governance Institute, Law Working No. 826/2025). https://papers.ssrn.com/sol3/papers.cfm?abstract_id=5120765 (accessed: 25.08.2025).

Locke, J. (1689). *Second treatise of civil government*. Awnsham Churchill.

Luttermann, C. (1993a). Die Rechtsprechung des Bundesfinanzhofes zur Anerkennung von Basisunternehmen im Internationalen Steuerrecht. *Internationales Steuerrecht (IStR), 2*, 153–160.

Luttermann, C. (1993b). Anlegerschutz und Bezugsrechtsausschluß bei Genußrechten. *Der Betrieb (DB), 46*, 1809–1813.

Luttermann, C. (1998). *Unternehmen, Kapital und Genußrechte: Eine Studie über Grundlagen der Unternehmensfinanzierung und zum internationalen Kapitalmarktrecht*. Mohr Siebeck.

Luttermann, C. (1999a). *Bilanzrecht in den USA und internationale Konzernrechnungslegung*. Mohr Siebeck.

Luttermann, C. (1999b). *Review of Alfred Rappaport, shareholder value* (2nd ed.). Verlag Schäffer-Poeschel. In *Die Aktiengesellschaft (AG), 45*, 143.

Luttermann, C. (2000). Mit dem ECJ (*Centros*) zum Internationalen Unternehmens- und Kapitalmarktrecht. *Zeitschrift für Europäisches Privatrecht (ZEuP), 8*, 907–921.

Luttermann, C. (2001). Aktienverkaufoptionsanleihen ("reverse convertible notes"), standardisierte Information und Kapitalmarktdemokratie. *Zeitschrift für Wirtschaftsrecht (ZIP), 2001*, 1901–1906.

Luttermann, C. (2003a). In B. Kropff & J. Semler (Eds.), *Münchener Kommentar zum Aktiengesetz* (Vol. 5/1, 2nd ed.). München.

Luttermann, C. (2003b). Unabhängige Bilanzexperten in Aufsichtsrat und Beirat. *Der Betriebs-Berater (BB), 58*, 745–750.

Luttermann, C. (2008a). Über Vertragsverhältnisse und Bewertungsrecht: Geld, Zeitwert und internationaler Goldstandard. *Finanz-Betrieb (FB), 9*, 193–204.

Luttermann, C. (2008b). Kreditversicherung (Credit Default Swaps): Vertrag, Restrukturierung und Regulierung (Hedge Fonds, Rating, Schattenbanken). *Recht der Internationalen Wirtschaft (RIW), 54*, 737–743.

Luttermann, C. (2008c). Die Erosion der Freiheit. *Frankfurter Allgemeine Zeitung (FAZ)*, 23.06.2008, p. 22.

Luttermann, C. (2009). Eigentum und Erbrecht als wertlose Garantien? *Zeitschrift für Steuer- und Erbrechtspraxis (ZErb), 11*, 77–85.

Luttermann, C. (2010a). Juristische Analyse von Ökonomie, Staat und Gesellschaft. *Zeitschrift für Rechtspolitik (ZRP), 43*, 1–4.

Luttermann, C. (2010b). Regulierungsperspektiven: War und ist die Finanzkrise die Folge von Hyperspekulation? *Österreichisches BankArchiv (ÖBA), 58*, 444–448.

Luttermann, C. (2011). Kopernikanische Wende zum Wahrheitsgebot oder eine europäische Ratingagentur nach US-Mustern? *Europäisches Wirtschafts-und Steuerrecht (EWS), 22*, 330–333.

Luttermann, C. (2012). Wirtschaftsstrafrecht: Zur prozessualen Lösung von Bewertungsfragen bei Vermögensdelikten als Freiheitsbasis. *Zeitschrift für Wirtschafts- und Steuerstrafrecht (wistra), 31*, 251–258.

Luttermann, C. (2013). Recht als praktizierte Ethik und unternehmerische Verantwortungskultur. In E. Weber (Ed.), *Albert Schweitzer – Hundert Jahre Menschlichkeit: Spital Lambarene (1913–2013)* (pp. 74–76). Deutscher Hilfsverein für das Albert-Schweitzer-Spital in Lambarene e.V.

Luttermann, C. (2014). Alibabas Wunderwelt: Perspektiven chinesischer Kapitalmarkt- und Gesellschaftsrechtspraxis. *Recht der Internationalen Wirtschaft (RIW), 60*, 777–784.

Luttermann, C. (2015a). Corporate Law and the Vermoegensordnung (Order of Assets). *European Business Law Review (EBLR), 26*, 31–48.

Luttermann, C. (2015b). Über Idee und Methodik eines internationalen Investitionsschutzes (Vermögensordnung) durch Privatrecht und Völkerrecht. *Zeitschrift für Europarecht, Internationales Privatrecht und Rechtsvergleichung (ZfRV), 56*, 274–282.

Luttermann, C. (2015c). Kapitalmarktrechtliche Information bei Finanzprodukten (PRIIP), Privatautonomie und Vermögensordnung. *Zeitschrift für Wirtschaftsrecht (ZIP), 37*, 805–814.

Luttermann, C. (2016a). Ist Panama überall: Mit Briefkastenfirmen über Hong Kong, USA, EU zu Transparenzgebot und internationalem Steuerrecht? *Recht der Internationalen Wirtschaft (RIW), 62*, 397–405.

Luttermann, C. (2016b). Persönliche prozessuale Haftungsverschärfung bei "Corporate Misconduct" (U.S. Yates Memorandum). *Der Betrieb (DB), 69*, 1059–1063.

Luttermann, C. (2019). Perspectives of infrastructure project finance: intercultural investment, connectivity and trust. *Finance: Theory and Practice (Финансы: теория и практика), 23*, 27–37.

Luttermann, C. (2022). Klimapartner einer kooperativen Weltvermögensordnung. *Recht der Internationalen Wirtschaft (RIW), 10*(October), p. I (editorial, *Die erste Seite*: https://online.ruw.de/suche/pdf/riw/riw-10-2022-i-d3f3bdcf9c541ac4fde57cadb3ca5968.pdf, accessed: 25.08.2025).

Luttermann, C. (2023). Unternehmensbewertung im Spannungsfeld von Rechts- und Wirtschaftswissenschaft. In K. Petersen, C. Zwirner, & G. Zimney (Eds.), *Handbuch Unternehmensbewertung* (3rd ed., pp. 163–202). Bundesanzeiger Verlag.

Luttermann, C., & Luttermann, K. (2021). Towards peace in Europe: On legal linguistics, prosperity and European identity – the European Reference Language System for the European Union. *International Journal of Legal Discourse, 6*, 7–41.

Luttermann, C., & Pöschk, M. (2014). Digitale Finanzkommunikation (XBRL/IFRS) für die Rechts· und Wirtschaftspraxis. *Wirtschaftswissenschaftliches Studium (WiSt), 43*, 663–666.

Luttermann, L. (2022). Klimawandel und Business Judgement: Nachhaltige Finanzierung als unternehmerisches Sorgfaltskonzept. *Recht der Internationalen Wirtschaft (RIW), 68*, 809–820.

Luttermann, L. (2023). Nachhaltigkeitsberichterstattung in den USA, Unternehmensbewertung und Copliance. *Recht der Internationalen Wirtschaft (RIW), 69*, 483–495.

Luttermann, L. (2024). Unternehmensführung: Nachhaltige Finanzinformation (U.S. SEC Climate Rules/EU), Wertschöpfung und Bankenfinanzierung. *Recht der Internationalen Wirtschaft (RIW), 70*, 410–422.

Luttermann, L. (2025). Nachhaltige Wirtschaftsaktivitäten: Eine europäische Eröffnungsbilanz aus Finanzdaten der Bankenregulierung. *Recht der Internationalen Wirtschaft (RIW), 71*, 26–43.

Maddaloni, A. M., & Scardozzi, G. (2022). *The new bail-in legislation: An analysis of European banking resolution*. Palgrave Mcmillan.

Mattli, W. (2019). *Darkness by design: The hidden power in global capital markets*. Princeton University Press.

Mayer, J. (2016). *Dark money: The hidden history of the billionaires behind the rise of the radical right*. Doubleday.

Mestmäcker, E.-J. (2007). *A legal theory without law: Posner v. Hayek on economic analysis of law*. Mohr Siebeck.

Milhaupt, C. J., & Pistor, K. (2008). *Law and capitalism: What corporate crises reveal about legal systems and economic development around the world*. University of Chicago Press.

Mishra, R. N. (2019). *Systemic risk and macroprudential regulations: Global financial crisis and thereafter*. SAGE Publications Pvt. Ltd.

Möschel, W. (2009). Die Finanzkrise: Wie soll es weitergehen? *ZRP, 42*, 129–133.

Morreale, M., Roisman, E., & Arnold, M. L. (2024). *A deeper dive into the SEC's landmark climate disclosure rules for public companies*, 05.04.2024. Harvard Law School Forum on Corporate Governance (www.corpgov.law.harvard.edu, accessed: 25.08.2025).

Morris, C. (2008). *The trillion dollar meltdown: Easy money, high rollers, and the great credit crash*. Public Affairs.

Muchlinski, P. T. (2021). *Multinational enterprises and the law* (3rd ed.). Oxford University Press.

Mumu, J. R., Saona, P., Russel, H. I., & Azad, A. K. (2021). Corporate governance and remuneration: A bibliometric analysis. *Journal of Asian Business and Economic Studies, 28*, 242–262.

Murray, J. H. (2020). Corporate purpose and the Business Roundtable. *Transactions: The Tennessee Journal of Business Law, 21*, 361–371.

Nemat, M., Rahat, B., Rossi, M., & Salloum, C. (2025). Global trade and financial turmoil: The Ukraine-Russia war's impact. *The Journal of Risk Finance, 26*, 516–529.

O'Neil, C. (2016). *Weapons of math destruction: How big data increases inequality and threatens democracy*. Crown.

Patterson, S. (2012). *Dark pools: The rise of the machine traders and the rigging of the U.S. stock market*. Random House.

Paulson, H. (2010). *On the brink: Inside the race to stop the collapse of the global financial system*. Hachette.

Pitkowitz, M. (2014). *Praxishandbuch Vorstands- und Aufsichtsratshaftung: Pflichten, Haftung, Ermessen und Versicherung in der AG in Deutschland und Österreich*. Verlag CH Beck.

Porter, M. E., Rivkin, J. W., Desai, M. A., & Raman, M. (2016). *Problems unsolved and a nation divided: The state of U.S. competitiveness*. Harvard Business School, September 2016.

Radin, S. A. (2009). *The business judgement rule: Fiduciary duties of corporate directors* (Vol. 1–4, 6th ed.). Wolters Kluwer.
Rathenau, W. (1917). *Vom Aktienwesen: Eine geschäftliche Betrachtung*. S. Fischer Verlag.
Roberts, R., & Kynaston, D. (2002). *City state: A contemporary history of the City of London and how money triumphed*. Profile Books.
Rogoff, K. (2022). *The long-lasting economic shock of war: Russia's invasion of Ukraine could upend fiscal and monetary policy in advanced economies*. IMF Analytical Series. https://www.imf.org/en/Publications/fandd/issues/2022/03/the-long-lasting-economic-shock-of-war (accessed: 25.08.2025).
Roth, M. (2001). *Unternehmerisches Ermessen und Haftung des Vorstands*. CH Beck Verlag.
Saad-Diniz, E., & Puppe, M. (2024). Corporations and the global backlash over privacy: Too big to regulate? In L. V. Sannikova (Ed.), *Digital technologies and distributed registries for sustainable development* (pp. 157–166). Springer.
Sandrock, O. (2016). Völkerrechtliche Grenzen staatlicher Gesetzgebung. *Zeitschrift für Vergleichende Rechtswissenschaft (ZVglRWiss), 115*, 1–94.
Schmalz, M. C. (2018). Common-ownership concentration and corporate conduct. *Annual Review of Financial Economics, 10*, 413–448.
Sen, A. (2007). *Identity and violence: The illusion of destiny*. Penguin Books.
Sen, A. (2009). *Introduction to Adam Smith: The theory of moral sentiments* (pp. VII–XXVI). Penguin Books.
Shiller, R. J. (2012). *Finance and the good society*. Princeton University Press.
Shirin, K. (2024). The role of financial stability of insurance companies in economic development. *American Journal of Economics and Business Management, 7*, 1100–1104.
Singh, M. (2025). Stargate or StarGatekeepers? Why this joint venture deserves scrutiny. *Berkeley Technology Law Journal*, upcoming in Vol. 41 (available at SSRN: https://ssrn.com/abstract=5184657 or https://doi.org/10.2139/ssrn.5184657, accessed: 24.11.2025).
Smith, A. (1759/1790[6]). *The theory of moral sentiments* (6th ed.). Penguin Books, 2009.
Stiglitz, J. (2010). *Freefall: America, markets, and the sinking of the world economy*. Norton.
Tabassum, S., & Yameen, M. (2024). Why do banks use credit default swaps (CDS)? A systematic review. *Journal of Economic Surveys, 38*, 201–231.
Taleb, N. N. (2007). *The black swan: The impact of the highly improbable*. Random House.
Talgo, C. (2024). You don't actually own the securities in your account. *Heartland Daily News*, 20.03.2024. https://heartlanddailynews.com/2024/03/you-dont-actually-own-the-securities-in-your-account/ (accessed: 25.08.2025).
Tomlinson, J. (2016). De-industrialization not decline: a new meta-narrative for post-war British history. *Twentieth Century British History, 27*, 76–99.
Tonello, M., & Tay, O. (2021). *CEO an executive compensation practices in the Russel 3000 an S&P 500*. https://corpgov.law.harvard.edu/2021/10/07/ceo-and-executive-compensation-practices-in-the-russell-3000-and-sp-500/ (accessed: 25.08.2025).
Tonti, J. (2022). On the 3rd anniversary of the Business Roundtable's redefined corporate purpose, corporations aren't living up to Americans expectations. *Just Report*. https://justcapital.com/reports/three-years-after-business-roundtable-redefines-corporate-purpose-americans-think-companies-are-lagging (accessed: 25.08.2025).
Tooze, A. (2019). *Crashed: How a decade of financial crisis changed the world*. Penguin Books Great Britain.
Trampusch, C., Linden, B., & Schwan, M. (2014). Staatskapitalismus in NRW und Bayern: Der Aufstieg und Fall von WestLB und BayernLB. *Zeitschrift für Vergleichende Politikwissenschaft, 8*, 129–154.
Uzialko, A. (2023). *The return of CDOs: Is another economic crisis on the horizon?* www.businessnewsdaily.com/10353-cdo-financial-derivatives-economic-crisis.html (accessed: 25.08.2025).
Vitali, S., Glattfelder, J. B., & Battiston, S. (2011). *The network of global corporate control*. http://arxiv.org/abs/1107.5728 (accessed: 25.08.2025).

Watanabe, H. (2020). *U.S. Business Roundtable new statement in August 2019: From the point of Japanese law*. https://doi.org/10.2139/ssrn.3689516 (accessed: 25.08.2025).

Wedel, J. R. (2009). *Shadow elite: How the world's new power brokers undermine democracy, government, and the free market*. Basic Books.

Williams, C. A. (2021). Fiduciary duties and corporate climate responsibility. *Vanderbilt Law Review, 74*, 1875–1916.

Wilson, W. (1913). *The new freedom: A call for the emancipation of the generous energies of a people*. Doubleday, Page & Co.

Xie, A. (2016), Don't listen to the ruling elite: The world economy is in real trouble. *South China Morning Post*, 02.03.2016. https://www.scmp.com/comment/insight-opinion/article/1919092/dont-listen-ruling-elite-world-economy-real-trouble (accessed: 25.08.2025).

Zhu, N. (2016). *China's guaranteed bubble: How implicit government support has propelled China's economy while creating systemic risk*. McGraw-Hill.

Zissu, A., & Stone, C. A. (2012). *The securitization markets handbook: Structures and dynamics of mortgage- and asset-backed securities* (2nd ed.). Bloomberg Press.

Zucman, G. (2015). *The hidden wealth of nations: The scourge of tax havens*. University of Chicago Press.

# Chapter 7
# Personal Responsibility and Valuation in Law and Practice (Compliance)

"Die wahre Verantwortlichkeit (...) ist souverän und bestimmt sich selbst."*

*Elias Canetti*

## Contents



*Canetti on Karl Kraus, *Schule des Widerstands*, in *Das Gewissen der Worte*, Essays, 2nd ed. Fischer, Frankfurt am Main 1981, translated: The true responsibility (...) is sovereign and determines itself.



C. Luttermann, *Human Corporation for Sustainable Development*,
https://doi.org/10.1007/978-3-032-07615-1_7

## 7.1 On Common Liberty

For if justice perishes, there is no longer any value in humans living on Earth: Thus writes Immanuel Kant,[1] referring to our nature as rational beings. Justice is the basis and function of the law. This is the aim of jurisprudence, as the science of what is just and what is unjust.[2] It provides the measure for practical reason, the basis for the order of our liberty in society and economy (*Vermögensordnung* – order of assets).[3] Personal responsibility and valuation, id est sustainability (see 5.2.4 and chapter 6), legally marks the original core function of responsible action, the basis of the imminent transformation processes worldwide.[4] In order for everyone to be able to build up an existence in an entrepreneurially individual way within a community (corporation, partnership, state), what is at stake is the presence and future of human dignity.

This liberty of ours is eroding massively, not only since the crackups of Enron Corp., WorldCom, Inc. and their auditor Arthur Andersen LLP at the dawn of the twenty-first century (2001/2002); and it cannot be limited to the globally ongoing debt crisis (*Weltschuldenkrise*) since the fall of the investment bank Lehman Brothers Holdings, Inc. (2008).[5] Basically, as we have already shown, human corporation is sustainably about the whole unit of "human, economy and environment", i.e. about peace and prosperity worldwide – virtually the present and future of humankind (see 1.2). Therefore, according to the juridical analysis of the economy,[6]

[1]German original Kant (1870) p. 332 (§ 52 E): "*(…); denn, wenn die Gerechtigkeit untergeht, so hat es keinen Wert mehr, daß Menschen auf Erden leben.*". – This chapter is based on my lecture at the Chinese University of Hong Kong in 2016, when brave people still carried the torch of freedom through the centre of a wonderful city.

[2]Ulpianus (1 reg.), Digesten 1.1.10.2: "*Iuris prudentia est divinarum atque humanarum rerum notitia, iusti atque iniusti scientia.*"

[3]Luttermann (2015a) and chapter 8.

[4]On this chapters 1, 2 and 9.

[5]On the erosion of freedom Luttermann (2008a) in a lead article for the Frankfurter Allgemeine Zeitung (FAZ, Germany), 23.06.2008 (note: insolvency of Lehman Brothers Inc. at 15.09.2008). Cf. Luttermann (2002), (2006) and (2007).

[6]See below 7.3.2, basically Luttermann (1998) pp. 465-485, and (2010a).

we will essentially focus on those persons who must act responsibly with other people' money in accordance with the law (due diligence),[7] in particular on corporate directors, auditors and regulators – on possibilities and limits.

Good corporate governance (compliance) is elementary for sound, sustainable corporations, business and markets, promoting prosperity and just communities. It grows out of the union of individual liberty (*Freiheit*) and responsibility (*Verantwortung*),[8] which has, however, been widely destroyed. This is evidenced by generations of innumerable corporate scandals, in particular massive manipulations of accounting (i.e. valuation, corporate finance and governance, financial reporting) and credit expansion, culminating in the world debt crisis, and beyond: justice (*Gerechtigkeit*) – the source of peace and prosperity – is being destroyed. That is not a natural phenomenon, but the work of humans. The financial reporting and auditing scandals before and after Enron, WorldCom and Lehman are numerous. Worldwide, the manipulation of corporate figures constitutes a blooming business.

Instead of accountability, id est sustainability (see chapter 4) regarding dealings with other people's money (see chapter 3), corporate directors are spreading a deadly virus: irresponsibility, the separation of liberty and responsibility. Greedy players with numbers and mathematical formulas, promoted by deregulation, paper money floods (fiat money) and massive transfers of assets (so-called shareholder value, quantitative easing),[9] are indulging in boundless financial speculation without any sanctions. Companies, states and citizens are sinking under chaos, debt and, meanwhile officially, inflation. We are experiencing a desaster economy. Obvious are the lack of values and the sense of a just balance in the human community. There is nebulous talk by actors of the failure of markets and "alternative-less" saving of banks, again and again (e.g., First Republic Bank, Credit Swiss in 2023).

Corporate governance is located in this rough terrain. It is time to establish financial reporting and auditing (valuation, *Bewertung*) for the human corporation as basic legal acts (*Rechtsakte*), not marketing.[10] Corporate directors must inform, id est, give a true and fair view of the material circumstances of the corporation (assets, liabilities, financial position and profit or loss, remuneration etc.)[11] in the sense of compliance on the basis of facts instead of hypotheses ("plausibility"). By complying with the imperative of truth (*Bilanzwahrheit*) and their duty of care

[7] On sustainable financial due diligence (duty of care) and wealth creation Luttermann, L. (2022) and (2024). Basically on environmental and human rights due diligence ICJ, Advisory Opinion: Obligations of states in respect of climate change, 23.07.2025 (https://www.icj-cij.org/sites/default/files/case-related/187/187-20250723-adv-01-00-en.pdf, accessed: 24.08.2025), paras. 280-300, on that see above 6.1.3. See Williams (2021).

[8] See above 1.5.1, 1.7 and 3.4.3.

[9] See below 7.2.2 and. e.g., 7.4.2, 7.8.2 and 3.6.5.

[10] Luttermann (2007), in the original German version: "*Rechnungslegung ist ein Rechtsakt, kein Marketing*".

[11] See below 7.8.1, Luttermann (2008c) and Luttermann (2009).

(*Sorgfaltspflichten*), they enjoy legal protection at court (see overall chapters 4 and 5),[12] while sustainability can take hold.

We will look holistically at the foundations and practical approaches in order to establish a reasonable concept. In a comparative perspective, with our previous findings it is about the balance that has to be obtained internationally in an "order of assets" (*Vermögensordnung*, see chapter 8), argued here with the necessary focus on personal responsibility.

## 7.2 Corporate Britain-America (Worldwide Inc.)

### *7.2.1 The Code of the City of London*

Let us start with Britain. This reflects the significance of "English" issues for our topic. It influenced the development for decades, overwhelmingly in practice through the actors of the financial industry in the City of London – even over centuries – and its modern outliers, especially in New York's Wall Street (see chapter 6, esp. 6.2.2), as global financial centres and hubs in a digitised world of corporate finance: "Money – New Lingua Franca?".[13] In May 1991, the private-economically organised Financial Reporting Council (FRC, meanwhile replaced),[14] the London Stock Exchange, and the accountancy profession founded a committee chaired by Adrian Cadbury to address the financial essentials of corporate governance. In December 1992, the result came out, the Report of the Committee on the Financial Aspects of Corporate Governance (so-called Cadbury Report).[15]

It defines corporate governance as "the system by which companies are directed and controlled" (Cadbury Report, 2.5). It is all about financial reporting and auditing. The Committee's sponsors "were concerned at the perceived low level of confidence

[12] Within the substantive civil-procedural concept above (chapter 5) on judicial practice (*Rechtsschutz* – legal protection), esp. 5.6 (with Fig. 5.3) with 4.6.5, 4.10.2 and 4.11.4. On the imperative of truth also in practical terms above, esp. 4.4.4, 4.5–4.6 with 4.11.4, 5.5–5.6 and below 8.4.

[13] Roberts and Kynaston (2002) p. 18. Cf. Tooze (2019) pp. 540-545. See above 3.3.2 and already Magna Carta Libertatum, 1215, no. 13: "Et civitas Londoniarum habeat omnes antiquas libertates et liberas consuetudines suas, tam per terras, quam per aquas." A basis, "to make money from trade", Carpenter (2015) p. 120, and even earlier, as he put it, p. 118, concessions were made to the Londoners by the king to form "a sworn, self-governing association" (commune), headed by its own elected mayor of London (one of the twenty-five 'barons' in the security clause) – "the 'ancient' liberties that Magna Carta confirmed". Cf. on associations above 2.3.3 and 3.7.

[14] By Financial Conduct Authority (FCA), see above 4.3.2 and 4.5.4. Private company limited by guarantee; on its private funding: https://media.frc.org.uk/documents/Proposals_for_future_arrangements_for_funding_the_FRCs_activities_in_relation_to_accounting_auditi.pdf (accessed: 24.08.2025).

[15] Cadbury Report: https://www.ecgi.global/sites/default/files/codes/documents/cadbury.pdf (accessed: 24.08.2025).

both in financial reporting and in the ability of auditors to provide the safeguards which the users of company reports sought and expected" (Cadbury Report, 2.1). It is emphasised: "The underlying factors were seen as the looseness of accounting standards, the absence of a clear framework for ensuring that directors kept under review the controls in their business, and competitive pressures both on companies and on auditors which made it difficult for auditors to stand up to demanding boards" (Cadbury Report, 2.1). This means there is a lack of clear, strict norms as well as corresponding control, in particular through really independent auditors (reasonable assurance), and sanctions (legal order). That sounds familiar right up to the present (see chapters 4, 5 and 6).

The Cadbury Report marks a "Code of Best Practice" for listed companies (UK Code of Corporate Governance). This is the beginning of a global movement to anchor privately formed "Codes of Corporate Governance". In terms of mere numbers, it has been a story of success: Nearly every developed country now has such a "Code".[16] They are accompanied by "standard setting" for financial reporting and auditing, also privately conducted by the International Accounting Standards Board (IASB, London). The "IFRS" propagated by this Board and its predecessors are employed by more than one hundred jurisdictions.[17] The so-called "standard setting" as a business basis was extended through the IASB in November 2021 by a so-called International Sustainability Standards Board (ISSB) in order to develop standards as a global baseline of sustainability disclosures – of course, "in the public interest".[18] The issue is a world monopoly of valuation of corporations and assets (*Vermögen*, see 4.11).

## 7.2.2 Meeting Reality

The numerical success of this private "standard setting" may be dazzling. However, numbers are merely "the sign of complete limitation" (Oswald Spengler).[19] The facts betray the catastrophic irresponsibility of the mathematically trimmed – so-called

[16]Overview: https://www.ecgi.global/publications/codes (accessed: 24.08.2025). However, note critically, e.g., above 4.5.4 (also from UK regulators).

[17]Overview: www.ifrs.org/Use-around-the-world/Pages/Jurisdiction-profiles.aspx (accessed: 24.08.2025).

[18]Formation of the ISSB announced on 03.11.2011 (https://www.ifrs.org/groups/international-sustainability-standards-board, accessed: 24.08.2025). See above 4.11.1. Cf. De Villiers and Dimes (2023), Hummel and Jobst (2024). On the Global Reporting Initiative (GRI) Pratama, Jaenudin, Anas (2022), Vigneau, Humphreys, and Moon (2015).

[19]See Spengler (1923/1998), esp. vol. 2, chapter 5. Cf. historically Fukuyama (1992). On the concept of numbers Courant and Robbins (2010), from pp. 42 and 70-71, quoting (p. 17) Carl Friedrich Gauss: *"Die Mathematik ist die Königin der Wissenschaften"* (Mathematics is the queen of sciences). Overall above chapter 3 (e.g., 3.6.3), chapter 4 (e.g., 4.2.1, 4.6: the "numbers game") and chapter 5. Luttermann (2010a) and (2010b).

"neoclassical" – economy, which can be experienced worldwide at the latest with the fall of Lehman Brothers (15.09.2008). Since then, we are witnessing massive distortions around the globe at the levels of the micro-economy and the macro-economy. This ranges from emergency programmes allegedly for saving states in the Eurozone (such as Greece, Ireland, Portugal, Cyprus), in fact, however, for saving companies and banks globally (e.g., US-Troubled Asset Relief Program, in Germany: *Sonderfonds Finanzmarktstabilisierung* – SoFFin) to the general glut of money: debt policy with unlimited money creation (fiat money and "quantitative easing").[20]

Only the symptoms are treated. Corporate scandals such as that of Volkswagen AG (2015, emissions violations) and the mismanaged retailer Arcandor AG (2009) in Germany and around the globe continue (see also in chapters 4 and 6). The Deutsche Bank AG was, among other things, involved in the manipulation of the London Interbank Offered Rate (LIBOR)[21] with the Bank of Tokyo-Mitsubishi UFJ, Citibank, HSBC, Rabobank, Royal Bank of Scotland, UBS. Worldwide, numerous cases of scandal have been discovered since 2008 in the course of the world debt crisis (so-called "financial crisis"). Particularly prominent are the tax avoidance schemes of multinational corporations (e.g., Apple, Google, IKEA: Luxemburg-Leaks) in tax oases (offshore leaks like the shocking Panama Papers)[22] and scandals in financial reporting such as those of Dynegy Inc. (USA), Olympus KK and Toshiba KK (Japan), Sino-Forest Corp. (Canada), Siwei/Caterpillar, NQ Mobile Inc. and Winsway Coking Coal Holdings Ltd. (China), Banco Espirito Santo SA (Portugal). – Who can still remember the names and cases, by now legion?

The Financial Times summarized the year 2015 with the following title: "Bankers strain against shackles: The financial world is way off recovering from the crash of 2008".[23] – Need more? – The Serious Fraud Office (London), an independent government department that investigates and prosecutes serious or complex fraud, and corruption, provides an overview: Its very substantial continuing investigations at that time included well-known actors ("big guns") like Rolls Royce, Barclays Bank, GlaxoSmithKline; among the new criminal investigations were Global Forestry Investments (investment scheme), Forex (manipulation of the FX benchmark), the Bank of England (conduct of liquidity auctions), Soma Oil and Gas (allegations of corruption in Somalia) and Quindell (accounting irregularities); more recent cases include, e.g., Glencore Energy, OpenText Axcelerate and, with 57,500 investors,

[20] See overall chapters 6 and 9.

[21] Gandhi, Golez, Jackwerth and Plazzi (2019), Huan, Previts and Parbonetti (2023).

[22] See: https://panamapapers.icij.org, also https://offshoreleaks.icij.org/ (both accessed: 24.08.2025). Cf. above 6.2.3.

[23] Financial Times, 09.12.2015, headline. Basically Stiglitz (2010).

London Capital & Finance Plc., Safe Hands Plans Ltd. and SHP Capital Holdings Ltd.[24] – An essentially never-ending story?

### *7.2.3 Critique and Focus*

The list of scandals is still growing worldwide – just take a look behind the scenes more recently at the Wirecard AG (Germany; see 4.9.4).[25] Sir Jonathan Thompson, Chief Executive of the former FRC, is headlined in 2022: "Stop complaining about audit fines and improve your work, UK regulator tells firms".[26] The range is wide, occasions and forms have manifold effects. Basically, however, there is always a lack of the diligence (*Sorgfalt*, ethic) necessary on the part of those responsible (see Fig. 7.1). In general, there seems to be hardly any sense of responsibility at all. At least this is the impression one gets, underscored by ways of public sanctioning. Look at Tesco PLC, the UK-based supermarket chain, with its 2015 accounting scandal (£263m overstatement of profits because of incorrectly booked payments from suppliers): Tesco agrees to a $12m payout to U.S. shareholders for settling a class action suit without admitting liability.[27]

Is there anybody who has done anything wrong? – This shows how cases are dealt with noiselessly. The USA stage show trials[28] and regulative politicking such as the Sarbanes-Oxley Act of 2002 (as a reaction to Enron, WorldCom)[29] and the Dodd-Frank Act of 2010 (as a reaction to Lehman and the crisis of the financial markets)[30] as variations of excess. What seems expedient are stipulations by the U.S. Department of Justice which has emphasised individual personal responsibility

[24]For data and more information www.sfo.gov.uk, particularly in the Annual Report & Accounts. Cf., e.g., Donelson, Ege and McInnis (2017), Tutino and Merlo (2019), Ratzinger-Sakel and Tiedemann (2022), Lokana and Sharma (2023), Adejumo and Ogburie (2025).

[25]More data on the United Kingdom: https://www.sfo.gov.uk/our-cases/case-archive/ (accessed: 24.08.2025). Cf. U.S. Securities and Exchange Commission (SEC) on enforcement (litigation releases): https://www.sec.gov/litigation/litreleases.htm; in Germany on financial reporting enforcement the Federal Financial Supervisory Authority (BaFin): https://www.bafin.de/EN/Aufsicht/BoersenMaerkte/Transparenz/Bilanzkontrolle/bilanzkontrolle_node_en.html; e.g., Australia with an individual structure (see above 4.8.6) and the Australian Prudential Regulation Authority (APRA): https://www.apra.gov.au/enforcement (all accessed: 24.08.2025).

[26]See FCA chief executive, reports, August 3, 2022, Financial Times (FT), cited already above in 4. 3.2.

[27]Guardian, 26.11.2015 (www.theguardian.com/business/2015/nov/26/tesco-makes-12m-payout-to-us-shareholders-over-accounting-scandal, accessed: 24.08.2025).

[28]E.g., Michael Milken ("junk bond king": sentenced to 10 years in prison, released after 22 months), Bernard Ebbers (WorldCom: 25 years); Bernard Madoff ("ponzi scheme mastermind": 150 years, in prison 2009–2021).

[29]Public Company Accounting Reform and Investor Protection Act (Senate) and Corporate and Auditing Accountability and Responsibility Act (House), Pub.L. 107–204, 116 Stat. 745.

[30]The Dodd–Frank Wall Street Reform and Consumer Protection Act, Pub.L. 111–203, H.R. 4173.

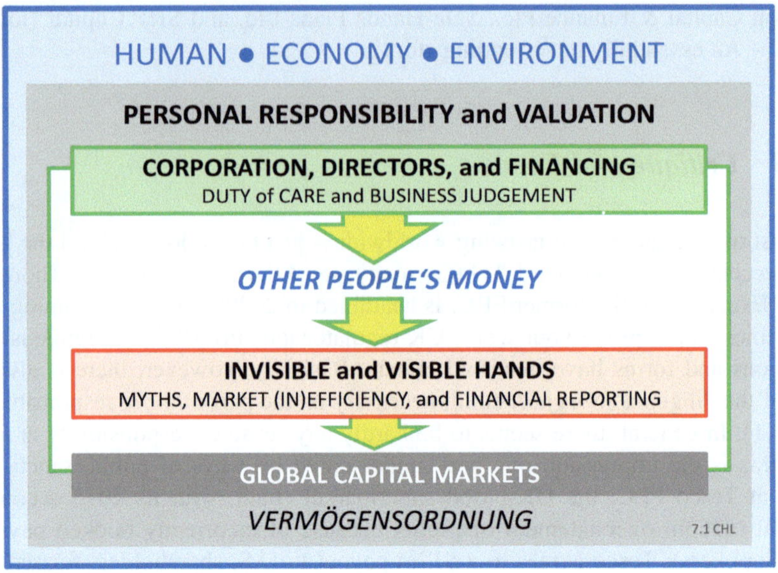


**Fig. 7.1** Personal responsibility of corporate directors for financing and valuation

in cases of "corporate misconduct" (the so-called Yates Memorandum).[31] – Generally the following holds: Private reign and state power fight for normativity and the prerogative of interpretation. This nicely illustrates the history of regulation for financial reporting and auditing in the USA – in spite of all the scandals.[32] It is all about power, private wealth and general prosperity, about legal protection of those involved, about the rule of law internationally. Corporate governance and measures for its good design are elementary.

Present practice appears to be a grandiose failure, intentionally shifting and accumulating gigantic assets (*Vermögenswerte*); concentration increases to the detriment of competition.[33] What is required in the relationship of economy and state is the description of a morally conceived "good economy":[34] the search for human meaningfulness for the individual and a just order overall. The world is in turmoil. The corporation – as a worldwide financial institution for entrepreneurial activity (see chapter 3) – is part of this, where in the process of transnational group formation

[31] Meanwhile further anchored in the U.S. Justice Manual, originally: DOJ, Individual Accountability for Corporate Wrongdoing, 09.09.2015. See on this Luttermann (2016b) and above 6.5.3.

[32] Luttermann (1999a) and (2006).

[33] See, e.g., Ghossoub, Reed (2015) and above 6.7.1; Vitali, Glattfelder, and Battiston 2011). Cf. on common ownership and control above in 6.2.3 and 6.5.1.

[34] Cf. Phelps (2007) 543, 554-558. In terms of "sustainability" above, e.g., 4.2 and 5.2.4. Basically Luttermann (1998) pp. 135-145.

(unitary business)[35] the attribution and sanctioning of responsibility becomes blurred, the connection with state and global economy erodes. We propose internationally establishing an order of assets (*Vermögensordnung*) that is based on freedom and the responsibility of individuals, structurally and methodologically secured as a sustainable concept.

## 7.3 Corporate Finance: Myths, the Law, and the Economics of Market Efficiency

### *7.3.1 The Corporation: Reality, Financial Instrument, and Information*

Good leadership is existential for any company. The discourse about good corporate governance internationally centres around the publicly held corporation (short: corporation). It is integrated into the stockmarket as a capital market, communicating the pricing for the securities (shares, bonds) of a corporation between supply and demand at short notice. Through this, it is the essence of the market model and practically the guiding example for regulation, its principles and rules being transferred to other types of companies. First the object of reference must be understood properly, which is still often not the case. So, once more the obviously widely forgotten core question for an adequate treatment: What is a corporation? – In the famous words of John C. Marshall it is "an artificial being, invisible, intangible, and existing only in contemplation of law":[36] a mere creature of law (*Rechtsgeschöpf*), embodied in the juridical person (cf. Latin *corporare*).[37]

The corporation is considered to be a fiction of law, attributed to the German champion of Roman law Friedrich Carl von Savigny (1779–1861, so-called *Fiktionstheorie*), as a construct of organisational law (bearer of the business, *Unternehmensträger*, with a special fund, *Sondervermögen*), usually designated in terms of so-called corporation law (*Gesellschaftsrecht*), of entrepreneurial "immortality".[38] A mystically working dimension, in modern diction standing for the discourse on the "separation of property and control" since Berle and Means (with

[35]Luttermann (1996). See § 297(3)(1) HGB (German Commercial Code), which stipulates by law that the assets, financial position and earnings of all group companies (*Konzern*) must be presented in the consolidated financial statements as if they were "a single company" (legal fiction): "*Im Konzernabschluß ist die Vermögens-, Finanz- und Ertragslage der einbezogenen Unternehmen so darzustellen, als ob diese Unternehmen insgesamt ein einziges Unternehmen wären.*". See above 4.7.

[36]*Trustees of Dartmouth College v. Woodward*, 17 U.S. 518, 636 (1819). Marshall had been Chief Justice of the U.S. Supreme Court (1801-1835).

[37]English to form the body (German *zum Körper bilden*), see above 2.1 and 2.4.1. Synonymous: legal person (German: *Rechtsperson*).

[38]See – also on Savigny – above 2.2.2, also 3.2.1 and 3.2.3.

big money managers even leading to "common control"),[39] most notably as a legally autonomous sponsor of assets (so-called principle of separation, see 2.4.3). Savigny, a leading legal scholar and Prussian Minister of State, with whom the modern science of the juridical person (*juristische Person*, legal person) begins, clarifies the juridical person holistically on the basis of its incapacity to act (*Handlungsunfähigkeit*), here translated as follows:

> Actions presuppose a thinking and volitional being, a single human person, which legal persons, as mere fictions, are not. And so here appears the inner contradiction of a subject capable of property rights, which nevertheless cannot fulfill the conditions for acquiring them.[40]

From this stem practically all questions of governance (*Unternehmensführung*), id est of good corporate governance regarding entrepreneurial freedom of development and duty of care (*Sorgfaltspflicht*), and the liability of those acting for the juridical person (*juristische Person*, corporation) in a personally responsible way (*Vertretung*, proxy by so-called "organs"). Werner Flume[41] clarified the controversy about the theory of the legal person in such a way that the legal person – already for Savigny – is indeed a reality which should be treated as a special "unit of effect" (*Wirkungseinheit*) that is provided and constituted by the legal order,[42] id est as the "ideal whole" (Savigny in German: *als das "ideale Ganze"*).[43] So through the liberal extension of the legal capacity (*Rechtsfähigkeit*), which is natural to any individual, to the legal person (e.g., the corporation),[44] the connection to the single human person (*natürliche Person, Menschen*) remains, due to the legal person requiring representation (*notwendige Vertretung*: corporate director). And therefore to his or her responsibility in acting for the legal person: in governance, financing and evaluating (duty of care) the corporation as life circumstances (*Lebensverhältnis*) – overall for financing sustainable business activity.[45]

---

[39] See on "common ownership" in more detail above 6.2.3 and 6.5.1.

[40] German original Savigny (1840b) p. 283: *"Allein Handlungen setzen ein denkendes und wollendes Wesen, einen einzelnen Menschen, voraus, was eben die juristischen Personen als bloße Fictionen nicht sind. Und so erscheint hier der innere Widerspruch eines der Vermögensrechte fähigen Subjects, welches doch die Bedingungen zum Erwerb derselben nicht erfüllen kann."*

[41] Flume (1983) pp. 1-31 (introduction) and from p. 31 on the German *Aktiengesellschaft* (AG, corporation). However, Flume (1983) p. 14, leaves out Savigny's central point of reference in the quotation, *"einen einzelnen Menschen"* (a single human person), see the correct quotation by Savigny in the preceding footnote and the respective translation in the text above.

[42] Ibid., see esp. p. 5 and p. 30.

[43] Savigny (1840b) pp. 244-245. See also above 3.2.3 and 3.6.1.

[44] Cf. Savigny (1840b) p. 3, under the essential starting point that all law exists for the sake of the moral freedom inherent in each individual human being; German original: *"Alles Recht ist vorhanden um der sittlichen, jedem einzelnen Menschen inwohnenden Freyheit willen."*

[45] Luttermann (1998), from p. 163 (financing of corporations, juridical person) with pp. 80-134 (participating rights – *Genußrechte*) and pp. 135-162 (venture community, appropriate risk bearing). Luttermann (2008d).

The law as the ordering factor of life sets benchmarks for legal dealings (*Rechtsverkehr*),[46] here for the corporation as a legal person. Basically, it is all about lawful financing and thus about real valuation and information under the imperative of truth.[47] The corporation is a financial instrument, traditionally one for large companies (see 2.5, 3.3.1): It collects many relatively small sums of capital permanently for the purpose of the company as determined in the statutes (financial function), independent of the identity of the capital providers (shareholders, bondholders, see 1.4.1, 3.5.4). They may dissociate themselves on their own motives from the investment at short notice via the stock or bond market, without any change in the amount of capital of the corporation. This is ingenious for directing short-term capital to long-term investments via the financial function of the corporation. And this is accompanied by the obligation to regularly provide sound information (facts) on the corporate financial situation to current and potential investors (real disclosure, see 3.3.3, and chapter 4: real financial reporting).

## 7.3.2 *Juridical Analysis of the Economy*

The cultural context and effective life connections for an adequate legal order remain open. The legal analysis of the economy forms a reasonable basis, reconciling humans as individuals and citizens with the state, society and the environment.[48] Business, economic thinking and working are the source of so-called "neoclassical", Anglo-American financial theories for companies and capital markets for the maximisation of profits. The valuation of the corporation and its emitted equity, debt and hybrid securities, is a function of the capital market. It is the institutions that require structures oriented towards efficiency (i.e., fair competition), for the negotiation of life conditions (*Lebensverhältnisse*) and their condensation in prices (contracts, see chapter 5). This is the field of the so-called "law and economics" movement.

Accordingly, economics attempts to provide a scientific theory of rational behaviour for the prediction of human reaction to law (incentives): to be a useful normative standard for the evaluation of law and politics. The "economic analysis of law" covers practically all fields of law (property, contract, tort, legal process), with power also the area of corporate governance. However, a market (considered "efficient") is neither necessarily rational nor precise in its information; individual investors may

[46]Luttermann (1998) p. 163, see also there p. 1: the economy as the "regulated matter" (*die "geregelte Materie"*). See above 2.6.1: market and corporation as orderly events.

[47]Ibid., and above, esp. chapter 4 on verified information for investors. On the elementary theory and practice of valuation see chapter 5 and below 8.4.2 (valuation statute – *lex aestimatio*).

[48]Basically above 1.2 and 6.1. See also 8.2.2, already above 6.7.3 and, e.g., 1.6.2, and 4.2.1 to 4.3.2. Fundamentally Luttermann (1998), esp. pp. 465-485, and Luttermann (2010a), Mestmäcker (2007).

be able to excel over others, if not permanently.[49] Judge Richard Posner, a main actor in the development and movement of the "economic analysis of law", said that economics, as the most advanced social science, "place the study of law on a scientific basis, with coherent theory, precise hypotheses deduced from the theory, and empirical tests of the hypotheses".[50] A rather questionable position, regarding which Posner himself already voiced some fundamental doubts (see 7.7.2).

Economics, mathematically-logically glossed over with so-called "market efficiency" and profit maximisation, thus gained primacy over the law regarding the formation of society. State regulation of the financial markets and rules made by business itself (so-called *lex mercatoria*) have widely taken hold. This can be observed in corporate governance (e.g., Corporate Governance Codes, see 7.5.1), in accounting and valuation rules (e.g., "IFRS", "IFRS-S", see chapter 4). This is a path along a slippery plane, in the course of which we have lost our measure, our centre – and thus, not only, but to a large extent, in economic terms: real values. Jurisprudence establishes the primacy of the law for the community of life ordered according to freedom, ethically founded with the help of the juridical analysis of the economy: The law prerogatively provides the measure for individual business activity (incl. environmental and human rights), necessary sustainability and general prosperity (see 6.1, 6.7.3 with Fig. 6.3).[51]

## 7.3.3 On Invisible Hands, Interests, and Order

This is not a renunciation or paternalism of the economy, but rather its admission and establishment for the purpose of a just order of liberty: a free-market order, to enable and encourage successful economic activity under fair competition. Adam Smith coined the metaphor of the "invisible hand" (of Jupiter, the ancient Roman deity) with great political effect: Every human being strives to invest his capital to the greatest advantage to himself (*Eigennutz*), at the same time, in striving for profit, unintentionally promoting public interest (*Gemeinnutz*, common good).[52] In this way, the individual, locally rooted and better informed, is able to optimise the increase in value. With all due criticism, this basically seems quite modern: Allover,

---

[49] Bernstein (1993) pp. 134-37. Luttermann (1998) pp. 210-237. On the limits of rational choice Mestmäcker (2007) pp. 46-49, fundamentally with the statement, p. 61: "The message is that there are philosophical ideas, values and insights that remain relevant beyond the disparate events of history." Cf. below 7.3.3.

[50] Cit. according to Cooter and Ulen (2016) p. 1. Overall see Posner (1979) and Posner (1973, 2014). Cf. basically Mestmäcker (2007), esp. from p. 26 (on efficiency: Posner v. Hayek); and note: "efficiency does not necessarily triumph", Coffee (2001) p. 4.

[51] See also Figs. 5.1 and 5.3. Luttermann (2010a). Cf. on judges, legislation and custom as sources of the law Mestmäcker (2007) pp. 29-32. Cf. on real disclosure above 3.3 (esp. 3.3.3). On corporate climate responsibility Williams (2021).

[52] Smith (1776/1789$^5$) pp. 571-573. Cf. Fig. 7.1.

it is about creation of value (*Wertschöpfung*), which is elementary in the sense of reason and sustainability.[53] Adam Smith, the moral philosopher, thought in the humanistic categories of integrity, jurisprudence and morals (i.e., virtues, *Tugenden*).[54] Thus, market-based private autonomy of the individual (freedom of contract) is superior to central state dirigisme.

This must be developed globally in the information age. Self-interest as the path to common interest: This function of the market, id est facilitating division of labour as far as possible and continuously adapting economic activities to millions of facts, is part of the core of a liberal society under the rule of law (*Rechtsstaat*). This ensures that the general rules for the limitation of individual activities can be determined, as Friedrich August von Hayek – in the sense of Friedrich Carl von Savigny – explains.[55] We call it: *Der Markt ist eine geordnete Veranstaltung* – the market is an orderly event.[56] As an institution of fair competition, it is particularly the requirement of individual fairness that counts for the actors. The law provides the yardstick (*das Maß*). Milton Friedman, an icon of capitalism, also considered this essential for individual freedom. With direct reference to Adam Smith, he tied profit maximisation to the "rules of the game", id est conformity with "the basic rules of the society, both those embodied in law and those embodied in ethical custom."[57] This provides the overall sense, which the apostles of Friedman, usually "neo-classically" stinted, have forgotten. The law determines the invisible boundaries within which humans as free beings meet, come into contact in business contracts and promote each other precisely in their own interest (Latin *do ut des*).[58]

That is the vital source of a civil society, socially harmonising the entrepreneurial striving of every human being into a prospering community. It should be remembered that Friedman also promoted a truly free market in gold (even before U.-S. President Richard Nixon closed the gold window in 1971).[59] A free society, as the

[53] See chapter 1 and 2.4.2, 4.11, overall chapter 9.

[54] Fundamentally Smith (1759/1790[6]), who summarises (p. 401), that the "two useful parts of moral philosophy (…) are Ethics and Jurisprudence"; and he testifies (p. 77): "the candidates for fortune too frequently abandon the paths of virtue". Cf. here chapter 6 and Galbraith (1994). See further below 7.8.

[55] Hayek (1991) p. 192. See Savigny, above 2.2.2, on the law, determining the "free, secure space" for everyone within society.

[56] See already above 2.6.1, 3.3.4 and Luttermann (2010a).

[57] Friedman (1970). Basically Friedman (1962, 2002) p. 133. Cf. Mestmäcker (2007) pp. 29-32. See in more detail 7.4.2 (shareholder value).

[58] Fundamentally Savigny (1840a) pp. 331-332. See below 7.6.1, 7.7.1 with 7.7.3 and above in 5. 3.3.

[59] And foreign exchange: Friedman (1962, 2002) pp. 69-70. On the "Nixon shock": Garten (2021). See on contractual relationships and valuation law (money, time value and internatl. gold standard): Luttermann (2008b). Cf. Krugman/Obstfeld/Melitz (2023), chapter 19 (internatl. monetary systems), esp. from p. 599 and pp. 640-646; Greenspan (2013), esp. chapter 13 (money and inflation), and Greenspan on central banks, stagnation, and gold, 10.11.2014: https://www.youtube.com/watch?v=_mmL8X_2Ces (from the 23:08 minute mark, accessed: 24.08.2025), see above 7.3.3; see also above 6.6.2, below 8.3.1 and 8.1 (on "the common good").

founding fathers of the USA timelessly affirm,[60] is based on substance (facts) precisely with the free-enterprise system (*freies Unternehmertum*). It is here that the universal mind of great life designs takes effect, whereas the phalanx of epigones loses itself in models, formulas and mathematical overshoot. Gerard Debreu, a champion of general equilibrium analysis, considered the great theory of unity unattainable.[61] But even that would not be a reason for giving up. Jurisprudence, with the law as the art of life (see 9.9), is essentially practical: constitutionally maintaining the balance between conflicting, also silently working forces (interests) within the diversity of a pluralistic community. In corporate governance and compliance, the main point concerns adequate information.

## 7.4 Corporate Management, Disclosure, and Valuation

### *7.4.1 Information: The Order of Assets and Accountability*

We are living in an information society, digitised with information as a new kind of "production factor" (*Produktionsfaktor*, see 4.12.3, 4.13), encompassing entrepreneurship, markets and corporations globally with the digital data flood ("big data", see 6.8.5). This easily undermines the age-old purpose forming the concept of "information", based on Latin *forma* for form, picture, and *informare* for designing, instructing, id est literally for "putting someone in the picture". Legally, that means providing – here: while reporting financially on the corporate positions – a fair view (German: *getreu Rechenschaft geben*) within the meaning of the general rule for financial reporting: the imperative of truth (*Bilanzwahrheit*, see chapter 4). This is also shown by the "comply or explain" approach in corporate governance. If behavior and explanation of the directors are unsatisfactory, the shareholders may make use of their right to hold the company and management "to account".[62]

This is the key: Any society (state) as a legal and economic order is an order of assets (*Vermögensordnung*, see 7.8 and chapter 8). Assets are legally (and thus from the perspective of accounting, financial reporting) connected to a legal subject (human being, juridical person) and thus at the same time separated from other spheres of assets (*Vermögenssphären*, legal subjects).[63] Materially, this is shaped by valuation law (*Bewertungsrecht*), namely accounting law (*Bilanzrecht*), which determines *what* is valued as assets or liabilities *in what way* (see chapters 4 and 5). This is

[60] See Art. I, sec. 10, clause 1 U.S. Constitution (also Art. I sec. 8, clause 2 and clause 5). Cf. Vandersteel, The constitution calls for gold and silver, The New York Times, 01.01.1986, sec. 1, p. 22; Vieira (2015). Overall above 7.3.3.

[61] Debreu (1991) 1, 3.

[62] Overall chapters 2, 3 and chapter 4 (esp. 4.4: accountability); esp. on duty of care see above 6.4, below 8.3.2 (due diligence), and Luttermann, L. (2022). Cf., e.g., UK FRC, https://www.frc.org.uk/about-us/ (accessed: 24.08.2025).

[63] See Luttermann (2012) and (2015a).

the essence of a juridical person (corporation) in financial terms, due to its financial function (see 2.2.2, 2.5). For economic practice, it establishes the legal structure of the organisation of the corporation and its financing by the "community of risk" (German: *Wagnisgemeinschaft*) of the investors (shareholders/equity and bondholders/debt).[64] It is the nucleus of corporate, capital market and insolvency law, highlighting the connection of property (liberty – *Freiheit*) and liability (responsibility – *Verantwortung*). Without it, no existence of the corporation and no participation of it in business would be possible at all (culture of responsibility – *Verantwortungskultur*).

For managers (corporate directors), this means accounting (financial reporting) for the way they deal with other people's money; cross-border (interculturally) and traditionally within national economies (*Volkswirtschaften*), it is also about the international order of assets (global *Vermögensordnung*, i.e., comparative law, *Rechtsvergleichung*).[65] This leads us right into the kind of discourse that begins with the inclusion of members from outside the family into the circle of the investors of a corporation (see 3.7). Alfred D. Chandler describes the development of the "visible hand" in the USA: the large modern business enterprise "administered by salaried managers replaced the small traditional family firm as the primary instrument for managing production and distribution".[66] The great private or governmental money managers (e.g., BlackRock, UBS Group AG, Government Pension Fund of Norway, Temasek Holdings) heighten the complexity.[67] – The underlying and leading principles of all good governance are generally valid: probity, accountability, transparency and sustainability.[68]

### 7.4.2 Concepts of Valuation and Manipulation

The "struggle for law" (Rudolf von Jhering: *Der Kampf ums Recht*, 1872),[69] id est here, the question as to how investors are to be informed, is highlighted by the two concepts of regulation and valuation in the corporation. The valuation of assets builds primarily on accounting data (cf. so-called "accounting model of the firm"), id est, systematically building on facts for the human corporation (see chapters 4

---

[64] Luttermann (1998), esp. from p. 135 and pp. 238-357. See above, e.g., 1.4.1 with 3.5.4 and 3.6.5.

[65] See chapter 8 and Luttermann (2015a).

[66] Chandler (1977) p. 1. See on "family business" and development above 1.3.3, 2.3.3, and 3.7, 3.8.

[67] See above 6.5.1, 6.9. Cf., e.g., Jo and Henry (2015), Gervais and Strobl (2023).

[68] Cf. UK CGC (September 2014, Governance and the Code 1.). It is of utmost importance: "Boards of directors are responsible for the governance of their companies." (UK CGC, January 2024, Introduction); with the principle (A of section 1, ibid.): "(…) generating value for shareholders and contributing to wider society."; see below in 7.5.1. Please note on "shareholder value" and bondholders above 3.4.4 and 3.6.2 with 3.6.5.

[69] English: The struggle for law, translated by John Joseph Lalor, 2nd ed. 1915, Callaghan & Company, Chicago.

and 5). According to economic theory, centered on efficiency, a well-organised, transparent market regularly generates a price between supply and demand (market price) that corresponds to or is close to the "fair value": This is in essence the efficient market hypothesis, the so-called neoclassical mantra of deregulation.[70] The manifold technically modelled constructions are shaped by a mechanical view of the world.

More recent approaches calculate cash values with prognosticated cash flows (so-called "economic model"). The reference point is thought to be what is considered an averagely acting "reasonable investor" (see 2.6.2 with Fig. 2.3). Under the condition of a relative scarcity of supply on the perfect market, he reacts to new information for the purpose of return on investment (ROI). Through his buying (selling), the price of a security (stock or bond market price) rises (falls). This is what the corporate managers are fixated on: Their model of management seeks to maximise the reported earnings per share (EPS, accounting model) or the reported free cash flow (economic model). "Creating shareholder value" has become their board maxim: a game of prognoses and models, vague expectations,[71] so-called hope values (*Hoffnungswerte*), id est "soft information" (see chapters 4 and 5). Institutionally, the U.S. Securities and Exchange Commission (SEC) has left standard setting for financial reporting to private organisations (FASB/AICPA etc.) to a large degree since 1938, thwarting the intention of the U.S. Congress.[72] Under the label "GAAP", these organisations provide patchwork: "too detailed" with "too many exceptions".[73]

The culmination is that the so-called "standard setters" (FASB, IASB) themselves regularly produce minority votes (dissents) in "standard setting". In practice, they provide "authoritative support" in proceeding in opposition to the so-called "standard".[74] Shame on him who thinks ill of it.[75] – Worldwide this mixture[76] led to the development of earnings management at Wall Street, described by Arthur Levitt 1998 as the SEC-Chairman as follows: "The numbers game" among market participants, a "game of nods and winks", where "the accounting is being perverted".[77]

[70] Fama (1970) and Fama (1991). Posner (1979).

[71] Rappaport (1986, rev. 2d 1997). Cf. Eccles, Herz, Keegan, and Phillips (2001). Koller, Goedhart, and Wessels (2020), Overall Mestmäcker (2007), esp. pp. 46-49 (limits of rational choice). On forecasting Greenspan (2013).

[72] See above 3.3.3 (on the "*coup de main*"). Overall Luttermann (1999a) pp. 34-57. See Chatov (1975), cf. Kripke (1979). Competitive Enterprise Institute, 04.10.2005, cei.org/studies-issue-analysis/public-company-accounting-oversight-board (accessed: 24.08.2025): PCAOB "quasi-private agency"; *Free Enterprise Fund v. PCAOB*, 561 U. S. 477 (2010). SEC-Chairman Ruder, quoted by: Seligman (2002) p. 473 (POB).

[73] FASB-Chairman Robert Herz, Wall Street Journal, 13.12.2007, p. 13: "Closing the GAAP". Cf. already, e.g. 3.4.6 and 3.5.2 to 3.5.5. Basically Luttermann (1999a).

[74] On this already Luttermann (1998) pp. 419-421. See below 7.6.6.

[75] German: *Ein Schelm, wer Böses dabei denkt.* Cf. Old French *Honi soit qui mal y pense*, the motto on a representation of a garter of the Royal coat of arms of the United Kingdom.

[76] See in more details above, esp. chapters 3 to 6.

[77] Levitt (1998), see for more below 7.6.1. Eisenberg (1976), chapter 12 (esp. pp. 188-195).

Systematically, massive accounting and market manipulation took place, as with Enron, WorldCom, then – leading to the "financial crisis" (*Weltschuldenkrise*) – Lehman Brothers, Goldman Sachs, Deutsche Bank: abuse of investment banking and structured finance products (CDO-Ponzi scheme), inflated credit ratings, high risk lending.[78] The varied list of scandals continues to the present. That means we are still teetering on the brink of the abyss.

### 7.4.3 Disclosure, Morals, and Independent Directors

"Sunlight is said to be the best of disinfectants", Louis D. Brandeis – a lawyer, who had a reputation as "the peoples' lawyer"[79] and presidential advisor, then an influential judge at the U.S. Supreme Court (1916–1939, see 7.6.5), – explained his position in 1914. Publicity was in his view justly commended as a remedy for social and industrial diseases.[80] This is why, in view of the deficiencies of the capital markets (financial oligarchy, manipulation, fraud), he demanded full disclosure to the investor (public) – instead of burdening the buyer (of securities) with the risk, as in Ancient Roman law (*caveat emptor*). At the time of Brandeis, after the turn of the century and, again, corporate scandals, the usual secrecy of corporate accounts was debated between "Main Street and Wall Street": the issue was better control of corporate management and possible liability of corporate directors to stockholders in corporate affairs.[81]

This led to the well-known discourse on "The modern corporation and private property" (Berle and Means, 1932), which shapes our topic at its modern root: the separation of ownership (atomistic shareholders) and control (of the corporate directors) with the well-known deficiencies (e.g., moral hazard). – What is, still and timelessly, required is fundamental fiduciary duty of the directors.[82] It is recognised that for the necessary balance there needs to be a comprehensive focus on people, markets and the law – of course, also according to environmental and human rights (see 7.3). Empirically, Corporate America is changing. Founding

---

[78] U.S. Senate, Subcommittee on Investigations: Wall Street and the Financial Crisis: Anatomy of a Collapse (13.04.2011). See above chapter 6.

[79] See Strum (1984), whose biography of Louis D. Brandeis (1856-1941), later an Associate Justice of the U.S. Supreme Court, is expressively subtitled: "Justice for the people". Groundbreaking (p. 406 there) his quote: "Liberty is the greatest developer". Cf. accordingly as judge: Brandeis, dissenting, in *Olmstead v. U.S.*, 277 U.S. 438, 479 (1928); on this with a quote below 8.2.3. Cf. also below 7.6.5, 7.6.6.

[80] Brandeis (1914) pp. 92 and 101-5 (cf. James Bryce, 1888, The American Commonwealth). See on Brandeis above 3.3.2 to 3.3.4 and below 8.2.3.

[81] Berle (1928) p. 177. See above 3.5.3 and 3.5.5 on the "discretionary power" of corporate directors.

[82] Ibid., p. 176. See above 7.2.3 (with Figs. 7.1 and 7.3) and, e.g., 3.4.4. According to environmental and human rights see Williams (2021) and above 6.1.

personalities of "big business" are being succeeded by the manager-directed corporation. In 1950, there were hardly 20% "independent directors" on their boards, in 2005 there were ca. 75%: a "powerful trend", thought to be due to the "shift to shareholder value as the primary corporate objective" and – interrelated through the overriding effect of the shareholder wealth-maximising strategy – "the greater informativeness of stock market prices".[83]

Disclosure ("informativeness") has in fact changed, becoming different, not better, changed with the neoclassically propagated profit dogma "shareholder value": Instead of information on the actual situation (substance), it is model calculations, prognoses, hoped-for values – all with their uncontrolled shifting of wealth (*Vermögensverschiebung*, see 7.7.3 with chapters 4 and 5) – that have gained the field. They are considered to be "fair value" and influence stock market prices, while they are in fact to a large degree precisely those instruments of market manipulation that have proven to be failures in the "numbers game" as it was and still is played on Wall Street. If, in particular, independent directors react to such "outside performance signals" (so-called "analysts' consensus earnings estimates"),[84] this is remarkable for the reform approaches of regulation; we will treat the framework of reference in more detail in the following.

## 7.5 Corporate Control ("Fair Value") and Approaches to Regulation

### *7.5.1 Reflections*

Good corporate governance means adequate protection of investors (equity and debt investors) for participation in sustainable business success. The UK Corporate Governance Code (1992, 1.) determines in its introduction: "The purpose of corporate governance is to facilitate effective, entrepreneurial and prudent management that can deliver the long-term success of the company". The following version (2018) underlines: "At the heart of this Code is an updated set of Principles that emphasise the value of good corporate governance to long-term sustainable success." Then (2024) it is: "A successful company is led by an effective and entrepreneurial board, whose role is to promote the long-term sustainable success of the company, generating value for shareholders and contributing to wider society."[85] Structurally this includes, as innumerable corporate scandals and the financial crisis

[83] Gordon (2007) p. 1563. Cf. Bonini, Deng, Ferrari et al. (2022), Banoo (2020). See above 2.3.2 and 3.6.2 ("big business"). See on personal responsibility chapter 6, esp. 6.8 and 6.3.3 ("independent directors").

[84] Gordon (2007) ibid. See below 7.6.1.

[85] UK CGC, January 2024, section 1, principle A. Cf. Fig. 7.2.

demonstrate, sound internal control (corporate law) and sound external control (capital market law, see Fig. 7.3).

Accounting, id est financial reporting and auditing, comprise both levels of control (see chapter 4). Overall, it is about reasonableness under the rule of law.[86] For corporate directors work with "visible hands" in the design of information (real disclosure).[87] This means: The regulation approach "comply or explain" aims at the flexibility of directors. Accordingly, the Corporate Governance Codes are voluntary ("soft law" approach, see 7.6.1). Experience shows this regulatory idea to have failed. Thus it seems time to move on to a so-called "hard law" or, better, to a reasonable statutory approach[88] to be delivered in terms of sustainability (*Nachhaltigkeit*, see 5.2.4). To legal experts socialised in Continental European law, this sounds like the long overdue conclusion[89] to legally regulate corporate and capital market law in a unified way. Aspects remaining for codes seem marginal, e.g. the so-called "*Entsprechenserklärung*" (declaration of conformity: § 161 AktG), where following the code does not hold contractually with institutional investors, being restricted to the signalling effect (*Signaleffekt*).

However, it would be wrong to adhere to mistaken notions of privately organised standard-setting belonging to an extra-legal zone (cf. *lex mercatoria*, so-called "custom").[90] With their unconditional declaration of conformity according to § 161(2) German AktG regarding future adherence to the recommendations of the German Corporate Governance Codex (German CGC), chairpersons and boards of directors make a voluntary self-commitment.[91] Fundamental, but hitherto only a poorly observed point is: The corporation (with a special fund – *Sondervermögen*, see 7.3.1) is constructed in terms of valuation law (*Bewertungsrecht*, see chapters 3, 5 and 8.4.2: *lex aestimatio*). Accounting law (*Bilanzrecht*, i.e. the law of financial reporting), characterised by corporate and capital market law, determines how the

[86] In international perspective Luttermann (2016a). Basically see chapters 2 and 3.

[87] Fundamentally 3.3.3; cf. above 7.3.

[88] On a general rule, not casuistry see above 3.5.5, also 4.2.4, 4.11.1 and 9.9.

[89] See 7.6.1. On rules of "just conduct" and "customary law" (custom) Mestmäcker (2007) pp. 29-42.

[90] Ibid. See above 7.3.2, below esp. 7.6.1 and 7.8.1; also on the *lex mercatoria* see Großmann-Doerth (1933), thereupon Blaurock, Goldschmidt, and Hollerbach (2005). Cf. Callies (2001) and overall Toth (2017).

[91] OLG München, 06.08.2008 (7 U 5628/07) <openjur.de/u/415881> recital 14. See BGH, 16.02.2009 (II ZR 185/07) BGHZ 180, 9, and BGH, 21.09.2009 (II ZR 174/08) BGHZ 182, 272, <openJur 2011, 1923> (German CGC 5.5.3, § 243(1) AktG). Cf. BGH, 09.10.2018 (II ZR 78/17) <openjur.de/u/2134876>, OLG Celle, 27.06.2018 (9 U 78/17) < openjur.de/u/2134886>. On breach of information obligations BGH, 23.02.2021 (II ZR 65/19) BGHZ 229, 27, <openJur 2021, 34958> recital 26: if the provision of information is necessary from the perspective of an objectively judging shareholder (*"eines objektiv urteilenden Aktionärs"*) for the proper assessment of the subject of the resolution (*Beschlussgegenstand*, § 243(4)(1) AktG).

corporation may and must be substantially present; it is the epitome of material justice in the respective legal circumstances, id est the legal relationships concerned (see chapter 4).[92]

## 7.5.2 *"Fair Value" as Appraisal of Business*

The valuation of the assets of the corporation is elementary in the governance concept, id est for the financing, disclosure and liability of the juridical person. Corporate governance is, says the UK CGC (1992, 3.), "about what the board of a company does and how it sets the values of the company"; the UK CGC (2024, 1.A.) emphasises "generating value for shareholders" as the boards' goal.[93] However, "value" is a colourful word also when it comes to the mentioned concepts of accountability, transparency and probity, that is, regarding "fair value". The designation is defined as "the price that would be received to sell an asset or paid to transfer a liability in an orderly transaction between market participants at the measurement date" (IFRS 13.9). However, such comparable transactions are only seldom to be found in reality, so that "fair value" is not the value "to be attributed" (*beizulegender Wert*), but the practically "attributed" (*beigelegter Wert*), as a rule under questionable assumptions, id est an arbitrary number.[94]

This mean that as a rule something is purported (i.e. widely feigned) that in reality is actually different. This needs to be observed in greater detail, in particular also as a control position (audit, assurance). Fair value measurements and disclosures remain problematical internationally.[95] This becomes clear in the treatment of assets and liabilities in a fair value hierarchy according to the so-called "International Financial Reporting Standards" (IFRS), which prioritise the inputs to the valuation techniques: (1) *Level 1* inputs are quoted prices (unadjusted) in active markets for identical assets or liabilities; (2) *Level 2* inputs are inputs other than quoted prices included within Level 1 that are observable for the asset or liability, either directly or indirectly (mark to market valuation); and (3) *Level 3* inputs are unobservable inputs for the asset or the liability (mark to model valuation).[96] – Obviously, this opens up a wide margin

---

[92] See below 7.8.1 and particularly 4.1, 4.4.1, and 6.3. Basically Luttermann (2003a) Einf BilanzR recitals 34-36 (26-43) and Luttermann (2003a) §§ 243, 342 recitals 30-72. Luttermann (2008c).

[93] See above 7.5.1. Cf. above 6.7.2, in the USA Business Round Table, Statement on the Purpose of a Corporation: "fundamental commitment to all of our stakeholders".

[94] See Fig. 7.2, below 6.6.5 and above 4.6.3, 4.8.3 and overall 4.9.

[95] IVS, ISA; IFRS 13.11, IAS 36.53A. Cf. "U.S. GAAP": FASB, ASC 820 (No. 2011-04; SFAS No. 157); *SEC v. KCAP Financial, Inc. et al.*, Release No. 34-68307 (AAER-3425, 28.11.2012). European Union, Fair Value Directive 2001/65/EC and Commission Regulation (EC) No 1864/2005 of 15.11.2005 ("fair value"-option, carve-out from IAS 39). See § 255(4) *HGB* (German Commercial Code).

[96] IFRS 13, technical summary: fair value measurement (2013; www.ifrs.org), IFRS 13.72-99; cf. IFRS 7.25-30 (Financial Instruments: Disclosure). Cf. Luttermann (2009).

of discretionary power to corporate directors (pricing models, see 7.4.3) precisely in those numerous areas where active markets (actual value, market price) are in fact largely non-existent.[97]

This is all the more true since the IFRS de-materialise valuation, commonly according to their model U.S. "GAAP".[98] The central accounting term "asset" highlights this, referring – originally – to any resource controlled by the corporation "from which future economic benefits are expected to flow to the entity" (IAS 38.8 (b)).[99] That might sound and be propagated even as the "concept" of financial reporting according to the IASB and its so-called "International Financial Reporting Standards", now even extended to global standards of sustainability disclosure (ISSB/IFRS S, see 7.2.1). It is obvious that this approach is oriented towards the future, based on the concept of probability ("degree of uncertainty").This also comprises the more recent phrasing presented by the IASB in the so-called "Conceptual Framework" (2018), describing "the objective of, and the concepts for, general purpose financial reporting" (CF SP1.1). According to this, an "economic resource" (asset) is a right "that has the potential to produce economic benefits" (IASB, CF4.4). That may sound good, generally.

However, it must be made clear: that is not a viable concept, it is not financial reporting (accounting) nor informing. Not even in the context of the decision usefulness theory, commonly used in financial affairs: "The investor must predict the future."[100] – Really? – And what's more, this is to be done on the basis of estimations (i.e., on a two-tiered hypothesis). Methodologically, the process seems like circular reasoning (*Zirkelschluss*). Not to mention sustainability, financial reporting and auditing (compliance) as legal acts (*Rechtsakte*, see chapter 4). Hopes, visions of the future: potential (from Latin *potentialis*), meaning possible or capable of coming into being or action.[101] Isn't it rather a glance into the crystal ball, a kind of fortune telling (*Wahrsagerei*) than "fair value"? Mathematically packaged in pretty numbers and models, of course. What is to be audited or assuranced here? – Muddy ground indeed.

[97] Basically on the discretionary power of corporate directors Berle and Means (1932, 1967) pp. 182 and 183; see in more detail above in 3.5.3 and 3.4.6.

[98] Cf. basically Luttermann (1999a) and, e.g., Onaran, 20.02.2013: www.bloomberg.com/news/articles/2013-02-20/u-s-banks-bigger-than-gdp-as-accounting-rift-masks-risk (accessed: 24.08.2025).

[99] For "liability" IAS 37.10. IASB, CF4.4(a) and CF4.38. Großfeld and Luttermann (2005) recitals 893-900. See above 5.6.1.

[100] Staubus (1999) p. 153. Cf. IASB, CF1.2 on "the objective of general purpose financial reporting". Cf. Greenspan (2013). How courts determine fair value, see Wertheimer (1998).

[101] Brown (1993) p. 2310 (potential).

### 7.5.3 Facts, Business Judgement Rule, and Fiduciary Duties

Good Corporate Governance (compliance, control) requires true information (real disclosure, see 3.3.3), id est facts in terms of sustainability as verifiability (*Nachprüfbarkeit*, see 1.3.2, 4.11.4). They are lacking under IFRS (U.S. "GAAP"), for nothing true can be known of the future – thus Friedrich Schiller describes the dubious seers in his tragedy *Die Braut von Messina.*[102] In the prognostically abbreviated "fair value", valuation and the "picture of the corporation" shown in its accounts (*Bilanzbild*) become arbitrary and pro-cyclically volatile: In the optimism of an economic boom, asset values rise (balance sheet assets), in a downturn – when financial power is desperately needed – they melt like ice in the sunshine (combustive agent). Suchlike is not enough for the hard, legal aspects of corporate governance (e.g., dividend calculation, accounting-based covenants/sustainability linked loans, duty of care, liability).

Legal experts are painfully experienced in abstaining regarding valuation issues, as at the U.S. Supreme Court: "Accountants long have recognized that 'generally accepted accounting principles' are far from being a canonical set of rules that will ensure identical accounting treatment of identical transactions. 'Generally accepted accounting principles,' rather, tolerate a range of 'reasonable' treatments, leaving the choice among alternatives to management."[103] – Extra-legal zones? – This is reminiscent of the corporate law concept of the Business Judgement Rule (cf. § 93(1) AktG). It lowers the liability risk in decisions for directors, who act on "an informed basis [i.e., with due care], in good faith and in the honest belief that the action taken was in the best interest of the company", in the sense of the presumption of due action.[104] If claimants show this presumption to be false on the basis of facts,

---

[102] *Isabella* in Schiller (1803) p. 136, the bride of Messina, a tragedy with elements of Greek tragedies and with choirs, German original: *"Nichts Wahres lässt sich von der Zukunft wissen"*; the whole paragraph (pp. 135-136) in translation reads:

The art of the seers is a vain nothingness,
They are deceivers, or are deceived.
Nothing true can be known of the future,
You draw down from the rivers of hell,
You draw from the source of light above. See on "U.S. GAAP" (and "IFRS") above, e.g., 4.5.1 and 4.8.5.

[103] *Thor Power Tool Co. v. Commissioner*, 439 U.S. 522, 544 (1979). Cf. *Shalala v. Guernsey Memorial Hospital*, 514 U.S. 87, 89 and 101-102 (1995): "GAAP is not a lucid or encyclopedic set of pre-existing rules". See above 7.5.2 and basically on the legal approach 3.5.3, 3.5.5, and 4.9.7.

[104] *Cede & Co. v. Technicolor*, 634 A.2d 345, 360 and 367 (Del. 1993). Radin (2009) vol. I, pp. 424-431. Luttermann (1998) pp. 251, 327-329, 424-427. Cf. overall above 3.2.1 and 3.5.2. Basically on environmental and human rights due diligence ICJ, Advisory Opinion: Obligations of states in respect of climate change, 23.07.2025 (https://www.icj-cij.org/sites/default/files/case-related/187/187-20250723-adv-01-00-en.pdf, accessed: 24.08.2025), paras. 280-300, on that above 6.1.3, 7.6.1. See fundamentally Williams (2021).

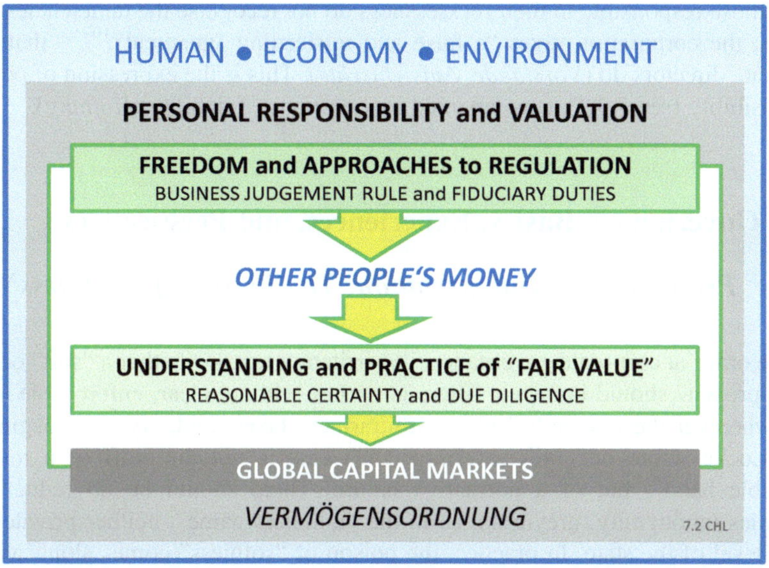


**Fig. 7.2** Freedom and duties of corporate directors: due diligence and "fair value"

the directors have to prove that they acted with due care (*gebotene Sorgfalt*, see Fig. 7.2).[105]

This does not reduce their obligation to inform comprehensively and truthfully on the transactions and results (financial *reporting*). According to the fiduciary duties of care and disclosure, individual cases may have to be examined – in the last instance by independent judges – as to whether the disclosure document "was materially misleading or omitted a material fact".[106] This holds all the more in the face of frequent corporate scandals (see chapter 6). Liability grounds include internal control weaknesses: If in financial instruments (securitisation plans etc.) there is an omission to report on valuation aspects (tax valuation allowance, deferred tax assets)

[105] E.g., *Smith v. Van Gorkom*, 488 A.2d 858, 872 (Del. 1985), *Hanson Trust PLC v. ML SCM Acquisition Inc.*, 781 F.2d 264, 273 and 275-276 (2d Cir. 1986), *In re Match Group, Inc. Derivative Litigation*, 315 A.3d 446 (Del. 2024) and, concerning Tripadvisor, Inc. et al.: *Palkon v. Maffei*, C.A. No. 2023-0449-JTL (Del. 2025). See also on the duty of care (business judgement rule) *Garfield v. Allen*, 277 A.3d 296 (Del. Ch. 2022), discussed by Wilson Corley (2024). Cf. for Germany (§ 93 AktG): BGH, 15.01.2013 (II ZR 90/11) NJW 2013, 1958, OLG Köln, 21.11.2023 (9 U 206/22) ZIP 2024, 20, <openJur 2023, 11783>; criminal law: BGH, 10.02.2022 (3 StR 329/21) ZIP 2022, 2435, <openJur 2022, 8539>.

[106] *In re Gen. Motors (Hughes) S'holder Litig.*, 2005 Del. Ch. LEXIS 65, at 26-28, *aff'd*, 897 A.2d 162 (Del. 2006). Cf. overall Luttermann (2008c).

and if those responsible in their recklessness do not recognise the deficiencies of the reports, the corporation gives "a false and misleading statement"[107] – that is, its corporate directors do (*Vorstände, Aufsichtsräte*). This is the expression of personal responsibility (see 7.3.1), accompanied by questions of liability (*Haftung*).

## 7.6 Governance: Basics, Experiences, and Perspectives

### *7.6.1 Prerogative of Interpretation: The Poison of "Softness"*

For the order of corporate governance, it is irritating to ask whether a "soft" or "hard law approach" should be taken. There is no law without clear, enforceable norms. For "wherever the law ends," id est arbitrariness takes hold, "tyranny begins", as John Locke wrote on civil government.[108] This is not the stuff of a mythical "invisible hand", but of a normative nature. There should be no reduction to quantities (anonymity, greyness), as in the "numbers game", neither privately nor at the level of the state. In practice, the poison of "softness" comes along with the process of so-called "standard setting" (see 7.4.2) and the prerogative of interpretation. The SEC Chairman Arthur Levitt, in his function as the key regulator and supervisor ("watchdog") on Wall Street,[109] describes the "numbers game" (*das Zahlenspiel*) as a commonly used practice by leading actors of the global financial industry:

> "Too many corporate managers, auditors, and analysts are participants in a game of nods and winks. In the zeal to satisfy consensus earnings estimates and project a smooth earnings path, wishful thinking may be winning the day over faithful representation. As a result, I fear that we are witnessing an erosion in the quality of earnings, and therefore, the quality of financial reporting. Managing may be giving way to manipulation (…)."[110]

The quality of the regulation has weight. Contractually, "fair value" stands for this, as the idea of a just price (Latin *iustum pretium*, see Fig. 7.2) already discussed by

---

[107] *In re Scottish Re Group Sec. Litig.*, 524 F.Supp. 2d 370 (S.D.N.Y., 2007). In *Thompson v. United States*, 604 U.S. ___ (2025) the Supreme Court ruled that title 18 U.S.C. § 1014 (loan and credit applications, a statute that rohibits "knowingly mak[ing] any false statement", here: to the FDIC) does not criminalise statements that are misleading but not false.

[108] (1689), chapter XVIII, sec. 202.

[109] The SEC, a federal so-called "administrative agency" established by the U.S. Congress, has broad legislative, administrative and even judicial powers. Adolf A. Berle (1938, p. 369) described the new SEC as a "synthetic czar in the accounting field". Overall on financial reporting as an area of law (*Rechtsgebiet*) Luttermann (1999a) pp. 34-101 (esp. pp. 34-37 on the SEC as an administrative agency), and pp. 113-136 (on international group accounting). See also above 4.11.4 and chapter 3, below 7.6.2. Cf. overall *Trump v. Wilcox*, 605 U.S. ___ (2025), on this above 3.3.2.

[110] Levitt (1998), see thereupon Luttermann (1999a), esp. pp. 3-7. Overall already earlier Luttermann (1998) and Luttermann (1997). Cf. basically Berle and Means (1932, 1967), Brandeis (1914) and others above, e.g., in 3.3.

Thomas Aquinas (born around New Year 1225–1274), the contractual consonance in value (*Wertungsgleichklang*) between performance (*Leistung*) and consideration (*Gegenleistung*), contractually agreed (Latin *do ut des*). That is the core of peaceful, sustainable economy, corporation and society. Valuation issues accompany business activities in a legal order (see 5.2–5.4). Things in general do not have a value "in themselves" (intrinsic value). Rather, they are given a value in business transactions according to specific features regarded as essential in transaction (e.g., material, durability, age, authenticity) and to actual or legal circumstances and relations to the environment – by our evaluation (*Bewertung*). Jurisdiction says: "'Value' is generally but an estimate of the worth of a thing, but 'valuation', when used in its passive signification (…) means the estimated value or worth placed on the thing.".[111] Basically, the prerogative of interpretation takes effect: How are values determined, valuations regulated, carried out and, in the last instance, controlled and sanctioned?

This affects all of corporate governance, audit and disclosure, id est investment as a whole (see chapter 5). Accordingly, the issue is the key element of the capital market order and society. As shown, the financial business of the human corporation is elementary in accounting and auditing (reasonable assurance). A special structural focus in the board of directors is on the audit committee. This conducts and monitors in particular:[112] the financial reporting process, the effectiveness of internal control (audit committee, see 4.12) and the risk management systems, the statutory audit of the annual and consolidated accounts, the independence of the statutory auditor and the provision of additional services to the corporation (see 4.9). In any case, it is facts that count, and, in Louis Brandeis' sunlight metaphor: the truth does not shun the light. – Let us take a closer look at some concrete elements in the "fair value"--paradise called USA.

### 7.6.2 *Regulated Industries and Interpretations*

From the perspective of the theory of equilibrium, "fair value" is a product of complete markets (general equilibrium theory).[113] Valuation as a process takes

[111] *State v. Central Pac. R. Co.*, 7 Nev. 99, 104 (1896). Under global climate change on environmental and human rights issues ICJ, Advisory Opinion, 23.07.2025 (https://www.icj-cij.org/sites/default/files/case-related/187/187-20250723-adv-01-00-en.pdf, accessed: 24.08.2025), on that above 6.1.3. Basically on valuation 5.3.

[112] Financial Conduct Authority, Handbook: https://beta-handbook.fca.org.uk/home (accessed: 24.08.2025), particularly DTR 7.1 (audit committees). For Germany, e.g., §§ 76, 91, 93 AktG (management board) and §§ 100, 107, 111 (supervisory board). Luttermann (2003b).

[113] Basically on market/fair value, efficient market hypothesis and valuation models (corporate leverage) Modigliani and Miller (1958) with correction (1963), Fama (1970) and 1991). See overall on *Finanzierungstheorie* (financial theory) Luttermann (1998) pp. 210-237 as well as pp. 465-485, pp. 486-539 and pp. 540-544 (*Rechtsordnung* – legal framework). Cf. Miller (1997), Stiglitz (2010) and Aliber, Kindleberger, McCauley (2023). See chapter 6.

place in many variations. In the USA, the illusionist cradle of "free markets", since the era of U.S. President Richard Nixon, this has included state regulation of key sectors such as banking (finance, investment) and the financial industry, the pharmaceutical industry as well as the energy sector and the telecommunications industry (so-called regulated industries). This applies to financial reporting and auditing (valuations). In the regulated industries, there are specific rules of accounting, making stock market corporations, e.g. Pfizer, Inc. (pharma) and Citigroup, Inc. (banking), hardly comparable in valuation.[114] Pricing and valuation are massively affected, as telecommunication shows.

The Federal Communications Commission (FCC) sets rules for adequate tariffs (prices) for services of public interest (pricing methodology). It operates with a Pricing Policy Devision "for administering the provisions of the Communications Act requiring that the rates and practices of telecommunications common carriers are just and reasonable, and non-discriminatory"; the division "develops competitive pricing policies and rules for telecommunications offerings" (incl. intercarrier compensation rates, interstate rates).[115] The FCC's jurisdiction, binding for the regulators in the federal states (*Bundesstaaten*), gives great discretionary power and is confirmed by the U.S. Supreme Court.[116] In regulation of the last century, the Federal Government divided the monopolist AT&T, Inc. in 1982 (see 3.2.1), then came the Telecommunications Act of 1996 (TA 1996). In order to promote competition, new providers (here: Verizon) may rent local networks from leading companies (top dogs) for joint use at "just and reasonable rates".

These rates have to be based, among other things, on "the cost (determined without reference to a rate-of return or other rate-based proceeding) of providing the (…) network element" (TA 1996 § 252(d)(1)(A)(i)). For the young Verizon Communications Inc., New York City (Verizon), this led to a fight about words and concepts. Here, the FCC specified "cost" in TA 1996 § 252(d)(1) as "forward-looking economic cost", thus valuating in a future-oriented way (47 CFR § 51.505). Thereby, it deviated from earlier interpretations that had proceeded from historically based costs for the tariff basis (*historische Kosten*).[117] The more recent approach according to the FCC encompasses "the total element long-run incremental cost of the element (TELRIC)". This means: "TELRIC should be measured on the basis of the most efficient technology currently available and the lowest cost network configuration" (47 CFR § 51.505).

[114] Luttermann (1999a) pp. 34-37. Cf. *Shalala v. Guernsey Memorial Hospital*, 514 U.S. 87 (1995). Generally Pierce and Gellhorn (1999), Awasthi, Yayavaram, George, and Sastry (2019).

[115] See – with more – Information and current data: https://www.fcc.gov/general/pricing-policy-division (accessed: 24.08.2025).

[116] *AT&T Corp. v. Iowa Utilities Bd.*, 525 U.S. 366, 385 (1999).

[117] *FPC v. Hope Natural Gas Co.*, 320 U.S. 591, 596-98 (1944).

### 7.6.3 Reasonable Certainty or Meaningless Rules?

The U.S. Supreme Court accepted the FCC's interpretation (see 7.6.2). The Supreme Court stated: Legally, the general use of "cost" did not clearly imply "past cost" (historical investment) and "has figured in contemporary state and federal ratemaking untethered to historical valuation"; "without any better indication of meaning than the unadorned term ["cost"], in 252(d)(1), as in accounting generally, is a 'chameleon,' a virtually meaningless term."[118] The judges did not consider the inadequacy of the regulation to be proven. The phrase "just and reasonable rates", the court ruled, provided wide discretionary power to the FCC, who focused on an adequate alternative with TELRIC instead of on "fixed-cost schemes". No constitutional rights were violated confiscatorily (*enteignend*).[119]

The crunchpoint in the Verizon case is: The judges do not criticise that "cost", in spite of being the core of the regulation, is an "unadorned term", even a "'chameleon', a virtually meaningless term".[120] They even emphasise the usualness of this practice ("as in accounting generally")[121] and do not find fault with it. – Where has the constitutional requirement of definiteness (vagueness doctrine)[122] gone to? And accordingly, let's remember Locke (see quote in 7.6.1): How are the foundation and the boundaries of the law to be determined? – This requires fair notice about the content of the rule (due process). This is true overall for corporate governance, disclosure and valuation, shaped by the corporate directors. Regarding this "powerful weapon", Berle und Means already remarked for the modern corporation: "So long as accounting standards are not hardened, and the law does not impose any specific canons, directors (...) may frame their figures, within limits, much as they choose"; Berle und Means recommend defining the accounting methods.[123] We have discussed this and integrated it into the financial function of the human corporation (see chapters 2, 3 and 4).

This applies in particular to profit-dependent equity securities and debt securities, which "are substantially meaningless", as long as no "provisions definitely

[118] *Verizon Comm. Inc. v. FCC*, 535 U.S. 467, at 500 (2002). Cf. *Shalala v. Guernsey Memorial Hospital*, 514 U.S. 87, 89 and 101-102 (1995). See also above 3.4.6 (distributions to shareholders).

[119] *Verizon Comm. Inc. v. FCC*, 535 U.S. 467, 523-28 (2002).

[120] *Verizon Comm. Inc. v. FCC*, 535 U.S. 467, at 500 (2002). Cf. in Germany BGH, 01.10.2020 (IX ZR 247/19) <openJur 2020, 75694>, recital 35-40, on the interpretation of legal terms (*Rechtsbegriffe*) according to their legal meaning (*"juristischen Fachbedeutung"*), here: profit-related interest for *Genußrechte* (profit participation rights) as hybrid financial instruments; see above 3.6.3 to 3.6.5.

[121] Ibid.

[122] See *Connally v. Gen. Constr. Co.*, 269 U.S. 385, 391 (1926) on due process of law and U.S. Const. Amend. V, XIV. Cf. on void for vagueness, e.g., *Grayed v. City of Rockford*, 408 U.S. 104, 108-110 (1972). *FCC v. Fox Television Stations, Inc.* 567 U.S. 239, 258 (2012). Cf. Asgeirsson (2020), Low and Johnson (2015), Scalia (1997).

[123] Berle and Means (1932, 1967) pp. 182-183; see already Berle (1928) pp. 176-188. Cf. above 7.5.2 and, e.g., 4.5.5, 4.6.3 and 4.8.3.

regulating the corporation's accounting" exist.[124] However, the whole field of the corporation and its good corporate governance (compliance, reasonable assurance) is covered; as shown, also with fiduciary relations between the corporate directors and the investors (*Kapitalgeber*). Basically, the requirement of definiteness (precision instead of loose terminology) applies to all branches of the law, in order to establish "reasonable certainty" against arbitrariness (*Willkür*), although – because of the inherent limitations of language – it may require a "delicate balance".[125] With foresight, and to be quoted here once again as a guiding motif, Berle wrote on the discourse about the general publicity of corporate accounts in the 1920s:

> "a corporate management which, as individuals, chooses to enter the open market and which at the same time exercises control over the release of information concerning corporate affairs, can deal with the current value of its securities, if not at pleasure, at least with tremendous effect; and the liquid value of the corporate securities held by the stockholders becomes a matter which the corporate management itself can determine."[126]

This is especially true in the dominance of "numbers" (corporate finance and accounts, credit ratings, mathematical models etc.) – instead of fact-specific information in clear language (*klarer Sprache*) under the imperative of truth[127] – shaping economic theory and practice, id est: the financial industry, which is neither regulated nor controlled in fact. That means in practical terms the shifting of wealth (*Wohlstand*): privatising profits, socialising losses – like in the ongoing "numbers game" on capital markets globally (see chapter 6). That is not initiated nor accomplished by an anonymous "invisible hand" of mystical powers. Manipulation by people responsible is at work (see 7.6.1). Regulation of valuation (financial reporting) and auditing (disclosure) in general is most urgently needed for the human corporation as a sustainable financial instrument.[128] But both remain rooted privately and uncontrolled in the USA, along with the prerogative of loose interpretation.

---

[124] Ibid., p. 183.

[125] See, e.g., *Nautilus, Inc. v. Biosig Instruments, Inc.*, 572 U.S. 898, 909 (2014) on the interpretation (clarity, definiteness) of patent claims in U.S. patents: "the definiteness inquiry trains on the understanding of the skilled artisan", ibid., at 911 ("reasonable certainty" standard, ibid at 910, so-called *Nautilus* test). Cf. basically Scalia (1997), esp. p. 23 on textualism: "A text should not be construed strictly, and it should not be construed leniently; it should be construed reasonably, to contain all that it fairly means." For comparative law Luttermann (1999b).

[126] Berle (1928) p. 180. See also below 7.8.2 and above 2.6.3, 3.5.5; esp. on due diligence and communication 8.3.3 and 5.3.4 (source of value), 5.5.5 (legal protection and valuation methods) and 5.6 (judicial practice). Cf. in European law the Corporate Sustainability Due Diligence Directive (EU) 2024/1760, 13.06.2024, OJ L, 05.07.2024.

[127] See above 2.6.2. In the multilingual context of the European Union Luttermann, C. and Luttermann, K. (2021).

[128] Luttermann (2011).

### 7.6.4 *Inflated Price Basis and Reasonable Rate*

Jurisdiction treated pricing (“reasonable rate”) by providers merely as tariff-based regulation. In the 1920s, U.S. Congress also recognised contracts between sophisticated buyers and sellers with negotiating power in the wholesale trade. Prices were condoned that brought less “than a fair return”,[129] without leading to discrimination. Prices that are too low affect “public interest”, by weakening the financial power of the providers, endangering service, excessively burdening consumers. Thus, retail prices come into play, taking effect in the federal states and locally. There, subsidising additions to the marginal cost are easy. That is why so-called “consumer protection” traditionally sets in here for the balancing of interests (conflict resolution). Regulators considered “a ‘just and reasonable’ rate” to be a task of “navigating the straits between gouging utility customers and confiscating utility property”.[130]

Provider prices (gas, electricity) are therefore subject to legal examination in order to ensure adequate valuation. The measure was “the revenue that would be a ‘fair return’ on certain utility property known as a ‘rate base’. The fair rate of return was usually set as the rate generated by similar investment property at the time of the rate proceeding”.[131] The alternative standard was the capital actually invested to provide the public service or good. The U.S. Supreme Court set the measure in *Smyth v. Ames,* linking the rate base to “fair value”. This was to be calculated as “the fair value of the property being used by [the utility] for the convenience of the public.”[132] The alternative on historical investment requires comprehensive considerations. The judges name criteria for determining “fair value” in an individual case:

(a) the original cost of construction,
(b) the amount expended in permanent improvements,
(c) the amount and market value of its bonds and stocks,
(d) the present as compared with the original cost of construction,
(e) the probable earning capacity of the property under particular rates prescribed by statute, and
(f) the sum required to meet operating expenses.

---

[129] *FPC v. Sierra Pacific Power Co.*, 350 U.S. 348, 355 (1956).

[130] *FPC v. Hope Natural Gas Co.*, 320 U.S. 591, 603 (1944).

[131] *Verizon*, 535 U.S. 467, at 481 (2002).

[132] *Smyth v. Ames*, 169 U.S. 466, 543-46 (1898). Cf. Fig. 7.2.

The list was conceived by the court as open, the criteria "are to be given such weight as may be just and right in each case".[133] The judges wanted to prevent excessive valuation and fictitious capitalisation, id est, abuse through artificial inflation of the price basis (cf. 7.7.3). This would have the effect that "the public (…) be subjected to unreasonable rates in order simply that stockholders may earn dividends."[134] This in general marks the field of tension. It should be noted that the issue in any case is precisely not to only maximise the return on investment (so-called „shareholder value", see 3.6.5) for the stockholders.

## *7.6.5 Critique of Immoderateness*

The U.S. Supreme Court in *Smyth v. Ames* did not fix a method of valuation for price control, but rather determined all "relevant" facts for each individual case. This seems problematic for providers with complex institutions and networks that are only rarely sold (completely). This means that a market of imagined free pricing – as for a large number of financial products – is lacking. Revenue (*Einnahmen, Umsatz*) as a reference point seems circulatory, as it is determined precisely by the prices (tariffs) that are subject to legal examination; what is yet again considered to be practicable are the current replacement or reproduction costs.[135] Overall, with the basic traits of corporate valuation, the problems of corporate governance, regulation and compliance also become obvious.

Louis D. Brandeis and Oliver W. Holmes, two great judges of the U.S. Supreme Court, have done groundbreaking work on this. Brandeis, in a minority opinion (dissent), which Holmes – also sitting on the bench – joined, shows the potential for conflict of "fair-value" in pricing under the constitutional barrier of dispossession. The (simplified) example:[136] The provider builds a complex for one million dollars with a promised return on equity of 90,000 dollars annually. Assuming at the time of price determination the value of the complex falls to 600,000 dollars with a return on equity of 6% for similar investments, *Smyth v. Ames* would then say a price is not confiscatory if it returns at least 36,000 dollars of the costs of capital to the provider,

[133] Ibid., at 546-547.

[134] Ibid., at 545, quoting *Covington & Lexington Turnpike Road Co. v. Sandford*, 164 U.S. 578, 596-597 (1896). Overall see *Verizon*, 535 U.S. 467, at 481-482 (2002), with the statement: "And the Court had no doubt who should make the sacrifice in that situation. "'If a corporation cannot maintain such a highway and earn dividends for stockholders, it is a misfortune for it and them which the Constitution does not require to be remedied by imposing unjust burdens upon the public.'" *Smyth v. Ames,* 169 U.S., at 545".

[135] See *McCardle v. Indianapolis Water Co.*, 272 U.S. 400, 417 (1926) and *Verizon*, 535 U.S. 467, at 483 (2002), with reference to Goddard (1928) 564, 570-571.

[136] Brandeis, dissenting from opinion, *Southwestern Bell Tel. Co. v. Public Serv. Comm'n*, 262 U.S. 276, 292 (1923), at 304-306, with whom – the equally brilliant – Justice Holmes concurs, ibid., at 289.

that is, 54,000 dollars less than planned. If, however, the value of the complex rises to 1.75 million dollars with a comparable return on equity of 8%, according to *Smyth v. Ames*, constitutionally prices would have to be set that would generate at least 140,000 dollars for the provider; that is, 50,000 dollars more than the capital costs (*Kapitalkosten*).

*Smyth v. Ames* is able to provide prices that are roughly inflated or roughly inadequate through their "galactic notion of fair value".[137] This promotes manipulation and the danger of corporations becoming insolvent not only by imprudent investment, but also by value loss in a general economic downswing. In a robust economic development, investment may bring on the accusation of predatory return. The judges Brandeis and Holmes therefore wanted to substitute "fair value". They gave the following advice for pricing and price control, as the *Verizon* court writes: "a calculation of rate based on the cost of capital prudently invested in assets used for the provision of the public good or service".[138] Basically, the issue is a substance-related valuation approach (see 7.3). Naturally on a sound and solid basis, a sustainable, as legally determined basis simultaneously in the sense of definiteness (*Bestimmtheit*, see 7.6.3 and 9.8). Brandeis, correspondingly, emphasised in his reasoning:

> "The adoption of the amount prudently invested as the rate base and the amount of the capital charge as the measure of the rate of return would give definiteness to these two factors involved in rate controversies (…). Such measures offer a basis for decision which is certain and stable."[139]

### *7.6.6 Investment and Price Determination*

Louis D. Brandeis nailed it, in substance and form. But the U.S. Supreme Court did not change its position until 1944. Then, in *FPC v. Hope Natural Gas Co.*,[140] the Supreme Court judges constitutionally refuted the sole legitimacy of "fair value" as the basis for calculating prices "justly and reasonably". As the U.S. Supreme Court in *Verizon* put it in 2002: although Justice Brandeis "did not live to enjoy success, his campaign against *Smyth* came to fruition".[141] – This is one of the outstanding cases

[137] *Verizon*, 535 U.S. 467, at 483 (2002), referring to Brandeis in *Southwestern Bell Telephone Co., supra,* at 304-306.

[138] *Verizon*, ibid., at 483.

[139] Brandeis, dissenting, *Southwestern Bell Tel. Co. v. Public Serv. Comm'n*, 262 U.S. 276, 292 (1923), at 306.

[140] 320 U.S. 591, 601-02 (1944). Cf. *Market Street Railway Co. v. Railroad Commission*, 324 U.S. 548 (1945).

[141] *Verizon*, 535 U.S. 467, at 483 (2002).

where the minority opinion of a mind that towered above his contemporaries becomes the majority in following generations.[142] In *Hope Natural Gas,* the U.-S. Supreme Court "disavowed the position that the Natural Gas Act and the Constitution required fair value as the sole measure of a rate base on which "just and reasonable" rates were to be calculated".[143]

At the federal level and the level of the federal states, valuation methods on the basis of "cost" have since been increasingly employed. "Fair value" held in particular in the market-conform investment rule: Capital investment – the original ratio of which has become useless through unforeseeable developments – may no longer be included (prudent-investment rule).[144] As explained for *Verizon* (see 7.6.2, 7.6.3) it was not – in the sense of Louis Brandeis – about a mere calculation of the capital "prudently invested" according to the accounting data at the point of valuation. This referred to the investments sensibly made for the service ("cost of service"). This comprises deductions for accrued depreciation (*Wertminderung*) and grants (*Zuschüsse*) for working capital. The monopoly-like providers, of course, kept the amortisations (*Abschreibungen*) low and the operating capital (*Betriebskapital,* including excess or outdated capacities) as high as possible, in order to optimise their basis of price calculation.

Lack of competition thus promotes manipulation ("fictitious capitalization") and monopoly prices. The supervisory authorities (regulators) were therefore often overchallenged under the prudent-investment rule (with, e.g., the "used and useful" qualification;[145] cf. the "fair value" concept, see 7.4.2 and 7.5). The regulators had no counterweight against the powerful utility companies (*Versorgungsunternehmen*). The introduction of price caps (*Preisobergrenzen*) seemed to be a solution. They were determined by different methods, proceeding from common cost formulas (cost of service formulas) with annually rising percentage rates for production growth.[146] The TA 1996 brought the reform already dealt with (see 7.6.2). Dennis L. Weisman summarises regarding the Court in *Verizon* that it had insufficient evidence on the record: (1) that the rate methodology at issue is confiscatory in violation of the *Hope* standard and (2) that it constitutes an

[142] See Luttermann (1998) pp. 419-421, comparing minority opinions of outstanding judges at the U.S. Supreme Court and corresponding, but questionable practice at the private FASB, which produces so-called "authoritative support" ("GAAP") instead of sound and clear standards; see already above 7.4.2 and 7.6.3 (definiteness). Overall chapter 4, also on so-called "U.S. GAAP"; on this Luttermann (1999a).

[143] *Verizon,* 535 U.S. 467, at 483-484, referring to *FPC* v. *Hope Natural Gas Co.,* 320 U. S. 591, at 601-602 (1944) and also to *FPC* v. *Natural Gas Pipeline Co.,* 315 U. S. 575, 602-606 (1942) with Black, Douglas, and Murphy, JJ., concurring.

[144] *Duquesne Light Co. v. Barasch,* 488 U.S. 299, 311-12 (1989).

[145] Id est, see *Verizon,* 535 U.S. 467, at 484 (2002): "that a utility can only recover prudently invested capital that is being "used and useful" in providing the public a good or service", with reference to the Pennsylvania rate statute upheld in *Duquesne Light Co.* v. *Barasch,* 488 U. S. 299 (1989).

[146] See *US Tel. Ass'n v. FCC,* 188 F.3d 521, 524 (D.C. Cir. 1999).

opportunistic change in regulatory schemes prohibited under *Duquesne*.[147] It is a wide field.

## 7.7 Governance: Adjusting Corporations, Governments, and Control

### *7.7.1 Market Theory, Freedom of Contract, and Legal Order*

With corporate governance (disclosure) and its regulation, the issue is a human corporation within a human society under the constitution of liberty and its proprietary, commercial order. The private autonomy of each individual market participant (human being) to act on his own responsibility (*Eigenverantwortung*) is elementary; at the same time, of course, with a view to sustainable business activity (see 5.2.4). This is the reciprocal expression of human dignity in community and education, which characterise the limits of state regulatory power.[148] Valuation law is, as has been shown (see chapter 5), micro-economically and macro-economically the backbone of the constitution of entrepreneurs, corporations and markets. The rule of law in the sense of reasonableness demands, in particular, clarity regarding possibilities and limits. The law in general must provide guidance, and it loses its honour and its sense where it ceases to serve the constitution of liberty.[149]

At the same time, the link to the economy, which independent judges ultimately decide on for a reasonable resolution in the event of conflict, remains effective. For the practice of market regulation, the following approach has been influential: "The Constitution does not bind rate-making bodies to the service of any single formula or combination of formulas".[150] Whether the regulators (such as the FCC, see 7.6.2, 7.6.3) choose the best way to fix the rates (prices) is "stuff of debate for economists and regulators versed in the technology of telecommunications and microeconomic

[147] Weisman (2019). See *Verizon*, 535 U.S. 467, at 539 (2002), Justice Souter, opinion of the Court: "The job of judges is to ask whether the Commission made choices reasonably within the pale of statutory possibility (…). The FCC's pricing and additional combination rules survive that scrutiny." See – with full quotation – below in 7.7 (with Justices Breyer and Scalia, dissenting). Cf. *Hope Natural Gas Co.*, 320 U. S. 591 (1944), *Duquesne Light Co.*, 488 U.S. 299 (1989). See, e.g., the FCC, Proposed Rulemaking, 15.09.2003 (03-224), and, more recently (www.fcc.gov), on the North American Numbering Plan (NANP) and the Telecommunications Relay Service (TRS).

[148] Groundbreaking Wilhelm von Humboldt (1792) and, building on this, Mill (1859). See above 1. 6.2, and 1.4.2, 8.2.3 ("green" paradigm shift, Trump US administration).

[149] Luttermann (1998) pp. 1 and 139-144. For the corporation (*Aktiengesellschaft*) Luttermann (2003a) Einf BilanzR recitals 19-43 and 107-133.

[150] *Natural Gas Pipeline Co.*, 315 U.S., 575, 586 (1942).

pricing theory".[151] This sounds like the expression of reticence on the part of the judges, which – traditionally – is constitutionally rooted in the parliamentary prerogative: "The job of judges is to ask whether the Commission made choices reasonably within the pale of statutory possibility in deciding what and how items must be leased and the way to set rates for leasing them."[152] – Well, this may suffice in the case in hand. But the position is questionable where "regulation", even privately driven, and private plenitude of power are taking wide hold precisely with the help of the financial industry (see chapters 3 to 6).

Justice Stephen Breyer[153] in his minority opinion in *Verizon* provides the following clarification: The legislator does indeed provide wide, but not unlimited power of discretion.[154] Breyer emphasises the purpose of law:[155] Deregulation for more competition on the market for telecommunication, and consequently lower prices, better products, more efficient production methods. This binds discretionary power, in order to prevent control-free areas. Legal vacuums in the economy have a counterproductive effect. Accordingly, it obtains that the judges "must review for rationality the substance of agency decisions, including technical decisions".[156] Irrespective of technical complexity, which can be translated into language in a way that is understandable for judges, Breyer noted,[157] "review by generalist judges is important" in order to secure "public control" (cf. 4.11.4, see chapters 3 to 6). A clear, sensible measure generally, which, however, has hitherto gone widely unnoticed.

### *7.7.2 Market, Appraisal, and Control*

We here see a guideline for the regulation of securities law and corporate governance. With reference to reforms, the market situation has to be fundamentally examined. The U.S. Supreme Court wrote in 2008: "The public information is reflected in the market price of the security." Consequently, the following rule of evidence applies: "Then it can be assumed that an investor who buys or sells stock at

[151] *Verizon*, 535 U.S. 467, at 539 (2002), Justice Souter, opinion of the Court. Cf. in the following Justice Breyer dissenting, joined by Justice Scalia.

[152] *Verizon*, ibid. Cf. Legg (2004).

[153] Dissenting, in *Verizon*, 535 U.S. 467, 539-563 (2002).

[154] See, e.g., Justice Breyer, dissenting, ibid., at 542, referring to "the scope of the statute" and "the need for the agency to show a "rational connection" between the regulations and the statute's purposes" he states: "We must determine whether, despite the leeway given experts on technical subject matter, agency regulations exceed these legal limits." On this basically 7.6.3, also above 5.5.5.

[155] See Justice Breyer, dissenting, ibid., esp. at 542-548, reasoning on the purpose.

[156] Justice Breyer, dissenting in *Verizon*, 535 U.S. 467, at 561 (2002), referring to *Motor Vehicle Manufacturers Assn. v. State Farm Mut.*, 463 U.S. 29, 56 (1983).

[157] Dissenting, in *Verizon*, ibid, at 561-562.

the market price relies upon the [financial] statement."[158] This strengthens the concept of disclosure and investors who cannot prove that they trusted in misleading financial statements (fraud-on-the-market presumption). This builds on market efficiency. Where it is lacking, the "fair value" of the investment is determined in the appraisal proceeding at court.[159] In principle, sustainable, id est verifiable information is what holds within the concept of trust (see 1.5.2): financial reporting as real disclosure (see 3.3.3).[160]

The key question remains as to whether judges examine and correct private economic arrangements (cf. 7.7.1). Legal scholar Richard Posner, federal appellate judge and co-founder of the "economic analysis of law",[161] remarked in 2008, astonishingly and largely unnoticed, that the market was ineffective for solving the problem of adequate pricing. His reasoning, dissenting: The majority judgement was based "mainly on an economic analysis that is ripe for reexamination on the basis of growing indications that executive compensation in large public traded firms often is excessive because of the feeble incentives of boards of directors to police compensation."[162] The panel opinion states that the compensation of the investment advisers (as trustees according to § 36(b) of the Investment Company Act of 1940) could be "so unusual that the court will infer that deceit must have occurred, or that the persons responsible for decision have abdicated".[163] The panel emphasises the fiduciary duty of the adviser to "make full disclosure and play no tricks", thereby refuting a "rate regulation" and the *Gartenberg* standard.

The U.S. Supreme Court reprimands this one-sidedness and confirms *Gartenberg* in a unanimous decision. According to this, liability obtains under § 36(b) of the Investment Company Act of 1940, if investment advisers "charge a fee that is so disproportionately large that it bears no reasonable relationship to the services rendered and could not have been the product of arm's-length bargaining"; and

[158] *Stoneridge Inv. Partners v. Scientific-Atlanta, Inc.*, 128 S.Ct. 761, 769 (2008), 552 U.S. 148; on this critically Gevurtz (2009). Cf. *Basic, Inc. v. Levinson*, 485 U.S. 224, 247 (1988). On *Stoneridge* restricting auditor litigation risk (secondary actor liability in class action suits) Bergman, Heron, Levy, and Zur (2023).

[159] *Cede & Co. v. Technicolor*, 684 A.2d 289, 296 (Del. 1996); 3 Model Bus. Corp. Act Annotated § 13.01, Official Comment at 13-7 (4th ed. 2008, rev. 2009). Cf. Luttermann (2009) and, specifically on minority discounts, Coates (1999), esp. p. 1352: "procedural rule".

[160] See above 5.2.4 (sustainability) and below 7.7.3. In theory and practical terms Luttermann, L. (2022) and (2024).

[161] See Posner (1973). See on the juridical analysis of the economy Luttermann (1998) pp. 465-485, and Luttermann (2010a). From a regulatory perspective Luttermann (2010b).

[162] Posner, dissenting, *Jones v. Harris*, 537 F.3d 728, 730 (7th Cir. 2008) and 731: Harris charged its captive funds more than twice what it charges independent funds. On "the efficacy of a law-and-economics orthodoxy" (William Birdthistle, https://www.theconglomerate.org/2009/03/judge-posner-and-behavioral-law-economics.html, accessed: 24.08.2025) see Posner (2009).

[163] *Jones v. Harris Assoc. L.P.*, 527 F.3d 627, at 632 (7th Cir. 2008), opinion by Easterbrook. Cf. on the fiduciary duty Johnson (2009). See also above in 7.3.2.

that "in light of all of the surrounding circumstances".[164] This standard "may lack sharp analytical clarity": But it reflects the position of U.S. Congress to rely mainly on the robust decision of the mutual fund board, with its disinterested directors "as 'independent watchdogs' of the relationship between a mutual fund and its adviser",[165] for the protection of shareholders, to approve an adviser's fee.[166] Judicial price-setting, thus say the judges, does not accompany fiduciary duties: Congress recognises "that courts are not well suited to make such precise calculations".[167] A questionable point of view, as shown.[168]

### 7.7.3 Sustainable Valuation Standards and Disclosure

This approach obtains in the way described in the determination of value ("fair price", Latin *do ut des*). The judges irritate with the statement that the "Court is institutionally unsuited to gather the facts upon which economic predictions can be made, and, professionally untrained to make them".[169] This is obviously a testimony of their own incompetence, at the same time for the office of a judge, as well as the infinite basis on which the market actors may act unchecked by effective control – as Justice Stephen Breyer put it: „to wrest themselves free of public control".[170] Reference should be made to the appraisal proceedings for the valuation of a corporation: They are, for example, to compensate fully investors affected by mergers according to the legislative intent, by "fair value" being determined in light of all relevant factors (substance).[171] That is "the most reasonable value", which the judge, in "a range of reasonable values" has to assign "in light of all the relevant evidence and based on considerations of fairness".[172]

That is indeed a wide terrain, a bumpy road. This means that "economic predictions" are all the more to be avoided and the facts to be clarified (cf. the legal principle of "substance over form"). This is no different in financial reporting

[164] *Jones v. Harris Assoc. L.P.*, 559 U.S. 335, 346 and 349 (2010), *Gartenberg v. Merrill Lynch Asset Management, Inc.*, 694 F.2d 923, 928 (2d Cir. 1982). Cf. Grospe (2011). Cf. on the business judgement rule (duty of care) *Garfield v. Allen*, 277 A.3d 296 (Del. Ch. 2022), discussed by Wilson Corley (2024).

[165] Referring to *Burks v. Lasker*, 441 U. S. 471 (1979), at 482 and 484.

[166] *Jones*, ibid., at 352: no "judicial second-guessing of informed board decisions".

[167] Ibid. at 352-53. Cf. *General Motors Corp. v. Tracy*, 519 U.S. 278, 308 (1997).

[168] See above in 7.6.5, 7.6.6 and 7.7.1. Basically in terms of the juridical analysis of economy, state and society Luttermann (2010a) and (2015a).

[169] *Jones*, ibid., at 352. *Verizon*, 535 U.S. 467, 539 (2002).

[170] Justice Breyer, dissenting, in *Verizon*, 535 U.S. 467, at 562 (2002): "because the law forbids agencies, in the name of technical expertise, to wrest themselves free of public control."

[171] *Weinberger v. UOP, Inc.*, 457 A.2d 701, 713 (Del. 1983). Cf. Fig. 7.3, overall see above in chapter 5.

[172] *Cede & Co. v. Technicolor*, 2003 Del. Ch. LEXIS 146, at *5-6 (*aff'd,* 884 A.2d 26 (Del. 2005)).

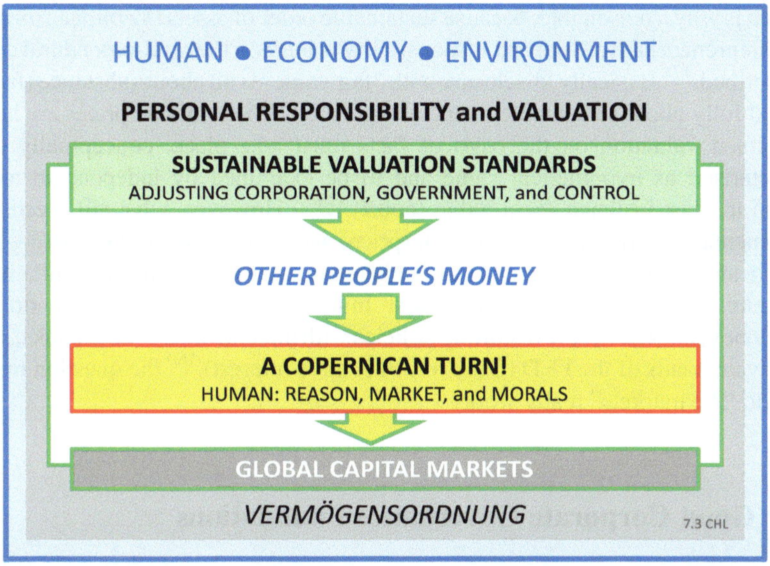


**Fig. 7.3** Sustainable valuation standards for the responsible actors on the capital markets

(disclosure) overall than in other areas of life (product liability, genetic patents etc.): The judge must investigate the relevant facts of the case under the imperative of truth (*Gebot der Wahrheit*) and weigh them for his or her decision ("fact-specific inquiry").[173] Sustainable norms of valuation and publicity (real disclosure, see 7.7.2 and Fig. 7.3) are necessary for good corporate governance (rules of law, *Rechtsregeln*). As early as 1928, Adolf Berle took the following focus: "Requirement of disclosure has to do with facts only, and not with prospects, hopes or estimates."[174] That is at the heart of our concept. Justice needs to establish a sustainable order for the process of creation and transfer of wealth.[175] The law, economy and society cannot tolerate haphazard estimations. That is why "presentations of future earnings, appraised asset valuations and other hypothetical data are to be discouraged".[176] For otherwise sham profits, id est the substance of the corporation, will ultimately be distributed according to the periodisation principle of accounting law – *caveat emptor*![177]

---

[173] *Basic, Inc. v. Levinson*, 485 U.S. 224, 240 (1988). Cf. Radin (2009) vol. II, pp. 1584-1648.

[174] Berle (1928), p. 181; cf. Berle and Means (1932, 1967) pp. 271-272. See also above 3.3.3, chapter 4 (esp. 4.5.3), and chapter 5 (esp. 5.2.4, 5.5.2: connecting facts – *Anknüpfungstatsachen*).

[175] Basically see chapter 1 (with 1.6 on a global wealth system), overall chapters 2 to 6. On a *Vermögensordnung* (order of assets) and complementarity for prosperity and peace through sustainable financial reporting see chapters 8 and 9.

[176] *Flynn v. Bass Bros. Enterprises, Inc.*, 744 F.2d 978, 986 (3rd Cir. 1984). Cf. Luttermann (2006) and (2015a).

[177] See above in 7.4.3 and 7.3 as well as already in 3.3.3 and 3.4.4. Overall Luttermann (1998).

That is why a reasonable, because sustainable order of assets (*Vermögensordnung*) for entrepreneurial freedom and responsibility is built on the civil-procedural concept as described.[178] Basically, disclosure with "fair value" is all about substance (facts), id est truthfully about sustainable financial reporting. Where market prices are lacking, disciplined valuation on the basis of facts must take place, conceptually clearly characterised as hypothetical value and to be examined by independent auditors and, in the last instance, by a judge (court).[179] – However, what still needs to be fundamentally clarified is: information (price) according to what standard? – That is the delicate question (see Fig. 7.3), not only regarding rating regime and inflation, but regarding the value basis (measure) itself. In the case of a worthless valuation basis (fiat money) and massively distorting policies with uncontrolled central banks, such as the private hands of the FED (QEs, zero-/negative interest),[180] the question remains: How do "the markets" really work?

## 7.8 Good Corporate Governance Foundations

### *7.8.1 Man: Reason, Market, and Morals*

We should break through the abstraction to reach the real core: How does good come into the world? – Man is in the centre: As in any area of life, the individual human being (*der Mensch*) decides autonomously, id est self-responsibly (*eigenverantwortlich*) whether good or bad comes into the corporate world. It is about reason and morals on which the law is based (duty of virtue or legal duty, see Fig. 7.3).[181] Related to this is the idea of the justice of a constitution of liberty, comprising corporate governance in general.[182] The sense of reasonableness according to the duty of loyalty (*Treuepflicht*), whereby self-interest commercially promotes public interest,[183] has to guide the acting person in each individual case. This obviously does not cover achieving financial result (personal gain) by manipulation (fraud). But such behaviour seems rational, in particular where it is institutionally promoted (e.g. executives' stock options, lack of sustainable standards and control).[184]

[178] Luttermann (2015a). See above 7.1, and in detail chapter 5.

[179] See chapter 5 and overall, on the juridical analysis of economy, state and society below 7.8, 7.9 and, e.g. 1.6.2 and 7.3.2 with chapters 2 and 9. Basically Luttermann (1998) and (2010a).

[180] See above 7.3.3 and chapter 6. Basically Luttermann (2008b) and (2011).

[181] Cf. Kant (1793) pp. 201-202 and 206-207.

[182] See above 7.3.1 and esp. chapters 1 and 2. Seminally Hayek (1991), esp. chapters 2 and 10; see also Luttermann (1998), esp. pp. 135-145 and 465-485 (juridical analysis of the economy).

[183] See about this with Adam Smith in 7.3.3.

[184] Gordon (2007) pp. 1537-1538. See Fig. 7.3.

Regulation is to provide practitioners with a measure and to keep measure itself, avoiding overregulation. The general assumption should be that the decent person is the normal case, also for disclosure standards. This may sound naïve, especially in the face of the experience of systematic manipulations and suchlike events: "Seven watchdog [FRC] members set to investigate KPMG are revealed as current and former employees".[185] Any rule may be perverted, any control instance (proctor, judge) may fail. Governance breakdowns such as Enron are even attributed unilaterally to the auditors ("enforcement side").[186] – Who watches the watchdog? – We ourselves shape value (worthlessness), humanity being "the ultimate source of value".[187] Reason as the guiding principle gains its content in thinking and acting, including the degree of regulation. Forcefully, Adam Smith, the moral-philosophical economic advisor, completely discarded casuistics, which, he believed, only feigned "nice exactness"; instead, he laid the emphasis on "justice, modesty, and veracity" as our, as it were, eternal principles of action.[188]

This reasonably brings people and markets together. The community establishes a sustainable order for human cooperation and fair competition, not individual circles that are only short-sightedly directed towards particular interests with excessive or unlawful practices. And that order is achieved through rules, "fixed by a standard of reasonable prudence, whether it usually is complied with or not".[189] They provide the necessary measure of care and liability (duty of care: "present fairly"). Economic circumstances and theories may provide incentives here. Edmund Phelps explains: "standard economics is not a guide to flourishing – it is a tool only for efficiency".[190] An unsuitable one, as we have seen. However, it may serve a system of law, a meaningful synthesis of "markets, morals, and law":[191] an order of assets (*Vermögensordnung*), in which we retain the ever fragile balance also in progress.

---

[185] Daily Mail, 19.04.2013, on KPMG's role in the collapse of HBOS.

[186] Bratton (2003) 1023, 1055. Cf. Seligman (2002) 449, 516: "a breakdown in corporate responsibility, that on occasion involved audit failure, auditor conflict of interest, porous generally accepted accounting principles, dysfunctional boards and audit committees, investment analysts conflict, and an overstretched SEC".

[187] Korsgaard, Christine in Raz (2008) p. 85. See above 5.3.4.

[188] Smith (1790) p. 401 (VII., sec. IV.). See above 7.3.3 with 3.5.5, 4.4.4 (general rule, complementarity), 4.8.4 and 4.11.1 (on the patchwork of "U.S. GAAP/IFRS"). Basically see chapter 9 on complementarity.

[189] Justice Holmes in *Texas & Pacific Railway Co. v. Behymer*, 189 U.S. 468, 470 (1903). On ("materiality") Luttermann (1999a) pp. 62-66 and Luttermann (2008c). Großmann-Doerth (1933) pp. 17-18: *"Verwilderung des Rechtsempfindens" durch "Tagesinteresse"* (interest of the day); cf. on this Blaurock, Goldschmidt, and Hollerbach (2005).

[190] Phelps, What is wrong with the West's Economies?, The New York Review, 13.08.2015 (www.nybooks.com/articles/2015/08/13/what-wrong-wests-economies, accessed: 24.08.2025).

[191] Eisenberg (1989) p. 1525.

## *7.8.2 Basics for a Reasonable Solution*

With these insights, we can focus on the just foundations. Good corporate governance is – micro- and macro-economically – elementary for prospering communities nationally and internationally. What is required is faithful business activity and faithful accounting in dealing with other people's money – id est equity *and* debt investors – in a sustainable order of assets (*Vermögensordnung*):[192] Truth is the imperative, procedurally built on facts (*Wahrheitsgebot*). This applies in particular in the face of dematerialisation that believes in the future ("soft information"), mega money managers (intermediaries),[193] high-frequency trading (speculation), dark pools, black box algorithms and the like (see chapter 6). For fundamentally it is about the effective control of power. That is why individual liberty (*Freiheit*) and individual responsibility (*Verantwortung*) are inseparable and must be followed up in practice in terms of sustainability (reasonable assurance) and liability (*Haftung*) for significant misconduct.[194]

Overall, the following – in the idea of justice (*Gerechtigkeit*) and in terms of sustainability (*Nachhaltigkeit*, see 5.2.4) – should be realised: The law relies on the private autonomy of each human being (*Mensch*) as the expression of humanity, the responsible power of judgement of the actor in a sound market order – also for the human corporation. To this end, the law determines mandatory rules as the yardstick in the sense of the *ratio legis*: (1) for the diligence and liability of corporate directors in general, (2) for their duty to inform (real disclosure), to present fairly the corporation in "the financial statements *taken as a whole*" (standard of fairness),[195] and (3) for the audit. For valuation, accounting and auditing are legal acts. They are, however, widely lacking, which shows the basic evil of the economy of catastrophe. Corporation law, the usual fuss about "shareholder value" and activism, decision usefulness etc. will come to nothing as long as: (1) the substance of corporate governance is not clearly and faithfully documented, and (2) an independent investigation has not taken place (financial *reporting* and *auditing*), and – in case of conflict – (3) this documentation has not been legally investigated according to the truth on a conclusively substantiated request of an investor.

This civil procedural concept of truth (*zivilprozessuales Wahrheitskonzept*) at the same time protects directors who act duly (avoidance of liability). Principally, the following applies: Where somebody responsible deviates from law and facts, he loses the protection of the legal system, which he himself avoids (see chapter 4). This depends on the understanding of norms. Both are lacking: Legal concepts distinguish between arbitrariness and the law (definiteness, see 7.6.3); like the general norm, the overriding imperative of truth ("a true and fair view", *Bilanzwahrheit*)

---

[192] Overall Luttermann (2015a).

[193] E.g., institutional investors and investor services, i.e. proxies like Institutional Shareholder Services Inc. (ISS: www.issgovernance.com). Strine (2014).

[194] See above, e.g., in 5.2.4 (sustainability) and 6.5.3 (liability).

[195] Eisenberg (1976) pp. 194 and 191. Overall on this see above, chapters 3 to 6.

provides the measure as the *ratio legis*, shaped by complementary individual norms (rules).[196] This does not mean retreating into vagueness (textualism)[197] or casuistics (see 3.5.5), into the "numbers game" according to „U.S. GAAP" (cooking the books), lacking the spirit of the law (*Bilanzmanipulation*). Corporate directors of human corporations should simply inform fairly, give a full and true account of the corporate affairs in clear language and numbers (real disclosure, see 4.4 to 4.6): the good, the bad, and the ugly.

### 7.8.3 Universality: Global Economy (Digitisation) and Legal Comparison

This concept is to be established comprehensively as a legal requirement of corporate governance (standard of care), in particular in their transnational dimension.[198] Corporations are globally instruments of business financing and international markets. Engagement of institutional investors (Stewardship Codes) may be an element,[199] while high aspirational goals, unenforced "best practices" (Codes of Conduct/Compliance) and the like have proved insufficient.[200] Instead of ideally conceived behavior, the norms of behaviour that are considered to be necessary must be practically implemented, id est, in the last instance institutionally enforced, no matter whether by statutory law (*lex scripta*) or case law. The guiding principle, in a global perspective, of the human corporation and worldwide capital markets should be comparative law (*Rechtsvergleichung*), that is, cultural comparison,[201] because we naturally only perceive one (our own!) segment of the world. What is sustainably effective is a dialogue of cultures (see chapter 9).

Personal responsibility and sustainability worldwide provide human universality (culture of responsibility, see 6.1.2). What is expedient in an overall view is systematic regulation, principled (general norm as the measure, *das Maß*) and specified, complementary rules (*ergänzende Einzelregeln*). Experience teaches us the fatal deficiencies of monolithic models ("one size fits all"). Political and technical development promote them massively: worldwide digitisation of companies and markets, computer business, advanced technical intelligence (like "Aladdin"/

[196] Overall chapter 4 (esp. 4.4.4) and above 3.3.3; Luttermann (2009) and (2015a).

[197] See above 7.6.3. Cf. Scalia (1997) p. 23, and *Connally v. Gen. Constr. Co.*, 269 U.S. 385, 391 (1926). Ribeiro (2004).

[198] Groundbreaking the International Court of Justice on environmental and human rights issues in its advisory opinion "Obligations of states in respect of climate change", 23.07.2025 (https://www.icj-cij.org/sites/default/files/case-related/187/187-20250723-adv-01-00-en.pdf, accessed: 24.08.2025), esp. paras. 405-457, on this see above 1.2 and 6.1.

[199] Çelik and Isaksson (2014).

[200] Radin (2009), vol. I, pp. 420-424. See, e.g., above 2.2, 2.3. Cf. Großfeld (2015) and Liu (2015).

[201] On comparative law and language Luttermann (2024) and (1999b). On multilingualism and legal language (*Rechtslinguistik*) Luttermann, C. and Luttermann, K. (2021).

BlackRock, singularity, AI: see 9.6) and standards such as the Xtensible Business Reporting Language (XBRL).[202] With "IFRS/IFRS S" they form a private world monopoly of valuation and information, which promotes dematerialisation. Regionally, counterpositions are forming (e.g., Australia, China, Japan, USA), apparently in the sense of the *ordre public* motivated like with "IAS/IFRS" in the European Union (the "European public good"),[203] particularly as obligations for publicity (disclosure) are less in the USA.[204] Regulation shapes international circumstances, global capital flows (investments): Where they flow, innovation, work and prosperity ensue.

Reason relies on the competition of visual diversity, on subsidiarity, on the law of nations (mutual recognition, international jurisdiction), and on common human values (*universalia*), in particular in view of global climate change, including scientific insights (*lege artis*), which characterise a human community. Confucianism, in a harmony of economics and ethics, sees virtue as the root, and wealth as the result. Practical reason (faithfulness) and justice are the foundation: riches acquired by injustice are "as a floating cloud".[205] This is what sustains good corporate governance. Regulated and protected in an international order of assets (*Vermögensordnung*) in a liberal way through the law (enforcement!) may then commercially serve the common good in the sense of an "invisible hand". At the individual level, the acting person remains responsible according to "the reason and spirit" of the law.[206]

## 7.9 A Copernican Turn!

We, the people, need a Copernican turn, especially of the financial actors, towards the imperative of truth (*Wahrheitsgebot*). It is about a reasonable order of assets in the idea of justice with sustainable financing and valuation (*Vermögensordnung*, see chapter 8) for a better world. This applies with regard to the personal responsibility

---

[202] See in more details above chapter 4, esp. 4.4.3 and 4.11. Cf. on the development of generative AI ("big data") 6.8.5.

[203] Art. 3(2) Regulation (EC) No 1606/2002, 19 July 2002, on the application of IAS see above 4. 4.3, 4.8.7 and 4.10.1.

[204] On accounting for non-listed companies under US laws, regulations, and accounting and auditing standards Siegel in Ebke, Luttermann, and Siegel (2007) pp. 95, 101-108 (cf. §§ 243, 264, 264a, 267 HGB). Cf. above 4.11.3 (on "IFRS for SMEs"). On the "green" paradigm shift, that the Trump administration in the USA is avoiding, see above 1.4.2 and below 8.2.3, 8.4.3; with regard to its sustainability regulations, the EU Commission is reducing the "complexity of EU requirements for all businesses, notably SMEs and small mid-caps (SMCs)", see: Omnibus simplification packages, 26.02.2025, COM(2025)80 and COM(2025)81.

[205] Confucius (Classics, vol. I, p. 200), quoted in: Huan-Chang (1911) p. 100. See also Confucius, Analects (Lunyü), book XII.2. Comparatively Luttermann (2015b), also Luttermann (2016a).

[206] Blackstone (1809) book I, § 72.5.

of the corporate directors (corporations) and the market participants in general. Mandatory financial information is at the heart of entrepreneurial organisation and business activity as real disclosure, id est, it "has to do with facts only, and not with prospects, hopes or estimates".[207] Accordingly, regulation of so-called "non-financial information" (whatever that may mean!) seems arbitrary ("nice to have"), not target-oriented in view of the worldwide climate change (see chapters 1, 2). The essence of the existence and development of a human corporation, its financing and valuation (i.e., financial *reporting* and *auditing*) along with the responsibility of the directors should not be built on quicksand (see chapters 3 to 6).

What is required is a paradigm change from economic-mathematical arbitrariness to the primacy of the law: Valuation and publicity, systematically-procedurally built on substance and facts (which in particular also includes scientific insight), strictly oriented towards the imperative of truth (*Bilanzwahrheit*).[208] The prerogative of standard-setting and interpretation belongs in the hands of independent legislators and – in case of conflict – independent judges instead of not democratically legitimised, uncontrolled private interest groups. Otherwise the corporation as an institution – and with it our markets and communities – will further degenerate into an "ingenious device for obtaining individual profit without individual responsibility" (Ambrose Bierce).[209] The unity of liberty (private autonomy) and responsibility (liability) need to be established for – quite self-interested – sustainability and the common good.[210] Reason as the key builds on education and research for the development of good corporate governance as the core element of an internationally just and sustainable order of assets (see chapter 8).

This may sound bold. However, Karl Llewellyn's metaphor of the Greek tragedy still holds: "Life struggling against form, or through form to its will – 'pity and terror'. Law means so pitifully little to life. Life is so terrifyingly dependent on the law."[211] This describes human existence, which has to be ordered in terms of liberty. The guiding principle for regulation, practice and control of corporate governance – as for all law – is the image of the scales (Latin *iustitia*): They require solid ground (justice as the idea of law) and clear measures (norms and facts). It is only then that each person responsible can use them, even when they are trembling, for measuring, for careful action (compliance). The imperative of truth sets a human yardstick[212] for corporate directors and good governance in a human corporation (including AI)[213]

[207] Berle (1928) p. 181, cf. Berle and Means (1932, 1967) pp. 271-272. Groundbreaking Brandeis (1914), see overall (esp. p. 104) and here above chapter 4.

[208] Overall chapters 4 (esp. 4.4.4) and 5, also with "a true and fair view"; see Luttermann (2009).

[209] Bierce (1911), corporation, *n.*

[210] See above 7.3 to 7.8, and esp. 5.6 to 5.7 with 5.2.4 (sustainability); see also 4.9.2 with 4.9.4, 4.10.

[211] Llewellyn (1931) p. 751.

[212] See above 4.4.1 and 4.13 (accountability) with 4.6.5 and 5.6, below 8.3.2 (against "depersonalisation").

[213] See chapter 9, esp. 9.6 to 9.9 also on the use and development of AI.

globally, procedurally secured by legal examination, executed by independent auditors and, in the last instance, at court by independent judges.[214] It is always about personal responsibility of the human.

## References

Adejumo, A., & Ogburie, C. (2025). Financial statement manipulation: Ethical and regulatory perspectives. *GSC Advanced Research and Review, 22*, 252–264.

Aliber, R. Z., Kindleberger, C. P., & McCauley, R. N. (2023). *Manias, panics and crashes: A history of financial crises* (8th ed.). Palgrave Macmillan.

Asgeirsson, H. (2020). *The nature and value of vagueness in the law*. Hart Publishing.

Awasthi, K., Yayavaram, S., George, R., & Sastry, T. (2019). Classification for regulated industries: A new index. *IIMB Management Review, 31*, 309–315.

Banoo, S. (2020). *Role of independent directors in a company: A concious keeper for corporate governance?* https://ssrn.com/abstract=3669220 (accessed: 24.08.2025).

Bergman Brown, A., Heron, N. M., Levy, H., & Zur, E. (2023). *StoneRidge Investment Partners v. Scientific Atlanta*: A test of auditor litigation Risk. *Journal of Business Ethics, 187*, 517–538.

Berle, A. A., Jr. (1928). *Studies in the law of corporation finance*. William S. Hein & Co.

Berle, A. A. Jr., & Means, G. C. (1932, 1967). *The modern corporation and private property* (2nd ed.). Harcourt, Brace & World.

Berle, A. A., Jr. (1938). Accounting and the law. *The Journal of Accountancy, 65*, 368–378.

Bernstein, P. L. (1993). *Capital ideas: The improbable origins of modern Wall Street*. Free Press.

Bierce, A. (1911). *The devil's dictionary*, first published by Doubleday, Page & Co. (in 1906, partly) and by Arthur F. Bird (in 1907 as: *The cynic's word book*).

Blackstone, W. (1809). *Commentaries on the Laws of England* (15th ed.). Printed by A. Strahan for T. Cadell and W. Davies.

Blaurock, U., Goldschmidt, N., & Hollerbach, A. (Eds.). (2005). *Das selbstgeschaffene Recht der Wirtschaft: zum Gedenken an Hans Großmann-Doerth (1894-1944)*. Mohr Siebeck.

Bonini, S., Deng, J., Ferrari, M., John, K., & Ross, D. G. (2022). Long-tenured independent directors and firm performance. *Strategic Management Journal, 43*, 1602–1634.

Brandeis, L. D. (1914). *Other people's money and how the bankers use it*. Frederick A. Stokes Company Publishers.

Bratton, W. W. (2003). Enron, Sarbanes-Oxley and accounting: Rules versus principles versus rents. *Villanova Law Review, 48*, 1023–1055.

Brown, L. (Ed.). (1993). *The new shorter Oxford English dictionary on historical principles* (2 Vols.). Clarendon Press.

Callies, G.-P. (2001). Lex Mercatoria: A reflexive law guide to an autonomous legal system. *German Law Journal, 2*(17) published online by Cambridge University Press: 06.03.2019, E4.

Carpenter, D. (2015). *Magna Carta with a new commentary*. Penguin.

Çelik, S., & Isaksson, M. (2014). Institutional investors and ownership engagement. *OECD Journal Financial Market Trends*, 93–114.

Chandler, A. D. (1977). *The visible hand: The managerial revolution in American business*. Harvard University Press.

Chatov, R. (1975). *Corporate financial reporting: Public or private control?* Free Press.

Coates, J. C. (1999). "Fair value" as an avoidable rule of corporate law: Minority discounts in conflict transactions. *University of Pennsylvania Law Review, 147*, 1251–1359.

[214] See above 7.6 with 4.6.4, 4.10.2 and, basically on theory and practise, Luttermann (2003a) Einf BilanzR recitals 1-45, 107-136 and Luttermann (2003a) § 264 HGB recitals 16-21, 119-169.

Coffee, J. C. (2001). The rise of dispersed ownership: The roles of law and the state in the separation of ownership and control. *Yale Law Journal, 111*, 1–81.

Confucius. (1914/2013). *Analects (Lunyü – Gespräche)*. German translation by Richard Wilhelm (3rd ed.). marixverlag.

Cooter, R., & Ulen, T. (2016). *Law and Economics* (6th ed.). Pearson.

Courant, R., & Robbins, H. (2010). *Was ist Mathematik?* (5th ed.). Springer (original in English since 1941: What is mathematics?, Oxford University Press).

Debreu, G. (1991). The mathematization of economic theory. *American Economic Review, 81*, 1–7.

De Villiers, C., & Dimes, R. (2023). Will the formation of the International Sustainability Standards Board result in the death of integrated reporting? *Journal of Accounting & Organizational Change, 19*, 279–295.

Donelson, D. C., Ege, M. S., & McInnis, J. M. (2017). Internal control weakness and financial reporting fraud. *Auditing: A Journal of Practice & Theory, 36*, 45–69.

Du Plessis, J. J., Großfeld, B., Luttermann, C., Saenger, I., Sandrock, O., & Casper, M. (2012). *German corporate governance in international and European Context* (2nd ed.). Springer.

Ebke, W. F., Luttermann, C., & Siegel, S. (Eds.). (2007). *Internationale Rechnungslegungsstandards für börsenunabhängige Unternehmen?* Nomos.

Eccles, R. G., Herz, R. H., Keegan, E. M., & Phillips, D. M. H. (2001). *The value reporting revolution: Moving beyond the earnings game*. Wiley.

Eisenberg, M. A. (1976). *The structure of the corporation: A legal analysis*. Little, Brown and Co.

Eisenberg, M. A. (1989). The structure of corporation law. *Columbia Law Review, 89*, 1461–1525.

Fama, E. F. (1970). Efficient capital markets: A review of theory and empirical work. *Journal of Finance, 25*, 383–417.

Fama, E. F. (1991). Efficient capital markets: II. *Journal of Finance, 46*, 1575–1617.

Flume, W. (1983). *Allgemeiner Teil des Bürgerlichen Rechts, Erster Band, Zweiter Teil: Die Juristische Person*. Springer-Verlag.

Friedman, M. (1962, 2002). *Capitalism and freedom* (40th Anniversary ed.). University of Chicago Press.

Friedman, M. (1970). A Friedman doctrine: The social responsibility of business is to increase its profit. *The New York Times*, 13.09.1970. https://www.nytimes.com/1970/09/13/archives/a-friedman-doctrine-the-social-responsibility-of-business-is-to.html (accessed: 24.08.2025).

Fukuyama, F. (1992). *The end of history and the last man*. Free Press.

Galbraith, J. K. (1994). *A short history of financial euphoria*. Viking Penguin.

Gandhi, P., Golez, B., Jackwerth, J. C., & Plazzi, A. (2019). Financial market misconduct and public enforcement: The case of Libor manipulation. *Management Science, 65*, 5268–5289.

Garten, J. E. (2021). *Three days at Camp David: How a secret meeting in 1971 transformed the global economy*. HarperCollins.

Gervais, S., & Strobl, G. (2023). *Money management and real investment*. https://ssrn.com/abstract=4325133 (accessed: 24.08.2025).

Gevurtz, F. A. (2009). Law upside down: A critical essay on *Stoneridge Investment Partners, LLC v. Scientific-Atlanta, Inc. Northwestern University Law Review, 103*, 448–455.

Ghossoub, E. A., & Reed, R. R. (2015). The size distribution of the banking sector and the effects of monetary policy. *European Economic Review, 75*, 156–176.

Goddard, E. C. (1928). The problem of valuation: The evolution of cost of reproduction as the rate base. *Harvard Law Review, 41*, 564–592.

Gordon, J. N. (2007). The rise of independent directors in the United States, 1950-2005: Of shareholder value and stock market prices. *Stanford Law Review, 59*, 1465–1571.

Greenspan, A. (2013). *The map and the territory 2.0: Risk, human nature, and the future of forecasting*. Penguin Press.

Grospe, N. (2011). Jones v. Harris Associates: Shareholders' consolation prize in the mutual fund fee debate. *Pace Law Review, 31*, 771–798.

Großfeld, B. (2015). Geography and semiotics in accounting: The challenge of globalization. *European Business Law Review (EBLR), 26*, 95–105.

Großfeld, B., & Luttermann, C. (2005). *Bilanzrecht* (4th ed.). CF Mueller.

Großmann-Doerth, H. (1933). *Selbstgeschaffenes Recht der Wirtschaft und staatliches Recht.* Wagner'sche Universitäts-Buchhandlung.

Hayek, F. A. von (1991). *Die Verfassung der Freiheit* (3rd ed.). Mohr Siebeck.

Huan, X., Previts, G. J., & Parbonetti, A. (2023). Understanding the LIBOR scandal: The historical, the ethical, and the technological. *Journal of Banking Regulation, 24*, 403–419.

Huan-Chang, C. (1911). *The economic principles of Confucius and his school* (Vol. I). Columbia University.

Humboldt, W. von (1792). *Ideen zu einem Versuch, die Grenzen der Wirksamkeit des Staats zu bestimmen*, first published by Eduard Trewendt, 1851.

Hummel, K., & Jobst, D. (2024). An overview of corporate sustainability reporting legislation in the European Union. *Accounting in Europe.* https://doi.org/10.1080/17449480.2024.2312145 (accessed: 24.08.2025).

Jo, T.-H., & Henry, J. F. (2015). The business enterprise in the age of money manager capitalism. *Journal of Economic Issues, 49*, 23–46.

Johnson, E. D. (2009). The fiduciary duty in mutual fund excessive fee cases: Ripe for re-examination. *Duke Law Journal, 59*, 145–181.

Kant, I. (1793). Über den Gemeinspruch: Das mag in der Theorie richtig sein, taugt aber nicht für die Praxis. *Berlinische Monatsschrift*, 201–284.

Kant, I. (1870). *Metaphysische Anfangsgründe der Rechtslehre* (Academy-Edition 1900-1901, Vol. VI).

Koller, T., Goedhart, M., & Wessels, D. (2020). *Valuation: Measuring and managing the value of companies* (7th ed.). Wiley.

Kripke, H. (1979). *The SEC and corporate disclosure: Regulation in search of a purpose*. Harcourt.

Krugman, P. R., Obstfeld, M., & Melitz, M. J. (2023). *International economics: Theory and policy* (12th Global ed.). Pearson.

Legg, M. (2004). Verizon Communications, Inc. v. FCC: Telecommunications access pricing and regulator accountability through administrative law and takings jurisprudence. *Federal Communications Law Journal, 56*, 563–585.

Levitt, A. (1998). *The "numbers game"*, 28.09.1998. https://www.sec.gov/news/speech/speecharchive/1998/spch220.txt (accessed: 24.08.2025).

Liu, J. (2015). Experience of internationalization of Chinese corporate law and corporate governance: How to make the hybrid of civil law and common law work? *European Business Law Review (EBLR), 26*, 107–128.

Llewellyn, K. N. (1931). What price contract: An essay in perspective. *Yale Law Journal, 40*, 704–751.

Locke, J. (1689). *Second Treatise of Civil Government*. Barnes & Noble, 2009.

Lokana, M. E., & Sharma, P. (2023). *Two decades of accounting fraud research: The missing meso-level analysis*. https://doi.org/10.1177/21582440231197305 (accessed: 24.08.2025).

Low, P. W., & Johnson, J. S. (2015). Changing the vocabulary of the vagueness doctrine. *Virginia Law Review, 101*, 2051–2116.

Luttermann, C. (1996). Besteuerung multinationaler Konzerne in den Vereinigten Staaten von Amerika. *Recht der Internationalen Wirtschaft (RIW), 42*, 935–948.

Luttermann, C. (1997). Zum Rechtsgebiet der internationalen Konzernrechnungslegung. In K.-H. Forster, B. Grunewald, M. Lutter, & J. Semler (Eds.), *Festschrift for Bruno Kropff* (pp. 485–506). IDW Verlag.

Luttermann, C. (1998). *Unternehmen, Kapital und Genußrechte: Eine Studie über Grundlagen der Unternehmensfinanzierung und zum internationalen Kapitalmarktrecht*. Mohr Siebeck.

Luttermann, C. (1999a). *Bilanzrecht in den USA und internationale Konzernrechnungslegung.* Mohr Siebeck.

Luttermann, C. (1999b). Dialog der Kulturen: Vergleichendes Handels- und Kapitalmarktrecht im Sprachspiegel. In U. Hübner & W. F. Ebke (Eds.), *Festschrift for Bernhard Großfeld* (pp. 771–789). Verlag Recht und Wirtschaft.

Luttermann, C. (2002). Der Fall Enron entzaubert die amerikanischen Bilanzregeln. *Handelsblatt*, 30.01.2002, p. 10.

Luttermann, C. (2003a). In B. Kropff & J. Semler (Eds.), *Münchener Kommentar zum Aktiengesetz* (Vol. 5/1, 2nd ed.). CH Beck Verlag.

Luttermann, C. (2003b). Unabhängige Bilanzexperten in Aufsichtsrat und Beirat. *Betrieb-Berater (BB), 58*, 745–750.

Luttermann, C. (2006). Unternehmenskontrolle und Bilanzmanipulation nach anglo-amerikanischen Mustern (IAS/IFRS und U.S. "GAAP"). *Die Wirtschaftsprüfung (WPg), 59*, 778–786.

Luttermann, C. (2007). Rechnungslegung ist ein Rechtsakt, kein Marketing. *Frankfurter Allgemeine Zeitung*, 26.02.2007, p. 20.

Luttermann, C. (2008a). Die Erosion der Freiheit (the erosion of freedom). *Frankfurter Allgemeine Zeitung*, 23.06.2008, p. 22.

Luttermann, C. (2008b). Über Vertragsverhältnisse und Bewertungsrecht: Geld, Zeitwert und internationaler Goldstandard. *Finanz-Betrieb (FB), 10*, 193–204.

Luttermann, C. (2008c). Wesentlichkeit (Materiality) als Haftungsvermeidung in den USA. *Recht der Internationalen Wirtschaft (RIW), 54*, 577–583.

Luttermann, C. (2008d). Juristische Person, Konzern und Existenzvernichtungshaftung. *Juristische Arbeitsblätter (JA), 40*, 833–838.

Luttermann, C. (2009). "Fair value": Mythos, Methoden und Maß international. *Recht der Internationalen Wirtschaft (RIW), 55*, 1–11.

Luttermann, C. (2010a). Juristische Analyse von Ökonomie, Staat und Gesellschaft. *Zeitschrift für Rechtspolitik (ZRP), 43*, 1–4.

Luttermann, C. (2010b). Regulierungsperspektiven: „War und ist die Finanzkrise die Folge von Hyperspekulation?". *Österreichisches Bank-Archiv (Zeitschrift für das gesamte Bank- und Börsenwesen – Journal of Banking and Financial Research, ÖBA), 58*, 444–448.

Luttermann, C. (2011). Kopernikanische Wende zum Wahrheitsgebot oder eine europäische Ratingagentur nach US-Mustern? *Europäisches Wirtschafts- und Steuerrecht (EWS), 19*, 330–333.

Luttermann, C. (2012). Internationale Vermögensordnung, Insolvenzrecht und Schulden(transfer)-systeme. *Zeitschrift für Wirtschaftsrecht (ZIP), 33*, 305–313.

Luttermann, C. (2015a). Corporate Law and the Vermoegensordnung (Order of Assets). *European Business Law Review (EBLR), 26*, 31–48.

Luttermann, C. (2015b). Ü ber Idee und Methodik eines internationalen Investitionsschutzes (Vermögensordnung) durch Privatrecht und Völkerrecht. *Zeitschrift für Europarecht, Internationales Privatrecht und Rechtsvergleichung (ZfRV), 56*, 274–282.

Luttermann, C. (2016a). German and Russian direct investment under the rule of international law. *Zeitschrift für Internationales Wirtschaftsrecht (IWRZ), 1*, 90–95.

Luttermann, C. (2016b). Persönliche prozessuale Haftungsverschärfung bei "Corporate Misconduct" (U.S. Yates Memorandum). *Der Betrieb (DB), 69*, 1059–1063.

Luttermann, C. (2024). Editorial on comparative law and language. *Comparative Law and Language I-II, 3*(1).

Luttermann, C., & Luttermann, K. (2021). Towards peace in Europe: On legal linguistics, prosperity and European identity – the European Reference Language System for the European Union. *International Journal of Legal Discourse, 6*, 7–41.

Luttermann, L. (2022). Klimawandel und Business Judgement: Nachhaltige Finanzierung als unternehmerisches Sorgfaltskonzept. *Recht der Internationalen Wirtschaft (RIW), 68*, 809–820.

Luttermann, L. (2024). Unternehmensführung: Nachhaltige Finanzinformation (U.S. SEC Climate Rules/EU), Wertschöpfung und Bankenfinanzierung. *Recht der Internationalen Wirtschaft (RIW), 70*, 410–422.

Mestmäcker, E.-J. (2007). *A legal theory without law: Posner v. Hayek on economic analysis of law*. Mohr Siebeck.

Mill, J. S. (1859). *On liberty*. John W. Parker and Son.

Miller, M. H. (1997). *Merton Miller on derivatives*. John Wiley & Sons, Inc.

Modigliani, F., & Miller, M. H. (1958). The cost of capital, corporation finance and the theory of investment. *The American Economic Revue, 48*, 261–297.

Modigliani, F., & Miller, M. H. (1963). Corporate income taxes and the cost of capital: A correction. *The American Economic Revue, 53*, 433–443.

Phelps, E. (2007). Macroeconomics for a modern economy. *The American Economic Review, 97*, 543–561.

Pierce, R. J., & Gellhorn, E. (1999). *Regulated industries in a nutshell* (4th ed.). West Publishing.

Posner, R. A. (1973). *Economic analysis of law* (1st ed.). Little Brown and Company (9th ed., 2014, Wolters Kluwer).

Posner, R. A. (1979). Utilitarianism, economics, and legal theory. *The Journal of Legal Studies, 8*, 103–140.

Posner, R. A. (2009). *A failure of capitalism: The crisis of '08 and the descent into depression*. Harvard University Press.

Pratama, A., Jaenudin, E., & Anas, S. (2022). Environmental, social, governance sustainability disclosure using international financial reporting sustainability standards S1 in Southeast Asian companies: A preliminary assessment. *International Journal of Energy Economics and Policy, 12*, 456–472.

Radin, S. A. (2009). *The business judgement rule: Fiduciary duties of corporate directors* (Vol. I and II, 6th ed.). Aspen.

Rappaport, A. (1986). *Creating shareholder value: The new standard for business performance*. Free Press (2nd ed. 1997: Creating shareholder value: a guide for managers and investors).

Ratzinger-Sakel, N. V., & Tiedemann, T. (2022). Fraud in accounting and audit research (1926-2019): A bibliometric analysis. *Accounting History Review, 32*, 97–143.

Raz, J. (2008). *The practice of value*. Clarendon Press.

Ribeiro, M. (2004). *Limiting arbitrary power: The vagueness doctrine in Canadian constitutional law*. The University of Chicago Press.

Roberts, R., & Kynaston, D. (2002). *City state: A contemporary history of the City of London and how money triumphed*. Profile Books.

Savigny, F. C. von (1840a). *System des heutigen römischen Rechts* (Vol. I). Veit.

Savigny, F. C. von (1840b). *System des heutigen römischen Rechts* (Vol. II). Veit.

Scalia, A. (1997). *A matter of interpretation: Federal courts and the law*. Princeton University Press.

Schiller, F. (1803). *Die Braut von Messina oder die feindlichen Brüder: ein Trauerspiel mit Chören*. J. G. Cotta'sche Buchhandlung.

Seligman, J. (2002). No one can serve two masters: Corporate and securities law after Enron. *Washington University Law Quarterly, 80*, 449–517.

Smith, A. (1759/1790$^6$). *The theory of moral sentiments, Edinburgh* (6th ed.). Penguin Books, 2009.

Smith, A. (1776/1789$^5$). *An inquiry into the nature and causes of the wealth of nations, London* (5th ed.). Bantam Classic Edition, 2003.

Spengler, O. (1923/1998). *Der Untergang des Abendlandes: Umrisse einer Morphologie der Weltgeschichte*. C.H. Beck Verlag (complete ed.)

Staubus, G. J. (1999). *The decision-usefulness theory of accounting*. Garland Publishing.

Stiglitz, J. E. (2010). *Freefall: America, free markets, and the sinking of the world economy*. W. W. Norton & Company.

Strine, L. E., Jr. (2014). Can we do better by ordinary Investors? A pragmatic reaction to the dueling ideological mythologists of corporate law. *Columbia Law Review, 114*, 449–502.

Strum, P. (1984). *Louis D. Brandeis: Justice for the people*. Harvard University Press.

Tooze, A. (2019). *Crashed: How a decade of financial crisis changed the world*. Penguin Books Great Britain.

Toth, O. (2017). *The Lex Mercatoria in theory and practice*. Oxford University Press.

Tutino, M., & Merlo, M. (2019). Accounting fraud: A literature review. *Risk Governance and Control Financial Markets & Institutions, 9*, 8–25.

Vieira, E. (2015). Gold and silver as constitutional alternative currencies. *Cato Journal, 35*, 209–232.

Vigneau, L., Humphreys, M., & Moon, J. (2015). How do firms comply with international sustainability standards? Process and consequences of adopting the Global Reporting Initiative. *Journal of Business Ethics, 131*, 469–486.

Vitali, S., Glattfelder, J. B., & Battiston, S. (2011). The network of global corporate control. *PLoS One, 6*(10), 1–6.

Weisman, D. L. (2019). Regulatory takings without confiscatory returns. *Yale Journal of Regulation, Bulletin, 36*, November 10, 2019. https://www.yalejreg.com/bulletin/regulatory-takings-without-confiscatory-returns/ (accessed: 24.08.2025).

Wertheimer, B. M. (1998). The shareholders' appraisal remedy and how the courts determine fair value. *Duke Law Journal 47*, 613–715.

Williams, C. A. (2021). Fiduciary duties and corporate climate responsibility. *Vanderbilt Law Review, 74*, 1875–1916.

Wilson Corley, K. M. (2024). *Garfield v. Allen*: The cat is out of the bag. *Tulsa Law Review, 59*, 169–192.

# Part V
# The World, and Beyond

# Chapter 8
# Global *Vermögensordnung*: Sustainable Valuation and Financial Reporting for Prosperity (Peace)

"Let there be light."

*Genesis* 1:3

**Contents**



## 8.1 Global Justice: Ecosystem, Humanity, and Economy (Corporation)

Reason is a gift for human prosperity. The law is its expression as practised ethics, the measure for each individual, for peace, prosperity and the common good, shaping and supporting an entrepreneurial culture of responsibility (*Verantwortungskultur*). Everybody, being a trustee of their world, is required to make use of their responsibility. Immanuel Kant classically describes the categorical imperative: Act according to the maxim that you would wish all other rational people to follow, as if it were a




C. Luttermann, *Human Corporation for Sustainable Development*,
https://doi.org/10.1007/978-3-032-07615-1_8

universal law.[1] Albert Schweitzer, in his search of self-perfection, takes this as the human principle of the veneration of life (*veneratio vitae*): I am life that wants to live, in the midst of life that wants to live.[2] The ethical idea of reason for peace. Basically, it is about the search for reasonableness (*Vernünftigkeit*, Greek *phrónesis*), for global justice, as undertaken as a whole with the human corporation (culture of responsibility, see 1.1 and 6.1.2).

At the human level, the global ecosystem and the economy as a whole have to be reconciled for this. It is the Enlightenment that makes a human as a rational being capable of reconciliation: *Sapere aude*! (Latin, in English: dare to know). It is the exit of man from his self-inflicted immaturity, id est the inability to use his intellect without the guidance of another. In this sense the human corporation may serve transnationally as a global model for human entrepreneurship and prosperity. Grounded in the rule of law (*Herrschaft des Rechts*), a constitution of liberty as a *Vermögensordnung* (an order of assets),[3] through individual entrepreneurship and fair competition, sensibly integrated into the great work of humankind (see chapter 9). Humanity, environment and economy make demands on us all, for ourselves and succeeding generations.[4] Let us take another look at the beginning, also of our journey (see 1.1). Since 1945, the United Nations Charta (see 1.2) reads:

> "to reaffirm faith in fundamental human rights, in the dignity and worth of the human person, in the equal rights of men and women and of nations large and small, and to establish conditions under which justice and respect for the obligations arising from treaties and other sources of international law can be maintained, and to promote social progress and better standards of life in larger freedom" (Preamble).

This denotes *de lege lata* in the community of nations, built with "Westphalian principles" after disastrous wars as a state-based international order,[5] the legal basis for people and the environment. The United Nations Framework Convention on Climate Change (Paris Agreement), entered into force on 4 November 2016, is a landmark of such a groundbreaking, also legally binding international treaty to which more than 193 Parties (193 states plus the European Union) have signed. The Paris Agreement sets long-term goals to substantially reduce global greenhouse

[1] Kant (1788) p. 54 (§ 7 *Grundgesetz der reinen praktischen Vernunft* – Basic law of pure practical reason).

[2] Schweitzer (1923) p. 330. See also Smith (1759/1790[6]) pp. 401-403 on justice (law) as a virtue, and Sen (2009), esp. pp. XIII-XVII, with comparison to Rawls theory on justice with "perfectly just institutions". Cf. Rawls (2001), and Savigny, above 2.2.2; also the "tractatus technologico-ethicus" by Jonas (1979).

[3] Please note: the term "asset" (*Vermögen*, *Vermögenswert*, Old French *asez*, modern *assez* enough to meet the debts) means not only items of property, but an ability (Latin *facultas* faculty *Fähigkeit*, e.g., to speak a language) is also an asset; see Brown (1993) p. 131 (asset). The German term *Vermögen* also encompasses both dimensions.

[4] Overall ICJ, Advisory Opinion: Obligations of states in respect of climate change, 23.07.2025 (https://www.icj-cij.org/sites/default/files/case-related/187/187-20250723-adv-01-00-en.pdf, accessed: 25.08.2025), on that see above 1.2, 6.1.

[5] See above 1.2 and 1.4, 1.6 with 8.2.1 and 8.5. Cf. Kissinger (2015) pp. 2-10.

gas emissions, to provide financing to developing countries to mitigate climate change and to adapt to climate impacts; it is also essential for the achievement of the seventeen Sustainable Development Goals (SDGs), set up to transform the world: to promote prosperity for the people while protecting our planet Earth (see chapter 1 and 8.2.1).[6] We, the people of the world, as her freeborn trustees, are called to act together for the common good.[7]

A human economy is needed to achieve this, as well as, first and foremost, peace. An economy that creates the innovations for sustainable economic activity through human creativity. Based and fostered on sound economic thinking (economics) for the people and the environment. The International Court of Justice affirms this and speaks of the need for urgent action; highlighting environmental and human rights, rules of due diligence and legal consequences, the judges emphasise "that climate change is a common concern of humankind".[8] The Court states:

> "The consequences of climate change are severe and far-reaching; they affect both natural ecosystems and human populations. Rising temperatures are causing the melting of ice sheets and glaciers, leading to sea level rise and threatening coastal communities with unprecedented flooding. Extreme weather events, such as hurricanes, droughts and heatwaves, are becoming more frequent and intense, devastating agriculture, displacing populations and exacerbating water shortages. Furthermore, the disruption of natural habitats is pushing certain species toward extinction and leading to irreversible loss of biodiversity. Human life and health are also at risk, with an increased incidence of heat-related illnesses and the spread of climate-related diseases. These consequences underscore the urgent and existential threat posed by climate change."[9]

Holistically, it is about our triad "human, economy and environment". But, as Edmund Phelps put it in his survey of the neoclassical "business of growth", governing previous thinking and acting: "In neoclassical economics, the objects of the theory were not human endeavor as we know it – only 'prices and quantities'. There was a *disconnect* from history and the humanities", its neoclassical growth theory "was conspicuous in having no people in it".[10] Phelps seeks the good economy with the conception of a good life as the classical theory of one's personal

---

[6]UN, Climate Action: www.un.org/en/climatechange/17-goals-to-transform-our-world (accessed: 25.08.2025); see above chapter 1.

[7]Earthtopia it may be called. Luttermann (1998a) pp. 135-145, 465-485 and (2010a) with Luttermann (2012), (2013) and (2015b) on law as practised ethics and a global *Vermögensordnung*; in English Luttermann (2015a) and chapter 9.

[8]ICJ, Advisory Opinion: Obligation of states in respect of climate change (https://www.icj-cij.org/sites/default/files/case-related/187/187-20250723-adv-01-00-en.pdf, accessed: 25.08.2025), para. 364. See on this above 1.2 and 6.1.

[9]ICJ, ibid., para. 74.

[10]Phelps (2007) p. 552. Cf. Sen (2009) pp. XI-XIII, accordingly on core deficiencies of modern economics with reference to Adam Smith. On sustainability and the common good Tirole (2019) p. 11: "The truth is that if we want to be green, we have to accept a small reduction in purchasing power and it is entirely worth it."; on intercultural investment and trust Luttermann (2019b), above 1.5.2 with 5.3.4, 4.2 and 4.3, 4.11.4 (valuation); on the "European public good" 4.4.4, 4.10.1.

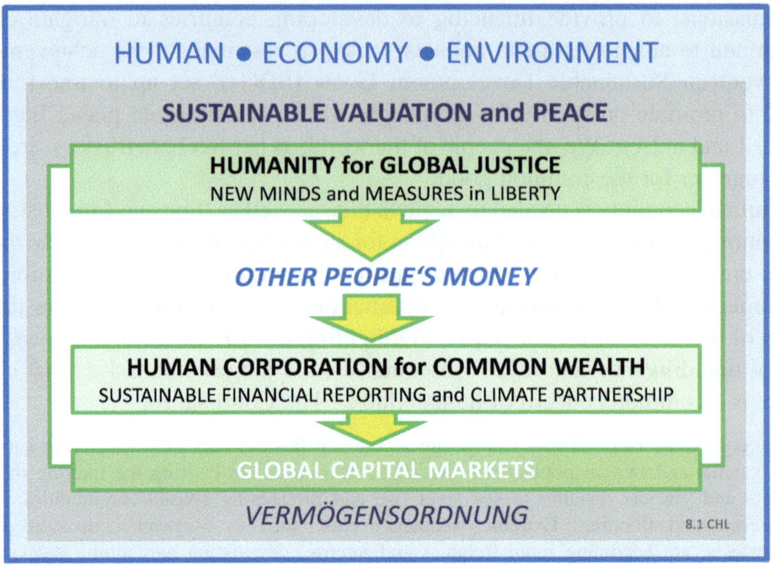


**Fig. 8.1** Sustainable valuation and financial reporting, id est human corporation for prosperity and peace (global *Vermögensordnung*; on the comprehensive meaning of "asset" see above footnote 3 and overall on the human corporation, esp. chapters 1 and 2)

development, originating in Europe (Aristotle).[11] Enlightenment is a sustained inspiration. Remember, especially in the categories of law around the globe, it is always "human conflicts that lie behind cases" that need to be reflected upon.[12] This is also true, if not even more so, when it comes to markets and corporations, because without people they are simply nothing worldwide (see chapter 6 and on corporate directors 7.3.1).

Human corporation means establishing sustainable corporate prosperity by good governance within a good economy, holistically conceived and lived in a philosophy of human affairs (*Philosophie und Praxis der menschlichen Lebensverhältnisse*, humanity, see Fig. 8.1). For that reason, we look back to win the future. As shown, the corporation is a product of human reason for the lasting financing of companies (or projects). We need to connect the corporation – back – to people (*Menschen*) and human life and its environment, back to the substance of qualities (real values) instead of just "prices and quantities" (cf. Phelps, see 9.7): elementary all around through science-based education (*Bildung*) and the law as practised ethics with sustainable valuation, financial reporting and auditing. As a whole, for a

[11] Phelps (2007) p. 555. See overall chapter 9.

[12] Strum (1984) p. 344, with reference to the work ethic of Alexis de Tocqueville and Louis D. Brandeis (on the latter below 8.2.3, above 3.3.3). On the "circumstances of life" (*Lebensverhältnisse*) below 8.3.3 and, e.g., 5.2.2, 7.3.2, 9.1, also Luttermann (1999b) pp. 3-5 on the "numbers game" and human destinies with Levitt (1998). On the dialogue of cultures Luttermann (1999a).

globally just order of assets of climate partners (*Klimapartner*, see 8.5, 6.1.1) who cooperate for individual wealth and the common good.[13] This can lead to prosperity and peace all over the world (i.e. global *Vermögensordnung*).

## 8.2 On New Minds and Measures

### *8.2.1 World Surveying: The Green Evolution of Capital*

The world has to be regauged, but: according to what measure? – With climate change, it is about a green paradigm change, about the sustainable restructuring of economy and society. In the course of initiatives of the United Nations (Paris Agreement 2015), the European Union has established the European Green Deal since 2019, designated as the "socio-ecological" transition of the economy – meanwhile along with a so-called Clean Industrial Deal.[14] In many places, also in the USA, people are becoming active.[15] The Green Deal is the first concrete programme worldwide, borne by the realisation that we are living beyond our means. "The Limits to Growth" (*Grenzen des Wachstums*, Club of Rome, 1972) have in fact been effective since humans are no longer living in harmony with nature and environment. Humankind keeps on growing with a global economic consumption of resources, as if there were no tomorrow.

For the human corporation and a good economy, let us first take a look at the recent genesis of the regulatory basis (see originally in chapter 1). For humankind, at the conference in Rio de Janeiro, in 1992, the United Nations formulated the concept for sustainable development that economic efficiency, social justice and securing the natural life foundations are equal interests that are essential for survival and

[13]Basically Luttermann (2022). See also 1.2, 8.5 and chapter 9. Cf. the debt economy (quantitative easing, high-debt deficit spending etc. – ever repayable?) based on fiat money in a banking system with "fractional reserve" lending, creating "debt" (so-called "money") through book entries, i.e. "free-lunch" (esp. with the dollar privilege) for some on account of many. See above 1.1, overall Galbraith (1994), esp. from p. 19 (leverage, paper money), Stiglitz (2010), Tooze (2019), e.g. pp. 84-90, from p. 422 and 480-482. See already Greenspan (1967) and chapter 6 (esp. 6.6.2): gold standard.

[14]See above 1.4.2. European Union: https://commission.europa.eu/strategy-and-policy/priorities-2019-2024/european-green-deal_en (accessed: 25.08.2025). Luttermann (2021). On the transition with a European opening balance for 2023 from regulatory data Luttermann, L. (2024) and (2025). Affirmative overall: ICJ, Advisory Opinion: Obligation of states in respect of climate change (https://www.icj-cij.org/sites/default/files/case-related/187/187-20250723-adv-01-00-en.pdf, accessed: 25.08.2025), para. 364. See on this above 8.1 with 1.2 and 6.1.

[15]E.g., Gerrard (2025), Franklin, MacDonald (2024), Luttermann, L. (2023) and (2024), esp. pp. 415-419. Current data: California Environmental Protection Agency (https://calepa.ca.gov), London School of Economics and Political Science (https://www.lse.ac.uk/granthaminstitute, both accessed: 25.08.2025).

condition each other reciprocally.[16] For the transformation of our world, the global community in 2015 formulated seventeen objectives for a socially, economically and ecologically sustainable development in the universal Agenda 2030 (so-called "Sustainable Development Goals" – SDGs, see 8.1 with Fig. 8.1). An action plan for people, planet and prosperity – as well as for peace and partnership (see 8.5) – which announces with regard to international law (*Völkerrecht*):[17]

> ***"People***
> We are determined to end poverty and hunger, in all their forms and dimensions, and to ensure that all human beings can fulfil their potential in dignity and equality and in a healthy environment.
>
> ***Planet***
> We are determined to protect the planet from degradation, including through sustainable consumption and production, sustainably managing its natural resources and taking urgent action on climate change, so that it can support the needs of the present and future generations.
>
> ***Prosperity***
> We are determined to ensure that all human beings can enjoy prosperous and fulfilling lives and that economic, social and technological progress occurs in harmony with nature."

This is what the Paris Agreement builds on. In it, following the Framework Convention on Climate Change (Kyoto protocol 1997), concrete goals have been formulated. In order to counter the dangers of climate change, global warming is to be kept markedly beneath 2 °C (if possible at 1.5 °C), the global culmination point of emissions of harmful greenhouse gases transcended and subsequently a rapid decrease of such emissions to be achieved. In the second half of the twenty-first century, an equilibrium between emissions and reduction is to be established. The developing countries are to be granted more time in this process. Overall, the efforts and measures for the good of all people are to be undertaken with the best available scientific insights (see 8.2.3).[18] The European Union, the largest internal market in the world and a signatory as a sui generis legal entity under international law,[19] is

[16] UN, General Assembly, Rio Declaration on Environment and Development, 12.08.1992 (www.un.org/en/development/desa/population/migration/generalassembly/docs/globalcompact/A_CONF.151_26_Vol.I_Declaration.pdf, accessed: 25.08.2025).

[17] UN, General Assembly, Transforming our world: the 2030 Agenda for Sustainable Development, 25.09.2015 (A/RES/70/1: https://www.un.org/en/development/desa/population/migration/generalassembly/docs/globalcompact/A_RES_70_1_E.pdf, accessed: 25.08.2025) p. 2. Further below 8.5.

[18] Overall UN Paris Agreement (FCCC/CP/2015/10/Add.1), see above chapter 1. Confirming ICJ, Advisory Opinion: Obligation of states in respect of climate change (https://www.icj-cij.org/sites/default/files/case-related/187/187-20250723-adv-01-00-en.pdf, accessed: 25.08.2025), paras. 222-270. See on this above 1.2 and 6.1.

[19] Council Decision (EU) 2016/1841 of 05.10.2016 on the conclusion, on behalf of the European Union, of the Paris Agreement adopted under the United Nations Framework Convention on Climate Change, EU OJ 19.10.2016, L 282/1. See also Charta of Fundamental Rights of the European Union.

fundamentally dedicated to humans, to human rights and the environment in its canon of values (Art. 2 and 3 TEU).

For the transformation, the European Union (EU) is placing "sustainable" financing for its internal market in the center of the financial system. In order to reach the environmental goals of the Paris Agreement by 2050, the economy is to be transformed "socio-ecologically" (so-called Green Deal). A core element is a classification system for "sustainable" activities with "technical" criteria of evaluation: According to the EU Taxonomy,[20] companies, projects and financial instruments are qualified and committed to disclosure, so that investors may orient their investment decisions accordingly and trillions of euros can flow into "sustainable" business activities. A gigantic instrument for directing capital flows, a unique system of valuation (*Bewertungsrecht*, see chapters 4 to 6): the green evolution of capital? – Sounds good. This needs to be monitored critically, scientifically sound in all disciplines.

### 8.2.2 *Juridical Analysis for a Sustainable Economy*

Who sets the new standards? – Already in the humanistically established European Union, this is a wide field, even more so in the global dimension of planet earth. Overall, jurisprudence searches for adequacy in the chaos of life, id est holistically reason and reasonableness (*Angemessenheit*) in a solution-oriented way, to secure the constitution of liberty as the personal responsibility of every human being (see 8.2.3).[21] It is about compatibility of international law.[22] In legal comparison, any order presents itself as the expression of a culture, as the balance of multiple processes of education, negotiation and acceptance. This is also the foundation of the human corporation in a sustainable economy, in general established for prosperity. A system of valuation directing capital flow essentially in certain business activities (see 1.3, 1.5.3) may have an alluring and massive effect, may create work through investment. – What about sustainability?

---

[20] Regulation (EU) 2020/852 of the European Parliament and of the Council of 18.06.2020 on the establishment of a framework to facilitate sustainable investment, and amending Regulation (EU) 2019/2088, EU OJ L 198, 22.06.2020, pp. 13-43. Luttermann (2021).

[21] See basically chapters 1, 2 and 7 (esp. 7.9). Generally Hayek (1960), Luttermann (1998a) pp. 139-143. Cf. Applebaum (2024), Kissinger (2015) p. 8: "America struggles to define the relationship between its power (still vast) and its principles." And – referring to the universal relevance of Westphalian order (cf. above 8.1) – success in an effort to "vindicate the legitimacy of any common system", he writes, "will require an approach that respects both the multifariousness of the human condition and the ingrained human quest for freedom."

[22] Basically on international law and climate change ICJ, Advisory Opinion: Obligation of states in respect of climate change (https://www.icj-cij.org/sites/default/files/case-related/187/187-20250723-adv-01-00-en.pdf, accessed: 25.08.2025), see on this above 1.2 and 6.1.

Juridical analysis, which sounds out the economy, the society and the state, provides the worldwide necessary framework: for a factually appropriate, intercultural community of responsibility (*Verantwortungsgemeinschaft*, see 8.5). The juridical analysis of the economy (*Juristische Analyse der Ökonomie*), founded in a comparative law perspective on the basis of holistic capital market research already at the end of the twentieth century in the face of severe financial rejections, sees humans and their environment in the center:[23] an ethically guiding alternative structure as opposed to the economically and regulatorily leading "economic analysis of law" (*Ökonomische Analyse des Rechts*), which is busily operating neo-classical efficiency models with wretched ideas of man as *"homo oeconomicus"* (see, e.g., 7. 3.2, 7.7.2). In such a disaster economy (*Katastrophenwirtschaft*), attested time and again (e.g., gigantic credit bubbles, leverage, shareholder value), capital markets and corporations have long been exposed as mathematical-speculative wasteland: Greed and "non-sustainable patterns of financial behaviour", a "boom-and-bust economy".[24]

The quake of the business world is man-made, not a natural disaster. The disaster economy reveals the lack of values (virtues) and consequently the significance of a just balance of a responsible community. Efficiency, the Holy Grail of so-called "economic analysis of the law", seems mechanically lifeless where there is a lack of reasonable measure. This was recognised even by the Chicago knight of the Holy Grail Richard Posner,[25] professor of law and judge, who, with reference to the failure of the market regarding consulting fees in the world debt crisis, made his colleague Judge Frank Easterbrook take to heart that the economic analysis was "ripe for reexamination".[26] Although Posner is considered a Keynesian, he has even confessed: "We have learned since [Lehman 2008] that the present generation of economists has not figured out how the economy works".[27] The limitation of economic theory on financing and valuation of companies is overlaid by the belief in a future that is calculable by a model mathematising guild, who also operate the regime of sham rationalism in the "analysis of law": grandiosely failed in innumerable accounting scandals and in the ongoing world debt crisis.[28]

Sustainable economy is different. It marks not the end of a scientifically based economy, but, on the contrary, that of its impostors and their phantasmagorias.

---

[23] Luttermann (1998a), esp. pp. 465-485. Luttermann (2010a) and (2015a), (2015b). See also Figs. 5.1 and 5.3 as well as Fig. 6.3.

[24] See above chapter 6. Aliber, Kindleberger, McCauley (2023), esp. pp. 1-15, 373-384. See also Stiglitz (2010), Tooze (2019) and basically Galbraith (1994). Cf. Sen (2009), from p. XI (on the "nature of the present economic crisis") and Greenspan (1967). Luttermann (2010c).

[25] Cf. Posner (2014).

[26] Posner, dissent, *Jones v. Harris,* 527 F.3d 627, 730 (7th Cir. 2008), majority opinion von Easterbrook, ibid., 727. On that Luttermann (2010a) 1, 4 and above 7.7.2; than *Jones v. Harris Associates L.P.*, 559 U.S. 335 (2010). Also, e.g., Swan (2011), Bollman and Andreu (2011) 717, 748-749.

[27] Posner (2009): how I became a Keynesian.

[28] See chapters 4 to 6. Luttermann (2010a) 1-4.

Pioneers issued early warnings. Therefore, once again: Frank Knight (1885–1972), one of the founders of the Chicago school of economics, saw "evil results" of the "theoretical character of economic speculation" even before the first world economic crisis "in every field of practical economics".[29] John von Neumann (1903–1957), a pioneer of modern game theory, warned against the alienation of a mathematical discipline to a purely aestheticising art through generations: a "disorganized mass of details and complexities".[30] We get a clear view. In particular at accounting, valuation and auditing as a domain of the law (financial reporting), often scorned and defamed as remote "numbers stuff" (*Zahlenkram*). The basis of capital markets and the human corporation as a sustainable financial instrument, which has to be filled with life with relation to the actual circumstances for careful governance and compliance (see 8.3); on capital markets that establish a much more sustainable economy and freedom instead of the "numbers game".

This promotes prosperity under the imperative of truth (see 8.4) in the rule of law (*Herrschaft des Rechts*) internationally.[31] Where this is lacking as a measure and mean (*Maß und Mitte*), arbitrariness ensues, which like anything too much or too little has a destructive force. It is not the capitalist idea of free markets that has failed. Immoderation, personal greed and ignorance have led to ruin. Jurisprudence demands enlivening the market economy of the human corporation in a sustainable way with scientific expertise:[32] The law provides measure and form in an ethically based way for the economy as a matter that has to be regulated reasonably. Accordingly, the boundaries have to be sounded out all around, in particular for the so-called "socio-ecological" transformation of the economy, in order for it to be soundly established sustainably. That is the necessary search for reasonableness[33] for a system of prosperity that entrepreneurially reconciles and supports humans, economy and nature in a sustainable way.[34]

### *8.2.3 Liberty: Regulation, Science, and Materiality*

Thus it is about a great, a sustainable goal. The Copernican turn, long since demanded for good corporate governance in economy and society (see 7.9),[35] paves the way for a

[29]Knight (1921/1971) pp. 11-12. Overall above 7.3.3, with Milton Friedman (2002/1962), chapter XIII (highlighting, p. 200, that the relevant interests "include the whole range of values that men hold dear and for which they are willing to spend their fortunes and sacrifice their lives"). See below 8.2.3 on Brandeis (in *Olmstead*) and accordingly Friedman (2002/1962) pp. 201-202.

[30]Cited after Dore, Chakravarty, and Goodwin (1989) p. XIV.

[31]Insightful on the international legal order Bingham (2010) pp. 110-129.

[32]See 8.2.3 and, on the character of sustainability (*Nachhaltigkeit*), above 5.2.4.

[33]See chapter 9. Luttermann (1998a) pp. 482-485.

[34]Overall see 8.1, 8.5 and chapter 9.

[35]Luttermann (2011), also Luttermann (2010a), (2019a).

reasonable order and practice. For this, the corporation need not be reinvented as the entrepreneurial wheel of incentive, but needs to be designed and made use of in a sensible way with sustainable financial reporting and auditing for further development (see 8.4). This requires new minds and measures that integrate the green paradigm change in a constitution of liberty. It lives in the spirit of humanism, such as the principles of the United Nations, through the culture of responsibility, to be practised every day individually, in a legal community, to which any business activity belongs. Sustainability is not a new-fangled phenomenon, but rather an intrinsic principle of human existence with jurisprudence and economy (see 5.2.4).

This is elementary for the human corporation and a good economy, as already described (see 8.1). It is about work of man, in natural imperfection and uncertainty, which requires order. The idea of constitutional liberty, the authority (*Herrschaft*) of reasonable rules, holds according to all experience: The law invisibly secures action spaces, where humans respect and support each other as free and equal.[36] John Stuart Mill described it as "the principal question in human affairs" what these rules should be, in terms of civil liberty against tyranny.[37] Basically, it is about the integration of power, about the unity of individual liberty and responsibility (see chapter 7), which aims at careful action in an orderly established ("effective") market:[38] Discernment and faith in the "invisible hand" (Adam Smith) while renouncing authoritarian direction that forces one's own values on other people; in particular here, palpable in the digital age of mass information patterns as boon and bane alike, where the progress of knowledge and science may open up new horizons (see 9.5).

This is what the green paradigm shift has a strong impact on, obviously on a global scale. The Commission of the European Union has presented its Green Deal as "a roadmap for making the EU's economy sustainable by turning climate and environmental challenges into opportunities across all policy areas and making the transition just and inclusive for all".[39] The President of the Commission Ursula von der Leyen has called this the "new growth strategy – for a growth that gives back more than it takes away" and it "shows how to transform our way of living and working, of producing and consuming so that we live healthier and make our businesses innovative."[40] – A brave new world? – The steering function of financial regulation (*Lenkfunktion*, see 1.5.3) is systematically conceived, for the so-called "false" allocation of resources to be avoided or corrected. U.S. President Joe Biden initiated a sweeping public climate and social spending program: the landmark

[36] On Savigny already above 2.2.2.

[37] Mill (1859) p. 22 (chapter I). Cf. above 6.7.3 with Locke.

[38] See above 2.6.1 (the market as an orderly event), Hayek (1960), esp. chapter 5, and Hayek (1991) pp. 481-497. See also above 7.3, 7.4.2, 7.7.2, chapter 6 and 3.3.4. Basically on "capital" Luttermann (1998a) pp. 5-30, and pp. 135-357 (corporation finance in view of comparative law), pp. 358-452 (valuation and accounting law in the USA); cf. Pistor (2019) p. 7, from p. 47 and from p. 158.

[39] European Commission, 11.12.2019: https://ec.europa.eu/commission/presscorner/detail/en/ip_19_6691 (accessed: 25.08.2025).

[40] Ibid.

clean-energy law cost about $1.2 trillion, meant to spur another $3 trillion investments in climate-friendly ventures.[41] U.S. President Donald Trump may propagate different roads,[42] whereas federal states in the US go further in climate protection.[43] Capital is thus to flow into sustainable economic activity (so-called "green projects") in a regulatory way.

Whichever way it is conceived: The qualification as "sustainable" (green) marks the distinction between "good" and "evil". A gigantic endeavour, one with substantial consequences, financially in particular and overall, also socially. How far will this go: generally or in fact aimed at applications, industries, research questions? – This is hardly predictable, however, the "social credit system" Chinese style acts as a warning.[44] Consequently, the triad "human, economy and environment" (Mensch, Wirtschaft und Umwelt) in the global economy and geopolitics is widened to where liberty and justice is hardly at home. Vigilance is required everywhere, also here with us for good regulation. This is part of the juridical analysis of the economy, the capital market and standardisation, so that well-meaning wishes for distributive or "social" justice do not mutate into state dirigism.[45] In any case, so-called "green" is no reason, not even an excuse, for arbitrariness or folly, for totalitarian or autocratic action. Let us remember Louis D. Brandeis, the people's lawyer (see 7.4.3):

> "Experience should teach us to be most on our guard to protect liberty when the Government's purposes are beneficent. Men born to freedom are naturally alert to repel invasion of their liberty by evil-minded rulers. The greatest dangers to liberty lurk in insidious encroachment by men of zeal, well meaning but without understanding."[46]

---

[41] Inflation Reduction Act of 2022, Pub.L. 117-169, according to Goldman Sachs Group Inc. (www.bloomberg.com/news/articles/2023-03-23/goldman-sees-biden-s-clean-energy-law-costing-us-1-2-trillion?leadSource=uverify%20wall, accessed: 25.08.2025). Cf. Bistline, Mehrotra, Wolfram (2023).

[42] U.S. President, Executive Order "Putting America first in international environmental agreements", Jan. 20, 2025, to withdraw the US from the Paris Agreement of 2015 (see above 1.4.2). Cf. basically Strine (2025), Lipton (2025).

[43] On California Franklin and MacDonald (2024). On climate change *Juliana v. United States* 947 F.3d 1159 (9th Cir. 2020) with *Juliana v. United States* 2024 U.S. Dist. LEXIS 71759 (D. Or., Apr. 19, 2024); on a SEC climate reporting rule *States of Texas, Louisiana, Utah and West Virginia v. SEC*, Litigation No. 23-60079 (5th Cir., May 5, 2024). On anti-ESG legislation: Padfield (2023); cf. Roe (2021) and Strine (2025). Basically *Loper Bright Enterprises v. Raimondo*, 603 U.S. 369 (2024), on this Malone and Holland (2024).

[44] See above 2.3.1 (with references).

[45] Luttermann (1998a) p. 482, on the EU "green deal" Luttermann (2021). Cf. above 6.6.1.

[46] Brandeis, dissenting, in *Olmstead v. U.S.*, 277 U.S. 438, 479 (1928). Accordingly Friedman (2002/1962) pp. 201 and 202. See above 7.3.3, 7.4.3. Cf. Applebaum (2024) p. 15: "the leaders of Autocracy, Inc., know that the language of transparency, accountability, justice, and democracy will always appeal to some of their own citizens. To stay in power they must undermine those ideas, wherever they are found." See 8.3.2, above 1.4.2 and overall chapters 6 and 7 (esp. 7.7).

The purpose of regulation (*ratio legis*), id est good regulation, is to safeguard liberty.[47] With this in mind, limitations of liberty – also in the environmental area – are always exceptions and must respect the essentials on all hands. The juridical analysis comprises the sciences, factually with the help of the best available insights (*Erkenntnisse*) for the concrete circumstances (*Lebensverhätnisse*). What is guiding for constitutional order are the imperatives of truth, materiality and transparency. This includes clear, scientifically based norms (regulation), democratically legitimised and independently controlled (separation of powers). This comprises the private and state actors as well as ideological reduction – of course also by so-called "scientists";[48] take a look, e.g., at the discourse on nuclear energy. The juridical analysis has only just begun – with all disciplines, for progressing balance worldwide (see chapter 9).

## 8.3 The Human Corporation for Common Wealth

### *8.3.1 Sustainable Finance Model of the Corporation*

The human corporation must be integrated in a sensible way into this evolving world. The corporation as a human creation (see 7.3.1) in its nature and development is, as we have shown,[49] an entrepreneurial venture community (*Wagnisgemeinschaft*): Its financing is elementary and contractually connects the capital providers (*Kapitalgeber* – investors) as a legal community (*Vermögensordnung*) in the unity of liberty and responsibility (*Freiheit und Verantwortung*, see 1.3.2); for this, market-based structures of careful leadership and valuation (duty of care, *Sorgfaltspflicht*) are at work, personal managerial responsibility lies on the corporate directors, id est good corporate governance as compliance (see 8.3.2). This is sustainably expressed and, particularly with regard to liability law, tangibly in financial reporting under the imperative of truth (see 8.4). This means that the corporation is a substantial instrument, with the help of which entrepreneurially sustainable business activity may be – globally – built (see 8.5).

For this, the sustainable financing model of the corporation forms a reasonable basis. It is market-based with contract law and secured civil procedures, as already explained (esp. chapters 2, 3 and 5). The investors jointly finance an enterprise

---

[47] Cf. controversial U.S. President Donald Trump: Kagan, J. (with whom Sotomayor and Jackson, JJ., join), dissenting, in *Trump v. Wilcox,* 605 U.S. ____ (2025), writes, the President has chosen "to take the law in his own hands" and not "leaving to this Court the prerogative of overruling its own decisions". Cf. Baude (2025), Gould (2025); generally Strine (2025). Basically on the limits of state regulatory power Humboldt (1792), Mill (1859). Cf. with *lex mercatoria* Schultz (2014) on stateless law and international arbitration (transnational legality).

[48] Hayek (1991) p. 489.

[49] In particular chapters 2, 3 and 4. Note esp. above 3.6 on the concept of the liable capital (*Haftkapital*) of the corporation.

(project). At the core, financing is about valuation questions, about sustainable financial reporting and auditing of the corporation: Accounting truth (*Bilanzwahrheit*, substance) and accounting clarity (*Bilanzklarheit*, transparency) have to be sustainably established.[50] This entails the rejection of insubstantial, one-sided value creation with the "numbers game" (i.e. "shareholder value") and accompanying financial theories. They are based on value-maximising management behaviour for the valuation of corporate equity (or debt) securities: phrased as an efficient market hypothesis in a multifarious network with puffy asset pricing and free cash flow models (so-called "economic model") or classically by investors in a balance-based way determined with the help of also ballooned reported earnings per share, capitalised in standard comparisons (so-called "accounting model of the firm").[51]

Overall with valuation of corporate assets (*Vermögen*), it is about the transfer of value (wealth), id est financially about realised risks (loss – *Verlust*) or realised chances (profit – *Gewinn*). The reasonable regulation of valuation (i.e. accounting and auditing), procedurally with reference to facts and materiality under the imperative of truth in financial reporting (*Bilanzwahrheit*, see 8.4), is the basis of an adequate order of assets (*Vermögensordnung*).[52] Accordingly, the corporate directors must act responsibly (see 8.3.2) and their practice has to be controlled, id est sustainability must be ensured through independent audit (auditors, judicial protection). This prevents one-sided valuations and valuation concepts (e.g., "shareholder value") and thereby too much shift of assets (wealth) between corporate debt and corporate equity (securities holders). In 2009, Detlev Vagts in the face of the global financial meltdown emphasised: The regulation of securities "consists of control over accounting and financial reporting" and "the world no longer looks to the U.S. GAAP as the global gold standard"[53] (see chapter 6).

This designates the core that finally needs to be cured. Questionable transfer of wealth is carried out systematically, at the micro- and the macro-economic level, with financial instruments and valuation patterns (so-called "fair value" in U.S. "GAAP", "IFRS", "IVS"); in addition, there is standard setting for "sustainability disclosure":[54] the massive monopolisation is progressing according to plan (see 4.11). Whether regarding the financing of companies with forms formally under the law of obligations (hybrid instruments), also dealt as investment products, or in high frequency trading of the derivate markets: Risks are still massively transformed (securitization, see 6.6.4, 6.8.5) and shifted. Globally, the private and state debt excesses, massive currency manipulations (fiat money) with zero interest policies or

[50]See above, esp. chapters 4 and 5. Luttermann (2004) and (2015a).

[51]See above 7.4.2. Donald Chew in: Stern and Chew (1992) p. XI. On this Luttermann (1998a) pp. 221 et seq.

[52]Luttermann (2015a), (2012) and (2010a).

[53]Vagts (2009) 684, 686. Cf. already Berle and Means (1932/1967) pp. 182-183: control over accounting. See chapter 3.

[54]See above 8.2.3, below 8.3.3 and 8.4.3; basically 5.2.4. Luttermann (2009a).

immoderate cash generation by the central banks are rampant, while the actors still pretend to be innocent. Inflationing is eating up savings, pension plans: confiscation (*Enteignung*) without a legal basis. Fraud, greed and arbitrariness are still dominant, as 2023 the fiasco of the Credit Swiss Group AG[55] and collapsing system-relevant banks in the USA (Silicon Valley Bank, Signature Bank)[56] far transcending companies and markets have again proven. A true gold standard is lacking.[57]

It was never a gold standard that U.S. "GAAP" and their offshoot "IFRS" constituted, as has early on been shown for adequate financing, valuation and disclosure of the corporation (good corporate governance).[58] The classically nationally focussed *corporation law* as organisational law is suitable only to a certain degree for reasonable regulation. What is decisive for the corporation is its material substance, which *valuation law* also regulates as capital markets law for financial reporting (see 8.4.2). Let us again return to Berle and Means, who warned: "So long as accounting standards are not hardened, and the law does not impose any specific canons, directors and their accountants may frame their figures, within limits, much as they choose".[59] The possibilities, including the creation of "hidden reserves", are manifold: "the directors may route the earnings by merely arranging that in certain years there shall be none, and in other years they shall be large."[60] – Reasonably, the corporation has to be understood as a permanent financial instrument (see chapter 3) and, hence, to be regulated in a sustainable way.

### *8.3.2 Accountability: A System of Corporate Valuation and Repersonalisation*

A reasonable law in general and particularly the sound solution of conflicts always require a comprehensive view. Here, the corporate directors are in the focus in particular as managing directors (e.g. in German: *Vorstände*, § 76 AktG), as has been shown (see chapter 7). They lead the corporation as a permanently organised financial instrument in personal responsibility (*Verantwortung*). They thus have at their disposal the financial means of the investors (securities holders), id est other people's money, acquired mainly through capital market contractual law (securities

[55] See, e.g. Bebchuck (2023), Rossi (2023). See above 7.1.

[56] Both classified by the Federal Reserve and the U.S. Treasury as systemic risk to the financial system; see also First Republic Bank, First National Bank of Lindsay, Pulaski Savings Bank. FDIC, 25.02.2025: U.S. banks held $482.4 billion in total unrealized losses on securities investments. Overall Bhagat and Laurion (2024), Shikha and Kapsis (2024). Gupta, French, Kelly (2025).

[57] See above 8.2.1 and 6.6.2, 7.3.3, below 8.4.3 and fundamentally Greenspan (1967), Luttermann (2008) and (2017).

[58] Overall Luttermann (1998a) and (1999b); in English: Luttermann (2007a, 3rd ed. 2017); see here chapter 4. Luttermann (2015a).

[59] Berle and Means (1932/1967) p. 182.

[60] Ibid.

as "risk constellations"), which is in manifold ways designed as debt, equity or hybrid securities.[61] For this, they owe accountability, financial reporting on the material business operations: the timeless protection to effectively prevent people from making the results seem better than in fact they are, the proof of good corporate governance (see chapter 4). A synonym for this sustainability is verifiability (*Nachprüfbarkeit*, see 5.2.4).

This shows the core of corporate law, which is founded in accounting law – remember, without financing there is no corporation at all. We have shown a capital market concept that is comprehensively designed,[62] in which the human corporation is integrated, in particular through its corporate directors: They have to act carefully as entrepreneurs and to inform the investors about their dealings under the imperative of truth (*Bilanzwahrheit*). This holds worldwide (see 8.4) and basically includes all questions of valuation. For it is about the appraisal of business (see chapter 5), value transfer and the marketable (profit-related) financial instruments: They are "substantially meaningless", as far as "provisions definitely regulating the corporation's accounting" do not exist.[63] This comprises the whole field of the corporation, financing and investment, also known as trust relationship between directors and investors. Already in 1928, even before the great Wall Street stock market crash (New York 1929), Adolf Berle wrote far-sightedly on the corporate accounts, which he was to reiterate later in his work with Gardiner Means on the modern corporation and private property,[64] as follows:

> "a corporate management which, as individuals, chooses to enter the open market and which at the same time exercises control over the release of information concerning corporate affairs, can deal with the current value of its securities, if not at pleasure, at least with tremendous effect; and the liquid value of the corporate securities held by the stockholders becomes a matter which the corporate management itself can determine."[65]

However, the responsibility (due diligence) of the corporate directors entails more. It relates to the corporation as a whole, in particular in its function as a financial instrument to be organised on a long-term scale. This is what it stands for in the real economy as a legal person, a fiction of the law, the limited liability and business foundation of which are materialised in its assets (see chapter 3). This means it is about the investors as a whole, responsibility of the corporate directors applying to all corporate securities held by stockholders or bondholders: this has to be determined under valuation law (see chapters 4 and 5). Every investor in the power structure of the market depends on this, even where there are protection mechanisms for shareholders. For in the publicly-held corporation, where the shareholders do not form a homogenous group either, they can hardly effectively bring up their interests

---

[61] See above 8.3.2, altogether 3.6.3. Basically Luttermann (1998a), esp. pp. 177-357.

[62] Luttermann (2003) Einf BilanzR, from recital 19, esp. 26-43. Overall see esp. chapters 3 to 5 and 7.

[63] Berle and Means (1932/1967) p. 183.

[64] As already quoted above in 8.3.1.

[65] Berle (1928) p. 180.

on the basis of corporate law. The asset component of the share property is dominant. They are addressed not as co-shareholders with easily transferrable standard products (shares), but predominantly as financiers of the company with a share in the profits ("shareholder value").[66]

This can in fact be of use. The basic structure corresponds to the function of the corporation as a financial instrument for larger, long-term enterprises (projects), as they are imminent at present with the transformation of the economy to sustainable business activity (see chapter 1). For the human corporation, this normatively presupposes a clear order of assets as a legal framework, providing adequate protection against unlawful transfer of assets (wealth) for all financiers of the corporation – among each other and with regard to further actors (see 8.3.1): This requires careful, sustainable action by the corporate directors, based on financial reporting, id est sound valuation law (see chapter 5).[67] This is mandatory, no matter what circumstances and theories may currently predominate. Accordingly, discourses have to be focussed that run along the usual categories concerning the corporation, e.g. "separation of ownership and control" (classically) or "separation of ownership from ownership" by institutional investors (pension funds, hedge funds) right up to "common ownership".[68]

Basically, it is about personal responsibility (see chapter 7), the control of power – no matter where it is based – in an adequate system of accountability: For power respects only counter-power. This is what a company law founded in accounting law (*Bilanzrecht*) is meant for, on which corporate law and capital market law order are based.[69] With this, the managing directors come to the forefront responsibly. This includes the supervisory directors, auditors and all persons bearing responsibility privately or officially in boards of control, legislation and standardisation, in law courts. It is about and – with the personalised responsibility – against the "depersonalisation" not only "of ownership",[70] but of the corporation as such. If this is understood as a financially organised instrument (legal person), acting solely through responsible humans (organs),[71] it must be established as a *Sondervermögen* (special fund, see 2.4.3) in valuation law terms: In an accountability system, that may lead "toward sustainable, sound long-term corporate growth",[72] and, to put it more clearly, to sustainable prosperity.

---

[66] Luttermann (2003) Einf BilanzR, esp. recitals 28-31. Note above 3.6 on the concept of the liable capital (*Haftkapital*) of the corporation. Cf. altogether above 3.7, also on new kinds of "corporation" (e.g., with AM and/or AI), also below 9.6.

[67] Ibid., recitals 32-39.

[68] See above 3.5.6 and 6.5.1.

[69] E.g., above 5.5 (legal objectives for proper valuation) and 5.6 (judicial practise). Luttermann (2003) Einf BilanzR, esp. recitals 34-43. Basically Luttermann (1998a) pp. 486-539 (511-512) on a hybrid financial instrument (*Investitionsgenußschein* – investment participation certificate).

[70] Already on this Walther Rathenau, *Von Kommenden Dingen*, Berlin 1918, cited by Berle and Means (1932/1967) p. 309.

[71] In detail above 7.3.1 on the structure of the corporation, and chapter 9.

[72] Strine (2014) 449. Cf. above in 3.7 (on the evolution of corporate structures). Overall above 2.6 (financial reporting for a better world), and chapter 9.

### 8.3.3 *Sustainability: Due Diligence of Corporate Directors and Communication*

Altogether, it is about sustainability in a holistic sense. The valuation of the corporation and its financial reality (equity, debt and hybrids) is not, though widely practised this way, arbitrary dealing with models, expectations and calculations in the "numbers game". A field of the law, valuation and financial reporting are legal acts, for which accountability stands as the proof of good corporate governance: verified information (see chapter 4). The life circumstances therefore have to be established with financial reporting (accounting and auditing) in an order of assets, the basis of the economy and society. Designed by humans as responsible entrepreneurs (see chapter 7) in the sense of a legal order sustainably, id est accountably. That classic legal character of sustainability coins the law dimension (human rights, environment).[73] This forms the true nature of sustainability (see 5.2.4), the due diligence of corporate directors and financial communication.

For the human corporation, in its economic substance as well as its legal determination (norm, contract), valuation is a communicative process.[74] For the market actors, corporate disclosure (financial reporting) constitutes the crucial element. Financial statements inform in a normative way, id est responsibly and verifiably signed by the corporate directors, on the circumstances of the undertaking (assets, liabilities, financial position, profit or loss). Practised thoroughly, the corporation thus becomes sustainably – and indeed at all – effective in its financing function: Investors can evaluate the corporate securities as the object of business on the basis of the financial statements, contractually as performance and consideration. For good management, financing and valuation of corporations, id est also for their digital and "socio-economic" transformation (see 8.4), the communication patterns (form, method) and the content have to be clarified with regard to sustainability (valuation law, law of evidence)[75] under the imperative of truth. This provides the measure for diligent action (due diligence) in all respects.

Accordingly, valuation (financial reporting) has to be structured communicatively, as required by the imperative of truth: clearly and sustainably. Working communication through truthful information of the corporate investors is fundamental for entrepreneurial creation of value in the legal order organised as a market economy and for the success of the corporation as a whole (cf. efficient-market

[73] See, e.g., in European law the Corporate Sustainability Due Diligence Directive (EU) 2024/1760, 13.06.2024, OJ L, 05.07.2024. Globally ICJ, Advisory Opinion: Obligations of states in respect of climate change, 23.07.2025 (https://www.icj-cij.org/sites/default/files/case-related/187/187-20250723-adv-01-00-en.pdf, accessed: 25.08.2025), on that see above 8.1, 1.2 and 6.1 (esp. 6.1.3).

[74] See chapter 5, above 4.12 (esp. 4.12.3 on information as creation of value), 5.3.4 and 7.6. Luttermann (2000a) 459, 464-465 (on valuation and accounting law as law of information). Luttermann (2023) recitals 91-95.

[75] Fundamentally chapter 5 with a civil-procedural concept. See also chapter 7.

hypothesis and 8.2.2);[76] right up to the avoidance of liability and legal sanctions, e.g. due to false or obscure presentation.[77] Law of evidence helps and supports here (see chapter 5) in financial reporting and generally in the financial spectrum of normative information relevant to valuation (disclosure), e.g., also in the key information documents (so-called *Basisinformationsblatt*) informing potential investors about the risk profile regarding investment products.[78] Good communication is therefore not an aim in itself, but a management programme of the directors of the human corporation (digital financial communication).

Information is conveyed by word and writing (image), by language that is as clear as possible: Truth and clarity are naturally paired.[79] They form good communication that is – normatively – adequate for the given context. What should be noted is: Numbers do not prove anything. It is only their explication (balance sheet item, note), as well as narrative elements that denote the given fact of life. According to the situation, information should be comprehensible regarding the actual circumstances, in general that is the value-creating factors, with the help of which valuation takes place (*verkehrswesentliche Eigenschaften*,[80] see 5.3.4): not fictions but facts (from Latin *factum* for a deed, reality, truth), id est "events or circumstances as distinct from their legal interpretation".[81] This is the basis of any valuation of the human corporation and its financial statements (disclosure) as the proof of good corporate governance; this only holds conditionally, under the fiction of a "unitary business", for consolidated financial statements.[82] As a whole, with the imperative of truth (*Wahrheitsgebot*) this provides a human measure.

It serves the corporate directors and market actors (auditors, investors, regulators, analysts) as a basis for carefully coordinating and sustainably securing their actions with regard to civil procedure (see chapters 5 and 7): A legal order as an order of

[76] Basically Fama (1970) and (1991). Altogether Luttermann (1998a) pp. 210-237.

[77] See above 7.5.3, 6.5.3 (U.S. Justice Manual: 6.8.2). In Germany: §§ 399, 400 AktG, § 82 GmbHG, §§ 331. 332, 340m, 341m HGB, § 266 StGB. Also 4.9 (EU).

[78] See Regulation (EU) No 1286/2014, 26.11.2014 on key information documents for packaged retail and insurance-based investment products (PRIIPs), OJ EU, 09.12.2014, L 352/1 (as updated). Originally proposed as a so-called *Risikopass* (risk passport) generally for securities by Luttermann (2001) 1901, 1904-1905. Overall Luttermann (2015c), from 810 on comprehensibility (*Verständlichkeit*).

[79] See above 7.6.3. Basically Luttermann (2003) §§ 243, 342 HGB recitals 7-20 and 73 et seq., also Luttermann (2003) § 244 HGB recital 20 et seq. On legal linguistics Luttermann, C. and Luttermann, K. (2020) pp. 201 et seq. On the iconic character (*Bildhaftigkeit*) Großfeld (2019) pp. 18-19, from p. 37 and p. 63.

[80] In practical terms, this means: characteristics, that are essential for valuation (pricing) on the free market.

[81] The New Shorter Oxford English Dictionary (Clarendon Press Oxford 1993) vol 1, p. 903 (fact).

[82] See chapters 4 (esp. 4.7) and 9. In Germany § 297(3)(1) HGB: *"Im Konzernabschluß ist die Vermögens-, Finanz- und Ertragslage der einbezogenen Unternehmen so darzustellen, als ob diese Unternehmen insgesamt ein einziges Unternehmen wären."*, i.e., as if these companies as a whole were a single company – but they are not, they are, each in their own right, separate legal entities, see above 4.7. Cf. above 3.7 and 6.5.1 (common ownership).

assets in the unity of liberty and responsibility, which is structured financially with the human corporation. Immoderation must not overlay this, neither through regulation-related nor green, technologically or econometrically operated hypes (see chapter 6, esp. 6.8.5). Rather, what is needed – holistically in the sense of the true character of sustainability (see 8.4.3) – is scientific excellence, factually applied to the actual circumstances. What is expedient is an appropriate (*sachgerechtes*) concept of diligence for the entrepreneurial process of decision-making.[83] Overall, sustainable financial reporting provides the necessary support for human weakness and a guideline for verifiability: the more a valuation departs from facts, the more the protection of the law that it is eschewing wanes (see 5.6.2, 5.6.3 with Fig. 5.3).

## 8.4 The Planetary Imperative of Truth

### *8.4.1 Human Imperative of Fidelity*

Holistically, it is about the planetary community (*Weltgemeinschaft*, see 8.5, 6.1: climate partners).[84] With the human imperative of truth the global dimension moves into focus in view of worldwide crises, violence, human rights violations and environmental destruction. It is about the work of human beings, which includes the corporation as the core element of entrepreneurial action (see chapters 1, 9). In progress, the sensible constitution of our liberty takes effect: individualism, as already described by Adam Smith in a system of regulated market forces, which is promoted by all humans in their diversity as far as possible.[85] The task is enormous. Basically, it is about war and peace worldwide.[86] Humans, the economy and the environment have to be reconciled sustainably.[87] A civil-humanistic, structured order, supported by international law, may globally mediate financially across the capital markets. The human corporation refers to this with sustainability in its true nature (see 8.4.3). Sensible investment protection serves the avoidance (resp. solution) of conflict and business success for overall prosperity.

---

[83] Innovative Luttermann, L. (2022), (2023) and (2024) with a concept of sustainable financial due diligence.

[84] Luttermann (2022) German original: *"Klimapartner einer kooperativen Weltvermögensordnung"*, on this see above 6.1 (esp. 6.1.1 with translation at the very end).

[85] See chapters 7 and 9. Fundamentally Hayek (1991) p. 486 (footnote 7).

[86] See above 1.2. Pioneering work during the Thirty Years' War Hugo Grotius, *De iure belli ac pacis libri tres* (1625). See also Keynes (1919) on economically sustainable conditions. Cf., e.g., Bingham (2010) chapter 10, with p. 114 ("self-interest of states"), p. 120-129 ("War"), and Kissinger (2015). On "Bretton Woods II" Luttermann (2009c). See also ICJ, 23.07.2025 (see following footnote).

[87] Groundbreaking ICJ, Advisory Opinion: Obligations of states in respect of climate change, 23.07.2025 (https://www.icj-cij.org/sites/default/files/case-related/187/187-20250723-adv-01-00-en.pdf, accessed: 25.08.2025), on that above 8.1, 1.2 and 6.1.

The legal concept of an international, global order of assets (*Vermögensordnung*) has been articulated.[88] Economy (prosperity – *Wohlstand*) and the law (justice – *Gerechtigkeit*) with its primacy condition each other in a consistent yet dynamic relation over time. In the perspective of a sustainably structured global commercial law (*Weltwirtschaftsrecht*), investments form the basis for a sustainable global economy, peace and prosperity. In the transnational capital movement, the financially effective element of sustainable development, it is – classically – about the protection of foreign direct investments: A foreign, private legal subject (humans or legal persons such as the corporation) invests in the sovereign territory of another state. The investment transfers assets (prosperity) of a nationally conceived and organised community (jurisdiction, national economy) to another jurisdiction (national economy, see 8.4.2). This means it is about a, nationally and internationally, state-coined order of assets (cf. on DAOs: 3.7). This affects private law and international law. The legal motif for business practice: establishing an adequate legal framework internationally, which promotes and protects private investments through sensible coordination – all in all, complementarily (see chapter 9).

This is a holistic conception, relating to the human being. The legal concept for a reasonable structure crystallises and lives in the imperative of fidelity (*Treuegebot*), integrated into an international order of assets[89] – for more to come (see 8.5). The life circumstances of people in the economy and the environment must be treated sensibly; this goes hand in hand with statecraft (*Staatskunst*, see 8.4.2). Whether transfer of capital and technology, jobs, export promotion, free capital movement and protection of property, as in international investment agreements:[90] In contracts between human beings, sustainability builds on reciprocity (Latin *do ut des*) and integrity, id est *bona fides* (see 8.4.3; cf. "fair and equitable treatment"). This comprises the procedural level formally and the content level materially. Both make reference to each other: Capital turns into assets through investment, which under the premise of accounting truth has to be fairly valued and protected nationally and internationally. The idea of justice takes effect here universally on a practical level in the imperative to act faithfully.

## *8.4.2 Measure of Valuation: Valuation Statute (*Lex Aestimatio*)*

For an international order of assets, private and international law have to be ordered with the necessary material content (substance). Statecraft (*Staatskunst*) is above all about recognising the limits of its effectivity. Here, private autonomy comes to the

---

[88] Luttermann (2012) and (2015b) with more references; in English Luttermann (2015a).

[89] Luttermann (2015b) pp. 274, 280-281.

[90] On this: https://unctad.org/topic/investment/international-investment-agreements (accessed: 25.08.2025).

fore as the core of human economic community for general prosperity: assets (private property, *Privateigentum*) are legally attributed to a legal subject (human, legal person), thereby at the same time being separated from other spheres of property (*Eigentumssphären*). This is the basis of a free society, in which everyone orders their affairs according to their own responsibility, entering into contractual relations with other asset holders (*Vermögensträger*).[91] The freedom of contract for personal development, which fundamentally includes the corporation, is thus, with the imperative of fidelity, integrated into the common whole of the human being as a social, entrepreneurial being, supported by the law. Of course, all fellow human beings (human rights) and the environment have to be integrated in their need for protection (see 8.4.3).

In the constitution of liberty, this is demanded by the imperative of truth, which is guiding for the law of the corporation and an order of assets. Sustainable valuations form its material core, without which any order is a fallacious facade: Technically, it is about its substance and that of each of the individual assets (facts, see chapter 5), for foreign investments, about the height of compensation claims (compensation, damages, restitution) right up to expropriation.[92] Legally, this is a wide field, which is internationally lying largely in a state of disorder and waste. In valuation, manifold ideas, as has already been shown,[93] and colourful approaches with so-called "fair value" as broadly arbitrarily arranged hope values (*beigelegte Zeitwerte*, see 7.5.2), are at work. They distort the actual circumstances of the corporation, promoting transfers of wealth (assets), flitting about in transnational capital markets around the globe: right up to a world monopoly of valuation of corporations and assets organised by private profiteers, established in digital form (eXBRL/IFRS) – uncontrolled systems (opinions) "embedded in code" and big data (artificial intelligence, AI, see 6.8.5).[94]

What about sustainability? – Important actors, the USA, remain reticent. Even where practice runs more or less officially under "IFRS", specifics have to be taken into account. In Australia, e.g., corporate law records strong reservations protecting national, economic interests,[95] China is striking out on its own.[96] – What sovereign would accept a foreign dictate, in particular regarding the order and valuation of assets (*Vermögen*), the core of economy and society? – The European Union, dedicated to its humanistic values (Art. 2 and 3 TEU), regulates on the basis of conflict of laws (*Kollisionsrecht*, international private law – IPR), with reference to the actual circumstances (*Lebensverhältnisse*, see *ordre public*: 4.4.4). This marks

[91] As individualistically already described (above 8.4.1) with Adam Smith; see also 2.2.2 (Savigny, Hayek).

[92] Overview: Marboe et al. in Bungenberg, Griebel, Hobe, and Reinisch (2015) chapter 9 on restitution, damages and compensation.

[93] See overall with examples and references chapters 4 to 7.

[94] See for quotation above 6.6.3 (O'Neil), see also 4.11 (world monopoly) and chapter 9 (esp. 9.6).

[95] On this Luttermann (2007b). Comparatively above 4.8.5 (China, Japan, USA).

[96] See above 2.1 and 2.3.1. Luttermann (2017).

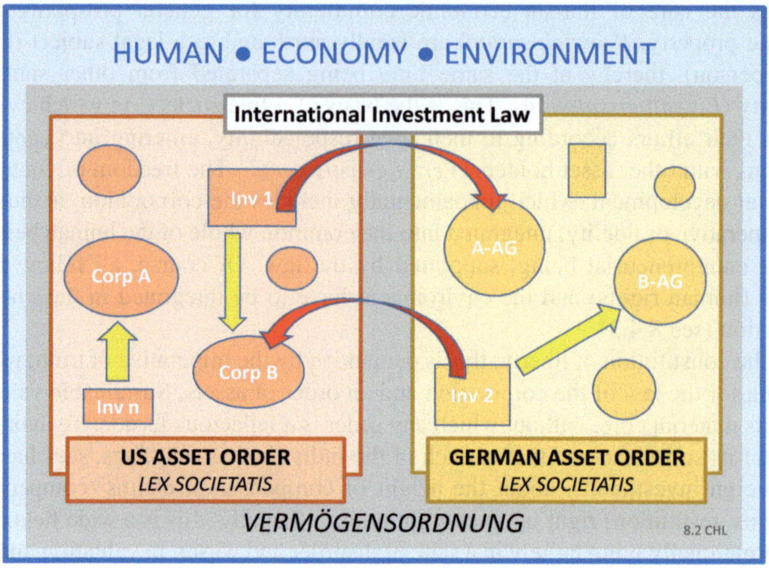


**Fig. 8.2** On the order of assets (*Vermögensordnung*) and transnational transfers according to *lex societatis*

the general norm of valuation law with the concept of the imperative of truth, as shown, on the basis of the law of evidence: International rules (such as the so-called "IFRS") are only allowed to be adopted in the Union if they correspond to the ethically founded general norm, the imperative of truth, and "the European public good".[97] The European Court of Justice fixes the general norm as "the primary objective" (*Hauptzielsetzung*) of making valuations and financial reporting.[98]

In the sense of sustainability (see 8.4.3), this marks a change of perspective. Hitherto, the corporation is conceived in the organisational framework of nationally informed corporation law, for transnational cases with conflict of laws with the according *lex societatis* (deed of partnership, *Gesellschaftsstatut*[99] – see Fig. 8.2). In economic terms, this goes hand in hand with a traditionally shaped economic view (v*olkswirtschaftliche Betrachtung*): transnational investment transfers capital across national borders from one national economy (*Volkswirtschaft* – nation, jurisdiction, e.g. USA) to another national economy (*Volkswirtschaft* – nation, jurisdiction, e.g. Germany, and vice versa). One economy (nation) thus suffers a disadvantage (capital outflow) – considerable in competition – while the other economy (nation)

---

[97] Art. 3(2) Regulation (EC) 1606/2002 of 19 July 2002 on the application of international accounting standards, with Art. 4(3)(1) Directive 2013/34/EEC (unchanged, formerly: Art. 2(3)(1) Directive 78/660/EEC). See above 4.4.3 to 4.4.6.

[98] ECJ, constant jurisdiction, e.g. judgment of 23.04.2020, C-640/18 (*Wagram Invest SA* – FR), ECLI:EU:C:2020:293, recitals 32, 34 (with further references).

[99] Großfeld in Staudinger (1998) recital 16 et seq.

gains an advantage (capital influx).[100] Under public international law, the principle of territoriality applies (*Territorialitätsprinzip*, *lex situs*), and taxation is also related to it.[101] On the whole, capital is the economic basis for investment, work and innovation, for prosperity and development.

The economic-national view emerges with the *lex societatis* for the corporation and, with it the nationally applicable company law (*Gesellschaftsrecht*),[102] which is formally characterised by organisational law. What is decisive for the legal relations of the corporation (e.g., claims to profit, taxation, liability) is, however, the estimation (from Latin *aestimo*, appraisal, German *Bewertung*). In legal dealings, the corporation becomes tangible only through its accounting picture (see 3.1). The corporation evolves, lives and ceases to be in the legal order as an order of assets according to certain valuation rules (*Bewertungsstatut*).[103] This holds respectively in other economic circumstances that have legal dimensions like network relations (see

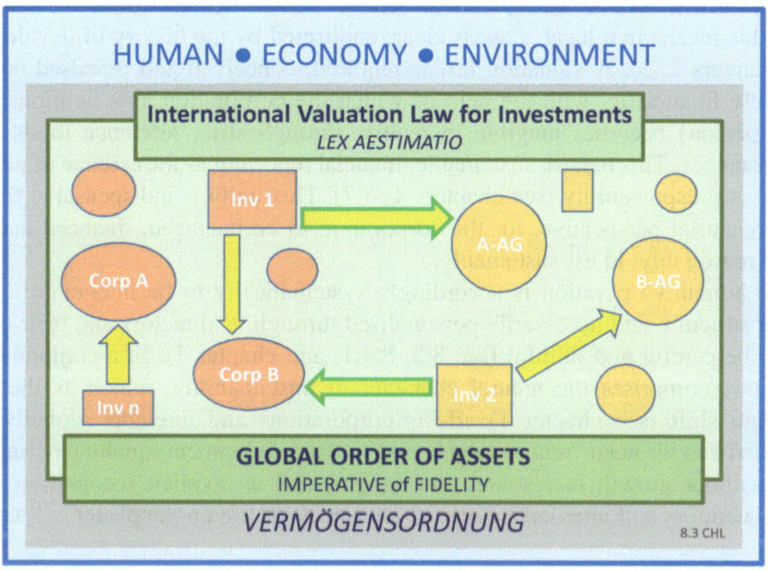


**Fig. 8.3** On the order of assets (*Vermögensordnung*) and international valuation law according to *lex aestimatio*

[100] See above 1.2 (on the "Westphalian system"), 1.3.1 and 1.6.2; cf. also 2.2.2 and 3.7, overall chapter 9. On the international allocation of assets (competition) and reform see 4.8.

[101] In Germany, e.g.: § 1(4) EStG, § 2 No. 1 KStG (*Quellenlandprinzip*, source country principle) and § 12 KStG (*Entstrickungs- und Wegzugsbesteuerung*, unbundling and exit taxation); cf. world income principle (*Welteinkommensprinzip*, in Germany: § 1(2) KStG). On the principle of territoriality for the European Union, e.g., Art. 4(2)(2) TEU. Also known as *lex rei sitae* or *lex loci*: the law of the place (country) where the property is situated.

[102] On the – traditionally national – creation of a corporation above 2.4.1 and 2.4.3 (legal characteristics of the modern corporation) with 7.3.1.

[103] Or *Bilanzstatut*: Luttermann (2010b) and Luttermann, Geißler (2012). See also above 7.6.

3.7: DAO). Altogether, it is thus about a holistic valuation law (*Bewertungsrecht*): A faithful picture of real values, which, as shown (see chapters 3 to 5, 7), are to be determined sustainably.[104] The law of valuation and financial reporting turns out to be – internationally in all of business life – the entrepreneurial core for legal dealings (i.e., business) with a human corporation (*lex aestimatio*, see Fig. 8.3).[105]

### 8.4.3 Exploring Sustainability's True Nature

Overall, for the human corporation and reasonable business activity, it is fundamentally about sustainability (*Nachhaltigkeit*, see 5.2.4). On this is based any order of assets as a legal order that may serve humans, the economy and the environment – also in the global dimension (see 8.5). The human corporation as a long-term financial instrument for enterprises (projects)[106] has to be established sustainably. What this means in a legal sense is clear, confirmed by the history of development (see chapters 2, 3). A valuation law is required, conceived and practised comprehensively financially, with the help of which the corporation as a fictitious entity (legal person) becomes tangible in reality, through strict reference to its actual circumstances. This means: sustainable financial reporting as the essence of personal liberty and responsibility (see chapters 4 to 7). This unity is indispensable from an entrepreneurial perspective, for the corporation to be managed, financed and controlled reasonably, id est sustainably.

The human corporation is accordingly systematically to be integrated into the market structure and necessarily personalised through its directors and their obligation to be careful and faithful (see 8.3, 8.4.1, and chapter 7). In a comprehensive view, this comprises the natural character of sustainability, which as the green paradigm shift (see chapter 1) affects corporations and directors globally. It is described that we need "real economic and social development (qualitative improvement without growth in resource throughput) and an explicit recognition of the interrelatedness and interdependence of all aspects of life on the planet".[107] Climate

---

[104] Cf. BVerfG, 26.07.2005 (1 BvR 782/94) NJW 2005, 2363, 2369-2370 (BVerfGE 114, 1, *Sachverständigengutachten*, expert opinion/testimony): This may be difficult, but as a rule it is "not practically impossible" (*"im Regelfall 'nicht praktisch unmöglich'"*). On "fair value" above 7.5 to 7.8 and Luttermann (2009a).

[105] Cf. Fig. 8.2. Basically on the *Bilanzstatut* (i.e. *Bewertungsstatut – lex aestimatio*) Luttermann (2010b). Also Luttermann (2015b) pp. 274, 280 (3.), Luttermann (2010d), Luttermann and Geißler (2012). For the European Union already Luttermann (2000b) on transnational financial reporting (valuation) instead of conflict of laws (*Kollisionsrecht*) with the ECJ, 09.03.1999 (C-212-97 – *Centros*, DA) ECLI:EU:C:1999:126.

[106] See in common perspectives above 2.3, 3.7, and 6.8.5. On permanence of the corporation (eternal asset holder, *ewiger Vermögensträger*) above 2.4.3.

[107] Costanza, Cumberland, Daly et al. (2015) p. 4 and pp. 116-119. Cf. above 2.1 (with translation) Goethe (1808), *Nacht* (night), Faust: *"Wie alles sich zum Ganzen webt! Eins in dem andern wirkt und lebt!"*.

risk as a financial risk must be integrated holistically.[108] The relation to the real economy corresponds to our concept of civil procedure, understanding the corporation in its financial function, its legal-factual circumstances and representing it with proof, id est in a sustainable way (see chapters 4, 5). This also holds for the accompanying life relations such as human rights und environment, which also have to be taken into consideration (due diligence).[109] So the concept is strengthened. What is and remains the yardstick are the facts. This demands a comprehensive scientific analysis.[110] The results form the sustainable basis for careful work (compliance, see 5.2.4).

This means that the imperative of truth (*Wahrheitsgebot*) as the measure, here as elsewhere in any life circumstance, sustains the entire governance, financing and valuation of the human corporation. It lives qualitatively in a system of capital market and information, designed by humans. This includes the valuation basis, financially reformed for a good economy (cf. public goods v. traditionally labor, land, capital), where the content of the real economy has long since evaporated (fiat money instead of sound money).[111] As shown, facts are largely lacking. The paradigm change is reminiscent of Niels Bohr, who made it clear for physics (the epitome of "exact" science) that it does not say what the world is like, but only what we can say about the world (see 4.6.5). This remains a guiding principle for our concept, which comprises all disciplines:[112] Information regarding the human corporation under the imperative of truth and fidelity includes everything those responsible are able to report substantially – the good, the bad and the ugly. This is what the law stands for in the constitution of liberty.

---

[108] Overall chapters 1, 2 (esp. 2.6.3, No. (3)). Fundamentally Williams (2021), e.g. Ortega (2023), Engen, Asdal (2024), Wetzer, Stuart-Smith, Dibley (2024); Luttermann, L. (2022), (2023) and (2024), (2025) first time with ECB supervisory data on sustainability: *Europäische Eröffnungsbilanz*; see also Luttermann, L. (2026). Cf. Bank for International Settlements (2021), EU Commission, Report on the monitoring of climate-related risk to financial stability, 28.06.2024 C(2024) 4372 final. See Lord Sales (2025).

[109] Corporate Sustainability Due Diligence Directive (EU) 2024/1760, esp. recitals 1 to 8 (SDGs) with 7: "All businesses have a responsibility to respect human rights, which are universal, indivisible, interdependent and interrelated.", and highlighting (recital 4), that it is "in the interest of companies to protect human rights and the environment, in particular given the rising concern of consumers and investors regarding these topics". See above 1.6.1 and Luttermann (2013). Groundbreaking globally ICJ, 23.07.2025 (see following footnote).

[110] Globally ICJ, Advisory Opinion: Obligations of states in respect of climate change, 23.07.2025 (https://www.icj-cij.org/sites/default/files/case-related/187/187-20250723-adv-01-00-en.pdf, accessed: 25.08.2025), paras. 72-87 (relevant scientific background), para. 300 with paras. 280-300 (due diligence standard), see overall on that above 8.1, 1.2 and 6.1.

[111] Luttermann (2008). This was obvious to Adam Smith, but hardly so to Berle and Means, see both (1932/1968) pp. 303-308, and their followers. Cf. Phelps (2007). See above 1.4.3, 1.5.2 and 7.3.3, below 9.7.

[112] Luttermann (2003) § 264 HGB recitals 125-128, Luttermann (2023) recitals 1-47.

## 8.5 Climate Partners of a Cooperative Global Asset Order[113]

Altogether, it is about humankind as the planetary community of the earth. Regauging the world for humans, the economy and the environment for a peace resting on the imperatives of reason, truth and justice. The juridical analysis of the economy, comprising the state, society and the environment, is meant for this purpose (see 8.2.2, 9.8). Jurisprudence provides the rules of ethical-practical reason, the concept of reason (*Verstandesbegriff*), which, accordingly, by subsumption in an act of judgement (*Aktus der Urteilskraft*) must be implemented reasonably. In this regard Immanuel Kant also underlines in cosmopolitan consideration: What applies to theory on the grounds of reason, also applies to practice.[114] Law is based on this in the idea of justice, as we have already described it as practised ethics (*Recht als praktizierte Ethik*, see 1.1). In this way, people, the economy and environment can be brought into harmony.

This is the framework that guides and supports every responsible person in individual cases (*Einzelfall*) and leads to the common good (*Gemeinwohl*). In the fundamental idea of justice, this triad sounds for the juridical analysis of the economy: power control (*Machtkontrolle*), wealth participation (*Wohlstandsteilhabe*) and the preservation of creation (*Schöpfungsbewahrung*). Correspondingly, with the human corporation and the financing (i.e., verifiable valuation and verified financial reporting) on global capital markets, it is about a globally reasonable, id est a sustainable architecture. This is needed in order to shape the world in a meaningful way through sustainable economic activity (*nachhaltige Wirtschaftstätigkeit*). In the climate change for human rights and the environment (so-called "green" paradigm shift, see 1.1), this has to be developed with the Charta of the United Nations (see 1.2) and its Agenda 2030 for Sustainable Development, which emphasises:[115]

> ***"Peace***
>
> We are determined to foster peaceful, just and inclusive societies which are free from fear and violence. There can be no sustainable development without peace and no peace without sustainable development.
>
> ***Partnership***
>
> We are determined to mobilize the means required to implement this Agenda through a revitalized Global Partnership for Sustainable Development, based on a spirit of

---

[113] Luttermann (2022).

[114] Overall Kant (1793) pp. 201-202 and 284. Cf. Luttermann (1998b).

[115] See – following on from above 8.2.1 – UN, General Assembly, Transforming our world: the 2030 Agenda for Sustainable Development, Resolution 25.09.2015, Preamble (A/RES/70/1: https://www.un.org/en/development/desa/population/migration/generalassembly/docs/globalcompact/A_RES_70_1_E.pdf, accessed: 25.08.2025), p. 2. Affirmative ICJ, Advisory Opinion: Obligations of states in respect of climate change, 23.07.2025 (https://www.icj-cij.org/sites/default/files/case-related/187/187-20250723-adv-01-00-en.pdf, accessed: 25.08.2025), paras. 140-142, 260-267 and 301-308, on this above 8.1, 1.2 and 6.1. Cf. already Luttermann (2022).

> strengthened global solidarity, focused in particular on the needs of the poorest and most vulnerable and with the participation of all countries, all stakeholders and all people.
>
> The interlinkages and integrated nature of the Sustainable Development Goals[116] are of crucial importance in ensuring that the purpose of the new Agenda is realized. If we realize our ambitions across the full extent of the Agenda, the lives of all will be profoundly improved and our world will be transformed for the better."

Integral thought conceives of the corporation in its financial function as an essential element of the solution, both in individual cases (microeconomics) and as a whole (macroeconomics). In the global economy, resources are used as if there were no tomorrow. Globally, we are all in the same boat, the Earth. This establishes the climate partnership, giving global incentives (cf. global commons). Common interest, to be developed as business ethics: sensibly cooperative with the principle of help for self-help[117] (*Hilfe zur Selbsthilfe*, see 1.3.3) and the sense for complementarity (*Komplementarität*, see chapter 9). Whoever has a special ability by nature (*Vermögen*, i.e. resource, talent resp. education) or by power (*Amt*, i.e. appointment) also bears a special responsibility. Human and environmental rights apply globally. This is underlined by the International Court of Justice[118] and recent jurisdiction (climate change litigation, see 8.4.3), establishing rights to life, health and clean environment. Accordingly, conflicts should be prevented, interests be harmonised. It is about transforming the economy, economic thinking and acting, sensibly in a reasonable way into a sustainable economy: a global *Vermögensordnung* (asset order).

The entrepreneurial culture of responsibility holds world-wide: fundamental for the corporation as well as overall for the financing of sustainable business activity. True and clear information, factual in the sense of sustainability – on a scientific basis according to the state of the art (*lege artis*) – carefully provided and checked (see chapters 4, 5), creates the necessary basis of trust among those involved;[119] without which the financial, capital-market concept of the corporation cannot work as set out in this book. Accordingly, regulation, currently undertaken in the course of the "socio-economic" transformation in the European Union and the USA,[120] has to be reasonably designed in a global perspective: Sustainable valuation and financial reporting, as verified (i.e. audited) information for investors of an enterprise. In a reasonable order of assets as a constitution of liberty, no state dirigisme, humans

---

[116] On the 17 Sustainable Development Goals (SDGs) of the United Nations: https://sdgs.un.org/goals and above 8.1, 8.2.1; overall chapters 1 and 2.

[117] Cf. above 1.6.1 (subsidiarity). On cooperation for environmental protection and human rights under the rule of law Bingham (2010) pp. 116-119, 129 (enforcement).

[118] See ICJ, Advisory Opinion: Obligations of states in respect of climate change, 23.07.2025 (https://www.icj-cij.org/sites/default/files/case-related/187/187-20250723-adv-01-00-en.pdf, accessed: 25.08.2025), paras. 371, 372-404; on this above 6.1.3.

[119] See above 1.5.2, chapter 6; Luttermann (2019b) and (2016), above 4.1 and 4.2.

[120] See above 8.2.3. Luttermann (2021) and, on sustainable financial due diligence Luttermann, L. (2024).

acting responsibly can create generally sustainable prosperity through sustainable financing (capital, investment).[121]

We, the trustees of the world, can built a better world. In a dialogue of cultures,[122] mindful of the limits of human cognition and law, yet with self-confidence within the manifold cultural spectrum as a creative force. United in a Copernican turn to the imperative of truth (*veritas*) and fidelity (*fides*)[123] urgently needed, id est facts (knowledge) and proof instead of illusions ("soft information"), where it is about life and justice. In a "philosophy of human affairs", designated by Aristotle, as ethically founded statecraft (Ancient Greek *politikē technē*).[124] Jurisprudence is the art of life, the law practised ethics.[125] This fundamentally includes the human corporation with its financing for a sustainable economic world, as shown, to restore the unity of freedom and responsibility (i.e. private autonomy and liability) by safeguarding sustainable valuation and financial reporting. For individual and general prosperity and lasting peace. Cooperatively.

## References

Aliber, R. Z., Kindleberger, C. P., & McCauley, R. N. (2023). *Manias, panics and crashes: A history of financial crises* (8th ed.). Palgrave Macmillan.

Applebaum, A. (2024). *Autocracy, Inc.: The dictators who want to run the world.* Random House.

Bank for International Settlements. (2021). *Basel Committee on Banking Supervision: Climate-related financial risks – measurement methodologies* (www.bis.org, accessed: 25.08.2025).

Baude, W. (2025). The Supreme Court ruled in favour of Trump, and that is ok. *The New York Times*, 23.05.2025. https://www.nytimes.com/2025/05/23/opinion/the-supreme-court-trump-executive-agencies.html? (accessed: 25.08.2025).

Bebchuck, L. A. (2023). *The Credit Suisse collapse and the regulation of Banking.* Harvard Law School Forum on Corporate Governance, 27.03.2023 (https://corpgov.law.harvard.edu/, accessed: 25.08.2025).

Belting, H. (2011). *Florence and Baghdad: Renaissance art and Arab science.* The Belknap Press of Harvard University Press.

Berle, A. A., Jr. (1928). *Studies in the law of corporation finance.* William S. Hein & Co.

Berle, A. A. Jr., & Means, G. C. (1932, 1967). *The modern corporation and private property* (2nd ed.). Harcourt, Brace & World.

Bhagat, S., & Laurion, H. (2024). Silicon Valley Bank demise: Causes and the path forward. *Review of Corporate Finance, 4*, 337–374.

Bingham, T. (2010). *The rule of law.* Penguin Books.

[121] See Luttermann (2015a) and (1998a) pp. 139-145.

[122] Luttermann (1999a), Belting (2011) and Jaspers (1919), see above 6.1.3 with Fig. 6.3, below 9.2; e.g., on Islamic finance Luttermann (2009b). Cf. Kissinger (2015) p. 373: "Yet world order cannot be achieved by any one country acting alone."; also above 8.2.3 with 1.6.3.

[123] See 8.4 and Luttermann (2004), (2011) and (2015b).

[124] See Aristotle, *Politiká* (Politics), which he introduces as a continuation of his ethics, esp. *Ēthika Nikomacheia* (Nicomachean Ethics). See below 9.1.

[125] See above 1.6.3. Luttermann (1998a) pp. 139-145, Luttermann (2013).

Bistline, J., Mehrotra, N., & Wolfram, C. (2023). *Economic implications of the climate provisions of the Inflation Reduction Act*. NBER Working Paper No. 31267, May 2023 (JEL No. E20,L94, Q54).

Bollman, R., & Andreu, M. (2011). Jones v. Harris Associates L.P.: The search for investor protection continues.... *University of Miami Law Review, 65*, 717–749.

Brown, L. (Ed.). (1993). *The new shorter Oxford English dictionary on historical principles* (2 Vols.). Clarendon Press.

Bungenberg, M., Griebel, J., Hobe, S., & Reinisch, A. (Eds.). (2015). *International investment law*. CH Beck/Hart/Nomos.

Costanza, R., Cumberland, J. H., Daly, H., Goodland, R., Norgaard, R. B., Kubiszewski, I., & Franco, C. (2015). *An introduction to ecological economics* (2nd ed.). CRC Press.

Dore, M., Chakravarty, S., & Goodwin, R. (1989). *John von Neumann and modern economics*. Clarendon Press.

Engen, S., & Asdal, K. (2024). The politics of climate risk: How the climate issue is turned into a risk issue through the little tools and operations of finance. *Journal of Cultural Economy, 17*, 1–14.

Fama, E. F. (1970). Efficient capital markets: A review of theory and empirical work. *Journal of Finance, 25*, 383–417.

Fama, E. F. (1991). Efficient capital markets: II. *Journal of Finance, 46*, 1575–1617.

Franklin, J., & MacDonald, G. M. (Eds.) (2024). Climate change and California sustainability-challenges and solutions. *Proceedings of the National Academy of Sciences, 121*(no. 32, Aug. 6, 2024: www.pnas.org, accessed: 25.08.2025).

Friedman, M. (2002/1962). *Capitalism and freedom*, with the assistance of R. D. Friedman, 1962 (40th Anniversary ed.). University of Chicago Press

Galbraith, J. K. (1994). *A short history of financial euphoria*. Viking Penguin.

Gerrard, M. B. (2025). Climate change litigation in New York. *New York Law Journal, 137*, March 11, 2025.

Goethe, J. W. von (1808). *Faust: Eine Tragödie, Erster Teil*. JG Cotta'sche Buchhandlung.

Gould, W. B. (2025). *Stanford's William B. Gould IV on the Supreme Court's decision in Trump v. Wilcox, 27.05.2025*. https://law.stanford.edu/2025/05/27/stanfords-william-b-gould-iv-on-the-supreme-courts-decision-in-trump-v-wilcox/ (accessed: 25.08.2025).

Greenspan, A. (1967). Gold and economic freedom. In A. Rand (Ed.), *Capitalism: The unknown ideal* (pp. 101–107). Signet (Penguin Random House). (already published 1966 in The Objectivist Newsletter: www.constitution.org/mon/greenspan_gold.htm)

Großfeld, B. (2019). *Schritte über Grenzen: Rechtsvergleichende Kulturerfahrung*. LIT Verlag.

Gupta, S., French, J., & Kelly, S. (2025). United States: First Republic Bank emergency liquidity program 2023. *Journal of Financial Crises, 7*, 623–653.

Hayek, F. A. von (1960). *The constitution of liberty*. University of Chicago Press.

Hayek, F. A. von (1991). *Die Verfassung der Freiheit* (3rd ed.). Mohr Siebeck.

Humboldt, W. von (1792). *Ideen zu einem Versuch, die Grenzen der Wirksamkeit des Staats zu bestimmen*, first published by Eduard Trewendt, 1851.

Jaspers, K. (1919). *Psychologie der Weltanschauungen*. Springer. Serie Piper 1985.

Jonas, H. (1979). *Das Prinzip Verantwortung: Versuch einer Ethik für die technologische Zivilisation*. Insel Verlag.

Kant, I. (1788). *Kritik der praktischen Vernunft*. Johann Friedrich Hartknoch.

Kant, I. (1793). Über den Gemeinspruch: Das mag in der Theorie richtig sein, taugt aber nicht für die Praxis. *Berlinische Monatsschrift*, 201–284.

Keynes, J. M. (1919). *The economic consequences of the peace*. Macmillan & Co, Ltd.

Kissinger, H. (2015). *World order: Reflections on the character of nations and the course of history*. Penguin Books.

Knight, F. (1921). *Risk, uncertainty and profit*. Houghton Mifflin Company. (here: Chicago 1971 with an introduction by Stigler).

Levitt, A. (1998). *The "numbers game"*, speech of 28 Sept 1998 at NYU Center for Law and Business. https://www.sec.gov/news/speech/speecharchive/1998/spch220.txt (accessed: 25.08.2025).

Lipton, A. (2025). The legitimation of shareholder primacy. *Journal of Corporation Law* (forthcoming, also: European Corporate Governance Institute, Law Working No. 826/2025). https://papers.ssrn.com/sol3/papers.cfm?abstract_id=5120765 (accessed: 25.08.2025).

Lord Sales. (2025). *Directors' duties and climate change: Navigating the shifting landscape of corporate environmental responsibility*, speech of 27 February 2025. https://supremecourt.uk/uploads/speech_lord_sales_270225_63efd97058.pdf (accessed: 25.08.2025).

Luttermann, C. (1998a). *Unternehmen, Kapital und Genußrechte: Eine Studie über Grundlagen der Unternehmensfinanzierung und zum internationalen Kapitalmarktrecht*. Mohr Siebeck.

Luttermann, C. (1998b). Der Sinn für das Europäische Recht: Eine zukunftsträchtige Aufgabe. *Juristenzeitung (JZ), 53*, 880–884.

Luttermann, C. (1999a). Dialog der Kulturen: Vergleichendes Handels- und Kapitalmarktrecht im Sprachspiegel. In U. Hübner & W. F. Ebke (Eds.), *Festschrift for Bernhard Großfeld* (pp. 771–789). Verlag Recht und Wirtschaft.

Luttermann, C. (1999b). *Bilanzrecht in den USA und internationale Konzernrechnungslegung*. Mohr Siebeck.

Luttermann, C. (2000a). Bewertungsrecht im Internetzeitalter: Über Finanzkommunikation, Börsenkurs, Wahrscheinlichkeit und "virtuelle" Aktiengesellschaft. *Die Aktiengesellschaft (AG), 45*, 459–469.

Luttermann, C. (2000b). Mit dem Europäischen Gerichtshof (*Centros*) zum Internationalen Unternehmens- und Kapitalmarktrecht: Kollisionsrecht in den Zeiten des Internet. *Zeitschrift für Europäisches Privatrecht (ZEuP), 8*, 907–921.

Luttermann, C. (2001). Aktienverkaufoptionsanleihen ("reverse convertible notes"), standardisierte Information und Kapitalmarktdemokratie. *Zeitschrift für Wirtschaftsrecht (ZIP), 20*, 1901–1906.

Luttermann, C. (2003). In B. Kropff & J. Semler (Eds.), *Münchener Kommentar zum Aktiengesetz* (Vol. 5/1, 2nd ed.). CH Beck Verlag.

Luttermann, C. (2004). Bilanzwahrheit international: Die Rechtsanbindung von Rechnungslegung und Wirtschaftsprüfung. *Zeitschrift für vergleichende Rechtswissenschaft (ZVglRWiss), 103*, 18–30.

Luttermann, C. (2007a). Accounting as the documentary proof of good corporate governance. In du Plessis, Großfeld, Luttermann, Saenger, & Sandrock (Eds.), *German corporate governance in international and European context* (1st ed., pp. 177–204). Springer. (3rd ed. 2017, pp. 329–400).

Luttermann, C. (2007b). Gesellschafts- und Bilanzrechtsreform in Australien: Perspektiven regionaler "IFRS" und Europäisches Bilanzrecht. *Recht der Internationalen Wirtschaft (RIW), 53*, 825–831.

Luttermann, C. (2008). Über Vertragsverhältnisse und Bewertungsrecht: Geld, Zeitwert und internationaler Goldstandard. *Finanz-Betrieb (FB), 10*, 193–204.

Luttermann, C. (2009a). "Fair Value": Mythos, Methoden und Maß international. *Recht der Internationalen Wirtschaft (RIW), 55*, 1–11.

Luttermann, C. (2009b). Islamic Finance: Ein Dialog über Recht, Weltwirtschaft und Religionen. *Juristenzeitung (JZ), 64*, 706–715.

Luttermann, C. (2009c). Weltwährungsreform: „Bretton Woods II"? In *7 Der Aufsichtsrat* (p. 25) (Stichwort – keyword).

Luttermann, C. (2010a). Juristische Analyse von Ökonomie, Staat und Gesellschaft. *Zeitschrift für Rechtspolitik (ZRP), 43*, 1–4.

Luttermann, C. (2010b). Das Bilanzstatut: Über Abkoppelungspraxis und Schadenersatz von Vorständen, Aufsichtsräten und Abschlussprüfern bei Bilanztatbeständen. *Die Aktiengesellschaft (AG), 55*, 341–350.

Luttermann, C. (2010c). Regulierungsperspektiven: War und ist die Finanzkrise die Folge von Hyperspekulation? *Österreichisches Bank Archiv (Zeitschrift für das gesamte Bank- und Börsenwesen – Journal of Banking and Financial Research, ÖBA), 58*, 444–448.

Luttermann, C. (2010d). Bilanzregeln und Finanzkrise: Die Besteuerung nach Leistungsfähigkeit und Bilanzwahrheit als Beweismaß. *Steuer und Wirtschaft (StuW) 87*, 346–355.

Luttermann, C. (2011). Kopernikanische Wende zum Wahrheitsgebot oder eine europäische Ratingagentur nach US-Mustern? *Europäisches Wirtschafts-und Steuerrecht (EWS), 22*, 330–333.

Luttermann, C. (2012). Internationale Vermögensordnung, Insolvenzrecht und Schulden(transfer)-systeme. *Zeitschrift für Wirtschaftsrecht (ZIP), 33*, 305–313.

Luttermann, C. (2013). Recht als praktizierte Ethik und unternehmerische Verantwortungskultur. In E. Weber (Ed.), *Albert Schweitzer – Hundert Jahre Menschlichkeit: Spital Lambarene (1913–2013)* (pp. 74–76). Deutscher Hilfsverein für das Albert-Schweitzer-Spital in Lambarene e.V.

Luttermann, C. (2015a). Corporate Law and the Vermoegensordnung (Order of Assets). *European Business Law Review (EBLR), 26*, 31–48.

Luttermann, C. (2015b). Über Idee und Methodik eines internationalen Investitionsschutzes (Vermögensordnung) durch Privatrecht und Völkerrecht. *Zeitschrift für Europarecht, Internationales Privatrecht und Rechtsvergleichung (ZfRV), 56*, 274–282.

Luttermann, C. (2015c). Kapitalmarktrechtliche Information bei Finanzprodukten (PRIIP), Privatautonomie und Vermögensordnung. *Zeitschrift für Wirtschaftsrecht (ZIP), 36*, 805–814.

Luttermann, C. (2016). German and Russian direct investment under the rule of international law. *Zeitschrift für internationales Wirtschaftsrecht (IWRZ), 1*, 90–95.

Luttermann, C. (2017). VR China: Neues Foreign Investment Law and Gold Trade Notes. *Recht der Internationalen Wirtschaft (RIW), 63*, 255–263.

Luttermann, C. (2019a). Die herrschende Meinung und Bewertungsrecht für Unternehmer. In W. A. Tönnes (Ed.), *Festschrift for Bernhard Großfeld* (pp. 245–256). C.F. Müller.

Luttermann, C. (2019b). Perspectives of infrastructure project finance: Intercultural investment, connectivity and trust. *Finance: Theory and Practice (Финансы: теория и практика), 23*, 27–37.

Luttermann, C. (2021). Grüner Paradigmenwechsel für Unternehmensfinanzierung, Vermögensanlage und Bewertungsrecht. *Recht der Internationalen Wirtschaft (RIW), 67*, 191–200.

Luttermann, C. (2022). Klimapartner einer kooperativen Weltvermögensordnung. *Recht der Internationalen Wirtschaft (RIW), 10*(October), p. I (editorial, *Die erste Seite*: https://online.ruw.de/suche/pdf/riw/riw-10-2022-i-d3f3bdcf9c541ac4fde57cadb3ca5968.pdf, accessed: 25.08.2025).

Luttermann, C. (2023). Unternehmensbewertung im Spannungsfeld von Rechts- und Wirtschaftswissenschaft. In K. Petersen, C. Zwirner, & G. Zimney (Eds.), *Handbuch Unternehmensbewertung* (3rd ed., pp. 163–202). Bundesanzeiger Verlag.

Luttermann, C., & Geißler, S. (2012). Haftungsfragen transnationaler Konzernfinanzierung (cash pooling) und das Bilanzstatut der Gesellschaft. *Praxis des Internationalen Privat- und Verfahrensrechts (IPRax), 32*, 55–62.

Luttermann, C., & Luttermann, K. (2020). *Sprachenrecht für die Europäische Union*. Mohr Siebeck.

Luttermann, L. (2022). Klimawandel und Business Judgement: Nachhaltige Finanzierung als unternehmerisches Sorgfaltskonzept. *Recht der Internationalen Wirtschaft (RIW), 68*, 809–820.

Luttermann, L. (2023). Nachhaltigkeitsberichterstattung in den USA, Unternehmensbewertung und Compliance. *Recht der Internationalen Wirtschaft (RIW), 69*, 483–495.

Luttermann, L. (2024). Unternehmensführung: Nachhaltige Finanzinformation (U.S. SEC Climate Rules/EU), Wertschöpfung und Bankenfinanzierung. *Recht der Internationalen Wirtschaft (RIW), 70*, 410–422.

Luttermann, L. (2025). Nachhaltige Wirtschaftsaktivitäten: Eine europäische Eröffnungsbilanz aus Finanzdaten der Bankenregulierung. *Recht der Internationalen Wirtschaft (RIW), 71*, 26–43.

Luttermann, L. (2026). Europäische Nachhaltigkeitsbilanz 2024: Evidenz der Bankenregulierung, unternehmerische Finanzdaten und Leistungsindikatoren (KPIs/KI). *Recht der Internationalen Wirtschaft (RIW), 72* (upcoming in 3/2026).

Malone, L., & Holland, E. (2024). *What the Supreme Court's Loper Bright Decision means for ESG and other key trends*. Harvard Law School Forum on Corporate Governance, July 4, 2024.
Mill, J. S. (1859). *On liberty*. John W. Parker and Son (here: Reclam, 2009).
Ortega, M. (2023). Finding a core of sustainability in directors' and officers' fiduciary duties. *Duke Environmental Law & Policy Forum, 34*, 49–89.
Padfield, S. J. (2023). An introduction to anti-ESG legislation. *Transactions: The Tennessee Journal of Business Law, 24*, 291–329.
Phelps, E. (2007). Macroeconomics for a modern economy. *The American Economic Review, 97*, 543–561.
Pistor, K. (2019). *The code of capital: How the law creates wealth and inequality*. Princeton University Press.
Posner, R. (2009). How I became a Keynesian. *The New Republic*, 23.09.2009. https://newrepublic.com/article/69601/how-i-became-keynesian (accessed: 25.08.2025).
Posner, R. (2014). *Economic analysis of law* (9th ed.) (first 1973, Little, Brown and Company). Aspen Publishing.
Rawls, J. (2001). *Justice as fairness: A restatement*. Belknap Press.
Roe, M. J. (2021). *Corporate purpose and corporate competition*. European Corporate Governance Institute Law Working Paper No. 601/2021 (July 13, 2021, available at SSRN 3817788).
Rossi, S. (2023). The banking crisis of Credit Suisse. *Investigación Económica, 82*, 21–36.
Schultz, T. (2014). *Transnational legality: Stateless law and international arbitration*. Oxford University Press.
Schweitzer, A. (1923). *Kultur und Ethik (Kulturphilosophie I and II)*. CH Beck Verlag, 1990.
Sen, A. (2009). *Introduction to Adam Smith, The theory of moral sentiments* (pp. VII–XXVI). Penguin Books.
Shikha, N., & Kapsis, I. (2024). Bank crisis management and resolution after SVB and Credit Suisse: Perspectives from India and the European Union. *International Insolvency Review, 33*, 55–88.
Smith, A. (1759/1790[6]). *The theory of moral sentiments, Edinburgh* (6th ed.). Penguin Books, 2009.
Staudinger, J. von (1998), Kommentar zum Bürgerlichen Gesetzbuch. In J. Kropholler (Ed.), *Internationales Gesellschaftsrecht* (Vol. 10). Sellier de Gruyter.
Stern, J. M., & Chew, D. (1992). *The revolution in corporate finance* (2nd ed.). Blackwell.
Stiglitz, J. E. (2010). *Freefall: America, free markets, and the sinking of the world economy*. W. W. Norton & Company.
Strine, L. E., Jr. (2014). Can we do better by ordinary investors? A pragmatic reaction to the duelling ideological mythologists of corporate law. *Columbia Law Review, 114*, 449–502.
Strine, L. E., Jr. (2025). Ignorance is strength: Climate change, corporate governance, politics, and the English language. *Journal of Law and Political Economy, 5*, 170–220.
Strum, P. (1984). *Louis D. Brandeis: Justice for the people*. Harvard University Press.
Swan, G. S. (2011). The law and economics of mutual fund investment-adviser fiduciaries: Jones v. Harris Associates L.P. *Nova Law Review, 35*, 394–474.
Tirole, J. (2019). Global challenges, the economist, and the common good. *Finance: Theory and Practice (Финансы: теория и практика), 23*, 6–12.
Tooze, A. (2019). *Crashed: How a decade of financial crisis changed the world*. Penguin Books Great Britain.
Vagts, D. F. (2009). The financial meltdown and its international implications. *American Journal of International Law, 103*, 684–690.
Wetzer, T., Stuart-Smith, R., & Dibley, A. (2024). Climate risk assessments must engage with the law: Legal actions determine the allocation and magnitude of climate-related financial risk exposures. *Science, 383*(6679), 152–154.
Williams, C. A. (2021). Fiduciary duties and corporate climate responsibility. *Vanderbilt Law Review, 74*, 1875–1916.

# Chapter 9
# The Nicomachean Question of Complementarity

"Panta rhei."*

*Heraclitus*

**Contents**



## 9.1 Happiness and Humanity: Law is Practised Ethics

Where everything is in flow, we need to go to the sources. It is about human life conditions (*Lebensverhältnisse*). Overall, the law is always practically about happiness and humanity, even with the "modern corporation" as a human corporation. Globally, it is the entrepreneurial instrument in the centre of society, economy and environment for sustainable action. Reasonableness is the ethical maxim of a culture of responsibility (*Verantwortungskultur*) comprehensively for just action (see 1.1, 8.1 with Fig. 8.1). The challenge, directed at everyone through all time, is to retain

*Old Greek πάντα ῥεῖ, English: everything flows (universal flux), attributed to Heraclitus of Ephesus (Ἡράκλειτος, around 500 BC) by Simplicius of Cilicia. Latin *cuncta fluunt*, see Ovid, Metamorphoses (8 CE), book XV, Speech of Pythagoras.

 
C. Luttermann, *Human Corporation for Sustainable Development*,
https://doi.org/10.1007/978-3-032-07615-1_9

the balance. For this reason, it is not a final accord that is sounded here, but rather we shall dare to proceed according to our complementary nature.

In the law, justice is ethically established by jurisprudence (from Latin *iuris prudentia*, i.e. reason). On this, we have already heard Aristotle with his "philosophy of human matters", which is regarded as statecraft (Greek *politikē technē*) and in general as rationality (Greek *phrónesis*).[1] It works through rationally (*vernünftig*) acting humans. The whole and its parts, they are insolubly correlated and interdependent – complementarily (see 4.6.4), as the essence of nature. Our time, where globally through the markets, egotisms and, even in Europe, war are massively gaining ground again, demands reason. Abstraction and inhumanity cannot endure with this. As the natural foundation of the laws of all nations,[2] the sense of justice shall prevail.

Let us place man (*den Menschen*) into the centre again, for it is only he who can bring good or evil into the world (see 3.9). Man strives for happiness borne by humanity. Through human community, which is liberally and responsibly founded in the sense of private autonomy (civil law)[3] as a universal order. The law, as the art of life, with this provides orientation for individual liberty (*persönliche Freiheit*) and the common whole (*gemeinsames Ganze*): law is practised ethics. Right action, adequacy in the one and the other, is preceded by right thinking. For peace (Latin *pax, pacis*), "the source of all human happiness".[4]

## 9.2 People, Human Corporation, and Sustainable Economics

For humans, the human corporation provides an individual basis for sustainable business activities worldwide (value creation), even through an investment. In addition, the human corporation in its financial function (see 2.5.1) globally opens a perspective for creating sustainable prosperity for humankind. A harmony and humanity in which – in fact evaluatingly based in thought – "a view of the world"[5] (cf. *Weltanschauung*) may be at work. This is also reciprocally conditioned, both on

[1] See above 8.5, overall Aristotle, *Politiká* (Politics) and *Ēthika Nikomacheia* (Nicomachean Ethics), Gadamer (1998) pp. 24-59 (VI), esp. pp. 33-45 (on *Vernünftigkeit* – reasonableness).

[2] Cf. Smith (1759/1790[6]) pp. 401-403, on international law Bingham (2010) chapter 10 (esp. p. 110). For European law Luttermann (1998b) and, towards peace, Luttermann, C. and Luttermann, K. (2021) with a concept for multilingualism.

[3] Fundamentally Großfeld (1977), Luttermann (1999) and (2015a).

[4] Erasmus of Rotterdam (1517) p. 1.

[5] See Belting (2011) p. 13, on perspective as a question of images (*Bildfrage*) and, pp. 13-54, with Arab mathematics, "paths between East and West" to the globalisation of perspective (also as a "betrayal"). Cf. Jaspers (1919) and on this Luttermann (1998) pp. 19-21 (about risk, from an entrepreneurial point of view). On humanity as the source of value above 5.3.4, on the dialogue of cultures Luttermann (1999).

a large scale (macroeconomics) as well as on a small scale (microeconomics), far beyond what is usually regarded as "economics". Conceived comprehensively, complementarily.

The human corporation is practically an ingenious instrument for sustainably financing a company. The corporation is regarded as an enduring creation of the law (legal person). It transforms – even transitory – capital (equity, debt) through securitised, marketable forms of participation (*Beteiligungsformen*: stocks, bonds, hybrids) into long-term investments: this means that the enterprise remains financed, whereas the capital investors may individually opt out. It is always people who found and/or lead a corporation (corporate directors), acting responsibly for it or accepting it as a business partner. Humans form a venture community (*Wagnisgemeinschaft*) as financers.[6]

This shows humans in their natural striving for happiness, which can be designated as wealth (*Wohlstand*). Also in terms of economics, though not – as Amartya Sen emphasises – in the limitations of the profit motive, as "a big part of modern economics gets (…) wrong in interpreting [Adam] Smith": Beyond self-love and alongside the outstanding, individually most helpful virtue of prudence, Smith argues that "humanity, justice, generosity, and public spirit are the qualities most useful to others".[7] Overall, sustainable community prospers with the right balance (measure, see 4.6.4, 9.4). Reasonable responsibility is the constitution of liberty.[8]

## 9.3 Financial Reporting and Auditing Under the Imperative of Truth

Financial reporting and auditing is about that responsibility in dealing with the corporate investments, id est with other people's money. This is what corporate directors regularly have to give an account of (*Rechenschaft*), id est inform truthfully. The law of accounting, valuation and auditing sets the rules that are to prevent succumbing to human weakness and making the results seem better than they are.[9] Louis D. Brandeis wisely states: "knowledge of the facts must be brought home" (real disclosure).[10] Otherwise the securities of the corporation, as Adolf A. Berle and Gardiner C. Means put it, "are substantially meaningless".[11]

---

[6] Overall Luttermann (1998). See above 1.3.2, 1.4.1 and 7.3.1.

[7] Smith (1759/1790[6]) p. 221, overall part IV, chapter II and (on Smith) Sen (2009) p. XI. Cf. Luttermann (2003) Einf BilanzR recital 130 (overall 123-133), arguing that the idea of man as a being who acts rationally only in an economic-material sense (*"homo oeconomicus"*) ruins the economic order itself.

[8] Basically Hayek (1991) with Gadamer (1998) on Aristotle, see Friedman (2002/1962), above 8. 2.2. On the ethical principle of reasonableness Luttermann (1998) pp. 139-144.

[9] Leffson (1987) pp. 152-153 and 55.

[10] Brandeis (1914) p. 104. On regulating information as a fiduciary duty Berle (1928) p.179: "disclosure has to do with facts only, and not with prospects, hopes or estimates." See overall chapters 4 and 5.

[11] Berle and Means (1932, 1967) p. 182. See overall chapter 3.

The imperative of truth – as the law as a whole – shapes the legal domain of entrepreneurial financing and valuation (general rule, *Generalnorm*). For those responsible, the imperative of truth designates the ethical tension necessary for financial reporting and auditing (culture of responsibility).[12] "True" (*wahr*) is no supernatural dimension, but a human measure. This is shown in the final instance in the formation of judicial conviction. In court, there is a standard of proof (*Beweismaß*) with a degree of certainty that suffices for practical life, which silences doubts without completely excluding them.[13] This reasonableness provides a guidance for practice to everyone (see 9.8).

With valuation (financial reporting, auditing), in practical life as in science, it is generally about knowledge (*Er-Kenntnis*), id est the actual conditions (*tatsächliche Verhältnisse*, facts) in present and past. It is these alone that provide connecting facts (*Anknüpfungstatsachen*) for prognostications, because the future is not open to proof (see 9.8). For the required information as an act of communication, it is about the greatest possible degree of objectification.[14] Niels Bohr describes for physics that it is not its task to say what nature is like but only what we can say about nature. This marks the duty of care also for financial reporting and auditing.[15]

## 9.4 Complementarity and an Economy of Climate Partners

For practical implementation, it is essential that the general rule (*Generalnorm*: imperative of truth) and specific rules (*Einzelregeln*) of law take effect methodologically in a relation of complementarity. This principle, basically applied in life conditions as a tension between parts (*Teilen*) and the whole (*Gesamtheit*), characterises any legal order. To complement something (Latin *complere* for "to accomplish") denotes opposing completion (*Vervollständigung*). What one has too much, the other has too little, what is crucial is continuous exchange:[16] a harmony of complementarity, as symbolised in the image of the scales in the law (*Waage*, see 9.9).

[12] See 9.8 (duty of care, *Sorgfaltspflicht*). Basically Luttermann (2003) § 264 HGB recitals 119-140 and Luttermann (2003) §§ 243, 342 HGB recitals 1, 7-20, 73.

[13] See above 4.6.4 with German original (e.g., BGH, 14.12.1993, VI ZR 221/92). Overall chapters 4 and 5.

[14] See above 8.3.3, 4.11.4 and 7.6, on connecting facts 4.11.4, 5.6.2.

[15] See below 9.8, above, e.g., 1.5, 4.6.5. Altogether Luttermann (2003) § 264 HGB recitals 119-135, 141-145, and Einf BilanzR recitals 37-39, Luttermann (2023) recitals 22-35 (28: connecting facts, instead of "prospects, hopes or estimates").

[16] Thus Erwin Chargaff on the pairing of the bases in our genetic substance (DNA): Luttermann (2003) § 264 HGB recitals 136-140; cf. in physics (there footnote 302) "complementary relationship" as "the capacity of two contrasted theories (e.g. the wave and particle theories of light) together to explain a body of phenomena, although each separately accounts for only some aspects". On the procedural law of faithful accounting see above 4.6.4, on subsidiarity 1.3.3.

The principle is to be practised in the sense of reasonableness. This becomes clear in particular for financial reporting. Conceptually, this applies already in the balance sheet (cf. Latin *bilanx*), which in Italian means "equilibrium of the scales". On the going concern basis in the human corporation, that is an ongoing challenge. In the application of the individual rules, also encompassing interpretation, estimation and prognostication,[17] the general rule (*Bilanzwahrheit*) binds and guides in a reciprocal relation between parts and whole, so that the responsible directors convey an image of the corporation that is factually faithful to the actual circumstances.

This comprehensive relation may shape the world, which perhaps holds it together at its core, and our reality (nature). With it, we may apprehend and order it. Better than we have succeeded so far. In relation to the whole as well as, also here complementarily, in the small things. A detail gains meaning in its connection to the whole. Life in the midst of lives, where the law provides humans their free space through invisible boundaries: With rational beings and their faculty (*Vermögen*) this may hold worldwide,[18] also between cultures (nations, see Fig. 9.1). As climate partners (*Klimapartner*) who accept their global responsibility in an economically cooperative way (see 8.5, 6.1.3).

## 9.5 Sustainability: Incorporating Trust and New Technologies

In the face of this global task of sustainable cooperation, it seems sensible to have recourse to realities. We have undertaken this, if incompletely, for the human corporation as a whole. What may guide us are the concept of trust (truth, fidelity, see 1.5.2), the necessary unity of personal freedom and responsibility. In particular in the connection of the human corporation and new technologies which are produced with the corporation entrepreneurially. We know the human ideals "goodness, truth and beauty", as well as abysses such as colonialism, pogroms and industrialisation right up to Auschwitz. Where there is much light, there is great shadow, Goethe[19] made us take to heart.

Goethe's Faust, the man striving for understanding nature, losing himself in abstraction, makes a pact with the devil, who entices him: No measure and no goal is set for you.[20] Demonical technological beacons (*Fanale*) are Chernobyl, Fukushima and originally the inferno of Hiroshima – applications of nuclear physics.

---

[17] See above 9.3 and, e.g., also 4.11.4 and 4.13, below 9.8 (at the end).

[18] Basically above 2.2.2 (Savigny) with 4.3.1, 1.2 and 8.1 (Schweitzer), also chapter 8, esp. 8.1, 8.2 with 1.7 (new "minds and measures"). On the organisational development of cooperation and common purpose (family, partnership, company, DAO etc.) above 3.7. Luttermann (1999) on the dialogue of cultures.

[19] German original: Goethe (1773), 1. act – Jagsthausen, Götzens *Burg* (castle), Götz: *"Wo viel Licht ist, ist starker Schatten".*

[20] With this, Mephistopheles encourages Faust, German original Goethe (1808), *Studierzimmer* (study room): *"Euch ist kein Maß und Ziel gesetzt. Beliebt's euch, überall zu naschen, im Fliehen etwas zu erhaschen, bekomm' euch wohl, was euch ergetzt. Nur greift mir zu und seid nicht blöde!".* Cf. above 4.6.5 and chapter 6.

Dürrenmatt describes them in a lunatic asylum, where the psychiatrist states that she has cautiously amassed capital in a powerful trust, in order to analyse the system of all sorts of inventions: the world formula for mastery of the world. Its inventor, a physicist, says resignedly: What has once been thought can no longer be taken back.[21]

Economy, science and technology belong to the whole, as parts of human life and aspiration in the sense of the Enlightenment (*Aufklärung*). They lose in mathematical limitation, as is the characteristic of weak works, which should not exhaust itself in the supposed calculability of life circumstances. Significant scholars have warned, epigones serve powerful interests, as the global financial crisis proves, and a general theory of equilibrium is lacking; modern game theory makes constructs with probability theory and nuclear physics.[22] The search for sustainable adequacy (*Angemessenheit*) remains a search for a reasonable consensus in problem solving.[23]

## 9.6 Man, AI, and Genetic Engineering: Creating New Entities?

The law, Oliver Holmes wrote, "cannot be dealt with as if it contained only the axioms and corollaries of a book of mathematics".[24] This may well serve as wisdom for the "life of the law" of the human corporation and beyond, also in the non-common law world. On a global stage, artificial intelligence (AI) is driving the old theme "man and machine" to new heights.[25] John von Neumann, involved in the construction of the atomic bomb, worked basically for the mathematisation of economics, with computer-based approaches.[26] Algorithms, quantum game theory, informatics (big data) and numerous real-world applications conquer our world (see 6.8.5).[27]

[21] Dürrenmatt (1962) p. 85 (Möbius: *"Was einmal gedacht wurde, kann nicht mehr zurückgenommen werden"*) and p. 83 (Frl. Doktor).

[22] See above 8.2.2, below 9.8, overall Luttermann (1998), esp. pp. 210-237, 465-482. Critical also Phelps (2007), Sen (2009) pp. XI-XIII; cf. Debreu (1991) and above 7.3.3, Fama (1991) p. 1610 and above 7.4.2. Overall chapters 6 and 7.

[23] Luttermann (1998) pp. 482-485. Interculturally Luttermann (1999).

[24] Holmes (1881) p. 5. Cf. Luttermann (1998) pp. 234-237 (on game theory, Neumann/ Morgenstern).

[25] See 9.7 as well as, e.g., above 3.8 and chapter 6.

[26] See above 6.6.3, 8.2.2. On game theory and economic behaviour Neumann/Morgenstern (1944), considered as the pioneering mathematical theory of economic and social analysis and organisation; on quantum mechanics already Neumann (1932). Overall Luttermann (1998) pp. 234-237, 466 and 195-233 (theory and practice of corporation finance in the USA).

[27] See also above 3.5.6 (big asset management), 4.11 (global monopolisation via "IFRS/XBRL") and, e.g., Orrell (2022), Herman, Googin, Liu et al. (2023), Pérez-Antón, López Sánchez, Corbi (2024); cf. Frąckiewicz (2014) on quantum cognition, option pricing, quantum economic modelling, quantum computation etc. working in economics and finance.

Machine and deep learning, generative AI can improve work with high energy input. Quantum technologies like quantum computing promise to solve even the most complex problems, creating gigantic financial value. AI is the magic word, multifariously leading to artificial general intelligence (AGI), surpassing human cognitive capabilities (artificial superintelligence, ASI). Geoffrey Hinton, though a trailblazer himself, surprised by the speed of development of computers outperforming humans, warns: "it's quite conceivable that humanity is just a passing phase in the evolution of intelligence", AI is an imminent "existential threat".[28]

AI may start manipulating people, spreading misinformation, gaining more control. Applications, complementarities are unlimited (cf. electronic person):[29] are they limitable at all? – Much good is possible, e.g. precision medicine (medical data analysis, drug and chemical research). However, more is at stake. Biophysics and computer science, virtual cells for designing biological systems that can be industrially used (cf. cyborgs), artificial life (synthetic biology).[30] The really alarming perspectives appear with the elementary structures of life, where advanced AI and genetic engineering are combined (genomic design, *sui generis*): Are we creating new "entities"?

## 9.7 Juridical Analysis of the Economy for Prosperity

In this, the human corporation is globally a remarkable instrument, which as such demands the juridical analysis of the economy even more.[31] Where natural borders are affected, where technological progress broadens the space of possibilities so dramatically, the prosperity of humanity and the world are at stake. The corporation seems like a spider in the net, peculiarly efficient. As a legal person, a fictitious but really powerful financial instrument beyond the lifetime of humans, practically immortal.[32] An infinite cluster of faculty (*Vermögen*), combined with incredible artificial intelligence (AI), which has the building blocks of life and beyond (universal person). – Who will own it?

The universality of man, established in personal responsibility and sustainability as a legal requirement of corporate governance (duty of care, see Fig. 9.1),[33] is challenged. AI as a black box, monstrous even to its inventors, is already running like BlackRock's "Aladdin" worldwide in finance (see 3.5.6), social media,

[28]Hinton, nobel laureate in physics 2024, interviewed by Metz (2023). Cf. call for a moratorium on the training of AI systems Bengio, Russel, Musk et al. (2023), Ienca (2023), Yudkowsky (2023). On "immediate risks" Hoes and Gilardi (2025).

[29]See 9.7 and, e.g., above 3.7.

[30]Luttermann (2011). On the corporation above 3.6.1 ("virtual realities") and Luttermann (2000). On quantum biology Fornés (2024).

[31]See 1.6, 7.3.2 and 8.2.2 with Figs. 5.3 and 6.3. Basically Luttermann (1998) pp. 465-485, and (2010).

[32]Fundamentally 1.4.1 and 2.4.3 (with 3.4), also 3.5.1 and chapter 6.

[33]See 4.11.4 (IFRS/XBRL) and 7.8.3 with 4.6.4, 4.6.5 (duty of care). On genetic engineering and civil liability system Luttermann (1998a). On depersonalisation ("*Entmenschlichung*") above 8.3.2. See further in 9.8.

technology and research (Alphabet/Google, Meta, Goldman Sachs, see chapter 6). Do those responsible know what they are doing? – Corporations have long since become the "virtual cells" (incubators),[34] in which in reality also – patentable[35] – these new dimensions are being developed. The corporation structurally functions as a gatekeeper to progress through information participation. It is about the knowledge and the prosperity of the world.

This characterises the demand of real disclosure in the modern corporation as a human corporation. Financial reporting and auditing, as comprehensive law of valuation (*Bewertungsrecht*), are further gaining in importance. For the common good, for the protection of humans and the environment, and as trustees for future generations. As shown, the human corporation provides an ingenious financial instrument under the imperative of truth if it is integrated into a sensible *Vermögensordnung* (order of assets). Elementary from a human perspective are self-interest and real values (substance) as a basis of trust.[36] This needs to be addressed globally in a time-adequate way for the best prosperity possible overall.

**Fig. 9.1** Dialogue of cultures (Luttermann (1999))

[34]Cf. 3.6.1 (financing, liability) and 6.8.5 (AI megahype, investors). Luttermann (2000) on valuation law and the virtual corporation in times of the internet.

[35]Basically *Assoc. for Molecular Pathology v. Myriad Genetics, Inc.*, 569 U.S. 576 (2013), on this Luttermann (2013).

[36]See above 1.5.2, 7.3.3 with Smith (1776/1789$^5$), book IV, introduction and chapters I, II; cf. Smith (1762/1982) pp. 340-355; also above, esp. 1.1, 1.6, 3.4.4 and 3.5.3, 3.6.3 (real estate) and 5.2.4, 5.6.1, 6.6.2 (substance, gold standard), 5.3.4 (*iustum pretium*), 4.10.2, 4.11.4, 6.6.2 and 7.7.3 (sustainability); overall chapters 5 and 8 (esp. 8.1). Basically Luttermann (2008) and (2015b).

## 9.8 Cooperation: Mutuality, Education, and Control

Prosperity (*Wohlstand*) is a shared dream and an imperative of peace for all. Experience shows that both blossom with cooperation. Economically as well as ethically founded. Man (state), who can augment his benefit through the assistance of others,[37] as a matter of course practices the principle of complementarity. From a market-economy perspective, this is based on mutuality, the contractual basis of private autonomy (Latin *do ut des*).[38] With the corporation, finance, financial reporting and overall, it is about real information (facts) and real values (energy). Cooperation can work this way for the people, societies and the environment.

The corporation, corporate finance (equity, debt, hybrid) and markets are based on this, and thus also sustainable business activity and the human corporation, as dealt with comprehensively. The change for the better, the transformation economic development for the protection of humans and the environment, also between peoples, can be effectively promoted in this way worldwide. This, however, sustainably requires control and education.[39] This metaphorically radiates in Raffael's "School of Athens" on the walls of the Vatican as an allegory of reason: the human being as a rational being, carefully acting entrepreneurially on the basis of scientific insights (duty of care).

This liberty, as any accountability, demands reasonable control. We have systematically shown this for the human corporation on the basis of accounting and auditing (law of valuation).[40] It is about the actual life circumstances, no "numbers game" (world monopoly). For those responsible (corporate directors, auditors) the following holds: their legal duty under the imperative of truth is not what the corporation (nature) is but what can be said about it (cf. on physics 9.3). Where someone who is responsible deviates materially from norms and facts, he accordingly loses the protection of the legal order, which he himself is evading.[41]

[37] Cf. basically Smith (1762/1982) p. 347 and seq. on the market principle (demand and supply, pricing).

[38] See the division of labour and above 5.3.3. On building investors' trust see 3.2 and overall chapters 4 and 6; in order to establish a global *Vermögensordnung* 1.6.1 (fidelity) and chapter 8.

[39] Note above 1.6.2 (education), on control in 3.3 (esp. 3.3.3), 4.9-4.10 and 5.2.4 (sustainability); overall chapters 4 and 5.

[40] Overall chapters 1 to 7 (esp. 4.10.2, 4.13). Luttermann (2003) Einf BilanzR recitals 1-45, 107-136 with 301-318, Luttermann (2003) § 264 HGB recitals 119-169.

[41] See above 9.3, 5.6 (esp. 5.6.2, 5.6.3 with Fig. 5.3), and 5.7 with chapter 4 (esp. 4.6.5), and 8.3.3.

## 9.9 The Art of Life and Practical Complementarity

In the book of life, new pages are opened, also for the human corporation. For a better world, sustainable corporate finance, financial reporting and auditing (i.e. valuation, good governance) comes to the fore in its elementary function. It is about information, which – also in the era of digitisation, genetic coding and AI[42] – simply has to be given (valuation law). By the responsibly acting human being, through real information (disclosure, facts), no matter in what language: clearly and comprehensibly under the imperative of truth (*Gebot der Bilanzwahrheit*, culture of responsibility). So that reasonable valuation can take place and inadequate transfer of wealth is inhibited.

In life circumstances, a complementarily designed community offers the basis for a just order. With reason and sustainability, including a trustworthy measure of value (precious metals, energy), this leads to successful cooperation, development and prosperity – born out of fidelity (*Treue*, universality).[43] Guided by the principle of rationality, instead of the blunt attempts at definitions of the reasonable (casuistry): "What is reasonable has to be determined with reference to times and places and circumstances".[44] This takes place in the complementary exchange between general rule (*Generalnorm*) and specific rules (*Einzelregeln*), to ensure justice.[45] In individual cases through sustainable weighing of the facts and arguments in the image of the scales (*Waage*, see 9.4, 5.5.5: Latin *judex non calculat*), which for that purpose must be solidly founded with a clear measure (*Maß*).[46]

This is what jurisprudence is directed at with the law as practised ethics. Accordingly, in the image of the scales, the centre (*Mitte*) is not the dictate of the mathematical average (mediocrity – *Mittelmäßigkeit*), but rather factual adequacy (*Optimum*, cf. 3.9). It is founded in law and practice as human reasonability (Greek *phrónesis*).[47] That is the art of life. It demands from everyone ethical tension in acting, with which humans distinguish evil from good (principle of reasonableness). Thus good and peace comes into the world, with the human corporation and cooperation. – How can we sustainably establish the harmony of human complementarity?

---

[42] See above 9.6 to 9.8. Cf. on co-operation (corporation, common purpose, AI) 3.7 to 3.9; on corporate finance and algorithms 6.2.3, 6.6.3.

[43] See 9.5, above 8.4.1, 7.7.3 and 7.8.3. Overall Luttermann (2015a).

[44] Pound (1954) pp. 10-11. See above 3.5.5. On the principle of reasonableness above 1.1, 2.2.2 and Luttermann (1998) pp. 139-145. See also Gadamer (1998) pp. 62-63, Smith (1759/1790$^6$) pp. 400-401 (overall from p. 388).

[45] See above 9.4 and 4.4 to 4.6, overall chapters 1 and 2.

[46] See above, esp. chapter 5 with chapters 4 and 8.

[47] See above, esp. 9.1, 1.6.1, 8.5 and 7.9. Cf. Aristotle (2024/1956, book VI, esp. from 1141b), see: Gadamer (1998) pp. 41-59, and afterword pp. 60-67. Cf. Confucius, Analects (Lunyü), book VI.27.

# References


Aristoteles. (1957). *Nikomachische Ethik* (Aristotle, *Nicomachean Ethics – Ēthika Nikomacheia*), translation by Franz Dirlmeier. Fischer Verlag.

Aristoteles. (2020). *Politik* (Aristotle, *Politics – Politiká*), translation by Eckart Schütrumpf. Felix Meiner Verlag.

Aristotle. (2024). *Ἠθικὰ Νικομάχεια (Ēthika Nikomacheia) – Nicomachean Ethics*, translation by Harris Rackham. Kaktos Publications (full text, 1956): https://archive.org/details/in.ernet.dli.2015.183333/page/324/mode/2up (accessed: 22.08.2025).

Belting, H. (2011). *Florence and Baghdad: Renaissance art and Arab science*. The Belknap Press of Harvard University Press.

Bengio, Y., Russel, S., Musk, E., et al. (2023). *Pause giant AI experiments: An open letter 22.03.2023*. https://futureoflife.org/open-letter/pause-giant-ai-experiments (accessed: 22.08.2025).

Berle, A. A., Jr. (1928). *Studies in the law of corporation finance*. William S. Hein & Co.

Berle, A. A. Jr., & Means, G. C. (1932, 1967). *The modern corporation and private property* (2nd ed.). Harcourt, Brace & World, 1967.

Bingham, T. (2010). *The rule of law*. Penguin Books.

Brandeis, L. D. (1914). *Other people's money and how the bankers use it*. Freederick A. Stokes Company Publishers.

Confucius. (1914/2013). *Analects (Lunyü – Gespräche)*. German translation by Richard Wilhelm (3rd ed.). marixverlag.

Dürrenmatt, F. (1962). *Die Physiker – Eine Komödie, Neufassung in zwei Akten, Neufassung 1980, Werkausgabe in dreißig Bänden* (Band 7). Diogenes (1985).

Debreu, G. (1991). The mathematization of economic theory. *American Economic Review, 81*, 1–7.

Erasmus of Rotterdam. (1517). *Querela pacis*. Johannes Froben (English: *The complaint of peace*), German: *Die Klage des Friedens*, translation by Brigitte Hannemann. Diogenes 2017.

Fama, E. F. (1991). Efficient capital markets: II. *Journal of Finance, 46*, 1575–1617.

Fornés, J. A. (2024). *Quantum processes in biology*. Springer Nature Switzerland.

Frąckiewicz, P. (2014). *Application of quantum computing to game theory*. LAP Lambert Academic Publishing.

Friedman, M. (2002/1962). *Capitalism and freedom*, with the assistance of Rose D. Friedman, 1962 (40th Anniversary ed.). University of Chicago Press.

Gadamer, H.-G. (1998). ed. and translated, *Aristoteles: Nikomachische Ethik VI*. Vittorio Klostermann.

Goethe, J. W. von (1773). *Götz von Berlichingen*. Printed anonymously.

Goethe, J. W. von (1808). *Faust: Eine Tragödie, Erster Teil*. JG Cotta'sche Buchhandlung.

Großfeld, B. (1977). *Zivilrecht als Gestaltungsaufgabe*. Müller Juristischer Verlag.

Hayek, F. A. von (1991). *Die Verfassung der Freiheit* (*The constitution of liberty*) (3rd ed.). Mohr Siebeck.

Herman, D., Googin, C., Liu, X., Sun, Y., Galda, A., Safro, I., Pistoia, M., & Alexeev, Y. (2023). *Quantum computing for finance*. https://arxiv.org/pdf/2307.11230 (accessed: 22.08.2025).

Hoes, E., & Gilardi, F. (2025). *Existential risk narratives about artificial intelligence do not distract from its immediate harms*. Proceedings of the National Academy of Sciences, April 14, 2025. https://www.pnas.org/doi/10.1073/pnas.2419055122 (accessed: 22.08.2025).

Holmes, O. W. (1881). *The Common Law*. Little, Brown, and Company, here: ed. by Mark DeWolfe Howe, Belknap Press of Harvard University Press 1963 (Back Bay Books).

Ienca, M. (2023). Don't pause giant AI for the wrong reasons. *Nature Machine Intelligence, 5*, 470–471.

Jaspers, K. (1919). *Psychologie der Weltanschauungen*. Springer.

Leffson, U. (1987). *Grundsätze ordnungsmäßiger Buchführung* (7th ed.). IDW-Verlag.

Luttermann, C. (1998). *Unternehmen, Kapital und Genußrechte: Eine Studie über Grundlagen der Unternehmensfinanzierung und zum internationalen Kapitalmarktrecht*. Mohr Siebeck.

Luttermann, C. (1998a). Gentechnik und zivilrechtliches Haftungssystem. *Juristenzeitung (JZ), 53*, 174–181.
Luttermann, C. (1998b). Der Sinn für das Europäische Recht: Eine zukunftsträchtige Aufgabe. *Juristenzeitung (JZ), 53*, 880–884.
Luttermann, C. (1999). Dialog der Kulturen: Vergleichendes Handels- und Kapitalmarktrecht im Sprachspiegel. In U. Hübner & W. F. Ebke (Eds.), *Festschrift for Bernhard Großfeld* (pp. 771–789). Verlag Recht und Wirtschaft.
Luttermann, C. (2000). Bewertungsrecht im Internetzeitalter: Über Finanzkommunikation, Börsenkurs, Wahrscheinlichkeit und "virtuelle Aktiengesellschaft". *Die Aktiengesellschaft (AG), 45*, 459–469.
Luttermann, C. (2003). In B. Kropff & J. Semler (Eds.), *Münchener Kommentar zum Aktiengesetz* (2nd ed., Vol. 5/1). CH Beck Verlag.
Luttermann, C. (2008). Über Vertragsverhältnisse und Bewertungsrecht: Geld, Zeitwert und internationaler Goldstandard. *Finanz-Betrieb (FB), 10*, 193–204.
Luttermann, C. (2010). Juristische Analyse von Ökonomie, Staat und Gesellschaft. *Zeitschrift für Rechtspolitik (ZRP), 43*, 1–4.
Luttermann, C. (2011). Synthetische Biologie: Bausteine für Leben und Jurisprudenz. *Juristenzeitung (JZ), 66*, 195–198.
Luttermann, C. (2013). Über Patentierung menschlichen Erbguts, Stammzellen(klone) und juristische Maßgaben. *Juristenzeitung (JZ), 68*, 934–937.
Luttermann, C. (2015a). Über Idee und Methodik eines internationalen Investitionsschutzes (Vermögensordnung) durch Privatrecht und Völkerrecht. *Zeitschrift für Europarecht, Internationales Privatrecht und Rechtsvergleichung (ZfRV), 56*, 274–282.
Luttermann, C. (2015b). Corporate Law and the Vermoegensordnung (Order of Assets). *European Business Law Review (EBLR), 26*, 31–48.
Luttermann, C. (2023). Juristische Anforderungen an eine ordnungsmäßige Unternehmensbewertung und an ein Bewertungsgutachten. In K. Petersen, C. Zwirner, & G. Zimney (Eds.), *Handbuch Unternehmensbewertung* (3rd ed., pp. 653–682). Bundesanzeiger Verlag. (chapter D.8.).
Luttermann, C., & Luttermann, K. (2021). Towards peace in Europe: On legal linguistics, prosperity and European identity – the European Reference Language System for the European Union. *International Journal of Legal Discourse, 6*, 7–41.
Metz, C. (2023). "The godfather of A.I." leaves Google and warns of danger ahead. *The New York Times*, May 5.
Neumann, J. von (1932). *Mathematische Grundlagen der Quantenmechanik*. In the book series: *Die Grundlagen der Mathematischen Wissenschaften*. Julius Springer.
Neumann, J. von, & Morgenstern, O. (1944). *Theory of games and economic behavior*. Princeton University Press.
Orrell, D. (2022). *Quantum economics and finance: An applied mathematics introduction* (3rd ed.). Panda Ohana Publishing.
Pérez-Antón, R., Sánchez, L., Ignacio, J., & Corbi, A. (2024). The game theory in quantum computers: A review. *International Journal of Interactive Multimedia and Artificial Intelligence, 8*(6), 6–14.
Phelps, E. (2007). Macroeconomics for a modern economy. *The American Economic Review, 97*, 543–561.
Pound, R. (1954). In H. Dölle, M. Rheinstein, K. Zweigert (Eds.), *Some thoughts about comparative law, Festschrift für Ernst Rabel* (Band I, pp. 7–16). J.C.B. Mohr.
Sen, A. (2009). *Introduction to Adam Smith, The theory of moral sentiments* (pp. VII–XXVI). Penguin Books.
Smith, A. (1759/1790[6]). *The theory of moral sentiments* (6th ed.). Penguin Books, 2009.
Smith, A. (1762/1982). In Meek, Raphael and Stein (Eds.), *Lectures on jurisprudence* (Report of 1762-3 and Report of 1766). Liberty Fund.

Smith, A. (1776/1789[5]). *An inquiry into the nature and causes of the wealth of nations* (5th ed.). Bantam Classic Edition, 2003.

Yudkowsky, E. (2023). *Pausing AI developments isn't enough: We need to shut it down*, 29.03.2023. https://empoweruohio.nyc3.cdn.digitaloceanspaces.com/Pausing%20AI%20Development.pdf (accessed: 22.08.2025).

# Epilogue

***Botticelli universale***

words, words, words fill the worlds
venus and mars, poet dreams, nerds
judgements melting, stones on grave

turn, turn, turn, see the cranes fly
venus and mars, dreams never die
the tune sounds, none ever safe

blue, blue, blue, the sky's colour turns
venus and mars, a kingdom burns
but look, the good you gave

CHL



C. Luttermann, *Human Corporation for Sustainable Development*,
https://doi.org/10.1007/978-3-032-07615-1

# Index




C. Luttermann, *Human Corporation for Sustainable Development*, https://doi.org/10.1007/978-3-032-07615-1

**N**



**O**

**T**

MIX
Papier aus verantwortungsvollen Quellen
Paper from responsible sources
FSC® C105338

If you have any concerns about our products,
you can contact us on
**ProductSafety@springernature.com**

In case Publisher is established outside the EU,
the EU authorized representative is:
**Springer Nature Customer Service Center GmbH**
**Europaplatz 3, 69115 Heidelberg, Germany**

Printed by Libri Plureos GmbH
in Hamburg, Germany